Handbook of Latin American Studies: No. 20

A SELECTIVE AND ANNOTATED GUIDE TO RECENT PUBLISHED MATERIAL
ON
ANTHROPOLOGY, ART, ECONOMICS, EDUCATION, GEOGRAPHY,
GOVERNMENT, HISTORY, INTERNATIONAL RELATIONS,
LABOR AND SOCIAL WELFARE, LANGUAGE
AND LITERATURE, LAW, MUSIC,
PHILOSOPHY, *AND* SOCIOLOGY

Advisory Board

HANDBOOK OF
LATIN AMERICAN STUDIES
No. 20

PREPARED IN
THE HISPANIC FOUNDATION
IN
THE LIBRARY OF CONGRESS
BY
A NUMBER OF SCHOLARS

●

FRANCISCO AGUILERA, *Editor*
PHYLLIS G. CARTER, *Assistant Editor*

1958
UNIVERSITY OF FLORIDA PRESS
GAINESVILLE

Contributing Editors

Lysia Maria Cavalcanti Bernardes, *Rio de Janeiro*, GEOGRAPHY

George Boehrer, *Georgetown University*, HISTORY

David Bushnell, *Holloman Air Development Center, N. Mex.*, HISTORY

Phyllis G. Carter, *The Library of Congress*, STATISTICS

Arnold Chapman, *University of California, Berkeley*, LITERATURE

Asher N. Christensen, *University of Minnesota*, GOVERNMENT

Helen L. Clagett, *The Library of Congress*, LAW

Mercer Cook, *Howard University*, LANGUAGE AND LITERATURE

Raymond E. Crist, *University of Florida*, GEOGRAPHY

Frank Dauster, *Rutgers University*, LITERATURE

Ralph Edward Dimmick, *Pan American Union*, LANGUAGE AND LITERATURE

Dirección de Investigaciones Económicas, Nacional Financiera, S. A., Mexico City,
ECONOMICS

Irene de Menezes Doria, *Instituto Nacional de Estudos Pedagógicos, Rio de Janeiro*,
EDUCATION

Robert C. Eidt, *Los Angeles State College*, GEOGRAPHY

Clifford Evans, *United States National Museum*, ANTHROPOLOGY

Carl H. Farman, *Department of Health, Education, and Welfare*, SOCIAL WELFARE

Ángel Flores, *Queens College*, LITERATURE

Siegfried Garbuny, *Washington, D. C.*, ECONOMICS

Arch C. Gerlach, *The Library of Congress*, CARTOGRAPHY

Charles Gibson, *State University of Iowa*, HISTORY

Charles C. Griffin, *Vassar College*, GENERAL

J. Leon Helguera, *North Carolina State College*, HISTORY

Roscoe R. Hill, *The National Archives* (retired), HISTORY

Roland D. Hussey, *University of California, Los Angeles*, HISTORY

Marjorie C. Johnston, *Department of Health, Education, and Welfare*, EDUCATION

Contents

CONTENTS

Editor's Note

INTRODUCTION

THE SELECTIVE bibliography offered in the present volume includes publications issued, in the majority of cases, in the years 1954, 1955, and 1956.

The new policy of coverage initiated last year in No. 19 is observed here for the second time. This policy consists in including all the important publications seen for the first time by the Contributing Editors during the year following the preparation of the last volume, regardless of their imprint date. *Handbook No. 19* included publications issued during 1953, 1954, and 1955. *Handbook No. 21* (in preparation) will include mostly 1955, 1956, and 1957 imprints.

This volume contains 3695 entries. For convenience in the preparation of the manuscript, a block of numbers was assigned to each section at the beginning of the work, each such block to be a safe margin larger than the expected number of items for the section. Thus, gaps of varying sizes in the item numbering appear between sections; and also, the numerical designation of the last entry (5073) is appreciably larger than the actual number of entries.

CONTRIBUTING EDITORS

Several new names appear in the present volume: Lysia Maria Cavalcanti Bernardes, Arnold Chapman, J. Leon Helguera, Richard Konetzke, Norman A. McQuown, Robert J. Mead, Jr., and Arturo Santana.

Mrs. Bernardes joined Dr. Sternberg in the preparation of the Brazilian geography section while Dr. James took a sabbatical from *Handbook* work.

Dr. Chapman is editor of the section on Spanish American Poetry of the nineteenth and twentieth centuries which Francisco Aguilera edited in Nos. 3-19.

Messrs. McQuown and Mead have assumed responsibility for two newly established sections, respectively: Linguistics (in the major division, Anthropology) and Essays (in the subdivision, Spanish American Literature: Nineteenth and Twentieth Centuries).

The acceptance on the part of Messrs. Helguera, Konetzke, and Santana of assignments in various fields of history has made possible a rearrangement of the divisions pertaining to Spanish America and Haiti. Mr. Helguera has joined Messrs. Bushnell and Kroeber in the preparation of the section dealing with Spanish South America of the nineteenth and twentieth centuries. Messrs. Santana and Gibson have relieved Dr. Hussey of part of his work (which he did in Nos. 6-14, 16, 18, and 19), namely, the sections on Colonial Middle America and Colonial West Indies, respectively. Dr. Hussey now devotes his efforts to the "General" section under Colonial Spanish America. Dr. Santana, in addition to his other commitment, has succeeded Robert E. McNicoll, who served in Nos. 11-19 as editor of the section on nineteenth- and twentieth-century West Indies. Finally, Dr. Konetzke is now in charge of the section on Spanish South America, Colonial period, which Dr. Gibson edited in Nos. 17-19.

The resignation of Manuel Cardozo, after serving as sole editor of Brazilian history in Nos. 13-18 and joint editor in No. 19, leaves Dr. Boehrer in full charge of this section.

J. H. Parry, who contributed notes on West Indies history to Nos. 18 and 19, has discontinued his collaboration now that he is located in Nigeria.

Robert S. Chamberlain (history), absent from this volume, will return next year.

Harold E. Wethey, whose section on Spanish American and Haitian art did not appear in No. 19, has resumed his work in the present volume with due attention to publications issued from 1953 on.

The contributions of Arch C. Gerlach, on cartography, and Roscoe R. Hill, on archival materials, are scattered under various headings according to their subjects.

ADVISORY BOARD

The death on March 13, 1957 of Miron Burgin, member of the Advisory Board, was a cause of profound grief to his colleagues and friends in the *Handbook* undertaking. He had been serving on the Advisory Board since 1948. For ten years prior to 1948 Dr. Burgin had been connected with the *Handbook* and the Hispanic Foundation in various capacities—as Contributing Editor (Nos. 5, 6, 8, 11, 12, 14), Associate Editor (No. 5), and Editor (Nos. 6-11). He resigned from the Library of Congress on February 9, 1948, to join the Department of State.

The Librarian of Congress appointed Charles C. Griffin to the Advisory Board to fill Dr. Burgin's vacancy (term ending July 1958). An eighth member, Robert C. Smith, was appointed for a term ending July 1960. With the latter action, the Board attains full membership. The members are appointed to definite, staggered terms, in compliance with the new policy explained in No. 19, page xii.

EXPLANATORY NOTES

AUTHOR INDEX. Includes names of individual authors ("Reyes, Alfonso") and names of corporate authors ("Rio Grande do Sul (state). Departamento Estadual de Estatística"). Under "Anonymous" are listed, alphabetically, author-less titles.

SUBJECT INDEX. Includes topics ("Architecture") and names of individuals ("Bolívar, Simón"), corporate bodies ("Organization of American States"), countries ("Haiti"), and areas ("West Indies"), when they are dealt with as subjects of study.

SPANISH ACCENTS. In the annotations in English, Spanish accents are used only for names of persons and organizations. Accents are no longer used in such annotations for names of places or geographical features, or for names of Indian tribes, because so many of these names have been incorporated into English without the accents.

ABBREVIATIONS. Attention is called to the "Key to Periodical and Other Title Abbreviations," which is self-explanatory. Throughout the bibliography various standard abbreviations are used ("v." for volume, "t." for *tomo*, "set." for *setembro*, etc.). "B. A.," "N. Y.," and "Rio" are used as abbreviations for Buenos Aires, New York, and Rio de Janeiro, respectively.

PERIODICAL CITATIONS. The following abbreviated citation is a typical one: 5:1, Mar. 1956, p. 93-99 (meaning, vol. 5, no. 1, March 1956, pages 93-99). Variations occur, such as: 2. época, 4, 1955 (segunda época, vol. 4, 1955); 24, out. 1956 (no. 24, outubro 1956); n.s., 45, 1956 (nouvelle série, no. 45, 1956).

FRANCISCO AGUILERA

The Hispanic Foundation
The Library of Congress
Washington, D. C.

Handbook of Latin American Studies

Anthropology

GENERAL

1. **Azevedo, Thales de.** Panorama demográfico dos grupos étnicos na América Latina (Am Indíg, 17:2, abril 1957, p. 121-139).
Comprehensive review, as of 1955, of the proportions and numbers of Indians, whites, Negroes, Asiatics, mestizos, etc., in the various Latin American nations, along with indications of demographic trends. The ethnic groups are carefully defined. [D. B. Stout]

2. **Barnett, Homer Garner.** Innovation: the basis of cultural change. 1st ed. N. Y., McGraw-Hill (Series in sociology and anthropology), 1953. 462 p., illus.
A penetrating theoretical treatment of the processes of innovation. Of great potential value to the students of culture change in Latin America. Reviewed at length in Spanish in *Ciencias sociales*, 6:33, junio 1955, p. 157-160. [D. B. Stout]

3. **Bird, Junius B.,** and **James A. Ford.** A new earth-shaking machine (Am Antiq, 21:4, Apr. 1956, p. 399-401, illus.).
Description of a simply constructed, power driven, portable sifter, for use in archaeological excavation where artifacts are too small to find by regular digging and must be passed over a screen. A useful, ingenious device worth constructing for any large-scale operation. [C. Evans and B. J. Meggers]

4. **Carter, George F.** The American civilization puzzle (Johns Hopkins Mag, 8:5, Feb. 1957, p. 9-13, 20-22).
Popular discussion of evidences for trans-Pacific pre-Columbian contacts, with a checklist of relevant traits. [R. Wauchope]

5. **Coluccio, Félix** (ed.). Antología ibérica y americana del folklore. Prólogo de Antonio Castillo de Lucas. B. A., Kraft, 1953. 320 p., 30 pl.
An excellent presentation of a number of themes or motifs in the folklore of Spain, Portugal, and the Americas. [D. B. Stout]

6. **Comas, Juan.** Aportaciones del sureste de Asia y de Oceanía al poblamiento de América (Yan, 3, 1954, p. 75-76).
Brief résumé of some theories regarding origins of American peoples and cultures. [R. Wauchope]

7. —————. Historia y bibliografía de los congresos internacionales de ciencias antropológicas: 1865-1954. México, Universidad Nacional Autónoma de México, Instituto de Historia (Publ., 1. serie, 37), 1956. 490 p., ports.
A detailed history of all the international anthropological congresses other than the International Congress of Americanists (for which see *HLAS, no. 19,* item 9A), with a general index to all of the volumes of proceedings, arranged by topic, nation and continent, and an author index for all of the papers in the various proceedings. The 24 plates are devoted to 80 portraits of leading prehistorians, physical anthropologists and ethnologists—a unique gallery for the profession. Pages 376-385 of the index deal with the Americas. [D. B. Stout]

8. **Disselhoff, Hans Dietrich.** Geschichte der altamerikanischen Kulturen. München, R. Oldenbourg, 1953. 376 p., illus., maps.
General discussion of the high culture areas of the New World, with chapters on Meso-America, the "Gold Lands" (Costa Rica, Panama, Colombia, and Peru). The author has consulted and used the up-to-date literature, with the exception of a few major works published in last ten years by North Americans, in developing a generalized account. [C. Evans and B. J. Meggers]

9. **Easby, Dudley T., Jr.** Ancient American goldsmiths (Nat Hist, 65:8, Oct. 1956, p. 401-409).
Magnificently illustrated account of prehistoric goldwork in Mexico and Central and South America. [R. Wauchope]

10. **Emery, Irene.** Notes on some of the basic requirements for a terminology of ancient and primitive textiles. Washing-

ton, Textile Museum (Workshop notes, Paper, 11), 1955. 10 p., illus.
Of extreme importance to anyone trying to describe aboriginal textiles. Enlarged photographs of the structures of fabrics made with a standard sized thread are easier to understand than the usual diagrams in textile articles. [C. Evans and B. J. Meggers]

11. **Evans, Clifford.** The cultural area concept in an exhibition of Latin American archaeology, United States National Museum, Washington (Museum, 9:4, 1956, p. 221-225, illus.).
Statement of the value of presenting exhibits of Latin American archaeology according to the classification of Julian Steward as proposed in the *Handbook of South American Indians,* using Marginals, Tropical Forest Tribes, Circum-Caribbean, Meso-American, Andean Civilizations. Also, specific information on opening a hall in connection with an important local event. French translation in same issue, p. 215-220. [C. Evans and B. J. Meggers]

12. ————. Tendencias actuales de la investigación arqueológica en América Latina (Cien Soc, 7:38, junio 1956, p. 85-95).
Published paper of a historiography session of the American Historical Association 1955 annual meeting for which the author was requested to outline for the historians the progress made in the last few decades by North Americans on the study of the prehistory of Latin America. The impact of two important research programs—Institute of Andean Research program of archaeological research 1941-1942 and Viru valley project in Peru in 1946—is emphasized. [C. Evans and B. J. Meggers]

13. **Gould, Harold.** The implications of technological change for folk and scientific medicine (Am Anthr, 59:3, June 1957, p. 507-516).
Sobre la interacción entre las prácticas médicas primitivas y modernas. Basado en trabajo de campo en el norte de la India, con referencias a América Latina. [A. Palerm]

14. **Hissink, Karin.** Vida y rebelión de los utensilios (Khana, año 4, 2:17-18, julio 1956, p. 266-274).
Examen de algunos paralelos mexicano-peruanos, relacionados con creencias relativas a los utensilios domésticos. [A. Palerm]

15. **Hoppenot, Hélène.** Mexique, magie maya. Introduction de Jacques Soustelle. Notice historique par Miguel Covarrubias. Lausanne, Switzerland, Guilde du Livre (212), 1954. 80 p. of illus., map.
Another collection of fine photographs of prehistoric ruins and contemporary native life in Mexico. [R. Wauchope]

16. **Muelle, Jorge C.** El Uhle que conocí (Cultura, Lima, 1:1, enero-marzo 1956, p. 4-10).

A very interesting account of Muelle's personal contacts with Uhle, written in honor of the 100th anniversary of Uhle's birth. [C. Evans and B. J. Meggers]

17. **National Geographic Society.** National Geographic on Indians of the Americas. A color-illustrated record [by] Matthew W. Stirling with contributions by Hiram Bingham [and others]. Illustrated with full-color reproductions of 149 paintings by W. Langdon Kihn and H. M. Herget. Foreword by John Oliver La Gorce. Washington, 1955. 431 p., illus., maps.
The magazine's past articles, assembled under these headings: North American Indians, Ancient life in New World, and Indians today. Fine illustrations. [R. Wauchope]

18. **Pan American Union. Social Science Section.** Guía del campo de investigación social. 1. parte. Antropología social. 1.-2. fascículos. Washington, 1956. 2 v. 101, 103-185 p. (Manuales técnicos, 3-4).
The first two of four projected fascicules in which are translated sections of the 1951 (6th) edition of *Notes and queries on anthropology,* the famous and long-established guide for ethnographers put out by the Royal Anthropological Institute of Great Britain and Ireland. The Pan American Union has done a signal service in making this methodological guide available in Spanish; the effect can only be salutary. [D. B. Stout]

19. **Sebeok, Thomas Albert.** Myth: a symposium. Philadelphia, American Folklore Society (Bibliographical and special series, 5), 1955. 110 p., diagrs.
Nine papers by as many authors who are all specialists in the study of myths and their relationship to other aspects of culture. Though the symposium does not result in firm and comprehensive agreement among the authors, yet it should serve as a provocative source of new insights for the numerous students of myths in Latin America. [D. B. Stout]

20. **Shepard, Anna O.** Ceramics for the archaeologist. Washington, Carnegie Institution of Washington (Publ., 609), 1956. 414 p., 59 figs., 11 tables.
A superb handbook for all archaeologists who classify pottery. Good explanations of temper, firing, paints, slips, polish, etc., in clear, semitechnical language. Regardless of area the book is of value, but the examples are mostly from the American Southwest (Pueblo) and Maya. [C. Evans and B. J. Meggers]

21. **Sociedad Mexicana de Antropología.** Estudios antropológicos publicados en homenaje al doctor Manuel Gamio. México, Universidad Nacional Autónoma de México, Dirección General de Publicaciones, 1956. 713 p., illus.
See items 86, 103, 108, 124, 148, 203, 755, 771, 773, 784, 795.

22. **Spindler, George D.** (ed.). Education and anthropology. Pref. by Lawrence K. Frank. Stanford, Calif., Stanford University Press, 1955. 302 p., diagrs.

The results of a four-day conference among 22 anthropologists and educators on the general issue of the application of anthropology to education, with many implications for the numerous *Indianismo* and applied anthropology programs presently being carried on in Latin America. [D. B. Stout]

23. **Titiev, Mischa.** The importance of space in primitive kinship (Am Anthr, 58:5, Oct. 1956, p. 854-864).

Énfasis sobre las consideraciones especiales y de comportamiento, más que sobre las lineales, en un análisis general del parentesco primitivo, con referencias a América Latina [A. Palerm]

24. **United States. Department of State. Office of Intelligence Research.** Area study programs in American universities. Washington, 1956. 58 p.

Systematic tabulation, based on responses to questionnaires, of area programs presently maintained in various universities in the U. S. 28 institutions have some degree of orderly and comprehensive study of Latin American culture and society, and of these 14 have fully developed programs with adequate staff, library holdings, degree programs through the Ph. D., etc. [D. B. Stout]

25. **Universidad Nacional Mayor de San Marcos de Lima. Escuela de Altos Estudios.** Homenaje al IV Centenario de la Fundación de la Universidad. Conferencia de Ciencias Antropológicas. I. Actas y trabajos. Lima, 1955. 233 p., illus., tables.

See items 757, 758, 787, 788, 789, 790, 792, 793, 798.

26. **Whorf, Benjamin Lee.** Language, thought, and reality; selected writings. Edited and with an introd. by John B. Carroll. Foreword by Stuart Chase. Cambridge, Mass., Technology Press of Massachusetts Institute of Technology (Technology Press books in the social sciences), 1956. 278 p., illus., port.

Most of Whorf's writings, with an introductory essay and bibliography. Whorf's brilliant contribution to linguistics in North America is hereby made available, in a single book, for the students of language in Latin America; they will find it of enormous value. [D. B. Stout]

27. **Willey, Gordon R.** (ed.). Prehistoric settlements patterns in the New World. N. Y., Wenner-Gren Foundation for Anthropological Research (Viking Fund publications in anthropology, 23), 1956. 202 p., illus., maps.

See items 43, 54, 57, 69, 72, 82, 250, 319a, 356.

28. **Winnick, Charles.** Dictionary of anthropology. N. Y., Philosophical Library, 1956. 579 p.

Generally successful, and certainly the most comprehensive dictionary of its sort yet to appear. Includes terms for all branches of anthropology. [D. B. Stout]

ARCHAEOLOGY: MIDDLE AMERICA

ROBERT WAUCHOPE

FROM THE viewpoint of their long-range importance, three developments during the past year are outstanding; one is bad news, the others, good. A long and important chapter in the history of Middle American archaeology drew near its close when the Carnegie Institution of Washington completed its last season of field investigations, and its staff concentrated on finishing their final reports. The Institution's withdrawal from this field will be a severe setback to Americanist research, for with the exception of the Mexican government itself, no organization has devoted so large a staff and such substantial funds to Middle American archaeology. The importance of its program is reflected in its publications: since 1920 the Division of Historical Research, later the Department of Archaeology, issued over 60 volumes of Middle American studies, plus about eight volumes of "Notes" and "Current reports." *HLAS* salutes the Carnegie Institution of Washington, its research associates, and the men who planned and directed its Middle American programs: the late Sylvanus G. Morley; Alfred Vincent Kidder, who inaugurated the multi-disciplinary approach to Mesoamerican research; and Harry E. D. Pollock, who has directed the important Mayapan project.

Good news, on the other hand, is that the University of Pennsylvania, in cooperation with the government of Guatemala, has begun a long-term program of excavation, repair, and restoration at Tikal, certainly the most famous and probably the greatest

Mayan ruin. Linton Satterthwaite, Jr., is Chief Archaeologist, and Edwin M. Shook is Field Director. Also encouraging is the progress being made toward a *Handbook of Middle American Indians*, a greatly needed set of volumes comparable to the very useful South American *Handbook*. A subcommittee of the National Research Council is consulting the various interested organizations both here and in Middle America, and has drawn up an outline, operating plan, and budget.

As usual, several important contributions were read at meetings and have not yet been published. Among these meetings were the XXXII International Congress of Americanists, which met in 1956 in Copenhagen; the International Congress of Anthropological and Ethnological Sciences, 1956, at the University of Pennsylvania, Philadelphia, with one session devoted to Mexican archaeology; a symposium on Middle American anthropology, 1955, in Cambridge, Massachusetts; and a special session on Middle American archaeology at the annual meeting of the American Anthropological Association in Boston, 1955. In 1956 the Sociedad Mexicana de Antropología held a seven-day symposium on calendar systems.

Most of the following items are reported in greater detail in Tatiana Proskouria-koff's news sections in *American antiquity*, and in the news reports of the *Boletín del Centro de Investigaciones Antropológicas de México*, to both of which I am indebted.

The late George W. Brainerd, University of California at Los Angeles, excavated at Cerro Portesuelo in the Valley of Mexico, aided by a Wenner-Gren Foundation grant, and at Peñitas, Nayarit, the latter work directed after Brainerd's death by C. W. Meighan. The Museum of Southern Illinois continued its summer excavations at the Schroeder site in Durango, under the direction of J. Charles Kelley. Walter W. Taylor, of the CIAM, excavated caves in northern Mexico. George E. Fay, Southern State College, Arkansas, continued his survey of western to northern Mexico.

The Instituto Nacional de Antropología e Historia de México carried on its usual vast program of excavation, repair, and restoration at important sites in Jalisco, Colima, Nayarit, and Michoacan; at Tlapocoya, Mexico, and Huapalcalco and Tula, Hidalgo; Tlatelolco and Tlatilco, Teopanzolco, and, in the Mayan area, at Palenque, Sayil, Labna, Kabah, and Uxmal. For the INAH staff members involved, see previous volumes of the *HLAS*. Plans were said to be under study for greater future concentration on Teotihuacan. Investigations were carried on by the Centro de Investigaciones Antropológicas at Coatlan, Oaxaca; by Mexico City College at Yagul, Oaxaca; and by the Departmento de Antropología del Estado de Veracruz in the Chicontepec region. A joint INAH-CIAM excavation on the Island of Jaina was scheduled for 1957.

Philip Drucker and Robert Heizer completed field work at La Venta for the Smithsonian Institution, the National Geographic Society, and the University of California, Berkeley. Frans Blom investigated ruins at Bolonchan in Chiapas. Robert L. Rands held a Guggenheim fellowship to study the pottery of Palenque and environs. Gordon F. Ekholm continued work at Comalacalco, Tabasco, for the American Museum of Natural History. The New World Archaeological Foundation concentrated on pre-Classic sites on the Grijalva River.

E. Wyllys Andrews of the Middle American Research Institute, Tulane University, carried on reconnaissance on the east coast of Yucatan with Loren M. Hewen of New York, and then returned to make more intensive investigations at the site of Xcaret. In 1957, Andrews began excavations at a major site, Dzibilchaltun, near Merida. Peabody Museum of Harvard completed its excavations in the Belize Valley, British Honduras, under the direction of Gordon R. Willey; and A. H. Anderson, Archaeological Commissioner of British Honduras, excavated for the Wenner-Gren Foundation at Caracol.

A group of University of Oklahoma students, under Stephen F. Borhegyi, excavated at Finca Samayoa, Kaminaljuyu, and Las Charcas, assisting Gustavo Espinosa of the Instituto de Antropología e Historia de Guatemala. Henry Lehmann dug at Chicol, near Zacueleu, and at Mixco Viejo, Chimaltenango. Wolfgang Haberland returned to Hamburg from archaeological reconnaissance in El Salvador.

News from Europe is scarce. In France, more archaeological attention has been directed lately to the Antilles and South America, but scholars like Henri Lehman, R. d'Harcourt, and Paul Rivet carry on some field work and publication. In Germany, Franz Termer and Guenter Zimmermann at the Hamburgisches Muzeum für Völkerkunde und Vogeschichte, and the University, were active in teaching and research, Termer planning to return to Central America and Mexico in 1958. The Société des Américanistes in Switzerland and in Paris continued programs, and the latter's *Journal* appears regularly.

Samuel K. Lothrop was the third Alfred Vincent Kidder medalist, an honor awarded every three years by the American Anthropological Association. A. V. Kidder, in whose honor this medal was created, was awarded the Order of the Quetzal, in grade of Commander, by the President of Guatemala, and he also received an honorary degree from San Carlos University.

The years reported here took a heavy toll of able scholars: George Walton Brainerd (1909-1956) (erroneously reported as 1955 in our last volume); Earl H. Morris (1899-1956), the second Alfred Vincent Kidder medalist who excavated the Temple of the Warriors at Chichen Itza; and Miguel Covarrubias (1904-1957).

GENERAL

40. Amábilis Domínguez, Manuel. La arquitectura precolombina en México. México, Orión, 1956. 250 p., illus., maps.
Mystical approach to the subject, from an Atlantis theory of origins to a Vitruvian-like "ad quadratum" analysis of architectural proportions. Profusely illustrated with inferior halftones.

41. Anderson, A. H. Archaeology in British Honduras today (Pro XXX Intl Cong Am, p. 32-35).
Recommends seven sites for future investigation.

42. Borhegyi, Stephen F. de. The development of folk and complex cultures in the southern Maya area (Am Antiq, 21:4, Apr. 1956, p. 343-356).
Reviews the history of cultural development in Middle America, distinguishing between domestic or folk elements and more formal, complex, and urban aspects.

43. ————. Settlement patterns in the Guatemalan highlands: past and present (*in* Prehistoric settlement patterns in the New World [see item 27], p. 101-106).
Suggests that the factors determining modern settlement patterns in Guatemala originated in prehistory.

44. Castillo Torre, José. Por la señal de Hunab Ku. Reflejos de la vida de los antiguos mayas. México, Manuel Porrúa (Biblioteca mexicana, 15), 1955. 286 p.
A varied selection of topics, from the origin of man in America to the tonolamatl, Quetzalcoatl,

and even epochs like "the New Empire," are discussed rather superficially. This book must be intended to interest the beginner rather than the advanced student of the Maya.

45. Coe, Michael D. The funerary temple among the classic Maya (SW J Anthr, 12:4, winter 1956, p. 387-394).
If, as seems increasingly unlikely, Middle American pyramids were funerary monuments, the political power of individuals was much greater than once supposed, possibly comparable to that of the divine royalty of ancient Egypt.

46. ————. The Khmer settlement pattern: a possible analogy with that of the Maya (Am Antiq, 22:4, pt. 1, Apr. 1957, p. 409-410).
The Khmer city was a cult center supported by the produce and labor of the hinterland, in a tropical forest civilization which had, however, intensive agriculture.

47. Comas, Juan. Principales contribuciones indígenas precolombinas a la cultura universal (Am Indíg, 17:1, enero 1957, p. 39-85).
The inventory includes agricultural techniques and crops, metallurgy, paper, calendar systems and mathematical concepts, religious beliefs, literature, and philosophy. Full and useful bibliography.

48. Díaz-Bolio, José. La serpiente emplumada. Eje de culturas. Mérida, México, Registro de Cultura Yucateca, 1955. 211 p., illus.
Considers all aspects of the plumed-serpent myth and its symbolism, which the author thinks is of Mayan origin.

49. Dressler, Robert L. The pre-Columbian cultivated plants of Mexico (Bot Mus Leaflets, 16:6, Dec. 4, 1953, p. 115-172).

Material drawn from the literatures of botany, ethnology, and archaeology. The species are listed alphabetically, with concise comments and bibliographic references.

50. Fernández, Justino. Coatlicue: estética del arte indígena antiguo. Prólogo de Samuel Ramos. México, Centro de Estudios Filosóficos (Ediciones del IV centenario de la Universidad Nacional, 15), 1954. 285 p., illus.

Reviews past critics of native American art, and offers his own appraisal of Coatlicue sculpture.

51. Freund, Gisèle. Mexique précolombien. Texte de Paul Rivet; photographies de Gisèle Freund. Neuchâtel, Switzerland, Éditions Ides et Calendes (Coll. des Ides photographiques, 8), 1954. 19 p. & 80 pl.

Superb photographs of Mexican antiquities. Rivet's introduction is brief and outdated, clinging to the old tripartite Archaic-Toltec-Aztec outline of Mexican prehistory, with Teotihuacan assigned to the Toltecs. French, English, and German texts.

52. Harrington, Richard. The glory that was Maya (Can Geog J, 51:6, Dec. 1955, p. 230-235).

Popular article with 11 photographs of ruins in Yucatan.

53. Iturribarría, Jorge Fernando. El papel de Oaxaca en la cultura precortesiana (Hist Mex, 5:3, enero-marzo 1956, p. 411-428).

Believes the Mixtecs excelled in ceramics, goldwork, drawing and painting of codices.

54. Kelley, J. Charles. Settlement patterns in north-central Mexico (in Prehistoric settlement patterns in the New World [see item 27], p. 128-139).

Settlement patterns in Zacatecas, Durango, and Chihuahua.

55. Krickeberg, Walter. Altmexikanische Kulturen. Berlin, Safari Verlag, 1956. 616 p., illus.

The best general text on Mexican prehistory yet published, this handsome book with over 500 illustrations presents both historical and theoretical data. An English edition would be enthusiastically welcomed.

56. Lizardi Ramos, César. La música precortesiana (Cuad Am, año 15, 85:1, enero-feb. 1956, p. 193-203).

Illustrated article inspired by Martí's book on this subject.

57. Macneish, Richard S. Prehistoric settlement patterns on the northeastern periphery of Meso-America (in Prehistoric settlement patterns in the New World [see item 27], p. 140-147).

Recognizes seven classes of settlement pattern in Tamaulipas and adjacent parts of Veracruz and San Luis Potosi.

58. Martí, Samuel. Instrumentos musicales precortesianos. México, Instituto Nacional de Antropología e Historia, 1955. 227 p., diagrs., illus., map, music.

Learned or inferred from archaeological and early documentary sources.

59. Martínez P., Domingo. ¿Qué significa Ch'ich'en Itzam? (Hist Mex, 4:3, enero-marzo 1955, p. 393-397).

Proposes the meaning "I am the plumed serpent" from "ch'ich'en" (soy pájaro); "itzam" [Huastec] (serpiente). Argues that there are no pozos at the site, and if cenote were meant, they would have used "Dzonoot Itzam."

60. México. Instituto Nacional de Antropología e Historia. Guía oficial del Museo Nacional de Antropología e Historia. México, 1956. 133 p., illus.

Minimum of text and maximum of pictures, some of the latter in color. The material, after the pre-Classic, is divided by regions.

61. México. Instituto Nacional de Antropología e Historia. El Instituto Nacional de Antropología e Historia. México, 1956. 28 p.

General account of the Institute's program, with some fine photographic illustrations of artifacts and ruins.

62. Noguera, Manuel G. Mitología, cultura y medicina en el México precortesiano. Prólogo de José F. Rulfo. México, Imer, 1954. 109 p. & illus.

Archaeological backgrounds somewhat debatable, but the examples and specimens themselves are useful.

63. Outwater, J. Ogden, Jr. The pre-Columbian stonecutting techniques of the Mexican plateau (Am Antiq, 22:3, Jan. 1957, p. 258-264).

Attempt to estimate the man years required to build various monuments, in order to test hypothesis concerning techniques of construction.

64. Piña Chan, Román. Las culturas preclásicas de la cuenca de México. México, Fondo de Cultura Económica, 1955. 115 p., illus.

Useful synthesis of Formative period life in Mexico, inferred from architecture, figurines, and other artifacts. Many drawings and halftones.

65. Pollock, H. E. D. Annual report of the director of the Department of Archae-

ology (*in* Carnegie Institution of Washington. Year Book, no. 54, for the year 1954-1955, p. 265-300).
Contains general statements on the Institution's program in the Maya area, with fairly detailed preliminary reports on individual projects.

66. **Proskouriakoff, Tatiana.** The death of a civilization (Sci Am, 192:5, May 1955, p. 82-88).
Results of Carnegie Institution of Washington's excavations at Mayapan, Yucatan, and their bearing on Mayan cultural decay.

67. **Puig, Pilar.** Los mayas en su esplendor. Colección de 29 dibujos originales del viejo imperio maya. México, Fournier, 1955. 21 p. & 29 pl.
The text on archaeological background is outdated and the drawings are not outstanding.

68. **Rands, Robert L.** Comparative notes on the hand-eye and related motifs (Am Antiq, 22:3, Jan. 1957, p. 247-257).
Reviews the details and art styles of these motifs in the southeast U. S., Middle America, and the Northwest Coast, and considers the possible problems of diffusion, independent invention, or common ancestry involved. Illustrated.

69. **Sanders, William T.** The central Mexican symbiotic region: a study in prehistoric settlement patterns (*in* Prehistoric settlement patterns in the New World [see item 27], p. 115-127).
Outlines the basic ecological factors of importance to human settlement in central Mexico, from archaeological and early historic or protohistoric native sources.

70. **Schroeder, Albert H.** Ball courts and ball games of Middle America and Arizona (Archaeology, 8:3, autumn 1955, p. 156-161).
Ball courts of Middle America and southwest U. S. are compared and contrasted, with implications regarding culture contacts between these areas.

71. **Séjourné, Laurette.** Burning water. Thought and religion in ancient Mexico. London, Thames & Hudson, 1956. 192 p.
Following some excellent cultural and historical background sections, the author discusses Nahuatl religion and symbolic language, with one entire chapter devoted to the leading deities. The area that this book covers most thoughtfully makes it a unique contribution.

72. **Shook, Edwin M.,** and **Tatiana Proskouriakoff.** Settlement patterns in Meso-America and the sequence in the Guatemala highlands (*in* Prehistoric settlement patterns in the New World [see item 27], p. 93-100).
Earliest ceramic remains in Middle America are from town settlements rather than purely agri-

cultural village communities. Describes three successive settlement patterns in Guatemala.

73. **Smith, Watson.** George Walton Brainerd, 1909-1956 (Am Antiq, 22:2, Oct. 1956, p. 165-168).
The career and bibliography of a leading archaeologist.

74. **Soustelle, Jacques.** Comment vivaient les Aztèques (R Paris, 62. année, janv. 1955, p. 31-48).
Some outstanding characteristics of the Aztecs, inferred from native sources.

75. **Spinden, Herbert Joseph.** Maya art and civilization. Indian Hills, Colo., Falcon's Wing Press, 1957. xliii, 432 p., illus., maps.
The first part is an offset reproduction of Spinden's 1913 Peabody Museum of Harvard Memoir; the second is an almost verbatim edition of his 1928 American Museum of Natural History Handbook.

76. **Swan, Michael.** Temples of the Sun and Moon. A Mexican journey. London, Cape, 1954. 288 p., illus.
Travel book, with a very readable non-technical text and fine photographic reproductions.

77. **Szekely, Edmond Bordeaux.** La filosofía del México antiguo. Tecate, México, Ediciones de la Academia de Filosofía, 1954. V. 1, 174 p.; v. 2, 183-347 p.
The second volume is a sort of dictionary of certain glyphs, symbols, and motifs found in the codices, arranged in groups relative to the author's ideas of native symbolism.

78. **Thompson, J. Eric.** El área maya norte (Yan, 3, 1954, p. 3-35).
A Spanish revised edition of the useful 1945 article in *American antiquity.* Text brought up to date and many excellent and only recently available drawings and photographs added.

79. ————. The character of the Maya (Pro XXX Intl Cong Am, p. 36-40).
Mayan personality and character traits inferred from archaeological remains. Chief among them was orderliness.

80. ————. Notes on the use of cacao in Middle America (Notes Mid Am Archaeol Ethn, 128, Nov. 1956, p. 95-116).
Cacao as currency and tribute, its representations in archaeology, its ritualistic importance, medicinal properties, and its part in cultural development. Exhaustive bibliography.

81. **Westheim, Paul.** La escultura del México antiguo. México, Universidad Nacional Autónoma de México, 1956. 124 p., illus.
A 29-page introduction analyzes the cultural background of ancient Mexican art, stressing its symbolic rather than representational nature. Many fine photographic illustrations.

82. **Willey, Gordon R.** Problems concerning prehistoric settlement patterns in the Maya lowlands (*in* Prehistoric settlement patterns in the New World [see item 27], p. 107-114).
Reviews what little evidence is available on this highly important subject.

83. ————. The structure of ancient Maya society (Am Anthr, 58:5, Oct. 1956, p. 777-782).
Village assemblages excavated in British Honduras suggest a prehistoric network of theocratic stations and substations, all supported by a peasantry whose archaeological remains indicate they were reasonably prosperous and participated in a cultural tradition not markedly different from their more urban contemporaries. Willey believes the notion of a great schizm between these classes has been overemphasized.

84. ————; **William R. Bullard, Jr.**; and **John B. Glass** The Maya community of prehistoric times (Archaeology, 8:1, spring 1955, p. 18-25).
Discuss the nature of the prehistoric Maya community in the light of excavations in the Belize Valley, British Honduras.

85. **Wolf, Eric R.**, and **Ángel Palerm.** Irrigation in the old Acolhua domain, Mexico (SW J Anthr, 11:3, autumn 1955, p. 265-281).
Late prehistoric irrigation systems in a region here described as once a key area, later undergoing a cultural decline.

EXCAVATIONS, ARTIFACTS, ETC.

86. **Acosta, Jorge R.** El enigma de los chac mooles de Tula (*in* Estudios . . . Manuel Gamio [see item 21], p. 159-170).
Believes that the chac mooles were not always gods, messengers to the gods, or receptacles for cardiac sacrifice, but that their function varied according to the rite.

87. **Armillas, Pedro; Ángel Palerm;** and **Eric R. Wolf.** A small irrigation system in the valley of Teotihuacan (Am Antiq, 21:4, Apr. 1956, p. 396-399).
Large storage dam, small diversion dam, dam for canal intake, and an irrigation canal, possibly pre-Columbian. These discoveries are of utmost importance to questions of the role of irrigation in the rise of high civilizations.

88. **Aveleyra Arroyo de Anda, Luis.** Contemporaneidad del hombre con fauna extinguida en el Pleistoceno Superior de México (A Inst Nac Antr Hist, 7, no. 36 de la colección, 1955, p. 29-39).
Reviews history of early man discoveries in Mexico, from Peñon to Tepexpan and Iztapan.

89. ————. The second mammoth and associated artifacts at Santa Isabel Izta-

pan, Mexico (Am Antiq, 22:1, July 1956, p. 12-28).
Abridged English translation of the 1955 article (see *HLAS, no. 19*, item 99).

90. ————; **Manuel Maldonado-Koerdell;** and **Pablo Martínez del Río.** Cueva de la Candelaria. Con la colaboración de Ignacio Bernal y Federico Elizondo Saucedo. V. 1. México, Instituto Nacional de Antropología e Historia (Memorias, 5), 1956. 217 p.
Thorough study of the geography, geology, vegetation, and artifacts of a Coahuila cave.

91. **Barba de Piña Chan, Beatriz.** Tlapacoya, un sitio preclásico de transición (Acta Anthr, 2. época, 1:1, 1956, 205 p.).
Chronological position and foreign relations, especially with Monte Alban II and Miraflores phase at Kaminaljuyu. Sees at Tlapacoya the beginnings of Mesoamerican urbanism and of Teotihuacan cultural development.

92. **Barbour, George B.** A note on jadeite from Manzanal, Guatemala (Am Antiq, 22:4, pt. 1, Apr. 1957, p. 411-412).
Visit to a source of pale green-gray jadeite.

93. **Berlin, Heinrich.** Apuntes sobre vasijas de Flores, El Petén (Antr Hist Guat, 7:1, enero 1955, p. 15-17).
Brief description of pottery.

94. ————. Late pottery horizons of Tabasco, Mexico (Contrib Am Anthr Hist, 59, May 1956, p. 95-153).
Description of Classic (Jonuta horizon) and late post-Classic (Cintla horizon) ceramics. Sees a shift toward Mexican influence in the latter.

95. ————. News from the Maya world (Ethnos, 20:4, 1955, p. 201-209).
Notes on sites briefly visited in Campeche, with photographs and transcriptions of inscriptions on sculptured monuments and other objects.

96. ————. Selected pottery from Tabasco (Notes Mid Am Archaeol Ethn, 126, Dec. 1955, p. 83-87).
Specimens not published in previous reports of this author's Tabasco survey.

97. **Beyer, Hermann.** La "piedra del sacrificio gladiatorio" del Museo Nacional de Arqueología (Méx Antig, 8, dic. 1955, p. 87-94).
Reprint of a 1920 article in *Revista de Revistas*, with an additional illustration.

98. ————. La "procesión de los señores," decoración del primer teocalli de piedra en México-Tenochtitlán (Méx Antig, 8, dic. 1955, p. 1-42).
Posthumously published, this describes a long stone beach excavated in Mexico City, repre-

senting a procession of warriors. From a temple erected by Itzcoatl.

99. Borhegyi, Stephen F. de. Incensario de Purulha, Guatemala (Antr Hist Guat, 9:1, enero 1957, p. 3-7).
From a Baja Verapaz cave, this censer probably represents Quetzalcoatl and is of estimated post-Classic age.

100. ————. El incensario de "tres asas" de Kaminaljuyu, Guatemala (Antr Hist Guat, 8:2, junio 1956, p. 3-7).
Another censer type, from Miraflores phase of the highland Formative period.

101. ————. Un raro cascabel de barro del período primitivo pre-Clásico en Guatemala (Antr Hist Guat, 9:1, enero 1957, p. 9-11).
From Las Charcas, these two rattles are of the Las Charcas or Providencia period.

102. Carnegie Institution of Washington. Ancient Maya paintings of Bonampak, Mexico. Washington, 1955. 36 p., illus., plates, map. (Supplementary publication, 46).
Excellent non-technical description and interpretation of the Bonampak murals.

103. Caso, Alfonso. La cruz de Topiltepec, Tepozcolula, Oaxaca (*in* Estudios. . . . Manuel Gamio [see item 21], p. 171-182).
Interpretation of the sculptures and inscriptions, including a Morning Star scaffold sacrifice.

104. Castellanos, Daniel. Hallazgos arqueológicos en la región de Chimalhuacan (Yan, 3, 1954, p. 51-53).
Pottery and stone artifacts.

105. Chowning, Ann. A round temple and its shrine at Mayapan (Cur Rept, 34, Feb. 1956, p. 443-462).
Includes description and discussion of interesting sculpture and stucco figure. Plans, sections, and photographs.

106. ————, and **Donald E. Thompson.** A dwelling and shrine at Mayapan (Cur Rept, 33, Jan. 1956, p. 425-441).
Another current report of excavations at Mayapan.

107. Coe, William R., and **Michael D. Coe.** Excavations at Nohoch Ek, British Honduras (Am Antiq, 21:4, Apr. 1956, p. 370-382).
Formative through Late Classic sequence at a minor ceremonial site.

108. Cook de Leonard, Carmen. Dos atlatl de la época teotihuacana (*in* Estudios . . . Manuel Gamio [see item 21], p. 183-200).
Most unusually well-preserved wooden spearthrowers from a site south of Cuautla, Morelos. Also describes apparently associated pottery and other artifacts.

109. ————. Dos extraordinarias vasijas del Museo de Villa Hermosa, Tabasco (Yan, 3, 1954, p. 83-104).
Magnificently illustrated in color as well as black-and-white, this article describes two remarkable ceramic specimens, a Tepeaca urn and a Tabasco (possibly Jaina) vase, together with abundant comparative material and suggested interpretations.

110. ————. Una "maqueta" prehispánica (Méx Antig, 8, dic. 1955, p. 169-191).
Suggests that rock carvings at Santa Cruz Acalpixcan may have been architectural plans for construction of ceremonial structures. Data and speculations regarding methods of planning buildings in prehistoric times.

111. Corona Núñez, José. Diferentes tipos de tumbas prehispánicas en Nayarit (Yan, 3, 1954, p. 46-50).
Stone cists, bottle- and Chultun-shape tombs.

112. Delgado, Agustín. La arqueología de la Chinantla (Tlatoani, 2. época, 10, junio 1956, p. 29-33).
Map of sites, photographs of artifacts, and a preliminary account of tombs and other discoveries.

113. De Pierri, Kate P. The Aztec corn goddess of Belle Meade (Tenn Archaeol, 12:1, spring 1956, p. 1-4).
Aztec stone image, of tuff presumably from the Mexican Plateau, said to have been excavated at a depth of three feet in a yard near Nashville, Tenn. Speculations regarding its history.

114. Di Peso, Charles C. A tubular stone pipe from Sonora (Am Antiq, 22:3, Jan. 1957, p. 288-290).
Experiments suggest that these artifacts could have been pipes, cloud blowers, or trumpets.

115. Dutton, Bertha P. A brief discussion of Chichen Itza (Palacio, 63: 7-8, July-Aug. 1956, p. 202-232).
Useful short but thorough review of the architectural remains, illustrated with photographs and a map.

116. Easby, Elizabeth Kennedy, and **Dudley T. Easby, Jr.** Apuntes sobre la técnica de tallar jade en Mesoamérica (A Inst Arte Am, 6, 1953, p. 11-37).
Brief description of jades from Kaminaljuyu and other Maya sites, from Oaxaca, the Valley of Mexico, and La Venta.

117. Fay, George E. Another cruciform artifact from Sonora (Am Antiq, 21:4, Apr. 1956, p. 410-411).

Polished obsidian cross of a type found in northwest Mexico and southeast Arizona.

118. ————. Peralta complex, a Sonoran variant of the Cochise culture (Science, 124:3230, Nov. 23, 1956, p. 1029).
An early lithic artifact assemblage.

119. ————. A preliminary archaeological survey of the western coast of Mexico (Am Phil Soc Year Book, 1955, p. 318-321).
Survey of sites and surface collections from Guerrero, Colima, Nayarit, Michoacan, Jalisco, and Sinaloa.

120. ————. Prepottery lithic complex from Sonora, Mexico (Science, 121:3152, May 27, 1955, p. 777-778).
Suggests that this is a Sonoran variant of the Cochise culture.

121. **Forster, James R.** Notas sobre la arqueología de Tehuantepec (A Inst Nac Antr Hist, 7, no. 36 de la colección, 1955, p. 77-100).
Posthumously published ceramic sequence.

122. **Foshag, William F.**, and **Robert Leslie.** Jadeite from Manzanal, Guatemala (Am Antiq, 21:1, July 1955, p. 81-83).
Chemical analysis of jadeite from Guatemala, Mexico, and Burma, and description of a probable local source near Manzanal.

123. **Franco C., José Luis.** Un caracol grabado de la Huasteca (B Cent Inv Antr Méx, 1:1, sept. 1956, p. 13-14).
Trumpet probably from the Mixquititlan, Hidalgo, area, carved to represent sexual union.

124. ————. Malcates del complejo Tula-Mazapan (*in* Estudios . . . Manuel Gamio [see item 21], p. 201-212).
Classification of spindle whorls from the Tula archaeological zone, Hidalgo.

125. ————. Un notable ejemplar de arte individual en cerámica azteca (Yan, 3, 1954, p. 105-113).
In an art so subject to conventions, this vessel is a notably typical specimen from Tula, Hidalgo.

126. ————. Representaciones del espejo humeante en cerámica azteca tipo M (B Cent Inv Antr Méx, 1:2, nov. 1956, p. 5-10).
Tezcatlipoca symbolism and representation.

127. ————. Sobre un molde para vasijas con decoración en relieve (Méx Antig, 8, dic. 1955, p. 76-84).
Stylized animal head mold from Acatlan, Puebla.

128. ————, and **Frederick A. Peterson.** Motivos decorativos en la cerámica azteca. México, Museo Nacional de Antropología (Serie científica, 5), 1957. 48 p.
Copiously illustrated description, classification, and placement of decorative motifs, with a section on the serpent motif by Peterson.

129. **García Payón, José.** La ofrenda del altar de la gran pirámide, Zempoala, Ver. (Méx Antig, 8, dic. 1955, p. 57-65).
Late protohistoric pottery representing Quetzalcoatl, Xochipilli, etc.

130. **Grebe, Willi Herbert,** and **Wolfgang Haberland.** Vorgeschichtliche Menschenfährten in der Küstenebene El Salvadors, C. A. (Zeit Ethn, 81:1, 1956, p. 83-94).
Estimates the age of these footprints as between 0 and 800 A.D.

131. **Helbig, Karl.** Antiguales (Altertümer) der Paya-Region und die Paya-Indianer von Nordost-Honduras. Hamburg, 1956. 40 p. (Beiträge zur mittelamerikanischen Volkerkunde, 3).
The first part describes artifacts, petroglyphs, and other remains encountered during geographical reconnaissance.

132. **Hughes, Jack T.** Stone crosses with a Cuicuilco burial (Am Antiq, 22:1, July 1956, p. 80-82).
Cruciform artifacts associated with an intrusive burial, excavated in 1942.

133. **Kidder, A. V.** Miscellaneous archaeological specimens from Mesoamerica (Notes Mid Am Archaeol Ethn, 117, Mar. 1954, p. 5-26).
Useful record of artifacts not hitherto described in the Carnegie Institution's archaeological program.

134. **Lehmann, Henri.** Différentes formes de sacrifices humains practiqués à Chicol (Guatemala) d'après les fouilles effectués en 1954 (A XXXI Cong Intl Am, v. 2, p. 673-682).
Decapitations, multiple burials and seated burials in couples at a site near Zaculeu.

135. **Lister, Robert H.** Cliff dwellings of the northern Sierra Madre Occidental (Méx Antig, 8, dic. 1955, p. 141-156).
Interesting excavations in northern Mexico, suggesting that Mogollon culture, which later influenced Casas Grandes, may have come up from Chihuahua and Sonora, rather than from the north as generally believed.

136. ————. The present status of the archaeology of western Mexico: a distributional study. Boulder, Colo., University of Colorado Press (University of Colorado

studies; Series in anthropology, 5), 1955. 183 p., illus., maps, tables.
General archaeological picture and history of research, listing 46 sites in 11 zones.

137. **Lizardi Ramos, César.** El dios reclinado (Pro XXX Intl Cong Am, p. 1-4).
The chac mool identified as a tlaloc, or rain god.

138. —————. Estatuaria tenek huasteca (Anda Mios, 15, junio-julio 1956, p. 4-5, 8).
Drawings and description of sculptures from Tamuin.

139. —————. La lápida de la cámara interior (Pro XXX Intl Cong Am, 1955, p. 27-28).
Describes and interprets the scene and associated hieroglyphs carved on the sarcophagus of the Palenque subterranean tomb, and deciphers the ninth cycle date.

140. **Longyear, John M., III.** Further notes on Copan incense burners (Am Antiq, 22:3, Jan. 1957, p. 287-288).
Correction of some errors and further discussion of some debatable points of Copan pottery.

141. **Lorenzo, José L.** Los concheros de la costa de Chiapas (A Inst Nac Antr Hist, 7, no. 36 de la colección, 1955, p. 41-50).
Further investigations of shell heaps of presumed early date (see *HLAS, no. 14, 1948,* item 150).

142. **Medellín Zenil, Alfonso.** Desarrollo de la cultura prehispánica central veracruzana (A Inst Nac Antr Hist, 7, no. 36 de la colección, 1955, p. 101-110).
Brief notes on archaeological remains at eight sites or zones in Veracruz. Many illustrations, including the unusual Quiahuiztlan tombs.

143. —————. Exploraciones en la Isla de Sacrificios. Informe. Jalapa, México, Gobierno del Estado de Veracruz, Dirección General de Educación, Departmento de Antropología, 1955. 100 p., illus., map.
Brief description of the ceramic types, profusely illustrated with color plates and inferior halftones.

144. **Médioni, Gilbert.** L'art tarasque du Mexique occidental. Paris, Paul Hartmann, 1952. Illus.
Excellent photographs of the famous Tarascan effigies.

145. **Milliken, William L.** Two pre-Columbian sculptures (B Cleveland Mus Art, 42:4, Apr. 1955, p. 59-61).
Description of Olmec-style jades.

146. **Müller, E. F. Jacobs.** Una efigie

femenina de madera de Cualac, Guerrero (Méx Antig, 8, dic. 1955, p. 135-139).
Unusual discovery in a cave, somewhat in the tradition of the Pueblo katcinas.

147. **Nicholson, H. B.** The temalacatl of Tehuacan (Méx Antig, 8, dic. 1955, p. 95-134).
A careful study of the symbolism carved on a monument from Puebla, possibly a gladiatorial stone or a ball game ring.

148. **Noguera, Eduardo.** Un edificio preclásico en Cholula (*in* Estudios . . . Manuel Gamio [see item 21], p. 213-224).
A Late Formative structure and its associated pottery and figurines.

149. —————. Extraordinario hallazgo en Teotihuacán (Méx Antig, 8, dic. 1955, p. 43-56).
Remarkable slab tripod cylinder vase decorated with onyx discs embedded in the core clay prior to firing, a technique known heretofore only in Ecuador. Teotihuacan III period.

150. —————. Un nuevo tipo de figurillas humanas (Yan, 3, 1954, p. 36-45).
Identifies and discusses the provenience of a particular type of effigy vessel.

151. **Orellana Tapia, Rafael.** Nueva lápida olmecoide de Izapa, Chiapas, Estela 21 (Méx Antig, 8, dic. 1955, p. 157-168).
Decapitation scene and a personage carried in a litter; blood is represented symbolically, in a style somewhat similar to Toltec ball-player beheadings at Chichen Itza and at Aparacio, Veracruz.

152. —————. El vaso de Ixtapa, Chiapas (Yan, 3, 1954, p. 114-118).
A tomb offering, decorated in champlevé and representing an historical or religious scene.

153. **Pérez Elías, Antonio.** Las cuevas del valle de México (Tlatoani, 2. época, 10, junio 1956, p. 34-38).
Ethnohistorical significance of the caves in this vicinity as described in early sources.

154. **Peterson, Frederick A.** Anthropomorphic effigy vessels from Chupicuaro, Mexico (Ethnos, 21: 3-4, 1956, p. 161-179).
Classification, description, and general considerations.

155. —————. A probable identification of the Sola god (Ethnos, 21:1-2, 1956, p. 143-146).
God typical of the Sola region, Oaxaca, found on clay plaque in central Veracruz associated with Late Classic materials, is the same deity as the feathered serpent of later periods.

156. **Pollock, H. E. D** The southern terminus of the principal sacbe at Mayapan:

Group Z-50 (Cur Rept, 37, June 1956, p. 529-549).
A late road constructed southward from a group of domiciliary structures to a partly ceremonial group. Interesting inferences and speculations regarding its history and purpose. Well illustrated.

157. Porter, Muriel Noé. Excavations at Chupícuaro, Guanajuato, México (Trans Am Philos Soc, n. s., 46:5, Dec. 1956, p. 515-637).
Late Formative and Early Classic remains, their temporal and geographic distributions, and cultural relationships. 27 pages of photographic reproductions. An important record of a still little known archaeological zone.

158. Proskouriakoff, Tatiana, and Charles R. Temple. A residential quadrangle; structures R-85 to R-90 (Cur Rept, 29, Nov. 1955, p. 289-362).
Excavations in an assemblage of structures at Mayapan, Yucatan.

159. Ramírez, Félix C. Ireti Khatape. Ensayo de una interpretación de la Relación de Michoacán. Personajes y dioses michoacanos. México, Casa Ramírez, 1956. 114 p.
New translation and interpretation of certain passages.

160. Romano, Arturo. Nota preliminar sobre los restos humanos sub-fósiles de Santa María Astahuascan, D. F. (A Inst Nac Antr Hist, 7, no. 36 de la colección, 1955, p. 65-77).
One of the skeletons is compared to Tepexpan.

161. Ruz Lhuillier, Alberto. Exploraciones en Palenque (Pro XXX Intl Cong Am, p. 5-22).
Architecture, sculpture, painting, and ceramics, with interpretations.

162. Sáenz, César A. Exploraciones en la pirámide de la cruz foliada. México, Instituto Nacional de Antropología e Historia, Dirección de Monumentos Prehispánicos (Informes, 5), 1956. 45 p.
Preliminary description of pottery and other artifacts, including some heavily ornamented clay cylinders, encountered in tombs and architecture at Palenque. Illustrated, with an appendix on hieroglyphic inscriptions by César Lizardi Ramos.

163. Séjourné, Laurette. Xochipilli y Xochiquetzal en Teotihuacán (Yan, 3, 1954, p. 54-55).
Attributes of these deities depicted in clay figurines and on pottery vessels.

164. Shook, Edwin M. Another round temple at Mayapan (Cur Rept, 27, Sept. 1955, p. 267-280).

Associated artifacts indicate ceremonial importance of this structure. Excellent plan, section, elevation, and photographs.

165. ————. Dentate and dentate rocker stamping from Tabasco (Am Antiq, 22:3, Jan. 1957, p. 285-287).
These techniques, although rare in Middle America, appear sporadically from Mexico to Honduras during the Formative and Late Classic periods. A possible important time marker.

166. ————. An Olmec sculpture from Guatemala (Archaeology, 9:4, winter 1956, p. 261-262).
Fragment of an unusual jade sculpture in Olmec or La Venta style, from the Pacific coast of Guatemala.

167. Smith, A. L., and Karl Ruppert. Ceremonial or formal archway, Uxmal (Notes Mid Am Archaeol Ethn, 116, Mar. 1954, p. 1-3).
Hitherto unreported ruined archway south of the Governor's Palace.

168. ————. Excavations in house mounds at Mayapan: IV (Cur Rept, 36, June 1956, p. 471-528).
Small assemblages, dwellings, altar shrine, and property wall. Four pages or architectural drawings and seven of photographed excavations and artifacts, including a jointed "doll."

169. Smith, Robert E. Ceramic sequence at Uaxactum, Guatemala. New Orleans, La., Tulane University, Middle American Research Institute (Publ. 20), 1955. 2 v. 214, 170 p.
Final and definitive report on Proto-Classic Formative through Late Classic pottery from the famous Carnegie Institution excavations in the Peten. The second volume contains the illustrations.

170. ————. A correction on "preclassic metal"? (Am Antiq, 20: 4, Apr. 1955, p. 379-380).
Doubt now cast on the provenience of sheet copper previously reported to be from a pre-Classic tomb in Guatemala (see *HLAS, no. 19,* item 87).

171. ————. Early ceramic horizons at Mayapan and Santa Cruz (Cur Rept, 26, Sept. 1955, p. 253-266).
Formative, Classic, Puuc, and Toltec period types.

172. ————. Pottery specimens from Guatemala: I (Notes Mid Am Archaeol Ethn, 118, Mar. 1954, p. 27-37).
Well-illustrated record of specimens not described elsewhere in Carnegie Institution's program.

173. ————. Pottery specimens from

Guatemala: II (Notes Mid Am Archaeol Ethn, 124, Dec. 1955, p. 75-78).
Description of pottery from Ilon, Panajachel, and La Flojera.

174. ————. Pottery vessels from Campeche (Notes Mid Am Archaeol Ethn, 125, Dec. 1955, p. 79-82).
Late Classic vessels from a Campeche mound.

175. **Sociedad de Arquitectos Mexicanos, and Colegio Nacional de Arquitectos de México.** 4000 años de arquitectura mexicana. México, Libreros Mexicanos Unidos, 1956. 330 p., plates.
The first 63 pages (47 plates) are splendid photographs of prehistoric structures.

176. **Sorenson, John L.** Preclassic metal? (Am Antiq, 20:1, July 1954, p. 64).
Two occurrences of metal, at Cuicuilco and San Miguel Ixtahuacan, which Sorenson suggests may have been of pre-Classic age.

177. **Stromsvik, Gustav.** Exploration of the cave of Dzab-na, Tecoh, Yucatan (Cur Rept, 35, Feb. 1956, p. 463-470).
Complex of caverns contained a wooden statuette, mushroom stone, milling stones, and pottery.

178. **Thompson, Donald E.** An altar and platform at Mayapan (Cur Rept, 28, Oct. 1955, p. 281-288).
Excavations in a small compact ceremonial group.

179. **Thompson, J. Eric S.** Mayapán, ultima etapa de una civilización moribunda, la maya (A XXXI Cong Intl Am, v. 2, p. 667-672).
Evidences for grave decadence during last centuries of Maya prehistory.

180. **Whitaker, Thomas W.; Hugh C. Cutler; and Richard S. MacNeish.** Cucurbit materials from three caves near Tamaulipas (Am Antiq, 22:4, pt. 1, Apr. 1957, p. 352-358).
Oldest specimens yet recorded for several species found in a sequence of eight cultural stages.

181. **Willey, Gordon R., and William R. Bullard, Jr.** The Melhado site, a house mound group in British Honduras (Am Antiq, 22:1, July 1956, p. 29-44).
One of the very few thorough excavations of a small cluster of little mounds grouped around a pyramidal mound. Possibly a village or hamlet with local religious and political functions, occupied from Formative through Classic periods.

182. **Winning, Hasso von.** Offerings from a burial mound in coastal Nayarit, Mexico (Masterkey, 30:5, Sept.-Oct. 1956, p. 157-170).
Pottery, alabaster, and copper from a mound

northwest of Tepic. Illustrated and described, with comparative notes.

183. ————. A two-part effigy from the Valley of Mexico (Méx Antig, 8, dic. 1955, p. 66-75).
Description and comparative material.

184. **Winters, Howard D.** Excavation of a colonnaded hall at Mayapan (Cur Rept, 31, Dec. 1955, p. 380-396).
Shrine contained altar and human effigy censers. Data on costumes.

185. ————. Three serpent column temples and associated platforms at Mayapan (Cur Rept, 32, Dec. 1955, p. 397-423).
Defines the basic, although not uniform, type of architecture for Mayapan serpent columns.

186. ————. A vaulted temple at Mayapan (Cur Rept, 30, Dec. 1955, p. 363-380).
Contained murals.

187. **Winzerling, E. O.** Aspects of the Maya culture. N. Y., North River Press, 1956. 109 p.
Superficial sketches of ancient Maya.

188. **Yeomans, William.** The musical instruments of pre-Columbian Central America (Pro XXX Intl Cong Am, p. 54-57).
Inferred from codices, artifacts, and other archaeological remains.

NATIVE SOURCES, EARLY HISTORY, EPIGRAPHY

189. **Agranovsky, Anatoli.** An adventure in research: deciphering the ancient Mayan inscriptions (USSR, Sept. 1956, p. 7, 58-59).
A great deal of boasting about Yuri Knorozov's discovering "the key" to Mayan hieroglyphic writing, but no actual examples or other data are provided.

190. **Barlow, Robert H.** El Códice de Tetelcingo, Guerrero (Yan, 3, 1954, p. 65-68).
Posthumously published, this is revised and edited by Fernando Horcasitas. The tribute pages reproduced in facsimile.

191. ————. Las joyas de Martín Ocelotl (Yan, 3, 1954, p. 56-59).
The treasures of a rich Indian who fell into the hands of the Inquisition, as depicted and described in early sources.

192. **Barthel, Thomas S.** Die gegenwaertige situation in der Erforschung der Maya-Schrift (J Soc Am, n. s., 45, 1956, p. 219-227).
Reviews attempts to translate Mayan glyphs,

especially the phonetic schemes, and makes some broad suggestions regarding the general nature of the written language.

193. ————. Maya epigraphy: some remarks on the affix "al" (Pro XXX Intl Cong Am, p. 45-49).
Proposes the phonetic value of "al" for the element 19.

194. **Berlin, Heinrich.** News from the Maya world (Ethnos, 20:4, 1955, p. 201-209).
Notes on sites briefly visited in Tabasco and Chiapas, with photographs and transcriptions of sculptured inscriptions.

195. **Beyer, Hermann.** El color negro en el simbolismo de los antiguos mexicanos (B Cent Inv Antr Méx, 1:1, Sept. 1956, p. 15-16).
Reprint of article in *Revista de revistas*, July 10, 1921.

196. **Blom, Frans.** La lápida de Chiapas (Ateneo, Chiapas, 5, enero-abril 1954, p. 41-44).
Believes that the stela fragment of 9th cycle date is from a Mayan site on the Lacanja or Usumacinta.

197. The book of the people: Popol Vuh, the national book of the ancient Quiché Maya. This English version made by Delia Goetz and Sylvanus Griswold Morley from the translation into Spanish by Adrián Recinos; with a pronouncing dictionary compiled by Lucille Kaufman Weil and with illus. by Everett Gee Jackson. Los Angeles, Calif., Limited Editions Club, 1954. 251 p., illus., col. plates.
A deluxe edition of a 1950 book. See *HLAS, no. 16, 1950,* item 207.

198. **Borgonio Gaspar, Guadalupe.** Organización militar de los tenochca (R Mex Estud Antr, 14:1, 1954-1955, p. 381-383).
Undocumented brief notes.

199. **Burland, Cottie A.** The Selden Roll; an ancient Mexican picture manuscript in the Bodleian Library at Oxford. Berlin, Verlag Gebr. Mann (Monumenta americana, 2), 1955. 51 p., with a German translation of the text, 16 p.
Reproduction and interpretation of the surviving portion of the late pre-Conquest or early post-Conquest codice.

200. ————. The Toltec-style calendar of Mexico (Pro XXX Intl Cong Am, p. 23-26).
Turns to Xochicalco sculptured monuments for evidence of the origins and nature of later Aztec calendars, and discusses in particular the intercalations necessary when astronomical corrections were applied at 52-year intervals of 20-day periods.

201. **Caso, Alfonso.** Los barrios antiguos de Tenochtitlan y Tlatelolco (Mem Ac Mex Hist, 15:1, enero-marzo 1956, p. 7-62).
Extent and location of the ancient city *barrios*, based on careful analysis of early maps and other sources. Two large folding maps, in color.

202. ————. El calendario mixteco (Hist Mex, 5:4, abril-junio 1956, p. 481-497).
The outstanding authority on the Mixtec calendar summarizes his findings in one general article.

203. ————. La cruz de Topiltepec, Tepozcolula, Oaxaca (Estudios . . . Manuel Gamio [see item 21], p. 171-182).
A cross, made of three unrelated sculptured stones, one of them depicting a Morning Star sacrifice.

204. ————. Der Jahresanfang bei den Mixteken (Baessler Arch, 3, 1955, p. 47-53).
List of 105 dates from the Nuttall Codex, suggests that the Mixtecs named their year from its first day, in Mayan fashion.

205. Catálogo de obras escritas en lenguas indígenas de México o que traten de ellas. De la biblioteca particular de Salvador Ugarte. Prólogo de Daniel Kuri Breña. 2. ed. México, Offset Vilar, 1954, i. e. 1955. 307 p., facsms.
Over 400 items arranged alphabetically by authors, with a brief description of the contents.

206. Chilám Balám de Chumayel. Livre de . . . Traduit de l'espagnol et présenté par Benjamin Péret. Paris, Denoël, 1955. 230 p., illus.
In addition to line drawings from the original, there are several photographic halftones of Chichen Itza and Uxmal.

207. **Comas, Juan.** Y eut-il des nègres en Amérique avant Colomb? (B Soc Suisse Am, 7:11, mars 1956, p. 10-12).
After summarizing Weitzberg's hypothesis that a Moslem expedition reached America in the early 14th century, Comas gives six early references to black-skinned people in the Antilles, southern Mesoamerica, and northern South America.

208. **Cook de Leonard, Carmen,** and **Ernesto Lemoine V.** Materiales para la geografía histórica de la región Chalco-Amecameca (R Mex Estud Antr, 14:1, 1954-1955, p. 289-295).
Early native sources and documents and field investigations bearing on this area.

209. **Crespo M., Mario.** Títulos indígenas

de tierras (Antr Hist Guat, 8:2, junio 1956, p. 10-15).

Three relatively short Indian titles from the Guatemala highland; it is from documents like these, however, that we have considerable information on protohistoric native towns, rulers, and families.

210. Dahlgren de Jordan, Babro. La Mixteca: su cultura e historia prehispánicas. México, Imp. Universitaria (Cultura mexicana, 11), 1954. 400 p.

Reconstruction of "prehistoric" culture, but based largely on early historic accounts.

211. Dávalos Hurtado, E. La alimentación entre los mexicas (R Mex Estud Antr, 14:1, 1954-1955, p. 103-118).

Food that was available, and foods mentioned in the early chronicles.

212. Dibble, Charles E. Los chichimecas de Xólotl (R Mex Estud Antr, 14:1, 1954-1955, p. 285-288).

References in the native sources.

213. ———— (ed.). Códice Xolotl. México, Instituto de Historia (1. serie, 22), 1951. 166 p., map, facsms., diagrs.

Scholarly and will-illustrated edition of an important codex by an eminent authority in this area.

214. Digby, Adrian. The maize god and the crossed band glyph (Pro XXX Intl Cong Am, p. 41-44).

Equates crossed band glyph with skull pendant and associates both with the maize god.

215. Fernández, Miguel Ángel. Drawings of glyphs of structure XVIII, Palenque (Notes Mid Am Archaeol Ethn, 119, Aug. 1954, p. 39-44).

The late artist's record of Palenque inscriptions, with notes by Heinrich Berlin.

216. Fischer, Hans. Eine "Guidonische Hand" in einer Maya-Handschrift (Zeit Ethn, 81:2, 1956, p. 301-302).

Picture of hand with fingers denoting notes of the hexachord, a medieval aid to music students, evidently copied from some European book into the Chilam Balam of Kaua in the belief that it treated of palm-reading or some other occultism.

217. Franco C., José Luis. Snares and traps in Codex Madrid (Notes Mid Am Archaeol Ethn, 121, Dec. 1954, p. 53-58).

Snares, deadfall traps, pitfalls, and nets.

218. ————. Trampas en el códice Madrid y discusión de glifos relacionados (Méx Antig, 8, dic. 1955, p. 193-218).

First part of this article previously published in English in 1954. The second part assembles glyphs associated with depictions of snares.

219. Gibson, Charles. Llamamiento general, repartimiento, and the empire of Acolhuacan (HAHR, 36:1, Feb. 1956, p. 1-27).

Thorough search of early documents reveals interesting differences between the scope of the ancient Texcocan dominion of the Aztec Triple Alliance and the Spanish colonial repartimiento area, with inferences regarding peonage and other socio-cultural developments.

220. Gillmor, Frances. Estructuras en la zona de Texcoco durante el reino de Nezahualcoyotl según las fuentes históricas (R Mex Estud Antr, 14:1, 1954-1955, p. 363-371).

Early references to temples, palaces, and other structures in this zone, with especial reference to large public works, the Chapultepec aqueduct, and the Tepetzinco defense wall.

221. Hernández Rodríguez, Rosaura. El Valle de Toluca (R Mex Estud Antr, 14:1, 1954-1955, p. 281-283).

Brief statements of archaeological background and notices in the native sources.

222. Jiménez M., Wigberto. Síntesis de la historia precolonial del Valle de México (R Mex Estud Antr, 14:1, 1954-1955, p. 219-236).

Concise summary of Mexican prehistory, prepared for the VI Mesa Redonda, whose studies concentrated on the Valley of Mexico. Useful chart.

223. Kirchhoff, Paul. Calendarios tenochca, tlatelolca y otros (R Mex Estud Antr, 14:1, 1954-1955, p. 257-267).

Finds that the Tenochcas and Tlatelolcas used calendars that were distinct, although based on the same principles. They differed in the month that began the year and in the day count as well.

224. ————. Composición étnica y organización política de Chalco según las relaciones de Chimalpahin (R Mex Estud Antr, 14:1, 1954-1955, p. 297-298).

Considerable information reduced to a brief outline.

225. ————. Land tenure in ancient Mexico: a preliminary sketch (R Mex Estud Antr, 14:1, 1954-1955, p. 351-361).

Three basic types of land tenure and three social groups that owned and/or tilled the land are described. To understand ancient Mexican society, one must be aware of these social groupings and their relation to common or private property.

226. Knorozov, Y. V. La antigua escritura de los pueblos de América Central. México, Fondo de Cultura Popular (Biblioteca obrera, 5), 1954. 38 p.

Spanish translation of an article in a Soviet ethnographic journal (1952).

226a. ————. La escritura de los antiguos mayas. Traducción del ruso de Adolfo S. Vásquez. México, Instituto de Intercambio Cultural Mexicano-Ruso (Col. Ideas), 1956. 79 p.

Spanish translation of another attempt to read Mayan hieroglyphs by combining morphemic elements.

226b. ————. New data on the Maya written language (J Soc Am, n. s., 45, 1956, p. 209-217).

Maya spelling employed regular and irregular phonetics, ideographic writing, and mixed phonetic-ideographic. In incomplete or defective spelling, some glyphs (representing phonemes or morphemes) were omitted. Notes changes from the ancient Maya of the codices to the present Maya. Differences between language of the manuscripts and that inscribed on stone are thematic.

227. León Portilla, Miguel. La filosofía nahuatl. México, Instituto Indigenista Interamericano, 1956. 344 p.

Treating the several Nahuatl-speaking tribes as one culture, this book examines early sources, particularly the codices, for clues to cosmology, theology, metaphysics, and Nahuatl views of man and nature.

227a. ————. El problema del albedrío humano en el pensamiento nahuatl (Tlatoani, 2. época, 10, junio 1956, p. 41-44).

Intellectual, philosophic, metaphysical, and theological aspects of Nahuatl thought, values, and world view, derived from early sources.

228. Lima, Oswaldo Gonçalves de. El maguey y el pulque en los códices mexicanos. México, Fondo de Cultura Económica, 1956. 278 p., illus., facsms.

Exhaustive compendium of the depictions and other occurrences of these ceremonial traits in native documents.

229. Linné, S. Radiocarbon dates in Teotihuacan (Ethnos, 21:3-4, 1956, p. 180-193).

Plausibility and significance of various dates relative to local stratigraphy and the correlation of calendars.

230. Lizardi Ramos, César. ¿Conocían el xihuitl los teotihuacanos? (Méx Antig, 8, dic. 1955, p. 219-223).

Glyph in a mural of Tetitla, Teotihuacan, contains the number 14, suggesting that it may belong to the 365-day xihuitl rather than the 260-day tonalpohualli.

230a. ————. La lápida de la cámara interior del Templo de las Inscripciones, Palenque (Pro XXX Intl Cong Am, p. 27-28).

Description and interpretation of the scenes and inscriptions.

230b. ————. Sincronología azteca-europea (R Mex Estud Antr, 14:1, 1954-1955, p. 237-255).

Further discussion of the difficulties in correlating the various Aztec chronologies with the European calendar.

231. Martínez Marín, Carlos. La "migración acolhua" del siglo XIII (R Mex Estud Antr, 14:1, 1954-1955, p. 377-379).

Dating, linguistic, and ethnic problems posed by the arrival of Tepanec, Otomi, and Acolhua peoples in the Valley of Mexico.

232. Molíns Fábrega, N. El Códice Mendocino y la economía de Tenochtitlan (R Mex Estud Antr, 14:1, 1954-1955, p. 303-335).

Analysis of tribute records, for example the relation between raw cotton and woven goods, suggests that Tenochtitlan was more a commercial than an industrial center.

233. Noriega, Raúl. Claves matemático-astronómicas del sistema calendárico de los antiguos mexicanos y demostración de la función astronómica del calendario de 260 días (R Mex Estud Antr, 14:1, 1954-1955, p. 269-280).

Problems of relating cycles of terrestial rotation around the sun to "weeks" and other planetary periods.

233a. ————. Homogeneidad del sistema calendárico del México antiguo con el cómputo de ocurrencias de eclipses (B Cent Inv Antr Méx, 1:1, sept. 1956, p. 11-12).

Synchronizes the Mexican calendric system with recurrences of solar eclipses and lunations.

233b. ————. Registro de eclipses de sol en dos monumentos del México antiguo (B Cent Inv Antr Méx, 1:2, Nov. 1956, p. 1-4).

Defines the recurrence of eclipses in periods of religious significance and suggests that the Mexican calendar was synchronized with these. Large folding charts and figures.

233c. ————. 3 estudios sobre la Piedra del Sol. Los signos del Nahui Olín. Función astronómica del calendario de 260 días. La gran flecha de Tonatiuh. México, 1954. Various paginations & illus.

The Piedra del Sol inscriptions relate to planetary observations; the 260-day calendar has an astronomical function; the large arrow motif has an astronomical value denoted in its infix.

234. Nowotny, Karl Anton. Restauración de las partes destruidas en el Códice Vindobonensis (B Cent Inv Antr Méx, 1:1, sept. 1956, p. 1-9).

Importance of filling in the damaged portions of this important manuscript.

235. **Olderogge, D. A.** The Maya hieroglyphic writing and its deciphering (VOKS B, 6:95, Nov.-Dec. 1955, p. 21-25).
Brief and somewhat inaccurate review of the history of Mayan epigraphic research, with a defense and explanation of the Knorozov method of deciphering the glyphs, which, the author states, was made possible by a "knowledge of the basic laws governing the development of society," as "adhered to by Soviet scientists."

236. **Olivera Sedano, Alicia.** Cuitláhuac (R Mex Estud Antr, 14:1, 1954-1955, p. 299-302).
Concise outline of events, dates, and rulers, taken from native sources.

237. **Palerm, Ángel, and Eric R. Wolf.** El desarrollo del área clave del imperio texcocano (R Mex Estud Antr, 14:1, 1954-1955, p. 337-349).
Interesting suggestions regarding the economic and political relationships of the Chichimecs and preceding "Toltec" populations in Acolhuacan, and the subsequent transformation of this area from a marginal zone of secondary importance to a key region of the Texcoco empire.

238. **Péret, Benjamin.** Nos traços dos grandes Itzás (Anhembi, ano 5, 20:59, out. 1955, p. 226-242).
The author has translated the Chilam Balam of Chumayel from Spanish to French (see item 206). This book tells of that document and the ruins of Chichen Itza.

239. **Río López, Antonio.** La historia maya escrita por los mayas (Hist Mex, 4:3, enero-marzo 1955, p. 377-394).
Events in Mayan history and suggested dates, as outlined in the Books of Chilam Balam.

240. **Romero Quiroz, Javier.** El dios Tolotzin. Toponimia de Toluca. Toluca, México, 1956. 120 p., illus.
Suggests a related etymology for the terms Toluca, Toloa, Tolotzin and Coltzin (place names, plant name, and god's name).

241. **Sahagún, Bernardino de.** Florentine codex. General history of the things of New Spain. Book 12. The conquest of Mexico. Translated from the Aztec into English, with notes and illustrations, by Arthur J. O. Anderson [and] Charles E. Dibble. Part 13. Santa Fe, N. Mex., School of American Research and University of Utah (Monographs of the School of American Research, 14, part 13), 1955. 122 p. & illus.
Continuation of this excellent series of translation, with the drawings reproduced.

242. **Schulz, R. P. C.** Dos variantes nuevas del calendário chinanteco (Méx Antig, 8, dic. 1955, p. 233-246).
From the village of Zapote, near the Veracruz frontier.

242a. ————. Sobre la antigüedad de los monumentos del llamado "antiguo imperio de los mayas": una nueva sincronología de los calendarios maya y europeo (Méx Antig, 8, dic. 1955, p. 225-232).
Presents sun-eclipse combinations and favors a 677723 correlation formula.

243. **Sejourné, Laurette.** Identificación de una diosa zapoteca (A Inst Nac Antr Hist, 7, no. 36 de la colección, 1955, p. 111-118).
Representations of Nohuichana, goddess corresponding to the Mayan Ixchel and the Aztecan Tlazolteotl.

244. **Spence, Lewis.** Folklore of the Popol Vuh (Pro XXX Intl Cong Am, p. 50-53).
Old World analogies with the mythological events and religious ideas in this Quiche bible.

245. **Thompson, J. Eric S.** Chronological decipherments from Uaxactun, Naranjo, and Ixlu, Peten (Notes Mid Am Archaeol Ethn, 127, Nov. 1956, p. 89-94).
Re-reading of a difficult inscription helps close a gap in recorded Uaxactun dates. New decipherments of other monuments clarify their associated lunar readings or altar proximity.

245a. ————. Memoranda on some dates at Palenque, Chiapas (Notes Mid Am Archaeol Ethn, 120, Aug. 1954, p. 45-52).
Further attempts to piece together the badly scattered and fragmentary Palenque inscriptions.

246. **Uribe de Fernández de Córdoba, Susana.** Las ideas morales y el derecho penal entre algunos pueblos prehispánicos del Valle de México (A Mex Estud Antr, 14:1, 1954-1955, p. 373-376).
Very brief summary, undocumented.

247. **Vargas Castelazo, Manuel.** La patología y la medicina entre los mexica (R Mex Estud Antr, 14:1, 1954-1955, p. 119-143).
Gods of medicine, knowledge of anatomy and physiology, teaching and practice of medicine, external pathology and surgery, diseases of the sensory organs, obstetrics.

248. **Wauchope, Robert.** Las fechas de carbón radioactivo y la arqueología americana (Cien Soc, 6:33, junio 1955, p. 161-179).
Spanish edition of a 1954 article (see *HLAS, no. 19,* item 92).

249. **Zimmermann, Günther.** La lista de los meses quichés según Domingo de Basseta (Yan, 3, 1954, p. 60-61).

Photograph and transcription of information apparently erroneously used by Brasseur from the Quiche dictionary now in Paris.

249a. —————. Notas para la historia de

los manuscritos mayas (Yan, 3, 1954, p. 62-63).

Interesting notes on the discovery and early fortunes of some famous codices.

ARCHAEOLOGY: THE CARIBBEAN AREA

IRVING ROUSE

WITH THIS number, the section previously entitled "West Indies, Venezuela, and Brazil" assumes a new form. The West Indies and Venezuela are retained as the core of the section, but the Guianas and Brazil are dropped and their place is taken by Colombia and the southern part of Central America, viz. Panama, Costa Rica, and Nicaragua. As in the past, items on the Spanish occupation of Florida are also included. Thus, the section now covers all lands bordering on or immediately adjacent to the Caribbean Sea, except for the Guianas and Mesoamerica, i.e., Mexico and the northern part of Central America.

Geographically, of course, this is a more logical division than the previous one, and it also makes better sense archaeologically. It corresponds to the culture area which some authors have called "Circum-Caribbean" (see, e.g., *HLAS, no. 19*, item 250). Others authors have questioned the validity of this concept (see, e.g., the present volume, item 250), but the fact that all parts of the area border on the Caribbean Sea does make for a certain cultural unity. For example, everywhere except in the mountains of the Andes and of the Greater Antilles, the Indians have relied as much upon fishing and upon shell fishing as upon agriculture and as a result we find that the sites consist primarily of shoreline shell heaps (cf. item 264). This maritime orientation is an outstanding characteristic of the area and one which differentiates it from other parts of Tropical America, especially Amazonia and Mesoamerica.

The Caribbean Sea has also lent unity to the area by serving as a major route of migration and cultural transmission. Too much should not be made of this point, however, for in reality there are other, equally strong lines of diffusion which lead outside or cut across the area. For example, evidence is accumulating that elements of Mesoamerican culture spread southward through Central America and Colombia into Ecuador and possibly also into Peru, by-passing the major part of the Caribbean area (items 278 and 283). Conversely, the Antilles and Venezuela are affiliated linguistically with Amazonia and the Guianas rather than with western South America (item 266). As a result, many authors look at diffusion through the Caribbean area in terms of a conception, originally proposed by Cornelius Osgood, of the letter *H*, in which one upright extends from Mesoamerica to Peru, the other from the Antilles to Amazonia, and the cross bar is formed by the north coast of South America (see *HLAS, no. 18*, item 137; also this volume, item 270, in which the theory of the *H* is cited with approval).

Treating the Caribbean as a single unit has the further advantage of permitting more efficient handling of the subject of Spanish-Indian relationships. From the standpoint of the Spanish discovery and colonization of the New World, the Caribbean forms a single unit and so it is more convenient to discuss Spanish-Indian contacts in the area as a whole rather than to split them up, as was the case under the former arrangement of the section.

Field work in the area during 1956 has been marked by continuation of previous research programs. The Caribbean Anthropological Program of Yale University has resumed activity in the West Indies with excavations by two graduate students. Paul Hahn dug a series of non-ceramic (Ciboney) sites in Cuba with the aim of establishing a chronological sequence and working out the nature of contacts with the ceramic (Arawak) Indians. Marshall McKusick initiated research on Dominica and St. Lucia in which he is attempting to locate sites occupied by the Carib Indians and, by working back from history into prehistory, to determine at what time the Carib seized the Lesser Antilles from the preceding Arawakan occupants.

On Jamaica, C. S. Cotter is investigating Sevilla la Nueva, a Spanish town of *ca.* 1510-1540, for the Institute of Jamaica. On Puerto Rico, the new Instituto de Cultura Puertorriqueña, directed by Ricardo E. Alegría, is planning to acquire the well-known Taino site of Capa and to preserve it as an archaeological monument. Another new institution, the Palacio de Bellas Artes in Habana, has added to the permanent exhibits of the area by opening a hall of Antillean archaeology, in which material from the important Grupo Guamá collection is displayed (item 256).

In Venezuela, J. M. Cruxent has continued his excavation and partial restoration of Nueva Cadiz, the first Spanish town in South America (item 272). He has also expanded his archaelogical survey of Indian remains by excavating in the state of Tachira in the high Andes, at Cerro Machado near La Guaira on the coast, and at Punta Gorda on Cubagua Island, near Nueva Cadiz. His surface discoveries at El Jobo in the state of Falcon must rank as one of the most important archaeological finds of the year, since it is the first definitely Paleo-Indian type of material to be found in Tropical America (item 273). Cruxent and the writer are completing a monograph entitled "An archaeological chronology of Venezuela" which will report the results of the survey and which is to be published by the Pan American Union.

In Colombia, Gerardo Reichel-Dolmatoff and his associates have continued excavating on the Caribbean coast. Carlos Angulo Valdés dug several refuse heaps on the lower Magdalena River, most of them belonging to a protohistoric-to-historic time level. At Malambo, a deep site with multi-period occupation was excavated, the lower strata containing Momil-type pottery and suggesting Venezuelan similarities. Graciliano Arcila Vélez made a detailed survey of petroglyphs in the central and eastern portions of the Department of Antioquia.

Reichel-Dolmatoff's report on his previous season's excavations at Momil in the Sinu Valley has just been issued. It is perhaps the most significant publication of the year, in that it establishes a succession of occupations with suggestive resemblances towards Mesoamerica (item 283).

Central American continues to lag behind the rest of the Caribbean area. Charles R. McGimsey III, a Harvard graduate student, completed his excavations at the important preceramic site of Cerro Mongote in Panama, but no other research in this region is known to the writer.

Among the publications of the year, mention should be made of an article by Douglas Taylor and the writer (item 266) introducing the technique of glottochronology into the archaeology of the area. Using this technique, Taylor has calculated an age of 150 A. D. for the original migration of Arawakan speakers from Venezuela into the Antilles. The writer correlates this migration with Period II of his relative chronology and thereby reaches the conclusion that Period II may have extended back to the time of Christ, which is considerably earlier than previous estimates based upon rates of refuse accumulation.

Both Reichel-Dolmatoff in Colombia and Cruxent and the writer in Venezuela have independently arrived at the conclusion that there are two major types of agriculture in the area, a tropical one based primarily upon the cultivation of bitter manioc and a temperate type based instead upon the cultivation of maize (see item 283). Cruxent and the writer theorize, in the monograph already cited, that these two types spread along eastern and western lines of diffusion respectively, corresponding to the two uprights of the letter *H* discussed above. In Venezuela, at least, manioc agriculture seems to be associated with pottery of Amazonian style whereas maize agriculture is accompanied by pottery with Mesoamerican affinities. If these theories are correct, it would be more accurate to refer to cultural relationships within the area as "Trans-Caribbean" instead of "Circum-Caribbean."

GENERAL

250. Rouse, Irving. Settlement patterns in the Caribbean area (in Prehistoric settlement patterns in the New World [see item 27], p. 165-172).
Classifies the cultures of the Caribbean (excluding Central America) according to Steward's three levels of development, Marginal, Tropical Forest, and Circum-Caribbean, and discusses the settlement patterns of each. A strong relationship is indicated with such aspects of the environment as sheltered beaches.

WEST INDIES

251. Alegría, Ricardo E. La tradición cultural arcaica antillana (in Miscelánea de estudios dedicados a Fernando Ortiz. Habana, 1955. V. 1, p. 43-62, map).
Summary of archaeological and ethnological evidence concerning the non-ceramic, non-agricultural Indians of the Antilles. Alegría assigns all these Indians to a single, Archaic tradition and suggests that it is derived from Florida, although he points out weaknesses in this hypothesis.

252. Álvarez Conde, José. Arqueología indocubana. Habana, Junta Nacional de Arqueología y Etnología, 1956. 329 p., illus.
Detailed and well-illustrated summary of Cuban archaeology. Includes biographical sketches of the principal workers and maps showing the sites investigated. The author favors Pichardo Moya's terminology for the cultures of Cuba (see item 263) but describes the remains by type of artifact rather than by culture.

253. Boyrie Moya, Emilio, and J. M. Cruxent. Muestras arqueológicas de Juan Dolio, República Dominicana (B Mus Cien Nat, 1:2, abril-junio 1955, p. 11-33, illus.).
Report on the excavation of a Taino habitation site containing pottery of the Boca Chica style. The authors date it in Periods IIIb and IV, in accordance with Rouse's chronology (see HLAS, no. 18, 1952, item 131).

254. Granberry, Julian. The cultural position of the Bahamas in Caribbean archaeology (Am Antiq, 22:2, Oct. 1956, p. 128-134, illus.).
Summary of the literature concerning the archaeology of the Bahamas, and an interpretation of the collections. The author sees an earlier, Period III, occupation of the Bahamas, marked by the Meillac style of pottery, and a later, Period IV, intrusion of the Carrier style from Haiti into the southern Bahamas. The Meillac style apparently survived into Period IV in the northern islands. This corresponds to Rouse's

chronology for the Greater Antilles (see item 264).

255. Hartog, Johannes. Aruba: zoals het was, zoals het werd; van de tijd der Indianen tot op heden. Aruba, Netherlands Antilles, Gebroeders De Witt, 1953. 480 p., illus., maps, ports.
Chapter 1 (p. 1-25) summarizes what is known about the Indians of Aruba from archaeology, ethnology, and history. Illustrated with maps of tribal distributions and a plate of artifacts.

256. Herrera Fritot, René. Los complejos culturales indo-cubanos basados en la arqueología (R Inst Nac Cult, 1:2, marzo 1956, p. 16-21, 42-45, illus.).
Summary of the archaeology of Cuba, written on the occasion of the opening of the Hall of Antillean Archaeology in the new Palacio de Bellas Artes. The author employs the Cuban terminology of Complejos I-III and, unlike most other current writers, believes that Complejo I originated in Venezuela rather than Florida. Well illustrated.

257. Howard, Robert R. The archaeology of Jamaica: a preliminary survey (Am Antiq, 22:1, July 1956, p. 45-59, illus.).
Summary of the archaeology of Jamaica, including the author's field work there in 1947 and 1948. The author concludes that the island was first occupied during Period III by the Sub-Taino Indians and that these survived there during Period IV, as in central Cuba.

258. Jesse, C. A. A note on Bequia (Carib Q, 3:1, 1953, p. 35-54).
Discovery of rock-cut basins, corresponding to those known to have been made by the Carib in other parts of the Lesser Antilles. Father Jesse was unable to locate refuse middens, and therefore he suggests that the island may have been uninhabited by the Arawak, who preceded the Carib elsewhere.

259. ———. Outlines of St. Lucia's history. St. Lucia, British West Indies, 1953. 83 p.
Includes (p. 15-19) a brief account of the prehistory and historic contacts of the St. Lucia Indians.

260. ———, and Harold F. C. Simmons. St. Lucia in the Lesser Antilles: a field for exploration (Archaeology, 9:2, summer 1956, p. 122-125, illus.).
Summary of the history and archaeology of the Indians of St. Lucia. Illustrated with a map and photographs of sites.

261. Maximilien, Louis. Considérations sur le précolombien haïtien (Formes Coul, 12:1, 1954, p. 81-88, illus.).

Notes on the archaeology of Haiti, illustrated with pictures of outstanding specimens.

262. ————. Quisqueya (Formes Coul, 12:1, 1954, p. 27-36, illus.).
Discussion of the historic, Taino Indians of Haiti and of their artifacts.

263. **Pichardo Moya, Felipe.** Los aborígenes de las Antillas. México, 1956. 140 p.
Synthesis of the archaeology and ethnology of the Indians of the Antilles, prepared for the general reader. Lacks illustrations.

264. **Rouse, Irving.** Areas and periods of culture in the Greater Antilles (SW J Anthr, 7:3, autumn 1951, p. 248-265, 3 figs.).
Establishes three major areas and four major periods of culture in the Greater Antilles, and organizes the preceramic phases and ceramic styles within this framework. It is noted that the preceramic (Ciboney) Indians were oriented towards the land, whereas the ceramic (Arawak) Indians had a maritime orientation, which shifted towards the land during the Period IV Circum-Caribbean development.

265. **Swadesh, Morris** (and others). Time depths of American linguistic groupings (Am Anthr, 56:3, June 1954, p. 361-377).
Includes Douglas Taylor's original glottochronological date for the migration of the Arawak into the Antilles, based upon the present languages of the Island Carib, which the latter apparently adopted from their Arawakan predecessors when they conquered the Lesser Antilles.

266. **Taylor, Douglas,** and **Irving Rouse.** Linguistic and archeological time depth in the West Indies (Intl J Am Ling, 21:2, April 1955, p. 105-115).
In the first part of this article, Taylor revises glottochronological date for the migration of the Arawak into the Antilles (see item 265). In the second part, Rouse applies Taylor's date of 150 A.D. to the archaeology, equating it with Period II in his relative sequence (see item 264).

PANAMA

267. **McGimsey, C. R., III.** Cerro Mangote: a preceramic site in Panama (Am Antiq, 22:2, Oct. 1956, p. 151-161, illus.).
Preliminary report on the first preceramic excavation in Central America. Resemblances are noted in pebble choppers and grinders with the preceramic, Loiza site in Puerto Rico (see *HLAS, no. 19,* item 280).

VENEZUELA

268. **Acosta Saignes, Miguel.** El poblamiento primitivo de Venezuela (*in* Miscelánea de estudios dedicados a Fernando Ortiz. Habana, 1955. V. 1, p. 1-9).
Restatement of the author's theories of four successive occupations of Venezuela in general and of the Peninsula of Guajira in particular (see *HLAS, no. 16, 1950,* item 238, and *no. 19,* item 292).

269. **Cruxent, José María.** Casacoima, reliquia histórica (R F Arm, 6:98, agosto 1954, p. 45-69, illus.).
Account of two expeditions to the Orinoco Delta, Venezuela, to study one of Bolívar's battlegrounds in the wars of independence. Includes (p. 55-56) a brief description of excavations in what is believed to have been the Libertador's headquarters; also, a photograph of petroglyphs.

270. ————. Descripción de una colección arqueológica del municipio Dabajuro, Edo. Falcón, Venezuela (Mem Soc Cien Nat La Salle, 15:41, mayo-agosto 1955, p. 89-113, illus.).
Description of a large collection of pottery and other artifacts received in the Museo de Ciencias Naturales, Caracas. The material, which dates from Periods IV and V, is much more varied than that of the same style previously published by Osgood and Howard (see *HLAS, no. 9, 1943,* item 448).

271. ————. Descripción de una colección de muestras de alfarería arqueológica del Caño del Oso, Hato de Calzada, Edo. Barinas, Venezuela (B Mus Cien Nat, 1:1, enero-marzo 1955, p. 89-110, illus.).
The first detailed account of excavations in the *calzadas* or earthworks of the western Llanos. The author dates his collection in Periods IV and V on the basis of similarities in its pottery with the Dabajuro style on the west coast of Venezuela, among others (see preceding item).

272. ————. Nueva Cádiz: testimonio de piedra (El Farol, 17:160, oct. 1955, p. 2-5, illus.).
Preliminary account of excavations at the first Spanish town in South America, inhabited during the first half of the 16th century.

273. ————, and **Irving Rouse.** A lithic industry of Paleo-Indian type in Venezuela (Am Antiq, 22:2, Oct. 1956, p. 172-178, illus.).
Preliminary report on the discovery of the El Jobo complex, characterized by leaf-shaped projectile points. Includes comments by Wormington, Davis, and Krieger, who suggest the possibility of relationships to the points found with the second mammoth of Santa Isabel Iztapan in the Valley of Mexico and with various late Paleo-Indian lanceolate-type projectile points on the U. S. plains.

274. **Rouse, Irving.** Archeological chronology of Venezuela (B Phila Anthr Soc, 9:2, 1956, p. 4-7).
Preliminary account of a five-period relative chronology for Venezuela which is being worked out by J. M. Cruxent and the author.

275. **Tavera-Acosta, B.** Los petroglifos de Venezuela. Caracas, Universidad Central de Venezuela, Instituto de Antropología e Historia, 1956. 103 p., 87 pl.

This is a posthumous publication, with an introduction by Miguel Acosta Saignes correcting the author's theory that Venezuelan petroglyphs are the result of migrations from the Old World. The body of the publication consists of a catalogue of the petroglyphs by area. Well illustrated.

COLOMBIA

276. **Angulo Valdés, Carlos.** Colecciones arqueológicas superficiales de Barranquilla y Soledad. Barranquilla, Colombia, Universidad del Atlántico, Instituto de Investigación Etnológica (Divulgaciones etnológicas, 3:5), 1954, p. 107-143, 6 pl.

Describes two ceramic complexes at the mouth of the Magdalena River. Their chronological position and relationships are not yet known.

277. **Arango Bueno, Teresa.** Precolombia. Introducción al estudio del indígena colombiano. Con 118 figuras en el texto y 51 figuras y mapas fuera de él. Revisado por el Instituto Colombiano de Antropología y por el Ministerio de Educación Nacional. Madrid, Sucesores de Rivadeneyra, 1954. 174 p., illus.

Textbook prepared for use in the Colombian schools. Describes the principal ethnological tribes and archaeological cultures.

278. **Cubillos, Julio César.** Tumaco (notas arqueológicas). Bogotá, Ministerio de Educación, Departamento de Extensión Cultural, 1955. 146 p., illus.

Description of material from six of ten sites excavated on the south Pacific coast of Colombia. The culture is closely related to that of Esmeraldas in Ecuador, and Cubillos also sees resemblances with Tres Zapotes and Teotihuacan in Mexico. He believes that the direction of movement was from north to south.

279. **Duque Gómez, Luis.** Colombia: monumentos históricos y arqueológicos. Libro 1. Monumentos y objectos arqueológicos. México, Instituto Panamericano de Geografía e Historia (Publ. 179; Comisión de Historia, 72; Monumentos históricos y arqueológicos, 10), 1955. 182 p. & illus.

Discusses laws for the protection of archaeological remains, the history of research on the remains, and some of the finds, particularly in central and southern Colombia.

280. **Escalante, Aquiles.** Los Mocaná: prehistoria y conquista del Departamento del Atlántico, Colombia. Barranquilla, Universidad del Atlántico, Instituto de Investigación Etnológica (Divulgaciones

etnológicas, 4:6), 1955. 150 p., 6 pl., 12 figs.

Utilizing both archaeological and historical sources, the author describes the culture of the Mocana tribe, which was situated just west of the mouth of the Magdalena river, and discusses that tribe's first contacts with Europeans.

281. **Ghisletti, Louis V.** Los mwiskas. Una gran civilización precolombina. Bogotá, Ministerio de Educación Nacional (Biblioteca de autores colombianos, 73, 74), 1954. T. 1, 525 p.; t. 2, 309 p.

Reconstruction of the culture and especially the language of the Chibcha and related tribes on the basis of their archaeology and the historical sources. The author follows Rivet in deriving the Chibchan linguistic stock from Malayo-Polynesian.

282. **Reichel-Dolmatoff, Gerardo,** and **Alicia Reichel-Dolmatoff.** Contribuciones a la arqueología del Bajo Magdalena (Plato, Zambrano, Tenerife). Barranquilla, Colombia, Universidad del Atlántico, Instituto de Investigación Etnológica (Divulgaciones etnológicas, 3:5), 1954, p. 145-162, 10 pl.

Continuation of the author's research program on the Caribbean coast of Colombia (see *HLAS, no. 17, 1951,* item 195, and *no. 19,* item 431). A new, protohistoric complex is described, and it is said to have some relationships with the Valencia pottery of Venezuela.

283. ————, and ————. Momil: excavaciones en el Sinu (R Colomb Antr, 5, 1956, p. 109-333, illus.).

Detailed report on a stratified site in the Caribbean lowlands of northwestern Colombia, the earlier occupation of which is thought to have been marked by cassava cultivation and the later occupation by maize agriculture. The authors see a strong relationship with Mesoamerica during both periods. A very important piece of work.

FLORIDA

284. **Aga-Oglu, Kamer.** Late Ming and Early Ch'ing. Porcelain fragments from archaeological sites in Florida (Fla Anthr, 8:4, Dec. 1955, p. 91-110, illus.).

Study of 27 fragments of Chinese porcelain from Florida Indian sites, to which is appended a general discussion of oriental porcelains in the New World. The author concludes that these materials were imported by the Spaniards from China by way of the Philippines and Mexico, and she predicts that additional Chinese and Japanese pottery will be found in Mexico, Peru, Chile, and U. S. (see following item).

285. **Smith, Hale G.** Archaeological significance of Oriental porcelain in Florida sites (Fla Anthr, 8:4, Dec. 1955, p. 111-116, map).

Brief description of three Florida Indian sites

in which Chinese porcelain has been found. This accompanies the article by Aga-Oglu (see preceding item) in which the Chinese porcelain is described.

286. ————. The European and the Indian. Gainesville, Fla., Florida Anthropological Society (Publ., 4), 1956. 150 p., illus., maps.

Summarizes our knowledge of the contacts between Europeans and Indians in Florida and Georgia between 1500 and 1800 A. D. Spanish and English influence is contrasted, and it is concluded that the former were less successful in acculturating the Indians than the latter. Contains good descriptions and maps of the historic sites in Florida.

ARCHAEOLOGY: SOUTH AMERICA
(EXCEPT COLOMBIA AND VENEZUELA)

CLIFFORD EVANS and BETTY J. MEGGERS

ALTHOUGH various publications are listed on the archaeology of Argentina, Chile, the Guianas, and Uruguay, none describe significant discoveries or new material that has not at least been mentioned previously in preliminary reports. It is, of course, useful to the scholar to have in detail the sequences of northwest Argentina established by Alberto Rex González, additional information on the El Molle culture of Chile by Francisco L. Cornely, and listings of the known petroglyphs of Chile by Jorge Iribarren Ch. and of the pictographs of British Guiana by H. J. Braunholtz.

In contrast to past years in Brazil, several major contributions indicate that an area heretofore lacking in archaeological research is gradually moving forward in this line. Peter Paul Hilbert's discussion of *Tripods in the Lower Amazon,* from sites near the mouth of the Trombetas and Jamunda rivers, is of great interest, for this is the first time that this Andean and Middle American trait has been reported from the Amazon. Fernando Altenfelder Silva and Oldemar Blasi, in an article appearing in the *Anais do XXXI Congresso Internacional de Americanistas,* discuss in detail their stratigraphic excavations in Parana, Brazil, an area heretofore unexplored from a scientific archaeological standpoint. Numerous articles appeared on the Brazilian shell middens (*sambaquis*), a problem that has deserved more scientific exploration than it has received in the past. It is interesting to note that the conclusions of the various investigations differ greatly. The articles by Emperaire and by Orssich and Orssich describe in detail their stratigraphic excavations in different *sambaquis,* and conclude that the middens appear to be the result of refuse accumulation from habitation, sometimes with burials scattered in the midden refuse. Paulo Duarte and José Loureiro Fernandes take the stand that the middens were built for burial places and interpret the ash as the result of large fires made for some elaborate ceremony. Luiz de Castro Faria emphasizes the need for more extensive research. Although comparative information on the formation of shell middens throughout the world is not discussed in detail in any of the articles, this lends support to the idea that the *sambaquis* were formed by the accumulation of refuse during habitation and occasionally used for burial. Perhaps Luiz de Castro Faria's conclusion that more research is necessary is the most timely statement on the problem.

Ecuador is represented by several significant archaeological publications, with Estrada's preliminary report of a new Coastal Formative culture (the Valdivia Period), which has a highly developed female pottery figurine complex, and his *Balsa and dugout navigation in Ecuador.* The latter article not only mentions the historical and ethnographic data on such navigation but tells of personal experience sailing the balsa raft by means of the center board off the Ecuadorian coast. The final report of Heyerdahl and Skjölsvold on *Archaeological evidence of pre-Spanish visits to the Galápagos Islands* appeared as a Memoir of the Society for American Archaeology. The report is excellently written and contains numerous good, clear illustrations. Without trying to prove a trans-Pacific movement beyond the Galapagos Islands, the authors describe their material and then compare it with aboriginal pottery from Ecuador and Peru to demonstrate conclusively that periodic fishing parties must have landed and camped on the Galapagos Islands from Coastal Tiahuanaco times through the Chimu and Inca Periods.

As in previous years, Peru and Bolivia lead the list in numbers of published articles and books on archaeology; however, many of these items unfortunately are a reworking of old data, stated in a slightly different way with a new title. Of major importance is the posthumous appearance of Julio C. Tello's notes and excavation data on the 1937 archaeological expedition to the Marañon with special emphasis on the Casma valley. This monograph, *Arqueología del valle de Casma*, appears as the first in a series of publications of the archives of Tello. It is of extreme significance to Peruvianists because for the first time the data of Tello's excavations and observations are collected in one volume with detailed illustrations and descriptions of the stone sculpture and pottery of the famous Cerro Sechin site.

A few other reports of special value to the scholar working in the archaeology of the Peru-Bolivia area should be singled out: *Curayacu—a Chavinoid site*, by Frederic Engel, describes magnificent Chavin materials from a site 52 kilometers south of Lima; Rowe's preliminary report of survey and excavations in the south coast and highlands is entitled *Archaeological explorations in southern Peru, 1954-1955;* and *Toward definition of the Nazca style*, by Alfred L. Kroeber, presents a revised version of Kroeber's Nazca pottery classification.

Although not dealing specifically with any country in this section of South American archaeology, two publications of extreme importance to archaeological analysis appeared in 1956. The first, *Ceramics for the archaeologist*, by Anna O. Shepard (see item 20), is an indispensable guide to the understanding of the mechanic of pottery-making and the techniques and criteria that can be used to analyze and describe the paste characteristics and the design elements of aboriginal pottery. Because it is based on her own experience, the illustrative material is mostly limited to the Maya of Guatemala and Yucatan and the Pueblo of southwestern U. S., but this in no way restricts the book to specialists in these areas. Many archaeologists in the past have described pottery features in terms either meaningless to the ceramic technician or without regard to an understanding of which ceramic traits have cultural significance. Study of certain chapters in this book, especially those dealing with temper and firing, should open new vistas and correct misconceptions.

The second general reference, *Prehistoric settlement patterns in the New World*, edited by Gordon R. Willey (see item 27), draws together in one volume the mass of archaeological data we now have available about the prehistoric settlement patterns in major American areas. The final essay in the volume is an appraisal of the other contributions by an ethnologist, Evon Z. Vogt. Of particular interest to those persons specializing in the archaeology of South America are the contributions by Alfred Kidder, II, on Peru and by Betty J. Meggers and Clifford Evans on the South American tropical forest.

GENERAL

300. **Fautereau, Éric de**. Études d'écologie humaine dans l'aire amazonienne (J Soc Am, n. s., 44, 1955, p. 99-130).
The author concludes, from an analysis of the amount of land needed to feed a person in the tropical forest of South America, that a semi-nomadic type of life is not required by the limitations of slash-and-burn agriculture. He shows that the area of impermanent settlement coincides with the distribution of the leaf cutting ant, *Atta s.*, and concludes that it is the invasion of these ants that requires the moving of villages to exploit new fields in uncontaminated areas.

301. **Lafon, Ciro René**. En torno a la integración de la cultura andina (Runa, 7, 1956, p. 113-120).
The traditional separation of Andean and Amazonian areas of South America should be abandoned in view of evidence of numerous highland influences, emanating from Ecuador and Colombia, which can be detected not only in isolated traits but also in larger complexes in the Amazon valley.

302. **Larrea, Carlos Manuel.** Homenaje a la memoria del sabio americanista profesor Max Uhle en el centenario de su nacimiento (B Inf Cient Nac, 8:75, marzo-abril 1956, 26 p.).
Data of interest to South Americanists. It emphasizes Uhle's work in Ecuador in light of the development of anthropological research of Uhle's day.

ARGENTINA

303. **Badano, Víctor M.** Caracteres del arte plástico indígena del Paraná inferior (A XXXI Cong Intl Am, v. 2, p. 777-800, illus.).
Descriptions and illustrations of aboriginal pottery art found on Rio Parana from its juncture with the Paraguay River to its mouth in the Rio de la Plata. Emphasis on bird modeling with roulette and stamped incision.

304. **González, Alberto Rex.** Contextos culturales y cronología relativa en el área central del N. O. argentino. (Nota preliminar) (A Arqueol Etnol, 11, 1950, i.e. 1955, p. 7-32, illus.).
Compares data and establishes sequences for northwest Argentina. Good interpretative and comparative article with good illustrative plates.

304a. —————. Contextos y secuencias culturales en el área central del N. O. argentino (A XXXI Cong Intl Am, v. 2, p. 699-725).
Identical text to article by similar title published in *Anales de arqueología y etnología* (see item above) but without plates.

304b. —————. La cultura condorhuasi del noroeste argentino. (Apuntes preliminares para su estudio) (Runa, 7, 1956, p. 37-85, illus.).
Brief description of the culture, followed by a detailed discussion of the problems of establishing cultural chronology in northwest Argentina.

305. **Márquez Miranda, Fernando.** Panorama general de la cultura diaguita (R Mus Inst Arqueol, 15, sept. 1953, p. 56-79, illus.).
Generalized summary discussion of Diaguita style, especially the material in provinces of Catamarca and La Rioja, Argentina.

306. **Menghin, Oswald.** Väinö Auer und die prähistorische Forschung in Fuego-patagonien (Acta Geog, 14:1, 1955, p. 7-14).
One of a series of articles written in honor of the Finnish geologist Auer's 60th birthday. Describes the dates he gave to glaciations in Patagonia which permit absolute dating of man's occupation in the area. In German.

307. **Rydén, Stig.** An Argentine-Egyptian archaeological parallel (Baessler Arch, 3, 1955, p. 137-141).
A peculiar object, composed of a rope with a loop at one end which terminates in a V-shaped wooden "hook," was used in northwestern Argentina, probably as a pack rope. A similar device also occurs archaeologically in Egypt. The author concludes that this similarity results from independent solution of the same problem rather than cultural connections between Egypt and Argentina.

308. **Schobinger, Juan.** El arte rupestre del territorio del Neuquén (Publ Mus Soc Arqueol La Serena B, 8, sept, 1956, p. 23-25, illus.).
Summary of results of investigation of 23 sites, 6 with petroglyphs, 14 with paintings, and 3 with both techniques. Designs are predominantly geometric. Several different time periods are believed to be represented.

309. **Serrano, Antonio.** La puntilla, una nueva cerámica de la región diaguita (A Arqueol Etnol, 11, 1950, i.e. 1955, p. 81-87, illus.).
At site of Puntilla near Belen, Catamarca, the author describes and illustrates a new type of painted (usually bicolor) pottery found with burials.

310. **Vignati, Milcíades Alejo.** Materiales para la arqueología de Patagonia (A Mus C Eva Perón, n. s., Antropología, 3, 1953, 38 p., illus.).
Well-illustrated dscription of polished axes, wooden handles, and shell containers of sites from Neuquen area.

BRAZIL

311. **Barata, Frederico.** Uma análise estilística da cerâmica de Santarém (Cultura, Rio, 3:5, dez. 1952, p. 185-205, illus.).
Discussion and illustration of five animal motifs found in Santarem pottery. They are snake, frog, owl, turtle, and jaguar.

312. **Duarte, Paulo.** Comentários à sessão de estudos de sambaquis (A XXXI Cong Intl Am, v. 2, p. 611-618).
Insists that in spite of Orssich's work showing that the middens are the result of refuse from habitation sites, he and others feel their work proves that the middens are burial grounds. Problems still need study.

313. **Emperaire, J.** Informations préliminaires sur les sambaquis du littoral de São Paulo (A XXXI Cong Intl Am, v. 2, p. 603-612).
Very brief descriptions of excavations.

313a. —————, and **A. Laming.** Les sambaquis de la côte méridionale du Brésil (J Soc Am, n. s., 45, 1956, p. 5-163, illus.).

Description of excavations conducted in several shell middens on the south coast of Brazil. The skeletal remains are discussed. Few artifacts are illustrated and their analysis is neither detailed nor complete. In the absence of Carbon 14 dates (samples are being tested), the problems of dating are summarized without clear-cut results.

314. Evans, Clifford. Filiações das culturas arqueológicas no Território do Amapá, Brasil (A XXXI Cong Intl Am, v. 2, p. 801-812, map).

Describes two earlier down river movements into the area, one late movement of Aruã from north along the coast. All aboriginal occupation of region is of short time span compared to Andean area. Cultures unrelated to islands of Marajo, Mexiana and Caviana except Aruã occupation.

315. Faria, Luiz de Castro. A formulação do problema dos sambaquis (A XXXI Cong Intl Am, 2, p. 569-577).

Reviews the history of shell midden investigation in Brazil and then outlines the need for careful scientific excavations, especially stratigraphic work.

316. Fernandes, José Loureiro. Os sepultamentos no sambaque de Matinhos (A XXXI Cong Intl Am, v. 2, p. 579-602, illus.).

Under direction of the Museu Paranaense, the shell midden of Matinhos, four kilometers north of entrance of Bay of Guaratuba, state of Parana, was excavated. Description of artifacts and skeletons. Insists that this and other shell middens were burial places where large fires were made for some ceremony.

317. Hilbert, Peter Paul. Tripods in the Lower Amazon (A XXXI Cong Intl Am, v. 2, p. 825-828).

Preliminary statement of archaeological excavations at sites between the lower Jamunda river and the Trombetas river. Black dirt the result of human occupation. Tetrapod and tripod vessels typical of this area; first definite occurrence of this Andean and Mesoamerican trait in Amazon.

318. Laming, A., and J. Emperaire. Découvertes de peintures rupestres sur les hauts plateaux du Paraná (J Soc Am, n. s., 45, 1956, p. 165-178, illus.).

Description of pictographs in the interior of the state of Parana, Brazil, consisting mainly of large animals and birds drawn with red or orange paint. The authors suggest that these paintings may have been left by the northernmost of the nomadic hunters that occupied the pampas in post-glacial times.

319. Meggers, Betty J. Filiações das culturas arqueológicas na ilha de Marajó (A XXXI Cong Intl Am, v. 2, p. 813-824, map).

Several simpler cultures precede the Marajoara occupation with its elaborate pottery and burial urns. Followed by Aruã from the north. Marajoara features suggest a movement down river from Colombia and/or Ecuador.

319a. ————, and Clifford Evans, Jr. The reconstruction of settlement pattern in the South American tropical forest (*in* Prehistoric settlement patterns in the New World [see item 27], p. 156-164, diagr.).

Settlement patterns as known from archaeological evidence in Brazil and British Guiana, with suggestions that the pattern is typical of the entire South American tropical forest environment. Of special significance if viewed in light of the entire volume.

320. Orssich, Adam, and Elfriede Stadler Orssich. Stratigraphic excavation in the sambaqui of Araujo II, Parana, Brazil (Am Antiq, 21:4, Apr. 1956, p. 357-369, illus.).

Excavation of a shell midden according to stratigraphic techniques by fully trained archaeologists. Description of results with excellent diagrams, profiles; fair plates of objects. Proof that middens are the result of habitation refuse with miscellaneous burials in the trash, and not constructed solely for ceremonial purposes or burial as believed by most Brazilians.

321. Pompeu Sobrinho, Th. Pré-história cearense. Ceará, Brazil, Instituto do Ceará (Col. Historia do Ceará, 3:1), 1955. 150 p.

Generalized discussion of the peopling of South America, based on reconstructions from physical anthropology and inferences about ethnic origins. Little use is made of strictly archaeological evidence. In the absence of detailed information about Ceara, little can be said specifically about the prehistory of that region. Instead, the author attempts to put Ceara in the larger American framework.

322. Silva, Fernando Altenfelder, and Oldemar Blasi. Escavações preliminares em estirão comprido (A XXXI Cong Intl Am, v. 2, p. 829-845, illus.).

At a site on the Ivai river, in Municipio de Prudentopolis, Parana, Brazil, the authors dug the site in levels. Materials described, pottery types set up. Excellent technique and interpretation.

CHILE

323. Bullock, Dillman S. Urnas funerarias prehistóricas de la región de Angol (B Mus Nac Hist Nat, 26:5, 1955, p. 73-157, illus.; also reprint issued as Publ. 4, Museo Dillman S. Bullock, Angol, Chile, mayo 1956, p. 73-157, illus.).

Detailed study of all the burial urns and related grave goods from Angol, Chile. Demonstrates that this trait came into Chile from Argentina and never penetrated further north in Chile than Bio-Bio.

324. **Cornely, Francisco L.** Alfarería de uso doméstico de los diaguitas chilenos (Publ Mus Soc Arqueol La Serena B, 8, sept. 1956, p. 1-6, illus.).
Description with line drawings of types of domestic pottery including several vessels with anthropomorphic features in low relief modeling.

324a. ————. Cultura diaguita chilena y cultura de El Molle. Santiago, Editorial del Pacífico, 1956. 223 p., illus.
Two separate works. The first is a revision and slightly longer version of an article of the same title (R Ch Hist Nat, 51-53, 1947-1949, p. 119-262); see HLAS, no. 18, 1952, item 181. The second is an expanded version of a publication of the same name appearing as a publication of the Museo Arqueológico de la Serena, 1953; see HLAS, no. 19, item 397.

324b. ————. The El Molle culture of Chile (Archaeology, 9:3, autumn 1956, p. 200-205, illus.).
Basically the same article, in English, printed originally in Spanish by the Museo Arqueológico de la Serena, Chile, 1953 (see HLAS, no. 19, item 397). Excellent illustrations.

325. **Gajardo-Tobar, Roberto, and Guillermo Rojas Carrasco.** Una clava cefalomorfa más (Publ Mus Soc Arqueol La Serena B, 8, sept. 1956, p. 7-9, illus.).
Descriptions of a stone object of unknown use, of a type now represented by 17 specimens from Chile and Argentina.

326. **Iribarren Ch., Jorge.** Investigaciones arqueológicas de Guanaqueros (Publ Mus Soc Arqueol La Serena B, 8, sept. 1956, p. 10-22, illus.).
Description of results of archaeological excavation in a cemetery site 40 kilometers south of La Serena. Objects of stone, bone, and shell were encountered.

326a. ————. Los petroglifos de las estancias Zorrilla y Las Peñas en el departamento de Ovalle y una teoría de vinculación cronológica (R U, Chile, 39:1, 1954, p. 193-197, illus.).
Trys to show that the petroglyphs were made by Inca. Evidence not too convincing.

327. **Mostny, Greta.** Culturas precolombinas de Chile. Santiago, Editorial del Pacífico, 1954. 125 p., illus.
A summary of the archaeology and ethnology of Chile before European contact. Written for the general public with line drawing illustrations. Arranged by such chapters as: geographical setting, agriculturists, diaguitas, inhabitants of central Chile, warriors, hunters, etc. References cited for majority of statements. For layman, not for the serious scholar.

327a. ————. El niño del Cerro "El Plomo" (A XXXI Cong Intl Am, v. 2, p. 847-863, illus.).
First good summary of history of the find, conditions upon discovery, and artifacts of the frozen child (Inca?) mummy from El Plomo in province of Santiago, Chile, found February 1954.

328. **Rydén, Stig.** Did the Indians in Chile know the use of sails in pre-Columbian times? (SW J Anthr, 12:2, summer 1956, p. 154-156, illus.).
In correction of statements made by Heyerdahl, who quoted an earlier reference of Uhle that the rafts of northern Chile used sails, Rydén indicates that the model on which the statement was based is actually a burial bundle of tortora mats and not a boat model.

ECUADOR

329. **Bushnell, Geoffrey H. S.** The stone carvings of Manabí, Ecuador (Pro XXX Intl Cong Am, p. 58-59).
Thinks the elaborate stone carvings of slabs and simple chairs are pre-Manteño Period, but chairs supported by figures are Manteño.

330. **Christensen, Ross T.** Una excavación, reciente, en la costa meridional del Ecuador (Cuad Hist Arqueol, año 5, 5:13-14, agosto 1955, p. 83-92, illus.).
Spanish translation of Christensen's "A recent excavation in southern coastal Ecuador" (B U Archaeol Soc, 5, Oct. 1954, p. 30-54 [see HLAS, no. 19, item 425]) with commentary and introduction by Olaf Holm and Francisco Huerta Rendón. Nothing of interest not already expressed in the English version; in fact Holm's and Huerta's comments are not always pertinent. Culture belongs to Evans, Meggers, and Estrada's Milagro Period.

331. **Cruxent, José M.** Noticia de una estación arqueológica de la hacienda Pucara en El Ángel, Ecuador (Antropológica, 1, sept. 1956, p. 33-39, illus.).
Brief notice of the archaeology of El Angel, Ecuador, where Jijón y Caamaño and Carlos Manuel Larrea had worked, and which was visited by Cruxent. Author sees relationships to Nariño culture in Colombia because of bottle-shaped tombs and the pottery, and possible connections with Bocono region of the state of Trujillo in the Andes of Venezuela.

332. **Cubillos, Julio César.** Tumaco, notas arqueológicas. Bogotá, Ministerio de Educación, 1955. 145 p., illus.
Archaeological excavations, in six sites in the southwest corner of Colombia adjoining the Ecuadorian border, in cultural material known in Ecuador as Esmeraldas, Atacamas, La Tolita. Tumaco and the above-mentioned sites all belong to the same cultural group. Report is well written in up-to-date archaeological style. Although Cubillos divides the material in two periods, he does not have any great time depth. He believes that Tumaco belongs to the same family as Upper Tres Zapotes in Mexico.

333. **Estrada, Emilio.** Balsa and dugout

navigation in Ecuador (Am Nept, 15:2, Apr. 1955, p. 142-149, illus.).
Excellent summary discussion of aboriginal navigation using the balsa and dugout and how this trait is still carried out today in Ecuador. Good diagrams. Estrada has actually sailed the balsa raft and proved how to steer and tack them by manipulations of the centerboards. In light of Heyerdahl's trips, the article is most significant.

333a. ————. Valdivia, un sitio arqueológico formativo en la costa de la provincia del Guayas, Ecuador. Guayaquil, Ecuador, Museo Arqueológico Víctor Emilio Estrada (Publ., 1), 1956. 11 p., illus.
Preliminary report of oldest culture in Ecuador related to Formative of Peru (Guañape Period) and Mesoamerica (especially Tlatilco). Pottery includes broad line incision, excision, appliqued ribs, pottery female figurines in great quantities. Extremely significant discovery.

334. Heyerdahl, Thor. Preliminary report on the discovery of archaeology in the Galapagos Islands (A XXXI Cong Intl Am, v. 2, p. 685-697).
Chimu period sherds from Peru and coastal Ecuadorian aboriginal pottery found on many sites on Galapagos. Recent experiments with centerboards of balsa rafts at Playas, Ecuador, show the possibility of sailing to these islands, now verified by archaeological remains.

334a. ————, and Arne Skjölsvold. Archaeological evidence of pre-Spanish visits to the Galápagos Islands (Am Antiq, 22:2, pt. 3, Oct. 1956, suppl. (Memoir, 12, Society for American Archaeology), 69 p., illus.).
Excellent account of archaeological investigations in 1953 of sites on four islands of the Galapagos. Sherds and artifacts described in usable, up-to-date manner. Comparative section indicates that, without any doubt, from Coastal Tiahuanaco through Chimu and Inca times, periodic fishing parties must have landed and camped on the Galapagos. Some contact from pre-Spanish cultures in Ecuador is also indicated. Of extreme importance to New World archaeology. Presented in an excellent manner within the limits of the data, and in no way tries to prove any other point, such as Pacific contacts, etc.

335. Nachtigall, Horst. Tumaco. Ein Fundort der Esmeraldas-Kultur in Kolumbien (Baessler Arch, 3, 1955, p. 97-121, illus.).
Description of archaeological remains from a site in Colombia that is related culturally to the well-known complex in the province of Esmeraldas, Ecuador, just to the south. This culture has intriguing Middle American affiliations. See report by Cubillos, item 332.

336. Pérez T., Aquiles R. Contribución al conocimiento de la prehistoria de los pueblos del norte del territorio de la república del Ecuador (Mus Hist, 8:24, agosto 1956, p. 27-65; 8:25, dic. 1956, p. 130-156).
Gives an archaeological background to study in Carchi and Imbabura provinces. Nothing new, just a reworking of writings of González Suárez and Jijón y Caamaño.

337. Vargas, José María. Ecuador: monumentos históricos y arqueológicos. México, Instituto Panamericano de Geografía e Historia (Comisión de Historia, 61; Monumentos históricos y arqueológicos, 9; Publ., no. 163), 1953. 144 p., maps, plates.
Only chapter 1 deals with archaeological monuments (p. 14-26), and in such generalized terms that it is of no use to the archaeologist and does not contribute anything not mentioned in Jijón y Caamaño's works or in the writings of González Suárez.

GUIANAS

338. Braunholtz, H. J. Rock paintings in British Guiana (A XXXI Cong Intl Am, v. 2, p. 635-647, illus.).
Summary of known rock paintings in British Guiana with brief descriptions.

339. Silva, Mauricio Paranhos da. Fouilles archéologiques en Guyane britannique (B Soc Suisse Am, 11, 1956, p. 14-16).
Summary of Meggers and Evans' preliminary report (Timehri, 34, 1955, p. 5-26) on British Guiana work. See HLAS, no. 19, item 289.

PERU AND BOLIVIA

340. Bellamy, H. S., and P. Allan. The calendar of Tiahuanaco. A disquisition on the time measuring system of the oldest civilization in the world. London, Faber & Faber, 1956. 440 p., illus., tables.
Although claimed to be different from the earlier book, Built before the Flood, it is the same unscientific data trying to point out that the Gateway to the Sun monument at Tiahuanaco is full of mathematical and astronomical data giving the monolith a date around 25,000 B.C. Fanciful and of no scientific value.

341. Canals Frau, Salvador. Sobre el período de la "agricultura incipiente" de la costa norte del Perú (Runa, 7, 1956, p. 121-128).
Rejects the interpretation that the inhabitants of the preceramic site of Huaca Prieta practiced rudimentary agriculture and attributes the presence of certain cultivated plants found in the site to trade with contemporary inland agricultural groups.

342. Chávez Ballón, Manuel. Una nueva cronología para la prehistoria peruana (R Mus Inst Arqueol, 15, sept. 1953, p. 119-125).

Restates the terminology of the archaeological sequences for Peru as recently defined by Bennett, Strong, Willey, etc.

343. Díez de Medina, Federico. Museos arqueológicos y colecciones culturales de La Paz. La Paz, Comité Organizador del III Congreso Indigenista Interamericano, 1954. 58 p., illus.

A discussion, with illustrations, of archaeological specimens in the various museums and private collections in La Paz, with special emphasis on the collection of the author.

344. Disselhoff, Hans Dietrich. Darstellung einer Kindertrage aus dem Nepeña-Tal (Ethnos, 18:1-2, 1953, p. 106-109, illus.).

Description of a pottery figurine lying in a cradle board, from Nepeña valley, Peru.

344a. ————. Gott muss Peruaner sein. Wiesbaden, Germany, F. A. Brockhaus, 1956. 253 p., illus.

Subtitled "Archaeological adventures between the Pacific and Lake Titicaca," this book recounts in a popular manner the problems and adventures surrounding visits to archaeological sites in various parts of Peru. Sites visited include chulpas in the vicinity of Lake Titicaca, Inca ruins at Machu Picchu and around Cuzco, Tiahuanaco and Inca pictographs at Toro Muerto in the Majes valley, and Batan Grande. Tombs were excavated at Cajamarca in the Lambayeque valley. Also included are information and observations on modern Peruvian Indian life.

344b. ————. Neue Fundplätze peruanische Felsbilder (Baessler Arch, 3, 1955, p. 55-73, illus.).

Description illustrated with many drawings and six photographs of pictographs from different parts of Peru.

345. Easby, Dudley T., Jr. Los vasos retratos de metal del Perú. ¿Cómo fueron elaborados? (R Mus Nac, 24, 1955, p. 137-153, illus.).

Very good discussion with clear diagrams of how metal cups or vases with faces on them were shaped by hammering and "stretching" the metal over wooden rods and forms. Diagrams printed in the wrong direction plus printing errors in the references make the article hard to follow at times.

346. Engel, Frédéric. Les amas de coquillages de la côte péruvienne (Ancón-Río Ica) (J Soc Am, n. s., 44, 1955, p. 39-47).

Generalized discussion of the importance of shell mounds in reconstructing prehistory in Peru. Shell mounds occur from preceramic to Inca in the Peruvian sequence.

346a. ————. Curayacu—a Chavinoid site (Archaeology, 9:2, summer 1956, p. 98-105, illus.).

Curayacu is a rocky peninsula 52 kilometers

south of Lima, Peru, with a site 300 x 400 meters and refuse averaging six meters deep. Top layers, Late Coastal with definite Inca influence; bottom layers, typical Chavin of the type from Ancon, Supe, highland valley of Chavin de Huantar and Cupisnique from north coast. Typical material includes rocker stamping, broad line incision, fanged cat motif, carved bone, etc. Peculiar (non-Peruvian) type of large pottery figurine from refuse. Of extreme importance but style of popular writing obscures the exact finds and their associations.

347. Espejo Núñez, Julio. Gotush. Nuevos descubrimientos en Chavín (Baessler Arch, 3, 1955, p. 123-136, illus.).

The author describes five carved stones in good Chavin style and various stratigraphic excavations revealing numerous walls and platforms, as well as some pottery, at the site of Gotush, six kilometers southwest of the famous site of Chavin de Huantar. Stresses the need for scientific excavation of area, now that the Chavin site has been covered by a landslide.

348. Fernández Baca, Jenaro. La cerámica inca-Cuzco y sus motivos de ornamentación (R Mus Inst Arqueol, 15, sept. 1953, p. 142-201).

Detailed description of the motifs of decoration of Inca pottery into geometric, botanical, zoomorphic, and anthropomorphic. Lack of illustrations makes the discussion hard to follow.

349. Flornoy, Bertrand. The world of the Inca. Translated by Winifred Bradford. N. Y., Vanguard Press, 1956. 212 p., illus.

Translation of L'aventure inca. Also published in London (Allen and Unwin, 1956) with title Inca adventure. In two parts: (1) Five chapters. Discusses the coming of the Spanish and the fall of the Inca empire. Done in first person with a fairly accurate use of Spanish chronicles, but often the romantic writing stretches the known facts slightly. Written in almost historical novel style. (2) Archaeological background, in 13 chapters. The poorest part of the book. The discussion reveals an amazing lack of knowledge of any literature written in English in last 20 years on scientific work done in Peru. This is verified by the bibliography. As a result the sequences are not up to date. To be used with extreme caution. Mainly repeats the ideas of Julio Tello and Rebeca Carrión Cachot about origin of Chavin in eastern South America, etc.

330. Garrido, José Eulogio. Descubrimiento de un muro decorado en la "Huaca de la Luna" (Moche) (Chimor, 4:1, nov. 1956, p. 25-31, illus.).

Description of new painted walls at famous Huaca de la Luna ruin in Moche valley, north coast of Peru, with colored plate illustrating the design.

350a. ————. Reconocimiento de carácter arqueológico en la hacienda Julcán (Chimor, 4:1, nov. 1956, p. 9-20).

On the hacienda Julcan, in the district of Salpo in the province of Otusco, there are six hills with ruins on them. Brief description of stone structures, but not enough information to give cultural affiliation.

350b. ————. La zona arqueológica de Trujillo (Chimor, 1:1, enero 1953, p. 3-21, illus.).
Summary article of the history of work in the region of Trujillo on the north coast of Peru.

351. Hernández, José Alfredo. Brujos y hechiceros del Perú antiguo (Fanal, 10: 42, 1955, p. 14-17, illus.).
Brief account of shamanism in prehistoric Peru, especially in the Inca period as described by the chroniclers.

352. Hollister, Victor F. Origin and significance of Chan Chan slags (Chimor, 3:1, dic. 1955, p. 37-39).
Analysis of slags found in furnace at Chimu ruin of Chan-Chan indicate that copper-silver ores were smelted in a primitive furnace lined with a mixed clay as a refractory. Smelting operations melted the clay and combined it with the impurities of the ores.

353. Horkheimer, Hans. 5 estilos fundamentales (Fanal, 10:42, 1955, p. 7-13, illus.).
Five major Peruvian cultures—Chavin, Nasca, Mochica-Chimu, Tiahuanaco, and Inca—are described briefly. Their evolutionary relationship to each other and to several different Peruvian cultures is shown on a chart.

354. Ibarra Grasso, Dick Edgar. Anciennes cultures du territoire bolivien (Avant Tiahuanaco) (Antiq Sur, 6, Feb. 1956, p. 501-510, illus.).
Expansion of ideas expressed in earlier article (A XXXI Cong Intl Am, v. 2, p. 561-568). Early stone culture called Viscachanense; second related to Ayampitin in Argentina; then a "Mesolithic" culture; then a fully developed agricultural culture called "cultura de los túmulos," with an Oceanic origin about 1000 B.C. This last culture has lots of small stone figures. The mixture of European terminology, lack of stratigraphic data, and fanciful interpretations make the article of limited scientific use.

354a. ————. Esquema de la arqueología boliviana (Zeit Ethn, 80:2, 1955, p. 192-199, illus.).
Summary of his past eight years of field work in non-Tiahuanacoid cultures. Wants to make clear that other cultures were of importance besides Tiahuanaco. Tiahuanaco culture never dominated over one third of the country. Inca unified the country politically but did not have time to impress its culture in Bolivia. Short but good summary of author's ideas on Bolivian archaeology.

354b. ————. Hallazgo de puntas paleolíticas en Bolivia (A XXXI Cong Intl Am, v. 2, p. 561-568, illus.).

Crudely chipped material from Viscachani, Bolivia, which Ibarra Grasso relates to Sandia types from U. S. and Ayampitin from Argentina. Use of Old World terminology confusing. Associated data and geological dating lacking.

354c. ————. Die letzte Eiszeit als notwendige Voraussetzung für die erste Besiedlung Amerikas (Zeit Ethn, 81:2, 1956, p. 258-269, maps).
Subtitle states that it is a new theory of the settlement of America. Actually nothing new is given. Ibarra Grasso, on the basis of a few chipped objects (see A XXXI Cong Intl Am, v. 2, p. 561-568), indicates Paleo-Indian was in Bolivia. Could be true, but his geological evidences and arguments are not revolutionary like the El Jobo finds of Cruxent in Venezuela.

354d. ————. A new mystery from Tiahuanacu (Antiq Sur, 1, May 1955, p. 64-66, illus.).
States that the designs of Tiahuanaco pottery and stone carving indicate that the Tiahuanacans wore pants, and this must have been derived from the Old World. Both his identifications and explanations are extremely tenuous.

354e. ————, and **Leonardo Branisa.** Nuevos estilos en la cerámica indígena de Bolivia (A XXXI Cong Intl Am, v. 2, p. 727-760).
A highly detailed description of a variety of pottery types of new cultures, of interest to a specialist but impossible to follow without illustrations.

354f. ————; **José de Mesa;** and **Teresa Gisbert.** Reconstrucción de Taypicala (Tiahuanaco) (Cuad Am, año 14, 79:1, enero-feb. 1955, p. 149-175, illus.).
Examination of the site of Tiahuanaco by an archaeologist and two architects resulted in the first general plan of the city. Two groups of pyramids and temples were distinguished, each with an avenue running through it. These avenues intersect at a right angle. Dwellings are presumed to have been of perishable construction. Architectural details of temples include square columns. The authors note that the Tiahuanaco center resembles Maya cities more closely than it does Inca ones.

355. Jiménez Borja, Arturo. La comida en el antiguo Perú (R Mus Nac, 22, 1953, p. 113-134).
Most of the article is of ethnological significance, but part of article illustrates Mochica pottery showing the role of food in feast scenes, modeled fruits, vegetables, etc. Of no importance to the archaeologist but of interest to an anthropological study of Peruvian Indians and their food habits, religion and food, superstitions, etc.

356. Kidder, Alfred, II. Settlement pattern —Peru (in Prehistoric settlement patterns in the New World [see item 27], p. 148-155).

Settlement pattern of the archaeological horizons of Peru. Article of most significance when viewed in comparative light with the whole volume.

357. King, M. Elizabeth. A preliminary study of a shaped textile from Peru. Washington, Textile Museum (Workshop notes, Paper, 13), 1956. 6 p., illus.
A textile woven to shape in the Textile Museum's collections is analyzed in detail, with excellent photographs of details of the garment (same specimen illustrated but not described by Bennett and Bird in *Andean culture history,* 1949, p. 284, fig. 56). Believed to be a cape-headdress of Inca-Spanish Colonial Period from south coast Peru, possibly Ica.

358. Kosok, Paul. Transport in Peru (Pro XXX Intl Cong Am, p. 65-71).
Classification, of aboriginal roads into five groups, which could be quite useful in descriptive work.

359. Kroeber, Alfred L. Toward definition of the Nazca style (U Calif Publ Am Archaeol Ethn, 43:4, p. 327-432, illus.).
Report divided into three parts: 1, explanation of errors and omissions in the first classification established in 1927; 2, revised classification of Nazca-style vessel shapes; 3, discussion of vessels illustrated. Both the line drawings and plates are excellent. For the scholar working in south coast Peru the report is invaluable, for it tries to explain in detail the good and bad of the old shape analysis and then proposes a new one. Will be most useful when compared with Strong's south coast stratigraphy and Kroeber and Collier's analysis of the Nazca collections at Chicago, both studies being in preparation.

360. Kutscher, Gerdt. Sacrifices et prières dans l'ancienne civilisation de Moche (Pérou du Nord) (A XXXI Cong Intl Am, v. 2, p. 763-776.).
From the scenes painted on Mochica pottery the author shows the role of prayer and of human sacrifice of victims obtained from war.

361. Lastres, Juan B. Dioses y templos incanos protectores de la salud (R Mus Inst Arqueol, 15, sept. 1953, p. 80-94, illus.).
Claims that most Inca medicine and curing was magical or appeal to the gods with offerings, prayer, etc.

362. Linné, Sigvald. Prehistoric Peruvian painting (Ethnos, 18:1-2, 1953, p. 110-123, illus.).
After a generalized discussion of Peruvian archaeological sequences, descriptions and photographs are given of painted textiles from Nazca, coastal Tiahuanaco sites, Pachacamac.

363. Lostaunau, Óscar. La zona arqueológica de Jequetepeque (Chimor, 3:1, dic. 1955, p. 4-9).
A generalized statement about the ruins and remains of irrigation works in north coast valley of Jequetepeque, Peru.

364. Lothrop, Samuel K. Peruvian pacchas and keros (Am Antiq, 21:3, Jan. 1956, p. 233-243, illus.).
Description of two types of wooden drinking cups of pre- and post-Conquest Peru, both with their counterparts in pottery, metal, or stone; paccha, a vessel with an outlet for drinking at the base; kero, a cup shaped like a tumbler. Useful, well-documented, and well-illustrated article.

365. Muelle, Jorge C. Del estilo Chavín (Baessler Arch, 3, 1955, p. 89-96).
Brief discussion of the chronological position of the Chavin style as it has been seen by various archaeologists.

366. Nogami, Toshiichi. On some ancient potteries of recent excavations in Peru, S. A. (Sci Pap Jap Antiq Art, 11, Oct. 1955, p. 1-7, illus.).
Compares the painted pottery of the pre-Tiahuanaco period of the Chillon valley as published by Stumer in *Archaeology* (6:1, spring 1953; 7:3, autumn 1954; 7:4, winter 1954) with Neolithic Japanese pottery. In Japanese, with short English summary. Of little scientific value in light of known time sequences in the two areas.

367. Pardo, Luis A. Informe sobre la apertura del fardo funerario de Paracas (R Mus Inst Arqueol, 15, sept. 1953, p. 202-208).
Describes the opening of an exhibit hall in Peru.

367a. ————. Los vestidos del inca y de la ccoya (R Mus Inst Arqueol, 15, sept. 1953, p. 3-55, illus.).
Discussion, with excellent drawings, of the dress of the Inca and his wives. Based upon the Chroniclers' accounts; the author expands and refines the discussions, on the basis of archaeological and historical data.

368. El problema de la conservación de las decoraciones murales prehistóricas (Chimor, 4:1, nov. 1956, p. 1-8).
Problem of preservation of painted walls, with a list of such walls known in Peruvian archaeology.

369. Reichlen, Henry. Le Pérou et la Bolivie (*in* Les sculpteurs célèbres. [Pierre Francastel, ed.] Paris, 1954, p. 122-125, illus.).
Illustration of one Chavin and two Tiahuanaco stone sculptures, with brief remarks on architectural achievements and sculpture of these periods. Pukara and Inca are also briefly commented on in the text.

370. Rossel Castro, Alberto. Figuras geométricas prehispánicas en Perú (Pro XXX Intl Cong Am, p. 60-64).

Classification of wide lines in desert areas of southern Peru. Says they are Nazca and mentions all the theories. No new ideas.

371. Rostworowski de Díez-Canseco, María. El apogeo del imperio (Fanal, 10:42, 1955, p. 18-23, illus.).
Brief account of major events during the reigns of Pachacutec and Tupac Yupanqui, and of the coronation of Waina Capac.

372. Rowe, John Howland. Archaeological explorations in southern Peru, 1954-1955. Preliminary report of the Fourth University of California Archaeological Expedition to Peru (Am Antiq, 22:2, pt. 1, Oct. 1956, p. 135-151, map, charts).
Two programs of field work—one out of Cuzco, one out of Ica on the coast. Rowe develops new sequences for south highlands and south coast, of extreme interest to the specialist. Good preliminary discussion of generalized finds. Main conclusion is that the Tiahuanaco horizon is not a homogeneous style all the way from central Bolivia to northern Peru, but a series of related styles. Evidence suggests Huari the capital, out of which a Tiahuanaco military conquest spread rather than from a center at Tiahuanaco or the Lake Titicaca basin.

373. Rydén, Stig. En arkeologisk forskningsresa i Bolivia 1951-52 (Årstryck 1953-1955, i.e. 1956, p. 43-60, illus.).
Article in Swedish on Rydén's archaeological survey and excavations in Bolivia in 1951-1952, especially in Muñecas where he dug over 100 stone-lined graves, from Late Tiahuanaco Period into Colonial Period.

373a. ————. A basketry technique from the Lake Titicaca region (Antiq Sur, 1, May 1955, p. 57-63, illus.).
Excellent descriptions and photographs of a basket purchased from an Aymara Indian on the Island of Taquiri, Lake Titicaca, which shows relationships to other illustrated materials of archaeological nature in Peru. A variation of coiled basketry and also of the wrapped twined basketry weaving technique.

373b. ————. The Erland Nordenskiöld archaeological collection from the Mizque valley, Bolivia (Etn Stud, 22, 1956, 143 p., illus.).
Nordenskiöld's excavations in Mizque valley in 1914 were never published in final form. Since no one to date has done work in the area, and scholars are publishing on the area and calling it "Mizque Tiahuanaco style," Rydén studied the collections and wrote this report. Lacking data on how the material was dug, etc., his analysis is based on style. Of extreme importance to South American archaeology. Well illustrated. No Classic Tiahuanaco pottery in this valley.

374. Shepherd, Dorothy G. An Inca poncho (B Cleveland Mus Art, 3, Mar. 1955, p. 48-50, illus.).
Description of a post-Spanish Inca poncho, with photograph.

375. Sivirichi, Atilio. Historia de la cultura peruana (R U, Cuzco, 42:104, 1. semestre 1953, p. 53-146).
More a philosophical discussion of the history of Peru viewed according to the anthropological concept of culture. Of interest to nonanthropologically trained persons. Archaeological summary does not utilize the up-to-date discoveries.

376. Soldi, Pablo L. Chavín en Ica. Ica, Perú, (privately printed), 1956. 8 p., illus.
Brief statement of a new classification of what is known in the conventional literature as Paracas Cavernas pottery. Establishes new types, "Juan Pablo" and "Ocucaje," based on style and painting technique. Nothing really fundamental added to an area where Strong's stratigraphy should shed some light on the problem. The new names merely confuse the issue.

377. Strömberg, Elisabeth. Textile fragments from a burial cave at Perez, Mizque valley (*appendix in* Rydén, Stig. The Erland Nordenskiöld archaeological collection from the Mizque valley, Bolivia [see item 373b], p. 139-143, illus.).
Detailed analysis of the textiles, with good photographs and measurements, thread counts, etc.

378. Szyszlo, Vitold de. La papa, la quínua y el maíz (Fanal, 10:42, 1955, p. 24-28, illus.).
Name (scientific for maize, Quechua for potato and quinoa) and description of varieties of the three major staple crops of Peru, with brief comments on their importance and their method of cultivation.

379. Tello, Julio C. Arqueología del valle de Casma. Culturas: Chavín, Santa o Huaylas Yunga y Sub-Chimú. Informe de los trabajos de la Expedición Arqueológica al Marañón de 1937. Lima, Universidad Mayor de San Marcos (Publ. antropológica del archivo Julio C. Tello, 1), 1956. 344 p., illus.
Posthumous appearance of Tello's notes and excavation data on the 1937 archaeological expedition to the Marañon, with special emphasis on the Casma valley. Of extreme importance to Peruvianists because the data of Tello for the first time are collected in one volume with illustrations of stone sculpture and pottery of Cerro Sechin given in great detail.

380. Ubbelohde-Doering, Heinrich. Bericht über meine dritte archäologische Expedition nach Peru (B Soc Suisse Am, 7, 1953, p. 9-11).
Investigations continued in Chicama and Jequetepeque valleys, north coast Peru, which had been begun in 1937, in search of further evidence of lithic culture belonging to early hunting groups. Also worked at Pacatnamu, Jequetepeque, where he thinks Gallinazo, Mochica, and Chavin cultures lived together, influencing each other.

381. **Valcárcel, Luis E.** La cultura antigua del Perú (Fanal, 10:42, 1955, p. 2-6, illus.).
General remarks about Peruvian culture and its investigation.

URUGUAY

382. **Acosta y Lara, Eduardo F.** Los chaná-timbues en la antigua Banda Oriental (A Mus Hist Nat, 2. serie, 6:5, 1955, p. 1-27, 12 pl.).
Excellent discussion of the historical evidence to show that a group called the Chana-Timbues lived in first part of 16th century along the Parana river and that they were the makers of

the modeled and incised-with-roulette pottery from the area. Excellent plates.

383. **Figueira, José Joaquin.** La pictografía del Cerro Pan de Azúcar en el departamento de Maldonado, Uruguay (A XXXI Cong Intl Am, v. 2, p. 627-633, illus.).
Description and history of exploration of pictographs of this one site.

383a. ————, and **Carlos A. de Freitas.** Pictografías en el territorio uruguayo (R Soc Ami Arqueol, 12, 1953, p. 189-213, 12 figs.).
Description and analysis of petroglyphs from various parts of Uruguay, with a review of the development of interest in their exploration.

ETHNOLOGY: MIDDLE AMERICA AND THE WEST INDIES

ANGEL PALERM AND SIDNEY W. MINTZ

AN INTRODUCTORY note covering the publications of 1952-1957 was prepared by the joint Contributing Editors. Because of its length, it was decided to omit it from the *Handbook*. It is expected to appear in an early issue of *Ciencias sociales,* published by the Pan American Union.

This year the Contributing Editors had the able assistance of Miss Susanne Albert, a student at Vassar College, in the preparation of this section.

GENERAL

400. **Adams, Richard N.** On the effective use of anthropology in public health programs (Hum Org, 13:4, winter 1955, p. 5-15).
Se examinan las ideas expuestas por George Foster en la misma revista (julio 1951), y se subraya la importancia de la aplicación de la antropología. Basado principalmente en trabajos del autor en Centroamérica. [A. Palerm]

401. **Arnoldo, Fr. M.** [i.e., **A. N. Broeders**]. Gekweekte en nuttige planten van de Nederlandse Antillen. Curaçao, (Uitgaven van de Natuurwetenschappelijke Werkgroep Nederlandse Antillen, 3), 1954. 149 p., illus.
Pages 10-141 contain a description of cultivated and useful plants in the Netherland Antilles, giving scientific, native, and Dutch names, and further references. This is no. 3 of the Publications of the Natural Science Study Group, Netherland Antilles. No. 4 will be by the same author, on the wild plants of Curaçao, Aruba, and Bonaire. [S. W. Mintz]

402. **Comas, Juan.** Influencia de la medicina azteca en la obra de Fr. Agustín Farfán (A XXXI Cong Intl Am, p. 27-40).
Síntesis preliminar. Se analizan las influencias

de la terapeútica indígena sobre la medicina europea. [A. Palerm]

403. **Gibson, Charles.** Llamamiento general, repartimiento, and the empire of Acolhuacan (HAHR, 36:1, Feb. 1956, p. 1-27).
Influencia de la estructura política prehispánica sobre la organización del repartimiento de trabajo en el centro del Virreinato de la Nueva España. [A. Palerm]

404. **Guerin, Daniel.** Un futur pour les Antilles? (Prés Afr, 6, fev.-mars 1956, p. 20-27).
The writer argues that certain cultural phenomena in the Caribbean—religious cults, patois—are forms of resistance to western culture. [S. W. Mintz]

405. **Hoetink, Drs. H.** Over de simadan (Chris, 1:9, Apr. 1956, p. 403-407).
The author discusses cooperative work groups with special reference to the Dutch Antilles, noting comparable groupings in Haiti and Curaçao, and speculating concerning African origins of the "simadan" or "Seoe" work groups in the Dutch Windward islands. [S. W. Mintz]

406. **Knorozov, J.** A brief summary of the studies of the ancient Maya hieroglyphic writing in the Soviet Union. Papers of the Soviet historians for the X International

Congress of Historical Science in Rome. Moscow, 1955. 53 p., illus. Sumario en inglés y ruso. [A. Palerm]

407. Le Page, R. B. The language problem of the British Caribbean (Carib, 8:7, Jan. 1955, p. 40-49). [S. W. Mintz]

408. Liscano, Juan. The feast of St. John (Américas, PAU, 8:5, May 1956, p. 14-19).
A discussion of this festival in Latin America, particularly where syncretic Afro-Catholic rituals have developed (e.g. Haiti). [S. W. Mintz]

409. Millon, René F. Trade, tree cultivation, and the development of private property in land Am Anthr, 57:4, Aug-1955, p. 698-712).
Basado en material mesoamericano, y particularmente en el cultivo del cacao, se estudia el desarrollo del comercio y de la propiedad privada del suelo. [A. Palerm]

410. Muller, Wim Statius. Enkele aantekeningen over de Antilliaanse dansmuziek (Chris, 1:11, Juni 1956, p. 500-505).
Some observations on Caribbean music dealing mainly with the merengue and waltz and their modifications. [S. W. Mintz]

411. Quigley, Carroll. Aboriginal fish poisons and the diffusion problem (Am Anthr, 58:3, June 1956, p. 508-525).
In debating the assumption that the New World is an independent area in terms of the use of fish poisons, the author discusses aboriginal fish poisons of the West Indies and their possible origins. [S. W. Mintz]

412. Rosenblat, Ángel. Un presunto africanismo: macandá, brujería (in Miscelánea de estudios dedicados a Fernando Ortiz. V. 2. Habana, 1956, p. 1291-1296).
The author attacks the claim that the term *macandá*, used in Puerto Rico and Colombia, is African in origin. [S. W. Mintz]

413. Taylor, Douglas. An additional note on the consonantal system of Island Carib (Word, 11:3, Dec. 1955, p. 420-423). [S. W. Mintz]

414. ————. A diachronic note on the consonantal system of Island Carib (Word, 11:2, Aug. 1955, p. 245-253). [S. W. Mintz]

415. ————. Island Carib. II. Word-classes, affixes, nouns, and verbs (Intl J Am Ling, 22:1, Jan. 1956, p. 1-44). [S. W. Mintz]

416. ————. Island Carib morphology. III. Locators and particles (Intl J Am Ling, 22:2, Apr. 1956, p. 138-150). [S. W. Mintz]

417. ————. Languages and ghost languages of the West Indies (Intl J Am Ling, 22:2, Apr. 1956, p. 180-183). [S. W. Mintz]

418. ————. Spanish huracán and its congeners (Intl J Am Ling, 22:4, Oct. 1956, p. 275-276). [S. W. Mintz]

419. Thompson, Roberto W. Duckanoo— a word and a thing (Carib, 9:10, May 1956, p. 218-219, 229).
A discussion of the etymology of the term "duckanoo" and of the diffusion of word and food in the Caribbean. [S. W. Mintz]

420. ————. The mushroom and the parasol (West Indische Gids, 36:2-4, May 1956, p. 162-164).
An attempt to establish an African origin for a riddle which occurs in both East and West Africa, and widely in the Antilles. [S. W. Mintz]

421. Trouillot, Henock. Les ouvriers de couleur a Saint-Domingue (R Soc Haïtienne Geog, 29:101, avril 1956, p. 33-60). [S. W. Mintz]

422. Wagenaar Hummelinck, P. Caribische beelden (West Indische Gids, 36:2-4, May 1956, p. 125-132).
Pictures accompanied by text taken in the Dutch Antilles and in Surinam. Include shots of petrographs and of grinding stones. [S. W. Mintz]

CUBA

423. Cabrera, Lydia (comp.). Refranes de negros viejos. Habana, Ediciones C. R. (Col. del Chicherekú), 1955. Unpaged.
A collection of Cuban proverbs, many of them with terms from African languages. [S. W. Mintz]

424. Fabelo, T. D. Lengua de Santeros, Guiné Góngorí. Habana, Adelante, 1956. 232 p.
A collection of words and definitions, religious terms, prayers, plant names, proverbs, etc., of the Afro-Cuban tradition. [S. W. Mintz]

425. Pereda Valdés, Ildefonso. Culinaria afroamericana (in Miscelánea de estudios dedicados a Fernando Ortiz. V. 2. Habana, 1956, p. 1205-1216).
Makes reference to Afro-Cuban cuisine. [S. W. Mintz]

426. Portuondo, José Antonio. Alcance a las "relaciones" (in Miscelánea de estudios dedicados a Fernando Ortiz. V. 2. Habana, 1956, p. 1237-1247).
The author claims that the now-disappearing dramatic poems (*relaciones*) of eastern Cuba are partly Bantu in origin. [S. W. Mintz]

427. **Rojas, María Teresa de.** Algunos datos sobre los negros esclavos y horros en la Habana del siglo XVI (*in* Miscelánea de estudios dedicados a Fernando Ortiz. V. 2. Habana, 1956, p. 1275-1287).
Contains some cultural data, as well as information on African origins of slaves. [S. W. Mintz]

DOMINICA

428. **Banks, E. P.** A Carib village in Dominica (Soc Ec Stud, 5:1, Mar. 1956, p. 74-86).
A brief ethnographic and sociological sketch of the Carib village of Bataka in Dominica. [S. W. Mintz]

429. **Hodge, Walter H.** Flora of Dominica, B. W. I. Pt. 1 [consisting of three parts] (Lloydia, 17:1, Mar. 1954, p. 1-96; 17:2, June 1954, p. 97-192; 17:3, Sept. 1954, p. 193-238).
Includes very brief notes on Carib agriculture (p. 13-14) in Dominica, and occasional notes on uses of wild plant varieties as foods and medicinals. [S. W. Mintz]

430. **Taylor, Douglas.** Names on Dominica (West Indische Gids, 36:2-4, May 1956, p. 121-124). [S. W. Mintz]

431. ————. Phonic interference in Dominican Creole (Word, 11:1, Apr. 1955, p. 45-52). [S. W. Mintz]

HAITI

432. **Aristide, Achille.** El problema del indio y sus supervivencias en Haití (Am Indíg, 16:3, junio 1956, p. 213-219).
The author feels that there are significant American Indian cultural survivals among the Haitian people today. However, he offers little evidence that is not already familiar. [S. W. Mintz]

433. ————. Los problemas demográficos de Haití (Am Indíg, 16:1, enero 1956, p. 35-39). [S. W. Mintz]

434. ————. Quelques aspects du problème de la population en Haïti. Communication présentée à la première conférence de l'hémisphère occidental sur les problêmes de la population et de la planification de la famille tenue à San Juan, Porto-Rico du 12 au 15 mai 1955. Port-au-Prince, 1955. 61 p.
Demography from the period of colonization to the present. [S. W. Mintz]

435. **Aubourg, Michel.** La divination dans le vodou (B Bur Ethn, série 2, 12, 1955, p. 36-46). [S. W. Mintz]

436. **Bourguignon, Erika.** Rorschachs of 75 Haitian children and 42 adults (Prim Rec Cult Pers, 1:26, 1956, microcard). [S. W. Mintz]

437. ————, and **Emily W. Nett.** Rorschach populars in a sample of Haitian protocols (J Proj Tech, 19:2, June 1955, p. 117-124).
An effort to interpret in preliminary fashion the significance of "popular" responses to Rorschach cards among a group of Haitian subjects. Hallowell has suggested that there may be varying degrees of universality in such responses—some almost unique to certain cultures, some common in several cultures, and others perhaps common in all cultural groups. This paper is inconclusive but suggests some special cultural emphases may be revealed in the Haitian protocols. [S. W. Mintz]

438. **Comhaire, Jean L.** El campesino haitiano y su gobierno (Cien Soc, 7:38, junio 1956, p. 96-100). [S. W. Mintz]

439. ————. The Haitian schism: 1804-1860 (Anthr Q, n. s., 4, 29:1, Jan. 1956, p. 1-10). [S. W. Mintz]

440. **Comhaire-Sylvain, Suzanne,** and **Jean Comhaire-Sylvain.** Survivances africaines dans le vocabulaire religieux d'Haïti (Étud Da, 14, 1955, p. 5-20).
A list of Haitian Creole religious terms collected by the authors and shown to be clearly derivative from African (West African and Congo) languages. Corroboration of the African origin of each term is provided by reference to specific works on Africa where the term is given. [S. W. Mintz]

441. **Courlander, Harold.** The loa of Haiti: New World African deities (*in* Miscelánea de estudios dedicados a Fernando Ortiz. V. 1. Habana, 1955, p. 421-444).
A valuable treatment of the Haitian *vodun* pantheon and an exhaustive list of its major gods (*loas*). Some note of syncretic change—as in tales combining *loas* and Christian saints —is taken. [S. W. Mintz]

442. **Denis, Lorimer.** Le cimetière (B Bur Ethn, série 2, 13, 1956, p. 1-16). [S. W. Mintz]

443. ————, and **François Duvalier.** La culture populaire (B Bur Ethn, série 2, 12, 1955, p. 1-29). [S. W. Mintz]

444. **Erasmus, Charles J.** Culture structure and process. The occurrence and disappearance of reciprocal farm labor (SW J Anthr, 12:4, winter 1956, p. 444-470).
The author makes frequent analytical reference to the reciprocal farm labor groups in Haiti. [S. W. Mintz]

445. **Hyppolite, Michelson Paul.** A study of Haitian folklore. Translated by E. Laforest and Pansy Hart. Port-au-Prince, Imp. de l'État, 1954. 51 p., illus. [S. W. Mintz]

446. **Métraux, Alfred.** La comédie rituelle dans la possession (Diogène, 11, juillet 1955, p. 1-24).
A contribution to the study of spirit possession, illustrated by the character of trance in Haitian *vodun.* [S. W. Mintz]

447. ————. Les dieux et les esprits dans le vodou haïtien (B Soc Suisse Am, 10, sept. 1955, p. 2-16; 7:11, mars 1956, p. 1-9). [S. W. Mintz]

448. ————. La noël vodou en Haïti (B Soc Neu Géo, n. s. 10, 51:5, 1954-1955, p. 95-118).
A comparison of two different Christmas ceremonies conducted by *vodun* group leaders, observed in Port-au-Prince and in Leogane, Haiti, in 1946. The author suggest these ceremonies are probably derived from others connected with the winter solstice and the "death" of the land. [S. W. Mintz]

449. ————. Rites funéraires des paysans haïtiens (Arts Trad Pop, 2:4, oct.-déc. 1954, p. 289-306). [S. W. Mintz]

450. **Paul, Emmanuel C.** Représentations religieuses dans le vodou (B Bur Ethn, série 2, 12, 1955, p. 47-54). [S. W. Mintz]

451. **Sylvain Bouchereau, Madeleine.** Haïti. Porträt eines freien Landes. Frankfurt-am-Main, West Germany, Waldemar Kramer, 1954. 119 p., maps, illus.
An introduction to Haitian culture and society which is clearly written and up to date. [S. W. Mintz]

452. **Viaud, Léonce.** Le houmfor (B Bur Ethn, série 2, 12, 1955, p. 30-35). [S. W. Mintz]

JAMAICA

453. **Cohen, Yehudi A.** A contribution to the study of adolescence: adolescent conflict in a Jamaican community (Samiksa, 9:3, 1955, p. 139-172).
The author hypothesizes that psychological isolation of the adolescent in Jamaican society, though anxiety-producing, serves to prepare the maturing individual for individualistic wealth accumulation when he becomes adult. The accumulation of wealth on a highly individualistic basis is viewed by Cohen as an immensely important goal in rural Jamaican society. [S. W. Mintz]

454. ————. Structure and function: family organization and socialization in a Jamaican community (Am Anthr, 58:4, Aug. 1956, p. 664-686). [S. W. Mintz]

455. **Cumper, George E.** Population movements in Jamaica, 1830-1950 (Soc Ec Stud, 5:3, Sept. 1956, p. 261-280).
Though primarily historical and demographic, this paper throws much light on the evolution of the Jamaican small land holder in the 19th and 20th centuries. [S. W. Mintz]

456. **Hogg, Donald W.** A West Indian shepherd (Context, 4:2, Mar. 1956, p. 12-15).
Brief notes on a Jamaican cult (Pocomania) leader. [S. W. Mintz]

457. **Ibberson, D.** Illegitimacy and the birth rate (Soc Ec Stud, 5:1, Mar. 1956, p. 93-99).
By a shrewd analysis of Jamaican census data, the author concludes that "increased acceptance of marriage by women at young ages would, in present conditions, raise the birth rate." [S. W. Mintz]

458. **Simpson, George E.** Jamaican revivalist cults (Soc Ec Stud, 5:4, Dec. 1956, p. iv, 321-442, xi, and 6 plates).
A ". . . study of revivalist cults in West Kingston, Jamaica . . . centred in a) the acculturative process as it is revealed in the Revival Zion-Pocomania-Obeah magico-religious complex, and b) the sociological and social psychological aspects of cult life as seen in cult organization, attitudes toward the cults and the functions of revivalism." Cult ideas and practices are related to other phases of West Kingston life, and are compared to those known in Haiti, Brazil, Trinidad, Cuba, the southern U. S., and the west coast of Africa. [S. W. Mintz]

459. ————. The Ras Tafari movement in Jamaica. A study of race and class conflict (Soc Forces, 34:2, Dec. 1955, p. 167-171).
The author attempts to fit the Ras Tafari movement on a continuum of religious adjustment developed by Yinger. [S. W. Mintz]

MEXICO

460. **Aguirre Beltrán, Gonzalo.** Antropología y educación (PH, 1:1, enero-marzo 1957, p. 7-14).
El nuevo rector de la Universidad de Veracruz examina algunos problemas de la educación en México desde el punto de vista antropológico. [A. Palerm]

461. ————. Programas de salud en la situación intercultural. México, Instituto Indigenista Interamericano, 1955. 191 p.
Describe los principios de la actividad sanitaria llevada a cabo por los Centros Coordinadores del Instituto Nacional Indigenista en varias regiones de México. [A. Palerm]

462. ————. Teoría de la investigación intercultural (Cien Soc, 7:37, marzo 1956, p. 1-26).
Examen de la teoría y metodología de la antropología social de México, consideradas como

resultantes de condiciones nacionales específicas y de sus tendencias hacia la aplicación práctica. [A. Palerm]

463. Burnight, Robert G.; N. L. Whetten; and B. D. Waxman. Differential rural-urban fertility in Mexico (Am Sociol R, 21:1, Feb. 1956, p. 3-8).
Análisis basado en el censo de 1950 del efecto diferencial del progreso de urbanización. [A. Palerm]

464. Caso, Alfonso. Los barrios antiguos de Tenochtitlán y Tlatelolco (Mem Ac Mex Hist, 15:1, enero-marzo 1956, p. 7-63, maps).
Documentado estudio de la localización, distribución y límites de los barrios indígenas de la vieja capital de México. [A. Palerm]

465. ————. El calendario mixteco (Hist Mex, 5:4, abril-junio 1956, p. 481-497, illus.).
El autor muestra que en la Mixteca y hasta el fin de la época Clásica se usó un sistema calendárico conectado estrechamente con el sistema de glifos zapotecos. [A. Palerm]

466. ————. Un experimento de antropología social en México (PH, 1:1, enero-marzo 1957, p. 15-22).
Breve exposición del programa de cambio dirigido de los grupos indígenas de México. [A. Palerm]

467. Foster, George M. Contemporary pottery techniques in Southern and Central Mexico. New Orleans, La., Tulane University, Middle American Research Institute, 1955. 35 p., illus., maps.
Técnicas de alfarería moderna, con referencias a prácticas precolombinas y coloniales; distribución geográfica y conclusiones. [A. Palerm]

468. Marino Flores, Anselmo. Indígenas de México: algunas consideraciones demográficas (Am Indíg, 16:1, enero 1956, p. 41-48).
Datos estadísticos basados en el censo de 1950, separando los grupos que hablan lenguas indígenas. [A. Palerm]

469. Marroquín, Alejandro D. Consideraciones sobre el problema económico de la región tzeltal-tzotzil (Am Indíg, 16:3, junio 1956, p. 191-203).
Examina los programas de desarrollo de las zonas indígenas de México a la luz de la existencia de centros de cultura nacional rodeados de constelaciones de lugares indígenas. [A. Palerm]

470. Rubel, Arthur J. Ritual relationships in Ojitlán, México (Am Anthr, 57:5, Oct. 1955, p. 1038-1040).
Comunicáción sobre algunos aspectos del parentesco ritual en un pueblo chinanteco de México. [A. Palerm]

471. Sayles, E. B. Three Mexican crafts (Am Anthr, 57:5, Oct. 1955, p. 953-973).
Descripción de tres artesanías populares en Oaxaca, México; alfarería, tejidos y joyería. Ocho láminas con ilustraciones. [A. Palerm]

472. Villa Rojas, Alfonso. Adiestramiento de personal (Am Indíg, 15:4, oct. 1955, p. 306-316).
Examen de los programas del Instituto Nacional Indigenista de México para la preparación de sus especialistas en el campo aplicado de la antropología. [A. Palerm]

473. Vogt, Evon Z. Some aspects of Cora-Huichol acculturation (Am Indíg, 15:4, oct. 1955, p. 249-263).
Informe preliminar. Compara tres grupos de México (coras, huicholes y mestizos) con dos del suroeste de Estados Unidos (zuñis y navajos) desde el punto de vista de la transculturación. [A. Palerm]

474. Wolf, Eric R., and Ángel Palerm. Irrigation in the old Acolhua domain, Mexico (SW J Anthr, 11:3, autumn 1955, p. 265-281).
Un sistema de regadío en el área de Texcoco. Estudio basado en fuentes documentales y reconocimiento arqueológico y etnográfico moderno. [A. Palerm]

TRINIDAD

475. Carr, Andrew T. Pierrot Grenade (Carib Q, 4:3-4, Mar.-June 1956, p. 281-314). [S. W. Mintz]

476. Crowley, Daniel J. The midnight robbers (Carib Q, 4:3-4, Mar.-June 1956, p. 263-274). [S. W. Mintz]

477. ————. The traditional masques of carnival (Carib Q, 4:3-4, Mar.-June 1956, p. 194-223). [S. W. Mintz]

478. Freeman, Linton C., and Alan P. Merriam. Statistical classification in anthropology: an application to ethnomusicology (Am Anthr, 58:3, June 1956, p. 464-472).
In outlining statistical device for classifying data in cultural anthropology, the authors compare songs of Trinidad Rada (a religious cult of African origin) and Brazilian Ketu. [S. W. Mintz]

479. Merriam, Alan P.; Sara Whinnery; and B. G. Fred. Songs of a Rada community in Trinidad (Anthropos, 51:1-2, 1956, p. 157-174).
Musicological analysis of 31 Dahomean-derived songs preserved in ritual by a cult group in Trinidad. [S. W. Mintz]

480. Ortiz Oderigo, Néstor R. El "calypso," expresión musical de los negros de Trinidad (*in* Miscelánea de estudios dedicados a Fernando Ortiz. V. 2. Habana, 1956, p. 1165-1172). [S. W. Mintz]

481. **Pearse, Andrew.** Carnival in nineteenth century Trinidad (Carib Q, 4:3-4, Mar.-June 1956, p. 175-193). [S. W. Mintz]

482. **Procope, Bruce.** The Dragon Band or Devil Band (Carib Q, 4:3-4, Mar.-June 1956, p. 275-280). [S. W. Mintz]

483. **Sampson, Mitto.** Mitto Sampson on Calypso legends of the nineteenth century (Carib Q, 4:3-4, Mar.-June 1956, p. 250-262).
Arranged and edited by Andrew Pearse. [S. W. Mintz]

OTHER

484. **Alegría, Ricardo E.** The fiesta of Santiago Apóstol (St. James the Apostle) in Loiza, Puerto Rico (J Am Folk, 69:272, Apr.-June 1956, p. 123-134). [S. W. Mintz]

485. **Biesanz, John,** and **Mavis Biesanz.** The people of Panama. N. Y., Columbia University Press, 1955. 148 p., illus.
Descripción de la población panameña en sus niveles diversos y actividades contemporáneas. Incluye los orígenes históricos. [A. Palerm]

486. **Crowley, Daniel J.** Naming customs in St. Lucia (Soc Ec Stud, 5:1, Mar. 1956, p. 87-92).
Includes discussion of *combosse* (address term for males sharing the same woman) and of godparenthood, and a general discussion of the confusion in names and naming which the author sees as protecting people against unpopular outside influences. [S. W. Mintz]

487. ————. Song and dance in St. Lucia (Ethnomus NL, 9, Jan. 1957, p. 4-14). [S. W. Mintz]

488. **Hoetink, Drs. H.** Over Braziliaanse en Curaçaose gezins-normen (Chris, 1:5, Dec. 1955, p. 220-223).
A comparative comment on Curaçaoan and Brazilian family norms. [S. W. Mintz]

489. **Nash, Manning.** The reaction of a civil-religious hierarchy to a factory in Guatemala (Hum Org, 13:4, winter 1955, p. 26-28).
Examen de la adaptación de la organización local tradicional a una fábrica textil (Cantel, Guatemala). [A. Palerm]

490. ————. The recruitment of wage labor and development of new skills (A

Am Ac Pol Soc Sci, 305, May 1956, p. 23-31).
Exposición de un caso de adaptación satisfactoria de una sociedad campesina (Cantel, Guatemala) al trabajo industrial. [A. Palerm]

491. **Newcomb, William W.** A reappraisal of the "cultural sink" of Texas (SW J Anthr, 12:2, summer 1956, p. 145-153, map).
El autor propone una nueva área cultural, denominada "Costa occidental del Golfo," en la que reúne grupos del sureste de Texas y noreste de México. [A. Palerm]

492. **Parsons, James J.** San Andrés and Providencia, English-speaking islands in the western Caribbean. Berkeley, Calif., University of California Press (University of California publ. in geography, 12:1), 1956. 83 p., illus., maps.
Includes some historical and sociological information. [S. W. Mintz]

493. **Redfield, Robert.** The relations between Indians and Ladinos in Agua Escondida, Guatemala (Am Indíg, 16:4, oct. 1956, p. 253-276).
Mantiene que indios y ladinos forman grupos culturales distintos en proceso de asimilación, pero a la vez tienen caracteres de clases sociales. [A. Palerm]

494. **Römer, Raúl.** De studie van het Papiamentu tot nu toe (Chris, 1:8, Maart 1956, p. 347-349). [S. W. Mintz]

495. **Rubio, Ángel.** La situación actual del indígena en Panamá (Am Indíg, 16:3, junio 1956, p. 205-212). [A. Palerm]

496. **Smith, Michael G.** The transformation of land rights by transmission in Carriacou (Soc Ec Stud, 5:2, June 1956, p. 103-138).
An analysis of land tenure and inheritance in Carriacou, largest of the Grenadines, over a 50-year period. The author argues that the forms of land tenure today can be understood only by a study of the processes of transmission. In Carriacou, legal rights in land have been transformed into customary rights, due to the congruence of local culture with changes in island demography. [S. W. Mintz]

497. **Steward, Julian H.** (and others). The people of Puerto Rico. A study in social anthropology. Urbana, Ill., University of Illinois Press (A Social Science Research Center Study, College of Social Sciences, University of Puerto Rico), 1956. 540 p., illus., maps.
An attempt to apply anthropological community study methods to a modern nation. Using Steward's area approach, four Puerto Rican rural

communities and the upper class subculture were studied and compared, and an effort made to fit the data into their historical and societal setting. Includes community studies by Manners, Wolf, Padilla Seda, Mintz, and Scheele. [S. W. Mintz]

498. **Torres de Ianello, Reina.** La mujer cuna (Am Indíg, 16:4, oct. 1956, p. 277-302, illus.).
Este trabajo forma parte de una investigación más extensa sobre la posición de la mujer en los grupos indígenas de América, llevada a cabo por el Instituto Indigenista Interamericano. Se detalla el ciclo de vida de la mujer cuna. [A. Palerm]

ETHNOLOGY: SOUTH AMERICA

D. B. STOUT

GENERAL

550. **Boglar, Luis.** Some more data on the spread of the blowgun in South America (Acta Ethn Ac Sci Hung, 1, 1950, p. 121-137, map).
Additional information on the occurrence of the several types of blowguns among the tropical forest tribes of South America which complements Jens Yde's study of 1948 which appeared in the *Journal de la Société des Américanistes,* v. 37.

551. **Dorsinnfang-Smets, A.** Contacts de cultures et problèmes d'acculturation en Amérique du Sud (R Inst Soc Solvay, 27:3, 1954, p. 647-666).
Comprehensive review of the varieties and degrees of acculturation among the Indians, whites and Negroes of the various South American nations and areas, with suggestions of future trends. Also published in Spanish with English summary (Am Indíg, 25:4, oct. 1955, p. 271-291).

552. **Hohenthal, W. D.,** and **Thomas Mc-Corkle.** The problem of aboriginal persistence (SW J Anthr, 11:3, autumn 1955, p. 288-300).
Comparative analysis of the acculturative process among the Fulnio Indians of Brazil and the Guayqueri of Margarita Island, Venezuela, with special emphasis on the contrasting outcome.

553. **Simmons, Ozzie G.** Popular modern medicine in mestizo communities of coastal Peru and Chile (J Am Folk, 68:267, Jan.-Mar. 1955, p. 57-72).
Excellent study of the role of popular medicine in folk communities, in which the nature of indigenous beliefs as a basis for the acceptance or rejection of scientific medicine is clearly brought out.

554. **Wilbert, Johannes.** Índice de las tribus sudamericanas (Antropologica, 2, enero 1957, p. 1-25).
Complete alphabetical index, by tribal name, to all of the tribes in the first four volumes of the *Handbook of South American Indians* (Steward, Julian H., ed., Washington, Smithsonian Institution, Bureau of American Ethnology, Bulletin 143, 1946-1950, 6 v.). This index is a great help in using the *Handbook* and will remain so for ethnologists until the Bureau of American Eth-nology is able to bring out an index volume of its own.

BRAZIL

555. **Carvalho, José Cândido de M.** Notas de viagem ao Javari-Itacoaí-Juruá. Rio, Museu Nacional (Publ. avulsas, 13), 1955. 81 p., illus.
Account of travels in 1950, mainly in the region of the Itacoai river, a southern tributary of the middle Amazon river. The author is a zoologist, but besides providing a wealth of data on the flora and fauna of the area, he also gives descriptions of the Indians (Tukuna and Catukina) and of the neo-Brazilians of this frontier area.

556. ————. Notas de viagem ao rio Paru de Leste. Rio, Museu Nacional (Publ. avulsas, 14), 1955. 82 p., 18 plates.
Account by a zoologist of travels in 1952 on the Paru de Leste river, a northern tributary of the Amazon in Brazilian Guiana. Contains incomplete data on the ethnography of the Apalai Indians.

557. **Cunha, Ayres Câmara.** Entre os índios do Xingu. São Paulo, Edições Melhoramentos, 1953. 74 p., illus.
Brief notes on the culture of the Kalapalos Indians and a paragraph or two on each of 14 other Xingu tribes.

558. **Diegues Júnior, Manuel.** Etnías e culturas no Brasil. Rio, Ministério da Educação e Cultura, Serviço de Documentação, 1956. 120 p.
Brief summary of the history and characteristics of the various ethnic groups of Brazil.

559. **Herskovits, Melville J.** Estrutura social do candomblé afrobrasileiro (B Inst Nabuco, 3, 1954, p. 13-32).
Much-needed analysis of the social patterns involved in the candomble cults, with suggestions for future research.

560. **Huxley, Francis.** Affable savages. An anthropologist among the Urubu Indians of Brazil. London, Hart-Davis, 1956. 285 p., illus.
Contains considerable data on the ethnography of the Urubu Indians of north central Maranhão state, but difficult to disengage from the travel-account aspect because most of the data occur

in the form of dialogues between the author and his Indian friends. As he refers to himself as an anthropologist, it is hoped that he will provide us with a systematic account of Urubu culture, for it would be a distinct contribution to Brazilian ethnology.

561. **Lévi-Strauss, Claude.** Tristes tropiques. Terre humaine, civilisations et sociétés. Paris, Librairie Plon, 1955. 462 p., 53 figs., 1 map, 63 plates.
A most engaging account of the author's travels in Brazil as an ethnographer, with portions devoted to descriptions of the culture and life of the Caduveo, Bororo, Tupi-Kawahib, and Nambikwara, of which the last is most complete. Excellent photographs.

562. **Murphy, Robert, and Yolanda Murphy.** As condições atuais dos Mundurucú. Belém, Brazil, Instituto de Antropologia e Etnologia do Pará (Publ., 8), 1954. 44 p., illus.
Brief description of the Mundurucu with emphasis on the results of acculturation. Based on field work done in 1952-1953.

563. **Ortiz Oderigo, Néstor R.** Notas de etnografía afrobrasileña: el "candomblé" (Cien Soc, 6:36, dic. 1955, p. 310-319).
Concise, but comprehensive, statement of the processes and nature of the development of the candomble, etc., cults.

564. **Pedrosa, Manuel Xavier de Vasconcelos.** A medicina dos índios brasileiros (A IV Cong Hist Nac, v. 8, 1951, p. 299-323).
Brief review of some 30 plant products used in folk medicine.

565. **Ramos, Arthur.** Introdução à antropologia brasileira. V. 1. 2. ed. As culturas não-européias. Rio, Casa do Estudante do Brasil (Col. Estudos brasileiros, série B, 1), 1951. 424 p. & illus.
First edition, 1943 (see *HLAS, no. 9, 1943, item 491*).

COLOMBIA

566. **Bernal Villa, Segundo.** Aspectos de la cultura páez: mitología y cuentos de la parcialidad de Calderas, Tierradentro (R Colomb Antr, 2. época, 1:1, junio 1953, p. 279-309).
26 myths and tales from the Paez rendered into Spanish but without accompanying original linguistic text.

567. ————. Bases para el estudio de la organización social de los páez (R Colomb Antr, 2. época., 4, 1955, p. 165-188).
Complete data on the kinship terminology of the Paez, with additional information on closely related aspects of their social organization.

568. ————. Economía de los páez (R Colomb Antr, 3, 1954, p. 291-367, 13 plates, charts, tables).
Thorough study of the subsistence economy and related economic patterns among the Paez.

569. ————. Medicina y magia entre los paeces (R Colomb Antr, 2:2, año 1954, p. 219-264).
Thorough study of the magical and folk medicine beliefs and practices among the Paez.

570. **Dussan de Reichel, Alicia.** Características de la personalidad masculina y femenina en Taganga (R Colomb Antr, 2:2, 1954, p. 87-113).
Excellent analysis of the culturally patterned personality differences between the sexes in fishing community of 800 persons near Santa Marta. The data were collected at various times over a period of four years.

571. **Fulop, Marcos.** Aspectos de la cultura tukana: cosmogonía (R Colomb Antr, 3, 1954, p. 97-137, 4 plates).

572. ————. Notas sobre los términos y el sistema de parentesco de los tukano (R Colomb Antr, 4, 1955, p. 121-164).
Complete data on the kinship terminology of the Tukano tribe.

573. **Price, Thomas J., Jr.** Estado y necesidades actuales de las investigaciones afro-colombianas (R Colomb Antr, 2:2, 1954, p. 13-36).
A panoramic view and soundly presented basis for the study of acculturation among the cultures and societies in Colombia, in which African, Indian, and Iberian elements are present.

PERU

574. **Maxwell, Thomas J., Jr.** Agricultural ceremonies of the central Andes during four hundred years of Spanish contact (Ethnohistory, 3:1, winter 1956, p. 46-71).
Based on field work done in 1949. Reviews and compares the whole complex of agricultural ceremonies from the 16th century to the present; the major conclusion is that the original ceremonies did not survive the fall of the Inca empire.

575. **Valcárcel, Luis E.** El conocimiento científico de los pueblos del Perú (R Mus Nac, 22, 1953, p. 3-16).
Comprehensive review of current and recent ethnological researches in Peru.

VENEZUELA

576. **Barker, James.** Memoria sobre la cultura de los guaika (B Indig Ven, año 1, 1:3-4, junio-dic. 1953, p. 433-490, illus., map).
Ethnographic notes on the Guaika tribe of the upper Orinoco area.

577. **Dupouy, Walter.** Algunos casos de postura nilotica (Nilotenstellung) entre indios de Venezuela (B Indig Ven, año 1, 1:2, abril-mayo 1953, p. 3-13, 8 plates, map).

Discussion and illustration of one-legged posture (in which the sole of one foot is placed against the ankle, knee on thigh of the other leg while standing up or leaning on an upright surface) in a number of Venezuelan tribes.

578. **Wilbert, Johannes.** Los instrumentos musicales de los warrau (guarao, guarauno) (Antropologica, 1, sept. 1956, p. 2-22).

Comprehensive study, based on field work and the study of museum collections, along with comparisons with previous writings and critical comments thereon.

579. ————. Notes on Guahibo kinship and social organization (SW J Anthr, 13:1, spring 1957, p. 88-98).

Full data on the kinship terminology and notes on family, band, etc., organization.

OTHER AREAS

580. **Butt, Audrey J.** "The burning fountain whence it came." A study of the system of beliefs of the Carib-speaking Akawaio of British Guiana (Soc Ec Stud, 2:1, Sept. 1953, p. 102-116).

Excellent study which aids greatly in understanding and settling the issues concerning the nature of Carib religious concepts. Based on field work done in 1951-1952.

581. ————. Ritual blowing: 'Taling'— a causation and cure of illness among the Akawaio (Man, 56:48-60, Apr. 1956, p. 49-55, illus.).

Full description and thorough analysis of the practice of ritual blowing, used both as a preventative and curative measure as well as to bring misfortune to others, among the Akawaio, a Carib tribe of British Guiana.

582. **Costales Samaniego, Alfred.** Los indios colorados. Quito, Instituto de Antropología y Geografía, 1956. 112 p.

Quite complete ethnographic monograph on Colorado Indian culture. Based on field work done in 1951, 1952, and 1955.

583. **Emperaire, José.** Les nomades de la mer. Paris, Gallimard (L'Espèce humaine, 11), 1955. 286 p., illus.

Excellent account of the Alakaluf, based on two years of field work.

584. **Rubio Orbe, Gonzalo.** Punyaro; [estudio de antropología social y cultural de una comunidad indígena y mestiza]. Quito, Editorial Casa de la Cultura Ecuatoriana, 1956. 422 p., illus.

Comprehensive description of a small community in southern Imbabura province, with comparisons to the culture of the inhabitants of Otavalo valley.

585. **Soler Bustamante, Eduardo.** La agricultura en la comunidad de San Pedro de Huancaire. Lima, Universidad Nacional Mayor de San Marcos, Instituto de Etnología (Publ., 23:9), 1954. 52 p., 5 figs., 2 maps.

Detailed study of the agricultural cycle and practices of a community of 561 inhabitants who are Indian racially but whose culture is mestizo.

LINGUISTICS

NORMAN A. McQUOWN

This number of the *Handbook of Latin American studies* initiates a new subsection on linguistics of the main subdivision of the *Handbook* devoted to anthropology. We shall attempt to survey the publications on Latin American indigenous languages, without pretence, however, to complete coverage. Such coverage may be sought in other publications in the field, such as the regular listings of works received in the *International journal of American linguistics,* the linguistics portion of the annual bibliographies published in the *Journal de la Société des Américanistes de Paris,* and the American Indian section of the periodic *Bibliographie linguistique* published, under UNESCO auspices, by the Comité International Permanent de Linguistes.

In general, we shall favor linguistic items with some wider import, but we shall not neglect sizeable publications of a straight descriptive nature, since these constitute the tools for application of linguistic knowledge to other areas. Articles of strictly linguistic theoretical import will, in general, not be included here.

In most recent years, of special interest to students of Latin American cultural history are (1) the promising attempt on the part of W. V. Knorozov to decipher the Maya hieroglyphic writing as embodied in the codices, (2) new publications, both of original documents and of careful and painstaking translation, in the series *Corpus codicum Americanorum medii aevi* and *Quellenwerke zur Geschichte des alten Amerikas* respectively, of documentary materials in Nahuatl and Maya, and (3) startling suggestions for North, Middle, and South American linguistic ties deriving in part from lexicostatical vocabulary comparison for time-depth estimates, in part from probabilistic comparative consideration for postulating common origin. Ernst Mengin is to be credited for the continuing *Corpus,* and translations by Walter Lehmann and Leonhard Schultze-Jena constitute major contributions to the *Quellenwerke.* Morris Swadesh is responsible for the more interesting and more startling suggestions on linguistic affinities. On the straight descriptive side, a steady stream of new materials continues to be supplied by workers among the Wycliffe Bible Translators, who now are working most actively with the indigenous languages of Mexico, Guatemala, Ecuador, and Peru. Some few studies are appearing from workers in Brazil, with a promise of increasing quantities to come.

650. **Agnew, Arlene,** and **Evelyn G. Pike.** Phonemes of Ocaina (Huitoto) (Intl J Am Ling, 23:1, Jan. 1957, p. 24-27).

650a. **Albisetti, César.** Nótulas morfemo-etimológicas de língua boróro (A XXXI Cong Intl Am, v. 2, p. 1073-1082).

651. **Alencastre G., Andrés.** Fonética, semántica y sintaxis quechua. Cuzco, Perú, Universidad Nacional, 1953. 41 p.

651a. **Álvarez, José.** Vocabulario mashco (Mis Dom Perú, 34:196, 1953, p. 99-100; 35:200, 1954, p. 19-20).

652. **Anaya, Rafael.** El acento y la entonación del qheshwa (Arte, 5:4, 1953, p. 27-28).

652a. **Andrade, Manuel José.** A grammar of modern Yucatec. Chicago, Ill., University of Chicago Library (Microfilm collection of manuscripts on Middle American cultural anthropology, 41), [1941] 1957. 462 p.
A thoroughgoing compilation based on a large accumulation of as yet unpublished texts.

653. **Ángeles Caballero, César A.** La gramática quechua de Juan de Aguilar (Mer Per, año 30, 36:335, feb. 1955, p. 113-124).

653a. **Ardissone, Romualdo.** Toponimias americanas (R Geog Am, año 20, 36:218-219, nov.-dic. 1953, p. 243-255).

654. **Arguedas, José María.** Breve antología de poesía india. Lima, Gran Unidad Escolar Bartolomé Herrera, 1953. 8 p.

654a. **Arroyo Ponce, Gamaliel.** Literatura oral de Tarma (Arch Per Folk, 1:1, 1955, p. 70-85).

655. **Ascásubi, Luis de.** Sobre un tipo de invasiones pre-colombianas del Continente americano por norasiáticos. Estudio de ciertas similitudes, entre los idiomas japonés-jívaro y japonés-quichua (B Ac Nac Hist, Quito, 34:84, julio-dic. 1954, p. 246-264).

655a. **Banks, E. P.** Island Carib folk tales (Carib Q, 4:1, Jan. 1955, p. 32-39).

656. **Barcelona, Fidel de.** Materiales toponímicos e hidronímicos del área Kamsá . . . según datos recogidos por el P. Marcelino de Castellví y Alberto Juajibioy (Amaz Colomb Am, 5:17-19, 1951-1953, p. 119-122).

656a. **Barlow, Robert H.,** and **Byron McAfee.** Diccionario de elementos fonéticos en escritura jeroglífica (Códice Mendocino). México, Instituto de Historia, 1949. 46 p.

657. **Barthel, Thomas S.** Versuch über Inschriften von Chich'en Itzá Viejo (Baessler Arch, n. f., 3, 1955, p. 5-33).

657a. **Bertonio, Ludovico.** Vocabulario de la lengua aymara (B Soc Geog La Paz, 64:71-72, 1954, p. 36-49).

658. **Brambila, David.** Gramática rarámuri. México, Buena Prensa, 1953. 645 p.
A Tarahumara grammar which, though cast in the Latin mold, contains a wealth of useful data.

658a. **Bright, William.** A bibliography of the Hokan-Coahuiltecan languages (Intl J Am Ling, 21:3, July 1955, p. 276-285).
Includes languages of Mexico and Central America; also Yurumangui of Colombia.

659. ————. Glottochronologic counts of Hokaltecan material (Language, 32:1, Jan.-Mar. 1956, p. 42-48).

Lexicostatistical counts confirm Sapir's Salinan-Seri grouping, tie Comecrudo more closely to Jicaque, and put into question the validity of Sapir's Coahuiltecan group.

659a. Burland, C. A. Ancient Mexican documents in Great Britain (Man, 57:83-97, May 1957, p. 76-77).
Brief account of Mixtec and Nahuatl codices in Great Britain.

660. Cartagena, Alberto de. Apuntes sobre danzas indígenas de algunas tribus de la Amazonia colombiana (Antr Etnol, 8, 1953, p. 83-113).

660a. ————. Cantos indígenas con su traducción y transcripción aproximada (Amaz Colomb Am, 5:17-19, 1951-1953, p. 95-102).

661. ————. Palabras indígenas relacionadas con los "Apuntes sobre el baile" de algunas tribus en la región sur-oriental de Colombia (Amaz Colomb Am, 5:17-19, 1951-1953, p. 26-33).

661a. Castellví, Marcelino de. La macrofamilia lingüística witoto y sus relaciones con la familia sabela y otras indoamericanas (Amaz Colomb Am, 5:17-19, 1951-1953, p. 9-16).

662. Castro Loayza, Arturo. Poesía quechua (Tradición, 5:12-14, 1953, p. 108-136).

662a. Catálogo de las voces usuales de aymara con la correspondencia en castellano y quechua. La Paz, Gisbert, 1953. 47 p.

663. Caudmont, Jean. Los fonemas del inga (R Colomb Antr, 2. época, 1:1, junio 1953, p. 357-389).
Unusually thorough treatment of the phonology of this Quechua dialect of Colombia.

663a. ————. Fonología del guambiano (R Colomb Antr, 3, 1954, p. 189-206).

664. ————. Fonología puinave (R Colomb Antr, 2:2, 1954, p. 265-276).

664a. ————. La influencia del bilingüismo como factor de transformación de un sistema fonológico (R Colomb Antr, 2:2, 1954, p. 207-218).
Mutual influence of Quechua and Spanish in the Inga language and in the Spanish of its speakers.

665. ————. La lengua chamí. I. Análisis de los fonemas (R Colomb Antr, 4, 1955, p. 273-283).

665a. ————. Materiales para el estudio

lexicográfico de la lengua inga (Div Etn, 3:5, junio 1954, p. 165-186).

666. Cisneros, Luis Jaime. La primera gramática de la lengua general del Perú (B Inst Riva Agüero, 1:1, 1951-1952, p. 197-264).

666a. Croft, Kenneth. Matlapa Nahuatl II: affix list and morphophonemics (Intl J Am Ling, 19:4, Oct. 1953, p. 274-280).

667. ————. Matlapa Nahuatl III: morpheme arrangements (Intl J Am Ling, 20:1, Jan. 1954, p. 37-43).
Phonology and morphology of a Northern Nahuatl dialect (Matlapa, San Luis Potosi).

667a. Cuestionarios lingüísticos (B Indig Ven, 1:2, abril-junio 1953, p. 309-324).
Swadesh lexicostatistical basic vocabulary adapted to Spanish.

668. Davis, Marjorie. Translating from FL Cuicateco to TL English (Intl J Am Ling, 20:4, Oct. 1954, p. 302-312).
Full analysis of a Cuicatec text.

668a. ————, and Margaret Walker. Cuicateco: morphemics and morphophonemics (Intl J Am Ling, 21:1, Jan. 1955, p. 46-51).

669. Díaz Romero, Belisario. El idioma aymara. Nuevas investigaciones gramaticales (Khana, año 3, 4:13-14, dic. 1955, p. 121-127).

669a. Dictionary of the Quechua language in two parts. First part: English-Quechua. Second part: Quechua-castellano-English. Cochabamba, Bolivia, Bolivian Indian Mission, 1952. 130 p.

670. Dony, Paul de. Une langue peu connue: le Guaraní (Vie Lang, 22, 1954, p. 37-41).

670a. Dozier, Edward P. Two examples of linguistic acculturation: the Yaqui of Sonora and Arizona and the Tewa of New Mexico (Language, 32:1, Jan.-Mar. 1956, p. 146-157).
Contrast between Yaqui (permissive) and Tewa (forced) acculturation as manifest in borrowed vocabulary.

671. Drumond, Carlos. Vocabulário na língua brasílica. V. 2. (I-Z). 2 ed., revista e confrontada com o ms. fg., 3144 da Bibl. Nacional de Lisboa. São Paulo, Universidade de São Paulo, Faculdade de Filosofia, Ciências e Letras (Boletim,

164; Etnografia e língua tupi-guarani, 26), 1953. 147 p.
Second volume of a Tupi-Guarani dictionary.

671a. **Dumézil, Georges.** Catégories et vocabulaire des échanges de services chez les indiens Quechua: *ayni* et *mink'a* (J Soc Am, n. s., 44, 1955, p. 3-16).

672. —————. Deux pièces "costumbristas" qhišwa de Killku Warak'a (Andrés Alencastre G.) (J Soc Am, n. s., 43, 1954, p. 1-84).
Quechua dramatic texts, some with Spanish, others with French translations.

672a. —————. Remarques complémentaires sur les six premiers noms de nombres de turc et du quechua (J Soc Am, n. s., 44, 1955, p. 17-37).
A proposed genetic relationship between Ural-Altaic and Quechua.

673. —————. Remarques sur les six premiers noms de nombres du turc (Studia Ling, 8:1, 1954, p. 1-15).
Comparison of Ural-Altaic and Quechua.

673a. Escritura de las lenguas quechua y aymara. Tres documentos sobre el sistema de escritura de estas lenguas, aprobado y recomendado por el III Congreso Indigenista Interamericano de la Paz, Bolivia (Cien Art, 1:1, 1954).

674. **Farfán, J. M. B.** Cronología quechua-aymara según el cálculo léxico estadístico (R Mus Nac, 23, 1954, p. 50-55).
Shows a time of separation 3,500 years ago.

674a. —————. Esquema para el estudio de antroponimias quechuas (R Mus Nac, 22, 1953, p. 52-60).

675. —————. Estudio de un vocabulario de las lenguas quechua, aymara y haqearu (R Mus Nac, 24, 1955, p. 81-99).

675a. —————. La intangibilidad de las toponimias aborígenes (R Inst Am Arte, 7:2, 1954, p. 7-9).

676.—————. Textos del haqe aru o kawki (R Mus Nac, 22, 1953, p. 61-74).
Materials on a sister language of Quechua.

676a. **Fernández Naranjo, Nicolás.** Notas sobre la lengua aymara (Kollasuyo, 10:67, julio-sept. 1951, p. 55-63).

677. **Flórez, Luis.** Algunas voces indígenas en el español de Colombia (R Colomb Antr, 4, 1955, p. 285-310).

677a. —————. El castellano y las lenguas indígenas de América (R Colomb Folk, 2, junio 1953, p. 287-292).
Reprinted with English translation in: B Indig, 14:2, junio 1954, p. 90-98.

678. **Forero, Manuel José.** Vestigios de la lengua muisca (Amaz Colomb Am, 4:12-16, 1946-1950, p. 39-49).

678a. **Friedrich, Johannes.** Kurze Grammatik der alten Quiché-Sprache im Popel Vuh. Mainz, Akademie der Wissenschaften and der Literatur (Abhandlungen der Geistes- und Sozialwissenschaftlichen Klasse, 1955:4), 1955. 143 p.
Exhaustive philological study of the language of the Popol Vuh. See also review by Morris Swadesh (in *Language*, 32:4, part 1, Oct.-Dec. 1956, p. 819-822) which gives a thumbnail sketch of Quiche as abstracted from Friedrich.

679. **Ghisletti, Louis V.** Los mwiskas. Una gran civilización precolombina. Bogotá, Ministerio de Educación Nacional, Ediciones de la Revista Bolívar (Biblioteca de autores colombianos, 73-74), 1954. 2 v. 535, 309 p.
Muisca grammar in v. 1, p. 205-500.

679a. —————. Los nombres de animales en mwiska y su aspecto semasiológico (R Colomb Folk, 2, junio 1953, p. 273-286).
Chibcha animal names.

680. **Gibson, Lorna F.** Pame (Otomi) phonemics and morphophonemics (Intl J Am Ling, 22:4, Oct. 1956, p. 242-265).

680a. **González Bravo, Antonio.** Poemas aymaras (Inti Karka, 1:1, 1952, p. 41-45; 2:3, 1953, p. 167-189).

681. **González Torres, Dionisio.** A língua guarani. São Paulo, Escola de Sociologia e Política, 1952. 152 p.

681a. **Greenberg, Joseph H.** An application of New World evidence to an African linguistic problem (Mém IFAN, 27, 1953, p. 129-131).

682. —————, and **Morris Swadesh.** Jicaque as a Hokan language (Intl J Am Ling, 19:3, July 1953, p. 216-222).
Evidence for membership of Jicaque in Sapir's Hokan linguistic family.

682a. **Grimes, Joseph E.** Style in Huichol structure (Language, 31:1, Jan.-Mar. 1955, p. 31-35).
Stylistics in an indigenous language.

683. **Gudschinsky, Sarah C.** The ABC's of lexicostatistics (glottochronology) (Word, 12:2, Aug. 1956, p. 175-210).

Essentials of lexicostatistical procedure illustrated with Mazatec and Ixcatec materials; the most conservative estimate of time of split is 1,887-2,269 years ago.

683a. ————. Lexicostatistical skewing from dialect borrowing (Intl J Am Ling, 21:2, Apr. 1955, p. 138-149).
Limitations on lexicostatistical dating illustrated by Mazatec dialects in contact.

684. Hamp, Eric P. Componential restatement of syllable structure in Trique (Intl J Am Ling, 20:3, July 1954, p. 206-209).

684a. Hanke, Wanda. Notas complementarias sobre los sirionos (R Cult, 1:1, junio 1954, p. 167-189).

685. ————. Parintintin y Boca Negra con sus idiomas (Kollasuyo, 12:70, marzo 1953, p. 29-47).

685a. ————. Vocabulário e idioma mura dos índios mura do Rio Manicoré (Arquivos, Manaus, 12, 1950, p. 3-8).

686. Hawkins, W. Neill. A fonologia da língua uáiuái. São Paulo, Universidade de São Paulo, Faculdade de Filosofia, Ciências e Letras (Boletim, 157; Etnografia e língua tupi-guarani, 25), 1952. 49 p.
Waiwai phonemics.

686a. Hellinga, Wytze Gs. Petroglyphes caraïbes: problème sémiologique. Amsterdam, North-Holland Publ. Co., 1954. 122-165 p., 4 plates, 9 fig.
Interpretation of Carib rock writing. Reprint from Lingua, 4:2.

687. Hickerson, Nancy P. Two versions of a Lokono (Arawak) tale (Intl J Am Ling, 20:4, Oct. 1954, p. 295-301).
A comparative study of phrasing.

687a. Hoff, B. J. The languages of the Indians of Surinam and the comparative study of the Caribe and Arawak languages (Bij Taal Land Volk, 111:4, 1955, p. 325-355).

688. Holmer, Nils M. Apuntes comparados sobre la lengua de los Yaganes, Tierra del Fuego (R Fac Hum Cien, 10, 1953, p. 193-223).
Yahgan linguistic relationship.

688a. ————. Contribución a la lingüistica de la Sierra Nevada de Santa Marta (R Colomb Antr, 2. época, 1:1, junio 1953, p. 311-355).
Grammatical and lexical materials on Cagaba and Sanha.

689. ————. Cuna chrestomathy. Göteborg, Sweden, Etnografiska Museet (Etnologiska studier, 18), 1951. 192 p., 9 illus.
Cuna linguistic texts with ethnographic content.

689a. ————. Ethno-linguistic Cuna dictionary. Göteborg, Sweden, Etnografiska Museet (Etnografiska studier, 19), 1952. 194 p., 34 figs.
Ethnographically useful data derived from uneconomically analyzed linguistic materials.

690. ————, and S. H. Wassen. Inatoipippiler, or The adventures of three Cuna boys, by Nils M. Holmer; New Cuna myths, by S. H. Wassen. Göteborg, Sweden, Etnografiska Museet (Etnologiska studier, 20), 1952. 106 p., plates.
Cuna texts.

690a. Huber, Konrad. Contribution à la langue mučik (J Soc Am, n. s., 42, 1953, p. 127-134).
Mochica loan-words in present day Peruvian coastal Spanish.

691. Ibarra Grasso, Dick Edgar. Lenguas indígenas de Bolivia (Khana, 4:7-8, marzo 1955, p. 36-49).

691a. Jackson, Frances, and Julia Supple. Vocabulario tojolabal. Breve coordinación alfabética de una lengua mayance del estado de Chiapas. México, Instituto Lingüístico de Verano [and] Dirección General de Asuntos Indígenas, 1952. 52 p.

692. Keller, Kathryn C. The Chontal (Mayan) numeral system (Intl J Am Ling, 21:3, July 1955, p. 258-275).

692a. ————, and Sol Saporta. The frequency of consonant clusters in Chontal (Intl J Am Ling, 23:1, Jan. 1957, p. 28-35).

693. Key, Harold. Algunas observaciones preliminares de la distribución dialectal del nahuatl en el área Hidalgo-Veracruz-Puebla (R Mex Estud Antr. 13:2-3, 1952-1953, p. 131-143).

693a. ————. Vocabularies of languages of the Uto-Aztecan family. Chicago, Ill., University of Chicago Library (Microfilm collection of manuscripts on Middle American cultural anthropology, 38), 1957. 473 p.
Vocabularies from 27 Nahuatl dialects, from Huichol, Cora, Tarahumara, Tepehuana, Taqui, Mayo, Varohio, Pima Bajo, Opata, and Tepecano in Mexico; from Comanche, Hopi (Oraibi), Papago, Southern Paiute, Hopi (Toreva), and Tübatulabal in the U. S.

694. Knorozov, Ürii Valentinove. Pisĭmennosti drevnix maiä: opyt rassifrovki (Sov Etn, 10:1, Jan.-Mar. 1955, p. 94-125).

Reprinted with a Spanish translation, "La escritura de los antiguos mayas," by the U.S.S.R. Academy of Sciences, 1955, 95 p. The most recent summary of results in Knorozov's attempt to decipher the Maya writing: 150 signs of which 110 are phonetic, the remainder either logographic or "determinant"; 200 words and phrases are interpreted, together with 30 sample sentences, all from the codices.

694a. Kroeber, Alfred Louis. Linguistic time depth results so far and their meaning (Intl J Am Ling, 21:2, Apr. 1955, p. 91-104).

Evaluation of lexicostatistical dating procedure; comment on length of separation indicated for (among others) certain North and Middle American languages.

695. Leal, Mary, and Otis Leal. Noun possession in Villa Alta Zapotec (Intl J Am Ling, 20:3, July 1954, p. 215-216).

695a. Loukotka, Čestmir. Les Indiens botocudo et leur langue (Ling Posnaniensis, 5, 1955, p. 112-134).

696. ———. Les langues non-tupi du Brésil du Nord-Est (A XXXI Cong Intl Am, v. 2, p. 1029-1054).

696a. McArthur, Harry, and Lucille McArthur. Aguacatec (Mayan) phonemes within the stress group (Intl J Am Ling, 22:1, Jan. 1956, p. 72-76).

First modern descriptive material on this Mayan language near the center of the Mayan-speaking area.

697. McKaughan, Howard P. Chatino formulas and phonemes (Intl J Am Ling, 20:1, Jan. 1954, p. 23-27).

First full statement of the phonemics of the Yatepec dialect.

697a. McQuown, Norman A. The classification of the Mayan languages (Intl J Am Ling, 22:3, July 1956, p. 191-195).

A suggested internal classification based on selected surviving phonological contrasts.

698. ———. Evidence for a synthetic trend in Totonacan (Language, 32:1, Jan.-Mar. 1956, p. 78-80).

Evidence for a Macro-Mayan family and for an analytic-polysynthetic cycle within it.

698a. Médiz Bolio, Antonio. Introducción al estudio de la lengua maya (Yikal, 15:173-174, 1954, p. 10-16; 15:175, 1954, p. 31-33).

699. Mejía Xesspe, M. Toribio. Lingüística del norte andino (Letras, 50-53, 1.-2. semestre 1954, p. 204-229).

699a. Mengin, Ernst (ed.). Memorial de Tecpán-Atitlán (Sololá). Anales de los Cakchiqueles. Historia del antiquo reino del Cakchiquel dicho de Guatemala . . . Copenhagen, Munksgaard (Corpus codicum Americanorum medii aevi, 4), 1952. 46 p., 96 plates, facsim.

Collotype plate reproduction of the original Cakchiquel manuscript.

700. Middendorf, E. W. Introducción a la gramática aymará. Directamente traducido del alemán por Fr. Tamayo (Khana, 3:5-6, oct. 1954, p. 7-31).

700a. Minor, Eugene E. Witoto vowel clusters (Intl J Am Ling, 22:2, Apr. 1956, p. 131-137).

Huitoto phonology (Muenane dialect on the Ampiyacu river a little above Pucuarquillo, Peru.)

701. Miranda Rivera, Porfirio. Florilegio keshua. Sucre, Bolivia, Don Bosco, 1953. 92 p.

701a. Miscelánea Padre Castellví (Amaz Colomb Am, 4:12-16, 1946-1950, no. extraordinario dedicado a . . . R. P. Marcelino de Castellví, misionero capuchino. 260 p.).

Articles on Colombian indigenous linguistics in honor of Father Castellví.

702. Mosoh Marka. Poema quechua (Inti Karka, 1:1, 1952, p. 46-56).

702a. Nimuendajú, Curt. Reconhecimento dos rios Içána, Ayarí, e Uaupés, março a julho de 1927. Apontamentos linguísticos (J Soc Am, n. s., 44, 1955, p. 149-197).

Vocabularies of varieties of Arawak, Tucano, Macu, Carib, and Tupi.

703. Noyes, Ernest. Grammar and lexicon of Black Carib and lexicon of Cholti and Chorti. Chicago, Ill., University of Chicago Library (Microfilm collection of manuscripts on Middle American cultural anthropology, 39), 1957. 370 p.

Field notes on Black Carib; supplementary descriptive and comparative notes on Chorti and on materials extracted from Fray Francisco Moran's *Arte y diccionario en lengua cholti* (1685-1695).

703a. Oblitas Poblete, Enrique. El Machchaj-Juyai o idioma callawaya (Khana, 5:9-10, julio 1955, p. 122-129).

704. Ortiz, Sergio E. El kechua y su expansión hacia el norte del imperio incaico (R Mus Nac, 22, 1953, p. 35-51).
Also published in *Letras*, 49, 1953, p. 229-232.

704a. Palavecino, María Delia Millán de. Lexicografía de la vestimenta en el área de influencia del quechua (Fol Ling Am, 1:1, 1954, p. 1-33).

705. Peeke, Catherine. Shimigae, idioma que se extingue (Perú Indíg, 5:13, dic. 1954, p. 171-178).

705a. ————, and Mary Sargent. Pronombres personales en Andoa (Perú Indíg, 5:12, dic. 1953, p. 103-112).

706. Philipson, J. La enseñanza del guaraní como problema de bilingüismo (J Filol, año 1, 1:1, julho-set. 1953, p. 45-58).

706a. Pickett, Velma. Isthmus Zapotec verb analysis (Intl J Am Ling, 19:4, Oct. 1953, p. 292-296; 21:3, July 1955, p. 217-232).
Thoroughgoing descriptive treatment.

707. Pierson, Esther. Phonemic statement of Popoloca (Lingua, 3:4, Aug. 1953, p. 426-429).
First modern descriptive material.

707a. Pike, Eunice V. Tonally differentiated allomorphs in Soyaltepec Mazatec (Intl J Am Ling, 22:1, Jan. 1956, p. 57-71).

708. Pinto, Estevão. Estórias e lendas indígenas. Recife, Brazil, Faculdade de Filosofia (Geografia e história, 15), 1955. 32 p.

708a. ————. Os Fulniô de Águas Bebas (A XXXI Cong Intl Am, v. 1, p. 181-194).

709. Pittman, Richard Saunders. A grammar of Tetelcingo (Morelos) Nahuatl. Baltimore, Md., Linguistic Society of America (Language dissertation, 50), 1954. 67 p.
Condensed presentation of the characteristics, both phonological and morphological, of a somewhat strikingly differentiated variety of Aztec.

709a. Pompeu Sobrinho, Thomaz. As origens dos índios cariris. Fortaleza, Brazil, Editôra Instituto do Ceará, 1954. 38 p.

710. Porras Barrenechea, Raúl. El primer vocabulario quechua (Letras, 49, 1. semestre 1953, p. 217-228).

710a. Pupiales, Mateo de. Palabras de origen kichua usadas en el castellano (Amaz Colomb Am, 5:17-19, 1951-1953, p. 17-25).

711. Rendón, Silvia. Ordenanza del señor Cuauhtemoc. Paleografía, traducción y noticia introductoria de Silvia Rendón. New Orleans, La., Tulane University, Middle American Research Institute (Philological and documentary studies, 2:2), 1952. 13-40 p.

711a. Rens, L. L. E. The historical and social background of Surinam Negro-English. Amsterdam, University of Amsterdam, Bureau for Linguistic Research in Surinam, 1953. 155 p.
Origins of a Creolized language.

712. Rivet, Paul. Les affixes classificatoires des noms de nombres (J Soc Am, n. s., 45, 1956, p. 179-187).
Numeral classifiers in Cholon compared with those of Bribri and Chiripo, as well as with other languages.

712a. ————. La langue mašubi (J Soc Am, n. s., 42, 1953, p. 119-125).
Bibliography, vocabulary, resemblances to Chibcha.

713. Rochereau, Enrique J. Textos tegrías: las uerjayas. Documentos en el dialecto de las tribus tunebas, radicadas en el triángulo Cubogón-Róyoto-Nevado de Chita, en Colombia (Amaz Colomb Am, 4:12-16, 1946-1950, p. 203-210).

713a. Rodrigues, Aryon Dall'Igna. As línguas impuras da família tupi-guarani (A XXXI Cong Intl Am, v. 2, p. 1055-1071).

714. Rowe, John Howland. Eleven Inca prayers from the Zithuwa ritual (Kroeber Anthr Soc Pap, 8-9, 1953, p. 82-99).

714a. ————. Linguistic classification problems in South America (*in* Papers from the Symposium on American Indian Linguistics held at Berkeley, July 7, 1951. Berkeley, Calif., University of California Press (University of California publ. in linguistics, 10), 1954, p. 13-26).

715. Sahagún, Bernardino de. Aztec manuscript dictionary. Chicago, Ill., University of Chicago Library (Microfilm collection of manuscripts on Middle American cultural anthropology, 37), [1590] 1957. 314 p.
Attributed, possibly erroneously, to Sahagún.

Nahuatl entries, Spanish and Latin equivalents in parallel.

716. Sanabria Fernández, Hernando. El idioma guaraní en Bolivia. Santa Cruz de la Sierra, Bolivia, Editorial Santa Cruz, 1951. 54 p.

716a. Schaden, Egon. Aculturação lingüística numa comunidade rural (J Filol, ano 1, 1:1, julho-set. 1953, p. 29-44).

717. Schultz, Harald. Vocábulos urukú e digüt (J Soc Am, n. s., 44, 1955, p. 81-97).
Two different languages spoken by groups of "Urucú" living on the banks of the Machado (Gy-Parana).

717a. Shedd, L. M., and E. A. Nida. A pedagogical grammar of the Quechua tongue. Cochabamba, Bolivia, Bolivian Indian Mission, 1952. 114 p.

718. Soria Lens, Luis. Pequeño vocabulario callawaya (B Soc Geog La Paz, 64:71-72, 1954, p. 32-35).

718a. Spicer, Edward H. Parentescos uto-aztecas de la lengua seri (Yan, 1, 1953, p. 37-40).

719. Spotts, Hazel. Some post-Conquest changes in Mazahua (Intl J Am Ling, 22:3, July 1956, p. 208-211).

719a. ————. Vowel harmony and consonant sequence in Mazahua (Otomí) (Intl J Am Ling, 19:4, Oct. 1953, p. 253-258).

720. Storni, Julio S. Diccionario toponomástico del Tucumán. Toponimias indígenas de la provincia del Tucumán. Tucumán, Argentina, Editorial La Raza, 1953. 95 p.

720a. ————. Disidencias con Leopoldo Lugones sobre voces indígenas. Tucumán, Argentina, Universidad Nacional de Tucumán, 1954. 38 p.

721. Sušnik, Branislava J. Sistema fónico y principios morfológicos del chulupí. Asunción, 1954. 90 p.

721a. Swadesh, Morris. Cuestionario para el cálculo lexicoestadístico de la cronología prehistórica (B Indig Ven, 1:3-4, julio-sept. 1953, p. 517-519).
Swadesh' lexicostatistical basic wordlist in Spanish.

722. ————. The language of the arche-

ologic Huastecs (Notes Mid Am Archaeol Ethn, 114, June 1953, p. 223-227).
Lexicostatistical time-depth count on Huastec and Yucatec yields 3200 years of separation and correlates with Ekholm's Tampico-Panuco Period II.

722a. ————. Perspectives and problems of Amerindian comparative linguistics (Word, 10:2-3, Aug.-Dec. 1954, p. 306-332).
Linking of Zoque and Totonac, Totonac and Yucatec, Totomayan and Huave; Aztec-Tanoan and Macrochibchan. Suggested affinities of Quechua; suggested relatives for Patagonian and Fuegian languages.

723. ————. Problems of long-range comparison in Penutian (Language, 32:1, Jan.-Mar. 1956, p. 17-41).
Lexicostatistical and probabilistic techniques lead to a suggested Penutian affiliation for Totonacan, Zoquean, Huave, Mayan, Coconucan, Quechumaran, and Tarasco.

723a. ————. Towards a satisfactory genetic classification of Amerindian languages (A XXXI Cong Intl Am, v. 2, p. 1001-1012).

724. Taylor, Douglas. Diachronic note on the Carib contribution to Island Carib (Intl J Am Ling, 20:1, Jan. 1954, p. 28-33).
Competition between men's (Cariban) and women's (Arawakan) speech in Island Carib.

724a. ————. [Island Carib I:] Phonemes of the Hopkins (British Honduras) dialect of Island Carib (Intl J Am Ling, 21:3, July 1955, p. 233-241).

725. ————. A note on some Arawak-Carib lexical resemblances (Intl J Am Ling, 19:4, Oct. 1953, p. 316-317).

725a. ————. A note on some Arawakan words for *man,* etc. (Intl J Am Ling, 23:1, Jan. 1957, p. 46-48).
Includes a rapprochement with Proto-Mayan *winaq.

726. ————. A note on the Arawakan affiliation of Taino (Intl J Am Ling, 20:2, Apr. 1954, p. 152-154).

726a. ————. A note on the identification of some Island Carib suffixes (Intl J Am Ling, 19:3, July 1953, p. 195-200).

727. ————. A note on the status of Amuesha (Intl J Am Ling, 20:3, July 1954, p. 240-241).
Amuesha is probably distantly related to Arawak.

LINGUISTICS

LINGUISTICS

727a. **Tovar, Antonio.** Semántica y etimología en el guaraní (B Inst Caro Cuervo, 5, 1949, p. 41-51).

728. **Trimborn, Hermann.** Ante una nueva edición del manuscrito quechua de Francisco de Ávila (Letras, 49, 1. semestre 1953, p. 233-239).

728a. **Uldall, Elizabeth.** Guaraní sound system (Intl J Am Ling, 20:4, Oct. 1954, p. 341-342).

729. **Ulsing, Tor.** Russian decipherment of the Maya glyphs (Intl J Am Ling, 22:2, Apr. 1956, p. 184-186).
Résumé of Knorozov's attempt.

729a. **Urioste-Herrero.** Gramática de la lengua quechua y vocabulario quechua-castellano, castellano-quechua de las voces más usuales. La Paz, Canata, 1955. 348 p.

730. **Vellard, J.** Contribution à l'étude des Indiens Uru ou Kot'suñs (Trav Étud And, 3, 1951, i.e. 1953, p. 3-39).
Continuation of article appearing in the same journal, 1, 1949, p. 145-209, and 2, 1950, p. 51-88.

730a. **Vocabulario mazateco.** México, Instituto Lingüístico de Verano [and] Dirección General de Asuntos Indígenas, 1952. 62 p.

731. **Wallis, Ethel.** Simulfixation in aspect markers at Mezquital Otomi (Language, 32:3, July-Sept. 1956, p. 453-459).
A demonstration that phonemic components have grammatical function and that item-and-process analysis is here more efficient.

731a. **Weitlaner, Roberto J.** El otomí de Ixtenco, Tlaxcala (A Inst Nac Antr Hist, 6:2, no. 35 de la colección, 1952, i.e. 1955, p. 11-14).
An indication of the possible conservative character of this isolated Otomi dialect.

732. **Whorf, Benjamin Lee.** A comparative decipherment of forty-one ancient Maya written words. Chicago, Ill., University of Chicago Library (Microfilm collection of manuscripts on Middle American cultural anthropology, 50), [1936] 1957. 10 p.

732a. ————. A contribution to the study of the Aztec language. Chicago, Ill., University of Chicago Library (Microfilm collection of manuscripts on Middle

American cultural anthropology, 42), [1928] 1957. 43 p.
A detailed linguistic and literary treatment of the second poem found in D. G. Brinton's *Ancient Nahuatl poetry* (Philadelphia, 1890).

733. ————. First steps in the decipherment of Maya writing. Chicago, Ill., University of Chicago Library (Microfilm collection of manuscripts on Middle American cultural anthropology, 49), [1935?] 1957. 112 p.

733a. ————. Notes on the oligosynthetic comparison of Nahuatl and Piman, with special reference to Tepecano. Chicago, Ill., University of Chicago Library (Microfilm collection of manuscripts on Middle American cultural anthropology, 44), [1928] 1957. 23 p.
Oligosynthesis viewed historically.

734. ————. The phenomenon of oligosynthesis in Nahuatl or Aztec. Chicago, Ill., Univeristy of Chicago Library (Microfilm collection of manuscripts on Middle American cultural anthropology, 43), [1928] 1957. 13 p.
The formation from a very small number of roots, by a process of combination and recombination, of a large complex vocabulary.

734a. ————. Recent determinations of phonetic characters in Maya writing. Chicago, Ill., University of Chicago Library (Microfilm collection of manuscripts on Middle American cultural anthropology, 47), [1933] 1957. 8 p.

735. ————. Stem series in Maya and certain Maya hieroglyphs. Chicago, Ill., University of Chicago Library (Microfilm collection of manuscripts on Middle American cultural anthropology, 45), [1930] 1957. 28 p.

735a. **Zimmermann, Günter.** Das Cotoque: die Maya-Sprache von Chicomucelo (Zeit Ethn, 80: 1, 1955, p. 59-87).
Additional material on Chicomuceltec; full comparison with Huastec, its closest relative within the Mayan family.

736. ————. Die Hieroglyphen der Maya-handschriften. Hamburg, 1956.

736a. ————. Über einige stereotype Wendungen and Metaphern im Redestil des Aztekischen (Baessler Arch, n. f., 3, 1955, p. 149-168).
Notes on Aztec stylistics.

PHYSICAL ANTHROPOLOGY

T. D. STEWART

TWO EXTENDED expeditions in 1956—one to Peru, the other to Brazil—helped clarify our understanding of man's reaction to his environment and man's antiquity in one part of the continent. At the end of July, Marshall T. Newman, Associate Curator of Physical Anthropology, U. S. National Museum, and various associates concluded a series of biological studies on Indians living at Vicos, an hacienda in the Callejon de Huaylas, Peru (Science, 124:3222, Sept. 28, 1956, p. 576). These Indians live at 10,000-12,000 feet altitude and subsist on a near minimal diet. Since there are prospects of improving the diet, the studies were designed to give an observational base in anticipation of discovering a response in physique. Besides anthropometric details, the studies included diet analyses, blood chemistry, and carpal X-rays. In general the population was found to be retarded in development and growth. Such a physique seems to represent a successful adaptation to the environment. It remains to be seen what will happen to the physique, if and when the diet is changed. The approach used here is somewhat different from that used by Carlos Monge and his followers (see item 790).

The expedition to Brazil, by contrast, was archaeological. However, the main objective was to investigate the antiquity of Lagoa Santa man. Leader of the expedition was W. R. Hurt, Director of the W. H. Over Museum, University of South Dakota. His Brazilian associate was the physical anthropologist, Luiz de Castro Faria. Field work ended on Oct. 3, 1956 (Mus News, 18:9-10, Sept.-Oct. 1956, p. 13-17). Of the eight caves and rock shelters in the areas of Cerca Grande and Matozinhos (Minas Gerais) in which work was done, none yielded evidence of occupation older than a few thousand years. There remains the problem of reconciling this finding with previous findings suggesting much more antiquity and also with the evidence from the fluorine test on the Confins skull reported in item 785.

Numerous cave burials (at least 20 in fairly good condition) were encountered by the expedition. These have been turned over to the Museum in Rio de Janeiro and will be described by Castro Faria.

In this connection it is noteworthy that Georg K. Neumann, Professor of Physical Anthropology at the University of Indiana, is one of the latest to examine the Lagoa Santa skeletal remains preserved in Copenhagen. Being an outstanding student of the craniology of North American Indians, Neumann's views on the Lagoa Santa type and its relationships are important. As yet, however, nothing is available but the titles of his papers read at the annual meetings of the American Association of Physical Anthropologists (April 1955) and of the Society for American Archeology (May 1956).

Only one major scientific meeting was held in the Western Hemisphere in 1956, namely, the V International Congress of Anthropological and Ethnological Sciences, Philadelphia, September 1-9. Although quite a few Latin Americans attended, the physical anthropology of this area was far from adequately represented. As a matter of fact, the only paper in this field actually read was unscheduled: Paul Rivet's "L'élément blanc et les pygmies en Amérique."

Earlier in the year Santiago Genovés of Mexico City completed his doctorate work at Cambridge University, England. His thesis runs to 555 pages and bears the title, "A study of sex differences in the innominate bone (os coxae), with special reference to the material from St. Bride's Church, Fleet Street, London, WC1" (obtainable in microfilm from the University Library, Ph. D. 2903).

In a belated report on anthropological activities in Peru (BBAA, 18:1, 1955, i. e. 1956, p. 139-148) it appears that C. Arturo del Pozo, Auxiliary Professor of Physical Anthropology at the Universidad Nacional del Cuzco, spent the months of February and March of 1955 in Lima studying cranial deformity at the Museo Nacional de Antropología y Arqueología. On March 10 he talked to the Asociación Peruana de Antropología e Historia on "Estudio de la cabeza ósea: género lama." Since the subject of cranial deformity is also of interest to Pedro Weiss of Lima (personal communication), it seems likely that new developments in this field will be forthcoming soon.

Some years back, this section included a statement of E. M. da Silva's plans to re-investigate the blood groups of the Caraja Indians of Brazil, together with an announcement of his death while returning from the expedition (*HLAS, no. 14, 1948,* p. 46 and footnote no. 4). As years went by without the publication of his results, it began to look as if da Silva's efforts had been in vain and the work would have to be done over again. Now, however, the record has been completed by P. C. Junqueira and P. J. Wishart (item 780), who show that da Silva succeeded in typing 113 Caraja Indians, finding less than 3% group B, rather than the 51% reported in 1930 by Golden.

GENERAL

750. **Arends, Tulio, and Miguel Layrisse.** Investigación del factor Diego en japoneses y chinos (Acta Cien Ven, 7:1, 1956, 7 p.).
Reports the finding of the factor in 12.3 percent of 65 Japanese and in 5 percent of 100 Chinese (Canton). Suggests that the factor is Mongoloid rather than Indian.

751. **Comas, Juan.** Los Congresos Internacionales de Americanistas. Síntesis histórica e índice bibliográfico general, 1875-1952. México, Instituto Indigenista Interamericano (Ediciones especiales), 1954. lxxxiii, 224 p.
118 items in physical anthropology are listed alphabetically.

752. ————. Historia y bibliografía de los congresos internacionales de ciencias antropológicas: 1865-1954. México, Universidad Nacional Autónoma de México, Instituto de Historia (Publ., 1, serie, 37), 1956. 490 p.
Subject classification includes physical anthropology of Eurasia and Africa: methods and techniques of work (53 items), paleontology and human evolution (148), genetics (48), eugenics (26), physical anthropology in general (113), craniometry and osteometry (114), somatometry and raciology (162), biotypology (36), and serology (56).

753. **Dupouy, Walter.** Dr. Eduardo Fleury Cuello, 1904-1954 (B Indig Ven, año 2, 2:1-4, enero-dic. 1954, p. 157-161).
Biographical sketch with photograph and bibliography of nine items.

754. **Eusebio Dávalos Hurtado** (1909-) (BBAA, 18:2, 1955, i.e. 1956, p. 314-318).
Bibliography from 1945 to date.

755. **Gini, Corrado.** Possono e devono i caratteri psichici e culturali essere tenuti presenti nella classificazione delle razze umane? (*in* Estudios . . . Manuel Gamio [see item 21], p. 59-62).
Cites the failure of the UNESCO statement on race to take into account the psychic and cultural aspects of mankind. Presents arguments on this score.

756. **Levine, Philip** (and others). The *Diego* blood factor (Nature, 177:4497, Jan. 7, 1956, p. 40-41).
General review of findings to date. Discusses problems of inheritance.

757. **San Martín, Mauricio.** Genética y antropología (*in* Conferencia de Ciencias Antropológicas [see item 25], p. 100-107).
Discusses the different approaches to race classification represented by the writings of Boyd (Genotypic) and the writings of Coon, Garn, and Birdsell (Phenotypic). Urges closer cooperation between the anthropologists and geneticists.

758. **Stewart, T. D.** El cuerpo humano y el ambiente (*in* Conferencia de Ciencias Antropológicas [see item 25], p. 108-116).
Discusses some of the difficulties connected with the study of man's physical adaptation to environment, particularly altitude. Uses for purposes of illustration his own anthropometric work done in 1947-1949 in the highlands of Guatemala.

MIDDLE AMERICA AND THE CARIBBEAN

759. **Aveleyra Arroyo de Anda, Luis.** Contemporaneidad del hombre con fauna extinguida en el Pleistoceno Superior de México (A Inst Nac Antr Hist, 7, no. 36 de la colección, 1955, p. 29-39).
General review of subject presented in a conference at the Royal Anthropological Institute of Great Britain and Ireland.

760. Dávalos Hurtado, Eusebio. La alimentación entre los mexicas (R Mex Estud Antr, 14:1, 1954-1955, p. 103-118). Reviews the writings on this subject and concludes that undernutrition was not present.

761. ————. Un ejemplo de patología ósea prehispánica de México (A Inst Nac Antr Hist, 7, no. 36 de la colección, 1955, p. 147-155, 14 pl.). Specimen excavated in 1951 by John L. Custer at San Francisco de Culhuacan, about 12 kilometers southeast of Mexico City. Young adult male buried in flexed position and accompanied by Aztec I cultural objects. Shows degenerative arthritis and healed fractures.

762. ————. Los restos de Hernán Cortés (Mem R Ac Nac Cien, 57:3-4, 1955, p. 431-457). Gives detailed measurements and photographs of bones exhumed on Nov. 25, 1946, in the Church of Jesús Nazareno, Mexico City. Concludes that the bones very probably pertain to Cortés and that the pathological lesions which they exhibit are not syphilitic but a combination of nonspecific osteitis and Paget's osteosis.

763. ————, and **A. Romano.** Las deformaciones corporales entre los mexicas (R Mex Estud Antr, 14:1, 1954-1955, p. 79-101). Distinguishes six forms and reviews the literature thereon. Most emphasis is on cranial deformity and dental mutilation. The only evidence on ear, nose, and lip mutilation, dental discoloration, and body scarification comes from the early chronicles.

764. Gates, R. Ruggles. Studies in race crossing. IV. Crosses of Chinese, Amerindians and Negroes, and their bearing on racial relationships (Zeit Morph Anthr, 47:3, März 1956, p. 233-315). Includes the following observations on 24 racially mixed Cuban families: hair form, eye color, skin color, ear form, eye folds, nose form, and characteristics of eyebrows and eyelashes.

765. Lehmann, Henri. Différentes formes de sacrifices humains pratiqués à Chicol (Guatemala) d'après les fouilles effectués en 1954 (A XXXI Cong Intl Am, v. 2, p. 673-681). Describes several burials from ruins some 12 kilometers west of Zaculeu. Argues, simply from the positions of the bones, that the individuals had been sacrificed. Four illustrations.

766. Montemayor, Felipe. La población de Veracruz. Historia de las lenguas, culturas actuales, rasgos físicos de la población. Veracruz, México, Gobierno de Veracruz, 1950-1956, i.e. 1956. 78 p. For purposes of greater distribution, the two-volume work of Faulhaber issued in 1955 (see *HLAS, no. 19,* item 875a) has been synthesized.

767. Muñoz, J. Antonio, and **Miguel Guzmán.** Reporte preliminar sobre pesos y estaturas en escolares de Guatemala (R Col Méd Guat, 4:1, marzo 1953, p. 60-69). Presents curves of growth in weight and stature for both sexes between the ages of 6 and 15-17 years for three groups: (1) 517 children from the Colegio Americano (upper class Guatemalans); (2) 1072 *ladinos;* and (3) 620 Indians from Sacatepequez, Totonicapan, and Huehuetenango. The first group matches Iowa standards and the second and third groups are 1-2 years and 3-4 years retarded, respectively, by the same standards. The retardation of the Indian children was also studied in 234 cases and from five areas by radiographs of the wrist. Three cases are illustrated.

768. Pompa y Pompa, Antonio. Nicolás León (6-XII-1859-24-I-1929) (BBAA, 18:2, 1955, i. e. 1956, p. 295-310). The first extended listing of the anthropological writings (210 items) of the founder of Mexican physical anthropology.

769. Romano, Arturo. Nota preliminar sobre los restos humanos sub-fósiles de Santa María Astahuacan, D. F. (A Inst Nac Antr Hist, 7, no. 36 de la colección, 1955, p. 65-74, 2 figs., 13 pl.). Detailed description of two skulls from site 1. Comparisons are with Tepexpan which is believed to be contemporaneous.

770. Romero, Javier. Aspectos psicobiométricos y sociales de una muestra de la juventud mexicana. México, Dirección de Investigaciones Antropológicas (Publ., 1), 1956. 63 p. Statistical analysis of biometric data on aspirants for admission to the Heroico Colegio Militar for the years 1953, 1954, and 1955. The total number of subjects is 1326; the average age is around 18 years.

771. ————. El laboratorio psico-biológico del H. Colegio Militar (*in* Estudios . . . Manuel Gamio [see item 21], p. 63-73). General statement about project. See item 770 for further details.

772. Schreider, Eugène. Étude de quelques signes de métissage dans une population amérindienne (B Mem Soc Anthr, 10. série, 6:4-5, 1955, p. 223-234). Identifies Negroid and Europoid types among Otomi Indians and shows that racial mixture has been going on for a long time. This is reflected in the blood group frequencies for the whole sample (29): 74.68% group O; 11.39% A; 8.86% B; 5.06% AB (7.5% *p,* 7.2% *q,* 86.4% *y*). (See also *HLAS, no. 19,* item 873.)

773. Stewart, T. D. Skeletal remains from Xochicalco, Morelos (*in* Estudios . . .

Manuel Gamio [see item 21], p. 131-156). In 1945 the skeletons of 22 individuals (16 adults, 6 subadults) were removed to the Museo Nacional de Antropología in Mexico City in blocks of earth. Burial position is reported along with detailed anthropometric observations. Tooth mutilation and cranial deformity are illustrated. The top of one skull had been cut as if for the removal of the brain.

ARGENTINA, BOLIVIA, AND BRAZIL

774. **Biocca, Ettore.** Sui gruppi sanguigni degli Amerindi dell' Alto Rio Negro (Amazzonia) (R Antr, Roma, 41, 1954, p. 375-376).
Author cites 12 papers which he has published since he went to Brazil in 1944. Only those dealing with blood groups are summarized here.

775. **Bórmida, Marcelo.** Recientes estudios sobre los antiguos habitantes de la Patagonia (A XXXI Cong Intl Am, v. 2, p. 939-963).
Based on 350 skulls from collections in B. A and from the author's recent expeditions. Considers deformity, measurements, cranial types, and reconstruction of racial history. A few types are shown in stereographic drawings.

776. **Faria, L. de Castro.** O estado atual da antropologia-física no Brasil (A XXXI Cong Intl Am, v. 2, p. 885-894).
Divides the history of physical anthropology in Brazil before 1930 into 2 periods: (1) construction (1860-1910), and (2) renovation (1910-1930). Regular and official teaching of the subject began in 1940. Discusses the deficiencies in instruction and the present status of research.

777. **Fernandes, José Loureiro.** Contribuição à antropometria e à hematologia dos Kaingang do Paraná (A XXXI Cong Intl Am, v. 2, p. 895-898).
Brief general statement based on 36 males from the Posto Fioravante Esperança in the município of Palmas. This population has a long history of racial admixture. Mean stature is 163 centimeters; mean cephalic index is 76.3. Blood groups are as follows: 88% group O; 10% B; 2% A; complete absence of Rh+.

778. **Imbelloni, José.** Sobre los constructores de sambaquí (3.ª contribución): yacimientos de Paraná y Santa Catarina (A XXXI Cong Intl Am, v. 2, p. 965-997).
Analyses of 64 skulls (31 male, 33 female) from 11 sambaquí in the collection of Guilherme Tiburtius in Curitiba. This is the first description of this material. Three types are defined and illustrated. The distribution of these types in this and other collections is presented.

779. **Junqueira, P. C.** (and others). The Diego blood factor in Brazilian Indians (Nature, 177:4497, Jan. 7, 1956, p. 41).

Reports an incidence of 46% for 48 Kaingang Indians living on a reservation near Palmas (state of Parana), and 36% for 36 Carajás living at Santa Isabel, Bananal Island. These groups belong to the Ge linguistic family but live 1100 miles apart.

780. ————, and **P. J. Wishart.** Blood groups of Brazilian Indians (Carajás) (Nature, 177:4497, Jan. 7, 1956, p. 40).
The findings of the late E. M. da Silva on 113 subjects: 92% group O; 0.9% A; 2.7% B; and 4.4% AB. This refutes the claim of Golden to 51% B in the Carajas.

781. **Pourchet, Maria Júlia.** Contribuição ao estudo antropofísico de descendentes de imigrantes portuguêses (A XXXI Cong Intl Am, v. 2, p. 899-910).
This is the first part of a project to study foreign elements in the Brazilian population. In the present sample of 500, both parents are immigrant Portuguese and the age range is 7 to 14 years. Among the findings reported in general is a tendency to brachycephalization. For further details see item below.

782. ————. Contribuição ao estudo antropofísico de escolares descendentes de portuguêses (B Inst Pesq Ed, 1:4, 1955, p. 5-54).
Based on a series of 500 students (259 males, 241 females) 7 to 14 years of age, of Portuguese parentage, from various parts of the Federal District. The first part deals with 24 characters of a general nature or relating to the body as a whole; the second part deals with 17 characters relating to the head. Age changes are stressed. Comparisons are made with a similar study in Portuguese India.

783. **Reichlen-Barret, Paulette.** Un crâne du sud de la Patagonie (J Soc Am, n. s., 44, 1955, p. 205-243 and pl. 6-7).
Extremely detailed description of a single undeformed male skull found in a rock shelter on Cape Porpoise, some 100 kilometers north of Punta Arenas. The specimen which is either Tehuelche or Alakaluf bears the number 20, 915-1948.I in the Department of Anthropology, Musée de l'Homme, Paris. 59 references.

784. **Sacchetti, Alfredo.** Abertura palpebral y párpados en los indios andinos aymara y uro (con una propuesta de clasificación) (in Estudios . . . Manuel Gamio [see item 21], p. 75-109).
Presents arguments against Aichel's (1932) eyefold classification and offers a new classificatory scheme. Various types of folds are illustrated.

785. **Stewart, T. D.,** and **H. V. Walter.** Fluorine analysis of putatively ancient human and animal bones from Confins Cave, Minas Gerais, Brazil (A XXXI Cong Intl Am, v. 2, p. 925-937).
Reviews history of finds of early man in the Lagoa Santa caves. Reports comparative fluo-

rine data, on bone specimens (human and animal) recovered in association by H. V. Walter in one of these caves, which seem to indicate a considerable antiquity.

ECUADOR AND PERU

786. Antropología física aplicada a la prehistoria peruana (Chimor, 2:2, mayo 1954, p. 18-29).
Reports that pottery vase no. 2006 from the Lizardo Vélez López collection — believed to represent a case of trephining—is now in the museum in Trujillo. Includes a reprinting of item 473, HLAS, no. 8, 1942.

787. Ericksen, Mary Frances. A preliminary report on late period crania from the central coast of Peru (in Conferencia de Ciencias Antropológicas [see item 25], p. 201-216).
Detailed measurements and observations on a series of 241 adult crania (72 females, 169 males) from the Incaic site of Makat Tampu in the Rimac valley. Comparisons are made with Newman's Late Chancay series from the Chancay valley and his Sub-Chancay series from the Chillon valley.

788. Guzmán Barrón, Alberto. La nutrición en el antiguo Perú (in Conferencia de Ciencias Antropológicas [see item 25], p. 229-233).
Concludes that various factors contributed to a balanced nutrition in ancient times, but admits that the subject needs more study. No documentation.

789. Hurtado, Alberto. El hombre en las grandes alturas habitadas (in Conferencia de Ciencias Antropológicas [see item 25], p. 24-31).
Concludes that adaptation to high altitude is acquired and proportional to the duration of exposure thereto.

790. Monge M., Carlos. Antropología fisiológica (in Conferencia de Ciencias Antropológicas [see item 25], p. 87-99).
Reviews the subject of man's adaptation to altitude from the following points of view: hematology, biochemistry, electrocardiography, radiology, and clinical data.

791. Obando V., Marcelo A. Lesiones de fluorosis dental endémica observadas entre los antiguos pobladores de la costa peruana (A IV Cong Nac Odon, 1956, 52 p.).
Illustrates and describes ten teeth in detail. Gives frequencies for fluorosis in the following series of skulls: 200 from Makat-Tampu (0%), 100 from Marquez (2%), 115 from Ancon (77.3%), 24 from Paracas (72.7%—all from "Las Cavernas"). Correlations are made with water analyses.

792. Pesce, Hugo. Lepra en el Perú precolombino (in Conferencia de Ciencias Antropológicas [see item 25], p. 171-187)

Review of 107 sources which leads to the conclusion that leprosy was introduced into Peru by the Spaniards.

793. Rotta, Andrés. El índice cardiotorácico en el habitante de las grandes alturas (in Conferencia de Ciencias Antropológicas [see item 25], p. 32-36).
Based on a selection of 276 radiographs of adults resident at 4,540 meters altitude. In the selected cases the transverse diameter of the chest was between 10 and 45% above North American standards. In this group the transverse diameter of the heart was also measured and expressed as the cardio-thoracic index of Danzer. Comparisons are made with a sample of 200 subjects from sea level.

794. Santiana, Antonio. Deformaciones del cuerpo de carácter étnico practicadas por los aborígenes del Ecuador (G Méd, Guayaquil, 10:5, sept.-oct. 1955, p. 691-712).
Considers the following subjects: skin coloring and decoration, tattooing, deformations of the ear lobes, deformations of the nose and lips, dental decoration, and head deformation. The last subject is expanded to include a review of the literature and the author's own investigations.

795. ————. Deformaciones del cuerpo, de carácter étnico, practicadas por los aborígenes del Ecuador (in Estudios . . . Manuel Gamio [see item 21], p. 111-129).
Slightly changed version of item above. Lacks illustrations and summary.

796. Stewart, T. D. Significance of osteitis in ancient Peruvian trephining (B Hist Med, 30:4, July-Aug. 1956, p. 293-320).
Based on 75 trephined skulls, mainly from the Central Coast and Central Highlands of Peru, in the U. S. National Museum. Shows that postoperative osteitis (septic or chemical) defined the limits of the scalp incisions and that a piece of scalp was completely removed at operation. In an addendum comments on item 913 in HLAS, no. 19.

797. Trulson, M. F.; C. Collazos Ch.; and D. M. Hegsted. Growth and development of Peruvian children. I. Carquin and San Nicholás (Pediatrics, 17:4, Apr. 1956, p. 510-523).
Analysis of height, weight, and physiological age (from carpal X-rays) for 109 children (51 girls, 58 boys) 5-14 years of age. Carquin is a fishing village on the Central Coast. San Nicholas is a nearby hacienda. The nutritional status of the samples is discussed.

798. Vellard, Jéhan. Antropología física del hombre del altiplano (in Conferencia de Ciencias Antropológicas [see item 25], p. 37-86).
Same as earlier version (see HLAS, no. 18, item 401), except for addition of a section on "Carac-

teres adaptativos a la vida en las altas regiones andinas" and a somewhat garbled version of the discussion by T. D. Stewart.

VENEZUELA

799. **Díaz Ungría, Adelaida G.; Sebastián Núñez Mier y Terán; and José Díaz Ungría.** Biotipología y medicina social (*in* Los guarao del Delta Amacuro. Caracas, Universidad Central de Venezuela, Facultad de Economía, Instituto de Investigaciones, Departamento de Sociología y Antropología Cultural, 1956, p. 63-99).

On p. 70 begins a section called "Pirámide biotipológica" in which are analyzed 32 measurements and indices on 75 male Guaraos. As indicated by the title, the approach is that of Nicola Pende (modified by Fernández Cabezas). Following the conclusions are a series of abstracts by the authors and others on unpublished papers on related subjects: blood groups, skin color, blood pressure, etc.

800. **Duggins, Oliver H., and Mildred Trotter.** Characteristics of hair of Yupa Indians (Pro Am Phil Soc, 100:3, June 1956, p. 220-222).

Data on 23 hair samples (14 males, 7-36 years of age; 9 females, 6 to 15 years of age) collected by Gusinde.

801. **Geipel, Georg.** Finger and palm prints of Yupa Indians (Pro Am Phil Soc, 100:3, June 1956, p. 219-220).

Brief general statement about the palm and finger prints of 19 Yupa Indians, obtained by Gusinde.

802. **Gusinde, Martin.** El concepto de "pigmeo" y los indios pigmeos "Yupa" (A XXXI Cong Intl Am, v. 2, p. 911-924).

A reduced version of item below.

803. —————. The Yupa Indians in western Venezuela (Pro Am Phil Soc, 100:3, June 1956, p. 197-219).

Reviews the history of studies on these so-called "pygmies" from the Sierra de Perija, discusses their culture, and gives details about their physique. Includes 69 body measurements and 49 head measurements for each of 23 males and 14 females (all adults). Good portraits.

804. **Layrisse, Miguel, and Tulio Arends.** High incidence of blood group found in Venezuelan Indians (Science, 123:3198, Apr. 13, 1956, p. 633).

Summary of studies on Diego factor made in Venezuela, including two pedigrees of Carib Indian families.

Art

SPANISH AMERICA
HAROLD E. WETHEY

The years 1953-1956 marked a high point in the field of research on Spanish American art, for in no other period of four years have so many important works appeared. V. 3 of the *Historia del arte hispanoamericano* by Angulo, Marco, and Buschiazzo (item 900) completed the study of the colonial period in that comprehensive publication. Dr. Erwin Palm's exhaustive study of the colonial art of Santo Domingo (item 1015) was produced in handsome form under the auspices of the government of the Dominican Republic. The first specific investigation in a little explored field distinguished Dr. Soria's book (item 917) on colonial painting of the 16th century in South America. Other general studies were Professor Giuria's on the colonial architecture of Uruguay (item 1012) and Busaniche's account of the ruins of the Jesuit missions in the tropics of Argentina and Paraguay (item 912). Thanks to the Pan American Union's guide to public collections of art in Latin America, edited by José Gómez Sicre (item 905), much little-known material is now called to the attention of the general public.

Manuel Toussaint's death on Nov. 22, 1955, cut short the distinguished career of Mexico's leading art historian. His last book was fittingly devoted to the churches of Puebla, his native city, and his bibliography (items 985 and 988) also includes two important articles. The colonial period continued to occupy the attention of scholars throughout Spanish America. The younger Mexican writers who added notably to the publications of these years included Francisco de la Maza with several studies (items 974-978), the most outstanding being the iconography of the Capilla del Rosario of Puebla, the colonial art of Chiapas, and his book on the nuns' choirs. The magnificent volume by Villegas on the history of the *estípite* throughout the ages, with particular reference to the late Baroque style in Mexico, is a major achievement (item 990). Moreover, Dr. Baird's thorough examination of the 18th-century retables of Querétaro and Salamanca (item 958) is one of the few significant pieces of research on the retable in Latin America.

In South America the well-known Peruvian Jesuit scholar, Padre Rubén Vargas Ugarte, added an appendix (item 1004) to his *Ensayo de un diccionario de artífices coloniales* (see *HLAS, no.14, 1948*, item 742), and he also issued a short monograph on the Jesuit church, San Pedro, at Lima (item 1005). At Cuzco the further publication of notarial documents under the direction of Dr. Jorge Cornejo Bouroncle (items 993-996) added important historical data on *cuzqueño* art of the 16th and 17th centuries. In addition, Dr. José Uriel García (item 997a) provided a substantial article on the Palacio del Almirante in Cuzco. The young Bolivian scholars, José de Mesa and Teresa Gisbert de Mesa, continued their high rate of productivity on the colonial art of their country with several articles and a fine book on Bolivian colonial painting (items 934-939).

As usual the majority of works devoted to contemporary paintings were concerned with the Mexican school. Dr. Bernard Myers contributed the first good general study of modern Mexico painting (item 1060) to appear in English in several years. That the wide enthusiasm for the art of Orozco remained unabated is demonstrated by the valuable monograph with much original source material written by Alma Reed; by Fernández's publication of articles and letters by the artist; and by McKinley Helm's book (items 1065, 1063, and 1055). The year 1955 marked an important exhibition of Latin American architecture at the Museum of Modern Art in N. Y., the catalogue (item 906) of which was prepared by Henry R. Hitchcock.

GENERAL

900. Angulo Iñiguez, Diego. Historia del arte hispanoamericano. T. 3. Los capítulos IV al XII por Enrique Marco Dorta. Los capítulos XIII al XVIII por Mario J. Buschiazzo. Barcelona, Salvat, 1956. 847 p., 778 illus.

This third volume of this comprehensive history of art in Latin America includes three chapters on Central America, Cuba, and Santo Domingo written by Professor Angulo, nine chapters on the northwestern parts of South America by Professor Marco Dorta, and a section on Argentina, Chile, Paraguay, and Brazil by Professor Buschiazzo. The material is largely concerned with the 18th century, except for Mexico which was treated in v. 2. The authors have handled this vast body of material in exemplary fashion, never losing sight of the main stylistic currents and tendencies. This work is indispensable to all students of Latin American culture.

901. Arts Council of Great Britain. Catalogue of the exhibition, Mexican art from 1500 B. C. to the present day. Illustrated supplement to the catalogue of an exhibition at the Tate Gallery. London, 1953. 68 illus.

This and the item below contain excellent photographs of selected works in the exhibition and a few examples of architecture.

902. ————. Exhibition of Mexican art from pre-Columbian times to the present day. Organized under the auspices of the Mexican government. The Tate Gallery. London, 1953. 103 p.

See also item above.

903. Boulton, Alfredo. Los retratos de Bolívar. Caracas. Tall. de Italgráfica, 1956. 176 p. & illus.

This useful iconography of Bolívar traces the revolutionary leader from youth to maturity. The documentation is extensive, being provided with dimensions and media, and an excellent index provides a key to the numerous data.

904. Fernández, Justino. Catálogo de las exposiciones de arte en 1955 (A Inst Inv Estét, 6:24, 1956, suplemento, 52 p.).

See also "Catálogo de las exposiciones de arte en 1952" (A Inst Inv Estét, 6:21, 1953, suplemento, 40 p.); ". . . 1953" (6:22, 1954, suplemento, 48 p.); ". . . 1954" (6:23, 1955, suplemento, 58 p.); all prepared by Justino Fernández.

905. Gómez Sicre, José. Guía de las colecciones públicas de arte en la América Latina. V. 1. Región del Golfo de México y del Caribe. Washington, Unión Panamericana, 1956. 191 p., illus.

This handsomely illustrated book is an indispensable guide to any traveler who wishes to see the museums of Latin America. The text gives a résumé of each collection as well as the days and hours when the museums may be visited.

906. Hitchcock, Henry R. Latin American architecture since 1945. N. Y., Museum of Modern Art, 1955. 203 p., illus.

The present volume was prepared in connection with an exhibition held at the Museum of Modern Art in N. Y. It consists largely of splendid photographs which comprise an excellent survey of the extensive developments in Mexico, Brazil, Uruguay, Cuba, etc.

907. Palm, Erwin Walter. New literature on Hispanic colonial art in South America, 1946-1952 (G Beaux Arts, 6. période, 95 année, 42:1014-1015, juillet-août 1953, p. 58-62).

The author not only surveys the recent books and articles in these fields, but he also touches upon general problems, contributing new ideas and information of his own.

908. Rubín de la Borbolla, Daniel Fernando. México: monumentos históricos y arqueológicos. Libro segundo. México colonial y moderno. México, Instituto Panamericano de Geografía e Historia (Publ., 145), 1953. 215 p., illus.

This collection of photographs in large format is accompanied by brief commentary. Unfortunately, the printing does not equal the quality of the photography. The subjects covered are architecture of the colonial period, the modern church at Monterrey, contemporary painting, and outstanding museums.

909. Sociedad de Arquitectos Mexicanos, and Colegio Nacional de Arquitectos de México. 4000 años de arqui-

tectura mexicana. México, Libreros Mexicanos Unidos, 1956. 330 p., illus.
This handsome picture book covers, as the title indicates, all phases of architecture from the pre-Columbian onward. The titles of the illustrations, given in Spanish, English, French, and German, consists of the briefest kind of identification. More than half of the plates are devoted to the 20th century.

910. Torralba Soriano, Federico B. Arte americano en la Bienal de Venecia (Estud Am, 5:17, feb. 1953, p. 177-182 & illus.).
Report on painting and sculpture shown at Venice in 1952.

911. Westheim, Paul. La calavera. Traducción de Mariana Frenk. México, Antigua Librerío Robredo (México y lo mexicano, 18), 1953. 123 p., illus., 30 plates.
A little volume devoted to the iconography of the death's head at it appears in pre-Columbian art and more specifically in the European tradition, as represented by Holbein's woodcuts of the Triumph of Death. The author shows how Manuel Mansilla and Posada turned the theme to comic and satirical uses, but he does not explore the full significance of the death's head in either Mexican culture or the Hispanic world in general.

COLONIAL

GENERAL

912. Busaniche, Hernán. La arquitectura en las misiones jesuíticas guaraníes. Santa Fe, Argentina, Castellví (El Litoral), 1955. 204 p., illus.
This monograph is one of the most thorough and up-to-date studies of the great Jesuit ruins which are located today within the borders of Argentina and Paraguay.

913. Géo, Charles. Art baroque en Amérique latine. Paris, Librairie Plon, 1954. 30 p., 66 illus.
A brief essay with vague references to Mexico, Brazil, and South American countries. It is difficult to understand why a reputable publisher should print such a worthless book.

914. Kelemen, Pál. The significance of the stone retable of Cristo Rey (Palacio, 61:8, Aug. 1954, p. 243-272, 12 illus.).
This provincial altar of the 18th century in New Mexico is the point of departure for a detailed iconographic study of the scenes represented and of the traditions and background out of which they grew.

915. Palm, Erwin W. Las capillas abiertas americanas y sus antecedentes en el occidente cristiano (A Inst Arte Am, 6, 1953, p. 47-64, 13 illus.).
The author makes a detailed survey of the European tradition in the use of chapels with outer openings, which he studies as background to the development of the "open chapel" for preaching to the Indians outdoors in Latin America. Many of the suggested relationships, such as lateral porches, Asturian treasure chambers, and the chapels of St. Michael, seem to have little to do with the American development. The article raises numerous questions of an arresting nature which merit further investigation.

916. Ramsey, L. G. G. Dress and customs of colonial Latin America in a series of unique paintings (Connoisseur, 133:537, May 1954, p. 162-167).
Here are reproduced 13 paintings of the late 18th century which illustrate the costumes and customs of the regions of La Plata (Sucre), Potosi, Chucuito, Cochabamba, Santa Cruz, Mojos, and Tucuman. They give an impression of considerable elegance among the highborn ladies, and they furnish some documentation of native traditions. Each picture has an explanatory legend.

917. Soria, Martin Sebastian. La pintura del siglo XVI en Sud América. B. A., Instituto de Arte Americano e Ideas Estéticas, 1956. 125 p., 82 illus.
This book constitutes the first detailed study of 16th-century painting in South America. It is thoroughly documented and it contains an exhaustive account of the mural (circa 1587-1607) in the house of Don Juan de Vargas in Bogota. Soria has demonstrated the source of various details in Flemish engravings of ornament. The major contribution of the book, however, is the reconstruction of the work of the Jesuit painter, Bernard Bitti. Born in Italy, he lived in Peru and Bolivia from 1574 until his death at Lima in 1610. Soria has discovered a large number of his paintings, which were hitherto unidentified, most notably a series of seven in the former Jesuit church of San Miguel at Sucre.

ARGENTINA

918. Altamira, Luis Roberto. Córdoba, sus pintores y sus pinturas, siglos XVII y XVIII (R U Nac, Córdoba, 40:2, mayo-junio 1953, p. 417-551; 40:3-5, julio-dic. 1953, p. 759-882, 35 illus.).
This long and ambitious study began in 1951 (*HLAS, no. 17, 1951*, item 417) and continues here in what appears to be the preparation of a book. The history of Spanish painting in the Baroque period is briefly sketched, and historical data on painters throughout South America have been culled from various sources. Since the author has done original research in the archives of B. A. and Cordoba, the sections on Argentina are the most valuable. The method is one of compilation rather than of study of the pictures themselves.

919. Carril, Bonifacio del. Acerca de las primeras pinturas sobre la Argentina (A Inst Arte Am, 8, 1955, p. 9-26, illus.).
Study of the maps and views of Argentina made for the Bauzá expedition of 1789-1794.

920. Dony, Paul. Orlas laterales en las

portadas andinas (A Inst Arte Am, 9, 1956, p. 99-105, 8 illus.).
This article consists of brief descriptions of the lateral strips of ornament on Baroque altars and portals. The author fails to distinguish even broad stylistic groups, such as the technique and ornamental motives of *mestizo* monuments. The documentation is superficial; he gives little or no indication of the source of his dating and no hint of the extensive bibliography on the subject.

922. **Ribera, Adolfo L.** La platería en el Río de la Plata. B. A., Domingo E. Taladriz, 1955. 110 p. & illus.
A thoroughly documented scholarly study based upon years of research in the archives of B. A. Included is an alphabetical list of biographies of silversmiths active in the 16th and 17th centuries.

923. ————. La platería en el Río de la Plata (A Inst Arte Am, 7, 1954, p. 12-17, illus.).
This study is the result of years of research in the archives of Argentina. The author has written a history of the silversmiths in his country and he includes the biographies of all known silversmiths, arranged in alphabetical sequence.

924. **Schenone, Héctor.** Tallistas portugueses en el Río de la Plata (A Inst Arte Am, 8, 1955, p. 40-56, illus.).
This documentary article reveals the surprising fact that a number of Portuguese sculptors were active in the B. A. region in the 18th century.

925. Tallistas, carpinteros y estatuarios, silleteros y toneleros, aserradores y peyneros (A Inst Arte Am, 6, 1953, p. 107-115).
Documents dated 1780.

926. **Torre Revello, José.** Arte popular en el antiguo Buenos Aires (A Inst Arte Am, 9, 1956, p. 91-97).
Various inventories of the late 18th century mentioning works of art bequeathed at times of death. The references to images made in Naples cannot always be taken at face value, since foreign importations were often claimed for local products.

927. ————. La Casa Cabildo de la ciudad de Buenos Aires. B. A., Instituto de Investigaciones Históricas (Publ., 97), 1951. 71 p., 8 illus.
An extensive monograph on the only important civil building of the colonial period which still survives in B. A.

928. ————. Datos relacionados con las artes plásticas en América durante la dominación española (A Inst Arte Am, 7, 1954, p. 118-135, illus.).
The extracts from letters of the bishops of Peru, preserved in the Archive of the Indies, contain valuable data about the building of churches. Much material is new, but some items have been previously published by the same author.

929. ————. Relaciones documentales (A Inst Arte Am, 7, 1954, p. 136-140).
Data on Enríquez, a sculptor born in Portugal but active in B. A. in the second half of the 18th century.

930. **Vázquez Basavilbaso, Roberto.** Sobre un cuadro de De Petris (A Inst Arte Am, 6, 1953, p. 104-106, 1 illus.).
On a late 18th-century portrait.

931. **Zapata Gollán, Agustín.** La construcción de la vivienda en Santa Fe la vieja (A Inst Arte Am, 9, 1956, p. 71-89).
A documentary article on the types of construction current in Santa Fe in the 17th century, wood and thatch being the chief materials.

BOLIVIA

932. **Buschiazzo, Mario J.** La arquitectura de las misiones de Mojos y Chiquitos (Südamerika, 4:3, Nov.-Dez. 1953, 14 p., 11 illus.).
A study of Jesuit missions in the tropics, many of which are now lost, using descriptions of travellers of the 18th and 19th centuries.

933. **Marco Dorta, Enrique.** El barroco en la arquitectura de la villa imperial de Potosí. Potosí, Editorial Potosí (Cuadernos de la colección de la cultura boliviana, 3), 1955. 53 p. & illus.
Reprinting of the article which originally appeared in *Arte en América y Filipinas* in 1949 (see *HLAS, no. 15, 1949,* item 540). The same article appeared in *Sur* (Potosí, 2, 1953-1954, p. 9-52).

934. **Mesa, José de,** and **Teresa Gisbert de Mesa.** El estilo mestizo en la arquitectura virreinal boliviana (Khana, 4:7-8, marzo 1955, p. 9-26).
A résumé of the subject with emphasis on Potosí. It is difficult to agree with the authors that La Compañía in Potosí, dated 1700-1707, is the earliest mestizo monument, since the school of Arequipa is slightly earlier, the façade of the Jesuit church there being inscribed 1698 and patently of an earlier phase of development. The dates given are in some cases incorrect, as in the case of San Agustín of Sucre which is documented *circa* 1585-1620 (not 1638), and La Merced in Sucre was nearly finished in 1630 rather than in 1650. The authors cite the works of earlier writers on the subject: Angulo, Marco Dorta, Schenone, and Wethey.

935. ————, and ————. Holguín y la pintura altoperuana del virreinato. La Paz,

Biblioteca Paceña, Alcaldía Municipal, 1956. 323 p., 102 plates.
The first history of colonial painting in Bolivia is a thoroughly documented work containing a vast amount of hitherto unpublished material. Although the authors make Pérez de Holguín the central figure, they give a survey of painting from the 16th through the 19th centuries. They have searched archives for documentary evidence and they reproduce signatures from numerous pictures. The authors have produced an important pioneer work in this field.

936. ————, and ————. La iglesia de Caquiaviri (Khana, 4:7-8, marzo 1955, p. 27-35).
A thorough study of a late Renaissance church in Bolivia (circa 1620) which is similar in type to those still extant in Peru on the shores of Lake Titicaca. Parts of the church have been rebuilt in the 18th century. The authors cite the existence of an atrium and posas, thus adding to the increasing number known of these peculiarly American features.

937. ————, and ————. La iglesia de las Carmelitas de Cochabamba (A Inst Arte Am, 7, 1954, p. 7-11, 9 illus.).
The authors have reconstructed the original and unusual polylobed plan of this little church, first designed in 1753 but rebuilt on a rectangular plan in 1791.

938. ————, and ————. Noticias para la historia del arte en La Paz (An Estud Am, 10, 1953, p. 171-208, 6 illus.).
This catalogue of the churches of La Paz and neighboring region is valuable as a compilation of material which has been studied very little. The authors have assembled historical data, and it is to be hoped that they will continue further with analysis of the architecture.

939. ————, and ————. La pintura boliviana en el siglo XVII (Estud Am, 11:52, enero 1956, p. 19-42).
An important survey of the subject in which the authors have assembled the names and works of all known painters of the colonial period in Bolivia.

CHILE

940. Benavides Rodríguez, Alfredo. Las pinturas coloniales del convento de San Francisco de Santiago. Discurso de incorporación a la Academia Chilena de Historia, pronunciado en Junta pública de 10 de septiembre de 1953. Santiago, 1954. 96 p., 21 illus.
A study of the series of pictures of the life of St. Francis in the Franciscan monastery at Santiago.

941. Iglesias B., Augusto, and Enrique Porta F. La catedral de Santiago de Chile. Santiago, Universidad de Chile, Facultad de Arquitectura, 1955. 71 p., illus.

A well-documented monograph on the cathedral, which is now largely of the 19th century.

942. Pereira Salas, Eugenio. La iglesia y convento mayor de San Francisco. Santiago, Consejo de Monumentos Nacionales (Cuadernos, 4), 1953. 25 illus., 1 drawing.
Short monograph based on documents in the monastic archives.

943. Secchi, E. La casa chilena hasta el siglo XIX. Santiago, Consejo de Monumentos Nacionales (Cuadernos, 3), 1952.
Brief introduction and drawings of houses and some plans.

COLOMBIA

944. Giraldo Jaramillo, Gabriel. Bibliografía selecta del arte en Colombia. Bogotá ABC (Biblioteca de bibliografía colombiana, 1), 1955. 146 p.
A useful list of bibliography on art in Colombia, although it does not give an adequate idea of the relative importance of various studies in the field.

945. ————. Francisco de Páramo, miniaturista y calígrafo santafereño del siglo XVII (Bolívar, Bogotá, 45, nov.-dic. 1955, p. 1075-1129, illus.).
The work of a provincial colonial illuminator of manuscripts.

946. ————. El Museo del Seminario Conciliar de Bogotá. Bogotá, Minerva, 1954. 16 p. & plates.
25 illustrations of works in the museum and a brief preface.

947. ————. Notas y documentos sobre el arte en Colombia. Bogotá, ABC (Academia Colombiana de Historia, Biblioteca Eduardo Santos, 9), 1954. 319 p., 53 plates.
Brief extracts from books and articles in periodicals relating to Colombian art of the colonial period and the 19th century. The book is curiously lacking in organization and in completeness.

948. ————. Pinacotecas bogotanas: La galería del Colegio Mayor de N. Sra. del Rosario (Bolívar, Bogotá, 38, mayo 1955, p. 635-668, illus.); La pinacoteca del convento de Santo Domingo (39, mayo 1955, p. 849-884); El Museo Metropolitano (40, junio 1955, p. 1017-1097); La galería del Colegio de San Bartolomé (41, julio 1955, p. 181-203); La galería del convento franciscano (42, agosto 1955, p. 397-407); Las colecciones de la Biblioteca Nacional (43, sept. 1955, p. 601-631); Artistas colombianos del siglo XIX (44, oct. 1955, p. 815-832).

Mostly portraits but also some religious pictures. The same articles have also been published as a book (Bogota, 1956, 379 p., illus.).

949. ————. Pinacotecas bogotanas: El Museo Colonial (Bolívar, Bogotá, 29, mayo 1954, p. 729-738 & illus.).
A brief description of the collection, with some illustrations.

950. Hernández de Alba, Guillermo. Arte hispánico en Colombia. Bogotá, Dirección de Información y Propaganda del Estado, 1955. 51 p. & 71 illus.
This booklet has the unusual virtue of being well printed and illustrated. The text is much too slight and undocumented, particularly since the author is a well-known scholar. In Spanish, English, and French.

951. Palm, Erwin W. Dürer's Ganda and a XVI century apotheosis of Hercules at Tunja (G Beaux Arts, 6. période, 98 année, 49:1054, nov. 1956, p. 65-74).
A well-documented study of an extraordinary series of murals containing an array of exotic animals in the Vargas house at Tunja. They demonstrate that Renaissance humanistic learning was well known in the Indies at this time. Dr. Palm interprets Hercules as symbolic of Philip II, and the union of Spain and Portugal in his person would explain representation of East Indian and African animals in this remote highland. (See also item 917).

952. Vásquez de Arce y Ceballos, Gregorio. Dibujos. Introducción de F. Gil Tovar. Bogotá, Dirección de Información y Propaganda del Estado, 1955. 10 p., 105 plates.
In this lavish publication the drawings by Vásquez de Arce (1638-1711) are reproduced on sepia paper. The format, although expensive, is provincial in the extreme in the use of colored paper with ragged edges on all four sides, mounted on black mats. No dimensions or other essential details of a good catalogue are included.

GUATEMALA

953. Markman, Sydney David. La arquitectura de la ciudad colonial, Antigua, Guatemala, 1543-1773 (A Soc Geog Hist Guat, año 27, 27:1-4, marzo 1953-dic. 1954, p. 37-53, illus.).
Survey of the architectural remains of Antigua.

954. ————. Santa Cruz, Antigua, Guatemala, and the Spanish colonial architecture of Central America (J Soc Archit Hist, 15:1, Mar. 1956, p. 12-19, 6 illus.).
Documentary study of an 18th-century church.

955. Rubín de la Borbolla, Daniel F., and **Hugo Cerezo.** Guatemala: monumentos históricos y arqueológicos. México, Instituto Panamericano de Geografía e Historia (Monumentos históricos y arqueológicos de América, 6; Comisión de Historia, 42; Publ., 144), 1953. 115 p., 34 illus.
Report on legislation and recent restorations to preserve national monuments.

956. Szécsy, János de. Santiago de los Caballeros de Goathemala en Almolonga; investigaciones del año 1950. Guatemala, Instituto de Antropología e Historia de Guatemala (Publ.), 1953. 172 p., illus.
This detailed report of the excavations of the first important settlement in Guatemala has led to confusing and somewhat indefinite conclusions. The chief sites investigated were the Capilla de Doña Beatriz, the Franciscan and Dominican monasteries, and the so-called house of Alvarado. Floor plans and photographs of excavated sites.

MEXICO

957. Arroyo, Esteban. El monumental convento de Santo Domingo de Oajaca. Oajaca, México, Camarena, 1955. 101 p., 6 illus.
A fairly detailed description of the church and monastery but without particular reference to the architecture or the works of art it contains.

958. Baird, Joseph A. Eighteenth century retables of the Bajío, Mexico: the Querétaro style (Art B, 35:3, Sept. 1953, p. 197-216, 20 illus.).
A thorough study of the retables of Queretaro and Salamanca is presented, this article being an extract from the author's doctoral dissertation on 18th-century retables in Mexico, Southern Spain, and Portugal. He believes that the *estípite* type of retable was originated by Jerónimo Balbás while still in Spain. Balbás migrated to Mexico, founding the 18th-century school there and passing his ideas on to Lorenzo Rodríguez, who established the same type of design in church façades. The author analyzes in detail, with ample documentation and footnotes, the altars of Santa Clara and Santa Rosa at Queretaro. He finds their antecedents in the monuments by Pedro Duque de Cornejo and Felipe Fernández del Castillo in Andalusia, but there are also rococo influences. In producing an important local school, the chief figures are Ignacio Mariano de las Casas and Mariano Perusquia. Pedro Joseph de Rojas, a close collaborator of Las Casas, is the leading master of the retables of San Agustín in Salamanca (Mexico).

959. ————. The ornamental niche-pilaster in the Hispanic world (J Soc Archit Hist, 15:1, Mar. 1956, p. 5-11, 13 illus.).
The author believes that important features of late Baroque altars in Mexico are developed from the work of Francisco Hurtado in Granada, Spain.

960. Berlin, Heinrich. La catedral de Morelia y sus artistas (A Soc Geog Hist

Guat, año 27, 27:1-4, marzo 1953-dic. 1954, p. 146-168, illus.).
Research in the notarial archives of Morelia and in the Archivo de la Nación in Mexico City has brought new data to light. The cathedral was begun in 1660 on the plans of a Spanish-born architect, Vicencio Varrocio Escallola. A document of 1660 shows that the same architect made the plans and began the church of La Compañía, also in Morelia. After his death in 1692, he was succeeded as *maestro mayor* of the cathedral by Juan de Silva Carrillo, native of Cadiz (1696-1702). The cathedral of Morelia was at last completed by the architect Joseph de Medina, of Puebla, who added the towers and lateral portals (1741-1746). The article contains a considerable amount of new documentary material on 18th-century architecture and architects of Mexico.

961. Blom, Frans. El retablo de Teopisca en Chiapas (A Inst Inv Estét, 6:23, 1955, p. 39-42, 6 illus.).
A Baroque retable (*circa* 1700) with spiral columns, statues, and paintings.

962. Calderón Quijano, José Antonio. Historia de las fortificaciones de Nueva España. Sevilla, Escuela de Estudios Hispano-Americanos (Publ., 60), 1953. xxxvi, 334 p., 183 figs.
This exhaustive study of a complex and difficult subject is illustrated with plans and drawings from the 16th through the 19th centuries and compared with photographs of the monuments in their present state. The appendices contain many documents transcribed from the Archives of the Indies in Seville, and the book is supplied with a usable index. The introduction was also published in *Estudios americanos* (6:21, junio-julio 1953, p. 37-53).

963. Carpenter, Edwin H., Jr. Copper engraving in Mexico in the late eighteenth century. An inventory of the engravers found in the New York Public Library (B NY Pub Lib, 57:6, June 1953, p. 263-272, 1 illus.).
A high point in Mexican copper engraving was reached in Mexico in the late 18th century when a few Spanish engravers emigrated to the New World. In addition to notes on the leading Mexican engravers of the period, the author gives a complete list of the signed engravings by Mexican which are in the collection of the N. Y. Public Library.

964. Carrillo y Gariel, Abelardo. Autógrafos de pintores coloniales. I. México, Universidad Nacional Autónoma de Méxi-co, Instituto de Investigaciones Estéticas, 1953. 168 p.
This important documentary study reproduces the signatures of colonial painting with citation of the exact source and complete statistical material. A small section contains written signatures transcribed from documents. In the appendix is an alphabetical list of Mexican colonial paintings with their dates, making this book an indispensable source of historical material.

965. Fernández, Justino. El ciprés de la catedral metropolitana (Hist Mex, 6:1, julio-sept. 1956, p. 89-98).
A study of the neoclassic high altar (1848-1851) by Lorenzo de la Hidalga in the cathedral of Mexico City.

966. Flores Guerrero, Raúl. El barroco popular de Texcoco (A Inst Inv Estét, 6:24, 1956, p. 35-51, 27 illus.).
An extremely interesting series of little-known Baroque monuments executed in provincial and primitive techniques. They are extraordinary for their originality in combining decorative motifs in stylized patterns.

967. ————. El convento de Charo y sus murales (A Inst Inv Estét, 6:22, 1954, p. 123-133 & 17 illus.).
Description of the interesting frescoes in the cloister of this fine Augustinian monastery built in the late 16th century. The author believes that European prints were used as models for the compositions.

968. González de Cossío, Francisco. Santa Águeda. Saint Agatha. Simón Pereyns. México, Porrúa, 1956. 19 p. & illus.
A well-illustrated booklet with an account of the 16th century painter, Simón Pereyns. Although born in Antwerp, he had lived in Spain before he accompanied the new viceroy Peralta to Mexico in 1566. Spanish and English text.

969. Grajales Ramos, Gloria. Influencia indígena en las artes plásticas del México colonial (A Inst Arte Am, 6, 1953, p. 77-100, 7 illus.).
The article seems to have been written by a student, since it consists entirely of lengthy quotations on the subject from the works of well-known historians.

970. Lucio, Rafael. Reseña história [sic] de la pintura mexicana en los siglos XVII y XVIII. México, Vargas Rea (Biblioteca de historiadores mexicanos), 1953. 42 p.
A short essay on Mexican colonial painting, writtten by a discerning critic in 1864. Unfortunately, there is no introduction or other explanation of the identity of the author.

971. McAndrew, John. Fortress monasteries? (A Inst Inv Estét, 6:23, 1955, p. 31-38).
The author shows that there is virtually no evidence to support the popular theory that Mexican monastic churches of the 16th century were used as fortresses in time of stress. The merlons on the churches and on the walls of the atria are purely decorative and not defensive.

972. MacGregor, Luis. Actopan. México, Secretaría de Educación Pública, Instituto Nacional de Antropología e Historia (Memorias, 4), 1955. 211 p., illus.
This long monograph on one of the most im-

portant monasteries of the 16th century in the New World is well illustrated and extensively described. The text consists, however, of a collection of notes without any pretense of even an elementary literary style. The bibliography includes only works in Spanish.

973. ————. El plateresco en México. México, Porrúa, 1954. 47 p., plates.
Revised version of the article published in the *Archivo español de arte y arqueología* in 1935. This list of 100 monuments has not been brought up to date to conform with recent research in the field, and bibliography is lacking.

974. **Maza, Francisco de la.** Arquitectura de los coros de monjas en México. México, Universidad Nacional Autónoma de México, Instituto de Investigaciones Estéticas (Estudios y fuentes del arte en México, 6), 1956. 11 p. & 90 illus.
A brief discussion of each of the important convents of nuns in Mexico City and the principal monuments in other cities with particular attention to the enclosed choirs.

975. ————. Arte colonial en Chiapas (Ateneo, Chiapas, 6, mayo 1956, p. 59-122, illus.).
This article is planned like a provincial catalogue and it includes a discussion of the Dominican church of Chiapas (*circa* 1554-1572), the famous 16th-century fountain of the same village, and various important buildings at San Cristobal las Casas including Santo Domingo whose façade must surely be dated in the 18th century, the Carmen, the Merced, etc. The author also discusses the works of art in the museum at Tuxtla Gutierrez.

976. ————. La decoración simbólica de la Capilla del Rosario de Puebla (A Inst Inv Estét, 6:23, 1955, p. 5-29, illus.).
An analysis of the complex iconography and symbolism of the decorations in the famous Chapel of the Rosary (inaugurated 1690) in Santo Domingo, Puebla.

977. ————. Las estampas de Alconedo (A Inst Inv Estét, 6:23, 1955, p. 69-74, 6 illus.).
Denunciation of a silversmith before the Inquisition for possessing French mythological prints.

978. ————. El urbanismo neoclásico de Ignacio de Castera (A Inst Inv Estét, 6:22, 1954, p. 93-101, 8 illus.).
Late 18th-century project for improving the plan of Mexico City.

979. **Obregón, Gonzalo.** El Real Convento y Santuario de San Miguel de Chalma (Estud Hist Am, p. 109-182).
An exhaustive historical study and description of the church and monastery at Chalma. The buildings, in large part of the 18th century, were partially restored in the past century.

980. **Orendain, Leopoldo I.** Los presuntos

Rubens de San Juan de los Lagos (A Inst Inv Estét, 6:23, 1955, p. 43-48, 6 illus.).
The author believes that these Rubenesque pictures on copper are Spanish, but it is probable that they are Flemish exports of the 18th century. The Forschoudt family of Antwerp conducted a large business in this sort of work.

981. **Pleasants, F. R.** Museum acquires collection of colonial Mexican portraits (Brooklyn Mus B, 14:3, spring 1953, p. 1-25).
An extremely interesting collection of Mexican portraits of the 18th and 19th centuries which previously belonged to the Algara family. Well illustrated.

982. **Reyes y Zavala, Ventura.** Las bellas artes en Jalisco (Et Caetera, 4:13, enero-marzo 1953, suplemento, p. 1-27).
Alphabetical lists of architects, painters, sculptors, and musicians born in Jalisco, with brief biographical notes.

983. **Rojas, Pedro.** Copándaro (A Inst Inv Estét, 6:22, 1954, p. 115-122, 6 illus.).
Study of the handsome church of Santiago and its cloister at Copandaro, dating from the third quarter of the 16th century.

984. **Romero de Terreros, Manuel.** El convento franciscano de Ozumba y las pinturas de su portería (A Inst Inv Estét, 6:24, 1956, p. 9-21, 34 illus.).
A study of the Franciscan monastery in general and of the 17th-century murals in the *portería* in particular.

985. **Toussaint, Manuel.** Apología del arte barroco en América (A Inst Arte Am, 9, 1956, p. 13-20).
This lecture, delivered at the University of Texas in 1943, is printed as a memorial to the famous author who died on Nov. 22, 1955.

986. ————. La catedral y las iglesias de Puebla. México, Porrúa, 1954. 247 p. & 244 plates, maps, plans.
This volume of small format is a handbook of all the churches and chapels of Puebla, including historical information as to dates of construction. The cathedral is most thoroughly studied, for the author summarizes the numerous problems concerned with its construction and gives the pertinent documentation and the opinions of various writers. In the substantial introduction Toussaint makes generalizations about the characteristics of the local school. He makes no pretense as to completeness, since much work still remains to be done in the archives and in the study of the stylistic development of the Puebla school.

987. ————. Huellas de Diego Silóee en México (A Inst Inv Estét, 6:21, 1953, p. 11-18 & 11 figs.).
In addition to the well-known dependence of the cathedrals of Mexico City, Puebla, and Guadalajara upon the Silóee School, Toussaint calls

attention to the interior of the Jesuit church at Puebla. He believes that Silóee influenced Claudio de Arciniega, Diego de Aguilera, and Juan de Alcántara, all of them Spanish architects who emigrated to Mexico in the middle of the 16th century. Most convincing is Toussaint's argument that the Renaissance portal of the Alhóndiga at Puebla shows close relationships to Silóee's style of ornament.

988. —————. Una joya de arte desconocida: el santuario de Tapalcingo (A Inst Arte Am, 6, 1953, p. 41-43, 6 illus.).
Attention is drawn to a remarkable late Baroque church (1759-1782) which has hitherto been unpublished.

989. Vargas Lugo, Elisa. La vicaría de Aculco (A Inst Inv Estét, 6:22, 1954, p. 103-114 & 9 illus.).
This hitherto unpublished monument still preserves its *posas* of the late 16th century, according to the author. She considers the church in large part of the 17th century, although much restored in the 19th and 20th centuries.

990. Villegas, Víctor Manuel. El gran signo formal del barroco. Ensayo histórico del apoyo estípite. México, Universidad Nacional Autónoma de México, Instituto de Investigaciones Estéticas, 1956. 241 p., 245 plates.
A monumental publication, splendidly printed, this work traces the history of the *estípite*, i.e., the tapering pilaster, which was so widely exploited in the late Baroque architecture of Mexico in the 18th century. The author discusses the *estípite* in antiquity, where it attained wide usage in connection with the herm. Borrowing from the antique, Italian Renaissance artists, particularly Michelangelo, employed it, and thus it passed into the body of late Renaissance and Mannerist design. From 1685 José Churriguera adopted the *estípite* in combination with the spiral column (*salomónica*). About the same time Sevillian and Granadine architects began to introduce them in retables and portals, and thenceforth the *estípite* spread like wild fire through Hispanic Baroque art. A few examples exist in Mexico prior to the 18th century, but nevertheless the true promoters of the *estípite* in Mexico were the Spanish-born Jerónimo Balbás and Lorenzo Rodríguez. The latter particularly made it a distinguishing feature of Mexico's florid and fanciful late Baroque style.

991. Zuno, José Guadalupe. Las llamadas lacas michoacanas de Uruapan no proceden de las orientales. Guadalajara, México, Instituto Tecnológico de Guadalajara, 1953. 28 p., illus.
The author rejects the theory of Chinese influence on colonial Mexican lacquer work.

PERU

992. Altar de plata de la catedral de Cuzco (R Arch Hist Cuzco, 8:8, 1957, p .130-138).
Inventories of 1806.

993. Cornejo Bouroncle, Jorge. Arte cuzqueño—III. Primera mitad del siglo XVII (R Arch Hist Cuzco, 4:4, 1953, p. 174-210).
Most of the works of art cited in the documents published here are lost, yet they make it possible to reconstruct to some degree the history of art in Cuzco before the great earthquake in 1650. Bartolomé Carrión is mentioned in 1604 as architect in charge of the cathedral. It is now clear that Martín de Torres was the leading sculptor and architect of retables in this period. A contract for two side altars (1633) in Santa Catalina in company with Bartolomé de Nápoles doubtless refers to those still in existence today. Of him were ordered the high altar of the cathedral (1637), the altar of the Immaculate Conception (1646) in the same church, the high altar of the Hospital de San Bartolomé (1642), works for the Franciscans and the Jesuits in Arequipa, etc. Another sculptor, Pedro de Mesa, appears as author of retables in La Merced, San Agustín, etc. The document for the monstrance of La Merced made by Ayala Olmos in 1610-1612 is published in full. Perhaps the most important single contribution is the contract of 1649, in which Francisco Domínguez de Chávez y Arellano was engaged to build 17 vaults in the nave and aisles of the cathedral. This enigmatic figure now becomes more concrete, for in the same year he received the contract to build the apse and three chapels in the new church of San Francisco. The importance of this archival work of the scholars of Cuzco today can scarcely be exaggerated.

994. —————. Arte cuzqueño—IV (R Arch Hist Cuzco, 5:5, 1954, p. 49-97).
The numerous documents cited in this article belong mainly to the late 16th and the first half of the 17th century, so that the original works were in great part lost in the earthquake of 1650. It is impossible to give even a résumé of the valuable historical data here contained. Works in La Merced, Santo Domingo, San Agustín, San Francisco, and the cathedral were particularly numerous. Martín de Torres, the important *retablero,* once more appears in the contract for the high altar of the hospital of San Bartolomé (1638) and there is reference to his pre-earthquake high altar in Santa Catalina (1643). Among the significant details are several references to Diego Arias de la Cerda as "administrador de la obra de la catedral", so that it should be settled once and for all that the canon Arias was never an architect but rather the administrator in the completion of Cuzco Cathedral. Published in full are the contract with Francisco Dominguez de Chávez y Orellano for the sanctuary of San Francisco and the agreement with Diego Martínez de Oviedo for the high altar of San Sebastián (1679). The article concludes with further material on the monstrance of La Merced (1804-1806).

995. —————. Arte cuzqueño. La custodia de la iglesia de la Merced (R U, Cuzco, 42:104, 1. semestre 1953, p. 183-194, 1 illus.).
The publication of notarial documents proves that the celebrated monstrance of silver, gold, and precious stones in La Merced at Cuzco is

the work of the silversmith Manuel Piedra, made in Cuzco in 1804-1806. It had been wrongly attributed to Ayala Olmos, the author of an earlier lost monstrance of 1610-1612.

996. ————. Informe sobre escrituras públicas existentes en el Archivo Notarial del Cuzco correspondientes al siglo XVI (R Arch Hist Cuzco, 4:4, 1953, p. 115-168).
An index of contracts, agreements, and wills made in Cuzco in the 16th century. Much important material relating to works of art is cited here. The construction of the church in Azangaro was ordered in 1572; gilding of the altar of the Merced in 1581; choir lectern for the Merced in 1581; foundation of a church of Nuestra Señora de la Cabeza at Sicuani to be like a church in Andujar in Spain, etc.

997. Cossío del Pomar, Felipe. El arte popular en el Perú (Cuad Am, año 12, 69:3, mayo-junio 1953, p. 232-242).
A popular account of Indian cultural survivals, illustrated by the author's portraits of Andean natives.

997a. García, José Uriel. Para la historia del arte del Cuzco: la Casa del Almirante (Cuad Am, año 14, 81:3, mayo-junio 1955, p. 143-161, 4 illus.).
This famous colonial palace is named after Almirante Francisco Aldrete Maldonado from Salamanca, Spain, who lived in Cuzco from 1595-1642. Since the palace is mentioned in his will, it can be dated in the early 17th century. The interior was extensively rebuilt according to the testament (1761) of a later owner, the canon Barrio y Mendoza.

998. Gutiérrez, Julio G. El Santuario de Nuestra Señora de Cocharcas (R Inst Am Arte, 7:2, 1954, p. 75-90).
This article is the first detailed study of the remote Jesuit church which has been reported only by the author and by Padre Rubén Vargas Ugarte. Gutiérrez dates the construction in the years 1618-1679. He gives much new and important information about the paintings and altars in the church. The high altar, a magnificent work, is related to the schools of Ayacucho and Cuzco and datable about 1700.

999. Harth-Terré, Emilio. Alonso de Morales. Alarife limeño. Biografía de un artífice del siglo XVI (Crónica, Lima, 41:18,618, feb. 1, 1953, p. 16-17).
A documentary study of the career of Alonso de Morales, an architect of Lima, who was active in the second half of the 16th century. He worked for the monasteries of San Francisco and La Merced, and he was consulted on the reconstruction of the cathedral in 1609.

1000. Mariátegue Oliva, Ricardo. Pintura cuzqueña del siglo XVII. Los valiosos lienzos del Corpus cuzqueño de propiedad de D. Carlos Peña Otaegue en Santiago. Lima, Alma Mater, 1954. 23 p., 3 plates.

Three paintings belonging to the famous series in Santa Ana at Cuzco were discovered by the author in a private collection in Chile.

1001. Mesa, José de, and Teresa Gisbert de Mesa. El pintor Diego Quispe Tito (A Inst Arte Am, 8, 1955, p .115-122).
Two signed and dated (1667) pictures by the Cuzco painter are in the collection of the Casa de Moneda at Potosi.

1003. Vargas Ugarte, Rubén. Archivo de la Beneficencia del Cuzco (R Arch Hist Cuzco, 4:4, 1953, p. 103-113).
Listing of documents from the archives of San Agustín, San Andrés, and other colonial establishments of Cuzco which contain historical information yet to be studied.

1004. ————. Ensayo de un diccionario de artífices coloniales de la América meridional: apéndice. B. A., A Baiocco, 1955.
Padre Vargas Ugarte adds valuable documentary information in this appendix to the earlier volume (see HLAS, no. 14, 1948, item 742). More complete citation of sources would increase the value of the work, since many documents mentioned here have been published in full elsewhere.

1005. ————. La iglesia de San Pedro de Lima. Lima, 1956. 54 p., 22 illus.
An excellent short monograph on this important Jesuit house by one of the leading Jesuit scholars in Latin America. Padre Vargas dates all of the altars before 1680 and several of them before 1640. In this matter it is impossible to agree with him, since only a few of the late Baroque type with spiral columns could be dated as early as 1680.

1006. Villanueva Urteaga, Horacio. La catedral de Cajamarca (R Inst Am Arte, 7:2, 1954, p. 103-134, 5 illus.).
The history of the church with new documentary material. An inventory of 1809, published in full, gives a vivid idea of the richness of Peruvian churches. Most of the treasure was confiscated in 1824 to support the War of Independence.

1007. Wethey, Harold E. Arte franciscano en el Perú (R Inst Am Arte, 7:2, 1954, p. 91-102, 4 illus.).
Spanish translation of following item.

1008. ————. Franciscan art in Peru (Americas, Franciscan Hist, 9:4, Apr. 1953, p. 399-411, 18 illus.).
This article is a slightly expanded version of a lecture given at the 1952 convocation at the Academy of American Franciscan History. It surveys the architecture of the Franciscan churches of Peru from the 16th through the 18th centuries. The chief monuments are located in Chiclayo, Cuzco, Lima, Cajamarca, and Sucre (Bolivia). Some attention is given to colonial choir stalls and to two pulpits and a lectern which were probably all made by a Franciscan friar, Padre Pedro Gómez, in the early 17th century.

PUERTO RICO

1009. Buschiazzo, Mario J. Estudio sobre monumentos históricos de Puerto Rico. San Juan, Junta de Planificación de Puerto Rico, 1955. 74 p.

A survey of the architectural monuments of Puerto Rico, preparatory to the formation of a National Commission for the preservation of historic monuments.

1010. ————. Los monumentos históricos de Puerto Rico (A Inst Arte Am, 8, 1955, p. 57-114, plans & illus.).

This important article is a survey of all architectural remains on the island of Puerto Rico. It is exemplary in its historical exactitude, and valuable in the inclusion of floor plans of all major buildings.

URUGUAY

1011. Campos, Alfredo R. La casa de Lavalleja. Su historia e importancia (R Nac, año 16, 60:178, oct. 1953, p. 29-36).

History and description of late 18th-century house.

1012. Giuria, Juan. La arquitectura en el Uruguay. T. 1. Época colonial. Montevideo, Universidad de la República, Facultad de Arquitectura, Instituto de Historia de la Arquitectura, 1955. 181 p. & 149 figs.

The author of this volume has devoted his life to the study of the architecture of his own country, and the result is a definitive work. Every building of the colonial period is studied and documented; in every case floor plans and elevations have been drawn and reproduced by the author. Unfortunately, the colonial architecture of Uruguay is limited in quantity, and it is restricted in date almost entirely to the 18th century. For a general understanding of Latin American domestic architecture, this volume also supplies considerable data.

OTHER

1013. Angulo Íñiguez, Diego. Planos y monumentos de América. Catedral, Santiago de Cuba, 1731-1784 (Arquit, Habana, 21:238, mayo 1953, p. 211-218).

Angulo reproduces nine important plans, preserved in the Archives of the Indies in Seville, which are projects for the rebuilding of the cathedral of Santiago in Cuba. He recounts the history of the documents which cover nearly a century of dispute and delay.

1014. Buschiazzo, Mario J. San Xavier del Bac, Arizona (A Inst Arte Am, 6, 1953, p. 67-73, 5 illus., floor plan).

Buschiazzo recounts the historical background of this famous site and then describes the present state of the late 18th-century church.

1015. Palm, Erwin Walter. Los monumentos arquitectónicos de la Española, con una introducción a América. Ciudad Trujillo, Universidad de Santo Domingo, 1955. 2 v. 209 p., 46 plans, figs. 1-46; 217 p., figs. 47-224.

This monumental and handsomely printed work ranks unquestionably at the very top of publications on Latin American architecture. The author approaches the subject from the broad point of view of general culture, and in his first chapters he prepares the setting with a discussion of the historical, literary, and philosophical background of Spain in the late 15th century. He then reviews the history of Española in a thorough fashion from the first settlement until the end of the 18th century.

In his discussion of urbanism Dr. Palm points out the fact that the city of Santo Domingo was the first in America to be laid out on the rectangular plan. After reviewing the history of urbanism he concludes that the literary tradition of ancient Rome accounts for the resurgence of the geometric scheme in America and in the city of Santa Fe in Spain. Closely related are the fortifications, a study of which he also includes.

The major portion of the book is devoted to the 16th century, the great age of architectural achievement in Santo Domingo. The plan of the cathedral, like so many others in America, is derived from that of Seville Cathedral, whereas the churches of the religious orders follow the Spanish Isabeline type or are simplifications thereof. The documentation and history of every ecclesiastical monument are studied exhaustively in a fashion which cannot be summarized in this brief bibliographical notice. The development of domestic architecture in Santo Domingo is examined with like thoroughness. The author has written this work against the broad background of European architecture in general and Spanish architecture in particular, and his bibliography is extraordinarily extensive and inclusive.

1016. Rubín de la Borbolla, Daniel F., and Pedro Rivas. Honduras: monumentos históricos y arqueológicos. México, Instituto Panamericano de Geografía e Historia (Comisión de Historia, 44; Monumentos históricos y arqueológicos de América, 8; Publ., 146), 1953. 98 p., 61 illus.

Report on legislation and recent restorations to preserve national monuments.

1017. Vargas, José María. Ecuador: monumentos históricos y arqueológicos. México, Instituto Panamericano de Geografía e Historia (Comisión de Historia, 61; Monumentos históricos y arqueológicos, 9; Publ., 163), 1953. 144 p., maps, 29 plates.

This check list of the principal colonial monuments of Quito is accompanied by the laws passed for the protection of historic monuments.

NINETEENTH
AND TWENTIETH CENTURIES

ARGENTINA

1018. Acquarone, Ignacio. Pintura argentina, colección Acquarone. Introducción: Córdova Iturburu; compilación: Mario Loza. B. A., Edición Aleph (Col. Ignacio Acquarone, 1), 1955. 21, 68 p. & 29 plates.
This book is a catalogue of the extensive collection of contemporary Argentine paintings which belong to Ignacio Acquarone. It includes a general introductory survey of Argentine developments, a catalogue raisonné of the pictures, and a brief biographical note on each painter. The small color reproductions are adequate. Spanish and French text.

1019. Eichelbaum, Manuel. Manuel Eichelbaum (su obra plástica). Textos de Rodrigo Bonome y Américo Abraham Balán. B. A., Perlado, 1953. 14 p., illus.
A very brief catalogue of paintings by a minor and conservative Argentine artist.

1020. Exposición C. Bernaldo de Quirós. Prólogo de Horacio Caillet-Bois. Santa Fe, Argentina, Museo Provincial de Bellas Artes, 1953. Unpaged, illus.
Exhibition of pictures of this contemporary (born 1879) Argentine Impressionist who is best known for his pictures of Gaucho life.

1021. Forner. B. A., Galería Bonino, 1954.
Six small color reproductions and a list of recent pictures exhibited in B. A. Her Surrealist pictures show the influence of Picasso's late work.

1021a. Gazaneo, Jorge O., and Mabel M. Scarone. Eduardo Catalano. B. A., Instituto de Arte Americano e Investigaciones Estéticas, 1956. 46 p., 63 illus.
This modern architect, born in B. A. and educated in the U. S., has worked widely throughout America. His masterpiece seems to be the auditorium of the city of B. A. (1947).

1022. González Capdevila, Raúl. Amancio Williams. B. A., Instituto de Arte Americano e Investigaciones Estéticas (Arquitectos americanos contemporáneos, 1), 1955. 37 p. & illus.
Some striking experimental architectural designs, particularly in the domestic field.

1023. Gudiño Kramer, Luis. Escritores y plásticos del Litoral. Santa Fe, Argentina, Castellví (El Litoral), 1955. 171 p., illus.
Literary appreciations of young Argentine painters.

1024. Merlino, Adrián. Diccionario de artistas plásticos de la Argentina, siglos XVIII-XIX-XX. B. A., 1954. 433 p.
A useful handbook of painters, sculptors, engravers, etc., whose biographies are alphabetically arranged. The emphasis is on the contemporary, and few bibliographical references are given except in the case of major figures.

1025. Mujica Láinez, Manuel. Victorica, 1884-1955. B. A., Ediciones Bonino, 1955. 95 p., 106 illus.
Well-illustrated catalogue of a commemorative exhibition of the work of a late Impressionist Argentine painter (1884-1954).

1026. Payró, Julio E. Contemporary Argentine sculpture (Studio, 147:735, June 1954, p. 170-175).
Brief notice on works of contemporary sculptors whose styles are dependent upon the French school.

1027. ————. Horacio Butler. B. A., Emecé (Monografías Van Riel), 1954. 35 p. & illus.
This booklet of recent pictures by the Argentine artist shows a trend to a more abstract decorative organization of his compositions. Some of the illustrations are in color.

1028. Pellegrini, Aldo (and others). Artistas abstractos de la Argentina. B. A., Cercle International d'Art, 1955. 121 p., illus.
Illustrations of abstract painting and sculpture, each artist explaining his theories about his own work. These men deal in pure non-objective art, i. e., with no reference to objects in nature.

1029. Pintores argentinos. 3. Orlando Pierri. Roberto Rossi. Raúl Russo. Marco Tiglio. Textos de Manuel Mujica Laínez. B. A., Pampa (Artes plásticas de América), 1953. 16 plates in color.
Competent color reproductions of young Argentine painters working in the modern idiom and brief notes on their careers.

1030. Schenone, Héctor. Acerca de una pintura de Manzoni (A Inst Arte Am, 6, 1953, p. 103-104, 1 illus.).
A picture of the Ecce Homo, dated 1862, in the church at Lujan.

1031. Storni, Eduardo Raúl, and Antonio Colón. Santa Fe en la plástica. 45 reproducciones en negro y 1 en color. Santa Fe, Argentina, Castellví, 1954. 103 p., illus.
A survey of painting and prints devoted to the streets of the city of Santa Fe, Argentina, with mediocre results.

1032. United State. National Gallery of Art. A century and a half of painting in Argentina. Sponsored by the Government of Argentina. Washington, 1956. 14 p.
Catalogue of an exhibition held in the National Gallery in Washington. Well illustrated, but the data on the artists and their pictures is incomplete. Compiled by Julio Payró.

1033. Valdés, Carmen. Argentine painting today (Panorama, 2:6, 1953, p. 30-41).
Illustrations of works by well-established artists, with slight journalistic text.

1034. Varela, Lorenzo. Luis Falcini. B. A., Ediciones Botella al Mar, 1954. 27 p. & illus.
Booklet on a contemporary Argentine sculptor.

BOLIVIA

1035. Fernández Naranjo, Nicolás. La vida y la obra de Cecilio Guzmán de Rojas (Khana, marzo 1956, p. 194-209, illus.).
A résumé of the career of the well-known Bolivian Indianist painter (1900-1950).

1036. Mariluz Urquijo, José M. Las escuelas de dibujo y pintura de Mojos y Chiquitos (A Inst Arte Am, 9, 1956, p. 37-51, 5 illus.).
A thoroughly documented article on the foundation of academies and the introduction of European academic methods of art instruction in these regions.

CHILE

1037. Droguett Alfaro, Luis. Agustín Abarca o el lirismo pictórico. Santiago, Universidad de Chile, Instituto de Extensión de Artes Plásticas, 1955. 37 p. & illus.
The contemporary painter, Agustín Abarca (1882-1953), produced landscapes more reminiscent of Corot than anyone else. He is another example of the conservatism of the Chilean school in general.

1038. Pereira Salas, Eugenio. La arquitectura chilena en el siglo XIX (A U Ch, 114:102, 2. trimestre 1956, p. 7-25, 32 illus.).
A substantial and well-documented article on the eclectic revivalist styles of architecture in Chile in the 19th century.

1039. ————. La arquitectura chilena en el siglo XIX. Santiago, Ediciones de los Anales de la Universidad de Chile (Serie verde, 2), 1955. 25 p. & illus.
A general survey of 19th-century architecture in Chile which is highly eclectic. Poorly printed.

1040. Zegers de la Fuente, Roberto. Juan Francisco González, el hombre y el artista, 1853-1933. Santiago, Universidad de Chile, 1953. 253 p., illus.
An extensive but journalistically vague biography of a Chilean painter (1853-1933). His studies in Europe led him to adopt the late Impressionistic style of Monet.

CUBA

1041. Kelly, John J. Arquitectura religiosa de la Habana en el siglo veinte. Habana, Imp. Úcar García, 1955. 155 p., illus.
After a summary review of the history of religious architecture since the time of the Egyptians, the author describes the contemporary ecclesiastical buildings of Habana, most of which are neo-Gothic and neo-Romanesque in design. The one modern building, San Agustín, is a weak adaptation of the famous dirigible hangar formerly at Orly in France, a work which has inspired the Brazilian architect, Niemeyer, to better results. The historical and scholarly value of this book is negligible, although it was written as a doctoral dissertation.

1042. Sánchez, Juan. El grabado en Cuba. Habana, Imp. Mundial, 1955. 104 p. & illus.
A well-compiled history of prints in Cuba, the work being mainly of the 19th and 20th centuries. The illustrations provide a survey with some emphasis on the contemporary.

1043. Torriente, Loló de la. Estudio de las artes plásticas en Cuba. Habana, 1954. 230 p., illus.
An historical account of painting in Cuba in the 19th and 20th centuries comprises the main interest of this modestly illustrated book.

ECUADOR

1044. Astudillo Ortega, José María. Escoplos, cinceles y pinceles. Cuenca, Ecuador, Casa de la Cultura Ecuatoriana (Núcleo del Azuay), 1955. 75 p.
Fragmentary résumé of painting in Ecuador, written in a poetic style.

1045. Guayasamín, Oswaldo. Huacayñan, el camino del llanto. The way of tears. Pinturas de Guayasamín. Quito, Casa de la Cultura Ecuatoriana, 1953. 45 p., 44 plates. Spanish and English text.
In the introduction the opinions of critics of various countries are quoted in respect to Guayasamín's pictures. The catalog lists the works illustrated, but it gives no dimensions, dates, or other data. The artist seems increasingly to be influenced by the Mexican school in general and by Tamayo in particular. The format of the book is large and the printing of the black-and-white plates is adequate.

HAITI

1046. Bastien, Lisa. Pintura popular de Haití (Panorama, 3:12, 1954, p. 56-79).
The writer gives a substantial account of modern primitivism as developed in the school of Haiti and discusses its relation to primitivism in contemporary art in general. Published also in *Cuadernos americanos* (año 13, 73:1, enero-feb. 1954, p. 215-232).

1047. Held, André. La peinture heureuse

(Formes Coul, 12. série, 1, 1954, p. 89-102).
A number of illustrations and some color prints of the contemporary primitivist school of Haiti.

MEXICO

1048. Cardoza y Aragón, Luis. Pintura mexicana contemporánea. México, Imp. Universitaria, 1953. 311 p., 124 plates.
A revised edition of the work published in 1940 under the title of *La nube y el reloj* (see *HLAS, no. 6, 1940*, item 775).

1049. Castellanos, Julio. Julio Castellanos, 1905-1947. Monografía de su obra con notas de Carlos Pellicer y de Salvador Toscano. México, Editorial Netzahualcoyotl, 1952 [i. e. 1953]. 35 p., 84 illus.
An exhibition catalogue and biographical and critical data on the Mexican painter, Castellanos (1905-1947).

1050. Catlin, Stanton L. Comments on the art of José Clemente Orozco (B Minneapolis Inst Arts, 42:24, Oct. 3, 1953, p. 118-123, illus.).
A review of the artist's achievement in connection with the Orozco exhibition.

1051. Charlot, Jean. Diego Rivera in Italy (Mag Art, 46:1, Jan. 1953, p. 3-10, 13 illus.).
Rivera's sketches after well-known painters of the Renaissance provide an insight into the artist's student years.

1052. Fernández, Justino. Un dibujo de Diego Rivera para el mural del anfiteatro Bolívar (A Inst Inv Estét, 6:23, 1955, p. 53-56, 3 illus.).
Study for the mural now in the library of the University of Mexico City.

1053. Forbes, W. Stanton. Orozco's Adam and Eve (Ariz Q, 10:4, winter 1954, p. 334-346).
An interpretative study of Orozco's work.

1054. Guerrero Lovillo, José. La pintura mejicana de hoy (Estud Am, 5:20, mayo 1953, p. 479-497).
An excellent résumé of the development of contemporary Mexican painting, in the light of pictures shown in Venice in 1950.

1055. Helm, McKinley. Man of fire: J. C. Orozco. An interpretative memoir. N. Y., Harcourt Brace, 1953. 245 p., 67 plates.
Written in a flamboyant style which is calculated to appeal to the general public, this book demonstrates, nevertheless, a thorough familiarity with the subject.

1056. Jaén, Ángel Benito. La nueva arquitectura mejicana (Estud Am, 6:26, nov. 1953, p. 473-489 & illus.).
One of the best short studies of the development of modern architecture in Mexico City, which culminates in the new Ciudad Universitaria.

1057. Ketchum, Morris. Mexican journey (J Am Inst Archit, 19:5, May 1953, p. 209-216, 5 illus.).
A popular report on the pre-Columbian elements in the modern University City in Mexico.

1058. Marrokin, Josel. México, capital mural del mundo (Humanismo, 2:15, nov. 1953, p. 70-87).
Article based on political concept of the movement and without interest in the artistic aspects.

1059. Monterde Fernández, Francisco. Francisco Monterde Fernández, 1921-1951. México, Imp. Universitaria, 1954. 219 p., illus.
This memorial volume is dedicated to a young Mexican artist who died at the age of 30. The brief text consists of a series of tributes by various critics, while the copious illustrations make it clear that his best work consisted of woodcuts which made him a successful book illustrator.

1060. Myers, Bernard S. Mexican painting in our time. N. Y., Oxford University Press, 1956. 283 p., 124 illus.
In this history of contemporary Mexican painting, the author follows a strictly chronological sequence. He devotes most of his attention to Rivera, Orozco, and Siqueiros, interspersing the non-muralists and minor figures. Dr. Myers has written the first good general book on the subject to appear in several years.

1061. ———. Tamayo versus the Mexican mural painters (College Art J, 13:2, winter 1954, p. 101-105, 3 illus.).
A sympathetic summary of the artist's career.

1062. Orozco, José Clemente. Obras de José Clemente Orozco en la colección Carrillo Gil. Complemento y notas del Dr. Alvar Carrillo Gil. México, 1953. 361 p. and addenda.
Catalogue of paintings, drawings, and prints in a de luxe edition lavishly illustrated.

1063. ———. Textos de Orozco. Con un estudio y un apéndice por Justino Fernández. México, Universidad Nacional Autónoma de México, Instituto de Investigaciones Estéticas (Estudios y fuentes del arte en México, 4), 1955. 157 p.
Justino Fernández, the leading Mexican critic and historian of modern painting in his country, has gathered together various articles by Orozco explaining his own art, and he publishes letters from Orozco to Fernández. He also adds two authoritative and profound studies of the painter's personality and art.

1064. Ortega Flores, Salvador. La escultura de Geles Cabrera (Arquitectura, 42, junio 1953, p. 117-122, 9 illus.).

Critical evaluation of the semi-abstract sculpture of a contemporary Mexican woman.

1065. **Reed, Alma.** Orozco. México, Fondo de Cultura Económica, 1955. 349 p., 189 illus.
This compendious biography is the most thorough and substantial yet written on the life of Orozco. Miss Reed, who first came to know him well in N. Y., gives a first hand personal account of the artist. His various sojourns in N. Y. and at Dartmouth College, his relations with other artists, collectors, and admirers are recounted in extensive detail. The book will unquestionably remain a primary source for a study of the life and art of Orozco. Although the book is a full-length biography, the author is most effective in dealing with the artist in the U. S. because of her personal knowledge of those years. The numerous illustrations, printed in offset, are unfortunately poor in quality.
The same book has been published in English (N. Y., Oxford University Press, 1956, 308 p., 16 illus.).

1066. **Romero de Terreros y Vinent, Manuel.** El barón Gros y sus vistas de México. México, Imp. Universitaria, 1953. 16 p., plates.
Jean Baptiste, the second Baron Gros, was son of the famous Napoleonic painter. He spent four years (1832-1836) as first secretary in the French embassy at Mexico City, and at this time he painted a number of interesting landscapes of Mexico, here published for the first time.

1067. **Sharp, Thomas.** Mexico University (Archit R, 114:683, Nov. 1953, p. 307-318, illus.).
Superb photographs and a description of the new University City.

1068. **Spilimbergo, J. E.** Diego Rivera y el arte en la revolución mexicana. B. A., Editorial Indoamérica (Biblioteca de la nueva generación, 2), 1954. 58 p.
A short biography with a decidedly ideological slant.

1069. **Whittet, G. S.** The Mexican exhibition. 2. Contemporary art (Studio, 145: 723, June 1953, p. 194-201).
Well-illustrated critical review of the exhibition at the Tate Gallery in London.

1070. **Zuno, José Guadalupe.** Orozco y la ironía plástica. México, Cultura (Cuadernos americanos), 1953. 85 p., illus.
This booklet gives a journalistic account of Orozco's political and social satire with particular reference to his early studies of prostitutes.

URUGUAY

1071. **Chiappini, Félix.** Para la historia de la pintura nacional. El pintor Queirolo

Repetto (R Nac, año 16, 58:177, sept. 1953, p. 405-413).
Short biography of the Uruguayan painter who died in 1947.

1072. **Figari, Pedro.** Pedro Figari, 1861-1938. Veinticinco obras del artista reproducidas en color. Textos de Oliveiro Girondo, Manuel Mujica Láinez, Julio Rinaldini, Jorge Romero Brest. B. A., Galerias Witcomb, 1953. 24 p. & 25 colored plates.
Adequate color reproduction, mounted in luxurious format, and accompanied by critical appreciation of his work.

VENEZUELA

1073. **Picón-Salas, Mariano.** Perspectiva de la pintura venezolana (Panorama, 3:11, 1954, p. 64-96).
A substantial survey of contemporary painting in Venezuela with introductory remarks on the colonial period and the 19th century. Traditionally, Venezuelan art has been conservative and based upon Spanish and French sources. The other influence today is that of the contemporary Mexican school, but the school of Paris predominates.

1074. ————. La pintura en Venezuela. Caracas, 1954. 85 p., 135 illus.
Well-illustrated booklet with emphasis on painting in the 19th and 20th centuries.

1075. **Planchart, Enrique.** El pintor Juan Lovera (R Nac Cult, 12:87-88, julio-oct. 1951, p. 64-82, 6 illus.).
Biography of a historical painter (1790-1840).

OTHER

1076. **Engel, Walter.** La pintura en Colombia (Panorama, 3:9, 1954, p. 67-90).
A good survey of the contemporary scene with more information than such articles usually supply, and a few illustrations. Reprinted from *Espiral, revista mensual de artes y letras,* Bogotá, 5:47, 1953.

1077. **Fernández Spencer, Antonio.** José Vela Zanetti. Ciudad Trujillo, La Española, 1954.
83 illustrations and brief text regarding the paintings and the drawings of this Spanish-born artist whose style is clearly inspired by the Mexican school of mural painting.

1078. **Velasco, Napoleón.** Cisneros, el pintor. San Salvador, Ministerio de Cultura, Departmento Editorial (Biblioteca popular, 11), 1955. 135 p.
Biography of a minor romantic painter, Juan Francisco Cisneros, who was born in Salvador (1823-1878), but who travelled widely in Europe and America.

BRAZIL
ROBERT C. SMITH

The year 1956 marked the 20th anniversary of the founding of the Diretoria do Patrimônio Histórico e Artístico Nacional (DPHAN) as a modest Serviço (SPHAN) of the Ministry of Education, charged with the preservation of old buildings. In these two decades this organization, under the leadership of its brilliant and devoted director, Dr. Rodrigo Melo Franco de Andrade, has restored countless colonial and 19th-century buildings all over Brazil (including almost the whole town of Ouro Preto), preserved and copied old archives, established museums, organized exhibitions, developed techniques of conservation, and conducted a program of publications which now includes 18 special monographs and 12 annual volumes of essays on the art of Brazil. DPHAN has developed the knowledge and taste of a generation of young Brazilians who have grown up since 1936, including a number of gifted artists who have received grants for study and other assistance from this important agency. To DPHAN and its great staff of historians, artists, and technicians of all sorts, this editor, who has accompanied their achievements since the beginning, offers his profound congratulations.

As though to commemorate this anniversary there appeared in Paris in 1956 the first comprehensive history of religious architecture and sculpture of colonial Brazil (item 1159). The work of a curator of the Louvre, who for over a decade had been studying the subject, this book is a monument comparable to such outstanding surveys of colonial art elsewhere in Latin America as the books of Professor Wethey on Peru, Kubler on 16th-century Mexico, and Erwin Palm on the Dominican Republic.

Another event of interest to students of colonial architecture in Brazil was the special issue of the *Journal of the Society of Architectural Historians* devoted to the art of building in the old Portuguese empire, in which Brazil was represented (item 1156) along with the mother country and Macau and Goa.

In the field of 19th-century art, Gilberto Ferrez's catalogue to his exhibition of old views of Recife (item 1173) deserves special attention. Publications on modern Brazilian art and architecture are headed by Henrique E. Mindlin's fine study of contemporary architecture since 1943. In São Paulo the periodical *Habitat* has provided a monthly issue so full of good criticism of the work of contemporary architects, painters, sculptors, and print makers that only a few articles could be considered individually in this bibliography.

Events of the year were the law passed in Salvador requiring the introduction of original works of art in new constructions, the law of Sept. 19 transferring the federal capital from Rio de Janeiro to the future city of Brasília, the decision to send the work of only one painter—Di Cavalcanti—to the Biennial Exhibition at Venice, and the exhibition of the new murals for the United Nations building in New York by Cândido Portinari (item 1181).

GENERAL

1150. Bardi, P. M. The arts in Brazil; a new museum at São Paulo. Milano, Edizione del Milione, 1956. 300 p., illus.
The Museu de Arte of São Paulo, like the city itself, has grown with amazing rapidity. Founded in 1947, it has become the outstanding "comprehensive" museum of Latin America, the only one in which can be seen Titians and Goyas beside paintings by Picasso and Cézanne, the only one, furthermore, which renders the kind of services in public education which are taken for granted in the U. S.

In this handsome and unconventionally written volume, the energetic, gifted Italian director explains the aims of his museum, describes its housing, installations and exhibits. He also presents, with many color plates, a selection of the European masterpieces it contains.
Because Bardi wants the world to know the problems he faces in creating a U. S. type of museum in Brazil, he has briefly sketched the background of the national art, from archaeology through colonial and 19th-century to contemporary expression, with reference also to folk art, photography, and the motion picture. With this goes a wealth of pertinent illustrations, vivid descriptions, and personal criticism, which

makes Bardi's history, though far from complete, for indeed it is merely a sketch, one of the essential statements of the growth of art in Brazil.

1151. 50 anos de paisagem brasileira (Habitat, 6:27, fev. 1956, p. 49-53, illus.).
Report of an exhibit at the Museu de Arte Moderna of São Paulo with many illustrations.

1152. Mueller, Bonifácio. Convento de Santo Antônio do Recife. Recife, Brazil, 1956. 179 p., illus.
For some time Father Mueller, with access to all existing source material, has been preparing this history of the Franciscan convent of Recife. It is therefore disappointing that he has apparently not been able to discover any information about the 18th-century rebuilding of this important structure. Furthermore, he does not even discuss the matter. Nor does he comment upon two early views of the primitive structure, dating from 1630 and 1644 respectively, although they contain differing details. Father Mueller does, however, publish the bill of F. M. Béranger for the woodwork of the interior which he replaced in 1849, together with a drawing by the sculptor for three altarpieces.

1153. Pinacoteca do Estado de S. Paulo. Catálogo. São Paulo, 1954. 174 p., plates.
A well-illustrated catalogue of the museum of the state of São Paulo, which is rich in the work of local artists of the 19th century. It is not to be confused with the more recently created museum of the city of São Paulo (item 1150).

1154. Pires, Heliodoro. Figuras do cenário religioso do Brasil (R Inst Hist Geog Br, 232, julio-set. 1956, 3-166).
Enmeshed in these notes on the religious history of Brazil are facts of interest through the cult to the history of religious art in Brazil.

1155. Schütz, Alfred (ed.). O mundo artístico do Brasil. The artistic world of Brazil. 1. ed. Rio, Pró-Arte, 1954. 402 p., illus.
This is an omnibus volume containing illustrated notices about the art institutions of Brazil (museums, schools, etc.) and some of the painters. It is a heterogeneous publication the exact arrangement of which is not easy to comprehend.

1156. Smith, Robert C. Nossa Senhora da Conceição da Praia and the Joanine style in Brazil (J Soc Archit Hist, 15:3, Oct. 1956, p. 16-23, illus.).
After telling the remarkable story of the sending of this major 18th-century church stone by stone from Lisbon to Salvador, the author discusses the origins of its plan and decoration in the architecture of Italy and Portugal. A stylistic consideration of the high altar and ceiling painting is also included. This is one of four articles, on aspects of architecture in the Portuguese-speaking world, comprising this issue.

1157. Vinte anos de atividades do SPHAN (Habitat, 6:32, julho 1956, p. 22-23, illus.).
In this anniversary statement more stress is laid upon the failures of the agency in the protection of old buildings than upon its great accomplishments.

COLONIAL

1158. Azevedo, Carlos de. Um artista italiano em Goa: Plácido Francesco Ramponi e o túmulo de S. Francisco Xavier. Lisboa, Ministério do Ultramar, 1956. 42 p., illus.
A new and important contribution to the colonial travel literature of Brazil. Ramponi, an Italian artist who escorted a marble sarcophagus to Goa, kept a diary which is now in London. On his return to Lisbon his ship stopped at Salvador, where he wrote a brief description of the city as it appeared at the end of the 17th century. Although his references to the arts are slight, they are significant, and his colored drawings are among the earliest representations of the flora and fauna of Bahia.

1159. Bazin, Germain. L'architecture religieuse baroque au Brésil. São Paulo, Museu de Arte; Paris, Librairie Plon (Éditions d'histoire et d'art), 1956. 2 v.
This book, divided into 2 volumes (the first— 378 pages—containing the text, the second the illustrations) goes far toward being the definitive work on this subject. The author has handled every aspect with thoroughness and authority, tracing the development of plans, façades and decorative devices from Portuguese and Italian sources, finding evidences of regionalism, classifying types and traditions. Much attention is given to the woodcarved altarpiece as the essential element of the Luso-Brazilian interior. In dealing with it, M. Bazin publishes for the first time a great deal of information, extracted from archives by the efforts of DPHAN, about specific sculptors. In presenting masses of minute detail he never loses sight of the main lines of stylistic development in Brazil, which he compares in masterful fashion to the evolution of the altarpiece in Portugal, the entire history of which is considered in a special chapter.

1160. Burland, C. A. O Brasil no mapa-mundi composto por Deceliers, em 1546 (Habitat, 6:27, fev. 1956, p. 61, illus.).
A map by Père Pierre Deceliers, vicar of Arques, dating from 1546, which is now at the John Rylands Library, Manchester, England, shows Indians and a thatched gabled shelter within a stockade.

1161. Dony, Paul. Kirchliche barockarchitektur in Portugal, Bayern und Brasilien (Münster, 10:1-2, Feb. 1957, p. 1-22, illus.).
Contains fine photographs stressing the resemblance in decoration and spatial composition between Portuguese, Brazilian, and Bavarian churches of the 18th century. Equally notable is the extraordinary similarity between the apses of the church of Miragaia at Oporto and that of São Francisco of Salvador.

1162. **Ferrez, Gilberto.** Um panorama do Rio de Janeiro de 1775 (R Inst Hist Geog Br, 233, out.-dez. 1956, p. 3-23, illus.).
A hitherto unknown anonymous pen and ink drawing of Rio de Janeiro seen from the harbor, with a map of the city and the Bay of Guanabara (Biblioteca Nacional, Iconografia e Mapoteca, no. 25, 6, 1B). The author finds that the view was copied by Luiz dos Santos from an unknown original, presumably for inclusion in his famous *Cartas*. The map, on the other hand, is a slight modification of that of André Vaz Figueira of 1750. The buildings, which are rendered in the greatest detail, are carefully documented in the text, which includes a bibliography.

1163. **Figueiredo, Napoleão.** O forte do castelo (Habitat, 6:26, jan. 1956, p. 63-66, illus.).
History of the old fort of Sto. Cristo of Belem, erected at the time of the founding of the city in 1616 and rebuilt on a number of occasions in the 18th and 19th centuries.

1164. **Freudenfeld, R. A.** Isto é Minas Gerais. São Paulo, Melhoramentos, 1955. 8 p. & 95 illus.
This unpretentious small volume presents the best-known colonial monuments of Minas Gerais. It is a picture book with a few pages of text, chiefly concerned with dates of settlement, practices of mining, etc. In these respects, and in the geographical arrangement of the plates, it resembles Edgar Falcão's sumptuous *Relíquias da Terra de Ouro* of 1946.
Both books have the same shortcomings. Neither ventures outside the limits of the five principal mining towns and the pilgrimage center of Congonhas do Campo, although some of the most impressive monuments are located elsewhere. Freudenfeld therefore missed a great opportunity to vary the monotonous repetition of material that characterizes publications on the architecture of Minas. Furthermore, the plates are poorly reproduced. This is a serious failing of all art publications in Brazil which could and must be remedied by compelling the printers to take more care with their work.

1156. **Géo, Charles.** L'art baroque au Brésil. Paris, Editions Inter-Nationales, 1956. 171 p., 77 illus.
An account of colonial art in Brazil arranged in guide-book form, according to regions and monuments. The book adds nothing to our knowledge of the subject and omits much that is known, especially concerning authors of buildings.

1166. **Germano, Manuel.** Desbrugando Ouro Preto (Habitat, 6:27, fev. 1956, p. 58-60, illus.).
Details of windows with bars, panes, and wooden lattices.

1167. **Jansen, D. Bonifácio.** Livro do gasto da sacristia do mosteiro de S. Bento de Olinda, 1756-1802 (R Pat Hist Art Nac, 12, 1955, p. 233-385, illus.).

This is the text of the very detailed account book of the Benedictine monastery of Olinda, transcribed by the 72nd abbot, D. Bonifácio Jansen, with a brief introduction by D. Clemente Maria da Silva Nigra, who points out the significance of the craftsmen mentioned in its pages.

1168. **Reis, José de Souza.** Arcos da Carioca (R Pat Hist Art Nac, 12, 1955, p. 9-108, illus.).
The aqueduct of Rio was constructed between 1719 and 1723. It therefore preceded that of Lisbon, which dates from 1729-1748, and is one of the outstanding works of engineering of the colonial period in Latin America, being still in use. The history of its construction is here presented together with that of the principal aqueduct of Portugal. The author did not have access to the great collection of unpublished material including early 18th-century drawings in the Arquivo Histórico do Ultramar at Lisbon.

1169. **Saia, Luiz.** A Casa Bandeirista (Habitat, 5:25, dez. 1955, p. 7-10, illus.).
A mid-century country house of São Paulo in the suburb of Butantã, restored and furnished on the occasion of the fourth centenary of the founding of the city, is here described by the local director of DPHAN, who was responsible for the work.

1170. **Trindade, Raimundo.** Ourives de Minas Gerais nos séculos XVIII e XIX (R Pat Hist Art Nac, 12, 1955, p. 109-149, illus.).
Notice of João de Lana, who came to Rio from Bayonne in France about 1695 and was appointed assayer of gold and silver at Ouro Preto in 1742, together with 104 other silversmiths of Minas Gerais.

NINETEENTH CENTURY

1171. **Benisovich, Michel.** Nicolas-Antoine Taunay às vésperas da Missão de 1816 (Habitat, 6:27, fev. 1956, p. 11-13, illus.).
A chapter of an important unpublished biography of one of the French painters invited to Brazil by the government to establish an academy in 1816 (see item 1175).

1172. **Debret, Jean Baptiste.** Viagem pitoresca e histórica ao Brasil. Aquarelas e desenhos que não foram reproduzidos na edição de Firmin Didot, 1834. Paris, R. de Castro Maya, 1954. 23 p. & 100 plates (in portfolio).
When Jean Baptiste Debret (1768-1848), a French painter of the Mission of 1816, published his famous 3-volume collection of lithographs, *Voyage pittoresque et historique au Brésil* (Paris, 1834-1839), he did not utilize all the water colors and drawings he had prepared. These were purchased by Raymundo de Castro Maya, a collector of Rio, who has published them in a sumptuous album in the same city of Paris, thus completing a work begun 120 years before. In fact he has improved upon the first undertak-

ing because modern processes have made it possible to publish the watercolors and drawings in their original colors. The work is superbly done. The folio contains 100 plates, some with short texts by Debret. These include such rare and informative subjects as a series of views of rooms in houses occupied by the artist, and panoramas of the towns of Laguna, Taubate, Areas, Sta. Catarina, in addition to the commoner street scenes of Rio, which fill the book of 1834. In a brief introduction to the volume Castro Maya provides brief biographies of all the artists who comprised the Mission of 1816. Since this material is available elsewhere, one would have preferred to find here more information on the making of this volume and its relation to the one of 1834.

1173. Exposição comemorativa. Iconografia do Recife, século XIX (Coleção Gilberto Ferrez e outros). Pernambuco, Brazil, Tricentenário da Restauração Pernambucana, Comissão Organizadora e Executiva, 1954. 59 p. & 200 plates.
A catalogue of 19th-century drawings, watercolors, and prints of the city of Recife, the life of its streets and suburbs. It was prepared by Gilberto Ferrez, the outstanding writer on the iconography of Brazilian cities, who also organized the accompanying exhibition, which was one of the official observances of the 300th anniversary of the departure of the Dutch from Brazil. The volume contains many hitherto unknown views found recently in the Biblioteca Nacional of Rio.

1174. James, David. Um pintor inglês no Brasil do primeiro reinado (R Pat Hist Art Nac, 12, 1955, p. 151-169, illus.).
Augustus Earle, the little-known subject of this article, was one of the most distinguished genre painters who worked in Brazil in the early 19th century. Nephew of the great Connecticut portrait painter Ralph Earl, he visited Rio and Recife in 1820-1824, where he made a series of watercolors, now in the National Library of Australia and the British Museum, which compare favorably with the work of J. B. Debret and M. Rugendas. Among them are the originals of three illustrations of Maria Graham's Journal of a voyage to Brazil (London, 1824).

1175. Taunay, Afonso de Escragnolle. A missão artística de 1816. Rio, Diretoria do Patrimônio Histórico e Artístico Nacional (Publ., 18), 1956. 351 p., illus.
One of the many extraordinary consequences of the coming of the Portuguese court to Brazil was the decision of John VI's government to invite a group of foreign artists to create an academy at Rio. Choosing Frenchmen instead of Italians, it was possible to secure first-rate figures whose former connection with the Bonaparte regime made them in 1816 unpopular with the new government of France. In spite of great difficulties, financial and political, the so-called Mission of 1816 was successful. The group was organized and conducted by Joachim Debreton, the academy was established in a handsome building designed by Grandjean de Montigny, where the neo-classic doctrines of the time were long expounded by the painters Taunay and

Debret and the sculptors Marcos and Zeferino Ferrez.
This is the story of the mission by a descendant of Taunay who is himself a patriarch of historical studies in Brazil. Using his already published biography of his ancestor as a nucleus, he has added new information about the formation and activity of the group, although he has not included all the details of political intrigue which are now known. There are biographies of the other artists as well as illustrations of their work.

CONTEMPORARY

1176. A atual fase do "Atelier Abstração" (Habitat, 6:31, junho 1956, p. 11-13, illus.).
Report on the third exhibition of a group of 12 young abstract painters of São Paulo.

1177. Brancante, E. F. Primeira exposição internacional de cerâmica moderna (Habitat, 6:32, julho 1956, p. 25-28, illus.).
Brazilian contributions to an international ceramics show held in 1955 at Cannes.

1178. Construction en pays chauds: Brésil (Archit Aujourd'hui, 27:67-68, oct. 1956, p. 152-167, illus.).
A report on current architecture in Brazil, in which are presented plans and photographs of the following new buildings: apartment house at Copacabana by M. and M. Roberto, office building at Rio by M. and M. Roberto, headquarters of the Lawyers' Association in São Paulo by Rino Levi and Roberto Cerqueira César, Museum of Modern Art at Rio by A. E. Reidy and R. Burle Marx, school theater at Campo Grande by A. E. Reidy, petroleum refinery at Rio by F. F. Saldanha, H. Kaulino and B. Fonyat, automobile showroom at Rio by R. A. Ribeiro, business center at Brooklin, São Paulo, by R. C. César and L. R. Carvalho Franco.

1179. Costa, Lúcio. Testimony of a carioca architect (Atl Month, 197:2, Feb. 1956, p. 137-139).
"Our architecture is important because it has succeeded in adding plastic lyricism and concern for human emotions to the structures in which we live and work." This is the explanation of the extraordinary appeal of contemporary building in Brazil as given by one of the leaders of the modern movement. Senhor Costa further states that this architecture is outstanding in the world for its brilliant use of reinforced concrete produced by the necessity to find a cheap substitute for steel in a non-industrialized country. To certain architects and engineers he gives credit for these developments but one has the feeling that the final explanation of Brazil's great achievement in contemporary architecture lies in certain intangibles which Lúcio Costa, the most modest of men, refrains from mentioning here.

1180. Ferraz, Geraldo. Individualidades na história da atual arquitetura no Brasil: I, Gregori Warchavchik (Habitat, 6:28, março 1956, p. 40-48); II, Affonso

Eduardo Reidy (Habitat, 6:29, abril 1956, p. 38-55); III, Rino Levi (Habitat, 6:30, maio 1956, p. 34-48); IV, M. M. M. Roberto (Habitat, 6:31, junho 1956, p. 49-66); V. Lúcio Costa (Habitat, 6:35, out. 1956, p. 28-47); VI, Roberto Burle Marx (Habitat, 6:36, nov. 1956, p. 12-24).

Profusely illustrated with plans and photographs, and fortified with biographical details, these critical studies of preeminent figures in contemporary Brazilian architecture are a major contribution to the study of the subject.

1181. Guerra e Paz de Portinari; paineis para a ONU. Rio, 1956. 8 p., illus.

A brief but useful publication issued in connection with an exhibition of the two huge oil paintings, War, and Peace, executed by Cândido Portinari for the Hall of Delegates of the United Nations building in N. Y. There is a chronological listing of the painter's achievements since his birth in 1903 and a critical statement by René Hughe, for whom Portinari is one of the greatest painters of our time.

1182. Hitchcock, Henry Russell. Latin American architecture since 1945. N. Y., Museum of Modern Art, 1955. 203 p., illus., plans.

This is the catalogue of an exhibition of photographs of contemporary Latin American buildings held at the Museum of Modern Art in N. Y. at the end of 1955. Brazil is represented by the work of 12 architects, for nine of whom brief biographies are given. In his introduction Professor Hitchcock finds that "Brazil . . . remains the country with the most solidly established modern tradition and provides the greatest number of individual buildings of distinction." He considers Le Corbusier, Costa, and Niemeyer's Ministry of Education in Rio "still perhaps the finest single modern structure in Latin America."

1183. Hôpital Sul América à Rio de Janerio (Archit Aujourd'hui, 26:50-51, nov. 1955, p. 76-80, illus.).

A superbly beautiful construction, by Oscar Niemeyer and H. Ochoa, for the great Sul América insurance company, which contains a number of innovations such as a "check-up clinic" borrowed from the U. S. The garden setting was designed by Roberto Burle Marx.

1184. House in Brazil (Arts Archit, 73:7, July 1956, p. 18-19, illus.).

A large house designed by S. W. Bernardes.

1185. Maison de week-end à Tijuca, Rio de Janeiro, Brazil (Archit Aujourd'hui, 26: 50-51, nov. 1955, p. 28-29, illus.).

A small house, characteristic of Brazil, by Afonso E. Reidy, with grounds laid out by Roberto Burle Marx.

1186. Mindlin, Henrique E. Modern architecture in Brazil. N. Y., Reinhold, 1956. 256 p., illus., plans.

In 1943 Philip Goodwin's *Brazil builds* disclosed the remarkable achievements of that country

following the historic visit of Le Corbusier in 1936. Since then the work of the thirties and forties has become classic and architectural journals the world over have been calling attention to spectacular developments of the last few years.

This volume is a successful effort on the part of a distinguished modern architect of Rio to present this new work against the background of what had preceded. Senhor Mindlin has selected some 108 buildings for inclusion in his book, the most recent of which date from 1955. These are divided into categories arranged chronologically. There are 59 houses and other living units; 25 public buildings; 15 purely commercial structures; 16 projects in urbanism and landscape architecture. Each is illustrated with several photographs and plans and is discussed in a short statement the objectivity of which is praised by the Swiss critic, Siegfried Giedion, in an introduction which is itself a model of clarity and concision.

1187. V Salão Nacional de Arte Moderna (Habitat, 6:31, junho 1956, p. 16-20, illus.).

A valuable survey of the most recent tendencies of Brazilian painting.

1188. V Salão Paulista de Arte Moderna (Habitat, 6:33, agôsto 1956, p. 2-6, illus.).

A general report.

1189. Secondary school, Rio de Janeiro (Archit Rec, 119:4, Apr. 1956, p. 251-252, illus.).

This beautiful and practical design by Eneas Silva is offered as a model for schools in the U. S.

1190. Valladares, José. The art of the tropics (Atl Month, 197:2, Feb. 1956, p. 125-136, illus.).

An admirably concise and penetrating statement by the director of the Museum of Bahia on a number of key figures in the contemporary painting and sculpture of Brazil. These are: the painters Cândido Portinari, Lasar Segall, Tarsila do Amaral, Alberto Guignard, Emiliano di Cavalcanti, José Pancetti, Djanira Heitor dos Prazeres, Cícero Dias, Alfredo Volpi, and the sculptors Victor Brecheret, Maria Martins, Bruno Giorgi, Mário Cravo. The article includes some photographs of contemporary architecture, four of which are in color.

1191. Vieira, José Geraldo. A arte "ingênua" (Habitat, 6:35, out. 1956, p. 2-11, illus.).

By means of many photographs the critic compares the "ingenious" work of French and Brazilian "Sunday painters" of genre, landscape, and history.

1192. ―――. Evolução do abstractionismo no Brasil (Habitat, 6:33, agôsto 1956, p. 7-10, illus.).

Points out that the abstract movement in Brazil is recent, dating from about 1930, since before that the modern movement, which goes back to about 1917, was dominated by Expressionist tendencies.

Economics

GENERAL

1250. **Alba, Víctor.** ¿Autarquía o división del trabajo? América como continente mal desarrollado (Cuad Am, 85:1, enero-feb. 1956, p. 33-61).
Análisis que parte del presupuesto de que el problema económico del continente no es de desarrollo insuficiente, sino de desarrollo desequilibrado, que debe enfocarse vía "ayudar a resolver" y no "ayudar a ayudarse" [Nacional Financiera]

1251. Informe del Seminario Interamericano del Ingreso Nacional, Santiago, Chile, enero 5-17, 1953 (Estadística, 11:40, suplemento).

1252. **Inter-American Economic and Social Council.** Reunión de Ministros de Hacienda o Economía en IV sesión extraordinaria del Consejo Interamericano Económico y Social celebrada en la ciudad de Petrópolis, Brasil, del 22 de noviembre al 2 de diciembre de 1954. México, Secretaría de Hacienda y Crédito Público, Dirección General de Prensa, 1955? 166 p.
The volume gives the historical background of the conference, with special details on the participation of the Mexican delegation. It also gives the various resolutions of the Conference. [S. Garbuny]

1253. **Inter-American Juridical Committee.** Ley uniforme sobre arbitraje comercial internacional. Washington, Unión Panamericana, 1955. 18 p.
The volume contains the comments of the governments of the U. S., El Salvador, Peru, and the Dominican Republic on the 1954 draft of an inter-American commercial arbitration code and submits on the basis of these comments a new draft for the consideration of the Inter-American Council of Jurists. See also item below. [S. Garbuny]

1254. ————. Proyecto de ley uniforme sobre arbitraje comercial internacional. Washington, Pan American Union, 1954. 22 p.
The Inter-American Council of Jurists resolved at its first meeting in Rio, May-June 1950, to prepare a draft code on international commercial arbitration, which is here presented. The volume also contains an explanation of the motives and the history of events that led to the draft project. See also item above. [S. Garbuny]

1255. **Jaszi, George,** and **John W. Kendrick.** Problemas y técnicas relacionados con la medición del volumen de la producción nacional. Washington, Pan American Union, 1954. 34 p.
This work, officially translated by the Pan American Union, served as a reference text for the first Inter-American Seminar on National Income, which met in Santiago de Chile in January 1953. It is a first approach to the problems of measurement of national income. [S. Garbuny]

1256. **Jones, Tom B.; Elizabeth Anne Warburton;** and **Anne Kingsley.** A bibliography on South American economic affairs. Articles in nineteenth-century periodicals. Minneapolis, Minn., University of Minnesota Press, 1955. 146 p.
A very meritorious and painstaking bibliography on articles on South American economic affairs. The authors list nearly 10,000 articles that appeared in 229 periodicals during the 19th century. The periodicals were published in the U. S., England, France, Austria, Germany, Belgium, Italy, Spain, Peru, Argentina, and Ireland. The articles deal principally with agriculture, commerce, communication, finance, immigration, labor, mining, and transportation. [S. Garbuny]

1257. **Mikesell, Raymond F.** Inversiones extranjeras en América Latina. Washington, Unión Panamericana, Departamento de Asuntos Económicos y Sociales (Serie de investigaciones económicas), 1956. 166 p.
A very important and valuable publication, originally presented by its author to the meeting of Finance or Economic Ministers at Rio in November 1954, it reviews now in revised form

the whole complex of private and public foreign investments in Latin America. The chapters on the investment climate, the World Bank and Export-Import Bank, and projects for other international financial institutions, rival in interest the presentation of the problems of foreign investment and international trade, economic development, and taxation of foreign investments. The statistical tables contained in this volume will be of equally great use to the reader. [S. Garbuny]

1258. Pan American Union. Selected economic data on the Latin American Republics. Washington, 1954. 43 p., tables.

A statistical compilation of 29 tables followed by a list of sources. The work consists of two parts, comparative international tables and country tables. The reference years are immediate pre-world-War-II years and the late 1940's and early 1950's. The last reported year is 1952. Valuable for a first approach to economic research on Latin America. [S. Garbuny]

1259. ————. Division of Economic Research. Fiscal receipts, expenditures, budgets and public debt of the Latin American republics. Washington, 1956? 180 p., tables.

A meritorious attempt to give a succinct survey of the revenues, expenditures, budgets, and public debt of each of the 20 Latin American republics, according to the available statistics. Data vary for the different countries, but all tables are for postwar years and the information in no case goes beyond 1954. A list of sources on which the tables are based permits further research. [S. Garbuny]

1260. Silva Herzog, Jesús. Homilía para futuros economistas (Cuad Am, 85:2, marzo-abril 1956, p. 7-18).

Ensayo sobre lo que es la economía como ciencia, su aplicación, qué es un economista y cómo debe ser el que trabaja para una economía nacional de un país en desarrollo. [Nacional Financiera]

1261. United Nations. Economic Commission for Latin America. A summary of preliminary study of the possibilities for the development of the pulp and paper industry in Latin America. Secretariat paper. N. Y., 1953. 24 p. (Doc. E/CN.12/ 294).

The slender volume is an attempt to appraise the need for pulp and paper in Latin America and to establish the available resources and productive capacity of the paper mills to meet the existing demand. Furthermore, the investigation considers future needs and the possibilities for developing the existing productive capacity of the region. Though statistical data are used to support the argument of the brief, the study is highly conjectural and of very conditional use to the studious reader. [S. Garbuny]

1262. Wilgus, A. Curtis (ed.). The Caribbean: contemporary trends. Gainesville, University of Florida Press (Publ. of the School of Inter-American Studies, series 1, 3), 1953. 292 p.

The first part, "Economic trends," p. 3-55, contains the following articles: Norton, E. A., "Conservation problems in the Caribbean area"; Burgin, Miron, "Some problems of economic development in the Caribbean area"; Loyo, Gilberto, and Raúl Ortiz Mena, "Problems of underdeveloped areas in the Caribbean"; Bell, Frank K., "Transportation in the Caribbean"; Akin, John, "Environment for United States enterprises in the Caribbean."

LATIN AMERICA (EXCEPT BRAZIL AND MEXICO)
SIEGFRIED GARBUNY

ARGENTINA

1300. Alende, Óscar E. Problemas fundamentales de la revolución del 16 de septiembre. B. A., Ediciones Signo, 1956. 57 p.

The author, long an opponent of the Perón regime, was deputy in the National Congress and, after Sept. 16, 1955, a member of the National Advisory Council of Argentina's provisional government. Though he principally agrees with Raúl Prebisch's thesis that the new Argentina must base its economy in the future on both agriculture and industry, he rather critically reviews in this booklet the Prebisch plans submitted to the provisional Argentine government. The critique consists of three parts, a general examination and criticism of the plan, a discussion of special problems, and a review of the wage proposals of the Prebisch program. The author then adds his thoughts on foreign capital investments in his country and on the legal status of his government.

1301. Argentina. Ministerio de Hacienda de la Nación. Política económica y atómica argentina. B. A., 1956. 59 p.

The first part of the pamphlet is a declaration by the Argentine Finance Minister on his country's economic policy, dealing essentially with foreign exchange and foreign trade problems. In the second part of the volume the Director of Argentina's Atomic Energy Council sums up for the press his country's resolve to buy atomic raw materials and machinery wherever it finds the most suitable bargain. Trade and financial statistics and graphs form the rest of the book.

1302. ————. President. Mensaje del Poder Ejecutivo e informe del Ministerio de Hacienda. Cuenta de inversión, ejercicio de 1953. B. A., Ministerio de Hacienda de la Nación, 1954. 180 p., tables.

Juan D. Perón's message to the Argentine Congress concerning the revenues and expenditures of his government during the fiscal year 1953, including a statement on Argentina's public debt as of the end of that year. Perón stresses the emergence of a balanced budget under his regime. The inserted statistical data and tables serve to illustrate the allegations of the message.

1303. ————. Secretaría de Asuntos Económicos. Producto e ingreso de la República Argentina en el período 1953-54. B. A., 1955. 164 p., graphs, tables.
Using the data, which before 1952 the Argentine Central Bank had compiled and after that year the newly created Ministry of Economic Affairs, this study attempts to give a comprehensive presentation of Argentine's gross national product and national income for the years 1934-1954. Conceptually and methodologically the investigation is based on the pertinent works of the American economists Simon Kuznets, Richard Ruggles, and Wassiby Leontief, as well as on the publications of Aukrust, Bjerve, and Frisch in Norway and of Richard Stone in the United Kingdom. Ample statistical material.

1304. Blanco, Eugenio A. La moneda, los bancos y la economía nacional. B. A., Ministerio de Hacienda de la Nación, 1956. 76 p., graphs, tables.
A lecture delivered in August 1956, by Argentina's Finance Minister in the Central Bank of the Argentine Republic. The lecture reviews the history of the Bank before and after its nationalization in 1946 and presents a résumé of its position and tasks since the fall of the Perón government. The Minister's statement contains moreover valuable references to monetary developments and to the very recent national and international banking policies of his country. Statistical tables and graphs conclude the slender volume.

1304a. ————. Política económica argentina. B. A., Ministerio de Hacienda de la Nación, 1956. 25 p., graphs, tables.
A brief radio address by Argentina's Finance Minister, delivered in October 1956 over the State network. The address analyzes very briefly the new Argentina's economic problems and the reforms undertaken by the provisional government. The sectors of agriculture, public finance, international lending and national corporation policies are of special interest. Includes statistical tables and graphs.

1304b. ————. Realidad económica argentina. B. A., Ministerio de Hacienda de la Nación, 1956. 58 p.
A lecture delivered in November 1956 by the Argentine Finance Minister before the faculty and the students of economics at the University of Buenos Aires. Referring briefly to the regained freedom of the University after the fall of Perón, the minister expanded mainly on Argentina's fiscal budget and monetary problems. Statistical tables and graphs are appended to and elucidate the lecture.

1305. Corominas, Enrique V. La lucha contra el coloniaje económico. B. A., Ediciones Hechos e Ideas, 1956. 96 p.
A pamphlet written after the fall of the Perón government about ways and means to obtain Ar-

gentina's economic freedom and independence. The author investigates his country's position in the American orbit and examines the role of the U. S. and the United Nations vis-à-vis his country. He thoroughly investigates the problems of Argentine agriculture and also discusses the national petroleum question and the function of foreign investments in his country.

1306. Guillén, Abraham. Monopolios y latifundios contra la economía argentina. Cómo salir de la crisis estructural. B. A., Comisión Nacional de Homenaje a Lisandro de la Torre (Cuadernos de cátedra de Lisandro de la Torre, 2), 1956. 128 p.
A polemic against monopolies, large estates, and big business, in Argentina and the world in general. The tract is quite unscientific, poorly documented, and written to appeal to the low income groups. The Prebisch plan for the post-Perón Argentina is severely criticized. Economic diversification rather than the intensification of agriculture and livestock production is counseled.

1307. Monti, Ángel F. Evolución y proposiciones para la economía argentina (R Cien Ec, 3. serie, 44:58, marzo-abril 1956, p. 91-142).
A very scholarly article on the development of the Argentine economy. Tries to discern clearly between what is desirable and what is possible given the status of the economy at the end of 1955. The author uses a good deal of economic analysis as nowadays applied to the complex of economic growth as well as comparative statistics. Though the analysis of the Argentine economy may be dated, it is doubtless an interesting and scholarly contribution.

1308. Prebisch, Raúl. Relatório preliminar da situação argentina (R Br Ec, 10:1, março 1956, p. 5-52).
After the fall of the Perón government in Argentina, Raúl Prebisch was called upon to submit to the successor government three reports on Argentina's economic situation: (1) "A preliminary report on the economic situation"; (2) "Sound money or run-away inflation"; and (3) "Plan for economic reconstruction." The first report is published here, in Portuguese, because it is of the greatest interest to the Brazilian reader. It contains the explanation of Argentina's economic difficulties in terms of shortages of foreign exchange, electric power, and transportation. It also cites the complications resulting from a neglect of agriculture in order to promote industry as well as from undesirable state controls of the economic process. The scourge of inflation is especially stressed.

1309. Salaberren, Raúl. Supplement No. 1 to the statement of the laws of Argentina in matters affecting business. 2d ed. Washington, Pan American Union, Division of Law and Treaties, 1954. 28 p.
This first supplement to the 1951 "Statement" contains the additions and changes that have occurred since issuance of the basic publication. Together, the statement and supplement present a summary of the pertinent constitutional, statutory, and regulatory provisions through early

1954. The reader should bear in mind that after the fall of the Perón government substantial changes took place in the laws affecting business.

1310. Sociedad Rural Argentina. Informe sobre la producción rural argentina. Año 3. B. A., 1955. 92 p., graphs, tables.
The third annual report of the Argentine Rural Society, a non-governmental organization. Mindful of the changes the Perón régime had brought, the report brings against that background extensive data on Argentine agriculture. It deals with the physical factors in agriculture and market problems, and discusses the labor force and the entrepreneurs' group. Questions of price formation are treated as well as problems of inventory and stockpiling. A brief review of population and income problems concludes the volume.

CHILE

1311. Banco Central de Chile. Departamento de Estudios. Inversiones extranjeras en Chile. Santiago, 1955. 120 p., tables.
After indicating the methods used for definitions and valuations, this publication surveys the foreign investments in Chile. It deals with both direct and portfolio investment, and private and public investments. The discussion of investments according to the parts of the economy in which they occur and according to the countries from which they come is especially interesting. Appendixes list laws and decrees, and there is a bibliography.

1312. Correa Prieto, Luis. Aspectos negativos de la intervención económica. Fracasos de una experiencia. Santiago, Zig-Zag (Obras de actualidad), 1955. 326 p.
A violent diatribe against any government interference in business. From the mercantilists and their policies the author goes on to the disturbances inflicted on private business by such legislation as the American N. R. A. or simple price and exchange controls such as are found in so many countries in the present time. The author even rejects foreign economic advisers for his country and calls those who advocate state interference in economic matters ignorant of the economic mechanism. The book is a totally negative polemic, as its title implies, and in spite of its many citations and statistics is not scholarly.

COLOMBIA

1313. Colombia. Caja de Crédito Agrario, Industrial y Minero. Departamento de Investigaciones Económicas. Producción nacional. Bogotá, 1955. lxxxvi, 253 p., graphs, tables.
An official account on the country's agricultural situation and the role of agrarian credit in it. A description of the development, activities, and credit conditions of the Agrarian Credit Bank (Caja de Crédito Agrario) is followed by a survey of agricultural costs. The volume also contains a presentation of the characteristics of the national agricultural products and of the country's livestock. A special part reviews agricultural and livestock conditions in the individual departments of the country.

1314. ———. Comité Nacional de Planeación. Plan del Norte de Santander. Bogotá, 1956. 99 p., tables.
A message concerning the economic development of the state of North Santander by the Secretary General of the Colombian National Planning Committee. With the help of United Nations agricultural and food experts, an investment plan for 130,000,000 pesos, which aims at the development of agriculture, transportation, education, electrification, and general public services, was drawn up.

1315. ———. Departamento Administrativo Nacional de Estadística. Muestra agrícola nacional. Bogotá, 1955.
Presents national data for Colombia's agriculture. The data are based on a scientific sample worked out with the help of United Nations Technical Assistance and FAO experts. The sampling method, originally tried in the Cauca Valley, is well explained, and followed by national and departmental statistics.

1316. ———. Dirección Nacional de Planeación Económica y Fiscal. Plan de Boyacá. Inversiones 1954-1958. Bogotá, 1953? 86 p., tables.
Contains the report of the National Economic and Financial Planning Board concerning economic development of the state of Boyaca. The report was submitted before the inauguration of the steel plant at Paz de Rio, but is actually based on the development of that steel-producing center. The plan provides for the investment of 360 million pesos over the period of five years, with the steel industry and related industries as main objects of the development policies.

1317. ———. ———. Plan del Valle del Cauca. Inversiones 1954-1958. Bogotá, 1954? 93 p., tables.
Contains the report of the national Economic and Financial Planning Board concerning economic development of the Cauca Valley. The report considers the region as especially well endowed with resources and good weather conditions. It envisages a rich agricultural and urban culture in the area in the future. An investment plan of 1180 million pesos to be spent in five years is submitted. The investments are to cover the mechanization of agriculture, irrigation, electrification, the construction of harbors and airports, the development of transportation, public services, education, and industrial surveys for the region.

1318. ———. División Nacional de Minas. Boletín de minas. Bogotá. Año 1, no. 1, abril 1954—.
The articles contained in the issue seen deal exclusively with mining problems. A large number of the articles are dedicated to Colombian copper.

1319. ———. Ministerio de Fomento. Fomento nacional. Publicación mensual destinada a difundir las actividades del

Ministerio. Bogotá. Año 1, no. 1, febrero 1954—.

The purpose of this review is to report monthly on the activities of the Ministry of Development. The first issue covers a number of diverse topics, but also contains several articles on cooperatives in Colombia which may be of special interest to the reader.

COSTA RICA

1320. **Agüero Sole, Omar.** Henificación de Jaragua en la zona de Liberia y su importancia para la ganadería guanacasteca. San José, Universidad de Costa Rica (Sección Tesis de Grado y Ensayos, 8), 1953. 62 p., 23 illus.

A technical agricultural study of how to produce with the means of modern agrochemistry enough hay to properly feed the cattle in the zone of Liberia, Costa Rica. Tables as well as photographs and diagrams elucidate the text.

1321. **Costa Rica. Dirección General de Estadística y Censos.** Comercio exterior de Costa Rica, 1955. San José, 1956. 175 p., tables.

A comprehensive statistical review of Costa Rica's foreign trade in 1955, giving detailed information as to commodity exports and imports and direction of trade. The U. S. and Germany emerge from the tables as Costa Rica's main markets. Costa Rica's balance of trade with the U. S. was unfavorable, with Germany favorable, in 1955.

1322. ————. **Ministerio de Agricultura e Industrias.** El MAI fortalece la riqueza del país. Memoria 1954. San José, Publicaciones MAI, 1955. 85 p., illus.

The annual report of the Ministry of Agriculture and Industries for the year 1954, submitted to the Costa Rican Legislative Assembly. The report, a combination of text, statistics and photographs, touches but lightly on a vast number of subjects. Research and improvements are reported for coffee, cacao, rice, maize, cattle raising, and veterinary medicine, among others. The brief notes on the meteorological service and on the administration of the Ministry are equally interesting.

1323. **Facio, Gonzalo J.** Estabilización de precios por el sistema de reservas. San José, Asamblea Legislativa de la República de Costa Rica, 1955. 26 p.

The pamphlet is a reprint of a speech by the President of the Costa Rican Legislative Assembly, delivered in July 1955. It is in defense of the author's motion to reconstitute the National Production Council as a Price Stabilization Council, and deals with the theoretical and practical aspects of price stabilization for Costa Rica.

1324. Ley orgánica del sistema bancario nacional. Capítulo VII. Sección de Juntas Rurales de Crédito Agrícola. Comentarios y observaciones. San José, 1955. 30 p.

The publication contains the seventh chapter of the organic law on the Costa Rican national banking system. The chapter consists of 17 articles (88-104) dealing with the Rural Agricultural Credit Boards, their composition, rights and obligations, administration, and the types of credit they may extend. The text of the law is augmented by a fairly extensive commentary and pertinent observations.

CUBA

1325. **Club de Rotarios de la Habana, and Club de Leones de la Habana.** Estado actual de las relaciones comerciales cubano-americanas. Exposición de datos históricos y estadísticos ante la sesión pública conjunta de los Clubes de Rotarios y Leones de la Habana, febrero 9, 1955. Habana, 1955. 72 p., graphs, tables.

The pamphlet is a joint publication of the Rotary and the Lions' Clubs of Habana, Cuba. It contains a historical and statistical review of U. S. and Cuban trade relations. Statistical tables and graphs show the development of this trade from the establishment of the Cuban Republic in 1902 up to 1954. Data are presented for the over-all trade as well as for individual commodities.

1326. **Cuba. Consejo Nacional de Economía.** La estimulación industrial en Cuba. Habana, 1956. 142 p. (Estudios e investigaciones económicas, 14).

The slender volume presents the proposals for economic development as given by the Cuban delegation at the meeting of the economic ministers in Petropolis, Brazil, at the end of 1954. The bulk of the book, however, is constituted by the text of the Cuban law no. 1038 of 1953 on industrial stimulation and the regulations pertaining to it.

1327. **López Sanabria, Hugo.** Clasificación industrial de las actividades económicas de Cuba. Habana, Tribunal de Cuentas, 1955. 138 p.

The present volume is published under the auspices of the Cuban General Accounting Tribunal. It contains a systematic classification of Cuba's economic activities each of which receives a code number. The work, undertaken to establish uniform and precise statistical records, is based on the Standard Industrial Classification Manual published by the U. S. Bureau of the Budget in 1945 and on the Uniform International Industrial Classification published by the Statistical Office of the United Nations in 1949.

1328. **Secretariado Permanente de Entidades Fiscalizadoras.** Boletín. Habana. Año 1, no. 1, 1. de julio de 1954.

The first number is a report on the first International Congress of Accounting Offices and Tribunals. It contains a speech of Cuba's president, General Batista, at the Congress, and a rather interesting description of the U. S. General Accounting Office. A list of the resolutions of the Congress concludes the issue.

1329. **Seiglie, Óscar.** Cuatro exposiciones sobre la industria azucarera de Cuba. Habana, Lex, 1955. 24 p.

The author has set forth his ideas on the Cuban sugar industry in four letters to the Director General of the Cuban National Association of Plantation Owners. They contain a multitude of ideas. Especially interesting for the author's comments on U. S.-Cuban relations and on President Franklin D. Roosevelt's and Agricultural Secretaries Wallace's and Anderson's policies vis-à-vis Cuban sugar.

ECUADOR

1330. **Ecuador. Junta Nacional de Planificación y Coordinación Económica.** Azuay y Cañar. Desarrollo económico. Situación agraria y forestal. Quito, Casa de la Cultura Ecuatoriana, 1956. 219 p., illus., tables.
In this volume the National Planning Board of Ecuador attempts an appraisal of the causes for the critical economic conditions of the provinces of Azuay and Cañar. Detailed data are listed. The economic development of the two provinces is traced and a study of their agricultural possibilities and limitations undertaken. Special observations on the utilization of the land and suggestions for conservation and better land usage complete the volume.

1331. ———. ———. Informe anual, 1955-1956. Quito, 1956. 315 p., tables.
The annual report of the National Planning Board of Ecuador for the period 1955-1956. The report deals in brief fashion with all phases of the economy, including developmental problems. It presents ample statistics, tables, graphs, and maps, and is therefore rather informative.

1332. **Inter-American Economic and Social Council.** Ecuador. Hacienda pública y política fiscal. Washington, Pan American Union, Department of Economic and Social Affairs, 1954. 205 p.
A case study of the fiscal policies of a still-underdeveloped country which, for its revenues, relies heavily on international trade. The first two parts of the book deal with government income and expenditures and the budget as well as with fiscal policies. The third part discusses the public debt, and the concluding fourth part reviews Ecuador's fiscal policies between 1938-1950 with special reference to the role of these policies as a countercyclical device.

1333. **Universidad Central del Ecuador. Instituto de Investigaciones Económicas.** Índice nacional de precios al por mayor. Quito. V. 1, no. 1, enero-mayo, 1953.
Attempts to present wholesale price statistics for the years 1952 and 1953. The commodities covered are foodstuffs, raw materials, and metals. Price developments in different geographic areas are well presented. Though the booklet reflects a meritorious effort, the statistical methods used are rather elementary.

1334. **Universidad de Guayaquil. Instituto de Investigaciones Económicas y Políticas.** Boletín de difusión económica.

Guayaquil, Ecuador. Año 1, no. 1, octubre 1954.
The bulletin is intended to publish the research of the Institute as well as other worthwhile economic papers issued in Ecuador. The first issue contains a wide variety of articles, including an interesting study of coffee statistics in Ecuador by a third-year economics student.

EL SALVADOR

1335. **El Salvador. Departamento de Estudios Económicos.** Leyes y disposiciones legales vigentes para el incremento y el nacimiento de industrias en El Salvador. San Salvador, 1954. Various pagings.
The volume contains a number of laws and decrees the purpose of which is to stimulate the growth of certain already existing industries or to bring about the foundation of others. Industries covered are, among others, the cement industry, canneries and food processing, and the amusement industry.

1336. ———. **Dirección General de Estadística y Censos.** Costo y condiciones de vida en San Salvador. San Salvador, 1956. 78 p.
Presents a rather interesting inquiry into the costs and living conditions of workers' families in El Salvador. The study is based on a comprehensive investigation of 300 workers' families in the city of San Salvador. The definitions and the statistical methods used in the inquiry are well explained in the volume. The presentation and the results of the obtained data are treated in a scholarly and critical review.

1337. ———. **Ministerio de Obras Públicas.** Obras públicas. Boletín. San Salvador. Año 1, no. 4-5, julio-diciembre 1953.
A special edition on its achievements by the Ministry of Public Works on the occasion of the fifth anniversary of the December Revolution of 1948. Essentially a propaganda issue which with its pictures and statistics tries to impress on the reader the success of various public projects of the revolutionary government.

1338. **Feltham, Percy M.** The textile industry in El Salvador. N. Y., 1954. 45 p. (UN Doc. ST/TAA/K/El Salvador/8).
A United Nations study for the purpose of technical assistance. The valuable slender volume gives detailed data on El Salvador's textile industry in all its aspects. The problems of a textile mill are well presented in the case of Fábrica de Hilados y Tejidos San Miguel. Of equal interest are the author's remarks on the employee training program.

1339. **Feuerlein, W. J.** Proposals for the further economic development of El Salvador. N. Y., 1954. 160 p., tables. (UN Doc. ST/TAA/K/EL Salvador/5).
A report prepared by an expert of the Technical Assistance Administration of the United Nations. After a brief presentation of general considerations, the author surveys the problems of agri-

cultural and industrial expansion. He also devotes space to social improvements in education, labor, housing, and medical services. He concludes with a review of the financial and foreign trade aspects of development.

GUATEMALA

1340. Guatemala. Ministerio de Gobernación. Estatuto agrario. Decreto número 559. Guatemala, 1956. 93 p.
The decree is the land tenure law passed by the Carlos Castillo Armas government. It regulates in 238 articles, for private and public lands, all direct or derived rights and duties inherent in land ownership or possession.

1341. ————. President. Informe del ciudadano Presidente de la República, Coronel Jacobo Arbenz Guzmán, al Congreso Nacional en su primer período de sesiones ordinarias del año de 1953. Este informe corresponde a la gestión administrativa del año de 1952 y al estado de la situación política al 1. de marzo de 1953. Guatemala, Tip. Nacional, 1953. xlvii, 637 p.
An account by ousted President Arbenz to the National Congress of Guatemala. The account is a detailed survey of the economic and budgetary conditions of Guatemala, essentially for the year 1952, as well as an appraisal of the political situation in that country as of March 1, 1953. The account reflects of course the attitudes of the Arbenz regime.

HONDURAS

1342. Cruz, René. Dinero y banca en Honduras. Reseña histórica y análisis de la situación originada por la legislación de 1950 y la creación del Banco Central de Honduras. Tegucigalpa, Banco Nacional de Fomento, 1954? 58 p., tables.
An evaluation of money and banking in Honduras, with special reference to the new situation created by the establishment of a Central Bank in 1950 and collateral monetary and financial legislation. The author gives a historical survey on Honduran finances since colonial times and ends his discussion with a review of the present problems of the Central Bank.

1343. Tosco, Manuel (and others). Ingresos del gobierno central, 1924/25-1951/52. Tegucigalpa, Banco Central de Honduras, 1953. 205 p.
A monograph prepared by staff members of the Central Bank of Honduras. It presents the revenue of the central government of Honduras in all its agencies with the exception of the Central Bank and the Development Bank. The study covers the years 1924-1952 and lists and briefly describes all sources of government revenues during the period under investigation. A useful fount of detailed information.

NICARAGUA

1344. Nicaragua. Consejo Nacional de

Economía. El desarrollo económico nicaragüense. Managua. Año 1, no. 10, dic. 31, 1953.
This official publication contains a number of brief reviews on the progress of the Nicaraguan economy. Developments in agriculture, education, sanitation, and credit and banking are briefly reported. Public works and public utilities as well as special services are also covered.

1345. ————. Instituto de Fomento Nacional. Apuntes sobre la economía azucarera de Nicaragua. Managua, 1954. 35 p., tables.
A description, supported by statistical tables, of the Nicaraguan sugar industry, essentially for the years 1947-1954. The production, distribution, internal consumption, and exports of sugar are reported. Questions dealing with the raising of the sugar cane are also treated. The last two chapters describe the National Bank's credit system serving the sugar industry and the general possibilities for the industry's development.

PERU

1346. Derteano Urrutia, Carlos. La libre empresa y la agricultura. Lima, Sociedad Nacional Agraria, 1954. 16 p. & tables.
A short but spirited essay to show the importance of free enterprise for agriculture in Peru. The author compares two periods, first the span between 1945-1948, when exchange, foreign trade, and price controls were particularly harsh, and secondly the period 1949-1953, when free enterprise prevailed. Ample statistical material helps to demonstrate that under free enterprise production rose, foreign trade expanded, and foreign exchange income grew—all of which secured greater revenue for the state, while the opposite effects, worsened by the ensuing scarcity of goods and by speculation, were the results in the period of controls.

1347. Hayn, Rolf. Cyclical exchange rate policy and real income: Peru (Interam Ec Aff, 8:1, summer 1954, p. 61-68).
Based on the author's unpublished doctoral dissertation at the University of Wisconsin. Discusses the theoretical issues of a cyclical exchange rate policy and its effects upon both real incomes and the balance of payments, using the Peruvian example. The policies of the 1930's and the exchange developments in Peru after the World War II are ably described, but the article is too brief to substantiate any scientific thesis.

1348. The Juan Carosio-Moyopampa power station (Water Power, 5:11, Nov. 1953, p. 402-409; 5:12, Dec. 1953, p. 457-464).
An article in two installments which appeared originally in German in the Swiss journal *Schweizerische Bauzeitung*, no. 3-4, 1953. It deals with a Peruvian development in which a 42 MW station on the Rio Santa Eulalia provides much-needed power to Lima and district. Essentially a technical article which with its graphs is of primary interest to the hydroelectrical engineer rather than to the economist.

1349. Ulloa, Alberto. A statement of the laws of Peru in matters affecting business.

2d ed. Washington, Pan American Union, Division of Law and Treaties, 1955. 133 p.

A second, revised and enlarged edition of a compilation of the laws of Peru, as they may affect the businessman. The volume includes a survey of the pertinent provisions of constitutional and administrative law. It deals with the problems of nationality and immigration, rights and duties of aliens, all aspects of commercial and business relations from corporation law to banking and insurance legislation. It also covers patents and trademarks and family relations as well as labor legislation and estate law. Ample references to the legal sources make the book a serious and dependable source of information.

URUGUAY

1350. **Cassinelli Muñoz, Horacio.** Statement of the laws of Uruguay. 2d ed. Supplement No. 1. Washington, Pan American Union, Division of Law and Treaties, 1954. 29 p.

The supplement and the original 1952 statement of the laws present a summary through Mar. 31, 1954. The reader must be warned that some parts of the supplement, e.g., the chapter on exchange controls, have been supplanted by legislation passed after 1954.

1351. **Faroppa, Luis A., and Israel Wonsewer.** La política económica del Uruguay. Montevideo, Facultad de Ciencias Económicas y de Administración, Instituto de Teoría y Política Económica, 1956. 61 p.

Two lectures delivered at the Institute of Theoretical and Political Economy at the University of Montevideo. Faroppa deals with the national economy of Uruguay in its historical development and present setting, and Wonsewer with the international economy in its effect on Uruguay. The lectures are a part of a lecture cycle on the "socio-economic reality of Uruguay." Scholarly as they are, they are too short to yield much information on their subjects.

1352. ————; Enrique V. Iglesias; and Israel Wonsewer. El nuevo régimen cambiario del Uruguay. Fundamentos, objetivos y efectos. Montevideo, Instituto de Teoría y Política Económicas (Facultad de Ciencias Económicas y de Administración, 9), 1956. 104 p.

The authors try to examine, each in one lecture, the contents and economic consequences of a comprehensive reform in Uruguay's exchange system. This reform is contained in a decree of August 1956 creating a new set of multiple exchange rates and of special export and import categories. The presentation of the authors' views is scholarly and based on theoretical reasoning.

1353. **Fernández, Alfredo; José Félix Bonsignore; and Julio Fitipaldo.** Los censos agropecuarios nacionales de 1946 y 1951. Comparación con los censos argentinos de 1947 y 1952. Montevideo,

Universidad de la República, Facultad de Ciencias Económicas y de Administración (Instituto de Estadística, 10), 1955. 74 p., tables.

A rather interesting and scholarly tract on the agricultural census of 1946 and 1951 in Uruguay by the director of the Statistical Institute of the University at Montevideo and two of his collaborators. After discussing the legal background of the census the authors present the results and then undertake a comparison of the findings with analogous data from the censuses of 1947 and 1952 in Argentina.

VENEZUELA

1354. **Banco Central de Venezuela. Departamento de Investigaciones Económicas y Estadísticas.** Desarrollo y perspectiva económica general. Informe para la X Conferencia Interamericana. Caracas, 1954. 109 p., graphs, tables.

A statement by the Central Bank of Venezuela presented at the X Inter-American Conference at Caracas, Venezuela, 1954. The brief volume deals with Venezuela's main economic activities: oil, ores, industry in general, and agriculture. It investigates the country's international financial positions and concludes with a review of the role of bank credit and budgetary measures and of the special problems of the business cycle.

1355. **González C., Ricardo.** La C. V. F. y su doctrina económica. Caracas, Grafos, 1956. 121 p.

The volume contains the ideas of the president of the Venezuelan Development Corporation. The contents embrace a presentation of the policies and objectives of the corporation, of the development plans and of the role of credit in these schemes. Furthermore, the book discusses the organization and the management of this agency as well as the special projects for electrification and agriculture.

1356. **Jankus, Alfred P., and Neil M. Malloy.** Venezuela, land of opportunity. N. Y., Pageant Press, 1956. 259 p.

A brief and useful personal account of Venezuela, its people and its land, as the authors saw and experienced them. Unpretentious and more journalistic than scholarly, the authors write a poignant and witty pen. They have compiled useful information and data on Venezuela's mores, history, politics, and economics, which the serious student may use with profit. Statistics, a bibliography of literature on Venezuela, and photographs enrich the presentation of the subject.

1357. **Rodríguez H., Ivan.** Política económica 1955. Petróleo, petroquímica, hierro, vivienda presupuesto, abastecimiento, electricidad. . . . Caracas, Cosmos, 1955. 162 p.

The author presents a collection of articles written in 1955, principally for the newspaper *El Universal*. The articles are not connected with each other but rather are independent essays on important issues in Venezuela's economy. They are written with more enthusiasm than scholarship. The author's thoughts on petroleum, tarchemistry, and iron will prove especially interesting.

1358. Venezuela. Consejo de Bienestar Rural. Estudio de los recursos agrícolas del estado Yaracuy y de partes de los estados Falcón y Carabobo. Parte 1. Estudio de los recursos agrícolas. Suplemento a los mapas de suelos, uso tenencia y clasificación de la tierra. Parte 2. Aspectos botánicos. Caracas, 1955. 2 v.; v. 1, 279 p. & illus.; v. 2, maps.

The agricultural resources of the state of Yaracuy and of ports of the states of Falcon and Carabobo. The study is essentially devoted to the physical aspects of the problem and to the types of products grown in the areas under survey. Characteristics of land tenure and agricultural techniques are also given. Pictures and geophysical maps enrich the volume.

1359. ————. ————. La industria ganadera en Venezuela. Caracas, 1955. 256 p., illus., charts.

An official survey of the Venezuelan cattle raising industry. The first part of the survey deals with technical problems of cattle raising such as the nutrition and feeds for cattle and the improvement of milk and meat production. The second part of the survey reports on marketing problems for cattle and meat; the third and last part contains an economic analysis and projection of Venezuelan cattle and meat supply to 1964.

OTHER COUNTRIES

1360. Dominican Republic. Dirección General de Estadística. Oficina Nacional de Censo. 4. censo nacional agropecuario, 1950. Ciudad Trujillo, 1955. 244 p., tables.

The fourth national agricultural census taken August 1950 by the National Census Bureau. The census appear to be comprehensive though the reader is warned in the introductory remarks of the inherent statistical weaknesses which permeate the tabular work. Statistical concepts and methods are in part explained in the introduction to the volume.

1361. Inter-American Economic and Social Council. International trade of the American states. Foreign trade of Haiti, 1945-1950. Washington, Pan American Union, Division of Statistics, 1954. 153 p., tables. (Bull., 1).

A comprehensive review of Haiti's foreign trade between 1945-1950. It briefly describes the general characteristics of the trade and then gives a full-length exposition on the Haitian exports and imports. A large number of statistical tables, including export price indexes, enhance the value of the discussion. The reader will also appreciate the bibliography which concludes the pamphlet.

1362. Peñaloza, Luis. Curso de economía política. Ingreso nacional. Desarrollo económico. Cochabamba, Bolivia, 1955. 307 p.

A report, prepared by an expert of the Technical Assistance Administration of the United Nations. The Bolivian author of this text is known for his economic history of Bolivia. The present book is a treatise on economics, particularly on national income and economic development. For the American reader, however, only the special sections on Bolivia's economic institutions and problems are of interest.

1363. United States. International Cooperation Administration in Latin America. The Industrial Development Center of the Institute for Economic Development. Facts for investors in Panama. Panama, 1956. 94 p. & maps.

The pamphlet is in the nature of an advertisement to attract foreign capital. It gives general information on the economy of Panama and on the incentives which the Panamanian government offers to foreign investors. Cost structures and labor conditions are briefly referred to. Some areas for investments are suggested, and a few pertinent legal provisions are cited in appendixes.

BRAZIL

HENRY WILLIAM SPIEGEL

1400. Acôrdos secretos sôbre os minerais estratégicos (Obs Ec Fin, 21:243, maio 1956, p. 47-60).

Strategic mineral deposits as the subject of international agreements.

1401. Banas, Geraldo. Os investimentos italianos no Brasil (Obs Ec Fin, 19:224, out. 1954, p. 102-105).

An up-to-date survey of Italian investments in Brazil.

1402. Banco do Brasil. Arquivos econômicos. No. 1, julho 1955-.

A new periodical with contributions by René Courtin (on economic theory), J. Jochman (on Brazilian standard of living), P. van der Meiren (on Brazilian investments), J. N. Guimarães (on inflation and soil conservation), and others. The principal articles are provided with English and French summaries.

1403. Bastos, A. de Miranda. A competição africana no mercado de madeiras duras (Obs Ec Fin, 18:215, jan. 1954, p. 31-34).

The Brazilian timber economy in the face of African competition.

1404. Berenhauser Júnior, Carlos. A importância das indústrias pesadas na atual conjuntura econômica do Brasil (Obs Ec Fin, 20:235, set. 1955, p. 22-35).
An official view concerning the role of heavy industry in the Brazilian economy.

1405. Borges, Pompeu Accioly. Pulverização da propriedade (Obs Ec Fin, 17:204, jan. 1953, p. 59-64).
A discussion of the statistical increase in the number of farms and its significance.

1406. Brasilien und Deutschland (Übersee-Rund, 6:9-10, Okt. 1954, p. 45-141).
Contains various articles in Portuguese and German on Brazil and Germany, setting forth ideas about commercial relations between the two countries.

1407. Brazil. Conselho Nacional de Economia. Exposição geral da situação econômica do Brasil, 1954. Rio, 1955. 150 p. & tables.

1408. ————. ————. Exposição geral da situação econômica do Brasil, 1955, Rio, 1956. 130 p.
An authoritative and well-documented survey of the Brazilian economy in 1955.

1409. ————. Contadoria Geral da República. Balanços gerais da União relativos ao exercício de 1952 . . . Rio, 1953. 2 v. V. 1, Contas financeiras e patrimoniais; balanços de autarquias, 356 p; v. 2, Análise da despesa orçamentária, 342 p.
Annual report of the general accounting office.

1410. Instituto do Açúcar e do Álcool. O Instituto do Açúcar e do Álcool em 1954. Relatório do Sr. Carlos de Lima Cavalcanti, como Presidente da Comissão Executiva, apresentado ao Sr. Presidente da República. Rio, 1955. 96 p.

1411. ————. Ministério da Viação e Obras Públicas. Relatório das atividades do primeiro semestre, 1956. Um plano em marcha, no. 5, Rio, Serviço de Documentação, 1956. 59 p.

1412. ————. Superintendência do Plano de Valorização Econômica da Amazônia. A SPVEA numa visão de conjunto. Belém-Pará, Brazil, 1955. 28 p.
A progress report of the Amazon river valley development board.

1413. Carli, Gileno dé. O Instituto do Açúcar e do Álcool em 1952. Relatório. Rio, 1954. 74 p. & graphs.
Activities of the sugar control board in 1952.

1414. César, Nirceu da Cruz. O mate no Brasil. Rio, Ministério da Agricultura, Serviço de Informação Agrícola (Serie estudos e ensaios, 5), 1952. 43 p. & illus.
An interesting and well-informed study of a lesser-known Brazilian product.

1415. Chacel, Julian Magalhães. O producto agrícola a preços constantes (R Br Ec, 10:1, março 1956, p. 71-87, graphs).
The volume of agricultural production.

1416. Comissão de Desenvolvimento Econômico de Pernambuco. Legislação institucional e atividades no período 54-56. Recife, Brazil, 1956. 52 p.
A progress report of the Pernambuco development board.

1417. A conjuntura tritícola no Brasil (Conjunt Ec, 10:4, abril 1956, p. 17-22).
The Brazilian wheat economy.

1418. Economics and business in Brazil. Conjuntura econômica. International edition. Year 1, no. 1, Apr. 1954-.
After two annual issues of an international edition of this periodical, this edition is now to be published monthly. Founded by Richard Lewinsohn, who now is its European correspondent, the periodical meets the need for concise and accurate reports on current economic affairs.

1419. Gomes, Anapio. Radiografia do Brasil. Rio, Irmãos Pongetti, 1955. 229 p.
Thoughts on the current situation of Brazil.

1420. Gordilho, Osvaldo. Os transportes no Brasil. Rio, Ministério da Viação e Obras Públicas, Serviço de Documentação (Col. Mauá, 7), 1956. 315 p.
The first 150 pages of this prize essay are devoted to a general and historical discussion of the role of transportation in the Brazilian economy. The remainder, of about equal length, treats the current transportation problem and the attempts at solution. The well-informed author is at his best when examining policy issues.

1421. Gudin, Eugênio. A formação do economista (R Br Ec, 10:1, março 1956, p. 53-70).
The teaching of economics in Brazil, as seen by the dean of Brazilian economists.

1422. ————. Orientação e programação de desenvolvimento econômico (R Br Ec, 10:3, set. 1956, p. 27-52).
An article by an eminent authority, on developmental planning. The author is critical of the usefulness of "programming."

1423. Indústria e transporte de gêneros alimentícios (Obs Ec Fin, 19:228, fev. 1955, p. 44-58).
Proposals for the improvement of transportation of foodstuffs.

1424. Lebret, Louis Joseph. Estudo sôbre

desenvolvimento e implantação de indústrias, interessando a Pernambuco e ao nordeste. Recife, Brazil, 'Comissão de Desenvolvimento Econômico de Pernambuco (Série planificação econômica, 3), 1955. 77 p. & illus.

An intelligent discussion of development possibilities in Pernambuco, with special emphasis on the human factor.

1425. Lima, Heitor Ferreira. Evolução industrial de São Paulo. Esboço histórico. São Paulo, Martins, 1954. 196 p. & illus.

The first four chapters treat of the industrial history of São Paulo, beginning with the colonial period and ending with a discussion of "industrial concentration and centralization of capital." The last chapter contains a number of appraisals of pioneering industrialists, including one (with portrait) of Roberto Simonsen, erstwhile editor of this section of *HLAS*.

1426. Loeb, Gustaaf F. O desenvolvimento da produção industrial em Minas Gerais (R Br Ec, 10:3, set. 1956, p. 61-82).

1427. Lopes, Lucas. O vale do São Francisco. Rio, Ministério da Viação e Obras Públicas, Serviço de Documentação (Col. Mada), 1955. 345 p., maps.

A comprehensive study of the important river valley development project.

1428. Monteiro, Fernando. Figuras do Banco do Brasil. Rio, A. A. B. B. (Cadernos, 8), 1955. 63 p.

Biographies of some leading Brazilian bankers of the 19th and 20th centuries.

1429. No mundo dos negocios—Krupp instala-se no Brasil (Obs Ec Fin, 20:239, jan. 1956, p. 81-84).

Activities of the German munitions concern in Brazil.

1430. Oliveira, Clovis de. A indústria e o movimento constitucionalista de 1932. São Paulo, Serviço de Publicações, 1956. 320 p.

A historical review of the activities of the São Paulo Association of Manufacturers in the early 1930's.

1431. Onody, Oliver. Nuevas tendencias del comercio exterior del Brasil. Madrid, Ediciones Cultura Hispánica, 1953. 115 p., tables.

Spanish translation of a survey of Brazilian foreign trade problems, providing facts and figures for a number of commodities.

1432. O papel no Brasil (Obs Ec Fin, 19:217, março 1954, p. 82-86).

The Brazilian paper economy.

1433. Potsch, Waldemiro. O Brasil e suas riquezas. Brasilogia. 27. ed. Rio, Livraria Francisco Alves, 1955. 380 p. & illus.

A well-produced and profusely illustrated edition of an eminently successful schoolbook, which has had over 300,000 readers.

1434. Reforma bancária (Obs Ec Fin, 17:205, fev. 1953, p. 55-60).

Problems of banking discussed by various authorities.

1435. Rio Grande do Sul (state). Secretaria de Estado dos Negócios da Fazenda. Gabinete de Orçamento e Finanças. Orçamento geral do estado e orçamentos das autarquias estaduais. Lei no. 2193, de 3 de dezembro de 1953. Orça a receita e fixa a despesa do estado para o exercício de 1954. Pôrto Alegre, Brazil, 1954. 207 p., tables.

1436. ————. ————. ————. Orçamento geral do estado e orçamentos das autarquias estaduais. Lei no. 2492, de 2 de dezembro de 1954. Orça a receita e fixa a despesa do estado para o exercício de 1955. Pôrto Alegre, Brazil, 1955. 557 p., tables.

1437. ————. ————. ————. Orçamento geral do estado e orçamento das autarquias estaduais. Lei no. 2752, de 1 de dezembro de 1955. Orça a receita e fixa a despesa do estado para o exercício de 1956. Pôrto Alegre, Brazil, 1956. 541 p., tables.

1438. Robock, Stefan H. Aspectos regionais do desenvolvimento econômico (Obs Ec Fin, 21:249, nov. 1956, p. 6-18).

Economic development of northern Brazil.

1439. Rodrigues, Eduardo Lopes. Aspectos do planejamento financeiro (R Serv Púb, ano 17, 66:1, jan. 1955, p. 30-53).

Fiscal policy for Brazil.

1440. Santos, Genival de Almeida. Renda social do nordeste 1947-1954 (R Br Ec, 10:2, junho 1956, p. 51-156).

Income in the northeastern part of Brazil.

1441. Schlesinger, Hugo. O Brasil não pode parar. Panorama e desenvolvimento da indústria nacional. Rio, Andes (Mundo brasileiro, 3), 1954. 167 p.

After a historical and geographical introduction, the author reviews such matters as the structure of Brazilian industry, the supply of capital and labor, and the raw-materials basis.

1442. Souza, Antônio José Alves de. A energia de Paulo Afonso e o nordeste.

Recife, Brazil, Gráf. Editôra do Recife, 1955. 42 p.

Problems of power supply for the northeastern part of Brazil.

1443. Storm and calm in Brazil (Economist, 168:5742, Sept. 12, 1953, p. 708-709).

1444. **Tourinho, Borba.** Petróleo do Brasil (Obs Ec Fin, 21:245, julho 1956, p. 20-26; 21:246, agôsto 1956, p. 42-47; and 21:247, set. 1956, p. 72-79).

The present status of the Brazilian petroleum economy.

MEXICO

DIRECCIÓN DE INVESTIGACIONES ECONÓMICAS, NACIONAL FINANCIERA, S. A.

La bibliografía económica mexicana correspondiente al año de 1956 refleja el momento actual del desarrollo económico del país. La etapa a que ha llegado la economía nacional exige el estudio constante de los problemas a que se enfrentan los distintos sectores para mantener y aumentar la tasa de crecimiento de la economía. De este modo la presente bibliografía abarca prácticamente todos los aspectos del sistema.

Junto a la elaboración de trabajos de un nivel teórico-académico cada vez más alto conducentes a la formación de una teoría del desarrollo económico derivada de la experiencia mexicana, continúa la realización de trabajos monográficos y de análisis globales y parciales de la actividad económica nacional y de las transacciones con el exterior. Los economistas mexicanos cumplen así con su función de informar y orientar a los diversos sectores productivos del país.

Como resultado del progreso alcanzado en el campo de la investigación económica, cada día son más necessarias las bibliografías. La presente se basa principalmente en una selección de la publicada mensualmente por la Dirección de Investigaciones Económicas en *El mercado de valores*, boletín semanal de la Nacional Financiera, S. A. Se han tomado también en cuenta las que formulan el Banco de México, S. A., a través de sus Departamentos de Estudios Económicos y de Investigación Industrial, la Secretaría de Hacienda y Crédito Público, el Banco Nacional de Comercio Exterior, S. A., el Instituto de Investigaciones Económicas de la Universidad Nacional Autónoma, adscrito a la Escuela Nacional de Economía, y otras instituciones oficiales, descentralizadas y privadas.

1450. **Acevedo Escobedo, Antonio.** El azufre en México; una historia documentada. México, Cultura, 1956. 218 p.

Historia y recopilación de datos sobre un tema de gran interés y actualidad para la minería y la economía de México.

1451. **Alanís Patiño, Emilio.** Demografía y economía de Yucatán. (Inv Ec, 16:4, 4. trimestre 1956, p. 489-504).

1452. —————. Los problemas del desarrollo industrial de México (Com Ext, México, 6:8, agosto 1956, p. 347-351; 9, sept. 1956, p. 418-421).

Estudio sobre el proceso de desarrollo económico de México y la superación de los obstáculos iniciales de la industrialización; necesidad de un aumento del ingreso per cápita para fortalecer el mercado interno y garantizar la madurez de la economía mexicana.

1453. **Albareda, José Daniel.** Las indus-

trias nuevas o necesarias (R Fisc Fin, 16:110, agosto 1956, p. 21-32).

1454. **Almacenes Nacionales de Depósito. Departamento Técnico.** Chiapas, esquema social y económico. México, 1956. 47 p., tables.

1455. —————. —————. Chihuahua, esquema social y económico. México, 1956. 47 p., tables.

1456. —————. —————. Colima, esquema social y económico. México, 1956. 40 p., map.

1457. —————. —————. Durango, esquema social y económico. México, 1956. 53 p.

1458. —————. —————. Hidalgo, esque-

ma social y económico. México, 1956.
56 p., map.

1459. ————. ————. Jalisco, esquema social y económico. México, 1956.
25 p., map.

1460. ————. ————. México, esquema social y económico. México, 1956.
46 p.
Estado de México.

1461. ————. ————. Morelos, esquema social y económico. México, 1956.
44 p.

1462. ————. ————. Nayarit, esquema social y económico. México, 1956.
77 p.

1463. Alva Martínez, Carlos. La industria
del calzado en México. México, Universidad Nacional Autónoma de México, Escuela Nacional de Economía, 1956. 107
p., graphs, tables.
Tesis profesional.

1464. Arango Rojas, José. El gasto federal en México. México, Universidad Nacional Autónoma de México, Escuela Nacional de Economía, 1956. 170 p., tables.
Tesis profesional.

1465. Banco de México. Trigésimacuarta
Asamblea General Ordinaria de Accionistas y Décimatercera Asamblea General Extraordinaria de Accionistas. México,
1956. 194 p., graphs, tables.
Informe del Consejo de Administración a la
Asamblea de Accionistas, correspondiente al
ejercicio de 1955. Comprende información y un
estudio de la situación económica general de
México, presentando en detalle el desarrollo
económico del país y sus relaciones económicas
con el exterior.

1466. Banco Nacional de México. La agri-
cultura nacional en 1955 (Examen Sit Ec
México, 32:362, enero 1956, p. 16-20).
Ediciones en español y en inglés.

1467. ————. Algunos efectos de la con-
centración demográfica en el Distrito Federal (Examen Sit Ec México, 32:363,
feb. 1956, p. 8-9).
Ediciones en español y en inglés.

1468. ————. El comercio exterior en
1955 (Examen Sit Ec México, 32:362,
enero 1956, p. 5-8).
Ediciones en español y en inglés.

1469. ————. La economía nacional en la
XXII Convención Bancaria (Examen Sit
Ec México, 32:366, mayo 1956, p. 3-5).
Ediciones en español y en inglés.

1470. ————. La ganadería mexicana,
algunos aspectos (Examen Sit Ec México,
32:363, feb. 1956, p. 12-16, tables).
Ediciones en español y en inglés.

1471. ————. Las importaciones de los
Estados Unidos (Examen Sit Ec México,
32:363, feb. 1956, p. 5-8).
Ediciones en español y en inglés.

1472. ————. Ingreso nacional y su desarrollo en 1950-55 (Examen Sit Ec México,
32:368, julio 1956, p. 12-15, tables).
Ediciones en español y en inglés.

1473. Benítez, Fernando. Ki; el drama de
un pueblo y de una planta. México, Fondo
de Cultura Económica (Vida y pensamiento de México), 1956. 291 p. & illus.
Good description of the social and economic
aspects of the henequen industry in Yucatan in
the 20th century. [W. V. Scholes]

1474. Bosch García, Pedro. Intervencio-
nismo de Estado. Un tema a discusión en
materia de política económica (Inv Ec,
16:3, 3. trimestre 1956, p. 279-283).

1475. Bravo Jiménez, Manuel. Planeación
económica (Inv Ec, 16:3, 3. trimestre
1956, p. 285-316).

1476. Bullejos, José. La bibliografía económica de México en 1954 y 1955. México, Banco de México, 1956. 119 p.

1477. Bustamante, Eduardo. Actitud reco-
mendable al gobierno federal frente a los
problemas hacendarios de los estados (Inv
Ec, 16:4, 4. trimestre 1956, p. 525-564).

1478. Cámara Nacional de la Industria
de Transformación. Comentario a las
tesis sobre inversiones extranjeras directas
de los oponentes de la CNIT. México,
1956. 17 p.

1479. ————. La inversión extranjera en
el servicio de teléfonos de México. México, 1956. 40 p.
Estudio por la comisión de la CNIT para el
estudio de las inversiones extranjeras.

1480. ————. Proceso ocupacional. Un
análisis del proceso en México. México,
1956. 229 p., tables.

1481. Campos Salas, Octaviano. La política comercial de los países poco desarro-
llados (Inv Ec, 16:3, 3. trimestre 1956,
p. 317-334).

1482. Carrillo Flores, Antonio. Discurso
pronunciado por el Secretario de Hacienda
y Crédito Público, A. Carrillo Flores, en

la sesión inaugural de la XXII Convención Nacional Bancaria celebrada en Acapulco, Gro., el día 23 de abril de 1956 (R Fisc Fin, 16:106, abril 1956, p. 13-24).

1483. Castro Ulloa, Guillermo. Los precios y el mercado interno (Pol Mex, 2, julio 1956, p. 36-37).
Trata el autor sobre la necesidad de una política de precios y salarios para mantener un mercado interno que responda al crecimiento económico de México.

1484. Cervantes, Manuel. La moneda en México. México, 1954. 99 p.
A good introduction to the monetary systems of Mexico. [W. V. Scholes]

1485. Cuspinera, Juan L. Préstamos y recuperaciones de avío por cultivos y ciclos (B Estud Espec, 4:46, marzo 6, 1956, p. 289-301, graphs, tables).
Análisis de los datos del Banco sobre las tasas de recuperación de los créditos de avío.

1486. Ekker, Martin H. La contabilidad del ingreso nacional; un curso introductorio. México, Banco de México, Departamento de Estudios Económicos, 1956. 311 p., graphs, tables.

1487. Elizondo, Juan Manuel. Monopolios y precios (Pol Mex, 2, julio 1956, p. 17-30).
Estudio en el que el autor atribuye el alza de los precios en México a la existencia de monopolios en los sectores de producción y distribución y no a otros factores del proceso de la actividad económica.

1488. Espinosa Olvera, René. Los recursos humanos en el desarrollo económico de México (Inv Ec, 16:3, 3. trimestre 1956, p. 335-349).

1489. Fayerweather, John. Las inversiones de Estados Unidos de América en México (R Esc Cont, 8:29, enero 1956, p. 1-34).
Puntos de vista y consideraciones sobre las inversiones estadunidenses dentro del marco del desarrollo económico de México, el criterio de los empresarios estadunidenses y las perspectivas de dichas inversiones.

1490. Fernández y Fernández, Ramón. México y su crédito agrícola (B Estud Espec, 6:64, julio 14, 1956, p. 65-80, graphs, tables).

1491. González, Enrique M. A diez años de plazo: se necesitan 6,000 millones para dar a México suficiente fuerza eléctrica (R Mex Construc, 2:18, enero 1956, p. 11-13).
Estimación de los recursos necesarios para financiar la electrificación de México de acuerdo con sus necesidades presentes insatisfechas y sus futuras inmediatas al ritmo de su crecimiento económico y demográfico.

1492. Gonzalez, Fernando. La industria siderúrgica en México. Notas para una planeación. México, Cámara Nacional de la Industria de Transformación, 1956. 227 p.

1493. González Gallardo, Alfonso. Desarrollo de la industria de la caña de azúcar en México (B Azuc Mex, 5:79, enero 1956, p. 10-16, tables).
Artículo sobre el crecimiento y progreso de la industria azucarera en México con datos ilustrativos de su capacidad de producción de acuerdo con las áreas de cultivo y la capacidad instalada.

1494. González Reyna, Jenaro. Riqueza minera y yacimientos minerales de México. 3. ed. México, Banco de México, Departamento de Investigaciones Industriales, 1956. 497 p., tables.
Estudio que recoge y sistematiza datos estadísticos proporcionados por el Departamento de Minas de la Secretaría de Economía.

1495. The International Bank for Reconstruction and Development. The economic development of Mexico. Report of the Combined Mexican Working Party. Baltimore, Md., John Hopkins Press, 1953. 392 p.
This report of the Combined Mexican Working Party, consisting of two Mexican economists and two economists of the International Bank for Reconstruction and Development, studies the major long-term trends in the Mexican economy with particular reference to Mexico's capacity to absorb additional foreign investments. A thorough analysis of Mexico's economy in all its aspects is undertaken with an eye on past and future investments. The report is accompanied by 153 tables and five appendices on selected topics. [S. Garbuny]

1496. Lamas, Adolfo. El pósito colonial (Trim Ec, 23:1, enero-marzo 1956, p. 73-89).

1497. Lavín, José Domingo. México descubre un sistema económico (Humanismo, 5:39, sept.-oct. 1956, p. 107-116).

1498. ————. El monopolio del crédito (Pol Mex, 2, julio 1956, p. 31-35).
Crítica a la forma en que opera el sistema bancario privado en México, como un obstáculo al financiamiento de la producción.

1499. López de la Parra, Manuel. Los caminos vecinales y su influencia en el desarrollo económico de México. México, Universidad Nacional Autónoma de México, Escuela Nacional de Economía, 1956. 133 p., graphs, map, tables.
Tesis profesional.

1500. López Munguía, Agustín. La nueva tarifa de importación (Com Ext, 6:1, enero 1956, p. 35-37).

Consideraciones sobre las necesidades que satisface la nueva tarifa de importación—basada en la Clasificación Uniforme de Comercio Internacional de las Naciones Unidas respecto a los cambios registrados por la economía mexicana en su proceso de desarrollo.

1501. López Rosado, Diego G. Las obras públicas de la Revolución (Cuad Or Pol, año 1, 1:3, marzo 1956, p. 31-47).

Relación histórica de las obras públicas, realizadas en México antes y después del movimiento revolucionario de 1910.

1502. Loyo, Gilberto. Política oficial en inversiones extranjeras (Com Ext, 6:8, agosto 1956, p. 344).

El Secretario de Economía de México, Gilberto Loyo, describe brevemente el clima económico de México para las inversiones extranjeras y define la posición del gobierno mexicano frente a dichas inversiones.

1503. Loyola Montemayor, Elías. La industria del pulque, cultivo y explotación del maguey, elaboración, transporte y comercio del pulque, aspectos fiscales, diversificación industrial, reseña histórica, estadísticas, patentes, reglamentación federal, bibliografía. México, Banco de México, Departamento de Investigaciones Industriales, 1956. 348 p., graphs, illus., tables.

1504. Luyando Martínez, Felipe. Los insecticidas y fumigantes en la agricultura mexicana. México, Universidad Nacional Autónoma de México, Escuela Nacional de Economía, 1956. 145 p., tables.
Tesis profesional.

1505. Mancera Ortiz, Rafael. Economía nacional. Presupuesto fiscal (R Fisc Fin, 16:109, julio 1956, p. 19-37, tables).

1506. Margain, Hugo B. La doble tributación en el campo internacional (R Fisc Fin, 16:112, oct. 1956, p. 5-57).

Publicado también en: R Banc, 4:5, sept.-oct. 1956, p. 790-811. Tesis para evitar la doble tributación en el campo internacional en materia de impuesto sobre la renta, basada en la teoría de la fuente del ingreso gravable.

1507. ————. Reformas al impuesto sobre la renta (Com Ext, 6:2, feb. 1956, p. 66-69; 6:3, marzo 1956, p. 117-120; 6:4, abril 1956, p. 159-161).

Consideraciones sobre las reformas a la ley del impuesto sobre la renta de 1954, vigentes a partir del lo. de enero de 1956, respecto a su justificación dentro del derecho fiscal, desde el punto de vista contable y su necesidad económica.

1508. Martínez Domínguez, Guillermo. La intervención del Estado en la economía. Tesis de la Revolución Mexicana (Cuad Or Pol, 1, 1956, 55 p.).

1509. Medina Mora, Raúl. La industria del petróleo en México (Humanismo, 5:39, sept.-oct. 1956, p. 90-106).

Estudio que comprende antecedentes de la industria petrolera mexicana y analiza cada uno de los aspectos que la estructuran, enmarcando sus conquistas dentro del apoyo que ha dado como industria nacionalizada al desarrollo económico de México.

1510. Meurs, Tjark A. Comercio entre los Países Bajos y México (Com Ext, 6:8, agosto 1956, p. 373-375, tables).

Artículo que registra el aumento del comercio entre los Países Bajos y México, tanto en volumen como en valor; análisis de su composición y del saldo favorable a México.

1511. México. Comisión Nacional de Valores. Los bancos y el mercado de valores en 1955 (B Mens Com Nac Val, 3:3, marzo 1956, p. 87-90).

1512. ————. ————. La economía nacional y el mercado de valores (B Mens Com Nac Val, 3:1, enero 1956, p. 5-9).

1513. ————. ————. Estado de la deuda interior (B Mens Com Nac Val, 3:1, enero 1956, p. 9-11).

1514. ————. ————. El mercado de valores dentro de la economía nacional (B Mens Com Nac Val, 3:2, feb. 1956, p. 49-54).

1515. Mondragón Moreno, Pablo Jesús. Transportes de las mercancías en México; incidencia de las tarifas en los precios. México, Universidad Nacional Autónoma de México, Escuela Nacional de Economía, 1956. 266 p., tables.
Tesis profesional.

1516. Mujica Montoya, Emilio. Consideraciones sobre el ciclo y el desarrollo económico. México, Universidad Nacional Autónoma de México, Escuela Nacional de Economía, 1956. 145 p., graphs, tables.
Tesis profesional. Segundo lugar, Premio Nacional de Economía del Banco Nacional de México.

1517. ————. Los salarios en la economía nacional (Inv Ec, 16:4, 4. trimestre 1956, p. 565-581).

1518. Nacional Financiera. Capital de E. U. de N. en México en 1956 (Merc Val, 16:14, abril 2, 1956, p. 157-158).

1519. ————. El control selectivo del

crédito en el desarrollo económico de México (Merc Val, 16:48, nov. 26, 1956, p. 565-566).

1520. —————. El crecimiento de las inversiones privadas directas de Estados Unidos en México y Canadá (Merc Val, 16:13, marzo 26, 1956, p. 145-146, tables).

1521. —————. El desarrollo económico y la empresa (Merc Val, 16:43, oct. 22, 1956, p. 510-511).

1522. —————. La industria textil en 1955 (Merc Val, 16:24, junio 11, 1956, p. 277-278, tables).

1523. —————. La industrialización impulsa el rápido desarrollo urbano de México (Merc Val, 16:47, nov. 19, 1956, p. 553-554).

1524. —————. Informe anual. Vigésima-segunda Asamblea General Ordinaria de Accionistas. México, 1956. 241 p., graphs, tables.
Informe del Consejo de Administración a la Asamblea de Accionistas sobre el ejercicio de 1955. Contiene un examen de la situación económica internacional y nacional, aspectos generales y específicos de la industrialización y el desarrollo económico del país, así como un estudio del mercado de capitales de México.

1525. —————. Mayores créditos a corto plazo para México (Merc Val, 16:8, feb. 20, 1956, p. 88).

1526. —————. México a la cabeza del desarrollo industrial de un grupo importante de países (Merc Val, 16:9, feb. 27, 1956, p. 97-98, tables).

1527. —————. México propugna la competencia libre en el problema del algodón (Merc Val, 16:21, mayo 21, 1956, p. 241-244).

1528. —————. La Nacional Financiera y los créditos de fomento, enero-septiembre de 1956 (Merc Val, 16:43, oct. 22, 1956, p. 505-506, tables).

1529. —————. Nuevas industrias de transformación (Merc Val, 16:45, nov. 5, 1956, p. 529-530, tables).

1530. —————. Oferta monetaria e ingreso nacional (Merc Val, 16:45, nov. 5, 1956, p. 533, tables).

1531. —————. El peso fiscal en 1956 (Merc Val, 16:8, feb. 20, 1956, p. 89, graphs).

1532. —————. Posible alivio a la doble tributación (Merc Val, 16:8, feb. 20, 1956, p. 90-91).
Información sobre negociaciones exploratorias realizadas en la ciudad de México respecto a un proyecto de tratado entre México y Estados Unidos de Norteamérica para limitar la doble imposición internacional concerniente a sus respectivos impuestos sobre la renta.

1533. —————. Progresos de la industria constructora de carros de ferrocarril en México (Merc Val, 16:52, dic. 24, 1956, p. 613-614).

1534. —————. Puntos de vista sobre la inversión extranjera (Merc Val, 16:7, feb. 13, 1956, p. 73-74).
Resumen de posiciones adoptadas por la Confederación de Cámaras Nacionales de Comercio, la Cámara Nacional de la Industria de Transformación y un punto de vista de un catedrático estadunidense.

1535. —————. Relaciones de México con el EXIMBANK (Merc Val, 16:12, marzo 19, 1956, p. 138-139, tables).

1536. —————. La reserva obligatoria de la banca comercial (Merc Val, 16:9, feb. 27, 1956, p. 102-103).

1537. —————. Sectores beneficiados con créditos del exterior (Merc Val, 16:7, feb. 13, 1956, p. 78-79).

1538. —————. Tendencias recientes de la economía mexicana (Merc Val, 16:46, nov. 12, 1956, p. 545).

1539. —————. Tres años de alza agrícola (Merc Val, 16:10, marzo 5, 1956, p. 109-110, table).

1540. —————. Departamento de Fideicomiso. Fondo de garantía y fomento a la industria mediana y pequeña. México, 1956. 64 p.
Folleto de información sobre forma de operación, recursos y operaciones del Fondo; importantes datos sobre un mecanismo más de la experiencia mexicana en el fomento al desarrollo económico.

1541. Navarrete, Alfredo, Jr. La inversión pública y el desarrollo económico de México (Merc Val, 16:36, sept. 3, 1956, p. 421-422).

1542. —————. Los precios, cuestión compleja (Pol Mex, 2, julio 1956, p. 55-56).
Consideraciones sobre la multiplicidad de factores que concurren en la formación de los precios y los riesgos de hacer un análisis parcial.

1543. —————. Productividad, ocupación y desocupación en México: 1940-1965

(Inv Ec, 16:3, 3. trimestre 1956, p. 395-406, graphs, tables).
Publicado también en: Trim Ec, 23:4, oct.-dic., 1956, p. 415-423. Análisis y proyecciones en relación a las tendencias de la economía mexicana en desarrollo, en sus aspectos de productividad y ocupación.

1544. ————. Los programas revolucionarios y el futuro progreso económico de México (Cuad Or Pol, año 1, 1:3, marzo 1956, p. 17-25).
Publicado también en: Paralelo, 20:10, enero 1, 1956, p. 14-17. Análisis cuantitativo y cualitativo de los programas de la Revolución Mexicana en sus efectos sobre el desarrollo económico del país y sus perspectivas.

1545. Navarrete, Ifigenia M. de. Política fiscal y desarrollo industrial (Com Ext, 6:1, enero 1956, p. 26-28, tables).
Análisis de la política fiscal de México como medio eficaz para fomentar, estabilizar y difundir equitativamente el desarrollo económico del país.

1546. Noyola Vázquez, Juan. El desarrollo económico y la inflación en México y otros países latinoamericanos (Inv Ec, 16:4, 4. trimestre 1956, p. 489-504).

1547. Petróleos Mexicanos. La industria petrolera y sus trabajadores, realizaciones y programas, 1955-1956. México, 1956. 23 p.

1548. ————. Minatitlán. México, 1956. 40 p., maps, photos.
Folleto ampliamente ilustrativo sobre las nuevas instalaciones de PEMEX en Minatitlán, su importancia por su localización, su moderna planta de desintegración catalítica y los problemas de producción y distribución que resuelve.

1549. ————. Refinerías de Petróleos Mexicanos. México, 1956. 86 p., illus.
Completo estudio sobre el sistema de refinerías de PEMEX realizado por técnicos de la empresa.

1550. Powell, Jack Richard. The Mexican petroleum industry, 1938-1950. Berkeley, Calif., University of California Press, 1956. 269 p., map, diagrs., tables.
A discussion of the oil industry after expropriation. Up to 1945 the industry was a failure. Since then there has been some improvement. The author concludes that expropriation was an economic mistake. [W. V. Scholes]

1551. Quintero Rivera, Nazario. El impuesto de la gasolina dentro del financiamiento de la construcción de caminos en México. México, Universidad Nacional Autónoma de México, Escuela Nacional de Economía, 1956. 157 p., tables.
Tesis profesional. Balance y análisis de la política de construcción de caminos carreteros en México y la aplicación de las recaudaciones del impuesto de consumo de gasolina al financiamiento de dichas obras. Apéndices sobre legislación al respecto.

1552. Ramírez Bonilla, Blanca Gloria. El seguro agrícola en México. México, Universidad Nacional Autónoma de México, Escuela Nacional de Economía, 1956. 110 p., tables.
Tesis profesional.

1553. Reyes Heroles, Jesús. Economía y política en el liberalismo mexicano (Cuad Am, 85:2, marzo-abril 1956, p. 180-202).
Ensayo histórico valorativo sobre el pensamiento liberal en México y su aplicación político-económica que habría de conducir a la Constitución de 1857.

1554. Robles, Gonzalo. La industria siderúrgica de México (Com Ext, 6:5, mayo 1956, p. 214-218; 6:6, junio 1956, p. 253-257; 6:7, julio 1956, p. 313-319).
Estudio que comprende todos los aspectos de la industria siderúrgica en México, incluyendo a industrias secundarias, política de fomento, aspectos económicos y perspectivas de desarrollo.

1555. Salinas Ramos, Alberto. La epopeya del trigo (Pol Agr, 5:56, agosto 1956, p. 6-11, illus.).
Progresos realizados en la producción de trigo en México en los últimos años, como resultado de las obras de riego, la modernización de los métodos agrícolas y la iniciativa de los agricultores.

1556. Sánchez Navarro, Juan. Ensayo sobre una política de inversiones extranjeras en México. 2. ed. México, CONCANACO, 1956. 90 p.

1557. Sandoval, Fernando B. La industria de la platería (Com Ext, 6:2, feb. 1956, p. 76-80, illus.).
Artículos sobre una de las artes más antiguas de México que ha resurgido como una industria de exportación importante; contiene antecedentes históricos, datos sobre producción, consumo, exportación y consideraciones sobre sus perspectivas.

1558. Sedwitz, Walter J. Mexico's 1954 devaluation in retrospect (Interam Ec Aff, 10:2, autumn 1956, p. 22-24, tables).
Ensayo alrededor de las causas de la devaluación del peso de 1954 y los efectos positivos que sobre la recuperación de la reserva monetaria tuvieron los aumentos de los precios de productos de exportación de México.

1559. Servín, Armando. Las finanzas públicas locales durante los últimos cincuenta años. México, Secretaría de Hacienda y Crédito Público, 1956. 142 p., graphs, tables.
Serie de trabajos monográficos de la Dirección General de Estudios Hacendarios, Secretaría de Hacienda y Crédito Público, no. 1.

1560. ————. Lo que sabemos y lo que no sabemos sobre nuestra marcha económica (Com Ext, 6:4, abril 1956, p. 167-168). Evaluación crítica de los instrumentos de medición de la actividad económica de México tomando como material las publicaciones que dan a conocer datos al respecto.

1561. ————. Las rentas derivadas de bienes muebles y nuestro impuesto sobre la renta (R Fisc Fin, 16:108, junio 1956, p. 13-17).

1562. Shaw, Carroll K. Bases para organizar el fomento de la investigación industrial en México (R Banc, 4:3, mayo-junio 1956, p. 657-661).

1563. Stringer, MacNeil. Aspectos prácticos de los problemas de mercados en México (R Esc Cont, 8:31, julio 1956, p. 271-278). Exhortación del autor al conocimiento más profundo de los mercados en México y la formación de vendedores.

1564. Torres Gaitán, Ricardo. El desequilibrio positivo (Inv Ec, 16:2, 2. trimestre 1956, p. 179-203).

1565. ————. Los desequilibrios de la balanza de pagos (Inv Ec, 16:3, 3. trimestre 1956, p. 461-488).

1566. ————. La política financiera de la Revolución (Cuad Or Pol, 2, 1956, 55 p.).

1567. Urquidi, Víctor L. El impuesto sobre la renta en el desarrollo económico de México (R Esc Cont, 8:31, julio 1956, p. 199-210). Publicado también en: Trim Ec, 23:4, oct.-dic. 1956, p. 424-437. Conferencia en la que se establece una relación entre las fuentes de ingresos del Estado Mexicano y el desarrollo de la economía como índice de progreso y se analiza al impuesto sobre la renta como el renglón más importante.

1568. Vaca Orozco, Alfonso. La organización del Banco Nacional de Crédito Ejidal en 1955 (B Estud Espec, 6:72, nov. 3, 1956, p. 273-291, graphs, tables).

1569. Villaseñor, Eduardo. Cambios recientes en la economía mexicana (Com Ext, México, 6:1, enero 1956, p. 13-15). Balance del desarrollo económico de México por sectores en los últimos 20 años y el impacto de su progreso en la estructura económica del país, así como su mayor interrelación con la economía mundial.

1570. Wiozeck, Miguel S. El comercio de productos básicos en 1955-56 (Com Ext, México, 6:3, marzo 1956, p. 106-110). Análisis de los productos básicos de exportación de América Latina y México sobre la base de sus precios más recientes en los mercados mundiales y algunas consideraciones sobre sus perspectivas inmediatas.

1571. Zamora, Fernando. Los recursos vivos del mar y la política económica de México (R Ec, México, 19:3, marzo 1956, p. 63-64). Consideraciones sobre la importancia que la explotación de los recursos vivos marítimos tiene para la integración económica de México.

Education

GENERAL

1650. **Conferência Regional sobre la Educación Gratuita y Obligatoria en América Latina, Lima, 23 de abril—5 de mayo de 1956. Recomendaciones.** Lima, 1956. (UNESCO/Reg. Conf./FCE/119). Recomendações: 1. A educação primária, para ser democrática, deve ser universal, gratuita e obrigatória, durante um período mínimo de seis anos para cada criança. 2. Há que associar a educação primária completa para tôda a população em idade escolar à educação fundamental para os adultos. 3. Planejamento da extensão da educação primária gratuita e obrigatória. 4. Devem os Estados recorrer aos auxílios externos, através dos organismos internacionais. 5. Revisão periódica dos sistemas e métodos de administração escolar. Conhecimento preciso do custo da educação obrigatória, de forma a dar uma previsão de aumentos periódicos, segundo o princípio de que a educação deve ter prioridade nos orçamentos. Os planos e programas devem dar lugar à criação de métodos de ensino adequados às necessidades do ambiente, afim de estar sempre em dia com a realidade econômica, social e cultural, contendo práticas de avaliação e promoção que estimulem o progresso contínuo dos alunos. A formação e aperfeiçoamento dos professores deve ser preocupação primordial a partir das escolas normais, fixando-se um tipo único, que considere, em todos os seus aspectos, de modo científico a formação do mestre, e incorpore aos seus objetivos a educação fundamental, reconhecendo-se-lhe a posição social como fator determinante da vida democrática da nação, requerendo para seu efetivo exercício a garantia de vida, o estímulo e as compensações justas. [I. Doria]

1651. **Costa Rica. Ministerio de Relaciones Exteriores.** Convenio de reconocimiento mutuo de validez de títulos profesionales y de incorporación de estudios con Colombia . . . San José, 1955. 5 p.
Terms of agreement between Costa Rica and Colombia concerning the validation of professional degrees from the two countries. [M. C. Johnston]

1652. **Gietz, Ernesto G.** (ed.). Bibliografía sobre reforma y autonomía universitarias. B. A., Universidad Nacional de Buenos Aires, Instituto Bibliotecológico, 1956. 87 p.
Mimeographed bibliography of 1168 entries on university reform, autonomy, and legislation in Argentina and Latin America. [M. C. Johnston]

1653. **Inter-American Seminar on Secondary Education, Santiago, 1954-1955.** Seminarios interamericanos de educación. La educación secundaria en América. Memoria del Seminario Interamericano de Educación Secundaria . . . Washington, Unión Panamericana, División de Educación, 1955. 466 p.
A compendium of work papers prepared by specialists in the field and of final reports of the six groups composing the Inter-American Seminar on Secondary Education: (1) nature and aims of secondary education, (2) organization and administration, (3) plans and programs, (4) methods and techniques, (5) the teaching staff, (6) relation of secondary education to professional and specialized education. [M. C. Johnston]

1654. **Key Ayala, Santiago.** Adolfo Ernst (1832-1899). Caracas, Ediciones de la Fundación Eugenio Mendoza (Biblioteca escolar; Colección de biografías, 18), 1955. 62 p., illus.
Attractive story of a young German scholar who went to Venezuela in 1861 to view the natural wonders described by Humboldt. He taught German and natural history at Central University, founded the National Library and National Museum, published the scientific journal *Vargasia*, in honor of Vargas, and participated in many patriotic endeavors, including the Bolívar Centennial. [M. C. Johnston]

1655. **Mac-Lean y Estenós, Roberto.** La crisis universitaria en Hispano-América. México, Universidad Nacional, Instituto de Investigaciones Sociales (Cuadernos de sociología; Biblioteca de ensayos sociológicos), 1956. 237 p.
From wide experience in Spanish American universities, the author, a Peruvian sociologist, an-

alyzes the status and needs of higher education in Mexico, Argentina, Chile, Uruguay, Venezuela, Bolivia, Paraguay, Peru, Colombia, and Central America. [M. C. Johnston]

1656. Pan American Union. Division of Education. La educación. Revista trimestral. Washington, D. C. Año 1, no. 1, enero-marzo 1956-.

Each issue of this new periodical contains articles on a theme of over-all interest, such as adult education, fundamental education, language teaching, and the like, plus brief accounts of current educational developments in each of the American republics. Other features of the journal are short bibliographies, commentaries on inter-American conferences, and book reviews. [M. C. Johnston]

1657. ―――. ―――. Estado actual de la educación secundaria en la América Latina. 2. ed., revisada y aumentada. Washington, 1957. 206 p.

Up-to-date and expanded edition of the workpaper prepared originally for the Inter-American Seminar on Secondary Education. Contains detailed information on secondary education in the 20 Latin American republics, including objectives, organization and administration, programs of study, methods, status of teachers, and the relation of the secondary school to the community. [M. C. Johnston]

1658. Seminário Sul-Americano para o Ensino Universitário das Ciências Sociais, I, Rio, 1956. Instituto Brasileiro de Educação, Ciência e Cultura, 1956. 75 p.

Plaquete dedicada à divulgação do Seminário, editada pelo IBECC, em que se inclui notícia das reuniões escrita pelo prof. Themistocles B. Cavalcanti, Presidente daquele Instituto, transcrição do temário e recomendações das diversas comissões bem como um relatório geral. Quanto

as conclusões mais objetivas e imediatas, exigem menção as que se dirigem no sentido de organizar, de pronto, em dois países da América Latina já escolhidos—o Chile e o Brasil—duas grandes instituições: uma de ensino, sendo a pesquisa apenas um elemento dêsse ensino, e outra especificamente de pesquisa, em tôda a área da América Latina. [I. Doria]

1659. Seminário Sul-Americano para o Ensino Universitário das Ciências Sociais, I, Rio, 1956. Mesa redonda sôbre la enseñanza de las ciências sociales. Documentos de trabalho e relatório. Paris, UNESCO, 1955. [Doc. 1-17].

A conferência sôbre o ensino universitário das ciências sociais na América do Sul, reunida no Rio de 6 a 14 de março de 1956, teve por agenda os seguintes itens: (1) ordenação dos estudos sociais nas universidades; (2) ensino; (3) investigação científica; (4) admissão e seleção de professôres; (5) recrutamento do corpo de professôres. Êsses itens foram tratados por vários colaboradores, que apresentaram informes sôbre a situação do ensino das ciências sociais nos diversos países da América Latina, inclusive o Brasil. [I. Doria]

1660. United Nations Educational, Scientific and Cultural Organization. Study abroad. International handbook. Fellowships, scholarships, educational exchange. VIII, 1956-1957. Paris, 1956. 719 p.

Valuable international reference work listing over 74,000 fellowship and scholarship opportunities offered by governments, universities, foundations and other types of organization in more than 100 states and territories. New features of this volume are chapters on "Teaching appointments abroad" and "Facilities for study abroad." A report for school year 1954-1955 is given of UNESCO's survey of foreign student enrollments at institutions of higher education throughout the world. [M. C. Johnston]

SPANISH AMERICA AND HAITI

MARJORIE C. JOHNSTON

ARGENTINA

1700. Mazo, Gabriel del. Reforma universitaria y cultura nacional. B. A., Raigal (Biblioteca Nuestra América, 4), 1955. 179 p.

12 essays and lectures from *La reforma universitaria*, first published in six volumes in 1926 and again in three volumes in 1941; six longer discourses, one given in Venezuela in 1945, the others before the Argentine Chamber of Deputies during 1946-1948. From student to vicerector, del Mazo's career is identified with the university reform begun in 1918 at the Universidad de la Plata.

1701. Miguez, Francisco. Porqué debe enseñarse religión. Política educativa. B. A., Ángel Domínguez e Hijo, 1956. 77 p.

Text and discussion of article 8 of the Argentine law 1420 referring to religious education.

1702. Piérola, Raúl Alberto. Aproximaciones al concepto de educación nacional. B. A., Nova (Biblioteca Nova de educación), 1956. 104 p.

General overview of the vital problems of national education.

CHILE

1703. Munizaga Aguirre, Roberto. Principios de educación. 2. ed., revisada. Santiago, Imp. Universitaria, 1954? 183 p.

A formulation of the central ideas of the author's course in philosophy of education given at the Instituto Pedagógico of the University of Chile.

1704. Silva Castro, Raúl. Fundación del Instituto Nacional. 1810-1813. Santiago, Imp. Universitaria, 1953. 33 p.
Documentary narrative of early efforts to establish the Instituto Nacional.

COSTA RICA

1705. Obregón Loría, Rafael. Los rectores de la Universidad de Santo Tomás de Costa Rica. Con una introducción de Rodrigo Facio. San José, Editorial Universitaria (Sección historia, 1), 1955. 181 p., illus.
The University of Santo Tómas de Costa Rica, founded in 1843 and closed in 1888, is linked in the national history with the University of Costa Rica, established in 1940. This book contains biographical sketches and photographs of its 15 titular rectors and 7 interim rectors.

1706. Pittman, Marvin S. Algunos problemas educativos de Costa Rica. Informe sobre la educación secundaria en Costa Rica. San José, Ministerio de Educación Pública, Misión de Asistencia Técnica de la UNESCO, 1954. 95 p.
Careful analysis of secondary education in Costa Rica, with recommendations for modernizing the curriculum.

CUBA

1707. Cuba. Instituto Nacional de Logopedia y Foniatría. Plan de estudios de las escuelas primarias para sordos de Cuba. Habana, 1956. 85 p., illus.
Description of materials and methods used in teaching deaf children during the 11 years required for completing the work of the kindergarten through grade 6.

1708. Fernández Concheso, Aurelio. El problema educacional cubano. Fundamentos y urgencias de una reforma. Habana, Instituto Cívico Militar, 1956. 60 p., illus.
Memorial publication consisting of five talks given by the Minister of Education in 1955. A clear exposition of the reforms he advocated in elementary, secondary, normal school, and industrial education.

1709. Guerra y Sánchez, Ramiro. La educación primaria en el siglo XX. Proceso histórico de la misma en Estados Unidos de América, Gran Bretaña y Cuba. Habana, 1955. 254 p. (Biblioteca cubana de educación, 4).
The system of primary education in Cuba is compared, because of historical influences, with the development of elementary education in the U. S. and Great Britain since 1900.

1710. Universidad de Santo Tomás de Villanueva. Universidad de Santo Tomás de Villanueva; contribución a la historia de sus diez primeros años. Habana, 1956. 189 p.
Interesting history of Cuba's first private university.

GUATEMALA

1711. Lanning, John Tate. The eighteenth-century enlightenment in the University of San Carlos de Guatemala. Ithaca, N. Y., Cornell University Press, 1956. 372 p.
Well-documented, highly readable study of the influence of the 18th century philosophers on academic life in the colonial University of San Carlos de Guatemala. In five parts: (1) the language problem—chairs of native tongues versus Castilian and "school Latin" versus Spanish, (2) academic reform, from within and from without, (3) changing intellectual standards, particularly in philosophy and science, (4) academic medicine, and (5) ethics, citizenship, government, and revolution.

1712. Martínez Durán, Carlos. Tiempo y substancia del estudiante eterno. Guatemala, Imp. Universitaria, 1956. 196 p. & illus.
Reminiscences of the author's student days in the Instituto Nacional Central de Varones, 1919-1923, and in the School of Medicine of Guatemala, 1924-1931. The sketches conclude with tributes to individual teachers and friends.

1713. Universidad de San Carlos de Guatemala. Reglamentos de la Facultad de Ciencias Jurídicas y Sociales. Guatemala, Imp. Universitaria, 1956. 63 p.
Statutes of the University of San Carlos de Guatemala applying to students, school year, admission, and examinations; complete laws and regulations governing the faculty and school of juridical and social sciences, including plans of study, professional examinations, the doctorate, technical training, prizes, library, journal, and work regulations.

MEXICO

1714. Cruz, Pacheco. Campaña alfabetizante i la educación indígena en el territorio de Quintana Roo. Bosquejo de la labor. Mérida, Yucatán, México, Zamma, 1956. 61 p.
Detailed report of literacy work directed by the author from 1948 to 1955. During this period 53 schools were established in Quintana Roo. The account is in three parts: (1) the organization of the literacy campaign, (2) a brief history of indigenous education in Yucatan, and (3) the present status of education in the Territory.

1715. Johnston, Marjorie C. Education in Mexico. Washington, U. S. Department of Health, Education, and Welfare (Bull., 1956, 1), 1956. 135 p., illus., tables.
Comprehensive study, offering background material on the people, economic conditions, and the political and educational history of Mexico

as well as the essential facts about school organization and the various levels of instruction from preschool through graduate study. Included are 25 sample programs of study leading to professional degrees, numerous statistical tables, and a selected bibliography in Spanish and English.

1716. Monroy, Guadalupe. La instrucción pública en México de 1867 a 1876. México, 1956. 633-743 p.

Reprinted from *Historia moderna de México,* by D. Cosío Villegas, v. 3. This thesis for the degree of *Maestra en Historia* in Mexico describes education in Mexico during the eventful decade of 1867-1876. The chapters discuss the historical setting, the educational ideas and laws of the Reform, elementary and secondary schools, and auxiliary institutions such as museums, libraries, and educational publications. Rich in statistical data.

1717. Zea, Leopoldo. Del liberalismo a la revolución en la educación mexicana. México, Biblioteca del Instituto Nacional de Estudios Históricos de la Revolución (4), 1956. 205 p.

Part 1 is a historical review of the educational ideas which inspired the generation of the Mexican Revolution and of the liberal antecedents of those ideas. Part 2 is an analysis of the various liberal positions with regard to positivist education and an exploration of the ideas of the precursors of education for freedom—Rébsamen, Carrillo, Torres Quintero, Joaquín Baranda, Justo Sierra, and others. The epilogue is a discussion of the ideas which prevailed in the framing of article 3 of the 1917 Constitution and their relation to liberalism and pre-Revolutionary thought in the field of education.

OTHER COUNTRIES

1718. Hernández, Ángel G. Problemas de la educación universitaria. Libros estimulantes para la juventud. Tegucigalpa, Ministerio de Educación Pública (Col. Ramón Rosa, 3), 1956. 165 p.

In three parts: (1) historical growth of the University of Honduras, (2) fundamental problems of university reform, the first necessity being autonomy, and (3) the university's sphere of influence.

1719. Rivera, Antonio, and Arturo Morales Carrión. La enseñanza de la historia en Puerto Rico. México, Instituto Panamericano de Geografía e Historia (Memorias sobre la enseñanza de la historia, 9; Comisión de Historia, 59; Publ., 161), 1953. 102 p.

Historical and descriptive account of the teaching of history in the high schools, the elementary schools, and the University of Puerto Rico, plus a brief discussion of the teaching of social studies and sociology in the Puerto Rico High School of Commerce. Apendices contain programs of study and lists of textbooks.

1720. Rodríguez Bou, Ismael. Estudio del sistema educativo de la República de Panamá. Informe para el plan de desarrollo económico. Panamá, Ministerio de Educación, 1956. 241 p., tables.

Comprehensive survey of education in Panama. Detailed information concerning finance, administration, instruction and supervision, private schools, and all types of public schools. The report ends with 51 recommendations. The apendices contain general statistical tables from the 1950 census and model forms for use in compiling educational statistics.

1721. Salazar Larraín, Arturo. San Marcos: entre la ley y el caos. Ensayo de interpretación. Lima, Mejía Baca & Villanueva, 1956. 139 p.

A study of the national university and its problems through an examination of the legal aspects of its institutional history.

1722. Uruguay. Consejo Nacional de Enseñanza Secundaria. Leyes fundamentales. Montevideo, 1954. 43 p.

Contains the following fundamental laws governing secondary education in Uruguay: organic law of secondary education, Dec. 11, 1935; statute of the teacher, Dec. 2, 1947; law for the teaching scale, July 2, 1949; supplementary law for the teaching scale, Mar. 22, 1953.

1723. Vegas, Rafael. Contribución al estudio de la situación económico-social del alumno caraqueño. Caracas, Universidad Central de Venezuela, Escuela de Educación, Facultad de Humanidades y Educación, 1956. 57 p., tables.

The Seminar in Sociology during school year 1954-1955 made adaptations of the Kerr and Remmers "American home scale" and applied it to 562 students in the Caracas schools.

BRAZIL

IRENE DE MENEZES DORIA

A partir de 1953, o Instituto Nacional de Estudos Pedagógicos vem sistematizando o levantamento da bibliografia brasileira de educação, trabalho êsse que havia sido iniciado em 1944, quando do aparecimento da sua publicação periódica *Revista brasileira de estudos pedagógicos,* na qual os itens eram apenas indexados, não contendo resumos analíticos.

Essa sistematização consiste em arrolar o que de mais representativo é publicado no país, no campo da educação, com o fim de registrar livros, folhetos, artigos de revistas, leis e regulamentos, bem como estudos que apareçam em revistas não especializadas e na imprensa diária. A bibliografia é publicada trimestralmente com o título de *Bibliografia brasileira de educação*. Os itens são analisados por especialistas que subscrevem os respectivos resumos.

Para realizar essa tarefa o INEP mantem um Serviço de Bibliografia, onde trabalho como orientadora técnica. Foi por êsse fato que passei a colaborar na secção do *HLAS*, (outróra tão bem selecionada pelo prof. Lourenço Filho), enviando o material contido nos v. 18 e 19, material que constituiu, tal como o deste vol. 20, uma seleção dos trabalhos publicados na *Bibliografia brasileira de educação*.

A bibliografia aqui reunida demonstra os resultados obtidos pela realização dos vários Congressos sôbre educação que se realizaram em 1956: a 12. Conferência Nacional de Educação, em Salvador, Bahia, o 1. Congresso Estadual de Educação, em Ribeirão Preto, São Paulo, o Seminário Sul-Americano sôbre o Ensino das Ciências Sociais, no Rio e a Conferência Regional sôbre Educação Gratuita e Obrigatória, realizada em Lima, Perú, onde várias teses de educadores brasileiros foram apresentadas.

Em 28 de dezembro de 1955, foi criado, por iniciativa do INEP, o Centro Brasileiro de Pesquisas Educacionais, com o objetivo de realizar pesquisa sôbre as condições culturais e escolares em tôda a extensão do território brasileiro, para elaboração de uma política educacional adequada às tendências do desenvolvimento de cada região. Merece destaque a publicação deste Centro, *Educação e ciências sociais,* boletim trimestral que divulga suas atividades e os estudos realizados por seus pesquizadores.

Outra publicação de importância como obra de referência educativa, é o indicador da CAPES (Campanha Nacional da Aperfeiçoamento do Nível Superior) *Estabelecimentos de ensino,* onde são relacionados nominalmente os estabelecimentos de nível superior, por estado e ramos de ensino.

Convem ressaltar ainda a *Mensagem* presidencial apresentada ao Congresso Nacional, onde é assinalada a administração dos sistemas públicos de ensino, e respectivo programa educacional.

Os trabalhos selecionados nesta secção foram analisados pelos colaboradores do Serviço de Bibliografia do INEP, Afrânio Coutinho, Cândida de Carvalho, Dagmar Furtado Monteiro, Generice Albertina Vieira, Nair Batista, Evandro de Oliveira Bastos e Regina Helena Tavares.

CONGRESSOS DE EDUCAÇÃO

1750. Conferência Nacional de Educação, XII, Salvador, Brazil, 1956. Conclusões, recomendações, moções e outros documentos resultantes dos relatórios e debates dos temas constantes do temário, conforme trabalho apresentado pela comissão prevista no número 16 do regimento da conferência. Rio, Associação Brasileira de Educação, 1956. 12 p.

1751. Congresso Estadual de Educação, I, Ribeirão Preto, Brazil, set. 16-23, 1956. Conclusões aprovadas. Rio, Instituto Nacional de Estudos Pedagógicos, 1956. 9 p.

Da discussão dos temas debatidos vale salientar as conclusões sôbre: necessidade de criação de um Serviço de Assistência e Orientação Pedagógica, no Departamento de Educação; elevação da duração do curso primário para mais de 4 anos e racionalização do sistema de exames; transformação da escola em centro social da comunidade; coordenação das matérias do curso normal em tôrno da cadeira de prática do ensino; incremento da correspondência inter-escolar, mesmo nas zonas rurais. [O. Bastos]

1752. ————. O temário do Congresso; relatório pronunciado na sessão solene de instalação [pelo] presidente da comissão diretora, A. Almeida Júnior. Ribeirão Preto, Brazil (Supl., Bol. do Congresso), 1956. 13 p.

Justifica a escolha dos temas debatidos no I Congresso Estadual de Educação, realizado em Ribeirão Preto de 16 a 23 de setembro, todos tendo por centro de interesse a criança. [O. Bastos]

EDUCAÇÃO DE BASE

1753. Como trabalha uma equipe de missão rural da C. N. E. R. (R Camp Nac Ed Rur, 2:2, 1956, p. 98-119).

Transcreve o relato apresentado na "Pasta de Campo" de uma missão rural da Campanha Nacional de Educação Rural relativo às atividades desenvolvidas durante o primeiro semestre de 1955 numa das seis áreas de trabalho que lhe estão confiadas—Tesourinha do município de Ipiaú. [O. Bastos]

1754. Conceição, Diamantina Costa. As deficiências de base na educação brasileira, especialmente nas zonas rurais (R Camp Nac Ed Rur, 2:2, 1955, p. 167-181).

Focaliza o estado de estagnação cultural do nosso meio rural, a falta de correlação da educação com a escola; a falta de preparação adequada do magistério rural; o aproveitamento de professôres leigos sem prévio preparo; a necessidade da criação de escolas normais rurais e os defeitos da legislação do ensino, encerrando o trabalho com uma informação sôbre o que vem fazendo a Campanha Nacional de Educação Rural do Ministério da Educação e Cultura para combater essa deficiência de base na situação cultural do nosso meio rural. [O. Bastos]

1755. Teles, J. F. de Sá. Problemas básicos da escola rural (R Prof, 14:28, 1956, p. 17-18).

Conclusão da série de artigos em que o autor analisa os problemas básicos da escola rural (no. 22, 24 e 27 da *Revista do professor*) detendo-se neste capítulo final sôbre as instituições complementares que cooperam com a escola primária rural na integração social do educando. Apresenta recomendações para a integração da escola no meio a que serve e para a formação de professôres. [O. Bastos]

1756. ————. O sentido pedagógico da Campanha Nacional de Educação Rural (R Camp Nac Ed Rur, 2:2, 1955, p. 182-190).

Mostra como a CNER procura atingir a educação de base através de métodos e técnica especiais, cujos princípios norteadores são os da educação ativa. Focaliza as diversas fases de organização e de trabalho de uma missão rural, para mostrar como a CNER estabelece princípios e normas de ação que visam e educação como objeto. [O. Bastos]

1757. ————. O treinamento em educação de base (R Ens, 5:36, 1956, p 71-72).

Descrição sucinta do VII curso de treinamento de educadores de base, promovido pela Campanha Nacional de Educação Rural em convênio com o govêrno do estado do Rio Grande do Sul e realizado na cidade de Osório. [G. A. Vieira]

EDUCAÇÃO PÚBLICA

1758. Azevedo, Fernando. A escola e a literatura (*in* Coutinho, Alfranio. A literatura no Brasil. Rio, Ed. Sul America, 1956, p. 129-153).

Estuda o problema das relações entre a educação e a literatura no Brasil. Salienta o papel das escolas e academias, a influência da escola de formação linguístico-literária, como fonte de uma tradição em que a literatura predominou, em detrimento do espírito científico. Por fim, menciona a ausência do ensino literário técnico. [A. Coutinho]

1759. Brazil. Conselho Nacional de Educação. Obrigatoriedade escolar. Rio, 1956. 69 p.

Diversos trabalhos que constituiram o debate empreendido pelo Conselho Nacional de Educação sôbre o problema da obrigatoriedade escolar. Ao lado dos discursos e pareceres e das conclusões aprovadas, figura um parecer do Conselheiro Celso Kelly relacionando as conclusões do Conselho em relação às doutrinas constitucionais e à legislação vigente. [A. Coutinho]

1760. Dines, Alberto. O ensino brasileiro em crise (Visão, 8:1, jan. 6, 1956, p. 30-32).

Comenta conclusões do recente inquérito realizado junto aos técnicos em educação do Instituto Nacional de Estudos Pedagógicos sôbre a atual situação do nosso ensino. Baseando-se em dados estatísticos, retrata ao vivo a situação educacional em todos os níveis. Informa como através, do INEP e suas campanhas, de outros órgãos ligados ao Ministério da Educação e Cultura e à Presidência da República, e, também, de algumas mais destacadas instituições educacionais, está se preparando a reestruturação educacional do país. [G. A. Vieira]

1761. Mariani, Clemente. A propósito dos processos de educação democrática. Conferência lida no quadro do temário da XII Conferência de Educação convocada pela Associação Brasileira de Educação e realizada em Salvador, sob os auspícios da Universidade da Bahia, em comemoração da passagem de seu primeiro decênio (EBSA, 9:105, 1956, p. 48-61).

Discute os diversos problemas da educação nacional, focalizando o projeto de lei de diretrizes e bases e defendendo os princípios que nortearam a sua elaboração quando da sua gestão no Ministério da Educação e Cultura. Divulga o memorando que dirigiu ao Prof. Lourenço Filho, com as observações e emendas segundo o ponto de vista do govêrno. [A. Coutinho]

1762. Moreira, J. Roberto. Aspectos atuais da situação educacional e cultural em Pernambuco (Ed Ciên Soc, ano 1, 1:3, dez. 1956, p. 21-75).

O autor faz um estudo da infra-estrutura econômica do estado de Pernambuco, salienta, o desajustamento entre a vida econômica rural e urbana e, como corolário, apresenta o problema educacional. Após analisar estatisticamente todos os níveis e graus da educação naquele estado (município por município) conclue afirmando a falta de possibilidades do próprio Estado como de todo o Nordeste, no sentido de um desenvolvimento mais acelerado para a solução dos seus problemas básicos. [C. Carvalho]

1763. **Oliveira, Juscelino Kubitschek.**
Ação do Estado no setor da educação e
cultura (Diário Cong Nac, 11:7, março
16, 1956, p. 79-86).
No capítulo referente à educação, fala da reestruturação dos processos pedagógicos, afim de
harmonizar a cultura técnica à humanística,
dadas as novas condições de desenvolvimento da
vida social e econômica do país. Essa reestruturação baseia-se em dois fatores essenciais: (1)
descentralização administrativa do ensino e (2)
flexibilidade dos currículos. Dá conta da situação dos vários ensinos e do programa do
govêrno para sua ampliação. No ensino superior
urge: (1) o preparo de profissionais e (2) formação de uma elite cultural. No ensino médio
há que ampliar o ensino técnico profissional pela
expansão e reerguimento da rêde escolar; pelo
aperfeiçoamento de professôres e administradores graças a cursos intensivos e bôlsas de
estudo; pela aprovação da lei que reajusta o ensino industrial; pela melhoria do material didático; pela orientação profissional e educacional; pela assistência técnica à indústria; pelo
prosseguimento de inquéritos sôbre mercado
de mão de obra; o ensino agrícola exige do Govêrno uma ação educativa ruralista a fim de
encaminhar êste setor para direções convenientes,
através de cursos regulares e extraordinários.
De referência ao ensino secundário, a medida
mais urgente é a reforma da sua lei orgânica, a
fim de corrigir o baixo rendimento da escola se-
cundária. No ensino primário é mister encaminhar a quota constitutional de 2% ao Fundo Nacional do Ensino Primário, a fim de que a União
contribua para o sistema escolar elementar. Mas
também é urgente que o ensino primário deixe
de ser exclusivamente intelectual, passando a
educar para o trabalho, integrando o homem na
vida económica e social de sua comunidade.
Fala do ensino emendativo e da educação física,
da assistência ao estudante, através de bôlsas,
material didático, merenda escolar, restaurantes
estudantis, assim como do aparelhamento das
instituições culturais do país, como institutos,
bibliotecas, museus, serviços de radiodifusão e
de cinema educativo e teatro. [A. Coutinho]

1764. **Teixeira, Anísio S.** A administração
pública brasileira e a educação (*in* A
educação e a crise brasileira, São Paulo,
Ed. Nacional (Col. BPB, sér. 3; Atualidades pedagógicas, 64), 1956, p. 100-
125).
O autor aborda, sob o ângulo da organização
estatal brasileira, o sistema de educação em vi-
gência entre nós. Mostra a alienação de que foi
vítima a administração pública brasileira em
consequência da falsa racionalização de seus
quadros operada pelo Estado Novo, cujos re-
flexos no processo educativo exprimem-se por
uma escola sem individualidade—instituição
desenraizada, imprecisa e flúida. [O. Bastos]

1765. ————. A educação e a unidade
nacional (*in* A educação e a crise brasileira. São Paulo, Ed. Nacional (Col. BPB,
sér 3; Atualidades pedagógicas, 64), 1956,
p. 3-51).
O autor defende a necessidade de uma escola
flexível e apaptável capaz de retratar, com fideli-

dade, os elementos dinâmicos da cultura que se
quer preservar e transmitir. Acusa os centra-
lizadores de se preocuparem menos com o
problema da unidade ou coesão nacionais do
que com o "contrôle das escolas para seus fins
próprios, defensivos de interêsses e preconcei-
tos." Conclui mostrando que a contribuição das
escolas para a unidade nacional só se fará
atuante quando nelas prevalecer o princípio fundamental de liberdade do Estado moderno, onde
a lei não é competente para decidir em questões
de saber ou de consciência profissional, pois o
"que se deve ensinar e como se deve ensinar
são questões a serem resolvidas pela escola
mesma e os que a servem, a não pelo legislador
comum." [O. Bastos]

1766. ————. Extensão do ensino primário brasileiro (B CBAI, 10:6, 1956,
p. 1614-1618).
Mostra o equívoco em que se assenta o sistema
educativo brasileiro—instrumento poderoso na
criação de privilégios—e o acerto das medidas
tomadas pelo atual govêrno acrescentando mais
dois anos à duração da escola primária com o
objetivo de promover uma educação fundamental para iniciação ao trabalho. O autor encarece
a necessidade de serem dadas aos novos cursos
(profissionais ou práticos) as mesmas consequências pedagógicas que damos aos cursos
ginasiais. [O. Bastos]

ENSINO

1767. **Almeida Júnior, A.** Repetência ou
promoção automática. Conferência pro-
ferida a 19 de setembro de 1956 no I Congresso Estadual de Educação, Ribeirão
Preto. São Paulo, Comissão Executiva
(Supl., Bol. do Congresso), 1956. 23 p.
Estuda o problema da repetência escolar, baseado em cálculo do volume da repetência, con-
frontando os dados estatísticos da sua ocorrência
no Brasil com os de outros países. Focaliza particularmente o caso do estado de São Paulo,
onde, em 1954, a proporção das aprovações nas
escolas primárias não ultrapassou 69.10%.

1768. **Belo, Rui de Aires.** Princípios e
normas de administração escolar. Pôrto
Alegre, Brazil, Globo, 1956. 283 p.
O livro destina-se a servir de fonte de informação para os estudos de administração escolar nas
Faculdades de Filosofia e também nas escolas
normais em cujo currículo seja a matéria in-
cluída. Situando devidamente os problemas da
matéria, apresenta no fim de cada capítulo,
temas para discussão e bibliografia do assunto.
[R. Tavares]

1769. **Freyre, Gilberto.** Em tôrno da
situação do professor no Brasil. Recife,
Brazil, Secretaria de Educação e Cultura
(Cad. de Pernambuco, 3), 1956. 28 p.
Ensaio inicialmente escrito em inglês, para o
Year book of education (1953). Na opinião do
autor, trata-se de um trabalho que poderá, dentro de seus limites, contribuir para um estudo
histórico-sociológico sôbre a situação do professor no Brasil atual em contraste com a que
foi no período colonial e imperial. Também

publicado na *Revista de educação e cultura*, 1:1, 1955, p. 5-37. [A. Tavares]

1770. Instituto Nacional de Estudos Pedagógicos. O método de projetos na escola experimental do INEP. [12. Conferência Nacional de Educação, Salvador, 1-9 de julho de 1956]. Rio, 1956. 25 p.
O assunto, é estudado tendo em vista a finalidade do método de projetos, mostrando-lhe as características, fundamentos e vantagens bem como as diretrizes gerais para a sua organização.

1771. Moura, Isnar de. Seis anos de verificação do rendimento escolar em Pernambuco. Recife, Brazil, Secretaria de Educação e Cultura (Cad. Pernambuco, 2), 1956. 97 p.
Trabalho publicado anteriormente, em dezessete capítulos, no *Jornal do commércio* de Recife com o objetivo de responder aos comentários feitos pelo prof. Nilo Pereira em sua coluna do *Jornal do commércio*, entre 30 de novembro e 3 de dezembro de 1955. A autora expõe minuciòsamente os trabalhos referentes à aplicação de testos objetivos levados a efeito pelo Serviço de Verificação do Rendimento Escolar da Secretaria de Educacão e Cultura de Pernambuco, pela qual é responsável. Apresenta a bibliografia consultada. [R. Tavares]

ENSINO ELEMENTAR

1772. Campos, Francisco. A escola ativa (B CBAI, 10:2, fev. 1956, p. 1553-1554).
Examina a função da escola primária, em face da criança como "um feixe de atividade à procura de expressão," destacando o sentido instrumental de noções e técnicas, em oposição ao conceito do conhecimento como fim em si mesmo. Focaliza o problema do programa de ensino, da formação e orientação técnico-profissional do professor primário e da administração educacional. [G. A. Vieira]

1773. Campos, Paulo de Almeida. A escola elementar brasileira e o seu magistério (tentativa de caracterização generalizada), [Conferência Regional Sôbre o Ensino Gratuito e Obrigatório na América Latina], Lima, 23 de abril—5 de maio de 1956. Rio, Instituto Nacional do Estudos Pedagógicos, Centro Brasileiro de Pequisas Educacionais, 1956. 44 p.
Estuda a escola primária brasileira e seu magistério, tendo em vista os condicionamentos históricos. Mostra as medidas que vêm sendo postas em prática, através de convênios, em obediência à determinação constitucional, no sentido de aumentar a rêde escolar, de melhorar o magistério primário, de desenvolver o ensino na zona rural.

1774. Cardoso, Ofélia Boisson. Alguns problemas do ensino da linguagem (R Br Estud Ped, 23:59, julho-set. 1955, p. 58-102; 23:61, jan.-março 1956, p. 35-90).
Analisa o problema do ensino da linguagem, detendo-se particularmente no exame da matéria

no nível primário. Tece primeiramente considerações sôbre psicologia da linguagem, estudando o caráter educacional da questão. [D. F. Monteiro]

1775. Instituto Nacional de Estudos Pedagógicos. Escola experimental. 12. Conferência Nacional de Educação, [Salvador, 1-9 de julho de 1956]. Rio, 1956. 68 p.
Relatório da Escola Guatemala, como centro experimental criado pelo INEP, e em funcionamento no Rio, desde 1955.

1776. ————. Centro Brasileiro de Pesquisas Educacionais. O problema do ensino primário no Brasil. Rio, 1956.
Partindo de um estudo da situação do ensino primário, o trabalho focaliza as medidas que o Ministério da Educação e Cultura pretende adotar para a ampliação e melhoria do sistema procurando articulá-lo melhor com o ensino médio. Para isso, seriam assinados convênios com os estados, a fim de estender a seis anos o curso primário, com seis horas diárias, sendo quatro de classe e duas de oficina.

1777. Melo, Orlando Ferreira de. O currículo da escola primária (R Ens, 5:37, 1956, p. 3-4).
Tece considerações sôbre o estudo *Introdução ao estudo do currículo da escola primária* do prof. J. Roberto Moreira publicado pela CILEME, órgão do Instituto Nacional de Estudos Pedagógicos em 1955 recomendando-o como leitura indispensável tanto para o professor primário como para os dirigentes dos órgãos educacionais que orientam e mantêm, nos estados, a escola primária.

1778. Moreira, J. Roberto. Os problemas do ensino primário no Brasil. 12. Conferência Nacional de Educação, Salvador, 1-9 de julho 1956. Rio, Instituto Nacional de Estudos Pedagógicos, Centro Brasileiro de Pesquisas Educacionais, 1956. 18 p.
Estudando os problemas do ensino primário no Brasil, passa em revista a conceituação da escola elementar, a questão dos currículos, da avaliação da aprendizagem e as reprovações, do tempo escolar e da divisão em turnos diários, da evasão escolar, trabalho e pauperismo. Lembra também certos problemas correlatos, como o da formação e recrutamento do pessoal docente, problemas êsses que exigem discussão e solução para a melhoria do sistema. [A. Coutinho]

1779. Oliveira Júnior, Ernesto Luis de. O ensino primário (B Inf CAPES, 42, 1956, p. 1-2).
Baseado em estatísticas, mostra que é mínima a percentagem de alunos que conseguem atingir o final do curso primário. Em face dêsse fenômeno grave, propõe um inquérito a fim de apurar as razões dessa fuga à escola, que parece evidenciar uma crise do ensino primário, de consequências para o secundário e o superior. [A. Coutinho]

1780. Silva, Caio Figueiredo. Processologia da escola primária. São Paulo, Ed.

do Brasil (Col. Didát. do Brasil; Sér. Bibl. pedag., 2), 1956. 380 p.
Livro de orientação metodológica para o professor primário. Contém processos experimentais e abrange tôdas as matérias do curso elementar. [R. Tavares]

1781. Teixeira, Anísio S. A escola pública universal e gratuita. Conferência pronunciada por ocasião do I Congresso Estadual de Educação, realizado na cidade de Ribeirão Preto, em setembro de 1956. São Paulo, Comissão Executiva (Supl., Bol. do Congresso), 1956. 45 p.
Assinala a coincidência de temas das mais recentes conferências de educação, que se dedicaram ao problema do ensino primário, e onde se defendeu a idéia de uma escola primária eficiente e adequada para todos, uma escola de seis anos e dias letivos completos. Expõe um plano de medidas a seram adotadas para fortalecer a escola primária e dotá-la dos recursos necessários, a fim de torná-la realmente a base do nosso sistema educacional. [A. Coutinho]

ENSINO SECUNDARIO

1782. Conner, S. Grant. Introdução ã educação profissional. Rio, CBAI, 1956? 150 p.
Monografia destinada ao professor-aluno dos cursos de treinamento de professôres de ensino industrial. Procura mostrar quais as relações existentes entre a educação profissional e os outros ramos da educação, assim como as relações entre êsse tipo de educação e os fatôres econômicos. [R. Tavares]

1783. Góes Filho, Joaquim Faria. Diretrizes atuais da aprendizagem industrial (B Cent Estud Roberto Mange, 1:2, 1956, p. 5-24).
Analisa o problema da formação da mão-de-obra em países de grande desenvolvimento e o papel do SENAI para a solução dêste problema no Brasil. Focaliza, em seguida, a organização, o currículo e o sentido dos cursos ministrados pelo SENAI, estabelecendo relações entre êstes e os ministrados na Inglaterra, França e nos Estados Unidos. [O. Bastos]

ENSINO SUPERIOR

1784. Campanha Nacional de Aperfeiçoamento do Pessoal de Nível Superior. Estabelecimentos de ensino. Rio, 1956. 74 p. (Ser. inform., 4).
Nova edição do indicador de estabelecimentos do ensino civil de nível superior incluindo: tabelas demonstrativas referentes ao número de estabelecimentos em 1955 discriminados por ramos de ensino; matrícula geral em 1955, conclusões de curso em 1954. Relação nominal dos estabelecimentos por estado e ramos de ensino com discriminação do número de matriculados em geral e na 1. série em 1955 e dos diplomados em 1954; cadastro dos estabelecimentos com dados sôbre seus nomes, ano da instalação, nome do diretor, endereço completo. [A. Tavares]

1785. Lima, H. da Rocha. Considerações sôbre o problema universitário brasileiro (Anhembi, ano 7, 25:73, dez. 1956, p. 12-17).
Conceituando dois tipos de universidade: a universidade de tipo clássico (francêsa e alemã) cuja finalidade é cultivar as ciências em suas formas mais elevadas e a universidade formada pela reunião de uma série de escolas profissionais, em que se adestram jovens para o exercício de uma profissão, considera que no Brasil deve se estudar minuciosamente a situação do ensino superior a fim de verificar-se qual o tipo de universidade adequada às nossas necessidades. [R. Tavares]

ESTATÍSTICA DA EDUCAÇÃO

1786. Brazil. Serviço de Estatística da Educação e Cultura. O ensino no Brasil em 1948-1950; ensino primário geral. Rio, 1956. 206 p.
Refere-se à organização do ensino primário geral no Brasil, contendo informações minuciosas dos principais resultados dêsse ensino, relativos ao triênio 1948-1950. Além disso, completa até o último dos anos citados, no que diz respeito à educação elementar não especializada, o farto material numérico constante da coleção de repertórios que desde 1932 vem publicando o Ministério da Educação e Cultura, sob o título *O ensino no Brasil*. [R. Tavares]

1787. Distrito Federal. Departamento de Geografia e Estatística. Situação cultural. Educação (An Est Dist Fed, Rio, 1951-1955, i. e. 1956, p. 170-212).
Quadros estatísticos sôbre o ensino municipal em seus diversos ramos e vários aspectos, abrangendo o período de 1951-1955. [R. Tavares]

FILOSOFIA DA EDUCAÇÃO

1788. Oliveira Júnior, Ernesto Luis de. Doze ensaios sôbre educação e tecnologia. Rio, Campanha de Aperfeiçoamento e Difusão do Ensino Superior (Sér. Estudos e ensaios, 7), 1956. 135 p.
Estudo sôbre educação e tecnologia, em que se põe em relêvo a noção da escola como agência de engenharia social, destinada a formar e distribuir os homens e mulheres pela imensa e diversificada rêde social de ocupações. O autor reúne fatos e provas, gráficos e estatísticas, que documentam a tese da finalidade da educação na organização da produção do trabalho. [A. Coutinho]

1789. Teixeira, Anísio S. Os processos democráticos da educação nos diversos graus do ensino e na vida extra-escolar. 12. Conferência Nacional de Educação, [Salvador, 1-9 de julho 1956]. Rio, 1956. 22 p.
Estuda o processo democrático da educação, como doutrina e orientação para tôdas as atividades escolares nos diversos níveis. Demonstra como a escola pode ser a fonte de vida democrática da sociedade.

FORMAÇÃO DE PROFESSORES E ADMINISTRADORES

1790. Caldeira, Eni. O problema da formação dos professôres primários. 12. Conferência Nacional de Educação, Salvador, [1-9 de julho de 1956]. Rio, Instituto Nacional de Estudos Pedagógicos, 1956. 19 p.

Baseada em ampla documentação, estuda a situação das escolas normais brasileiras, cujo funcionamento e prestígio não estão à altura da missão e das necessidades, oferecendo uma série de recomendações para a melhoria do ensino normal brasileiro. [A. Coutinho]

1791. Rangel, Wellman Galvão de Franca. A formação de administradores escolares. O que é e o que deve ser. Trabalho apresentado ao I Congresso Estadual de Educação, reunido em Ribeirão Preto, estado de São Paulo, de 16 a 23 de setembro de 1956. Campinas, Brazil, 1956. 18 p.

Analisa os termos do projeto de lei no. 515/56, que reforma o ensino normal paulista, apontando-lhe as principais deficiciências; como contribuição apresenta esquema de ante projeto de lei, cuja aplicação atenderia melhor às exigências atuais do Curso de Administração Escolar do Estado. [N. Batista]

ORIENTAÇÃO EDUCACIONAL E PROFISSIONAL

1792. Alambert, Sílvia B. A orientação profissional no curso secundário (Arq Br Psico, 8:1, 1956, p. 111-114).

Reproduzindo questionários, testes e tipos de entrevista, expõe o que se vem fazendo no terreno da organização profissional com os alunos do 1. ciclo do curso secundário da Escola Normal e do Ginásio Estadual Anhanguera, da capital paulista. [O. Bastos]

1793. Neder, Matilde. Centros de estudos e orientação (B Psico, 7-8:25-27, 1956, p. 25-27).

Estuda o papel dos Centros de Estudo e Orientação, como instituições auxiliares da escola, a fim de atender à necessidade de conhecimento, formação e orientação dos alunos dos cursos primário e normal. Analisa a natureza, objetivos e organização dos Centros, e mostra como êsses Centros ajudariam o professor primário a conhecer e compreender a criança. [A. Coutinho]

PSICOLOGIA EDUCACIONAL

1794. Bauzer, Riva. Caminhos que levam à aprendizagem (R Br Estud Ped, 23:61, jan.-março 1956, p. 132-139).

Indica a autora alguns caminhos que conduzem mais facilmente à aprendizagem, vinculados todos à boa atuação do professor.

1795. Matos, Luís Alves de. A aprendizagem como objeto de ensino (R Ped, ano 2, 2:1, 1956, p. 79-87).

Expõe sumàriamente os fatos fundamentais da aprendizagem nas diversas ciências e sua importância na didática. Conclui com uma série de considerações sôbre a natureza da aprendizagem e as doutrinas que a interpretam. [O. Bastos]

OBRAIS GERAIS

1796. Ferreira, Tito Lívio. O ensino público no estado do Brasil (R U Campinas, 3:10-11, 1956, p. 44-55).

Refuta falsas interpretações da história do Brasil colônial, segundo as quais não era devidamente atendida a cultura literária do país, por parte de seus colonizadores. Analisa o papel da assistência concedida pela Côrte aos jesuítas e o problema da proibição da impressão de livros no Brasil nos séculos XVII e XVIII.

1797. Instituto Nacional de Estudos Pedagógicos. Bibliografia brasileira de educação. Rio. V. 1, no. 1, out.-dez. 1953-.

Trimestral. Divulgação da bibliografia pedagógica brasileira, selecionada em livros, revistas e jornais, organizada pela classificação decimal de Dewey, com índices remissivos de autor e assunto.

1798. ————. Centro Brasileiro de Pesquisas Educacionais. Educação e ciências sociais; boletim. Rio, ano 1, v. 1, no. 1, 1956-.

Boletim trimestral cujo objetivo é a divulgação periódica das realizações do Centro Brasileiro de Pesquisas Educacionais no setor dos estudos e pesquisas sociais relacionados à educação. Em seu número inicial: (a) informa sôbre "as razões históricas e técnicas e os problemas" que motivaram a instituição do referido Centro; (b) expõe seu plano de ação; (c) relata atividades já iniciadas. [G. A. Vieira]

1799. Luz Filho, Fábio. Cooperativismo e educação (Div Coop, 63:65, 1955, p. 2-3).

O autor aprecia o problema do ponto de vista da América Latina, e particularmente, no caso do Brasil, o de projetos pilotos, afim de satisfazer a expansão do cooperativismo escolar e extra-escolar.

Geography

GENERAL

1900. **Asamblea Latinoamericana de la Ciencia del Suelo, I, 1953.** [Informe]. México, Secretaría de Agricultura y Ganadería, Oficina de Estudios Especiales (Folleto misceláneo, 5), 1955. 318 p.

A mine of information on the nature of soils and the development of soil science in many Latin American republics. An extremely valuable work for that growing body of scientists interested in soil science and related studies, basic to agricultural development. [R. E. Crist]

1901. **Rubio, Ángel.** Geografía y planificación regional. Panamá, Universidad de Panamá, 1953. 51 p.

A paper which brings out the importance of sound, basic training in physical and cultural geography for all those who think in terms of regional planning. [R. E. Crist]

THE CARIBBEAN AREA

RAYMOND E. CRIST

Various government agencies in Venezuela, especially the Corporación Venezolana de Fomento and the Consejo de Bienestar Rural, continue to do basic work in cultural geography and in allied fields. Geographic investigations in Puerto Rico continue to be vigorously pushed by the Planning Board, whose distinguished President, Dr. Rafael Picó, has become Secretary of the Treasury. Professor Levi Marrero has given a great impulse to geographic studies and research all over Latin America with the publication of *La tierra y sus recursos* (see *HLAS, no 19,* item 2361). This volume was so well received that it was sold out in a few months, and a new, augmented, and much larger edition appeared in the fall of 1956. Its success has been phenomenal. Professor Marrero has just published a charmingly written and illustrated volume for grade school and high school students entitled *Viajemos por América* (Publicaciones Culturales, Habana, 1957). This is a really new book, in presentation and content.

MIDDLE AMERICA

1950. **Aguilar Pinel, Carlos.** Geografía de Honduras. 3. ed. Tegucigalpa, Carlos Aguilar Pinel (Col. de textos nacionales), 1955. 248 p., illus.

1951. **Bradomin, José María.** Toponimia de Oaxaca. Crítica etimológica. México, Camarena, 1955. 262 p.

A most scholarly treatise on the place names derived from the Nahuatl language to be found throughout the state of Oaxaca.

1952. **Castillo Cordero, Clemente,** and **Juan Alfredo García O.** Atlas político-administrativo de la república de Guatemala. Guatemala, Ministerio de Educación Pública, 1953. 62 p.

Each of the 22 departments of Guatemala and the Territory of Belice are mapped at small scale (about 5 x 5 inches) to show department boundaries, *municipios,* drainage, roads, and railroads. For each map there is a page of text and tables with descriptive geographical information and population statistics. [A. C. Gerlach]

1953. **Comité Coordinador del Levantamiento de la Carta Geográfica de la República Mexicana.** Atlas de México. México, 1956. [Maps]

This atlas consists of 22 sheets at 1:500 000

Most of them were prepared in 1947-1949, but were assembled in atlas form in 1956. They show relief by contours at a 200-meter interval, plus drainage, roads and railroads, pipelines, airports, cities, towns, villages, ruins, mines, etc. [A. C. Gerlach]

1954. El Salvador. Ministerio de Obras Públicas. Dirección de Cartografía. ₊City plans₎. 1:1,000. San Salvador, 1956? ₊Maps₎

Ozalid reproductions have been made for large scale city plans of Ciudad de San Miguel (3 sheets, 38 x 76 in.), San Vicente (5 sheets, 38 x 38 in.), Sonsonate (6 sheets), and "Ciudad de Nueva San Salvador, Santa Tecla y alrededores" (6 sheets). Buildings are outlined to scale and some are named. Street names are indicated, but not block numbers. There is background contouring at a vertical interval of one meter. The same authority has prepared a map of Santa Ana at 1:2,000 without contours. [A. C. Gerlach]

1955. ————. Servicio Metereológico Nacional. La lluvia y Boletín meteorológico de El Salvador. Año 1, no. 1, junio 1954-.

No. 2 dated May 1954. With v. 2 changes to *La lluvia de El Salvador*. Useful for the climatologist.

1956. Fabila, Alfonso (and others). Tlaxcala. Tenencia y aprovechamiento de la tierra. México, Centro de Investigaciones Agrarias, 1955. 136 p., maps, tables.

This is an outstanding contribution to the body of literature on land tenure and its influence on land use practices. Great progress in the organization of agricultural cooperatives has been made since 1912, when the abject peons revolted against intolerable conditions imposed on them by great landlords. Many *ejidatarios* even today occupy and cultivate minuscule agricultural plots, and some proprietors, by holding a number of dispersed plots or by obtaining certificates showing that their land is "unaffected" by the Código Agrario, still have properties in excess of 1000 hectares. However, it is obvious that, in the words of President Ruiz Cortines, the Revolution has forged "a new juridical and economic structure in the process of liberating and bestowing dignity on the rural population."

1957. Gerencia de Exploración de Petróleos Mexicanos. Carta Geológica de la República Mexicana. 1:2,000,000. México, 1956. ₊Map₎

Compiled by Santiago Hernández Sánchez Mejorada for the XX Session, International Geological Congress. Shows the areal distribution of rocks according to geologic age, mode of occurrence and formation names, in relation to roads, railroads, national and state boundaries, cities and rivers. [A. C. Gerlach]

1958. Gutiérrez B., Federico. Expedición del doctor Richard Weyl al macizo del Chirripó. Bosquejo geológico de la Cordillera de Talamanca. San José, Instituto Geográfico de Costa Rica, 1955. 56 p., illus.

A preliminary report on a geological and physiographic reconnaissance of the Cordillera de Talamanca. Many features showing glacial action were found in Cerro Chirripo, made up of intrusive rocks to the very summit.

1959. México. Secretaría de Comunicaciones y Obras Públicas. Atlas de la República Mexicana. México, 1952. ₊Maps₎

This is a group of state maps, varying in scale from 1:490,000 to 1:2,555,000 and showing roads in eight categories plus numerous place names. The location value of the maps is enhanced by the inclusion of a geographical grid at intervals of one degree or less. Road data provided by the Dirección Nacional de Caminos. [A. C. Gerlach]

1960. Riquelme Vértiz de Rejón, Dolores. Geografía de Guanajuato. México, Universidad Nacional Autónoma de México, 1953. 157 p.

A brief treatment of the physical and human geography of this little-known region, where the Agrarian Revolution has been quietly at work. 30 per cent of the farmers live in *ejidos*, which entities own 39 percent of the *total* area of Guanajuato, but 51 percent of *all* cultivated land.

1961. Sáenz Maroto, Alberto. Los forrajes de Costa Rica. San José, Editorial Universitaria (Sección de ciencias naturales, 1), 1955. 606 p., illus., tables.

A monumental work on the many aspects of growing forage crops in the tropics, with particular emphasis on the influence of the several altitudinal climatic zones of Costa Rica. This volume should be invaluable for the thousands of ranchers all over tropical Latin America who are interested in improving their pastures, to be used for direct grazing, or as a soilage crop for stall feeding, or in the making of hay.

1962. Tromp, Solco Walle. Development of geological resources in El Salvador. Prepared for the government of El Salvador. N. Y., United Nations, Technical Assistance Programme, 1954. 100 p., diagr. (Doc. ST/TAA/K/El Salvador/2).

A well-organized mining department should be established in El Salvador to bolster this important part of the country's economy. A detailed survey of the northeast area is highly recommended, and possible deposits of petroleum, lignite, iron ore, etc., are discussed. Appendices, on creation of a geological institute for El Salvador; on stratigraphy of Central America; on tectonic structure of El Salvador and surrounding areas; and a bibliography of geologic and geographic reports for El Salvador and neighboring countries. [R. C. Eidt]

1963. United States. Board on Geographic Names. British Honduras. Official standard names approved by the United States Board on Geographic

Names. Washington, U. S. Govt. Print. Off., 1956. 25 p. (Gazetteer, 16). Useful for the cartographer.

1964. ————. ————. Mexico. Official standard names approved by the United States Board on Geographic Names. Washington, U. S. Govt. Print. Off., 1956. 750 p. (Gazetteer, 15). Useful for the cartographer.

1965. **Visintin, L.** Estados Unidos Mexicanos. 1:2,500,000. México. Printed in Italy for Artesania y Propaganda, 1956. ₁Map₁ Designed for lecture illustration, the map emphasizes relief by combining form lines and shading, and contains many place names for its scale. State boundaries are shown and main roads are in white. An inset shows air routes. [A. C. Gerlach]

WEST INDIES

1966. **Augelli, John P.** The British Virgin Islands: a West Indian anomaly (Geog R, 46:1, Jan. 1956, p. 43-58). ₁S. W. Mintz₁

1967. **Isnard, Hildebert.** La Réunion et la Martinique (Cahiers d'Outre-Mer, 9:33, jan.-mars. 1956, p. 58-69). A geographical comparison. [S. W. Mintz]

1968. **Machatschek, Federico.** Terminología geomorfológica. Tucumán, Argentina, Universidad Nacional de Tucumán, Instituto de Estudios Geográficos (Serie didáctica, 4), 1951. 204 p. A handy and much-needed glossary of the most frequently used geological and geomorphological terms, with their French, German, and English equivalents. The Spanish terms are briefly defined.

1969. **Parsons, James J.** San Andrés and Providencia; English-speaking islands in the western Caribbean. Berkeley, Calif., University of California Press (University of California publ. in geography, 12:1), 1956. 83 p., illus., maps (part fold.). A careful weighing of the physical and historical factors operative in creating the seemingly anomalous situation of these islands which, inhabited by 6000 contented, English-speaking Protestant islanders, are owned and administered by the republic of Colombia, although the inhabitants' cultural affinities are with the British West Indies and North America, and the position of the islands suggests that they should belong to Nicaragua.

1970. **Roig y Mesa, Juan Tomás.** Diccionario botánico de nombres vulgares cubanos. 2. ed. ampliada y corregida. T. 1-2. Habana, Ministerio de Agricultura, Dirección de Estaciones Experimentales (Boletín, 54), 1953. 589, 597-1128 p., illus. The author of this definite work has done for

Cuba what Pittier did for Venezuela. This is an invaluable reference book for the ecologist, botanist, geographer, and soils scientist.

1971. **United States. Board on Geographic Names.** British West Indies and Bermuda. Official standard names approved by the United States Board on Geographic Names. Washington, U. S. Govt. Print. Off., 1955. 157 p. (Gazetteer, 7). Useful for the cartographer.

1972. ————. **Bureau of the Census.** Census atlas maps of the Greater Antilles. Washington, 1956. ₁Maps₁ This series of seven maps is subdivided into regional maps of the Greater Antilles at 1:4,000,000, showing land forms, climatic regions, natural vegetation, and roads and railroads, plus separate maps at larger scales showing the urban and rural population distribution in Cuba, Hispaniola, and Puerto Rico. The maps show enough detail to be valuable for both teaching and research use. [A. C. Gerlach]

COLOMBIA

1973. **Acevedo Latorre, Eduardo.** Panorama geo-económico del departamento del Cauca (Ec Est, 4. época, 12:82, p. 3-48). An exhaustive, well-organized paper on the climatic, historic and geologic factors, and of the physiographic and economic regions of the department of Cauca, Colombia. In spite of the gradual decrease in number and influence of great landed estates, or *latifundia,* some 120 persons still control units of land ranging in size from 1000 to 2500 hectares—and this frequently some of the very best land—against 11,000 who work less than 1 hectare—often on steep, infertile slopes. Education, transportation, and housing are admirably treated.

1974. **Barcelona, Fidel de.** Geografía del Caquetá (Amaz Colomb Am, 4:12-16, 1946-1950, i. e. 1953. p. 211-223). The geographic highlights of this little-known region appear in a volume dedicated to the memory of Father Marcelino de Castellví, who selflessly labored for 20 years among the Sibundoy Indians. The volume contains many articles of interest, including one on gold working in Colombia and another on phytogeographic regions of northeast Amazonas—to name but two.

1975. **Caro Molina, Fernando** (ed.). De Agustín Codazzi a Manuel María Paz. Cali, Colombia, Editorial La Voz Católica, 1954. 318 p. A selection from the fascinating and valuable letters and reports—hitherto available only in manuscript—of the great cartographer and geographer, Codazzi. A wide range of topics is covered, the tone is serious, and the style is highly readable. This volume is excellent background reading for the social historian and the cultural geographer. Document no. 17, written in 1853, for example, is a detailed account of the many advantages that would accrue to Barbacoas, Pasto, and Tuquerres were they connected by good roads—a forecast amply borne out by the event.

1976. Colombia. Ministerio de Obras Públicas. Mapa vial del departamento del . . . . 1:500,000. Bogotá, Tall. Gráf. del Banco de la República, 1955. [Maps]
A series of high quality road maps has been prepared under the editorship of the Ministry of Public Works. Each map covers a department, and shows roads in six or more categories, railroads, many place names, detailed drainage, minor civil divisions, tables of distances, and spot heights. The maps result from cooperative efforts by the Institute Geográfico de Colombia, the Ministry of Public Works, and various agencies within the respective departments. All were printed by the Bank of the Republic. Maps known to be complete include those for the departments of Antioquia, Atlantico-Bolivar y Cordoba, Boyaca, Caldas-Tolima y Valle, Cauca y Nariño, Choco, Cundinamarca, Huila, Magdalena y Guajira, and Santander y Norte Santander. [A. C. Gerlach]

1977. Cubillos, Julio César. Tumaco. (Notas Arqueológicas). Bogotá, 1955. 145 p.
A well-illustrated volume based on detailed field work in what has been a little-known area. The author concludes that this area was culturally influenced from the north. The archaeological finds show cultural affinities with Central American material, notably with the material from Upper Tres Zapotes in Veracruz, Mexico. The coastal cultures of both Colombia and Ecuador in turn influenced pre-Columbian cultures of the interior of those countries. Future investigations will throw light on the degree and geographic extension of this influence.

1978. Escalante, Aquiles. Geoeconomía del algodón (R Geog, Barranquilla, 1:1, dic. 1952, p. 65-104).
A discussion of some of the aspects of the raising of cotton by the pre-Conquest Indians of northern Colombia, followed by an analysis of the present status and the future prospects of cotton production and manufacture in Colombia.

1979. ————. Notas sobre el palenque De San Basilio, una comunidad negra en Colombia (Div Etn, 3:5, junio 1954, p. 207-358).
A penetrating study of the elements of material and non-material culture of a Negro community in Colombia, by a brilliant young anthropologist whose writings are based on many years of painstaking work in the field.

1980. Friede, Juan. Conceptos geográficos durante el descubrimiento del Nuevo Reino de Granada. Madrid, Real Sociedad Geográfica (Publ., serie B, 346), 1955. 13 p.
This and the study below deal with the same topic. The second is the lengthier and is a well-documented report of 16th-century geographic notions concerning the discovery and occupation of the Chibcha altiplanos (*sabana* of Bogota, Ubate, etc.) in Colombia, and the role they were supposed to play in developing a route to the viceroyalty of Peru. The fact that Jiménez de Quesada had started exploration overland and via the unknown Magdalena river with (perhaps) as many as 800 men has long been considered poor judgment. Yet if the 16th-century ideas of geography are considered, it becomes clear that it was believed possible to reach the area of Peru within a short time via the Magdalena. García de Lerma, governor of Santa Marta, felt that the equator was to be encountered some 50 leagues south of the terminus of the Magdalena. Pedro de Heredia wrote in 1534 of the nearness of the coast of Colombia to the land of Peru. The author discusses concepts held by Belalcázar and Federmann, both of whom arrived in Chibcha territory while on the lookout for new "dorados." The thesis that Belalcázar was headed east from Popayan to look for an El Dorado beyond the Andes, i.e., far from the Chibcha territory, is supported. Finally, Pedro de Heredia, governor of Cartagena, had still other concepts of location which placed the Magdalena entirely under his supervision—an erroneous belief stemming from the impression that the Cauca was really the main path of the Magdalena. Such false notions of geography account for numerous "errors" made by the conquistadors, and have influenced settlement and political development considerably. [R. C. Eidt]

1981. ————. Las ideas geográficas en la conquista del Nuevo Reino de Granada (R Indias, Madrid, 15:61-62, julio-dic. 1955, p. 523-551).
See item above.

1982. Guhl, E. Colombia: fisiografía-clima-vegetación. Bogotá, 1956. 17½ x 13 inches. [Map]
For a small map this contains a wealth of information. Line boundaries and area patterns in black and white show the areal distribution of five natural regions, with several subdivisions of climate, relief, and vegetation in each. [A. C. Gerlach]

1983. Instituto Colombiano de Antropología. Gráfico que muestra la ubicación de los grupos indígenas actuales de Colombia. 1956? 17 x 13 inches. [Map]
The distribution of native groups is shown pictorially, with some indication of their activities and housing. [A. C. Gerlach]

1983a. ————. Gráfico referente a la habitación popular colombiana. 1956? [Map] 17 x 13 inches.
The areal distribution of some 35 house types is shown pictorially in black and white. Housing details are remarkably clear for the size. [A. C. Gerlach]

1984. Instituto Geográfico de Colombia. Ciudad de Pasto. 1:5,000. Bogotá, 1956. [Map]
Although this is an excellent, detailed map of a city, its more general value is in demonstrating

cartographic techniques for modern city plans. It is highly colorful, with shaded relief in brown and green, white streets with black names, and red for buildings. [A. C. Gerlach]

1984a. ————. Departamento del Magdalena. 1:250,000. Ed. preliminar. Bogotá, 1956. ₍Map₎

This is one of a series of shaded relief maps of the individual departments of Colombia, but it is more spectacular as an illustration of mapping techniques then accurate in detail. A list of control points is given, but relief features drawn by different cartographers do not always match in style or detail in various parts of the map. Roads, railroads, pipelines, aqueducts, *municipio* boundaries, and population centers are shown. The drainage pattern is detailed, but river names are conspicuously absent. [A. C. Gerlach]

1984b. ————. Mapa básico de suelos, distrito de irrigación del Río Coello. 1:20,000. Bogotá, 1955. ₍Map₎

25 soil types are mapped in five groups and shown in relation to roads, railroads, drainage, houses, and farm boundaries in the irrigation district. [A. C. Gerlach]

1984c. ————. Mapa preliminar del departamento de Cundinamarca. 1:250,000. Bogotá, 1954. ₍Map₎

This is one of the more accurate in a series of shaded relief maps of the individual departments of Colombia because contours supplement the relief shading. The drainage pattern is detailed, but very few rivers are named. Populated places, roads, railroads, and other cultural features of the landscape are shown. An inset of Bogota at 1:75,000 does not show enough detail to include street names. [A. C. Gerlach]

1984d. ————. República de Colombia, mapa histórico-político, descubrimiento, conquista e independencia. 1:1,500,000. Bogotá, 1955. ₍Map₎

This colorful map, nearly 4 x 5 feet, contains a wealth of information. The departments are shown in colors, and district boundaries are also delineated. There is a background of delicately shaded relief, a detailed drainage pattern, and many place names to aid orientation of historical places and routes of discovery which also appear on the map. The distribution of natives is shown, battlefields are marked, and routes of conquest are emphasized. Scores of notes explain the historical significance of many locations, and the margin of the map contains three-inch portraits of some 25 heroes and as many more historical scenes. An inset indexes the rulers and their principal campaigns in chronological order. [A. C. Gerlach]

1985. República de Colombia. 1:1,700,000. Barcelona, Seix Barrall, 1956? ₍Map₎

Relief and drainage are presented in striking colors. Little other information is given, but the map is very effective for illustrating the major relief and drainage features of the country. It is essentially a classroom or wall map. [A. C. Gerlach]

1986. Valle (department). Oficina de Tu-

rismo. Mapa vial del departamento del Valle. 1:200,000. Cali, Colombia, 1956. ₍Map₎

Although this is a blue-line print, it is a carefully compiled road map showing roads in four categories, railroads, waterways and watershed boundaries, electric power plants, pipelines, airports, and departmental boundaries. [A. C. Gerlach]

VENEZUELA

1987. Compañía Shell de Venezuela. Mapa del norte de la república de Venezuela. 1:500,000. Caracas, 1954. ₍Map₎

This is not an ordinary gas-ad road map. It is a detailed road map over a physical base which shows drainage plus relief by means of layer coloring between contours at sea level, 100 meters, 200 meters, and succeeding intervals of 1000 meters. The map also shows state and district boundaries, railroads, and airports. [A. C. Gerlach]

1988. Jones Parra, Juan. Atlas de bolsillo de Venezuela. 8. ed. Caracas, Lito. Miangolarra, 1954. 145 p.

This is a very convenient and informative little atlas (4½ x 6 in.) for Spanish-reading tourists and others who want a pocket-edition summary of information on Venezuela. There are numerous photographs, tables of statistical data, and maps of the individual states in addition to a brief but scholarly text. [A. C. Gerlach]

1989. Lasser, Tobias; John S. Penny; and Vernon L. Marsh. Aspectos de la vegetación de la parte occidental de la cuenca del lago de Maracaibo (B Soc Ven Cien Nat, 17:85, 1956, p. 47-70).

A discussion of the processes of soil formation on the various geological formations of the western sector of the Lake Maracaibo basin, under tropical conditions inherent in a wet and dry season rhythm. The xerophytic, deciduous forest and tropical rainforest belts are delimited on the basis of edaphic conditions.

1990. Tavera-Acosta, Bartolomé. Rionegro; reseña etnográfica, histórica y geográfica del Territorio Amazonas. 3. ed. Caracas, 1954. 309 p., illus.

Third edition of a deservedly famous book on a region that has for too long been an "underdeveloped" area, due largely to cultural rather than to physical factors. The author insists that an energetic program providing roads, schools, public health measures, non-corrupt officials, and immigrants with a little capital and modern farming techniques, would go a long way toward bringing the area out of the moral, social, economic, and political doldrums.

1991. Venezuela. Consejo de Bienestar Rural. Problemas económicos y sociales de los Andes venezolanos. Parte 2. Caracas? 1956? 136 p.

V. 1 (See *HLAS, no. 19,* item 1462) and 2 of the monumental treatise on the physical and cultural aspects of the Venezuelan Andes, by a U. S.-

Venezuelan team of social scientists, under the direction of Professor Sterling of the University of Wisconsin and Professor Lorenzo Monroy of the Universidad Central de Venezuela. This beautifully illustrated volume, based on intensive field investigation, is a model of cooperative research.

Especial attention is given in v. 2 to the cultural factors operative in overcoming human inertia and in inducing local changes or migration. These volumes are a mine of information for the rural sociologist, social anthropologist, and economist, as well as for the cultural geographer and the historian. It cannot be too highly recommended.

1991a. ————. ————. Recursos agrícolas del Guárico Occidental. 1:250,000. Caracas, 1955. ₁Maps₁

These are carefully constructed, detailed maps of the western part of the state of Guarico, showing soils, vegetation, land use, and land ownership. [A. C. Gerlach]

1991b. ————. Ministerio de Minas e Hidrocarburos. Dirección de Geología. Mapa geológico de la república de Venezuela. 1:1,000,000. Caracas, Dirección de Cartografía Nacional, 1955. ₁Map₁

Prepared for presentation at the IV World Congress on Petroleum in Rome, 1955, this map shows in colors and symbols some 27 geological formations throughout Venezuela. Even small tributary streams are named in blue, and there are many cities, towns, and villages named in black. [A. C. Gerlach]

1991c. ————. Ministerio de Obras Públicas. Carta aeronáutica seccional. 1:500,000. Caracas, Dirección de Cartografía Nacional, 1954. ₁Map₁

In addition to navigational information, this 26-sheet map shows roads, railroads, drainage, and altitude tints separated by contours at 500 meter intervals. [A. C. Gerlach]

1992. Vila, Marco-Aurelio. Aspectos geográficos del estado Cojedes. Caracas, Corporación Venezolana de Fomento, Sub-gerencia de Servicios Técnicos (Monografías económicas estadales, 7), 1956. 219 p., illus., maps (part fold., part col.).

This is the seventh in the series of geographies of the several states of Venezuela to be published by the Corporación Venezolana de Fomento.

The chapters on agriculture, ranching, population, and transportation are especially meaty. The author of this extremely well-illustrated volume concludes that human resources should be added to by immigration, that housing and nutrition should be improved, and that educational facilities should be enlarged.

SURINAM

1993. Dahlberg, H. N. Kaart van Suriname. 1:1,000,000. Utrecht, Topografische Dienst, 1956? ₁Map₁

Very good general reference map, with legend in German and English. It shows roads and railroads, telecommunication lines, population centers, Indian villages, district boundaries, mining areas, and the major relief features. [A. C. Gerlach]

1994. Kaart van Suriname. 1:500,000. Zeist, Netherlands, Dijkstra's Uitgeverij Zeist N. V., 1956. ₁Map₁

This is a relief map, with layer tints between generalized contours at 200, 500, and 1000 meters. It also shows geological formations of clay, sand, and mixed clay and sand near the coast. It is a wall map, with bold coloring and few place names, but rivers are named and internal political subdivisions are bounded and named. Areas in the southwest and southeast of the country are clearly indicated as disputed territory. [A. C. Gerlach]

SOUTH AMERICA (EXCEPT BRAZIL, COLOMBIA, AND VENEZUELA)

GEORGE McCUTCHEN McBRIDE AND ROBERT C. EIDT

Now that all major boundary problems of mainland South America are settled, the countries are giving less attention to frontier disputes and are carrying out more detailed mapping and other research activities within their borders. Geographical agencies both private and official are devoting their efforts to projects concerning soils, vegetation, climates, distribution of population, and development of resources. Argentina is advancing her cartographic work rapidly, and leads the list for home research publications. The *Ministerio de Agricultura y Ganadería* has produced several excellent studies, as have various private individuals. Peruvians and Chileans have made valuable contributions to knowledge of their countries, particularly in the realms of mapping and of human geography. Growing numbers of semitechnical reports have been written about Bolivia, Uruguay, Ecuador, and Paraguay, and this would seem to be a hopeful sign. Several good travel books in German, Spanish, and English have also appeared for most of the countries covered in this section. [R. C. Eidt]

GENERAL

2000. Chebataroff, Jorge. Esquema general de la evolución de las costas platenses; con algunas referencias acerca de las costas uruguayas y riograndense del Atlántico (A Assoc Geóg Br, 7:1, 1952-1953, i. e. 1955, p. 56-95, maps).

2001. Lockwood, Agnes Nelms. Indians of the Andes (Intl Conc, 508, May 1956, 78 p., map).

2002. Szyszlo, Vitold de. La naturaleza en la América ecuatorial. Descripción de la naturaleza de la región amazónica del Perú, Brasil, Bolivia, Ecuador, Colombia, Venezuela y de la Guayana; observaciones hechas durante doce viajes en los años 1904 a 1953. Lima, Sanmartí, 1955. 528 p., illus.
A naturalist's varied observations as a result of many expeditions to the upper Amazon regions. [G. M. McBride]

2003. Tschopik, Harry, Jr. At home in the high Andes (N Geog Mag, 107:1, Jan. 1955, p. 133-146, illus.).

ARGENTINA

2004. Acevedo Díaz, Eduardo. La República Argentina. Parte física. B. A., Tall. Gráf. Didot, 1955. 322 p., illus., maps.
A good discussion of the physical geography of Argentina, for use in high schools, terminating with a description of six natural regions: the Andes, the plains of the Chaco and Pampa, Mesopotamia, Patagonia, non-Andean Tierra del Fuego, and the Falkland Islands. [R. C. Eidt]

2005. Argentina. Administración General de Parques Nacionales. Natura. B. A. T. 1, no. 1, 1954-.
Articles of interest in various phases of plant ecology in the several national parks of the country. [R. E. Crist]

2005a. ————. Dirección General de Navegación, Hidrografía, Faros y Balizas. Derrotero argentino. Parte 4. Ríos Paraná, Paraguay y Uruguay. 5 ed. actualizada hasta el 31 de diciembre de 1953 (Folleto no. 24 de Avisos a los navegantes, inclusive). B. A., 1954. 229 p., diagrs., illus., maps.
Latest revision of the Maritime Ministry's navigation series on Argentine rivers. Includes general description of port facilities with maps, magnetic declination tables, etc., and somewhat more detailed information regarding pluvial regimes, river gradients, and routes to be followed by seagoing and river vessels. [R. C. Eidt]

2005b. ————. Ejército. Reseña histórica del Instituto Geográfico Militar; su misión y su obra. B. A., 1951. 143 p., maps.

2005c. ————. Instituto Geográfico Militar. Carta topográfica de la República Argentina. B. A. ɾMaps, various dates, various scales and editions꜀.
High quality topographic maps of Argentina are being continuously prepared and revised at scales of 1:25,000, 1:50,000, and 1:100,000. Although many of the basic surveys date back to 1915-1917, the new sheets are based on modern air photography and excellent geodetic controls, and revisions bring the cultural data up to 1953-1957. Coverage of the country is not complete at the larger scales, but indexes showing the status of mapping to date may be obtained from the publisher. These are the basic maps of the country. [A. C. Gerlach]

2005d. ————. ————. República Argentina. 1:2,500,000. 3. ed. B. A., 1957. ɾMap꜀
Published in two sheets, each 34 x 42 inches, this is of wall-map proportions but is filled with detail for desk research. Relief is shown by layer tints, including ocean depths. The drainage pattern is detailed but only principal streams are named. Provinces are named and conspicuously delineated. Population centers are numerous, and are shown in seven categories, including those with less than 500 people. Railroads are in eight classes and roads in four. Insets show Argentina's claims in the Antarctic and a map of world trade routes. [A. C. Gerlach]

2005e. ————. Ministerio de Agricultura y Ganadería. Cartilla agrícola-forestal de la provincia de Buenos Aires. B. A., 1953. 285 p., maps. (Publ. miscelánea, 370).
This book divides the province of Buenos Aires into 16 zones based on varying ecologic conditions. In a general section, climates, soils, crops, and domestic animals are discussed for each zone. In a more specific section, crop varieties, acreages, yields, etc., are given. Some 30 colored maps include climates and crops for each zone. [R. C. Eidt]

2006. Bonelli, Juan M. República Argentina: mapa general de los ferrocarriles y caminos principales. B. A., 1956. 72 by 56 inches. ɾMap꜀
Detail of roads and a multitude of place names are the chief characteristics of this map, and ribbon colors emphasize province boundaries. Locational accuracy is doubtful because there is no scale or grid of geographical coordinates. [A. C. Gerlach]

2007. Burnet-Merlin, Alfredo R. Nombres de Chascomús; topónimos de ayer y de hoy. Prólogo de Francisco L. Romay. Chascomús, Argentina, Editorial del Lago (Biblioteca de Chascomús, 5), 1954. 39 p.
Study of the place names in one of the *partidos* into which the province of Buenos Aires is divided. [G. M. McBride]

2008. **Daus, Federico A.** Reseña geográfica de las islas Malvinas. B. A., Universidad Nacional de Buenos Aires, Instituto de Geografía (Serie A, 19), 1955. 51 p., maps.

2009. **Domicelj, Sergio.** Ascensión al Ojo del Salado (R Geog Am, año 23, 40:240, abril 1956, p. 258-268, map).

2010. **Fina, Armando L. de (and others).** Difusión geográfica de cultivos índices en la provincia de Tucumán y sus causas. B. A., Instituto de Suelos y Agrotécnica (Publ., 50), 1956. 47 p., maps.

2011. **Fochler-Hauke, Gustavo.** La conquista de la Puna por el hombre (R Geog Am, año 19, 35:205-207, oct.-dic. 1952, p. 151-157).

2012. **Frenguelli, Joaquín.** Loess y limos pampeanos. La Plata, Argentina, Universidad Nacional de la Plata, Facultad de Ciencias Naturales y Museo de La Plata (Serie técnica y didáctica, 7), 1955. 88 p. Originally published in 1925.

2013. **González, Carlos.** Actualidades pesqueras en la República Argentina y posibilidades de incrementar el consumo de pescado. B. A., Ministerio de Agricultura y Ganadería, Departamento de Investigaciones Pesqueras (Publ. Miscelánea, 415). 43 p.

A bulletin which discusses fish consumption in Argentina, estimated at three kilograms per person per year, compared with beef consumption which is some 60 kg per person per year. 1953 fish production was 77,241 metric tons. 90% of this catch was from ocean fishing. 60% of the amount was used fresh, 34% for canning or curing, and 6% for oils and fertilizer. Most of the fish was consumed near the coast, but shipments as far away as Jujuy, Mendoza, Carmen de Patagonia, etc., were made from B. A. A map of fish shipments over the country is included. [R. C. Eidt]

2014. **Harrington, Richard.** Sheep ranchers of Patagonia (Can Geog J, 52:2, Feb. 1956, p. 64-71, map).

2015. **Hueck, Kurt.** Urlandschaft, Raublandschaft und Kulturlandschaft in der Provinz Tucumán im nordwestlichen Argentinien; ein Beispiel für die Bedeutung der ursprünglichen Pflanzendecke beim Werden einer subtropischen Landschaft. Bonn, Germany, Im Selbstverlag des Geographischen Instituts der Universität Bonn (Bonner geographische Abhandlungen, 10), 1953. 102 p., illus., maps (2 fold. col. in pocket).

2016. **Ostrowski, Wiktor.** Más alto que los cóndores; sobre los "techos" de los cerros Mercedario, Ramada, Alma Negra, La Mesa y Aconcagua. ₍Traducción por la señora Yadviga del Prado₎. B. A., Albatros, 1954. 339 p., illus.

The account of a Polish expedition to the Argentina Andes in 1934. Landscape descriptions are good, particularly with regard to the snow pinnacles found in the vicinity of El Mercedaria peak. A summary is given of Andean peaks above 6000 meters, and of world peaks 7000 meters or higher that have been climbed. Numerous photographs. [R. C. Eidt]

2017. **Pendle, George.** Argentina. London, Royal Institute of International Affairs, 1955. 159 p., illus.

Brief summary of geography, history, and politics of Argentina. Useful appendices on demography, and the San Nicolas steel project. [R. C. Eidt]

2018. **Pla, Guí.** Buenos Aires, Capital Federal y Gran Buenos Aires. B. A., General San Martín, 1955. 163 p.

This is an excellent atlas of B. A., showing street names (indexed), block numbers, and transportation lines for the capital city as well as 159 suburban areas. Former names of streets are also listed in a separate table. [A. C. Gerlach]

2019. **Stura, Ángel C., and Jorge Alfredo Luque.** Estudio general del problema del riego y su técnica en la provincia de Mendoza. B. A., Ministerio de Agricultura y Ganadería (Publ. miscelánea, 395), 1954. 47 p.

This is a technical bulletin dealing with irrigation methods and their applicability in the province of Mendoza. Of interest to the geographer are soil and water analyses, and climatological data involving the 320,000 hectares of irrigated land in this province. [R. C. Eidt]

2020. **Tortorelli, Lucas A.** La lucha por la vida en los bosques argentinos. B. A., Ministerio de Agricultura y Ganadería de la Nación (Publ. técnica, 1), 1954. 19 p., illus.

Study of the struggle among species reaching toward a climax vegetation in the few forested areas of the Argentine. Published also in Natura, 1:1, 1954, p. 5-20. [G. M. McBride]

2020a. ————. Maderas y bosques argentinos. Pref. por Ph. Guinier. B. A., Acme (Ciencias biológicas y agronómicas), 1956. 910 p., illus. (part col.), map, diagrs.

A comprehensive volume which divides Argentina into several forest zones: the Selva (Misiones, Tucuman-Bolivian Gallery Types), Subantartic forests (Chaco, Pampa-Puntano, Mesopotamian), and Western forests. Chapters on wood classification, uses, geographic distribution, etc., are useful. Many photographs, over 350 references, and index are included. [R. C. Eidt]

BOLIVIA

2021. Fain, Cynthia. Bolivie. Grenoble, France, Arthaud (Col. Les clefs de l'aventure, 9), 1955. 248 p., illus.

2022. Forster, Walter. Die Yungas (Kosmos, 52:11, Nov. 1956, p. 514-524, map).

2024. Monheim, Felix. Klimatologie und Hydrologie des Titicacabeckens. Heidelberg, Germany, Selbstverlag des Geographischen Instituts der Universität Heidelberg (Heidelberger geographische Arbeiten, 1), 1956. 152 p., maps.

2025. United States. Board on Geographic Names. Bolivia. Official standard names approved by the United States Board on Geographic Names. Washington, U. S. Govt. Print. Off., 1955. 269 p. (Gazetteer, 4).
About 18,000 entries for places and features in Bolivia. Scale of map coverage from which data taken approximately 1 to 1 million. Four Bolivian maps listed in bibliography. [R. C. Eidt]

CHILE

2026. Chile. Instituto Geografico Militar. Anuario del Instituto Geográfico Militar, no. 7, 1951-1954. Santiago, 1955. 179 p., maps.
Report of cartographic work done in this period for the army and other government agencies, such as the boundary commission and property surveys (catastro). Detailed maps illustrate accomplishments. [G. M. McBride]

2028. Hardee, Jay H. The forestry phase of the United States technical assistance program in Chile (Carib For, 17:1-2, Jan.-June 1956, p. 28-36).

2029. Klapp, Ernst. Futterbau und Futterwirtschaft in Chile zwischen dem 30 und 42° s Br (Bonn Geog Abhand, 17, 1956, p. 87-137).
Spanish summary: "Cultivo y economía de las plantas forrejeras en Chile, entre los 30° y los 42° de latitud sur."

2030. Marchant, Roberto. Oil at the end of the earth; a visit to the Chilean wells in Tierra del Fuego (Américas, PAU, 7:12, dic. 1955, p. 12-16, map).

2031. Schwabe, G. H. Die ökologischen Jahreszeiten im Klima von Minico (Chile) (Bonn Geog Abhand, 17, 1956, p. 139-183, map).
Spanish summary: "Aportación al conocimiento ecológico del año 1953/1954 en Mininco (Chile); a base de promedios mensuales meteorológicos y microclimáticos."

2032. Silva, Euzébio Flôres. Comentarios sobre unos mapas de densidade de población de Chile (R Geog Inst Pan Am, 16:42, 1. semestre 1955, p. 39-131, maps).

2033. United States. Board on Geographic Names. Chile. Official standard names approved by the United States Board on Geographic Names. Washington, U. S. Govt. Print. Off., 1955. 351 p. (Gazetteer, 6).
Contains some 23,750 entries of "places and features in Chile and her outlying possessions." Approved standard names and unapproved variant names are given. Useful cartobibliographical material included. [R. C. Eidt]

ECUADOR

2034. Acosta Solís, Misael. La forestación artificial en el Ecuador central; [especies ensayadas y técnicas de plantación experimentadas en áreas secas]. Quito, Escuela Politécnica Nacional, 1954. 85 p., illus.
An important study, by a noted botanist, of afforestation already carried on mainly with eucalyptus (introduced in 1865 and now widely grown in large groves) with a few other species suited to altitude, soil, and climate on the high inter-Andean basins. [G. M. McBride]

2034a. Banfield, A. F.; Charles H. Behre; and David St. Clair. Geology of Isabela (Albemarle) Island, Archipiélago de Colón (Galápagos) (B Geol Soc Am, 67:2, Feb. 1956, p. 215-234, maps).

2034b. Blomberg, Rolf. The naked Aucas. An account of the Indians in Ecuador. London, Allen and Unwin, 1956. 192 p., maps, photographs.
An account of the author's travels in the Oriente of Ecuador. House descriptions, crops, utensils, hunting equipment, etc., of the Aucas, briefly treated. [R. C. Eidt]

2034c. ——— (ed.). Ecuador; Andean mosaic. With 212 photos. Stockholm, Geber, 1952. 319 p., illus., map.
A sketchy review of historical, geographical, and other aspects of Ecuador in 10 articles by several authors. Selected bibliography of English language books about Ecuador. [R. C. Eidt]

2035. Naveda, Bolívar H. Galápagos a la vista. Quito, Casa de la Cultura Ecuatoriana, 1952. 570 p.
Description of the islands, their topography, fauna and flora, together with an account of the part played by them during the recent war and of the efforts being made toward their colonization. [G. M. McBride]

2035a. Platt, Raye Roberts. Ecuador. [Prepared with the cooperation of the American Geographical Society] Garden

City, N. Y., Doubleday (Around the world program), 1956. 64 p., illus. (part mounted col.).

Authentic, penetrating, selective, condensed description, well illustrated with colored prints. [G. M. McBride]

2035b. Terán, Francisco. Geografía del Ecuador. Texto para los colegios secundarios. 3. ed. Quito, Imp. del Ministerio de Educación, 1955. 374 p., illus.

A high school text with the usual approach: location of Ecuador, boundaries, racial composition of the people, history, natural regions (Sierra, Coast, Oriente), and economy. Maps and photographs are especially poor. [R. C. Eidt]

PARAGUAY

2036. Crist, Raymond E. Paraguay (Focus, 7:3, Nov. 1956, 6 p.).

Brief, up-to-date description of the land and its development. [G. M. McBride]

2036a. Paraguay. Estado Mayor General. Sección Cartográfica. Mapa de la República del Paraguay. 1:1,000,000. Asunción, 1956. ₁Map₁

Revised from 1939 edition. This is a single-sheet general reference map showing departments in color, a detailed drainage pattern, mountain ranges by "woolly worm" technique, many place names, roads, railroads, and airports. [A. C. Gerlach]

2037. Raine, Philip. Paraguay. New Brunswick, N. J., Scarecrow Press, 1956. 443 p., illus., map.

A good general description of a country about which little satisfactory recent literature exists. [G. M. McBride]

2037a. United States. International Cooperation Administration. Operations Mission to Paraguay. Centro Audiovisual. República del Paraguay. 1:500,000. Asunción, 1956? ₁Map₁

As a base map for plotting other data, this blueline print is useful. Being on poor paper and in two very large sheets (each 40 x 60 in.), it is difficult to use, and contains so few place names that location relationships cannot be ascertained. The map also lacks longitude or latitude references and a grid, but it does show departmental and district boundaries and capitals, roads in three classes, railroads, and forts. [A. C. Gerlach]

PERU

2038. Alayza y Paz Soldán, Luis. Geografía concertada del Perú. Fragmentos de una obra inédita (B Soc Geog Lima, 72, 3.-4. trimestre 1955, p. 5-27, maps).

2039. Cole, John P. The economic possibilities of the selva region of Peru (Tijd

Ec Soc Geog, 47:10, Oct. 1956, p. 237-242, map).

2039a. —————. Un esperimento di colonizzazione nel Perù orientale (B Soc Geog It, serie 8, 8:9-10, settembre-ottobre 1955, p. 470-476, maps).

2939b. —————. Geografía urbana del Perú (R Mus Nac, 24, 1955, p. 50-80).

2039c. —————. Huarochiri, une petite région des Andes du Pérou (R Géog Alp, 44:3, 1956, p. 445-462, maps).

2039d. —————. Ports and hinterlands in Peru (Tijd Ec Soc Geog, 47:6-7, Juni-Juli 1956, p. 173-177, maps).

2040. Dorst, Jean. L'exploitation du guano du Pérou: la protection de la nature au service de l'économie humaine (Terre Vie, 103:2, avril-juin 1956, p. 49-63, maps).

2040a. Egeler, Cornelis Geoffrey, and T. de Booy. Challenge of the Andes; the conquest of Mount Huantsán. Translated from the Dutch by W. E. James. N. Y., McKay, 1955. 203 p., illus.

Translation of Naar onbestegen Andes-toppen.

2041. Eiselen, Elizabeth. A tourist-geographer visits Iquitos, Peru (J Geog, 55:4, Apr. 1956, p. 176-181).

2041a. González Tafur, Oswaldo B. Perú; población y agricultura. Lima, Librería Internacional del Perú, 1952. 288 p., illus.

2042. Guevara Velasco, Agustín. Apuntes sobre mi patria, volumen del Departamento de Puno. Pref. de Víctor J. Guevara. Colofón de Alejandro Quesada. Cuzco, Perú, Rozas (Biblioteca de la Revista de filosofía y derecho), 1954-1955. 3 v. 1462 p., illus.

Elaborately detailed description, province by province and district by district, hence valuable for reference. [G. M. McBride]

2042a. Kropp, Miriam. Cuzco: window on Peru. N. Y., Studio Publications, 1956. 143 p., illus.

2043. López Albújar, Carlos. Bosquejo monográfico de la provincia de Morropón (B Soc Geog Lima, 73, 1.-2. trimestre 1956, p. 18-30, maps).

2043a. Mapa del Perú. 1:800,000. Barcelona, Seix Barral, 1956. ₁Map₁

This is an effective political map, with departments in vivid colors. For classroom use other details are too cluttered for good visibility. Relief is shown by hachures; drainage features and many populated centers are named in fine print; and roads, railroads, airports, department and province boundaries are also shown. A similar map with softer colors and the same detailed information is also available at 1:3,250,000. It would be more suitable for desk or office use. [A. C. Gerlach]

2044. Murphy, Robert Cushman. El guano y la pesca de anchoveta; informe oficial al Supremo Gobierno. Lima, Compañía Administradora del Guano, 1954. 147 p., port.

"Documentos oficiales en pro de la conservación de las especies productoras del guano y su base alimenticia," p. 41-147.

2044a. Nicholson, Carlos. La estructura en la geografía económica del Perú (B Soc Geog Lima, 73, 1.-2. trimestre 1956, p. 43-48).

2044b. Österreichischer Alpenverein. Cordillera Huayhuash, Perú. Ein Bildwerk über ein tropisches Hochgebirge. Hrsg. von der Anden-Kundfahrt 1954 des Österreichischen Alpenvereins. Innsbruck, Austria, Tiroler Graphik, 1956? xlii p., map, 64 plates (part col.).

Contains a geographical description of the Cordillera Huayhuash of Peru, a section on mountain climbing in this region (with incomplete translations in Spanish and English). [R. C. Eidt]

2045. Orbegoso Rodríguez, Efraín. Consideraciones en torno de la tierra y el hombre del Perú (R Geog Inst Pan Am, 16: 42, 1. semestre 1955, p. 133-150, map).

2045a. Sayle, John. Along the Peruvian Andes. A travel adventure. N. Y., Vantage Press, 1953. 201 p., illus.

Sketchy notes about areas visited, including forested region about Quince Mil and Maldonado. [G. M. McBride]

2045b. Ulloa, Bolívar. La geografía del Perú y sus fronteras (B Soc Geog Lima, 73, 3. trimestre 1956, p. 19-27, map).

2046. Villarejo, Avencio. Así es la selva. Estudio monográfico de la Amazonia nororiental del Perú. Maynas-Loreto-Requena. Lima, Sanmarti, 1953. 307 p., maps, photographs.

Well-prepared geographical study of three provinces in Peru's northeast: Maynas, Loreto, and Requena. The total area involved is 283,080 square kilometers. It has an estimated population of 140,800 (1951). The region is described as a lowland with gently undulating character (local relief 5-50 meters). Its soils are principally reddish semi-lateritics with low fertility and little agricultural future. Climate is continuously hot and humid. During June and early July cold winds (Fríos de San Juan) occur, and are believed to be associated with Brazil's *fria-*

gem. They may cause temperature drops of 15 degrees C. within a few hours. The terms *invierno* and *verano* are associated mainly with rise and fall of rivers, or with continuity of rainfall or lack of it. Separate sections deal with phytogeography, human geography, and political geography. Bibliography. Insert map of area at scale of one to one million. [R. C. Eidt]

URUGUAY

2046a. Dyer, Donald R., and **Raymond E. Crist.** Uruguay (Focus, 7:8, 1957, 6 p., maps).

2046b. United States. Board on Geographic Names. Uruguay. Official standard names approved by the U. S. Board on Geographic Names. Washington, U. S. Govt. Print. Off. (Gazetteer, 21), 1956.

Involves some 8600 places and features in Uruguay. Entries include approved standard names as well as unapproved variant forms. Useful cartobibliography of official maps. [R. C. Eidt]

2047. Ureta Martínez, Horacio. Mapa de la República del Uruguay. 1:400,000. Montevideo, Barreiro y Ramos, 1956. ₁Map₁

This is a good general reference map with emphasis on drainage. Background relief is shown by hachures, population centers are in four categories, roads show distances in kilometers from Montevideo, and railroads, airlines, and minor civil and judicial boundaries are shown. The two sheets of this map, each 29 x 48 inches, are bound in a folder 15½ x 13½ inches. [A. C. Gerlach]

2047a. Uruguay. Ministerio de Obras Públicas. Dirección de Topografía. Carta del departamento de . . . 1:200,000. Montevideo, 1951-1956. ₁Maps₁

This series of general reference maps covers at uniform scale the departments of Cerro Largo (1951), Paysandu (1955), Rivera (1956), and possibly others. The maps show drainage, major relief features by form lines, population centers, railroads, roads in several categories, military and civil airports, minor civil divisions, judicial districts, etc. [A. C. Gerlach]

2047b. Vidart, Daniel D. La vida rural uruguaya: escenario geográfico, proceso histórico, caracteres socioculturales. Montevideo, Departamento de Sociología Rural (Publ., 1), 1955. 196 p., diagr., tables.

OTHER AREAS

2048. Great Britain. Colonial Office. Report on the Falkland Islands and dependencies for the years 1952 and 1953. London, H. M. Stationary Office, 1954. 52 p., maps, photographs.

This is an informative booklet dealing with the geography, history, and management of the

Falkland Islands and their dependencies to the south. The Falklands produce wool, skins, tallow, and, since 1953, frozen mutton for export. Whaling and sealing are the only industries in the dependencies. Good bibliographies included with each section as a rule. [R. C. Eidt]

2049. Sent, Guillermo W. La Patagonia austral y Tierra del Fuego; impresiones de carácter económico-social recogidas durante viajes de estudios realizados en 1952-1953. B. A., Albatros, 1955. 60 p.

BRAZIL

LYSIA MARIA CAVALCANTI BERNARDES
AND
HILGARD O'REILLY STERNBERG

This volume of *HLAS* covers items published in 1956, the year when the Eighteenth International Geographical Congress met in Rio. Particular note should be made of the guidebooks prepared especially for the nine excursions held in connection with the Congress. Five of these were published both in English and French, two were published in English, and two in French. The volume *Abstracts of papers* contains abstracts of no less than 58 papers, on different aspects of Brazilian geography, submitted to the Congress, and furnishes a foretaste of the numerous geographical papers on Brazil to be published *in extenso* in the proceedings.

The first volume of the *Bibliografia geográfica do Brasil*, published by the Centro de Pesquisas de Geografia do Brasil, covers the year 1951 and contains brief summaries of more than 800 titles of writings which contribute to the knowledge of Brazilian geography. In addition to a general index and a list of abbreviations giving the name of the publishing institution and the place of publication, the volume includes an author index and an extensive subject index.

PHYSICAL GEOGRAPHY

2050. Ab'Sáber, Aziz Nacib. Contribuição à geomorfologia do estado do Maranhão (An Fac Fil, São Paulo, 1955-1956, 12 p.). Following a comparison of the so-called Maranhense Embayement, in the state of Maranhão, with the Amazonian estuary and the Parnaíba-Longa delta, the author considers the geomorphic evolution of the Golfão Maranhense, analyzing the main features of the fluviomarine lowland and of the surrounding hills of Tertiary age. Certain residual features found further inland are attributed to pediplanation. Finally, attention is directed to the tabular forms of the central and southern parts of the state.

2050a. ——. Contribuição à geomorfologia do litoral paulista (A Assoc Geóg Br, 8:1, 1953-1954, i. e. 1956, p. 67-131). Morphogenetical problems of the coast of the state of São Paulo.

2050b. ——. Depressões periféricas e depressões semi-áridas no nordeste do Brasil (B Paulista Geog, 22, março 1956, p. 3-18). According to the author, a special Brazilian type of interior drainage basins or "bolsones," obtaining during the Pleistocene epoch and the site of regional pediplanation, may still be observed, despite posterior rejuvenation which established outlets for the interior drainage.

2050c. ——. État actuel des connaissances sur les niveaux d'érosion et les surfaces d'aplanissement au Brésil (*in* Premier rapport de la Commission pour l'Étude et la Correlation des Niveaux d'Érosion et des Surfaces d'Aplanissement autour de l'Atlantique. V. Recherches en Amérique du Sud. N. Y., Office of the Secretary-Treasurer, International Geographical Union, 1956). A review of studies bearing upon the problem of erosion levels and planation surfaces in Brazil.

2050d. ——. Relêvo, estrutura e rêde hidrográfica do Brasil (B Geog, Rio, 14:133, maio-junho 1956, p. 225-268). A review of the structure, relief, and hidrography of Brazil, accompanied by a substantial bibliography. Mineral resources of different formations are examined in connection with structure. The morphology of each of the major physiographic units is considered separately, and the relations between morphology and land use are indicated in the Parana-Uruguay basin. The influence of relief on surface transportation is also brought out. In addition to the general characteristics and hydraulic potential of the Brazilian river basins, the author takes up the problem of fluvial transportation and that of the connection between the centripetal pattern of some basins and the establishment of towns.

2050e. ——. Significado geomorfológico da rêde hidrográfica do nordeste oriental brasileiro (An Fac Fil, São Paulo, 1956-1957, p. 69-76). Geomorphology of the eastern section of the northeast region of Brazil, with special reference to the drainage network.

2051. Almeida, Fernando F. M. O planalto basáltico da bacia do Paraná (B Paulista Geog, 24, out. 1956, p. 3-34).
After having considered the paleogeography and structure of the basaltic Parana river plateau, the author examines the various geomorphic units into which he divides the province, *viz.* (1) Upper Parana Basin, (2) Araucaria Plateau, (3) Missões zone, and (4) *Haedo cuesta.* In addition to maps and photographs, the study is enriched by a number of sections across the different subdivisions of the province.

2052. Andrade, Gilberto Osório de. Quelques niveaux de terrasses eustatiques sur le littoral nord-oriental et nord du Brésil (*in* Premier rapport de la Commission pour l'Étude et la Corrélation des Niveaux d'Érosion et des Surfaces d'Aplanissement autour de l'Atlantique. V. Recherches en Amérique du Sud. N. Y., Office of the Secretary-Treasurer, International Geographical Union, 1956, p. 57-64).
Study of terrace levels along the Pernambuco coast, on the islands of São Luis (Maranhão) and Mosqueiro (Para), as well as at several points along the lower Amazon and Solimões.

2053. Brasil sul: carta dos estados de Paraná, S. Catarina, e Rio Grande do Sul. 1:1,000,000. Pôrto Alegre, Brazil, Sacres, 1952. ₁Map₁
This map names 836 cities and towns. An inset for each of the three states lists the names of populated places, and also the old and modern names for places which have changed. It is an unusual map which looks like a brown ozalid with hand coloring, and is probably difficult to obtain. [A. C. Gerlach]

2054. Brazil. Conselho Nacional de Geografia. Carta do Brasil. 1:500,000. Rio, 1950-. ₁Map₁
A topographic map in 45 sheets, showing relief by contours, detailed hydrography, roads in three categories, railroads in nine, cities in six population groups, and national, state, district, and municipal boundaries. [A. C. Gerlach]

2055. ————. ————. Carta geográfica: estado do Espírito Santo. 1:400,000. Rio, 1954. ₁Map₁
Representative of a new series of general maps being prepared on the states of Brazil. Contours, transportation facilities, drainage, populated centers, and minor civil divisions are shown. [A. C. Gerlach]

2056. ————. ————. Mapa de vegetação do sudeste do Planalto Central. 1:-900,000. Rio, 1952. ₁Map₁
This map folds into an explanatory booklet by S. Faissol, *Vegetação e solos no sudeste do Planalto Central,* and shows the distribution of forest and grassland, without further details about either. [A. C. Gerlach]

2057. ————. ————. Mapa do Brasil. 1:5,000,000. Rio, 1954. ₁Map₁
This is an excellent general reference map. It shows many rivers and names them, the states are in colors, roads and railroads are distinctive, there are many place names, and insets show the climate, geology, relief, natural vegetation, and population of Brazil. [A. C. Gerlach]

2058. ————. ————. Mapa do Território do Amapá. 1:1,000,000. Rio, 1953. ₁Map₁
Although the map shows little but one road and a railroad plus drainage and a few place names, it represents more than has been mapped previously in that area just north of the mouth of the Amazon. [A. C. Gerlach]

2059. ————. ————; and Rio de Janeiro (state), Departamento Geográfico Estadual. Carta corográfica do estado do Rio de Janeiro. 1:400,000. Rio, 1953. ₁Map₁
Shows *municípios* (counties) in color, drainage, contours at 100 meters, detailed transportation, and many place names. [A. C. Gerlach]

2060. ————. Divisão de Geologia e Mineralogia. Carta geológica do Brasil. 1:100,000. Rio, 1954. ₁Map₁
At least two sheets of this detailed geological series were issued in 1954, covering the Campos-São Tome and Lagoa Fei-Xexe areas. Several additional sheets were planned. They show in colors the types of rocks as well as the structures and geologic ages of materials. [A. C. Gerlach]

2061. ————. Ministério da Guerra. Diretoria do Serviço Geográfico. Carta do Brasil. 1:50,000. Rio, 1948-. ₁Map₁
Many new sheets of this series are being published each year to supplement or revise the scores that were previously published for the more populous areas of Brazil. The contouring is not smoothly done, resembling form lines on some sheets, but the cultural information is carefully plotted and up to date for each new sheet as it is printed. For detailed information this series is of basic value. (A. C. Gerlach]

2062. ————. Ministério da Viação e Obras Públicas. Plano rodoviário nacional. ca. 1:12,000,000. Rio, 1952. 15 x 20 inches. ₁Map₁
The map presents a comprehensive highway program for Brazil, including existing roads, those under construction, and those planned for the future. The map is colorful and shows route numbers, state names and boundaries, and a table of distances. [A. C. Gerlach]

2063. Forest, J. Estados Unidos do Brasil. 1:4,000,000. Paris, Girard, Barrère & Thomas, 1956. ₁Map₁
This is a political map for lecture illustration. Color ribbons mark state boundaries. Rivers and tributaries are named. Major relief features are shown by form lines. Place names are numerous, giving the map a cluttered appearance. but adding to its reference value. Roads, rail-

roads, and airports are shown. Product names scattered over the map indicate the general regional distribution of agricultural and mineral resources. An inset shows the distribution of indigenous races. [A. C. Gerlach]

2064. **Freitas, Ruy Ozório de.** Considerações sôbre a tectônica e a geologia do vale do Paraiba (Engenh Min Met, 24:143, nov. 1956, p. 276-283).
Written as a guide to the Paraiba valley field trip, which took place during the 10th annual meeting of the Sociedade Brasileira de Geologia. The introduction presents the eastern section of the Brazilian shield, which, in the states of Rio de Janeiro and Minas Gerais, forms a tectonic plateau. After considering the characteristics of the Serra da Mantiqueira, attention is directed to the tectonics and sedimentation of the Paraiba valley, judged to be one of the best Brazilian examples of a rift valley. The author briefly reviews the precambrian formations and devotes some attention to the alkaline eruptives and the Tertiary and Quarternary deposits. A geologic itinerary of the field trip is provided.

2065. ————. Sedimentologia e paleogeografia de depósitos piemônticos na Usina de Peixotos (R Br Geog, 18:3, julho-set. 1956, p. 37-86).
Sediment analysis in and paleogeography of a portion of the Rio Grande valley on the São Paulo-Minas Gerais boundary.

2066. **Hueck, Kurt.** Mapa fitogeográfico do estado de São Paulo (B Paulista Geog, 22, março 1956, p. 19-25).
A contribution to the vegetation map of the state of São Paulo.

2067. **Instituto de Biologia e Pesquisas Tecnológicas. Serviço de Geologia.** Mapa geológico do estado do Paraná. 1:750,000. Rio, 1953. [Map]
Fairly detailed for its scale, this map also has structure sections to illustrate sub-surface geology. [A. C. Gerlach]

2068. **Instituto Geográfico de Agostini.** Brazil: political map. 1:4,000,000. Novara, Italy, 1956. [Map]
This is a wall map which covers, in addition to Brazil, all of Venezuela, the Guianas, Paraguay, Bolivia, and much of Argentina, Chile, Colombia, and Peru. The states of Brazil are in colors, population centers are in four categories, the drainage pattern is fairly complete for this scale, and relief is shown by subdued, generalized form lines. An inset shows the economic development and products of the states. [A. C. Gerlach]

2069. **Ira, Rudolf,** and **Edgar Klettner.** Atlas do Brasil Globo. Índice remissivo e descritivo dos topônimos por Lourenço Mario Prunes. Rio, Editôra Globo, 1953. 67 p. 12½ x 17 inches.
The index is noteworthy because it is annotated at length for each place listed, giving geographical coordinates, altitude, population, and political and commercial significance. The physical

and political maps are at a scale of 1:17,500,000 and maps of the states and territories vary from 1:5,500,000 to 1:3,250,000. The delineation of roads and railroads is poor because both are shown as plain red lines, distinguished from each other only by their width. [A. C. Gerlach]

2070. **King, Lester C.** A geomorfologia do Brasil oriental (R Br Geog, 18:2, abril-junho 1956, p. 147-265).
A valuable contribution to the geomorphology of eastern Brazil by the well-known African morphologist, in an unsatisfactory translation from the original English typescript. Abstracts in French, Spanish, English, German, and Esperanto.

2071. **Kuhlmann, Edgar.** Os tipos de vegetação do Brasil; elementos para uma classificação fisionômica (A Assoc Geóg Br, 8:1, 1953-1954, i. e. 1956, p. 133-180).
A physiognomic classification of the vegetal cover of Brasil is attempted, the following subdivisions being recognized: (1) forest types (perennial broadleaf forest, semideciduous broadleaf forest, and subtropical conifer forest); (2) the *caatinga;* (3) the *cerrado;* (4) mixed types (*restinga,* mixed forest and grasslands, Pantanal complex); (5) *campos* types (*campo limpo, campo sujo*).

2072. **Oliveira, Avelino Ignacio de.** Brazil (B Geol Soc Am, Memoir 65, June 1956, p. 1-62).
Written to accompany the Brazilian section of the Geologic Map of South America, this geological text, accompanied by well-chosen geological sections, should prove invaluable to geographers.

2073. **Oliveira, Paulo Erichsen de,** and **J. R. de Andrade Ramos.** Geologia das quadrículas de Recife e Pontas de Pedra. Rio, Divisão de Geologia e Mineralogia (Boletim, 151), 1956. 60 p.
Geological column and mineral resources of the area covered by two quadrangles of the geological map of Brasil, which accompany the text: Recife and Pontas de Pedra (Pernambuco).

2074. **Pardé, Maurice.** Quelques aperçus relatifs à l'hydrologie brésilienne. Edité par *La Houille blanche* a l'occasion du XVIII Congrès International de Géographie. Rio, 1956. 51 p.
The effect of climate and topography on the behavior of stream-flow in the Brazilian river basins is examined in the introduction. Separate chapters are devoted to average annual volume, seasonal variations, droughts and floods. Attention is directed to the normal values of run-off and to the variability of same, for the different basins. These are grouped according to characteristics of stream flow, as follows: tropical austral type, modified tropical boreal type, subequatorial or equatorial types, subtropical types with two maxima and variable complex types of great rivers, such as the Amazon and Parana. The author occupies himself with droughts in the southeast, Uruguay, and Amazon basins, but makes no mention of the northeast, possibly for

lack of data; the study of floods covers, among others, the Amazon, Parana, Paraguay, and Jacui basins. A final chapter is devoted to fluvial dynamics: the longitudinal and transverse profiles of Brazilian rivers are examined cursorily, as is the mention of their load.

2075. Rio Grande do Sul (state). Departamento Estadual de Estatística. Rio Grande do Sul. São Paulo, 1956. 20 x 20 inches. ₁Map₁

Drawn by F. P. Freitas. This is an outline map showing only the new administrative boundaries and centers for *munícipos* in Rio Grande do Sul. [A. C. Gerlach]

2076. Ruellan, Francis. Les caractères des aplanissements du relief brésilien (*in* Premier rapport de la Commission pour l'Étude et la Corrélation des Niveaux d'Érosion et des Surfaces d'Aplanissement autour de l'Atlantique. V. Recherches en Amérique du Sud. N. Y., Office of the Secretary-Treasurer, International Geographical Union, 1956, p. 73-79).

Planation surfaces in Brazil, with special emphasis on the effects of different types of climate.

2077. ————. Contribuição ao estudo da Serra do Caraça (A Assoc Geóg Br, 4:2, 1949-1950, i. e. 1956 p. 77-106).

Morphological and biographical results of field work conducted under the direction of the author in the Caraça massif (altitude over 2000 meters), which rises above the surface that acts as a divide between the São Francisco and Doce river basins.

2078. São Paulo (state). Instituto Geográfico e Geológico. Carta geográfica, estado de São Paulo. 1:1,000,000. São Paulo, 1954. ₁Map₁

This state map has an unusually detailed drainage pattern with names also in blue, and a good road and railroad net. In the margin is a table of distances, in kilometers, from São Paulo, including altitudes in meters for approximately 300 places. [A. C. Gerlach]

2079. Senna Sobrinho, Mariano. As estiagens na faixa de fronteira (B Geog Rio Grande do Sul, 1:3, março-abril 1956, p. 58-68).

Consideration of the normal values of rainfall in the state of Rio Grande do Sul and of the droughts which have occurred there.

2080. Setzer, José. A natureza e as possibilidades do solo no vale do rio Pardo entre os municípios de Caconde (S. P.) e Poços de Caldas (M. G.) (R Br Geog, 18:3, julho-set. 1956, p. 1-36).

Characteristics and agricultural potentialities of soils in the Pardo valley, at the São Paulo-Minas Gerais boundary. Geology, climate, topography, and man stressed as soil-forming factors.

2081. ————. Os solos do município de São Paulo (B Paulista Geog, 20, julho 1955, p. 3-30; 22, março 1956, p. 26-54; 24, out. 1956, p. 35-56).

A comprehensive study of the soils of the *município* of São Paulo and of their requirements. Measures are proposed to lower production costs in agriculture and to increase productivity per unit area.

2082. Touring Club do Brasil. Carta rodoviária do Brasil. 1:2,000,000. Rio, 1954. ₁Map₁

Shows detailed road network in six categories, minor political boundaries, and numerous place names. [A. C. Gerlach]

ECONOMIC GEOGRAPHY

2083. Abreu, Sílvio Fróes. Produção de diamantes (Dig Ec, 12:130, julho-agôsto 1956, p. 58-69).

Diamond production in Brazil.

2084. Araujo Filho, J. R. de. O café, riqueza paulista (B Paulista Geog, 23, julho 1956, p. 78-135).

After indicating the importance of coffee in the Brazilian economy and the foreign buying markets for this commodity, the author touches upon the problem of the agricultural labor force and proceeds to examine the spread of this crop from the lands of the state of Rio de Janeiro and of the São Paulo section of the Paraiba valley to the western plateau of the latter state. The techniques of coffee production are described in considerable detail and the role of coffee in shaping the rural landscape, as in the emergence of urban centers, is highlighted.

2085. Balanço agropecuário de 1955 (Conjunt Ec, 10:1, jan. 1956, p. 15-34, tables).

Statistical data on agricultural production in 1955.

2086. Bastos. A. de Miranda. Manganês do Amapá (Obs Ec Fin, 21:248, out. 1956, p. 40-50, illus., map).

Importance of the manganese deposits for the development of the Territory of Amapa, in Amazonia.

2087. Brochu, Michel. Cartes économiques des villes et régions de Rio de Janeiro et São Paulo (R Can Géog, 10:1, jan.-mars 1956, p. 17-39).

Different branches of industry in the cities of São Paulo and Rio de Janeiro, as well as in the surrounding area, represented according to annual power consumption. Comparisons drawn are somewhat misleading since São Paulo city is considered to comprise all the industry of greater São Paulo (including São Caetano and Santo Andre), and the same criterion is not adopted in the case of Rio de Janeiro, where not even all of the Federal District is included (Bangu, for instance, is placed outside Rio de Janeiro). The fact is that the industrial regions considered in the paper are not at all well defined.

2088. **Carvalho, Daniel de.** A evolução econômica Minas Gerias (Obs Ec Fin. 21:243, maio 1956, p. 22-27, illus.).
Economic evolution of the state of Minas Gerais.

2089. Comércio (Conjunt Ec, 10:1, jan. 1956, p. 47-56).
Brazil's foreign trade, with particular emphasis on coffee.

2090. Diminuição do ritmo de expansão industrial (Conjunt Ec, 10:1, jan. 1956, p. 37-46).
Indices of industrial production, 1944-1955.

2091. **Geiger, Pedro Pinchas, and Myriam Gomes Coelho Mesquita.** Estudos rurais da baixada fluminense. Rio, Conselho Nacional de Geografia (Biblioteca geográfica brasileira), 1956. 211 p., illus.
A series of studies dealing mainly with the economic geography of the coastal area of the state of Rio de Janeiro, the so-called "baixada fluminense." In the final chapter, "Conclusions," an attempt is made to characterize four economic regions (Guanabara, Lagoons, Central, and Campos), subdivided into zones according to the predominant economic activity.

2092. **Köhler, Günther.** Verkehrsgeographische Übersicht von Südamerika (Petermanns Geog Mitteilungen, 100:2, 1956, p. 115-121).
Contains a map on the transportation geography of South America, at 1:10,000,000.

2093. **Leonardos, Othon Henry.** Recursos minerais do Triângulo Mineiro (Engenh Min Met, 24:140, agôsto 1956; 24:141, set. 1956; 24:142, out. 1956; 19 p., illus., maps).
Mineral resources of the so-called Triângulo Mineiro, the triangular panhandle of western Minas Gerais, wedged in between the Paranaiba and Grande rivers.

2094. **Lima, Rubens Rodrigues.** A agricultura nas várzeas do estuário do Amazonas. Belém, Brazil, Instituto Agronómico do Norte (Boletim técnico, 33), 1956. 164 p., illus.
Flood-plain agriculture at the mouth and lower course of the Amazon and Para rivers and lower sections of tributaries. Tidal influence on sedimentation. Agricultural practices and results.

2095. **Magnanini, Ruth Lopes da Cruz.** Condições climáticas das regiões cafeeiras do Brasil (R Br Geog, 18:3, julho-set. 1956, p. 136-152).
Climatic conditions of the various coffee-producing areas of Brazil. Special consideration is given to the São Paulo-Parana plateau and to the nucleus formed by the so-called Zona da Mata of Minas Gerais, the state of Espirito Santo, and the northern section of the state of Rio de Janeiro, but reference is also made to areas of scanty production such as the Bahia plateau, the Borborema region, the Minas Gerais panhandle (Triângulo Mineiro), south central Goias, and southern Mato Grosso.

2096. **Pinto, Maria Magdalena Vieira.** Contribuição ao estudo da pesca na região do rio Arari, ilha de Marajó (R Br Geog, 18:3, julho-set. 1956, p. 87-122).
Fresh water fishing on Marajo, the large island at the mouth of the Amazon. Seasons, fishing techniques and equipment, processing of the catch, commerce, as well as way of life of the fishermen, are dealt with.

2097. Recuperação de um vale (Obs Ec Fin, 21:240-241, fev.-março 1956, p. 80-108, illus., maps).
Plans for the development of the São Francisco Valley.

2098. **Rezende, E. da Motta.** O plano brasileiro de eletrificação e as possibilidades da energia atômica (Aguas En El, 7:25, março 1956, p. 3-13, table).
National plan for electrification. Atomic energy in Brazil.

2099. **Ribeiro, Paulo de Assis.** Estrutura, economia e política dos transportes. Rio, Instituto Nacional do Livro (Biblioteca de divulgação cultural, série B, 1), 1956. 216 p., illus.
After considering the general technical and economic aspects of transportation, in the first half of the book, the author occupies himself with the problem of transportation in Brazil. Geographical, socio-economic, technical, economic, and other aspects are considered. Suggestions are brought forward for a national transportation policy. Maps and graphs are included.

2100. **Rio Grande do Sul (state). Comissão Estadual de Energia Elétrica. Diretoria dos Serviços Auxiliares. Estatística.** Rio Grande do Sul: situação das usinas em funcionamento construidas, encampadas e instalações de emergência. 1:2,000,000. São Paulo, 1954. [Map]
Power lines are in seven categories of voltage, and power plants or generators are classified according to stage of completion and source of power (water, coal, mixed). [A. C. Gerlach]

2101. ————. **Departamento Estadual de Estatística.** Rio Grande do Sul, produção agrícola. São Paulo, 1953. [Maps]
A series of 7 x 7-inch maps shows the area, production, and value of flax, grapes, kidney beans, onions, potatoes, rice, soy beans, tobacco, and wheat. [A. C. Gerlach]

2102. **Rocha, Domingos Fleury da.** Preservação dos recursos naturais, reflorestamento e eletrificação (Engenh Min Met, 23:136, abril 1956, p. 191-198).
Need for conservation of natural resources stressed; effect of industry on deforestation. De-

velopment of hydroelectricity, an important factor in the preservation of forests.

2103. Santos, Milton. Zona do cacau. Introdução ao estudo geográfico. Bahia, Brazil, Artes Gráf., 1955. 114 p.
An excellent introduction to one of Brazil's important and little-known regions. Chapters are devoted to the geographic setting, the relation of cacao culture to climatic and other natural features, cacao culture, the settlement process and population, the problems of the rural and urban habitats, transportation, diet, the human types found in the zone, and to monoculture. [T. L. Smith]

2104. Schröder, Rudolf. Einige tropische Nutzpflanzen Brasiliens in ihrer Abhängigkeit vom Klima (Staden-Jahrbuch, 4, 1956, p. 19-30).
Climatic controls of certain tropical crops in Brazil.

2105. ————. Die klimatischen Bedingungen für den Kaffeeanbau auf der Erde, insbesondere in Zentral und Südamerika (Petermanns Geog Mitteilungen, 100:2, 1956, p. 122-136, 2 maps).
Relationships of coffee production and climate by a technician working with the Instituto Agronômico at Campinas (São Paulo).

2106. Strauch, Ney. Observações relativas ao minério de ferro e à siderurgia no planalto de Minas Gerais (A Assoc Geóg Br, 8:1, 1953-1954, i. e. 1956, p. 313-341).
Iron ore and iron industry in the state of Minas Gerais, with suggestions for future planning.

2107. Tourinho, Borba. Petróleo do Brasil (Obs Ec Fin, 21:245, julho 1956, p. 20-26, illus., tables).
Magnitude of reserves in the Bahian oil fields.

POPULATION AND SETTLEMENT

2108. Avila, Fernando Bastos de. L'immigration au Brésil. Rio, Agir, 1956. 223 p.
Whereas the first of the three parts of the book is devoted to a discussion of the problem of migrations, within its doctrinal context, and the final chapters attempt to establish a sound immigration policy for Brazil, the student of the cultural geography of this country will find much interesting materials in the second part, e.g., the demographic, economic, and social impacts of immigration. Many interesting items may be culled in the extensive bibliography.

2109. Azevedo, Aroldo de. Vilas e cidades do Brasil colonial; ensaio de geografia urbana retrospectiva. São Paulo, Universidade de São Paulo, Faculdade de Filosofia, Ciências e Letras (Boletim, 208; Geografia, 11), 1956. 96 p., illus.
By describing the centers of population in each century since the beginning of European settlement, the writer makes an attempt to depict the evolution of urban life in Brazil. Some of the characteristics of the colonial centers, such as preferred sites, origin, ground plan, and functions are examined, and attention is directed to what the writer calls an anti-urbanizing tendency of colonial Brazil.

2110. Bernardes, Lysia Maria Cavalcanti. Problemas da utilização da terra nos arredores de Curitiba (R Br Geog, 18:4, abril-junho 1956, p. 127-134).
An analysis of present conditions of land utilization in the area of European, non-Portuguese settlements around Curitiba, state capital of Parana, which brings out the predominance of backward agricultural systems, notwithstanding the proximity of the consuming center. Natural conditions (forests, open grassland), characteristics of the immigrants, as well as advantages and disadvantages of the proximity to the urban center are examined.

2111. Causas e efeitos do êxodo rural (R Br Mun, 9:35-36, julho-dez. 1956, p. 198-208).

2112. Dozier, Craig L. Northern Paraná, Brazil. An example of organized regional development (Geog R, 46:3, July 1956, p. 318-333).
Opening up of the newest and richest coffee-producing area in Brazil.

2113. Figueiredo, Áureo Pinto de. Distribuição territorial dos alemães e dos austríacos presentes no Brasil em 1950 (R Br Est, 17:67, julho-set. 1956, p. 237-240, tables).
Geographical distribution of German- and Austrian-born persons enumerated in the 1950 census.

2114. Geiger, Pedro Pinchas, and Ruth Lyra Santos. Notas sôbre a evolução da ocupação humana na baixada fluminense (A Assoc Geóg Br, 8:1, 1953-1954, i. e. 1956, p. 233-264).
Three phases in the economic evolution of the Guanabara lowlands, based respectively on sugar cane, on citrus, and on industrial and urban development. Relations with transportation. Attention is directed to the persistence of the old agrarian structure.

2115. Immigrant colonization in Brazil, as seen by European experts (Migr Dig, 3, 1956, 36 p.).
Multilingual issue with articles in English, French, or German, followed in some cases by summaries in Portuguese. Reprints, articles and excerpts which have already appeared (e. g., Leo Waibel, Herbert Wilhelmy) and contains a few new articles written especially for this issue.

2116. James, Preston E., and Speridião Faissol. The problem of Brazil's capital city (Geog R, 46:3, July 1956, p. 301-317).

Reasons for and against moving Brazil's capital analysed. Stock is taken of some of the problems of the Central Plateau, to which the capital is to be removed. Principles adopted in the selection of a site are reviewed and the conclusion is reached that the establishment of the capital in the interior will not change the basic pattern of population and settlement.

2117. Magnanini, Ruth Lopes da Cruz. Possibilidades de povoamento da bacia do São Francisco (A Assoc Geóg Br, 8:1, 1953-1954, i. e. 1956, p. 265-311).
General characteristics of the São Francisco basin examined in connection with the possibilities for settlement. Emphasis is given to the need for soil and water conservation through sound agricultural practices. Various obstacles to settlement are considered.

2118. Menezes, Adriano. O problema da colonização na Amazônia (R Br Mun, 9: 30, jan.-março 1956, p. 18-33).
The problem of settlement in Amazonia.

2119. Mortara, Giorgio. Distribuição territorial dos japonêses no Brasil (R Br Est, 17:65, jan.-março 1956, p. 1-3, tables).
Geographical distribution of Japanese-born persons enumerated in the 1920, 1940, and 1950 censuses.

2120. Petrone, Pasquale. O homem paulista (B Paulista Geog, 23, julho 1956, p. 39-77).
An analysis of the population of São Paulo state: density by areas, growth, sex, age, race and nativity, religions, educational and occupational composition. The paper comprises a review of the settlement and a cursory survey of the urban network of São Paulo and is concluded with the presentation of what the author calls geo-human regions of the state.

2121. Valverde, Orlando. O uso da terra no leste da Paraiba (A Assoc Geóg Br, 8:1, 1953-1954, i. e. 1956, p. 181-232).
Presenting a regional division of the eastern section of the state of Paraiba, the author makes a separate analysis of the prevailing land use in the Mata, in the Agreste, and with greater detail, in the Brejo zones. A land use map of the region and suggestions for rural development are presented.

REGIONAL GEOGRAPHY

2122. Ab'Sáber, Aziz Nacib. A terra paulista (B Paulista Geog, 23, julho 1956, p. 5-38).
An analysis of the physical basis of the geography of São Paulo state: geology, main aspects and morphological development of relief, soils, climate, vegetation.
The author concludes with the physical basis of *paulista* wealth. Several maps, sections, and a morphological map of São Paulo state accompany the text.

2123. ————, and **Nilo Bernardes.** Excursion guidebook, no. 4: Paraiba valley,

Serra da Mantiqueira, and São Paulo city and surroundings. Rio, Eighteenth International Geographical Congress, I. G. U., Brazilian National Committee, 1956. 269 p.
English translation by Richard P. Momsen, Jr., and John Knox; a French translation by Annette and Francis Ruellan was published simultaneously. A general description of southeastern Brazil, the "core area" of the country, including a summary of the morphology and tectonics, climate, soils, and vegetation, and, especially, settlement and present-day occupance patterns, prepares the reader to understand apparently contradictory aspects of the cultural landscape. Separate chapters are devoted to the physical and human geography of the various regions to be traversed. A final chapter directs attention to points of interest along the itinerary.

2124. Almeida, Fernando Flávio Marques de, and **Miguel Alves de Lima.** Excursion guidebook, no. 1: The west central plateau and Mato-Grosso "Pantanal." Rio, Eighteenth International Geographical Congress, I. G. U., 1956. 129 p., illus., maps.
English translation by Richard P. Momsen, Jr. Opens with an extensive chapter dealing with the geomorphology of west central Brazil. The crystalline plateaus, the Araguaia peneplain, the Parana river sedimentary basin, the basaltic and sedimentary plateaus, and, finally, the Paraguay "depression" with its Cuiaba peneplain, paleozoic massifs, and "Pantanal" floodplain, are taken up separately. This morphological analysis is rounded out with a study of the origin and evolution of the regional drainage pattern. The chapter on climate directs attention to the effects of air masses and closes with a description of the types of climate found in the region. Stock is taken of the different types of forest to be seen during the field trip (equatorial, tropical, and subtropical), the origin and distribution of the *cerrado* and *campo* formations are discussed, and the characteristics of the Pantanal vegetational complex are described. A short chapter is devoted to general aspects of the region's soils. A cursory study of the opening up and settlement of the region follows this rather extended description of the physical aspects of the region. A final chapter considers the main points of interest along the scheduled itinerary.

2125. Barros, Gilberto Leite de. O Território Federal do Amapá (Dig Ec, 13:132, nov.-dez. 1956, p. 136-149).
Physical, historical, and economic data on the Federal Territory of Amapa, at the mouth of the Amazon river.

2126. Bernardes, Lysia Maria Cavalcanti. Excursion guidebook, no. 5: The coastal lowlands and sugarcane zone of the state of Rio de Janeiro. Rio, Eighteenth International Geographical Congress, I. G. U., 1956. 195 p., illus., maps.
English translation by John Knox; a French translation by Pierre and Juliette P. Mombeig was published simultaneously. A panoramic

treatment of the Baixada Fluminense precedes the examination of the regions traversed during the excursion. The physical characteristics which give the Baixada its individuality while creating a variety of landscapes are analyzed. In all of these landscapes, the initial process of occupance was the same and the spread of settlement is attributed to the so-called sugarcane cycle. The succeeding chapters are devoted to the coastal massif and the lowlands east of Guanabara Bay, the region of Araruama-Cabo Frio, the Barra de São João and Macae region, and the sugarcane producing area of Campos. Numerous illustrations. Special mention may be made of the geomorphic interpretations of the region in general and of the Cabo Frio area in particular.

2127. Domingues, Alfredo José Porto, and Elza Coelho de Souza Keller. Livret-guide, no. 6: Bahia. Rio, XVIIIème Congrès International de Géographie, U. G. I., 1956. 256 p., illus., maps.

French translation by Michel and Regina Rochefort. An excursion guidebook dealing with the eastern half of the state of Bahia, from Ilheus in the south to Paulo Afonso in the north. The first of four parts considers physical and cultural geography of the southern littoral and the eastern slopes of the Bahian plateau, highlighting three areas dominated respectively by coconut, cacao, and cattle economy. In a similar fashion, the second part takes up the Bahian plateau, subdivided into various sections (Conquista, Itiruçu, Cruz das Almas), separated by the Contas and Paraguaçu valleys; careful attention is directed to the pastoral economy of the Conquista section and the Contas valley, to farming in the Itiruçu section, and, especially, to the tobacco growing area of Cruz das Almas. The third part is devoted to the Reconcavo and the city of Salvador (position and function, site development and urban physiognomy). The fourth part considers the semi-arid *sertão*, four subdivisions being recognized: the Feira de Santana, Caatinga, and Cicero Dantas section, and the Agua Branca and Tacaratu ranges. Additional details are given in the appended itinerary.

2128. França, Ary. Guide of excursion, 3: The coffee trail and pioneer fringes. Rio, XVIII International Geographical Congress, I. G. U., Brazilian National Committee, 1956. 255 p.

English translation by David Maybury Lewis and Renata Hamond. A French translation by Fr. Nicole Lépine was published simultaneously. Guidebook for an excursion over the same itinerary followed in southeastern Brazil by the migration of coffee production from the Rio de Janeiro coast to western São Paulo and northern Parana. Relief, geology, climate, soil, and vegetation are considered, and the influence of natural factors on the expansion of coffee cultivation is brought out. Each of the individual areas successively invaded by the coffee bush, in its westward march, is examined separately: the lowlands of the state of Rio de Janeiro, the crystalline and sedimentary plateaus, and the north of Parana state. In the chapter dealing with the crystalline plateau, special attention is devoted to the two great urban centers of São Paulo state which are so closely dependent upon each other:

the metropolis of the plateau, São Paulo, and Santos.

2129. Geiger, Pedro Pinchas. A região setentrional da baixada fluminense (R Br Geog, 18:1, jan.-fev. 1956, p. 3-69).

A regional study of the northern section of the state of Rio de Janeiro including the Paraiba plain. Following an account of the general features of the physical setting, the major morphological units of the region are described: the argillaceous plan, the strip of beaches, the *taboleiros* and the crystalline hills. After delineating the main lines of human occupance, an account is rendered of the regional economy, and separate consideration is given to the sugar economy, livestock breeding, coffee and small-time agriculture (grain and manioc). The work is all the better for good maps dealing with morphological features, soils, and economic regions.

2130. Lima, Miguel Alves de. Contribuição ao estudo da campanha gaucha (A Assoc Geóg Br, 8:1, 1953-1954, i. e. 1956, p. 343-375).

Relief, climate, vegetation, and economy of the Campanha region of the state of Rio Grande do Sul, with emphasis on controversial problems and on aspects hitherto not studied.

2131. Melo, Mario Lacerda de. Excursion guidebook, no. 7; North-East. Rio, XVIIIth International Geographical Congress, I. G. U., 1956. 256 p., illus., maps.

English translation by Rod W. Horton; a French translation by Pierre and Juliette P. Mombeig was simultaneously published. A study of the major regional units of the eastern section of the northeast of Brazil as defined in terms of their climatic, phytogeographic, and/or morphologic features. Land use and economic organization are brought out in the characterization of each region. Thus, fishing and coconut planting keynote the littoral zone, whereas sugar cane plantations and the sugar industry are inseparable from the so-called Zona da Mata. In considering the complex area designated as the Agreste, the author notes the great regional significance of the humid Brejos, more densely settled and more intensively farmed; the special case of the Brejo of Paraiba is considered in detail. In the chapters dealing with the *sertões*, the effects of semi-arid climate on the vegetation and morphology as on cattle raising and cotton planting is duly emphasized; the area of Triunfo, an island of humidity, is dealt with separately. Urban life is focused within regional frameworks, devoted to Caruaru, Arcoverde, and Campina Grande trading centers, and Pesqueira, food processing center. The regional importance of Recife, the great metropolis of the northeast, justifies the special chapter dedicated to it.

2132. Moreira, Eidorfe. Conceito de Amazônia (R Br Mun, 9:34, abril-junho 1956, p. 105-110).

Different criteria for delimiting the area of Amazonia.

2133. Müller, Nice Lecocq. Contribuição

ao estudo do norte do Paraná (B Paulista Geog, 22, março 1956, p. 55-97).

A regional study of the northern part of Parana state, settled in consequence of the pioneer front advancing from São Paulo state. The southern limits of the region are taken to be those of possible coffee production. The physical individuality of the region arises from the presence of a transitional climate, of a broadleafed forest, and, except for the southeastern section, of fertile "terra roxa" soil.

The pattern of land occupance is presented in the light of the dynamics of settlement. Coffee is the common denominator in the regional landscape, within which differentiation springs from the degree to which coffee is preponderant, from the dominance of small or large landholdings and the way in which this is reflected in the rural habitat, and from the smaller or greater age of settlement. The economic significance of northern Parana is highlighted by an analysis of its capacity to produce coffee. Here are to be found the *municípios* which boast the highest production rates in the entire country; total production is continually increasing and the production per unit of land far exceeds that of São Paulo state.

2134. Soares, Lúcio de Castro. Excursion guidebook, no. 8: Amazônia. Rio, Eighteenth International Geographical Congress, I. G. U., 1956. 216 p., illus., maps.

English translation by Richard P. Momsen, Jr. A definition of the area known as the Brazilian Amazon (or Amazonia) and an indication of its boundaries precede a review of the general physical and cultural geography of the region. Another chapter deals with the first five-year plan for the development of the Amazon region. The fourth chapter is devoted to the study of selected areas to be visited during the field trip (Manaus and its environs, the so-called lower Amazon, Amapa Territory, Belem, and the strip along the Belem-Bragança railway.) An itinerary indicates points of major interest to be visited during the excursion.

2135. Sternberg, Hilgard OReilly. A água e O homem na Várzea do Careiro. xii, 29 p., illus.; portfolio containing 17 maps, 1 cross section. Private lithoprinted edition.

Human occupance of a section of the Amazon flood-plain, in respect to the geomorphic activity (extensively discussed) and yearly floods of the river. Among the cartographical materials is a geomorphic map at 1:60,000 of the area, which lies in the vicinity of Manaus.

2136. ⸺. Geography's contribution to the better use of resources (*in* The future of arid lands. Washington, American Association for the Advancement of Science, 1956, p. 200-220).

In showing how the work of geographers can contribute to the better use of the resources of arid and semi-arid lands, the paper considers some aspects of the dry section of northeastern Brazil, afflicted with recurring periods of drought. The creation of man-made desert landscapes, it is pointed out, leads to confusion concerning the true extent of the so-called "drought-polygon." After reviewing various criteria for the delimitation of the area, the utility of large surface storage reservoirs is examined and the conclusion is reached that development schemes should make every effort to promote full and competent use of the humid *serras* and tablelands, natural cores of more intensive land occupancy.

2137. Strauch, Ney. Livret-guide, no. 2: Zone métallurgique de Minas Gerais et vallée du Rio Doce. Rio, XVIIIème Congrès International de Géographie, U. G. I., 1956. 161 p., illus., maps.

French translation by Lucian Pouesselle. The area considered embraces a section of the coastal plain, the coastal ramp of the plateau, the Rio Doce valley, and the iron mining and manufacturing section of the plateau of Minas Gerais. General considerations about the eastern littoral strip precede a more detailed examination of the coast at Rio and Vitoria. In considering the Atlantic ramp of the plateau, the Serra do Mar, the Paraiba valley, and the so-called Zona da Mata (i. e., forest zone) of Minas Gerais are taken up separately, special attention being given to the city of Juiz de Fora. Although the Rio Doce valley may be considered to be part of the coastal ramp, the fact that it was to be one of the main features to be considered during the field trip, explains why it was made the object of a chapter to itself; in this, physical aspects, settlement patterns, and types of land use of the different sections of the valley are analyzed. The chapter dedicated to the area characterized by iron mining and manufacturing deals with the site and position of Belo Horizonte: general aspects of the human geography as well as special problems stemming from the exploitation of the iron ores. A final chapter directs attention to points of special interest along the itinerary chosen for the excursion.

2138. Valderde, Orlando. Excursion guidebook, no. 9: Southern plateau. Rio, Eighteenth International Geographical Congress, U. G. I., 1956. 298 p., illus., maps.

English translation by Richard P. Momsen, Jr., and John Mulholland; a French translation by Michel and Regina Rochefort was published simultaneously. The first part, after delimiting the region, deals in a general way with its relief, structure, climate, vegetation, settlement, and, in relation to the latter point, the subject of regional agricultural systems. The second part describes the main characteristics of the smaller area units to be traversed, *viz*, in the state of Parana, the so-called Northern Parana section, the Apucarana-Castro section, the Campos Gerais, the Curitiba plateau, the Serra do Mar, and the coastal plan; in Santa Catarina, the Itajai, Itapocu, and other small valleys, the littoral, the island of Santa Catarina, and the Campos of Lajes; in Rio Grande do Sul, the campos of Vacaria, the area of Italian and German settlement on the plateau and on its slopes, the state capital of Porto Alegre, the section between this city and Santa Cruz, and, finally, the tobacco growing area around this center. An outline of the itinerary, making references to the text, concludes the guidebook.

URBAN GEOGRAPHY

2139. Azevedo, Aroldo de. Barão de Cocais; estudo geográfico de um pequeno centro siderúrgico de Minas Gerais (A Assoc Geóg Br, 4:2, 1949-1950, i. e. 1956, p. 41-76).

Study of a small urban center (state of Minas Gerais), where the iron industry is dominant and which got started as a result of gold mining activity. Its origin and present function are revealed by the physiognomy and structure of the town. The author, in charge of a group committed to the study of the region, examines the small urban nucleus, the activities related to the iron industry, the agricultural possibilities of the rural zone, and the relations obtaining between the latter and the manufacturing center.

2140. Mattos, Dirceu Lino de. Principais aspectos da geografia urbana de Belo Horizonte (A Assoc Geóg Br, 4:2, 1949-1950, i. e. 1956, p. 11-35).

Report of a study group on the geography of Belo Horizonte, state capital of Minas Gerais. An analysis of site and location is followed by a description of the urban panorama. Special chapters are devoted to truck-farming zones on the outskirts of the city and the manufacturing satellite town, planned to incorporate the growing industry of Belo Horizonte.

2141. Santos, Elina O. Ponta Grossa, capital regional do oeste do Paraná (B Paulista Geog, 24, out. 1956, p. 57-80).

After giving an account of the principal urban centers in Parana and of the general characteristics of the western part of this state, the author proceeds to the study of Ponta Grossa. The establishment and site of this regional center are analyzed, as are its trading functions, which result from its position at the intersection of the north-south and east-west axis of transportation. This is followed by a description of Ponta Grossa and an appraisal of the outlook for this modern city.

2142. Santos, Milton. O papel metropolitano da cidade do Salvador (R Br Mun, 9:35-36, julho-dez. 1956, p. 185-190).

The metropolitan function of Salvador, state capital of Bahia.

2143. Sette, Hilton. Pesqueira. Aspectos de sua geografia urbana e de suas interrelações regionais. Recife, Brazil, 1956. 104 p.

Urban geography of Pesqueira, a town of the *agreste* section of Pernambuco. Following a description of the physical aspects of the region, the author considers the reasons for the choice of the site, and the development, present-day physiognomy, and functions of the town. Manufacturing overshadows other activities, for Pesqueira is prominent in the production of jellies and other canned foods.

Government

ASHER N. CHRISTENSEN

This year's listings, like those of no. 19 of the *Handbook*, contain many items relating to what might be called the more basic and fundamental factors influencing the government and politics of Latin America. Users of No. 20 will find books, monographs, or pamphlets on the nature of Latin American revolutions, the causes of the all-too-prevalent dictatorships, the nature of Latin American presidential governments (one writer labels them "legalized dictatorships"), and how and why the politics of Latin America differ from politics in the U. S. A few of the publications discuss the role of the armed forces in the political life of the nation; two noteworthy ones come from Chile and Paraguay.

The more traditional political subjects are also well covered. Several monographs on political parties are listed; public administration and municipal government are among the other topics discussed. A book on municipal government from Brazil has a splendid bibliography on local government in that country. In general, it is the opinion of the editor that the writers of this year's publications have given more attention to the inclusion of a bibliography than has been the case in past years. If this trend should be continued, all scholars in the field of Latin American government will be grateful.

With reference to more current political events, the MNR (Movimiento Nacionalista Revolucionario) in Bolivia has now been in power long enough to warrant publications discussing its ideology, its legislative program, and its accomplishments. Almost all of the items from Guatemala relate to that nation's internal difficulties; as yet there seems to be little consideration of what must be done to confront basic social and economic problems in order that the nation may return to a fuller democratic way of life. The fall of Perón naturally loosed a flood of publications in Argentina. They seem to fall into three categories: condemnations of the former regime; the task of liquidating the confusion, not to say the chaos, emanating from that era; and the basic problems with which Aramburu—or any of his successors—must deal. An excellent discussion of these almost innumerable books and pamphlets, and their relation to the politics of Argentina, is found in Fritz L. Hoffman's "Peron and after: a review article" (HAHR, 36:4, Nov. 1956, p. 510-528).

GENERAL

2200. Carril, Bonifacio del. Problemas de la revolución y la democracia. B. A., Emecé (Cuadernos de ensayos), 1956. 77 p.

Four very good essays are contained in this little brochure. They deal with "Liberty and law"; "Revolution and legitimacy"; "Politics and force"; and "Democracy and authenticity." The third is concerned with the question, so pertinent for the region, of when recourse to force to overthrow a regime is justified.

2201. Fitzgibbon, Russell H. Catholicism, Protestantism, and politics in Latin America (Hanover F, 2:1, winter 1956, p. 3-13).

Another of Professor Fitzgibbon's concise and excellently written studies. In general, the subject is the changing political position of the Church in Latin America.

2201a. ————. Revolutions: Western

127

Hemisphere (South Atl Q, 55:3, July 1956, p. 263-279).
A brief but incisive essay on eight revolutions of the recent past or present. The author thoughtfully considers what the eight changes of regime had in common.

2201b. ————. A statistical evaluation of Latin American democracy (West Pol Q, 9:3, Sept. 1956, p. 607-619).
A careful statistical study, and an evaluation of the status of democracy in Latin America based upon a "poll" taken by the author in 1945, 1950, and 1955. Most of those polled are from academic circles; all are known specialists in the area.

2202. Gaxiola, Federico Jorge. La crisis del pensamiento político, y otros ensayos. México, Porrúa (Biblioteca mexicana, 17), 1956. 256 p.
This is a collection of very good essays on political theory in general; it is especially good in the discussion of federalism. The treatment is general, and it is not oriented to Latin America specifically.

2203. Livingston, William S. Federalism and constitutional change. Oxford, Clarendon Press, 1956. 380 p., tables.
This volume is concerned with constitutional change in federal systems in general, and most of the material in it refers to the U. S., Canada, Australia, and Switzerland. One chapter, however, has a short discussion of the process of constitutional amendment in the other federal systems of the world; it includes those of Latin America.

2204. Pierson, William Whatley, and Federico G. Gil. Governments of Latin America. N. Y., McGraw-Hill, 1957. 514 p., maps, tables.
This new college text discusses government topically rather than country by country. It begins with good, and informative, "background" chapters on the people, the land, and the economy. These are followed by the chapters on the political organization; the executive, legislative, and judicial branches, etc. A considerable portion of the book is devoted to the functions of government, with very fine chapters on labor and social legislation, education, and public finance. Most of the chapters have a short but a very well selected bibliography.

2205. Public Administration Clearing House. La administración pública en la América Latina. Un informe al Consejo Interamericano Económico y Social de conformidad con la resolución 49/53. Washington, Unión Panamericana, 1955. 87 p.
Although brief, this is a fine analysis of the general trends in public administration in the entire region, and a discussion of its present needs and probable future developments. Issued also in English: Public administration in Latin America, 1955, 74 p.

2206. Ravines, Eudocio. América Latina, un continente en erupción. B. A., Claridad (Biblioteca Hombres e ideas, 1. serie, 36), 1956. 263 p.
This is a very thought-provoking volume which has as its point of reference the unique nature of politics in Latin America. The chapters on industrialization, agrarian reform, and "The forging of a democratic regime" are very well done.

2207. Telles Júnior, Goffredo. Resistência violenta aos governos injustos (R Fac Dir, 50, 1955, p. 192-219).
Interesting as a Latin American (in this case a Brazilian) theory of when violent resistance to government is justified.

2208. Waiss, Óscar. Nacionalismo y socialismo en América Latina. Santiago, Prensa Latinoamericana (Col. América libre), 1954. 168 p.
The author, a lawyer whose political orientation is socialist, makes an analysis of Latin American revolutions in Marxist terms. Of most value to the student of government are chapters 2, "Agrarian roots"; 3, "The basic problems—landowners and peasants"; 6 and 7, which contain a brief discussion of the socialist parties of the major Latin American states; and 9 and 10, which have as their central theme the character of Latin American revolutions. The author includes a very short bibliography; there are no footnotes.

2209. Wilgus, A. Curtis (ed). The Caribbean: its political problems. Gainesville, Fla., University of Florida Press (School of Inter-American Studies, 1:6), 1956. 324 p.
An excellent collection of papers on the politics, political organization, and political problems of the Caribbean area. Similar collections on the politics of the other major regions of Latin America would indeed be welcomed by all students of Latin American political institutions.

ARGENTINA

2210. Argentina. Cámara de Diputados de la Nación. División Archivo, Publicaciones, y Museo. Composición de la Cámara de Diputados de la Nación por partidos políticos y distritos electorales, 1912-1943. B. A., Imp. Congreso de la Nación, 1956. 43 p.
The composition of the Argentine Chamber classified by party and by electoral district for each of the sessions from the adoption of the Sáenz Peña law in 1912 to the end of the Castillo administration in 1943. A very useful publication.

2210a. ————. President. Mensaje del Presidente de la Nación Argentina General Juan Perón al inaugurar el 89. período ordinario de sesiones del Honorable

Congreso Nacional. Conceptos doctrinarios. B. A., 1955. 62 p.

This annual message of the President is of more than normal interest. It was the last delivered by Perón to the Congress. In it he notes the great gains made in the years 1946 to 1955.

2210b. ————. ————. Mensaje del Presidente de la Nación Argentina General Juan Perón al inaugurar el 89. período ordinario de sesiones del Honorable Congresa Nacional. II. Reseña general de actividades. B. A., 1955. 417 p.

This volume supplements President Perón's last message to the Argentine Congress (see item above). Each of the ministries makes its annual report. That of the Ministry of Finance has valuable data on the budget, new taxes, and other fiscal material.

2211. Castelli, Elena. Segunda tiranía. Mendoza, Argentina, Tall. Gráf. D'Accurzio, 1955. 116 p.

The second tyranny (the first being that of Rosas) is of course the Perón administration. The preface notes that the book was written in 1953 but that it could not then be published. There is a good chapter on the presidency.

2212. Confalonieri, Orestes D. Perón contra Perón. B. A., Antygua, 1956. 398 p.

The author points out the contradictions of Perón and the Perón ideology by quoting from the speeches of Perón and following these quotations by citing decrees and other governmental actions which contradict the spoken word. The book is a good source of documentary materials on the Perón administration.

2213. Cúneo, Dardo. Juan B. Justo y las luchas sociales en la Argentina. B. A., Alpe, 1956. 469 p.

This is the second, and a much fuller edition, of a book first published in 1942. It is a full account of the life and political action of Justo; the author makes a careful evaluation of Justo's contribution to government and politics in Argentina.

2213a. ————. El romanticismo político: Leopoldo Lugones, Roberto J. Payró, José Ingenieros, Macedonio Fernández, Manuel Ugarte, Alberto Gerchunoff. B. A., Ediciones Transición, 1955. 139 p., illus.

Biographical essays, mostly of prominent Argentine socialists who were politically active at the turn of the century. Of interest to students of the Argentine socialist movement.

2214. Estrada, José María de. El legado del nacionalismo. B. A., Gure, 1956. 94 p.

The writer quite objectively discusses the general theory of nationalism, and why Argentina is nationalistic in a broad and general, as contrasted with a narrowly political, sense.

2215. Frondizi, Arturo. La lucha antiimperialista; etapa fundamental del proceso democrático en América Latina. B. A., Ediciones Debate, 1955. 96 p.

This essay was originally published as an introduction to the author's Oil and politics. It concerns the whole problem of the development of Argentina's oil productive capacity. It is strongly "nationalistic" and sweepingly condemns the "schemes" of the international oil cartels. It is of greater interest because its author will play a prominent role in the forthcoming presidential election.

2215a. ————. Ni odio ni miedo: reconstruir el país. [Discursos de Arturo Frondizi y declaraciones de la Mesa Directiva del Comité Nacional de la Unión Cívica Radical del 17 de junio de 1955 al 25 de junio de 1956]. B. A., Servicio Editorial y Periodístico Argentino (Col. SEPA, 2), 1956. 92 p.

A collection of speeches by Frondizi, who is now prominently mentioned as a presidential candidate, and statements on party policy issued by the executive committee of the Radical party (Unión Cívica Radical). Now that the elections for the constituent assembly have been held, the position of the party with reference to this question is of interest. There are several references to the petroleum industry; the party, as is well known, is opposed to any foreign exploitation.

2216. Frondizi, Silvio. La realidad argentina. Ensayo de interpretación sociológica. 1. El sistema capitalista. B. A., Praxis, 1955. 267 p.

The author, in a highly "intellectual" study, looks at Argentine politics within the context of world capitalism.

2217. Galíndez, Bartolomé. Apuntes de tres revoluciones: 1930, 1943, 1955. B. A., Castro Barrera, 1956. 188 p.

Running through this little volume on recent Argentine political history are some incisive comments on Argentina's three revolutions of the 20th century.

2218. Greco, Rafael. Frondizi no puede ser presidente. B. A., Ediciones FB, 1956. 62 p.

Given the political tensions of the moment, this is a notably objective discussion of why Frondizi "cannot" be president of Argentina. The author is most concerned over the danger of a return to the "personal" politics of the second Yrigoyen administration.

2219. Guemes, Gontrán de. Así se gestó la dictadura. B. A., Ediciones Rex, 1956. 142 p.

This little book has much important material in it. It is primarily concerned with GOU (Grupo Oficiales Unidos), the nationalists, and the immediate backgrounds of the revolution of June 1943. No footnotes or bibliography.

2220. López Basanta, J. Cultura ciudadana. B. A., Fides, 1953. 2 v. V. 1, La sociedad argentina, 174 p.; v. 2, El jus-

ticialismo social; el justicialismo económico, 263 p.
This is a sort of political catechism for secondary-school use in Argentina; it is naturally in complete sympathy with the political ideas and actions of Perón. V. 1 has data on the composition of the Argentine people and where and how they live.

2221. **Lubertino, José.** La tragedia de las dictaduras latinoamericanas y cuatro problemas argentinos. B. A., Gure, 1956. 273 p.
Part 1 of this book deals with Latin American dictatorships in general, part 2 with Argentine problems. As the author sees it, the attainment of democracy in Argentina is dependent upon reforms in the educational program, and the finding of some program by which the moral and spiritual level of those who work the land may be elevated.

2222. **Mazo, Gabriel del.** El radicalismo; notas sobre su historia y doctrina, 1922-1952. B. A., Raigal (Biblioteca histórico-política argentina; Formato mayor, 2), 1955. 450 p.
An excellent and very full account of Argentine politics, and especially the role of the Unión Cívica Radical in the years 1922 to 1952. Significantly, there is almost no reference to the position of the party after Perón came to power. The book does not include a bibliography.

2223. **Palacios, Alfredo Lorenzo.** Mensaje a la juventud. B. A., Ediciones Populares Argentinas, 1956. 110 p.
There are three "messages" in this little volume; one to the youth of Argentina—primarly concerned with problems of education; one to the workers; and one to the young army officers. The last named is most important for those concerned with the role of the army in Argentine politics.

2224. **Pendle, George.** The land and people of Argentina. N. Y., Macmillan, 1957. 88 p.
This is the first of a projected series of short books about the land and people of other nations. Although written for a lay, and possibly a young, audience, it contains much information useful in the understanding of the political life of the country.

2225. **Perón, Juan Domingo.** La fuerza es el derecho de las bestias. La realidad de un año de tiranía. Caracas, Ediciones Garrido, 1957. 246 p., illus.
The tyranny is that of the post-Perón governments in Argentina; the force, that employed to suppress the Argentines since June of 1955. Chapter 3 has considerable information on Perón's policy toward the Church, and some on the coups which ousted him. To the author, the greatest infamy, among many, of the Aramburu government was the destruction of the Eva Perón Foundation.

2226. **Petrocelli, Héctor Benjamín.** El concepto de orden económico en la constitución nacional de 1949. B. A., Arayú, 1954. 54 p.
A good study of what the author labels the political and economic theory underlying the 1949 Argentine constitution. The author contrasts this theory with the "false" economic basis of the 1853 constitution.

2227. **Pinedo, Federico.** El fatal estatismo. 2. ed. B. A., Kraft, 1956. 190 p.
The author presents a vigorous argument against state intervention in economic affairs, and a strong plea for support of the conservative party (Partido Demócrata). The book contains a great deal of information on the Argentine economy of the past two decades.

2228. **Puiggrós, Rodolfo.** Historia crítica de los partidos políticos argentinos. B. A., Argumentos, 1956. 482 p.
A most important contribution to the literature on political parties in Latin America. There is little reference to the political parties of Argentina prior to 1890 and none after 1945. The author is as much concerned with political history as with party history. Footnotes, but no bibliography.

2229. **Reissig, Luis.** El fin de un ciclo histórico en Argentina. Función y perspectiva de la oligarquía, clase media y clase obrera frente a los problemas nacionales. B. A., Servicio Editorial y Periodístico Argentina (SEPA, 1), 1956. 62 p.
The author presents the thesis that the fall of Perón marked the end of a cycle of land-owner oligarchy in Argentina. He optimistically looks forward to the next era which, in his view, will be a progressive development of agriculture, industry, and mining, but with no special privileges to any one of them.

2230. **Romero, José Luis.** Las ideas políticas en Argentina. 2. ed., corr. y aumentada. México, Fondo de Cultura Económica (Col. Tierra firme, 25), 1956. 268 p.
The second edition of an excellent book on the development of Argentine political thought from the colonial period down to the outbreak of World War II. There are scanty references to the Perón era. A bibliography is included.

2231. **Romero Carranza, Ambrosio.** Qué es la democracia cristiana. B. A., Ediciones del Atlántico, 1956. 236 p.
This is an explanation of the Christian Democratic ideological position; it is the author's firm conviction that this movement will become a major political party force in Argentina. The volume includes a very full bibliography.

2232. **Sánchez Viamonte, Carlos.** El último caudillo. Juicio crítico por Aníbal Ponce; epílogo por Deodoro Roca. B. A., Devenir, 1956. 87 p.
This is the second edition of a 1930 book; it contains brief vignettes on the politics and personalities of the second Yrigoyen administration.

2233. Solari, Juan Antonio. Doce años de oprobio [itinerario de la dictadura]. Prólogo del Dr. Nicolás Repetto. B. A., Bases Editorial (Bases, 7), 1956. 259 p.

An important book, by a competent observer, on the effects of the Perón dictatorship, and on what must be done in Argentina in order to make possible the return to a democratic way of political life.

2234. Uruguay. Biblioteca del Poder Legislativo. Alfredo L. Palacios. Montevideo, 1955. 102, 66 p., port. (Referencia, 27).

This collection is in honor of Alfredo Palacios, now Argentine ambassador to Uruguay. It contains much reference material on the Socialist party in Argentina, and Palacios' activities in that party. The last section is a bibliography of the published works and writings of Palacios.

2235. Whitaker, Arthur Preston. Argentine upheaval; Perón's fall and the new regime. N. Y., Praeger (Foreign Policy Research Institute series, 1), 1956. 179 p.

An excellent account and analysis of events in Argentina from the events of June 1955 until early 1956. Part 2, "Classes, power groups and parties," is essential reading for those who are following the hoped-for return of democracy in Argentina.

2236. Zamboni, Humberto. Peronismo, justicialismo; juicio crítico. Córdoba, Argentina, Assandri, 1956. 140 p.

An attack on the inconsistencies of the Perón administration and its political ideology, and a condemnation of the graft and corruption attending the Perón era. It was written and published after the fall of Perón.

BOLIVIA

2237. Duin, Juan. Bolivia y la revolución de liberación nacional. La Paz, Universo, 1953. 53 p.

In this study the author traces all of Bolivia's ills to capitalist imperialism. The book does contain, however, some valuable data on the alliances and coalitions of the left-wing parties of that republic.

2238. Fellman Velarde, José. Trabajos teóricos. La Paz, Juventud (Biblioteca de orientación social, 2), 1955. 82 p.

Although it is brief, this study has good material on the evolution of the ideology of MNR (Movimiento Nacionalista Revolucionario).

2239. Fernández Larraín, Sergio. El comunismo en Bolivia. Santiago, Unión Democrática Boliviana, 1956. 71 p.

This pamphlet, published by the Bolivian Democratic Union Party in Chile, maintains that the Bolivian Movimiento Nacionalista Revolucionario follows a Communist party line. The author is a Chilean who has been a member of both the Chamber and the Senate. He names Communist party members who are active in MNR. It has a fairly extensive bibliography.

2240. García, Antonio. La rebelión de los pueblos débiles. Nacionalismo popular y anti-imperialismo. La Paz, Juventud, 1955. 135 p.

The author, who is the head of the Socialist party in Colombia, dedicates this volume to "the people of Bolivia who are building the road to the revolution for Indo-America." The book is replete with such cliches as "imperialism," "capitalist-imperialism," "counter-revolutionary tactics," etc. The author attempts a theory of revolution in backward countries in the opening chapter.

2241. Llosa, J. A. Revolución agraria. Análisis doctrinal, tesis de la Central Obrera Boliviana, Decreto ley de reforma agraria, Reglamento del Servicio de R. A. Con autorización oficial. La Paz, Ediciones Nueva Bolivia, 1953. 98 p., ports.

This is a study of the agrarian reform program of the Movimiento Nacionalista Revolucionario. It is not critically done but despite this the volume makes a significant contribution. Chapter 1, for example, presents a good short synthesis of the nature of the land reform problem. The last chapter contains the full text of the decree law of agrarian reform (Aug. 2, 1953) and the supplementary decree of Aug. 27 of that year.

2242. Muñoz-Paz, José. La realidad de Bolivia. Caracas, Ancora, 1956. 68 p.

The author is, in his own words, one of "the anti-Marxist old guard members of MNR [Movimiento Nacionalista Revolucionario]," the only group which continues to maintain the true party position (this member is doing so now in Venezuela). Despite the bitterness of this book —Víctor Paz Estenssoro is the principal target— it is an important source of material on recent Bolivian politics.

2243. Paz Estenssoro, Víctor. Discursos parlamentarios. Prólogo de José Cuadros Quiroga. La Paz, Canata, 1955. 324 p., illus.

This volume contains 12 long speeches—they are in fact oral essays—on Bolivian politics and the Movimiento Nacionalista Revolucionario. The period covered is 1938-1944.

2243a. ————. Mensaje al pueblo . . . , 6 de agosto de 1955. La Paz, Subsecretaría de Prensa, Informaciones y Cultura, 1955. 70 p.

This very long message to the people is mainly concerned with economic matters; its longest section deals with the agrarian reform program of MNR.

2244. Siles Salinas, Jorge. La aventura y el orden. Reflexiones sobre la revolución boliviana. Prólogo de Roberto Prudencio. Santiago, Imp. Bustos y Letelier, 1956. 200 p.

There is much good material in this book; the chapters on nationalism, indigenism, and on the social structure of Bolivia merit special commendation.

BRAZIL

2245. Alves, Francisco M. Rodrigues. Democracia corrompida; ou, Golpe de estado? São Paulo, Gea, 1955. 59 p.

In general, the subject of this volume is the role of the armed forces in the political life of the nation from the death of Vargas to the presidential election of 1955.

2245a. ――――. Um homem ameaça o Brasil. A história secreta e espantosa da "caixinha" de Ademar de Barros. São Paulo, 1954. 216 p., illus.

A political indictment of former Governor Barros of São Paulo. There is considerable material referring to the "ring" which had, according to the author, a vast political and economic power which extended far beyond the boundaries of the state.

2246. Barros, Jacy Rego. Do baronato á democracia brasileira. 2. ed. Ensaio sôbre entidades e instituições brasileiras. Rio, Gráf. Editôra Souza, 1953. 174 p.

First edition published under title *Do baronato ao estado novo.* The author fails to make any serious study of the transition from colony to democracy in Brazil.

2247. César, Afonso. Política, cifrão e sangue. Documentário do 24 de agôsto. Rio, Andes (Col. Asa-branca, 3), 1955. 291 p.

An account, with many accompanying documents, of the events of August 1954 which culminated in the suicide of Getúlio Vargas. One of the persons quoted blames the Standard Oil Company and other American oil interests for the *golpe.* The author was closely associated with Vargas and remains a staunch admirer of the man and his works.

2248. Harris, Marvin. Town and country in Brazil. N. Y., Columbia University Press (Columbia University contributions to anthropology, 37), 1956. 302 p., illus., maps, tables.

One of the chapters of this study of life in a small Brazilian town is on the government and politics of the community. It will aid in the understanding of municipal government not only in Brazil but in all Latin America.

2249. Instituto Brasileiro de Administração. Divisão de Pesquisas. Evolução do Ministério das Relações Exteriores. Rio, 1954. 209 p., diagrs.

A very fine administrative study on the origins and development of one of the national ministries. It includes a few charts on the internal organization of the Ministry of Foreign Affairs.

2250. Lima, Alceu Amoroso. Obras completas . . . XXII. Política. 4. ed. rev. et anotada. Rio, AGIR, 1956. 279 p.

Part 1 of this book, p. 11-150, is a general treatise on the theory of the state; part 2 is more directly related to the political organization of Brazil. Chapters 6, 7, and 8 deal with: "The political problems of Brazil"; "The economic problems of Brazil"; and "The spiritual problems of Brazil."

2251. Lima, Cláudio de Araujo. Mito e realidade de Vargas. Rio, Editôra Civilização Brasileira, 1955. 130 p.

An account of Vargas' rise to power, and the kind of person he was in the exercise of the vast powers which he held.

2252. Machado, F. Zenha. Os últimos dias do govêrno de Vargas. A crise política de agôsto de 1954. Rio, Lux, 1955. 194 p.

The writer addresses himself to the question: Why did Getúlio Vargas take his own life? He includes many statements of military officers who were connected with the *golpe* of August 1954.

2253. Martins, Rue Nogueira. Tentativas para organizar o Brasil. São Paulo, Instituto de Sociologia e Política da Federação do Comércio do Estado de São Paulo, 1956. 81 p.

Chapter 2 of this short monograph contains an informative and fairly complete discussion of the present electoral system in Brazil, with some data on its origins and legislative development.

2254. Medeiros, Océlio de. Problemas fundamentais dos municípios brasileiros; planejamentos intergovernamentais como instrumentos de solução: política de valorização de áreas e projetos da Operação-Município. Rio, Departamento Administrativo do Serviço Público, Serviço de Documentação (Ensaios de administração, 6), 1956. 123 p.

This is an excellent monograph on the structure and the problems of local government in Brazil. Its value is increased by an 18-page bibliography on virtually all phases of municipal government in that republic.

2255. Mesquita, Julio de. *Memórias de um revolucionário*, notas par um ensaio de sociologia política. São Paulo, Anhembi, 1954. 41 p.

The revolution referred to is the one of 1930 which brought Vargas to power. Despite its title, there is little "sociological" in this account.

2256. Mourão, Milcíades M. Dutra. História de um govêrno. Rio, 1955. 211 p.

A good account of the Dutra administration; 1946 to 1951. A chapter on the election of 1946 is included; it contains brief accounts of the party alignments in that election. The book also includes references to the political party affiliations and backing of the Ministers in the Dutra administration. The author is highly critical of Dutra, and blames him for the later election of Vargas. There are no footnotes and no bibliography.

2257. Olivetti, Benedicto. Municipalismo caótico. São Paulo, Atena Editôra, 1955. 131 p.

A good critique of the lack of a sound and consistent program with reference to the status and role of local governments in Brazil. No bibliography.

2258. Paupério, A. Machado. Presidencialismo, parlamentarismo e govêrno colegial. Rio, Revista Forense, 1956. 158 p.

In the first three chapters of this book the author discusses the presidential system in general. He then turns to the presidential system in Latin America, which he calls legalized dictatorship, and in Brazil. He follows the same general approach in his treatment of parliamentary and collegial executive systems. In the appendix he has included proposed amendments to the Brazilian constitution by which either the parliamentary or the collegial executive system could be established in Brazil.

2259. Viana, Arízio de. D. A. S. P., an institution at the service of Brazil. Rio, International Institute of Administrative Sciences, Brazilian Section (Serviço de Documentação do D. A. S. P., Publ. avulsa, 486), 1955. 130 p., diagrs.

A good account of DASP, how it is organized, and what its objectives are. One section contains very useful information on the budget, administrative organization of Brazil, and personnel administration.

2259a. ————, and Araújo Cavalcanti. Completed staff work; a concise bulletin. Rio, Documentation Service of the D. A. S. P. (Serviço de Documentação do D. A. S. P. Seção de Publicações, Publ. avulsa, 465), 1955. 35 p.

Chapter 3 of this little brochure has a brief but very good description of the special characteristics of Brazilian administrative organization.

CHILE

2260. Araneda Bravo, Fidel. El arzobispo Errázuriz y la evolución política y social de Chile. Prólogo de Emilio Rodríguez Mendoza. Santiago, Editorial Jurídica de Chile, 1956. 248 p.

An excellent biography of one who was very influential in Chilean thought. Especially noteworthy are the chapters on "Churchman and politics" and "Separation of Church and State."

2261. Bello Codecido, Emilio. Recuerdos políticos. La Junta de Gobierno de 1925; su origen y relación con la reforma del régimen constitucional. Santiago, Nascimento, 1954. 239 p.

A very good account of events in Chile from the end of the parliamentary system in 1925 to the presidential election of 1952. Students of Latin American government will find chapter 1, "The crisis of the parliamentary regime," and chapter 10, which deals with the constitutional reform, extremely valuable.

2262. Bravo Ríos, Leónidas. Lo que supo un auditor de guerra. Santiago, Editorial del Pacífico, 1955. 307 p.

The author of this most interesting book held many administrative posts in defense departments. The book is not only good for its detail on public administration but also because the writer has included many comments on the role of the army in political affairs—both the normal and in the golpes de estado.

2263. Edwards, Alberto. La organización política de Chile. Santiago, Editorial del Pacífico, 1955. 137 p.

This very good monograph is limited to the period from Independence to the adoption of the Constitution of 1833. Chapter 2, "The elements of government in the early nineteenth century," is especially noteworthy.

2264. Fernández Larraín, Sergio. Informe sobre el comunismo rendido a la convención general del Partido Conservador Unido, el 12 de octubre. Santiago, Zig-Zag, 1954. 180 p.

This report, presented to a convention of the Conservative party, can hardly be called an objective study. Nevertheless, it contains a great deal of valuable information. One will find chapters on the history of the Communist party in Chile, its organizational structure, communist infiltration tactics, and the relations between the Communist party and the popular front. In chapter 9 the author lists the newspapers and magazines which he states are eigther communist directed or influenced.

2265. Frei Montalva, Eduardo. La verdad tiene su hora. Santiago, Editorial del Pacífico, 1955. 165 p.

This volume is mainly concerned with the economic problems of Chile; chapter 1, however, deals with the general problem of state intervention in economic affairs. Chapter 4, "America has a destiny," has some thoughtful comments on the differences in the politics of Latin and non-Latin America.

ECUADOR

2266. Ecuador. Secretaría General de la Administración Pública. 4 años de trabajo (1952-1956). Quito, 1956. 292 p., illus., ports., diagrs.

A review of the administration of President José María Velasco Ibarra. The sections on education, public works, and foreign relations are well done; that on public finance contains very full data on Ecuador's foreign trade.

2267. Maldonado Estrada, Luis. Una etapa histórica en la vida nacional. Quito, Rumiñahui, 1953, i. e. 1954. 271 p.

The author was formerly the head of the Socialist party of Ecuador. He includes a considerable amount of material on the politics and the political parties of Ecuador for the years 1948-1952. There is no bibliography.

2268. Miranda Ribadeneira, Francisco. Política cristiana. Quito, Editorial Fray Jodoco Ricke (Col. Pensamiento católico, 7), 1955. 259 p.

A very thoughtful, and very Catholic, view of the relations between religion and politics, and especially as they exist in Ecuador. The author strongly condemns the false, and Protestant, liberalism of Latin America. It has a fine section on ecclestiastical public law.

GUATEMALA

2269. Comité de Estudiantes Universitarios Anticomunistas. El calvario de Guatemala. Guatemala, 1955. 397 p., illus.

At head of title: Páginas de horror y crimen. A well-documented account including many photographs of the "reign of terror" which took place in the last year of the Arbenz administration. It names Communist party members who held posts in the government, and also lists the names of anti-communists who were tortured or murdered.

2270. Una era de labor constructiva en Guatemala. Gestión administrativa del régimen democrático que preside el coronel Carlos Castillo Armas, 1954-1956: período preconstitucional. Guatemala, Tip. Nacional, 1956. 440 p.

A report based upon the annual summaries of the ministries and other major government departments. It is perhaps significant that there is almost no reference to any land or agrarian reform program.

2271. Guatemala. Secretaría de Divulgación, Cultura y Turismo. Así se gestó la liberación. L. A. H. A. Guatemala, 1956. 434 p., illus., ports.

Documents published by the government of Castillo Armas on how it organized and fought the previous administration. The book has some lurid photographs. [W. V. Scholes]

2271a. ————. ————. Historia de un golpe rojo. Guatemala, 1956? 84 p., illus.

An official government account of the *golpe* of June 25, 1956. Much of it is devoted to the relationship of the university students to this attempt to overthrow the Castillo regime. It contains a list of those who were arrested and those who were wounded in the disturbances.

2272. James, Daniel. Tácticas rojas en las Américas. Prólogo de David Vela. México, Editorial Intercontinental, 1955. 245 p.

A Spanish edition of the author's *Red design for America* (see HLAS, no. 19, item 2919).

2273. Marroquín Rojas, Clemente. Crónicas de la constituyente del 45. Guatemala, Imp. La Hora Dominical, 1955. 112 p.

A collection of news reports on the work of the constituent assembly of 1945. Some of these are full and detailed, such as those referring to the articles of the proposed constitution which dealt with the executive, the powers of the Congress, and the suffrage.

2274. Martz, John D. Communist infiltration in Guatemala. N. Y., Vantage Press, 1956. 125 p.

A chronology of the events of 1954 in that country. It contains a short but not very critically selected bibliography.

2275. Nájera Farfán, Mario Efraín. Los estafadores de la democracia; hombres y hechos en Guatemala. B. A., Glem, 1956. 301 p.

A discussion of the politics of Guatemala in the years 1945-1955. The author is obviously very anti-Arévalo in his point of view, and maintains that the Arévalo administration was the intended prelude for the communist infiltration which followed.

2276. Samayoa Chinchilla, Carlos. El quetzal no es rojo. Guatemala, Arana Hermanos, 1956. 268 p.

The author strongly maintains that the communist infiltration in no way represented the real desires of the Guatemalan people. Among the more informative chapters are those related to Dr. Juan José Arévalo; Arévalo and the communists; Jacobo Arbenz Guzmán; and agrarian reform.

MEXICO

2277. Cosío Villegas, Daniel. La Constitución de 1857 y sus críticos. México, Hermes, 1957. 199 p.

A very important book, especially for those who are interested in Mexican constitutional history. The author makes an evaluation of the critiques of the 1857 constitution.

2278. González Luna, Efraín. Humanismo político. Preámbulo, selección y notas de Luis Calderón Vega. México, Jus, 1955. 382 p.

The subject of this book *is* Efraín González Luna, principal member of the Partido Acción Nacional of Mexico and the candidate of that party for the presidency in 1952. It is of some importance because it presents the political views of a party leader who is not affiliated with PRI (Partido Revolucionario Institucional).

2279. Guisa y Azevedo, Jesús. Estado y ciudadanía. México, Polis, 1957. 282 p.

The three sections of this volume are: "Advice to the citizen"; "Advice to the authorities"; and "Advice to the Mexicans."

2280. Mexico. President. Informe que rinde al H. Congreso de la Unión el C. Presidente de la República Adolfo Ruiz Cortines . . . correspondiente a su gestión del 1. de septiembre de 1954 al 31 de

agosto de 1955. México, Secretaría de Gobernación, 1955. 93 p.
The president summarized the plans and accomplishments of his administration in the preceding year.

2281. Román Celis, Carlos. El estado administrativo como forma política del mundo moderno. México, Universidad Nacional Autónoma de México, Facultad de Derecho, 1953, i. e. 1956. 172 p.
This thesis contains a brief and a very sketchy study of centralization in the Mexican federal system. The bibliography is short and does not include many well-known existing works.

2282. Scott, Robert E. Budget making in Mexico (Interam Ec Aff, 9:2, autumn 1955, p. 3-20).
The budget is under the close personal control of the president. Congress has little or no control over it. [W. V. Scholes]

2283. Tucker, William T. The Mexican government today. Minneapolis, Minn., University of Minnesota Press, 1957. 484 p.
A very fine and informative book. Almost half of the pages are devoted to the functions and activities of the Mexican government. The 38-page bibliography is exhaustive and complete.

2284. Zuno, José Guadalupe. Nuestro liberalismo. Guadalajara, México, Imp. Fénix, 1956, i. e. 1957. 185 p.
A general history and criticism of liberal thought and action in Mexico. It is the author's thesis that the Church has, in general, given support to—or at least has not opposed—really liberal programs of economic and political reform.

PARAGUAY

2285. González Merzario, Américo. Política y ejército; consideraciones sobre problemas político-militares del Paraguay. B. A., Yegros, 1955. 145 p.
The author, a naval officer, has written on a subject of great significance in the study of Latin American government. Some of the chapters are primarily military history, or are concerned with the formulation of military policy. However, chapter 5, which is concerned with the army and internal politics, rather fully discusses the political role of the army in Paraguay.

2286. Raine, Philip. Paraguay. New Brunswick, N. J., Scarecrow Press, 1956. 443 p., illus.
The source material for this book is principally Paraguayan. It contains much information about a nation which is little known in the U. S.

2287. Stroessner, Alfredo. Mensajes y discursos. Asunción, Presidencia de la República, Sub-secretaría de Informaciones y Cultura, 1955. 255 p., illus.

The main contribution of this volume is found in the scattered observations of its author on the role of the Colorado party in the politics of Paraguay in the last two decades.

PERU

2288. Haya de la Torre, Víctor Raúl. Enfoque aprista de imperialismo, antimperialismo y marxismo. México, Ediciones Humanismo (Política de América, 5), 1955. 10 p.
Much too brief an explanation of the position of APRA (Alianza Popular Revolucionaria Americana).

2288a. ————. Treinta años de aprismo. México, Fondo de Cultura Económica, 1956. 247 p.
A summary of the origins and evolution of the political principles of this very important movement. The author makes a strong argument for an economic unification of Latin America as a means of avoiding the danger of foreign economic imperialism.

2289. Hernández Urbina, Alfredo. Los partidos y las crisis del Apra. Lima, Ediciones Raíz, 1956. 119 p.
A collection of newspaper articles on the current (1955-1956) politics of Peru. The appendix contains the platforms, or official party policy statements, of the following parties: People's Party, Revolutionary Union Party; Socialist party; and Communist party.

2290. Kantor, Harry. Ideología y programa del movimiento aprista. México, Humanismo, 1955. 247 p.
This is a Spanish edition of the author's *The ideology and program of the Peruvian Aprista movement* (see *HLAS, no. 19,* item 2932).

2291. Martin, César. El preludio de la democracia. Una campaña periodística por la legalidad de los partidos proscritos y el retorno de los desterrados. Lima, 1956. 158 p.
Mostly a collection of short biographical essays of leading political figures in Peru who are members of and active in several political parties. Representatives of APRA are not included.

URUGUAY

2292. Ferreira, Santos E., and Edison Gnazzo. Naturaleza financiera de los proventos y su tratamiento en nuestro régimen positivo. Montevideo, Universidad de la República, Instituto de la Hacienda Pública (Cuaderno, 10), 1955. 23 p.
Because of the brevity of this pamphlet it can do no more than present a short outline of the tax system.

2293. Gros Espiell, Héctor (ed.). Las constituciones del Uruguay (exposición, crítica y textos). Madrid, Ediciones Cul-

tura Hispánica (Las constituciones hispanoamericanas, 8), 1956. 462 p.
This volume, like the similar ones for other Latin American republics published in the past by Ediciones Cultura Hispánica, is excellent. It is well footnoted. An appendix contains the principal constitutional texts; those of 1830, 1918, 1934 (including the changes of 1936 and 1938), 1942, and 1952. There is no bibliography; an index is also lacking.

2294. Rodríguez Araya, Agustín. Génesis constitucional de la República Oriental del Uruguay (Asamblea General Constituyente y Legislativa del Estado, 1828-1830). Prólogo de Juan J. Carbajal Victorica. Montevideo, 1955. 412 p.
An excellent constitutional history, covering the period from Independence to the adoption of the Constitution of 1830. There are a few footnotes; a bibliography is lacking.

OTHER

2294a. Costa Rica. Ministerio de Gobernación. Constitución política de Costa Rica, 7 de noviembre de 1949. San José, 1955. 146 p.
The full text of the 1949 constitution, made the more useful by the inclusion of a very fine analytical index.

2295. El Salvador. Ministerio de Defensa. Principios y objetivos del Gobierno de la Revolución. San Salvador, Departamento de Publicaciones e Información, 1955. 75 p.
This is a review of how well the junta, which came to power December 1948, has accomplished the objectives of political, social, and economic reform to which it was pledged.

2295a. Esquenazi Mayo, Roberto. Fundamentos para un partido nuevo. Habana, Alfa, 1954? 16 p.
The author argues that Cuba's most pressing need is a new political party—new in ideology and program as well as in name. He offers no suggestions as to how this party realignment might be accomplished.

2296. Gabaldón Márquez, Joaquín. Archivos de una inquietud venezolana. Caracas, Ediciones EDIME (Autores venezolanos), 1955. 486 p.
This substantial book has a good analysis and discussion of the basic economic problems of Venezuela and the author includes a consideration of the political repercussions of these economic factors. The sections dealing with agri-

culture, agrarian reform, and petroleum are noteworthy. Part 4 is concerned with the politics of the nation, and emphasizes the political events and developments of the 1930's and early 1940's.

2296a. Gil Fontana. Trujillo y su obra, 1930-1952. La Romana, Dominican Republic, Romana, 1954. 189 p.
The preface of this laudatory biography tells us that "the spontaneous affection for and admiration of the Benefactor of the Fatherland is felt unanimously by all the Dominican people."

2297. Gonzáles Herrera, Julio. Trujillo, genio político. Ciudad Trujillo, Editora del Caribe, 1956. 361 p.
Like almost all books published now in the Dominican Republic, this one is fulsome in its adulation of the Benefactor of the Fatherland.

2297a. Liga Espiritual de Profesionales Católicos. Costa Rica, un estado católico. Por un círculo de abogados de la Liga . . . San José, Imp. Nacional, 1955. 202 p.
A thoughtful discussion of the intent and meaning of article 76 of the Costa Rican constitution, and of the other articles and clauses which refer to the relationships between Church and State.

2298. Lugo-Silva, Enrique. The Tugwell administration in Puerto Rico, 1941-1946. Río Piedras, Puerto Rico, Editorial Cultura, 1955. 185 p., ports.
Dr. Lugo-Silva wrote this study as his Ph. D. thesis at Ohio State University. After two introductory chapters, the emphasis is on the political, social, and economic policies of the Tugwell administration. The author has included a most complete bibliography, and an appendix contains a brief digest of the most important laws adopted during the administration.

2298a. Santos, Eduardo. La crisis de la democracia en Colombia y El Tiempo. México, Gráf. Panamericana, 1955. 236 p.
The subject of this volume is the closure of El Tiempo, Aug. 3, 1953. It includes an account of the events leading to the closure, a tribute to Dr. Eduardo Santos, and comments from the press of the free world. There is a very fine "biography" of El Tiempo written by Germán Arciniegas.

2299. Vega Cobiellas, Ulpiano. Batista y Cuba; crónica política y realizaciones. Habana, Publ. Cultural, 1955? 280 p.
A most laudatory account of the rise and works of Fulgencio Batista. It includes a very full account of the social and economic measures (listed as "accomplishments") of the Batista administrations.

History

GENERAL

2300. Acosta, Roberto. La hacienda de beneficio de Santa María de Guadalupe de Thobaca y sus fundadores: la familia Campoy (Mem Ac Mex Hist, 14:1, enero-marzo 1955, p. 5-17).
The hacienda, for silver working, was established in the early 18th century and abandoned in the early 19th. The archives used include those of the parish of Los Alamos, the site of the hacienda. [R. D. Hussey]

2301. Andrews, K. R. Christopher Newport of Limehouse, mariner (Wm Mary Q, 3. series, 11:1, Jan. 1954, p. 28-41).
A study of the hitherto obscure years before Newport's voyages of 1606 and 1611 to Virginia. Born in 1560, he made a voyage to Brazil in 1581, served under Drake at Cadiz, and then in the "service of the London privateering entrepreneurs" made several voyages to the Spanish West Indies, 1596-1605. [R. D. Hussey]

2302. Ayón, Tomás. Historia de Nicaragua desde los tiempos más remotos hasta el año de 1852. Madrid, Escuela Profesional de Artes Gráficas, 1956. 3 v. 460, 443, 542 p.
New edition. First published in 1882. [W. V. Scholes]

2303. Bachiller y Morales, Antonio. Galería de hombres útiles. Habana, Instituto Nacional de Cultura (Grandes periodistas cubanos, 12), 1955. 289 p.
Collection of articles originally published in 19th-century Cuban and Spanish periodicals by Antonio Bachiller y Morales (1812-1889), Cuban biographer and bibliographer. Contains biographies of 14 Cubans prominent in public affairs, some in the 18th century and others in the first half of the 19th century. There is an introduction with a biography and a study of Bachiller y Morales by the present day Cuban biographer and bibliographer Fermín Peraza Sarausa. [A. Santana]

2304. Bibliografía de la historia de México,

1956 (Mem Ac Mex Hist, 16:1, enero-marzo 1957, p. 76-92).
The compiler, Manuel Carrera Stampa, states: "Para la elaboración de esta bibliografía nos hemos valido de listas mensuales de libros hechas por don Rafael Porrúa Estrada; de la *Bibliografía de la historia de México* (1956) que abarca hasta octubre del año pasado, que hizo para *Historia mexicana* Susana Uribe de Fernández de Córdoba; de las bibliografías que traen la *Revista de historia de América* (hasta junio, que es el último número aparecido a la fecha), la *Revista interamericana de bibliografía* y la *Hispanic American historical review*, y de una búsqueda por bibliotecas y librerías." [Ed.]

2305. Brønsted, Johannes (ed.). Vore gamle tropekolonier. København, Westermann Verlag, 1952-1953. 2 v., illus., maps.
A cooperative work by a number of excellent Danish scholars, under way for some seven years. V. 1 deals with the Danish East Indies, 1616-1835, and Danish Guinea, and v. 2 with the Danish West Indies to 1917. Although the authors make no effort to recognize the possible value of the Spanish and Portuguese sources and story, Latin Americanists could benefit greatly by using this volume. In any case, the many maps and illustrations and tables of statistics should interest them. Bibliophiles will wish to add this to the list of printed labors of love which are said to have ruined their sponsors. In this case the splendid specially commissioned water colors were the main culprit. [R. D. Hussey]

2306. Cabanillas, Berta. Orígenes de los hábitos alimenticios del pueblo de Puerto Rico (Trab Conf, 6, 1955, p. 199-215).
Brief essay on the evolution of the dietary habits of the Puerto Rican people from pre-Columbian times up to the 19th century. Contains some bibliographical notes. [A. Santana]

2307. Carmichael, Gertrude. The archives of Trinidad and Tobago, British West Indies (Arch, Brit Rec Assoc, 1:8, Michaelmas 1952, p. 39-41).
The Trinidad records are few before 1816, but

there are a few from 1810, and a manuscript index to the non-existent Spanish records of 1787-1813. Those of Tobago are fairly numerous from 1793. [R. D. Hussey]

2308. ————. Some notes on Sir Ralph James Woodford, Bt., Governor of Trinidad, 1813 to 1828 (Carib Q, 2:3, 1952, p. 26-38).
There are a good many references to, or sidelights on, the Spanish period of the island, or relations with Spanish areas. [R. D. Hussey]

2309. **Castro de Morales, Lilia.** Impresos relativos a Cuba editados en los Estados Unidos de Norteamérica. Habana, Biblioteca Nacional, 1956. 370 p.
A praiseworthy compilation covering from the 18th century; the first entries in this chronological list date from 1762. It includes government documents, travel books, histories, archaeological reports, botanical studies, novels, poems, reminiscences, and the extensive number of Cuban revolutionary writings published in the U. S. The volume, built upon the previous inventory made in 1898 by the then Assistant Librarian of Congress, A. P. C. Griffin, ends with a list of 75 Cuban newspapers edited in the U. S. and a very useful alphabetical index. [A. Santana]

2310. **Chaunu, Huguette, and Pierre Chaunu.** Autour de 1640. Politiques et économies atlantiques (A Éc Soc Civ, 9:1, jan.-mars 1954, p. 44-54).
The result of long research on Spanish trade with the Indies, but especially combines that with a sort of review of Boxer's *Salvador de Sá,* London, 1952 (see *HLAS, no. 18, 1952,* item 2160). [R. D. Hussey]

2311. **Costa Rica. Archivos Nacionales.** Revista de los . . . San José. Año 19, no. 1-6, enero-junio 1955; año 19, no. 7-12, julio-dic., 1955; año 20, no. 1-6, enero-junio 1956; año 20, no. 7-12, julio-dic. 1956.
These numbers contain historical documents from the Archive, including especially presidential messages and proclamations, documents regarding events of 1823, documents regarding the campaign against Walker in 1856-1857, and other matters. Each number has an installment of the index of documents of the national period. [R. R. Hill]

2312. **Cruz de del Pino, Mary.** Camagüey, biografía de una provincia. Habana, Academia de la Historia de Cuba, 1955. 257 p., illus.
Covers the history of the province of Camagüey from pre-Columbian days to the present. Matters primarily of local interest are emphasized: the founding and growth of towns, the development of educational and charitable institutions, the careers of notable personages, and the province's participation in Cuba's wars for Independence. Too little attention is devoted to developments in the 20th century. Based largely on printed primary and secondary sources, these are indicated in the bibliography. [A. Santana]

2313. **Cuba. Archivo Nacional.** Catálogos de los mapas, planos, croquis y árboles genealógicos existentes en el Archivo Nacional de Cuba. Prefacio . . . Joaquín Llaverías y Martínez. Habana, 1954. T. 3, D-H, 377 p., t. 4, I-O, 311 p.
A full listing of maps, plans, and genealogical trees for the names from D to O which are at present in the Cuban National Archives. For each item the date, a complete identification, and the location within the various collections are given. T. 1 appeared in 1951 and t. 2 in 1952. All four maintain a high standard of printing and editing. Very important for the historical evolution of architecture and land distribution and division in the island of Cuba. [A. Santana]

2314.————. ————. Memoria correspondiente al año de 1954. Habana, 1955. 29 p. (Publ., 43).
A brief account by the director, Joaquín Llaverías, of the activities during the year. [R. R. Hill]

2315. **Debien, Gabriel.** Les travaux d'histoire sur Saint Domingue. Chronique bibliographique, 1950-1952 (R Hist Colonies, 40, 2. trim. 1953, p. 313-357).
A detailed and critical discussion of a large number of publications in book or periodical form, many of which have not been listed in any *HLAS.* "Les bibliothèques," p. 317-319, is the best brief note on the history and character of the major Haitian libraries that is known to this reviewer. [R. D. Hussey]

2316. Documentos de la época colonial comprados por el Archivo Nacional (B Arch Nac, Habana, 51-52, enero 1952-dic. 1953, i. e. 1954, p. 116-255).
Transcription of the text of some Colonial documentation purchased by the Archivo Nacional. It comprises some *décimas,* a collection of documents belonging to the years 1851 and 1852, and a series of letters written between 1776 and 1783. [A. Santana]

2317. **Elliott, Claude** (comp.). A check list of theses and dissertations in Texas history, 1907-1952 (SW Hist Q, 57:3, Jan. 1954, p. 336-388; 57:4, Apr. 1954, p. 475-505; 58:1, July 1954, p. 98-142; 58:2, Oct. 1954, p. 249-288; 58:3, Jan. 1955, p. 372-404).
555 items, gathered through the cooperation of 51 colleges and universities, and listed alphabetically. There are summary statements of content. Another installment is announced, to complete the work. [R. D. Hussey]

2318. **Ezell, Paul H.** The conditions of Hispanic-Piman contacts on the Gila river (Am Indíg, 17:2, abril 1957, p. 163-191).
Detailed chronology of forms of contact between Spaniards and Gila Pimas from the 17th century to the middle of the 19th century. Operation of Spanish mission policy under Jesuits

and Franciscans and of Mexican policy toward Indians after Independence. [C. Gibson]

2319. Fernández de Córdoba, Joaquín. Sumaria relación de las bibliotecas de Michoacán (Hist Mex, 3:1, julio-agosto 1953, p. 134-156, 6 plates).

An excellent discussion of libraries, public, private, and semi-public, extant or no longer so, from the colonial era to date, with some information upon the fate of some of the collections. [R. D. Hussey]

2320. Fernández del Castillo, Francisco. El Hospital de San Lázaro, 1571-1862 (G Méd Méx, 82:2, marzo-abril 1952, p. 87-105).

The Hospital for lepers founded by Cortés having soon failed, Dr. Pedro López (1527-1597) established this one. It was taken over by the Brothers of San Juan de Dios in 1721. Economic problems led to the closure in 1862, but not before it had done good work even in the 19th century. Dr. Ladislao de la Pascua reported discovery there, in 1844, of spotted leprosy, and this was described by others of the hospital in detail, seven years later. [R. D. Hussey]

2321. Franklin, John Hope. From slavery to freedom; a history of American Negroes. 2d ed., rev. & enl. N. Y., Knopf, 1956. 639 p., illus., ports.

The revisions from the first edition, of 1947, seem to be confined to the chapters at the end. The several excellent chapters of interest to Latin Americanists are unchanged, and still excellent. (See also *HLAS, no. 13, 1947*, item 1136). [R. D. Hussey]

2322. Fúrlong, Guillermo. The influence of Benjamin Franklin in the River Plate area before 1810 (Americas, Franciscan Hist, 12:3, Jan. 1956, p. 259-263).

Electricity, lightning-rods, and maxims. [D. Bushnell]

2323. ————. Lázaro de Ribera y su *Breve cartilla real* (Humanidades, La Plata, 34, Sección Historia, 1954, p. 15-69).

Sound research on a representative of Spanish enlightened despotism who served different posts in the Viceroyalty of La Plata, 1784-1809. While Governor of Paraguay he published his *cartilla*, a catechism of absolutism. [D. Bushnell]

2324. Gay-Calbó, Enrique. Las banderas, el escudo y el himno de Cuba. Habana, Sociedad Colombista Pan Americana, 1956. 76 p., illus.

Brief undocumented essay, published for popular information, on the different flags which have fluttered over Cuba from colonial to republican days, and the present seal and national anthem, with an appendix on the legal statutes involved and instructions on the proper flag display. [A. Santana]

2325. Giraldo Jaramillo, Gabriel. Estudios históricos. Bogotá, Ministerio de Educación Nacional (Biblioteca de autores colombianos, 86), 1954. 387 p.

Collected articles on various topics, the largest single group referring to Colombian intellectual history. [D. Bushnell]

2327. Gorbea Trueba, José. La fortaleza de San Juan de Ulúa (A Inst Nac Antr Hist, 6, pt. 1 (34), 1952, i. e. 1955, p. 135-150, illus. & 6 plans).

A survey of the history from the 16th century to the present, important to specialists for the plans and illustrations. Some of these are from 16th-century and 18th-century originals, but have apparently been redrawn for clarity, and enlarged from only a portion of the original. Others are modern architects' drawings. [R. D. Hussey]

2328. Grullón y Julia, Eliseo. Acerca del Archivo Nacional (B Arch Gen, Ciudad Trujillo, año 18, 18:84, enero-marzo 1955).

New annotated edition of an article originally published in the *Listín diario* (Ciudad Trujillo, June 22, 1907) and later republished in the *Boletín del Archivo General de la Nación* (Ciudad Trujillo, no. 36-37, 1944). On the vicissitudes of the official archives of the Dominican Republic from Spanish colonial times up to the present. [A. Santana]

2329. Iguíniz, Juan B. Monseñor Valverde Téllez, bibliófilo y bibliógrafo (B Bib Nac, México, 2. época, 4:2, abril-junio 1953, p. 39-51).

A note upon the late bishop-scholar's works, and on his library, now in the University of Monterrey. [R. D. Hussey]

2330. Índices de la *Revista de Indias*, 1940-1952, números I-L (R Indias, Madrid, 13, 1953, supl., 123 p.).

A highly classified arrangement of articles, by type and by periods and/or other subdivisions. [R. D. Hussey]

2331. Instituto Colombiano de Estudios Históricos. Historia. T. 1, no. 1, enero 1955-.

A quarterly review, organ of the Instituto Colombiano de Estudios Históricos, founded in 1955. The issues contain the following sections: Articles, documents, texts, "nota bene" (about history), notices regarding historical activities and publications, activities of the Institute, book reviews, and bibliography. A valuable contribution to the cultural life of Colombia. [R. R. Hill]

2332. Iturribarría, Jorge Fernando. Oaxaca: la historia y sus instrumentos (Hist Mex, 2:3, enero-marzo 1953, p. 459-476).

A valuable discussion of scholarly institutions, libraries, and archives of the area, and a list of books about the area published in recent years. [R. D. Hussey]

2333. Larrazábal Blanco, C. Familias de Santo Domingo (Clío, 23:104, julio-sept. 1955, p. 150-156).
Genealogical notes, covering from the late 18th to the early 20th century, on the ancestors, descendants, and relatives of the *prócer* Francisco del Rosario Sánchez. [A. Santana]

2334. Martin, Michael Rheta, and Gabriel H. Lovett. An encyclopedia of Latin-American history. Supervisory editor: Henry Bamford Parkes. N. Y., Abelard-Schuman, 1956. 392 p.
Broadly conceived and well handled, though perhaps it depends too much upon English language accounts, and gives less full coverage, proportionately, to the colonial period than to that of Independence and later. Few serious errors occur, but a few definitions or interpretations might be quarrelled with by specialists, and the omission of a few men (such as Luiz Prestes) is hard to understand. [R. D. Hussey]

2335. Millares Carlo, Agustín. Notas bibliográficas acerca de archivos municipales, ediciones de libros de acuerdos y colecciones de documentos concejiles. Adiciones y rectificaciones (R Hist Am, 35-36, junio-dic. 1953, p. 175-208).
Additions to his book of 1951 (see *HLAS, no. 17, 1951*, item 1426). These 1953 notes have some additions or corrections for almost any part, but are strongest on Spain, Argentina, Cuba, and Peru. [R. D. Hussey]

2336. Miller, Thomas L. A note on the Spanish and Mexican ceremony conveying possession of land (Agr Hist, 28:4, Oct. 1954, p. 168-170).
Data concerning various Texas cases, 1794-1831, from the Texas archives and a note on the ceremonies elsewhere. [R. D. Hussey]

2337. Nieto y Cortadellas, Rafael. Documentos sacramentales de algunos cubanos ilustres (R Bib Nac, Habana, 4:4, oct.-dic. 1953, p. 142-159; 5:2, abril-junio 1954, p. 115-132; 5:3, julio-agosto 1954, p. 199-211; 5:4, oct.-dic. 1954, p. 69-82; 6:2, abril-junio 1955, p. 209-221; 6:3, julio-sept. 1955, p. 121-136).
Textual transcriptions from Cuban ecclesiastical archives of baptismal, marriage, and death records of prominent 18th- and 19th-century Cubans. [A. Santana]

2338. Parry, John Horace, and Philip Manderson Sherlock. A short history of the West Indies. N. Y., St. Martin's Press, 1956. 316 p., illus.
An excellent popular survey of the history of the West Indies, presenting in its 18 chapters a balanced account of the history of the Spanish, British, and French islands and covering the development of the whole area, showing it to be an interrelated process, part of the process of European expansion to this continent. It covers the period from the discovery until the latest current developments, touching every different aspect of this evolution: political, administrative, social, economic, and institutional. In spite of some minor omissions and errors, the best book in its field yet to appear. [A. Santana]

2339. Patterson, Jerry E. Spanish and Spanish American manuscripts in the Yale University Library (Yale U Lib G, 31:3, Jan. 1957, p. 110-133).
A brief historical account of the Del Monte purchase, the gifts of Hiram Bingham, and the gifts of Henry Raup Wagner to Yale University, together with a listing of the collections of Spanish and Spanish American manuscripts divided by subject and date. Each entry describes the manuscript, giving the author, the date, an indication of the subject, the pages and other pertinent data. [R. R. Hill]

2340. Paul, C. Questions d'histoire. (Études critiques). Port-au-Prince, Imp. de l'État, 1955. 64 p.
Contains several studies, among them a discussion of the ideas presented by Dr. E. Charlier in his *Aperçu sur la formation historique de la nation haïtienne*, and a study of the recognition of Haitian Independence by France and the role played by President Boyer in these negotiations. [A. Santana]

2341. Peraza Sarausa, Fermín. La obra del P. Zulaica en Cuba (RIB, 5:4, oct.-dic. 1955, 275-289).
Documented biographical data on the Spanish Franciscan Father José Román Zulaica y Gárate, who died in 1943, and his most important historical works, dedicated mainly to the beginnings of the printing press in Spanish America and the intellectual contributions of the Franciscan Order in Mexico during the 16th century. The author discusses at length Zulaica's work on the introduction of the printing press in Santiago de Cuba, which occurred, according to him, in 1799. [A. Santana]

2342. Perú. Archivo Nacional. Memoria del director del Archivo Nacional del Perú, Dr. Óscar Malca Olguín, correspondiente al año 1953 (R Arch Nac Perú, 20:1, 1956, p. 206-241).
An account of the activities and progress of the Archive during 1953. [R. R. Hill]

2343. ————. ————. Revista del Archivo Nacional del Perú. T. 19, entrega 1-2, 1955; t. 20, entrega 1, 1956.
This review was established in 1920 and suspended publication with t. 18 in 1947. Publication was resumed with t. 19 in 1955. These numbers contain documents from the Archive, with introductory notes, information about the Archive, and an index to the first 18 volumes. [R. R. Hill]

2344. Phelan, John Leddy. The Philippine collection in the Newberry Library (Newberry Lib B, 3:8, Mar. 1955, p. 229-236).

A revealing survey of the very large body of materials, manuscript and printed, which has been brought together in the Newberry Library, Chicago, by additions in recent years of microfilm and various transcripts to the treasures of the older Ayer and Greenlee collections. Some separate items are mentioned, but there is no intention of presenting a list or a guide. [R. D. Hussey]

2345. **Pressoir, Catts; Ernst Trouillot; and Henock Trouillot.** Historiographie d'Haïti. México, Instituto Panamericano de Geografía e Historia (Publ., 168; Comisión de Historia, 66; Historiografías, 1), 1953. 298 p.
Essential biographical data on the best-known Haitian historians, together with a summary and evaluation of their work. It is divided into three parts, on the Spanish, the French, and the national periods, the last two receiving a more detailed treatment. Aside from one section on English travellers in the early part of the 19th century, the volume deals mainly with books written in French and Spanish. Contains also a brief section on historical manuals, compilations of laws, and bibliographies. [A. Santana]

2346. **Quintana, Jorge.** Algunas noticias sobre masonería en el Archivo Nacional de Cuba (B Arch Nac, Habana, 51-52, enero 1952-dic. 1953, i. e. 1954, p. 23-41).
A study of the origins and early growth of masonry in Cuba, based mainly on documentary data from the Archivo Nacional at Habana. After briefly sketching the earliest masonic activity in the island, during the British occupation of Habana in 1763, the author studies the formal establishment of the first masonic lodge in 1793 at Santiago de Cuba by French emigrés from St. Domingue, and the subsequent development in Cuba of the movement. Direct masonic influence from Spain was a late arrival. The author considers there is enough data for an affirmative assertion on the masonic origins of the revolutionary movement of 1868; he describes the Spanish persecution of Céspedes, Aguilera, and other patriots because of their masonic activities. Most of the documentary material presented is from the 19th century. [A. Santana]

2347. **Remos, Juan J.** Historiadores de Cuba (R Bib Nac, Habana, 2. serie, 6:1, enero-marzo 1955, p. 45-92).
Brief analysis and synthesis, with critical commentary and bibliography, of Cuban historiography from the 18th century to the present, devoting its main attention to the 19th and 20th centuries. Presents toward the end a good panorama of the present state of Cuban historiography. [A. Santana]

2348. **Rodríguez Demorizi, Emilio.** Apuntes y documentos (Clío, 22:98, enero-abril 1954, p. 25-43; 22:100, julio-sept. 1954, p. 121-132; 22:101, oct.-dic. 1954, p. 226-251; 23:102, enero-marzo 1955, p. 50-57; 23:105, oct.-dic. 1955, p. 194-204).

Brief data on a variety of subjects: several historical figures from both the colonial and republican periods in the history of the Dominican Republic; the shipbuilding industry in Española from the 15th to the 18th century; the different names held throughout its history by the city of Concepción de la Vega Real; the cession of the western part of the island to France by the treaty of Ryswick; the state of Santiago de los Caballeros in 1813; plus a miscellany of material on the state of convents in the island at different periods. Extensive bibliography citations. Based on documentary material from the Archivo General de Indias, the editor's private collection, and printed primary sources. [A. Santana]

2349. ———— (ed.). La era de Francia en Santo Domingo; contribución a su estudio. Ciudad Trujillo, Academia Dominicana de la Historia, (2), 1955. 311 p.
A collection of documents and articles dealing with the French occupation of Santo Domingo (1795-1809). [R. R. Hill]

2350. **Rodríguez Vicente, María Encarnación.** El comercio cubano y la guerra de emancipación norteamericana (An Estud Am, 11, 1954, p. 61-106).
Documented article on the effect on Cuban commerce and general economic life of the American Revolutionary War. The trade between the island and the rebellious Anglo-American colonies is only part of the story presented here. After offering a general panorama of Cuban economic life at that moment and the structure of trade between Spain and her Caribbean colonies, the author describes the effect of the war on Cuban life and trade, touching incidentally on other aspects of Spanish trade in the Gulf and Caribbean region. During the war period it became necessary to enlarge the scope of Cuban trade, as the island became the supply center for the Spanish armies engaged against the British throughout the whole region. It became necessary to import food and supplies from the U. S. and from other Spanish colonies in the Caribbean. In this connection the author analyzes the fiscal, legal, and institutional transformation resulting from this increased trade. Based on a limited number of published primary and secondary sources and an extensive documentary research at the Archivo General de Indias. [A. Santana]

2351. **Roig de Leuchsenring, Emilio.** Algunos viejos edificios coloniales de La Habana (Cuad Inst Interam Hist Mun Inst, 11, dic. 1954, p. 29-59).
Notes on the history of various buildings, mostly of the 18th and 19th centuries. Apparently based upon local records. [R. D. Hussey]

2352. **Rubio Sánchez, Manuel.** El añil o xiquilite (A Soc Geog Hist Guat, 26:3-4, sept.-dic. 1952, i. e. 1955, p. 313-349).
An excellent study, from the Guatemalan Archives, of "the agricultural product about which the economy of Guatemala [e. g., Central America] revolved from . . . the mid 16th century to the start of the 19th." The study is based upon laws and general accounts for earlier period,

with much statistical information for the 18th and 19th centuries. [R. D. Hussey]

2353. ————. Breve historia del desarrollo del cultivo del café en Guatemala (A Soc Geog Hist Guat, 27:1-4, marzo 1953-dic. 1954, p. 169-238).

A valuable collection of data, to about 1900 in this installment. Coffee was known in Guatemala as a beverage by 1743, and apparently the Jesuits introduced its cultivation about 1760. Small scale commercial activity began about 1835, as *grana* (cochineal) met with trouble (as had its predecessor, anil) and coffee exporting was placed on a firm foundation by the second half of the century. Detailed figures are given from about 1860. To be continued. [R. D. Hussey]

2354. Seminario Relativo a la Enseñanza de la Historia, San Juan, marzo 4-9, 1954. Documento VIII. México, Instituto Panamericano de Geografía e Historia, 1955. 53 p.

Reports and *ponencias* presented at the Seminar. Among the subjects covered are the ends of history, its relation to the social sciences, its methodology and the preparation of teachers, texts, and programs. [A. Santana]

2355. Sociedad de Geografía e Historia de Honduras. Revista de la . . . Tegucigalpa. T. 34, no. 1-9, julio-marzo 1956, p. 437-904, xxxviii p.

This is the new title and continuation of the *Revista del Archivo y Biblioteca Nacionales,* the organ of the Society of Geography and History of Honduras. This issue is devoted to a homage to Dr. José Trinidad Reyes, the founder of the National University and spiritual father of Honduran culture, on the occasion of the centenary of his death. Included are tributes to, articles about, and documents regarding Reyes. [R. R. Hill]

2356. Stimson, Frederick S. The beginnings of American Hispanism, 1770-1830 (Hispania, AATSP, 37:4, Dec. 1954, p. 482-489).

A handy survey of literary allusions to Spain in the writings of the U. S., interpreted and evaluated essentially by intuition. [R. D. Hussey]

2357. Stone, Doris. Estampas de Honduras. México, 1954. 252 p., illus.

A survey history from the Conquest through the 19th century. [W. V. Scholes]

2358. Teixidor, Felipe. Bibliografía del agrarismo en México hasta 1930 (B Bib Nac, México, 2. época, 6:4, oct.-dic. 1955, p. 3-40).

Unannotated, and alphabetically by authors; very extensive on the colonial period—when few of the items were upon *agrarismo* as such—as well as on the 19th and 20th centuries. [R. D. Hussey]

2359. Tió, Aurelio. Fundación de San Germán y su significación en el desarrollo político, económico, social y cultural de Puerto Rico. San Juan, Biblioteca de Autores Puertorriqueños, 1956. 274 p.

Series of essays on the foundation, history, and significance of the town of San German in the history of Puerto Rico. The town, the second in age on the island, was, according to Sr. Tió, the place at which the most important events in the history of the island have somehow or other happened most of the time. Based on rather flimsy evidence (selected transcriptions from the Archivo General de Indias and published primary and secondary sources) and a generous use of the adverb "probablemente," he makes a series of sweeping controversial assertions: Columbus' discovery of Puerto Rico at what was later to be the early site of San German, the establishment of San German as the first urban settlement on the island, etc. The book has no continuity of exposition but is rather a storehouse of unconnected data, some of them unpublished until now, on a wide variety of subjects. [A. Santana]

2360. Torre Villar, Ernesto de la. Notas para una historia de la instrucción pública en Puebla de los Ángeles (Estud Hist Am, p. 563-684).

A study based largely upon printed works, and dealing largely with the colonial period. But a few manuscripts are used and some data appear on the 19th century. 16 teaching institutions and the Biblioteca Palafoxiana are discussed. [R. D. Hussey]

2361. Trens, Manuel B. Historia de la H. Ciudad de Veracruz y de su ayuntamiento. México, Tall. Gráf. de la Nación, 1955. 178 p., illus.

Sweeping survey from the colonial period down to the present. [W. V. Scholes]

2362. Troncoso Sánchez, Pedro. Las guerras europeas de Santo Domingo (Clío, 23:102, enero-marzo 1955, p. 1-12).

Originally delivered as a lecture before the Academia Dominicana de la Historia. The author discusses at length the main works by Dominican historian Manuel Arturo Peña Batlle, commenting at length on one of the subjects dealt with by the latter writer; the repercussion in the Dominican Republic of the main European wars, from the 16th to the 20th century. Brief undocumented essay. [A. Santana]

2363. Uprimny, Leopoldo. ¿Capitalismo calvinista o romanticismo semi-escolástico de los próceres de la independencia colombiana? (Universitas, Cien Jur, 6, 1954, p. 87-148).

Describes Spanish American (not just Colombian) Independence as a "conservative" reaction against Bourbon absolutism and *afrancesado* liberalism; "Calvinist capitalism" is mentioned only casually, in reply to another article. This essay is not necessarily convincing, but representative of what seems to be a growing school of thought. Cf. Guillermo Fúrlong, "Causas y caracteres de la Independencia Hispanoamericana" (Hist, B A, 1:4, abril-junio 1956, p 25-

43), a convenient analysis of the book by the same title (*HLAS, no. 19*, item 3021) that contained the proceedings of a historical congress on causes of Independence. Fúrlong points out with approval that the Spanish and Spanish American historians participating paid far more attention to the "fuentes ideológicas hispanas"— e. g., Francisco Suárez—than to French Encyclopedists. [D. Bushnell]

2364. Utrera, Cipriano de. Los sínodos del Arzobispado de Santo Domingo (Clío, 22:100, julio-sept. 1954, p. 141-162).
Data and documentation from the Archivo General de Indias and the Archivo de Palacio in Madrid on the different synods held by the Roman Catholic Church in Santo Domingo from 1539 to 1938. [A. Santana]

2365. Valle, Rafael Heliodoro. Químicos mexicanos (Hist Mex, 4:1, julio-sept. 1954, p. 115-123).
A study, from printed but often uncommon sources, of a large number of Mexican chemists of the late 18th and earlier 19th century. Many were connected with the great Escuela de Minería. [R. D. Hussey]

2366. Venezuela. Archivo General de la Nación. Boletín del . . . Caracas. T. 42, no. 165, oct.-dic. 1954; t. 42, no. 167-169, enero-sept. 1955; t. 43, no. 170, oct.-dic. 1955; no. 171-173, enero-sept. 1956.
Each issue contains installments of the indexes of the various sections of the Archive. Also, there are selected documents and news items. [R. R. Hill]

2367. ————. Comisión Indigenista. Fuero indígena venezolano. Caracas, 1954. 2 v. Parte 1, Período de la Colonia (1552 a 1783); compilación y prólogo . . . Joaquín Gabaldón Márquez, 277 p.; parte 2, Período de la República (1811 a 1954) (Recopilación de leyes, decretos, resoluciones, reglamentos, convenios y aclaraciones sobre la materia); compilación . . . Cesáreo de Armellada; prólogo de Walter Dupouy, 396 p.
A collection of laws, regulations and other documents treating the legal situation of the Indians of Venezuela and the functions of the State and other organizations in reference to the problems involved. Part 1 covers the colonial period, 1552-1783, and part 2, the period of the republic, 1811-1954. The latter volume includes laws, decrees, resolutions, regulations, agreements, and clarifications regarding the subject. [R. R. Hill]

2368. Vivanco, Julián. Crónicas históricas de San Miguel de los Baños. Habana, El Sol, 1955. 33 p.
Local history with an overriding parochial viewpoint covering many matters from archaeology to literature but without relating to the larger historical picture of Cuba or the Caribbean. [A. Santana]

2369. Weymuller, François. Histoire du Mexique. Paris, Presses Universitaires de France ("Que sais-je?" Le point des connaissances actuelles, 574), 1953. 126 p., illus.
One of a lengthy series of good popularizations of knowledge. [R. D. Hussey]

2370. Wickberg, Edgar B. Spanish records in the Philippine National Archives (HAHR, 35:1, Feb. 1955, p. 77-89).
Shows that a large amount is still extant from the 18th century on, but very little for the earlier years. The report is the outgrowth of the Bancroft Library microfilming mission, and gives some idea of what has been copied for that library. [R. D. Hussey]

SPANISH AMERICA AND HAITI: THE COLONIAL PERIOD

GENERAL

ROLAND D. HUSSEY

A section on the colonies-as-a-whole is unlikely to have much concentration of topic, and, unfortunately, part of what concentration there is comes from a deplorable rehashing of worn out subjects and polemics. Nevertheless, one can point to several notable additions to scholarly resources.

Modesto Bargalló has done much to satisfy the long felt need of a study of colonial mining. The *Cedulario americano del siglo XVIII* is a happy departure from the common emphasis on laws of the 16th century, and valuable in itself.

Words fail with which properly to praise the study of trans-Atlantic shipping which is now appearing, by Pierre and Hugette Chaunu. And the study in early colonial policy by Juan Pérez de Tudela, though on a very long-worked period, is equally necessary for future students of colonial policy.

As in every year, worthwhile bibliographies, and reprints of books that have been neglected because of their rarity, are included, and studies in the field of religious history, of good quality even if largely in rather familiar aspects of the subject, continue to pile up. In addition, the centenary of the establishment of the dogma of the Immaculate Conception, in 1854, called forth a great body of writings of interest for the 16th century and later. (It must be recalled that the doctrine was practically official in the Spanish realms two centuries before it became dogma). Only two of these studies have been listed, and these because they especially pertained to America but many others appeared, especially in Spain, which might be worth the time of specialists.

2400. Academia de la Historia. Biblioteca. Catálogo de la colección de don Juan Bautista Muñoz. Madrid, 1954-1956. 3 v., port.

The prologue by Antonio Ballesteros Beretta includes a bio-bibliography, and a group of Múñoz' letters connected with his work is published in v. 3. The *Catálogo* lists in great detail, with good indices, the contents of this valuable and well-known collection of documents in extenso or abstract, including so far as possible the contents of many volumes which have never been in the Real Academia de la Historia. Many of the latter have never been transferred from their original depository, the present-day Biblioteca del Palacio; some cannot be found at all.

2401. Álvarez Mejía, Juan. La cuestión del clero indígena en la época colonial (R Javeriana, 44:220, nov. 1955, p. 224-233).
To be continued. Thoroughly documented discussion of an almost entirely neglected subject. The basic civil or ecclesiastical laws would have made no difference among races, as to entry into sacerdotal status. But pride of blood, and doubts about legitimacy and ability to fill the positions with honor—because of faulty background—barred practically all Indians and mestizos from ordination. This was originally by administrative practice, but later had the support of law.

2402. Anuario de estudios atlánticos. No. 1. Madrid-Las Palmas, Patronato de la Casa de Colón, 1955-.
Has not been seen, but according to dependable mentions elsewhere, this new periodical is a scholarly review of high quality, devoted to the history of the Canaries, especially in their conjunction with the American colonies.

2403. Arciniega, Rosa. En torno a una célebre polémica. La libertad del historiador (Cuadernos, 16, enero-feb. 1956, p. 74-80).
Good popular treatment of the well-known dispute between the *cronista* Antonio de Herrera, and the Conde de Puñonrostro, over the former's account of the acts of Pedrarias Dávila, grandfather of the Conde.

2404. Armas Medina, Fernando de. Notas historiográficas sobre la Iglesia en Indias (Estud Am, 10:46, julio 1955, p. 63-69).
Another belaboring of the wornout theme of the *leyenda negra* and the reaction against it.

2405. Arrubla, Juan Manuel. Colón y América (B Hist Antig, 42:487-488, mayo-junio 1955, p. 265-273).
A rather shallow *discurso de recepción* concerned with geographical ideas and concepts of ancient days, especially as to Plato's story of Atlantis.

2406. Ballesteros-Gaibrois, Manuel. ¿Quienes acompañaron a Colón en el Descubrimiento? (Mundo Hisp, 8:91, oct. 1955, p. 18-19, 60-61).
A popularized account of the work of a few investigators of the subject named, and especially of that of Miss Alicia B. Gould y Quincy, to give that deceased Bostonian the form of name by which she was revered for some 40 years throughout Spanish scholarly circles. It is of interest to learn that her notes have not been dispersed, but remain in the custody of Señor José de la Peña, director of the Archivo General de Indias.

2407. Bara, Modesto. La patria de Colón (Mundo Hisp, 8:91, oct. 1955, p. 11-12, 51-60).
Without troubling to expound his documents—which presumably are the same as those that have long ago been discredited by most scholars—the author claims that the Discoverer was a Galician, he being different from the weaver and vintner of the name who lived in Italy.

2408. Bargalló, Modesto. La minería y la metalurgia en la América Española durante la época colonial; con un apéndice sobre la industria del hierro en México desde la iniciación de la Independencia hasta el presente. México, Fondo de Cultura Económica, 1955. 442 p., illus. (part col.), ports., maps (part. fold.), facsims.
An enormously valuable compilation of facts about all areas and the whole three centuries of the colonial era. The appendix on the Independence era has only 12 pages. Bibliography, p. 367-401.

2409. Bataillon, Marcel. L'idée de la découverte de l'Amérique chez les espagnols du XVIᵉ siècle, d'après un livre récent (B Hisp, 55:1, 1953, p. 23-55).
Discusses and disputes with Edmundo O'Gorman's *Idea del descubrimiento de América* (Mexico, 1951). O'Gorman replied in 1954 (see item 2467) and Bataillon replied to him with *Sur l'idée de la découverte de l'Amérique*, in this same periodical, 56:4, 1954, p. 364-365.

2410. ———. Pour l' "Epistolario" de Las Casas. Une lettre et un brouillon (B Hisp, 56:4, 1954, p. 366-387).
A photograph and transcription (which is fortu-

nate for readers of this printed version) of a letter found, out of place, in the Guatemala series of the Archivo de Indias. It is not dated or signed, but Bataillon establishes a near certainty that it was written by Las Casas in 1549, probably to Domingo de Soto. It mentions both North and South America, in expounding ideas which are already familiar to anyone who keeps up with the Lascasiana canon.

2411. ————, and **Eduardo O'Gorman.** Dos concepciones de la tarea histórica, con motivo de la idea del descubrimiento de América. México, Imp. Universitaria, 1955. 115 p.

Reprints two articles which are listed separately here (see items 2409 and 2467), the first published by Bataillon in 1953, the other by O'Gorman in reply in 1954, and adds an extensive correspondence between the two, in 1954. But does not reprint Bataillon's reply of 1954, also mentioned above, to the O'Gorman article.

2412. Blanco Castilla, Fidel. Hernando de Soto, el centauro de las Indias. Madrid, Carrera del Castillo, 1955. 358 p.

A popular history, rather eulogistic and mostly from printed sources. But recounts his life in both South and North America.

2413. Blanco-Fombona, Rufino. El conquistador español del siglo XVI. Ensayo de interpretación. Prólogo de Joaquín Gabaldón Márquez; estudio bibliográfico por Edgar Gabaldón Márquez. Caracas, Ediciones Edimé (Grandes libros venezolanos), 1956. 292 p.

The first edition of this well-known essay appeared in Madrid in 1922.

2414. Bonet de Sotillo, Dolores. El tráfico ilegal en las colonias españolas. Caracas, Universidad Central de Venezuela, 1955. 28 p.

A handy résumé of information from the well-known works of such specialists as Haring and Arcila Farías.

2415. Borah, Woodrow. The New World (Americas, Franciscan Hist, 12:3, Jan. 1956, p. 246-257).

A useful essay, not documented but by an expert, upon autonomous institutions of government in the New World, and their crushing by the Spanish government. Part 3 of "Representative institutions in the Spanish empire in the sixteenth century."

2416. Borges, Pedro. El sentido trascendente del descubrimiento y conversión de Indias (Miss Hisp, 13:37, 1956, p. 141-177).

An interesting essay on the theoretical or philosophical interpretations of the American discovery and acts of religious conversion. Explores contemporaneous and colonial answers to such questions as: "Why was America discovered?", "Why were the discovery and conversion entrusted to Spain?", and "What have been the effects of discovery and conversion?" Catalogues the answers under such headings as "The theory of the punishment of Indian sins," and "The impending end of the world as the cause of discovery and conversion." [C. Gibson]

2417. Borome, Joseph A. Winsor's *History of America*, 1880-1881 (Boston Pub Libr Q, 5:3, July 1953, p. 119-139).

A valuable article on the origins of the idea of the eight-volume cooperative history named—which had so much of value in it for the history of Latin America—and on its writing, publishing, and the reviews which followed. Based upon extensive correspondence of the people concerned, found in libraries all the way from Boston to San Marino, California. No specific attention is given to the Latin American aspects.

2418. Bromley, J. S., and A. Goodwin. A select list of works on Europe and Europe overseas, 1715-1815. Edited for the Oxford Eighteenth Century Group. Oxford, Clarendon Press, 1956. 132 p.

Unannotated, short title, classed catalogue. No value for specialists, but a handy check list for people working in unfamiliar fields, and has sections on the French, Spanish, and Portuguese colonies.

2419. Carande, Ramón. Das westindische Gold und die Kreditpolitik Karls V (Ges Auf Kult Span, 10, 1955, p. 1-22).

An advance product of research for the author's third volume of *Carlos V y sus banqueros*. It surveys the loans made 1519-1556, "as a means of clarifying the value and destination of the treasure exported from Spain." The treasure, of course, came mostly from America. Carande gives much data upon this treasure, claiming that the real flood started with the return of La Gasca's fleet from Peru in 1550.

2420. Carcer, M. de. ¿Se llamó alguna vez patata a la papa en el siglo XVI? (Arch Hispalense, 20:63, 1954, p. 73-77).

Erudite notes, showing that the potato was introduced into Sevilla sometime in the second half of the 16th century, and was always called *papa* in that century, although it has been known as the *patata* since the 19th.

2421. Casa de los Duques de Frías. Archivo de los Duques de Frías. Introducción de José Fernández de Velasco, Duque de Frías. I. Casa de Velasco. Madrid, Dirección General de Archivos y Casa de los Duques de Frías, 1955. xxxv, 615 p., illus.

The privately owned and controlled, recently organized archive of the Dukes of Frías is open to the public in the Castillo de Montemayor, near Montilla (Cordoba). Its documents in this first series, which includes the titles of Dukes of Frías and of Uceda, Condestable de Castilla, and Marques de Villena, stretch from the 13th century to 1851. American value is probably not large, but surely will be extensive for the archive as a whole, as more inventories are published.

2422. Castro Seoane, José. Aviamiento y catálogo de las misiones que en el siglo XVI pasaron de España a Indias y Filipinas según los libros de Contratación (Miss Hisp. 13:37, 1956, p. 83-140).

Documentation on supplies for missions and financial disbursements granted by the Casa de Contratación in the 16th century. Contains valuable information on the material aspect of missionary preparation. [C. Gibson]

2423. Cedulario americano del siglo XVIII . . . Parte I. Cédulas de Carlos II (1679-1700). Edición, estudio y comentarios por Antonio Muro Orejón. Sevilla, Escuela de Estudios Hispanamericanos (Publ., 99), 1956. xcvi, 834 p.

The lengthy introduction discusses the sources of such *cedularios* as are used, and their earlier exploitation, and also, by subjects, their content for the period. There follow, chronologically, 437 texts from Feb. 28, 1679, to Nov. 18, 1700, indices of persons, places, and subjects, and a brief title list of the cedulas.

2424. Chaunu, Huguette, and Pierre Chaunu. A la recherche des fluctuations cycliques dans l'économie des XVIᵉ et XVIIᵉ siècles. Crises de tonnage. Cris de fret (*in* Hommage à Lucien Febvre, v. 2, Paris, 1953, p. 389-407).

2425. Chaunu, Pierre, and Huguette Chaunu. Économie atlantique. Économie mondiale, 1504-1650. Problèmes de fait et de méthode (Cahiers d'Hist Mond, 1:1, juillet 1953, p. 91-104).

The above two studies are anticipations of the long-awaited multi-volume statistical study, "L'Atlantique espagnol de 1504-1650," but have value of themselves. The full study is said to have gone to press in Paris in 1955, but has not been seen for use in this *HLAS*.

2426. ————, and ————. Séville et l'Atlantique, 1504-1650. Paris, Colin, 1955-. T. 1-5.

There are to be eight tomes, in ten volumes, of this amazing work. T. 1 is on methodology. T. 6-8 (v. 6-10) are to be statistical tables, charts, and interpretation.
T. 2-5 present data on shipping, for the whole period under discussion. Tables list, by year and fleet or *navio suelto*, each vessel that sailed in either direction between America and Spain. Details are given, so far as available, as to name of craft, shipmaster, owner, type, tonnage, crew, age, and port to or from which sailing. Extensive notes add much specialized information upon these points, and a great deal about background factors that explain the voyage, or details of the voyage when those were other than routine. Data are not usually given on cargo or prices, but some even of those appear. References are carefully made to the probative documents, mostly in *Contratación* or *Contaduría* of the Archives of the Indies. Even were no further volumes to be published, scholars could mine these five for data upon a host of subjects, for years to come.

2427. Clissold, Stephen. Sarmiento de Gamboa and Sir Walter Raleigh (Atlante, 2:2, Apr. 1954, p. 78-83).

A poorly documented article, really upon the whole life of the never quite fortunate Sarmiento de Gamboa. But points out that the latter was taken by Raleigh's ships, off the Azores, while on his way to Spain after colonizing the Straits of Magellan, and that he apparently had a considerable influence upon Raleigh by his talk about El Dorado.

2428. Cobo, Bernabé. Obras. Madrid, Biblioteca de Autores Españoles (81, 92), 1956. 2 v.

There is an excellent introduction by the editor, Padre Francisco Mateos. Texts are then reprinted of Cobo's till now very scarce and costly *Historia del Nuevo Mundo* (4 v., Sevilla, E. Rasco, 1890-1893) and *Historia de la fundación de Lima* (Lima, Imp. Liberal, 1882) and some lesser items.

2429. Commissione Scientifica del Comitate Onoranze ad Amerigo Vespucci. Mostra Vespucciana. Catálogo. Prefacio de Alberto Giraldo. Firenze, 1955. 188 p., 67 plates and maps.

An exhibition, gathered up from various sources, concerning the discovery of America and commemorating the 500th anniversary of the birth of Vespucci. The catalogue lists some 300 items, including manuscripts, books, maps, atlases, and nautical instruments. The exhibit was at the Palazzo Vecchio from June 1954 to September 1955.

2430. Cummins, Lejeune. Antonelli the younger, first engineer of the Indies (Mid Am, 38:1, Jan. 1956, p. 3-14).

A good straightforward account of the work of Antonelli in fortifying the major harbors of the Caribbean at the end of the 16th century, but entirely from printed sources.

2431. Domínguez Company, Francisco. Bibliografía de las instituciones locales de Hispanoamérica (época colonial) (RIB, 6:3, julio-sept. 1956, p. 209-223).

A lightly annotated list, with usually abbreviated but adequate data, of sources and studies upon municipal government and Indian pueblos, arranged under the following headings: Relaciones; Peticiones y consultas; Leyes y ordenanzas; Colecciones de documentos; Actas capitulares; Protocolos y sentencias; Crónicas e historias generales; Tratados; Estudios actuales; Bibliografías; Revistas.

2432. Dornic, François. Le commerce des français à Cadiz d'après les papiers d'Antoine Granjean, 1752-1777 (A Éc Soc Civ, 9:3, juillet-sept. 1954, p. 311-327).

A discussion based upon the papers of a Lyons silk merchant who was active in Cadiz, for himself and as the agent of others. He had dealings in such commodities as cloves and beaver hats, as well as in textiles, and much of his trade was American.

2433. **Durand, José.** Baquianos y chapetones, criollos y gachupines. Albores de la sociedad americana colonial (Cuad Am, 87:3, mayo-junio 1956, p. 148-162).

Examination of the forms of rivalry between Peninsulars and the local Creole aristocracy in colonial times. Traces the rivalry from the 16th century and identifies the varieties of factionalism. [C. Gibson]

2434. ————. El lujo indiano (Hist Mex, 6:1, julio-sept. 1956, p. 59-74).

An essay on ostentation in architecture, dress, and behavior, with examples drawn from many parts of colonial Spanish America. Ostentation is seen as a provincial habit in distinction from that of Spain. [C. Gibson]

2435. **Esquemeling, John.** The buccaneers of America. N. Y., Macmillan, 1953. 272 p.

Appears to be a reissue of the London 1893 version of the 1684 English.

2437. **Gesammelte Aufsätze zur Kulturgeschichte Spaniens.** Münster-Westfallen, Germany, Aschendorffsche Verlagsbuchhandlung (Spanische Forschung der Görresgesellschaft, Erste reihe, 10, 11), 1955. 2 v.

Band 10 revives a series last published in 1940. Published by a society named for Guido Görres (1805-1852), the great German Catholic historian, the series specializes in European aspects of history, and on matters at least cognate to religion. But occasional articles with American value are being published.

2438. **González Ruiz, Felipe.** Juan de la Cosa y el primer mapa de América (R Geog Am, año 21, 38:226, julio-oct. 1954 p. 35-42).

A good popularized treatment, which includes a reproduction of the American portion of the well-known map of 1500.

2439. **Goslinga, C. Ch.** Emancipatie en emancipator. De geschiedenis van de slavernij op de benedenwindse eilanden en van het werk der bevrijding. Assen, Netherlands, Van Gorchum, 1956. 187 p.

As might be supposed from its title, primarily concerned with slavery in Aruba, Bonaire, and Curaçao, and especially the legal status of the slaves and the emancipation movement. Covers 1634-1863, and in chapter 1, "Historical survey of the slave trade in Curaçao" (1634-1778), and a few other places, there are scraps of information that might interest students of the slave trade of the Spanish Caribbean.

2440. **Greepe, Thomas.** The true and perfecte newes of the woorthy and valiaunt exploytes, performed and doone by that valiant knight Syr Frauncis Drake, not onely at Sanoto Domingo, and Carthagena, but also nowe at Cales and uppon the coast of Spayne, 1587. Now reproduced in facsimile from the original ed. in the private library of Henry C. Taylor. With an introd., notes, and a bibliography of English military books by David W. Waters. Hartford, Conn., Printed for H. C. Taylor by C. P. R. (Americanum nauticum, no. 3), 1955. 95 p., facsim., ports., fold. maps.

The American value is from the text on the Caribbean raid of 1585-1586, and the notes on the related printed account by Walter Bigges, and the map by Baptista Boazio. 500 copies were printed, for distribution only by the London and New York firm of Henry Stevenson and Stiles.

2441. **Gutiérrez de Arce, Manuel.** Regio patronato indiano. Ensayo de valoración histórico-canónica (An Estud Am, 11, 1954, p. 107-168).

Well-documented general essay on the royal patronage, its historical characterization, canonical validity, and the various interpretations made upon it. Concludes that the cedulas and other enactments proceeding from the patronage constituted authentic and legitimate ecclesiastical legislation. [C. Gibson]

2442. **Hanke, Lewis.** Was Bartolomé de las Casas a scholar? (*in* Miscelánea de estudios dedicados al Dr. Fernando Ortiz. Habana, 1956, 6 p.).

Answers a charge of the Franciscan historian Antonine S. Tibesar, in the latter's review (Cat Hist R, 38:4, Jan. 1953) of Hanke's *Bartolomé de las Casas, bookman, scholar, and propagandist,* 1952 (see *HLAS, no. 18, 1952,* item 1707).

2443. **Hernández y Sánchez Barba, Mario.** La participación del Estado en la estructuración de los grupos humanos en Hispanoamérica durante el siglo XVI (R Estud Pol, 55:84, nov.-dic. 1955, p. 193-225).

A summary of the laws which affected the various racial groups as to such things as landowning, chance for holding office or receiving honors, or restrictions upon the lower classes. Like most such articles, fails to deal much with the actual application or to prove the effects, but the sources are detailed and the treatment is thoughtful.

2444. **Hussey, Roland Dennis.** America in European diplomacy, 1597-1604 (R Hist Am, 41, junio 1956, p. 1-30).

An effort to deal with the subject named from the sources of Spain, France, and England and, to a lesser degree, the Netherlands. "An advance product of thirty years of research upon the Caribbean as a center of international rivalry, 1492-1789."

2445. **Jos, Emilio.** Las Casas, historian of Christopher Columbus (Americas, Franciscan Hist, 12:4, Apr. 1956, p. 355-362).

A defense of Las Casas against charges that he tampered with Fernando Colon's history of his father.

2446. Juderías y Loyot, Julián. Leyenda negra. Madrid, Editora Nacional, 1954. 407 p.

First edition, Madrid, 1917; second edition, revised and augmented by the author, Madrid, *ca.* 1921.

2447. Junco, Alfonso. Inquisición sobre la Inquisición. Figuras y episodios de la historia de México. 2. ed. México, Campeador, 1956. 140 p.

An unchanged reprint of the book published in 1950 (see *HLAS, no. 16, 1950,* item 1525). The suggestion in the title of this second edition, that it is of special value for Mexico, is unjustified.

2448. Kratz, Guillermo. El tratado hispano-portugués de límites de 1750 y sus consecuencias. Estudio sobre la abolición de la Compañía de Jesús. Versión directa del alemán por Diego Bermúdez Camacho. Roma, Institutum Historicum S. I. (Bibliotheca Instituti Historici S. I., 5), 1954. 312 p.

An excellent study of the events of 1750-1761, which brings out Minister Wall's anger over the breakdown of the treaty and his anti-Jesuit policy. A final chapter discusses the era of 1761-1767. But in spite of the title, and some suggestions here and there as to the author's beliefs, there is no proof, or effort to offer proof, of his claim that this was the real cause of the expulsion of 1767.

2449. Lejarza, Fidel de. Expansión de las Clarisas en América y Extremo Oriente (Arch Ib Am, 14:54, abril-junio 1954, p. 129-190; 14:55, julio-sept. 1954, p. 265-310; 14:56, oct.-dic. 1954, p. 395-455; concluirá).

Notes toward a history of the little-known but important functions, in teaching, caring for orphans, and similar capacities, of the Second Franciscan Order of cloistered nuns. These reached Mexico, Santo Domingo, and Peru in the middle of the 16th century. Their story is carried to the 18th century. The conclusion will presumably discuss the Philippines, but had not appeared in the serial through 1955.

2450. Lobsiger, Georges. Deux mythes rajeunis par la découverte de l'Amérique: le bon sauvage et la cité utopique (B Soc Suisse Am, 12, sept. 1956, p. 1-17).

Catalogue, with commentary, of utopian and noble-savage concepts in European literature as affected by knowledge of America. [C. Gibson]

2451. Lohmann Villena, Guillermo. Cifras y claves indianas. Capítulos provisionales de un estudio sobre criptografía indiana (An Estud Am, 11, 1954, p. 285-300, 24 plates).

Discussion, in varying detail, of 44 examples of cryptographs used in connection with America, from the time of Cortés to the early 19th-century. The early ones are very simple substitution ciphers; later ones are mostly codes, for words or for syllables or for both. One involved the use of the cut out shield, with the *ventanas* revealing the significant words. The only faintly complicated cipher is that of the Jesuits, 1601, which seems to be a reflection of the Porta system, used in the Papal Curia well before that date.

2452. ——————. Documentos cifrados indianos (R Indias, Madrid, 15:60, abril-junio 1955, p. 255-282).

Transcription in clear of 12 documents in the Archivo de Indias (1533-1818) of which important parts were enciphered. Nine are of the 16th century, mostly written in Mexico but some in Panama or Habana. These deal mostly with trade and/or foreign dangers. Two are of the 18th century, dealing with Colonia or the Malvinas, and the last one is by Viceroy Apodaca in Mexico, referring to the danger of an attack from the U. S.

2453. Madariaga, Salvador de. El auge del Imperio Español en América. B. A., Editorial Sudamericana, 1955. 527 p., illus.

See item 2455. [C. Gibson]

2454. ——————. L'essor de l'empire espagnol d'Amérique. Traduction de Marcelle Sibon. Paris, A. Michel, 1955. 490 p., illus., port., map.

Apparently a straightforward translation of Book 1 of the Spanish of 1945 (see *HLAS, no. 11, 1945,* item 1971).

2455. ——————. El ocaso del Imperio Español en América. B. A., Editorial Sudamericana, 1955. 553 p.

This and Madariaga's *El auge del Imperio Español en América* (see item above) constitute a new edition of a work first published in 1945 under the title *Cuadro histórico de las Indias* (see *HLAS, no. 11, 1945,* item 1971). [C. Gibson]

2456. Martínez, Manuel María. Fray Bartolomé de las Casas, "El gran calumniado." Madrid, Imp. La Rasa, 1955. 210 p.

Refutes all the attacks that anyone has ever made upon, and lauds all of the work of, Las Casas. For earlier version, in articles, see *HLAS, no. 18, 1952,* item 1717a, and *HLAS, no. 19,* item 3166.

2457. ——————. Fray Bartolomé de las Casas y la patria de Colón (R Indias, Madrid, 15:61-62, julio-dic. 1955, p. 555-567).

Combats the thesis of Padre Tomás Barreira, S. J., that Colón was a *gallego.*

2458. Martínez Cardós, José. La política económica indiana de las Cortes de Castilla (R Estud Pol, año 15, 54:82, julio-agosto 1955, p. 173-192).

A useful résumé of the facts and episodes recorded in the *Actas* of the Cortes, from the early 16th to early 17th centuries. Readers will not be surprised to learn that the Cortes supported about the same policy as did the merchants of

Sevilla and Cadiz, nor that Charles and Philip II paid little attention to the protests of the Cortes when that body's views ran counter to those of the monarchs.

2459. Mateos, Francisco. Los Loyola en América (Razón y Fe, 154:702-703, julio-agosto 1956, p. 60-76; 154:704-705, sept.-oct. 1956, p. 153-176).
Genealogical study of the relatives of St. Ignacio de Loyola in America, including Martín García de Loyola, Governor of Chile; Martín Ignacio de Loyola, bishop of Paraguay; and many others. To be continued. [C. Gibson]

2460. ——————. Pensamiento ignaciano sobre misiones de América (Razón y Fe, 153:696-697, enero-feb. 1956, p. 129-148).
Shows that from the first approval of the Order by Paul III, in 1539, there were thoughts of missionary work in the New World, but that the Council of the Indias held up any approval during the life of the founder.

2461. Melis, Federico. Il commercio transatlantico di una compagnia fiorentina stabilita à Siviglia à pochi anni dalle imprese di Cortes e Pizarro (*in* Fernando el Católico e Italia, Zaragoza, Spain, 1954, p. 129-206, fold. tables, facsims.).
From the Strozzi archives (in the State Archives of Florence) relates the work of Francesco Lapi i Campagnia, founded in Florence in 1532 and established in Sevilla and Cadiz from 1534. It did much business with the New World.

2462. Millares Carlo, Agustín, and José Ignacio Mantecón. Álbum de paleografía hispanoamericana de los siglos XVI y XVII. México, Instituto Panamericano de Geografía e Historia (Publ. 148; Comisión de Historia, 46; Manuales de técnica de la investigación de la historia y ciencias afines, 3), 1955. I, Introducción, 187 p., illus.; III, Transcripciones, 132 p.
A paleographical guide and source book containing summary histories of Spanish and colonial calligraphy with bibliography and many examples of writing styles. V. 3 contains transcriptions of documents from the 12th to the 17th centuries, with a heavy concentration upon colonial Spanish America. Apart from their application as a paleographic guide, the documents are noteworthy as contributions to historical knowledge on many different subjects. [C. Gibson]

2463. Moore, John Robert. Defoe and the South Sea Company (Boston Pub Libr Q, 5:4, Oct. 1953, p. 174-188).
A critical article which shows that Defoe was not, as has usually been supposed, the inspirer or the main spring behind the actions of 1711 which brought the company into being, and that he had some reservations about their wisdom.

2464. Muñoz Pérez, José. Los proyectos sobre España e Indias en el siglo XVIII:

el proyectismo como género (R Estud Pol, año 15, 54:81, mayo-junio 1955, p. 169-195).
Shows that the many "projects" which—under various names—were suggested as a means of regenerating Spain, mostly assigned a prominent role to reforms in America. The article concentrates upon the second half of the century, but has some information upon *proyectos* even of the later 17th century.

2465. Museo del Ejército. Catálogo. Madrid, Ediciones Ares, 1953-1955. 3 v., illus. (part col.), ports. (part col.), plans.
This museum, established in its present form in 1940, amalgamates the collections of the various service museums, of which that of *Artillería* was founded in 1803. These three sumptuous, folio-size volumes list thousands of objects, mostly for the period from the 16th century on. Some have a direct American connection; many of course illustrate things that were true in America as elsewhere.

2466. Novoa, Emilio. Las Sociedades Económicas de Amigos del País. Su influencia en la emancipación colonial americana. Prólogo de José García Goldara. Madrid, Prensa Española, 1955. 141 p.
Deals with the societies of Madrid, Vizcaya, Guatemala, and Habana in some detail, and mentions others. The author seems curiously impressed with the necessity of proving that the *Sociedades* were not related to Freemasonry and were not anti-Church, and has by no means exhausted the possible treatment of many other angles. But barring something more scholarly, worth reading.

2467. O'Gorman, Edmundo. Marcel Bataillon et l'idée de la découverte de l'Amérique (B Hisp, 56:4, 1954, p. 345-363).
Part of a polemic. See item 2409.

2468. Ortiz Fernández, Fernando. Los primeros técnicos azucareros de América. Habana, Imp. Universitaria, 1955. 21 p., port.
An address to the Asociación de Técnicos Azucareros de Cuba, without scholarly apparatus, but apparently a sort of abridged and specialized treatment of the material used by the author in his *Contrapunteo cubano* (Habana, 1940).

2469. Padden, Robert Charles. The Ordenanza del Patronazgo, 1574: an interpretative essay (Americas, Franciscan Hist, 12:4, Apr. 1956, p. 333-354).
As background for the *Ordenanza* itself, discusses many related aspects of history, such as the relations from 1474 between the newly absolutist Crown and the Church, the conflicts between the secular and regular clergy, and questions involving the tithes.

2470. Parks, George B. Ramusio's literary history (Stud Philol, 52:2, Apr. 1955, p. 127-148).
A useful discussion of the origins and develop-

ment of the well-known *Navigationi et viaggi,* and of the relations of the author with various savants and Americanists of the day. The viewpoint of the discussion is "literary" or "humanist" rather than critical in historical terms, but is well worth every historian's time.

2471. Pérez de Tudela Bueso, Juan. Las armadas de Indias y los orígenes de la política de colonización. Madrid, Instituto Gonzalo Fernández de Oviedo, 1956. 265 p.

Four articles, each with its own title, published in the *Revista de Indias* during 1954 and 1955 (for the first one, see *HLAS, no. 19,* item 3182). A critical re-examination of the history of the Spanish overseas development to 1505, actually in La Isla Española but the basis for later colonization elsewhere. Regards the story as one involving a conflict between two concepts: the *factoría-fortaleza* or *mercantilista* system, favored by Colón and by others who were members of, or influenced by, the merchant groups of Italy and Portugal and including many New Christians; and the *poblamiento* system or tradition, an expansion of the pattern and ideas of settlement and assimilation as a national enterprise which had been developed in Castile during the *Reconquista.* Points out that the Crown would benefit under either, but that the greatest benefit, an economic resource susceptible to State control and fiscalization, would come from the mercantilist viewpoint rather than from expansion of settlement and *señorio* alone.

The story is related in great detail. Perhaps partly for this reason it does not, as told, always clearly bring out the conflict between the two policies, or that the solution consisted in a sort of compromise by the Crown between the two, with gradual destruction of the monopoly and the essentially feudalistic system created under Colón, in favor of settlement and private enterprise under State controls. This was relatively complete by 1505.

But in spite of the fact that the reader will have to do some of the organizing and interpreting for himself, he will benefit greatly. Even the few specialists upon the period and area will learn many new facts, and get many new viewpoints, from this important work.

2472. ————. La quiebra de la factoría y el nuevo poblamiento de la Española (R Indias, Madrid, 15:60, abril-junio 1955, p. 197-252).

Third of a series of articles devoted to an analysis of the main trends and significance of Spanish colonization in America from 1493 to 1505. Studies the fall of Christopher Columbus as the head of the Spanish colonizing effort in Hispaniola and the events that led up to this process. Analyzes the changes introduced immediately afterwards, as exemplified especially in the new "capitulaciones." Based on an extensive bibliography of printed and secondary sources and original research in the Archivo General de Indias. [A. Santana]

2473. Perkins, Bradford. Toussaint, Miranda, Alliance (*in his* First rapprochement: England and the United States, 1795-1805. Philadelphia, Pa., 1955, p. 106-115).

Using excellent British and U. S. sources, though none of importance of a Spanish or Haitian origin, shows that although the interests of the two English-speaking nations were recognized to be divergent as early as 1793, the two tried sincerely to cooperate regarding relations with Haiti or projects by Miranda, especially 1797-1799.

2474. Peterson, Harold Leslie. Arms and armor in colonial America, 1526-1783. Harrisburg, Pa., Stackpole Co., 1956. 850 p., illus., ports.

A scholarly work, profusely illustrated with photographs from examples of arms and armor in various collections. It includes a considerable amount of material directly upon the Spanish parts of the present U. S. In addition, because of the highly international character of the arms trade in the period, much that is specifically relevant to English parts of America is also valuable for Spanish America.

2475. Reguera Sierra, Ernesto. El mapa de Piri Reis. Examen y valorización del pintoresco y desconcertante portulano ejecutado por el almirante turco Piri Reis, en 1513 y, presumiblemente, la primera carta geográfica turca que se refiere al hemisferio de Colón (R Geog Am, año 21, 38:226, julio-oct. 1954, p. 43-46).

A good semi-popularized discussion. Cites two Turkish writers but probably adds nothing to knowledge for the specialist.

2476. ————. Mapas de la Casa de Contratación de Sevilla (Hist, B A, 1:1, agosto-oct. 1955, p. 41-60).

A study of six maps made between 1525 and 1529. All have previously been known and published.

2477. Saltillo, Marqués de. La nobleza española en el siglo XVIII (R Arch Bib Mus, 60:2, julio-dic. 1954, p. 417-449).

Shows that a condition of being "noble" (possessed of a title, or of *hidalguía*) even in the 18th century was good descent, not the possession of material wealth. (Even artisans or *guardas de ganado vacuno* are registered on the *padrones.*) Also, that service to the Crown is always listed among the qualifications of those newly honored in the 18th century. Among the 200 *vitae* offered, many had served, *et al,* in the Consejo de Indias, or the Casa de Contratación, or in civil or military government in the Indies.

2478. Sandoval, Alonso de. De instauranda aethiopum salute; el mundo de la esclavitud negra en América. Bogotá, Empresa Nacional de Publicaciones (Biblioteca de la Presidencia de Colombia, 22), 1956. xxxvii, 598 p., facsim.

A reprint of the 1627 Sevilla first edition of this famous but little-used book.

2479. Severino de Santa Teresa, P. La Inmaculada en la conquista y coloniaje de la América española. Vitoria, Ediciones El Carmen, 1954. 338 p.

Has not been seen. Apparently a group of essays, rather than a synthesized history, which deal with many aspects of the doctrine of the Immaculate Conception in the history of America, with some emphasis on the work of the five brothers of Santa Teresa de Jesús who went to the colonies, and upon the devotion in Nicaragua.

2480. Silva Tena, María Teresa. Las Casas, biógrafo de sí mismo (Hist Mex, 4:4, abril-junio 1955, p. 523-543).

An interesting effort at interpreting the facts about his life which Las Casas reveals in his *Historia de las Indias*.

2481. Straet, Jan van der. New discoveries; the sciences, inventions, and discoveries of the Middle Ages and the Renaissance as represented in 24 engravings issued in the early 1580's by Stradanus. Norwalk, Conn., Burndy Library (Publ., 8), 1953. 6 p., 24 plates., illus., port.

Reproductions of the rare plates issued originally as *Nova reperta* and *America detectio.* These have little real value as Americana, but several do depict Vespucci and one plate shows four animals of the New World. (The real value of the works is for the depiction of how people lived, and especially how artisans worked, in Europe.)

2482. Tentori, Tullio. I manoscritti di interesse americanistico esistenti nella biblioteche ed archivi italiani: I manoscritti della Biblioteca Nazionale Central di Roma (Rend Cl Sci Mor St Mil, ser. 8, 8:5-6, maggio-giugno 1953, p. 262-277).

Lists 40 items (which vary from one document to a big series) from the Jesuit, Sessoriano, and S. Apostoli *fondi.* They are strongly ethnological and/or theological in character, and strongly 18th century and South American. But there is much for North American areas (including a little on the area of the present U. S.) and for "history," and the dates range from the 16th to the 19th centuries.

2483. Trimborn, Hermann. Pascual de Andagoya; ein Mensch erlebt die Conquista. Hamburg, Universität Hamburg (Abhandlungen aus dem Gebiet der Auslandskunde, 59, Reihe B; Völkerkunde, Kulturgeschichte und Sprachen, 33), 1954. 315 p., illus., maps (part fold.), facsims.

A scholarly work upon Andagoya's whole life, in Central America as well as in Colombia and Peru, and upon his work as a trader as well as a conqueror. Appendix of 10 documents.

2484. Tudisco, Anthony. América en la literatura española del siglo XVIII (An Estud Am, 11, 1954, p. 565-585).

Bibliography and commentary of 18th-century Spanish writings on the following subjects: America in general, Columbus and the Discovery, Cortés and the Conquest of Mexico, Pizarro and the Conquest of Peru, other discoverers

and conquistadores, and the *leyenda negra* and its antithesis. [C. Gibson]

2485. ————. The land, people and problems of America in eighteenth-century Spanish literature (Americas, Franciscan Hist, 12:4, Apr. 1956, p. 363-384).

A different article from the one just above by the same author.

2486. University of Minnesota. Library. The James Ford Bell Collection; a list of additions, 1951-1954. Compiled by John Parker. Minneapolis, Minn., University of Minnesota Press, 1955. 69 p.

The original collection was catalogued in *Jesuit relations and other Americana in the library of James Ford Bell* (Minneapolis, 1950). Since then the collection has been expanded into the field of the rise and growth of European commerce overseas in the colonial period, but without American emphasis. But the 393 added titles in this supplementary catalogue will still have value to Latin Americanists.

2487. Uribe, Ángel. La Inmaculada en la literatura franciscano-española (Arch Ib Am, 15:57-58, enero-junio 1955, p. 201-495, 6 illus.).

An excellent bibliographical essay on the many works upon various aspects of the doctrine of the Immaculate Conception, written by Franciscans of 16th- to 18th-century Spain and Spanish America.

2488. Vigil de Quiñones, José María. Polizones en la carrera de Indias (R Gen Marina, Madrid, 147, sept. 1954, p. 373-379, illus.).

A scholarly study of the problems of immigration, to some degree, as well as of that of stowaways in particular. Most detail is for the 18th century.

2489. Whitaker, Arthur P. La historia intelectual de Hispano-América en el siglo XVIII (R Hist Am, 40, dic. 1955, p. 553-573).

Interpretative and bibliographical essay on the intellectual history of the 18th century and especially of the Enlightenment in America. Remarks on recent historiography dealing with this subject. [C. Gibson]

2490. Zavala, Silvio. Aspectos económicos y sociales de la colonizacion en América (Mem Col Nac, 3:10, 1955, p. 73-88).

Generalized observations on colonial agriculture, mining, commerce, industry, communication, urbanism, and society. [C. Gibson]

2491. ————. Ojeada a la historia de México (Hist Mex, 5:4, abril-junio 1956, p. 498-505).

Summary sketch of the totality of Mexican history by one of its foremost interpreters. A French version appeared in *Nouvelles du Mexique* (Paris), no. 1, 1955. [C. Gibson]

MIDDLE AMERICA

CHARLES GIBSON

The list of items on colonial Mexico includes several works of importance. John L. Phelan's study of Gerónimo de Mendieta and the Franciscan "millennial kingdom" is an original, brilliant interpretation of the ideology of mysticism that attended Spanish imperial thinking in the 16th century. C. Harvey Gardiner's careful examination of Cortés' brigantines adds detailed information to the narrative of the Mexican conquest. José Joaquín Izquierdo contributes a revealing study of Montaña, and Jorge Ignacio Rubio Mañé has published the first volume of his large viceregal history. Some notable contributions appear in local history, in the work of Alfonso Caso and Delfina López Sarrelangue on Tenochtitlan and Tlatelolco and of others on Chalco Amecameca, San Luis de la Paz, Jacona, and Zamora. Northern New Spain in its mission and frontier aspects receives new documentation in the writings of John Francis Bannon and Mario Hernández y Sánchez-Barba on 17th- and 18th-century Sonora and in James M. Daniel's translation of Pedro José de la Fuente's diary. The amount of detailed material on colonial Chiapas is noteworthy. Materials on Guatemala and the remainder of Central America are, as is customary, far slimmer than those on Mexico. Among them the work of Roberto Trigueros on the defenses of the Rio de San Juan is outstanding.

Mexico and the North

2500. Acta de la fundación de Chihuahua (B Soc Chihua Estud Hist, 9:4, oct. 1955, p. 835-836).
Text of the act of foundation of Chihuahua, dated Oct. 12, 1709.

2501. **Bannon, John Francis.** The mission frontier in Sonora, 1620-1687. Edited by James A. Reynolds. N. Y., United States Catholic Historical Society (Monograph series, 26), 1955. 160 p., map.
Scholarly and detailed account of Jesuit labors in 17th-century Sonora.

2502. **Brand, Donald D.** The development

of Pacific coast ports during the Spanish colonial period in Mexico (*in* Estudios . . . Manuel Gamio [see item 21], p. 577-591).
Useful summary of fundamental data on the Pacific coast ports of New Spain, from the Colorado river to the Isthmus of Tehuantepec. Identifies principal ports and periods of activity and lists pertinent fields for future research.

2503. **Butterfield, Marvin E.** Jerónimo de Aguilar, conquistador. University, Ala., University of Alabama Press (University of Alabama studies, 10), 1955. 54 p.
Short biography of the interpreter of the Cortés expedition, with citations of sources and bibliography.

2504. **Carreño, Alberto María.** Luis de Carvajal, el Mozo (Mem Ac Mex Hist, 15:1, enero-marzo 1956, p. 87-101).
Biographical and bibliographical notes on a 16th-century victim of the Mexican Inquisition.

2505. **Caso, Alfonso.** Los barrios antiguos de Tenochtitlán y Tlatelolco (Mem Ac Mex Hist, 15:1, enero-marzo 1956, p. 7-63).
An important study for the pre-colonial and colonial periods of Tenochtitlan-Mexico. Examines the problem of the local barrios in the city, utilizing for the first time the material of the Plano de Alzate of 1789. Identifies and maps a large number of toponyms inside the city.

2506. Catálogo general de documentos (B Arch Gen Chiapas, 3:4, abril-junio 1955, p. 156-157).
Section of a continuous publication of documentary titles from the Archivo General de Indias relating to colonial Chiapas. A variety of subjects.

2506a. **Cook de Carmen, Leonard,** and **Ernesto Lemoine V.** Materiales para la geografía histórica de la región Chalco-Amecameca (R Mex Estudios Antr, 14:1, 1954-1955, p. 289-295).
Lists and describes a number of little-known codices and historical documents of colonial Amecameca.

2507. **Daniel, James M.** (trans., ed.). Diary of Pedro José de la Fuente, Captain of the Presidio of El Paso del Norte, January-July, 1765 (SW Hist Q, 60:2, Oct. 1956, p. 260-281).
Translation of a private diary, the original of which is in the Archivo General de Indias. Records of Indian attacks, military inspections, and other events in the life of an 18th-century frontier garrison.

2508. **Dávalos Hurtado, E.** La morfología social de Nueva España, móvil de su Independencia (*in* Estudios . . . Manuel Gamio [see item 21], p. 593-603).
Contemplative essay on the ethno-cultural va-

rieties of Mexican society in the colonial and early revolutionary periods.

2509. Dávila Garibi, José Ignacio Paulino. El capitán D. Diego de Ochoa Garibay, conquistador de Nueva Galicia y poblador muy antiguo en la provincia de Michoacán, avecindado en Zamora, y relación genealógica entre éste y el Lic. D. Guillermo Romo Celis. Estudio leído en la Academia Mexicana de Genealogía y Heráldica, en la sesión del 12 de mayo de 1954. México, Cultura, 1955. 26 p., illus.
Brief biographical and genealogical jottings on the conquistador of Nueva Galicia.

2510. Designación de un Protector de Indios para las alcaldías mayores de Tuxtla y Ciudad Real, año 1782 (B Arch Gen Chiapas, 4:6, enero-junio 1956, p. 55-74).
Series of documents concerning the nomination, instruction, and appointment of Joseph Canales as Protector de Indios in the two *alcaldías mayores.*

2511. Despoblación de Xiquipilas, Tacoasintepec, Las Pitas, Coneta, Suchiltepeque, Popocatepeque, Ecatepec, Bachajón, San Andrés, Ixtapilla y Sacualpa, 1733-1734 (B Arch Gen Chiapas, 3:4, abril-junio 1955, p. 25-66).
Data on the redistribution of populations in 11 Chiapas towns and their merger with other towns in the 18th century. Includes material on tribute and the internal subdivision of towns.

2512. Díaz del Castillo, Bernal. The discovery and conquest of Mexico, 1517-1521. Edited from the only exact copy of the original ms. (and published in Mexico) by Genaro García. Translated with an introd. and notes by A. P. Maudslay. Introd. to the American ed. by Irving A. Leonard. N. Y., Farrar, Straus, and Cudahy, 1956. 478 p., illus., maps.
An abridged edition of the well-known but rare Maudslay translation of Bernal Díaz.

2513. Diller, Aubrey. A new map of the Missouri river drawn in 1795 (Im Mundi, 12, 1955, p. 175-180, fold. map).
Discusses and reproduces the "Idée topographique des hauts du Mississippi et du Missouri" of Antoine Soulard and Francisco Bouligny. This reflects the Spanish expedition of 1794 to the Mandans, which was a reaction to recent British expeditions from Canada. The original of the map is in the Service Hydrographique in Paris, and has not been entirely unknown. [R. D. Hussey]

2514. Dunne, Peter Masten, and **Ernest J. Burrus.** Four unpublished letters of Anton Maria Benz, eighteenth century missionary to Mexico (Arch Hist Soc Iesu, 24:48, Iul.-Dec. 1955, p. 336-378).

Text of four letters, 1750-1752, written by the German Jesuit Anton Maria Benz to his parents and a fellow Jesuit. Perceptive and detailed observations on the ocean crossing, Mexico City, and mission experiences in northern Mexico.

2515. Fernández de Recas, Guillermo S. Aspirantes americanos a cargos del Santo Oficio. Sus genealogías ascendentes. Prólogo de Manuel Romero de Terreros. México, Porrúa, 1956. 253 p.
Over 1000 short genealogies of applicants for Inquisition offices in Mexico. Arranged chronologically and alphabetically. The material is derived from the Ramo de Inquisición of the Archivo General de la Nación.

2516. Gardiner, C. Harvey. Naval power in the conquest of Mexico. Austin, Tex., University of Texas Press, 1956. 253 p., illus., maps.
Thorough examination of the role of the brigantines on Lake Texcoco in the conquest of Mexico. Data on their construction, form, commanders, and strategic utility, and especially on their principal builder, Martín López. Illustrations from Mexican codices.

2517. Gemelli Careri, Giovanni Francesco. Viaje a la Nueva España. Traducido por José María Agreda y Sánchez. Introducción de Fernando B. Sandoval. México, Libro-Mex (Biblioteca mínima mexicana, 13-14), 1955. 2 v. 302 p., illus.
Reprint of the edition of the Sociedad de Bibliófilos Mexicanos, Mexico, 1927, which was the first complete Spanish translation. This 1955 edition is enriched with the plates from the first edition, of 1700. [R. D. Hussey]

2518. Gibson, Charles. Llamamiento general, repartimiento, and the Empire of Acolhuacan (HAHR, 36:1, Feb. 1956, p. 1-27).
Establishes a continuity in geographical limits between the pre-Conquest Acolhua "empire" in the vicinity of the Valley of Mexico and the 16th-century labor repartimiento.

2519. —————. The transformation of the Indian community in New Spain, 1500-1810 (Cahiers d'Hist Mond, 2:3, jan. 1955, p. 581-607).
Summary and generalized history of Indian towns in highland New Spain during the colonial period.

2520. Gómara, Francisco López de. Historia general de las Indias, "Hispania Vitrix," cuya segunda parte corresponde á la conquista de Méjico. Modernización del texto antiguo por Pilar Guibelalde, con unas notas prologales de Emiliano M. Aguilera. Barcelona, Edit. Iberia (Col. de obras maestras), 1954. 2 v.
Has not been seen, but it is said that the "modernization" applies to the words as well as to their orthography. [R. D. Hussey]

2521. **González Obregón, Luis.** Cuauhtémoc; rey heroico mexicano. México, Libro-Mex (Biblioteca mínima mexicana, 6), 1955. 94 p., illus.

Reprint of a eulogy first published in 1922. Lacking in historical value save as an instance of 20th-century interest in the heroism of Cuauhtemoc.

2522. ————. Rebeliones indígenas y precursores de la Independencia mexicana. México, Ediciones Fuente Cultural, 1953. 495 p.

Republication of a well-known work first issued in 1906-1908, with some additional extracts from the *Rebeliones indígenas en la Nueva España* of Vicente Casarrubias (1945). The treatment is serious but not exhaustive and is weakest in the 18th century. It remains a useful summary source of information on the Cortés conspiracy, Guillén de Lampart, and various popular demonstrations and tumults of the colonial period.

2523. **González Valadez, Guillermina.** Cristóbal de Oñate y su actuación en el noroeste de México. México, Universidad Nacional Autónoma de México, 1954. 141 p.

Recapitulation of the biography of Cristóbal de Oñate with particular attention to the Nuño de Guzmán expedition and the Mixton War. Thesis.

2524. **Guerra, Francisco.** Iconografía médica mexicana; catálogo gráfico descriptivo de los impresos médicos mexicanos de 1552 a 1833, ordenados cronológicamente. México, Imp. del Diario Español, 1955. ccclxxviii p., facsims, Issued in portfolio.

A handsome bibliography of Mexican medical publications from the 16th century to 1833, with facsimiles of over 800 title pages. Lacks critical commentary.

2525. Hambre y explotación indígena en 1771 (B Arch Gen Chiapas, 3:4, abril-junio 1955, p. 111-154).

Interesting details on famine and the distribution of maize in Chiapas towns in the late 18th century.

2526. **Hernández y Sánchez-Barba, Mario.** Frontera, población y milicia. Estudio estructural de la acción defensiva hispánica en Sonora durante el siglo XVIII (R Indias, Madrid, 16:63, enero-marzo 1956, p. 9-49).

An informative study of frontier conditions in Sonora in the 18th century. The imperial task, complicated by English and Russian ambitions, and the task of maintaining internal order against Indian attack and uprising are studied in their relationship to three topics: human geography, social groups, and military organization. Data on natives, towns, population, classes, militias, and other subjects.

2527. **Houdaille, Jacques.** Frenchmen and francophiles in New Spain from 1760 to 1810 (Americas, Franciscan Hist, 13:1, July 1956, p. 1-29).

An article of importance for the intellectual origins of the revolutionary movement in New Spain. Examines French residents of New Spain and their activities and attitudes during the 50 years preceding the revolution, the sympathy that they aroused among Mexicans, and the influence of the Napoleonic agents in 1808 and after. Documents from the Archivo General de la Nación, Mexico.

2528. **Howe, Jane.** Spanish bells in New Mexico (New Mex Hist R, 31:2, Apr. 1956, p. 148-153).

Catalogue, description, and reproduction of some inscriptions of bells in New Mexico missions or dating from the Spanish colonial period in New Mexico.

2529. Información de méritos y servicios de Alonso García Bravo, alarife que trazó la ciudad de México. Introducción de Manuel Toussaint. México, Universidad Nacional, Instituto de Investigaciones Estéticas (Estudios y fuentes del arte en México, 3), 1956. 133 p., fold. maps (part col.).

The document from the Archive of the Indies relating the services of the men whom Cortés chose to draw a plan for the city of Mexico, together with an introductory study. [R. R. Hill]

2530. Informe rendido por la Sociedad Económica de Ciudad Real sobre las ventajas y desventajas obtenidas con el implantamiento del sistema de intendencias, año 1819 (B Arch Gen Chiapas, 4:6, enero-junio 1956, p. 7-53).

Portion of an important local evaluation of the intendancy system in Chiapas, with population figures, financial statistics, and the testimonies of witnesses comparing pre- and post-intendancy conditions.

2531. Informe sobre el incidente habido entre el justicia mayor de Chiapas y el discreto provisor del obispado, en los autos de competencia jurisdiccional, en la reposición del presbítero José Ordóñez y Aguilar, en el curato de Chamula, 1785 (B Arch Gen Chiapas, 4:6, enero-junio 1956, p. 75-99).

A characteristic instance of conflict of authority between ecclesiastical and secular authorities.

2532. **Izquierdo, José Joaquín.** El brownismo en México. México, Imp. Universitaria (Cultura mexicana, 14), 1956. 311 p.

Brief description of the known circumstances surrounding the translation of John Brown's *Elementa medicinae* by Luis José Montaña *ca.* 1800, and the text of the translation.

2533. Jiménez Moreno, Wigberto. La conquista: choque y fusión de dos mundos (Hist Mex, 6:1, julio-sept. 1956, p. 1-8).
Generalized commentary on the Conquest as the meeting of two distinct cultures.

2534. Lamb, Ursula. Religious conflicts in the conquest of Mexico (J Hist Id, 17:4, Oct. 1956, p. 526-539).
Analysis of the spiritual and social tensions created by the convergences of Catholicism and the Aztec religion. Sections on the creed, sacraments, status of the Indian convert, and extent of conversion.

2535. Lascurain, Vicente. Los grandes caudillos en la conquista de México (B Inst Am Estud Vas, 7:25, abril-junio 1956, p. 101-111; 7:27, oct.-dic. 1956, p. 219-238).
A biographical listing of the principal figures in the Mexican Conquest and its aftermath. Adds nothing to known materials.

2537. López Sarrelangue, Delfina. Los tributos de la parcialidad de Santiago Tlatelolco (Mem Ac Mex Hist, 15:2, abril-junio 1956, p. 129-224).
An important and detailed study of Indian tribute payments in colonial Tlatelolco. Classifications and amounts of tribute, methods of collection, changes through time, and many related subjects are authoritatively discussed and documented. Depends essentially upon new archival research in Mexico and Spain. A part of a major forthcoming work on colonial Tlatelolco.

2538. Marín-Tamayo, Fausto. Nuño de Guzmán: el hombre y sus antecedentes (Hist Mex, 6:2, oct.-dic. 1956, p. 217-231).
Sketch of the early life of Nuño de Guzmán in Spain and until his arrival in the New World. The first section of a forthcoming volume, *Nuño de Guzmán, gobernador de Pánuco y Nueva España.*

2539. Montejano y Aguiñaga, Rafael. La fundación de San Luis Potosí; opiniones sobre su fecha. San Luis Potosí, México, Editorial Universitaria, 1955. 33 p., illus.
Summary recapitulation of the statements of various 16th-century authorities on the date of foundation of San Luis Potosi. The several versions, ranging from 1576 to 1594, are analyzed and traced. The correct date is probably 1592.

2540. Motolinía, Toribio [i. e., Fray Toribio de Benavente]. Relaciones de la Nueva España. Introducción y selección de L. Nicolau d'Olwer. México, Universidad Nacional (Biblioteca del estudiante universitario, 72), 1956. 208 p.
Selections from the *Relaciones* of Motolinía, with an introductory study by Nicolau d'Olwer. [R. R. Hill]

2541. El obispo de Chiapas Illmo. Severiano de Salazar y Frías, sobre la excomunión que impuso al alcalde mayor, año 1624 (B Arch Gen Chiapas, 3:4, abril-junio 1955, p. 7-23).
Documents relating to a conflict between civil and ecclesiastical authority in Chiapas in 1624, from the Archivo General de Indias.

2541a. Phelan, John Leddy. The millennial kingdom of the Franciscans in the New World; a study of the writings of Gerónimo de Mendieta (1525-1604). Berkeley, Calif., University of California Press (University of California publ. in history, 52), 1956. 159 p.
A perceptive and profound study in intellectual history. Though centering upon Mendieta, it illuminates also an entire tradition of Spanish colonial mysticism as regards the New World. Chapters on the Hapsburg universal monarchy, the apocalypse in the age of discovery, Cortés as the Moses of the New World, the "millennial kingdom," the Indian as *genus angelicum,* as well as a thorough analysis of the mind of Mendieta. A work of major importance for an understanding of Spanish imperial attitudes.

2542. Provincia de Sayula. México, Vargas Rea (Biblioteca de historiadores mexicanos), 1954. 38 p.
One of the series of 18th-century *relaciones,* concerning Sayula (Avalos) province, from the Francisco del Paso y Troncoso collection.

2542a. Ramírez, Esteban. Díaz de Gamarra; biobibliografía. México, 1955. 146 p., illus.
Commentary and documentation on the life and thought of Juan Benito Díaz de Gamarra y Dávalos (1745-1783), native of Michoacan and author of *Elementa recentioris philosophiae* (1774). A substantial contribution to the intellectual history of 18th-century New Spain.

2543. ———. Estudio histórico de San Luis de la Paz. Guanajuato, México, 1952. 272 p., illus.
Review of the colonial history of San Luis de la Paz, including much miscellaneous material, especially of the 16th century.

2544. Reeve, Frank D. Seventeenth century Navaho-Spanish relations (New Mex Hist R, 32:1, Jan. 1957, p. 36-52).
Carefully documented history of relations, mainly military and hostile, between Navahos and 17th-century Spaniards.

2545. Relación de Cualcoman. México, Vargas Rea (Biblioteca de historiadores mexicanos), 1954. 36 p.
A 16th-century *relación geográfica* of a town in the Colima region, published from the copy in the Francisco del Paso y Troncoso collection.

2546. Rodríguez Zetina, Arturo. Jacona

y Zamora; datos históricos, útiles y curiosos. México, Jus, 1956. 173 p., illus.
Documents and commentary on the colonial history of the towns of Jacona and Zamora, Michoacan; original location, early friars and settlers, political officials, land grants, and details of the local histories.

2547. Royer, Fanchón. Tehuacán—Franciscan outpost (Americas, Franciscan Hist, 13:3, Jan. 1957, p. 269-286).
Account of the 16th-century history of Tehuacan, Mexico, and especially of its Indians' devotion to the Franciscan friars.

2548. Rubio Mañé, Jorge Ignacio. El cronista maya Gaspar Antonio Chi, 1531-1610 (Mem Ac Mex Hist, 15:1, enero-marzo 1956, p. 102-108).
Documentation on the Maya chronicler who aided Landa in the preparation of the *Relación de las cosas de Yucatán* and collaborated in a number of Yucatecan *relaciones geográficas* of 1579-1581.

**2549. ————. **Introducción al estudio de los virreyes de Nueva España, 1535-1746. 1. Orígenes y jurisdicciones, y dinámica social de los virreyes. México, Universidad Nacional Autónoma de México, Instituto de Historia (Publ., 32), 1955. 310 p., illus., ports., fold. maps.
Sophisticated examination of viceregal government in New Spain to the middle 18th century. Treats the creation of the viceroyalty, its subdivisions, viceregal powers and relations with the Audiencia, viceregal voyages and receptions, the viceroy's salary and social position. Contains a useful chronology and bibliography.

2550. Sáenz de Santa María, Carmelo. Bernal Díaz del Castillo: historia interna de su crónica (R Indias, Madrid, 16:66, oct.-dic. 1956, p. 585-604).
Notes on manuscripts and editions of Bernal Díaz' history of the conquest of Mexico, preliminary to the critical edition to be published by the Instituto Gonzalo Fernández de Oviedo. Modifies and amplifies the author's previous article, "Importancia y sentido del manuscrito Alegría," published in the *Revista de Indias* in 1951.

2551. Sahagún, Bernardino de. Historia general de las cosas de Nueva España, escrita por Bernardino de Sahagún y fundada en la documentación en lengua mexicana recogida por los mismos naturales. La dispuso para la prensa en esta nueva edición, con numeración, anotaciones y apéndices Ángel María Garibay K. México, Porrúa, 1956. 4 v., illus. (part col.), port., maps, facsims.
A new edition of the Spanish text of Sahagún, with some innovation in internal subdivision of paragraphs but without other major textual variation from standard versions. Though edited by a prominent Nahuatl scholar, this text is not a new translation of any of the Nahuatl originals of Sahagún. A glossary of Nahuntl terms employed in the Spanish text is added.

2552. Sodi de Pallares, María Elena. Historia de una obra pía, el Hospital de Jesús en la historia de México. Illus. de Manuel Holguín. México, Ediciones Botas, 1956. 343 p., illus.
Documented history of the Hospital de Jesús in Mexico City, from its 16th-century foundation to modern times. Adds numerous details to the known history of the hospital with data from the archives of the Hospital and the Archivo General de la Nación. Not a definitive institutional study.

2553. Spell, J. R. The historical and social background of *El Periquillo Sarniento* (HAHR, 36:1, Nov. 1956, p. 447-470).
Detailed identification of buildings, local toponyms, towns, and other names in and about Mexico City at the end of the colonial period, as they occur in the novel *El Periquillo Sarniento* by José J. Fernández de Lizardi.

2554. Street, J. The G. R. G. Conway Collection in Cambridge University Library: a checklist (HAHR, 37:1, Feb. 1957, p. 60-81).
Titles and brief descriptions of transcripts and translations from the Conway papers in Cambridge. Documents mainly on the Inquisition in Mexico in the 16th century, with other papers on Martín López and the Luna y Arellano family and some miscellaneous items.

2555. Taylor, Virginia H. (trans., ed.). Calendar of the letters of Antonio Martínez, last Spanish governor of Texas, 1817-1822 (SW Hist Q, 60:1, July 1956, p. 80-99; 60:2, Oct. 1956, p. 292-305; 60:3, Jan. 1957, p. 387-400; 60:4, Apr. 1957, p. 533-547).
Continuous calendar of précis of the governor's correspondence, consisting principally of official military reports.

2556. Thornton, A. P. The G. R. G. Conway MS. Collection in the Library of the University of Aberdeen (HAHR, 36:3, Aug. 1956, p. 345-347).
Lists of transcripts, facsimiles, and translations in the Aberdeen portion of the Conway collection. Documents on Martín López, Cortés' lawsuits, and persons and events of Mexico in the 16th and 17th centuries.

2557. Torre Revello, José. El viaje de Yáñez Pinzón y Díaz de Solís, 1508 (Hist Mex, 6:2, oct.-dic. 1956, p. 233-246).
Establishes the approximate itinerary of the voyage of Vicente Yáñez Pinzón and Juan Díaz de Solís to the Yucatecan coast in 1508, after statements by Hernando Colón and Bartolomé de las Casas. Convincingly criticizes the version of Antonio de Herrera y Tordesillas, who dated the Yucatan voyage in 1506 and introduced a "falso viaje" to the Rio de la Plata in 1508.

2558. True, David O. Some early maps relating to Florida (Im Mundi, 11, 1954, p. 73-84).

Maps mostly from 1500 to 1601 (a few of the 18th century) discussed especially as to errors in latitude and such matters as the maps' proper datings. [R. D. Hussey]

2559. Valle-Arizpe, Artemio de. Papeles amarillentos. México, Editorial Patria (Tradiciones, leyendas y sucedidos del México Virreinal, 10), 1954. 242 p.

Essays on a variety of subjects relating primarily to the festivals, social life and external aspects of Mexico City in the colonial period.

2560. Vindel, Francisco. En papel de fabricación azteca fue impreso el primer libro en América; apuntes que comprueban la falta de veracidad en un dictamen de la Academia Mexicana de la Historia. Madrid, 1956. 42 p., illus., facsims.

An item in the historical-literary dispute between Francisco Vindel and the Academia Mexicana de la Historia. The work reproduces and comments on photomicrographs in support of the thesis that the alleged first volume printed in America was printed on native paper. A continuation of the argument proposed in Vindel's *El primer libro impreso en América fué para el rezo del Santo Rosario* (1953).

2561. Zafarrancho en el cabildo de Ciudad Real entre el alcalde mayor y los capitulares, 1751 (B Arch Gen Chiapas, 3:4, abril-junio 1955, p. 67-109).

Details on a series of acts of insubordination against the *alcalde mayor* of Ciudad Real in the middle 18th century.

2562. Zertuche, Francisco M. Las cartas de relación de Cortés a Carlos V (Universidad, Monterrey, 13, agosto 1955, p. 63-83).

Light bibliographical and literary glosses on Cortés' letters.

CENTRAL AMERICA

2563. Documentos para la historia de Nicaragua. Madrid, Imp. Juan Bravo (Col. Somoza), 1954-. T. 9, 1544, 768 p.; t. 10, 1544, 747 p.; t. 11, 1544-1545, 561 p.; t. 12, 1543-1546, 550 p.

Documents from Archive of the Indies relating to the colonial history of Nicaragua, 1544-1546. Of the 85 items in the four volumes, four lengthy documents deal with *residencias* of Rodrigo de Contreras, governor, and Luis de Guevara, lieutenant governor,; and four others are judicial proceedings in various complaints. These occupy the major portion of the volumes. The remaining documents are royal cedulas, letters from officials and others of the colony, petitions and information on various subjects. A continuation of item 3056, *HLAS, no. 19.* [R. R. Hill]

2564. Fundación del pueblo Sabana de Tulijá, 1816 (B Arch Gen Chiapas, 4:6, enero-junio 1956, p. 101-132).

Interesting data on the founding and financing of an early 19th-century *reducción*, established at Indian request.

2565. Gutiérrez y Ulloa, Antonio. Estado general de la provincia de San Salvador: Reyno de Guatemala (Anaqueles, 5. época, 5, mayo 1954-agosto 1955, p. 149-175).

Installment of a continuing series, a general description and identification of places in the province of San Salvador, 1807.

2566. Historia Belemitica. Vida ejemplar . . . del Padre Pedro de San José Betancur. V. 19. 2. ed. Prólogo de Carmelo Sáenz de Santa María. Guatemala, Biblioteca Goathemala (19), 1956. 662 p., illus.

Faithful re-edition of the biography of P. Pedro de San José Betancur first published in Seville in 1723.

2567. Mérida, Martín. Origen de la imprenta en Guatemala; su desarrollo hasta la Independencia. Guatemala, Edición de la Biblioteca Nacional y de la Editorial del Ministerio de Educación Pública, 1956. 66 p., illus.

Notes on the history of printing and on individual printers of colonial Guatemala. Originally written ca. 1890 but never before made available.

2568. Molina Argüello, Carlos. Misiones nicaragüenses en archivos europeos. México, Instituto Panamericano de Geografía e Historia (Publ. 223; Comisión de Historia, 85; Misiones americanas en los archivos europeos, 12), 1957. 163 p.

A description of the seven official and private missions from Nicaragua to Spain and Europe to locate and study records of the colonial period. The major portion of the volume is devoted to the official mission of Dr. Andrés Vega Bolaños, which includes a listing of the documents in the first 10 volumes of the *Colección Somoza.*

2569. Sáenz de Santa María, Carmelo. La tradición lascasiana y los cronistas guatemaltecos. El caso del cronista Fray Antonio Remesal, O. P. (R Indias, Madrid, 16:64, abril-junio 1956, p. 267-285).

A study of the tendencies of Fray Antonio Remesal, O. P. (author of the *Historia de la provincia de San Vicente de Chiapas y Guatemala* . . .) to criticize the conquistadores after the manner of Las Casas, and the opposition he encountered from Creole defenders of the conquistadores. Notes that the Creole-peninsular positions in this 17th-century case were the opposite, in respect to the conquest theme, of those of Americans and Spaniards in the 20th century.

2570. **Smith, Robert S.** Forced labor in the Guatemalan indigo works (HAHR, 36:3, Aug. 1956, p. 319-328).
A repartimiento document of 1784 from the Archivo General del Gobierno, Guatemala, authorizing compulsory Indian labor on Guatemalan indigo plantations after a long period during which Indian labor had been prohibited. Rules of employment, wages, the employers' obligations, and other requirements are specified.

2571. **Termer, Franz.** Die Marschroute des Pedro de Alvarado durch El Salvador im Jahre 1524 (B Soc Suisse Am, 8, sept. 1954, p. 3-13).
A reconsideration of traditional versions of Alvarado's route in El Salvador, particularly with reference to the site of Cuscatlan (here provisionally identified as La Bermuda).

2572. Testimonio del cuaderno de diligencias e instrumentos de los gastos hechos en la conquista y misión de los indios xicaques en las montañas de Lean y Yoro (R Arch Bib Nac, 29:9-10, marzo-abril 1951, p. 326-333).
Letters on the efforts are expended to reduce the resistant Indians of central Honduras, 1749-1750.

2573. **Trigueros, Roberto.** Las defensas estratégicas del Río de San Juan de Nicaragua (An Estud Am, 11, 1954, p. 413-513).
A thoroughly documented study of 17th- and 18th-century defenses of the Rio de San Juan, with 21 plates of contemporary plans of the fortifications.

WEST INDIES

ARTURO SANTANA

GENERAL

2574. **Malagón, Javier.** Un documento del siglo XVIII para la historia de la esclavitud en las Antillas (*in* Miscelánea de estudios dedicados a Fernando Ortiz. Habana, 1956. V. 2, p. 953-968). [S. W. Mintz]

2575. **Parsons, James J.** English speaking settlement of the western Caribbean (Y Assn Pac Coast Geog, 16, 1954, p. 3-16).
A mainly historical comment on the settling of San Andres and Providencia Islands. [S. W. Mintz]

CUBA

2576. **Lage, Guillermo.** El primer hospital de la Habana. Prólogo del Dr. E. Saladrigas. Habana, 1955. 43 p., 5 plates (Col. Cuadernos de historia sanitaria).
A historical account of the first hospital established at Habana during the early period of

Spanish colonization. The author digresses to retrace briefly the origin of similar institutions in other parts of Spanish America. Presents short biographical sketches of the earliest physicians established in Cuba during Spanish colonial times.

2577. **Lavin, Arturo G.** El capitán de artillería don Francisco de Garro y Bolíbar (R Bib Nac, Habana, 5:3, julio-agosto 1954, p. 93-102).
Biographical and genealogical notes on the Spanish artillery officer Don Francisco de Garro y Bolíbar, who lived in Cuba during the 17th century.

2578. **Ramírez Corría, Filiberto.** La primitiva colonización de la Isla de Pinos (R Bib Nac, Habana, 5:3, julio-agosto 1954, p. 33-54).
Brief documented essay on the history of the Isle of Pines from its discovery up to the first Spanish attempts at colonization towards the end of the 16th century. Genealogical data on persons and families who received land grants in the island during the 17th century. Based on extensive library and archival research in Cuba, the work contains bibliography and textual transcription.

DOMINICAN REPUBLIC AND HAITI

2579. **Alfau Durán, Vetilio.** D. Simón Bolívar y el Santuario de Higuey (Clío, 22:101, oct.-dic. 1954, p. 202-208).
Data on Bolívar's ancestor who in the second half of the 16th century helped toward the reconstruction of the Sanctuary at Higuey. Based on a document dated 1569, from the Archivo General de Indias, which is here transcribed in full.

2580. **Chiriboga Navarro, Ángel L.** Alexandre Petion (B Ac Nac Hist, Quito, 35:85, enero-junio 1955, p. 121-128).
Lecture given by the author, historian, and ambassador of Ecuador to Argentina in the Instituto Mitre in B. A., Mar. 29, 1955, in an "homenaje to the Haitian statesman." Sketches the history of Haiti's emancipation and Pétion's relations with Bolívar.

2581. Colección Lugo. Recopilación diplomática relativa a las colonias española y francesa de la isla de Santo Domingo (B Arch Gen, Ciudad Trujillo, año 16, 16:77, abril-junio 1953, p. 125-138; 16:78, julio-sept. 1953, p. 235-257; 16:79, oct.-dic. 1953, p. 354-378; año 17, 17:80, enero-marzo 1954, p. 47-64; 17:81, abril-junio 1954, p. 231-250; 17:82, julio-sept. 1954, p. 309-326; 17:83, oct.-dic. 1954, p. 379-399; año 18, 18:84, enero-marzo 1955, p. 35-55; 18:85, abril-junio 1955, p. 138-156).
Textual transcriptions from this important documentary collection preserved in the Archivo

General de la Nación at Ciudad Trujillo, a collection which is made up of transcripts from Spanish and other European archives. Contains important documentary material for the 17th- and 18-century diplomatic history of the Spanish and French colonies in the island of Hispaniola. A great bulk of the material is on boundary and other jurisdictional conflicts between the two areas. Of great value to students of international relations in the West Indies during this period.

2582. Fouchard, Jean. Plaisirs de Saint-Domingue. Port-au-Prince, Imp. de l'État, 1955. 181 p.

An introduction to the work by the same author, *Le théâtre à Saint-Domingue* (see item 4453). The author studies the artistic and literary life enjoyed during the French colonial period by the upper classes of St. Domingue. Of great interest for the social history of the West Indies.

2583. Franco, José Luciano (ed.). Documentos para la historia de Haití en el Archivo Nacional. Habana, Archivo Nacional de Cuba (Publ., 37), 1954. 259 p.

Published by the Archivo Nacional de Cuba as an "homenaje" to the Republic of Haiti on her 150th anniversary. Contains the literal transcription of 268 documents, the bulk of them unpublished so far, drawn principally from the "Capitanías generales" and "Asuntos políticos" collections of the Archivo Nacional, covering the years 1790-1804, and representing, in the main, correspondence of Spanish officials in Cuba with others in the mother country, the French and English colonies in the Caribbean, and the U. S. Arranged chronologically and preceded by a 60-page introduction on the revolt, from 1789 to 1804, of the French colony of St. Domingue. Presents an excellent picture of the influence of the Haitian revolution on Cuba and other regions of the Caribbean and the interrelations of these areas of this region during the Latin American struggle for Independence. Although centering on the Haitian rebellion there is material on many other tangential topics such as American and European politico-economic activities in the Caribbean during this period. There is a 26-page appendix of documents on the 1803 commission of "Oidor" Francisco de Arango y Parreño representing the Real Consulado of Habana, to Haiti and Santo Domingo. An indispensable book for students of Caribbean diplomatic history.

2584. Giménez Fernández, Manuel. Las cortes de la Española en 1518 (A U Hispalense, 15:2, 1954, p. 47-154).

A detailed account of the meetings in Santo Domingo City from April to June, 1518, of the proctors named by the cities and towns of the island, to discuss and urge plans of reform. There is much information also upon related matters, such as the history of the opposing factions in the island, and the breakdown of unanimity over the choice of the proctor to be sent to Spain. [R D. Hussey]

2585. Lugo Lovatón, Ramón. Reconstrucción del Alcázar de don Diego Colón (B

Arch Gen, Ciudad Trujillo, año 17, 17:83, oct.-dic. 1954, p. 375-378).

Brief undocumented synthesis of the history of Don Diego Colón's "Alcazar" in Ciudad Trujillo, devoting especial attention to its construction.

2586. Peña Batlle, Manuel Arturo. Orígenes del estado haitiano. Prólogo de H. Incháustegui Cabral. Ciudad Trujillo, 1954. 99 p.

A study rendered incomplete due to the author's untimely death. His purpose is not to retell the story of the Haitian rebellion but "determinar con precisión y con la mayor claridad posible el contenido social e ideológico de aquel movimiento para relacionarlo con el proceso de la formación nacional dominicana." The story scarcely finishes the year 1792. The sources utilized are in the main scanty and obsolete.

2587. Relación de los documentos de asuntos políticos de Santo Domingo, procedentes del Archivo Nacional de Cuba (B Arch Gen, Ciudad Trujillo, año 17, 17:80, enero-marzo 1954, p. 65-81).

An inventory of the 29 volumes of textual transcription (in photocopy) of documentary material for the history of the Dominican Republic preserved in the Asuntos Políticos section of the Archivo Nacional de Cuba. They cover both the colonial and national periods.

2588. Rodríguez Demorizi, Emilio. Invasión inglesa de 1655 (B Arch Gen, Ciudad Trujillo, año 19, 19:88-89, enero-junio 1956, p. 6-161).

A collection of accounts, some original and some reproduction of printed pamphlets, of the English invasion of Santo Domingo in 1655, which was unsuccessful. There is an introductory study with a bibliography of Spanish and English publications of the epoch. The explanatory notes are extensive, with additional notes by Fray Cipriano de Utrera. [R. R. Hill]

2589. Utrera, Cipriano de. Episcopologio dominicopolitano. Selección de los números 86 y 87 del Boletín del Archivo General de la Nación. Ciudad Trujillo, Tip. Franciscana, 1956. 56 p.

Catalogue, with biographical data, of the bishops and archbishops of Santo Domingo from the creation of the diocese in 1511 and its elevation to an archdiocese in 1546 up to the present time. As indicated by the author, the data are based on documentary material from the Archivo General de Indias and published primary sources; there are, however, no footnotes on sources throughout the text.

2590. ————. La Inmaculada Concepción en Santo Domingo (Clío, 22:102, enero-marzo 1955, p. 32-38).

Brief documented essay with data on mass worship of Our Lady of the Immaculate Conception in the Dominican Republic, from the 15th to the 18th century. Contains transcribed documents from the Archivo General de Indias.

PUERTO RICO

2590a. González García, Sebastián. Tres tormentas olvidadas (Hist, Río Piedras, 4:2, oct. 1954, p. 235-236).
Brief data on three hurricanes, one occurring during the 17th century, the other two during the 18th, which are not included in Luís A. Salivia's *Historia de los temporales en Puerto Rico* (San Juan, 1950). Based on material obtained from the Actas Capitulares of the San Juan Cathedral, as reproduced in v. 2, p. 213 ff., of the now defunct *Boletín de historia puertorriqueña* and the *Actas del cabildo de San Juan, 1751-1760* (San Juan, 1950). [A. Santana]

2591. Miyares González, Fernando. Noticias particulares de la Isla y Plaza de San Juan Bautista de Puerto Rico. Río Piedras, Puerto Rico, Universidad de Puerto Rico, Publicación de la Revista Historia, 1954. 146 p.
Introduction by Eugenio Fernández Méndez. Textual reproduction of a general account and description of Puerto Rico written by a Spanish army officer during his sojourn in the island from 1769 to 1779 and unpublished till now. Brief descriptions of the main cities and towns, folkways and customs, trade, agriculture, and administration. The statistics presented give an indication of the remarkable progress of the island under Bourbon reformism. The 26 pages of introduction offer us a panorama of the author's life and times and a brief analysis of his *memoria*. Unfortunately, there are no critical or explanatory annotations throughout the text.

2592. Murga, Vicente. Historia documental de Puerto Rico. V. 1. El concejo o cabildo de la ciudad de San Juan de Puerto Rico (1527-1550). Río Piedras, Puerto Rico, Editorial Plus Ultra, 1956. lxxxviii, 449 p., illus.
First in a projected 25-volume *Historia documental de Puerto Rico*. Presents selected records, from the Archivo General de Indias, of the cabildo sessions held in San Juan from 1527 to 1550, a most critical period in the island's early history, when the attraction of the new continental empire and the gradual impoverishment of the island threatened ruin to the struggling settlement and menaced its continued existence as a Spanish colony. The documentary selections are preceded by an extensive introduction by the editor covering the history of Puerto Rico prior to 1527 and commenting upon several of the actions and measures of the cabildo as revealed through the documents themselves. Contains extensive notes and indexes.

2593. ————. Historia documental de Puerto Rico. V. 2. El juicio de residencia, moderador democrático. Juicio de residencia del Licdo. Sancho Velázquez, juez de residencia y justicia mayor de la isla de San Juan, Puerto Rico, por el Ldo. Antonio de la Gama (1519-1520). Río Piedras, Puerto Rico, Editorial Plus Ultra, 1957. cxvii, 568 p.

Presents a textual reproduction of the complete *expediente*, preserved in the Archivo General de Indias, of the *juicio de residencia*. The *expediente*, with all the witnesses' testimonies and depositions, is an important historical source for the early days of Spanish colonization in the island. As in the case of v. 1 in this series (see item above), there is an extensive introduction by the author on the historical background of the documentary selections presented, and also a list of the *juicios de residencia* of the different governors of Puerto Rico up to the beginnings of the 19th century, a list unfortunately marred by many errors in names and dates.

2594. Perea, Pedro L. Nueva luz sobre nuestro siglo XVII (Hist, Río Piedras, 6:1, abril 1956, p. 59-70).
Brief commentary on the relevance for the history of Puerto Rico of two recent Spanish products in the field of Spanish American historiography: L. A. Vignera's documented article "El viaje de Samuel Champlain a las Indias Occidentales" (An Estud Am, 10, 1953, p. 457-500) and Francisco Morales Padrón's *Jamaica española* (Sevilla, 1952, 497 p.) The first contains data on the reception in Spain of the news about the capture of Puerto Rico in 1598 by a British expedition under the Earl of Cumberland and the fitting out of an impressive expedition for the recapture of the island, a step which proved unnecessary, as the British soon abandoned Puerto Rico. Señor Morales Padrón's book brings extensive information on Puerto Rico's military contribution during the campaign led by Spain from 1657 to 1660 for the reconquest of Jamaica from the British.

2595. Torres Reyes, Ricardo. El Mariscal O'Reilly y las defensas de San Juan, 1765-1777 (Hist, Río Piedras, 4:1, abril 1954, p. 3-36).
Important study on the military reforms and construction works undertaken in San Juan de Puerto Rico after the inspection in 1765 by Field Marshall Don Alejandro O'Reilly and following his plans and suggestions. The central figure, rather than O'Reilly, is Col. Tomás O'Daly, Chief of Military Engineers and the man who, after collaborating with O'Reilly in the plans, directed their execution from 1765 to 1777. At the end the author analyzes the impact on the fiscal structure and socio-economic evolution of the island. Unpublished documentary sources from the Archivo General de Indias and the Archivo de Cuba have been utilized for this study.

SOUTH AMERICA (EXCEPT BRAZIL)

RICHARD KONETZKE

Of collections of documents, those from the Archivo General de Indias of Seville, mainly relating to the 16th century, are of special importance. Of these, the publications for the New Kingdom of Granada (edited by Friede), and the second series for Chile (edited by Medina), and for the Jesuit missionary activities in Peru (edited by Egaña), supply us with new material for a better understanding of many important aspects of colonial life. For the 18th century, in which research in recent times has been especially strong, the publication of the correspondence of the viceroys (edited by Moreyra y Paz-Soldán and Céspedes del Castillo) and of the papers of the Lima Consulado (edited by Moreyra) provide a new documentary basis for research of Peru. These various publications of source material all have good indices which, unfortunately, are lacking in older publications.

No critical editions of chronicles were published during the last years. Simple reprints—useful as they may occasionally be—are not sufficient. As long as historians restrict themselves to quoting from such chronicles indiscriminately and regardless of the real source value, erroneous interpretations cannot be avoided.

Several thorough studies were, however, written by R. Porras Barrenechea and other Peruvian authors about the life and work of the Inca Garcilaso, the South American chronicler.

With regard to individual South American regions, a general history of Peru has been published by Vargas Ugarte. And yet, we are still far from being able fully to understand the structure and formation of South American historical regions.

Among the studies relating to the discovery and conquest of the South American continent, Gil Munilla's *Descubrimiento del Marañón* and Emilio Robledo's *Vida del Mariscal Jorge Robledo* should be mentioned. Hermann Trimborn's life of Andagoya tried to show how a conquistador reacted to the foreign surroundings, whereas Mellafe's and Villalobos' studies about Diego de Almagro emphasize the economic and social elements of the Conquest.

Problems of Indian life and labor in Chile and the New Kingdom of Granada are successfully treated by Huneeus Pérez and Ots Capdequí. Moore and Zorraquín Becu concentrate on the question of the cabildos in Peru and Argentina. Various aspects of the Bourbon reforms are examined by Comadrán Ruiz, Robledo, and Lynch. Further studies in this particular field are to be expected from several young Argentinian and Peruvian scholars who worked in the Archivo General de Indias.

Problems of economic history in Peru are treated by Céspedes del Castillo and Moreyra y Paz-Soldán, those in Chile by Riveaux Villalobos and Inge Wolff, in the Río de la Plata by Fúrlong and Rodríguez, and in Venezuela by Morales Padrón. Vasquez-Machicado's study about South American highways is a first step in the neglected field of South American transportation. Amongst the very few works in the field of social history, González Echenique's book on the profession of law in colonial Chile should be mentioned.

Very numerous are the publications in the field of church history. Barriga and Tibesar concentrate their interest on the Mercedarians and Franciscans respectively. Echánove gives a documented study of early Jesuit missions in Peru; Kratz and Mateos re-examine the so-called Paraguayan "Jesuit State" as well as the reasons for the expulsion of the Jesuits. Several important contributions to the knowledge of the Jesuit activities in the River Plate district we owe to the never failing endeavours of P. Fúrlong. The aspect of the missions as frontier institutions in the Chaco is dealt with by Acevedo. A thorough investigation of the rôle of the frontier in South American colonization is still lacking.

The studies of Fals-Borda, Lohmann Villena, Rowe, and Service show how successfully local archives can be used for examining the social and cultural changes of Indian tribes which resulted from the Spanish colonization.

Puente Candamo points out that Latin American nationalism may be traced back to the intellectual climate and the way of life of the Creoles during the 18th century. A more methodical investigation of these questions might yield very valuable results.

Smaller contributions dealing with local questions should always be welcomed. More important and desirable, however, would be a general re-orientation of Latin American historiography towards the modern trends of universal historiography.

Several historical academies as well as other research centers in various countries are publishing historical documents, but plans for research on a larger scale apparently have not yet been made. A series of monographic studies, however, published by the University of Chile, seems to indicate that research there is methodically directed in the right way.

GENERAL

2700. **Carvajal, Gaspar de.** Relación del nuevo descubrimiento del famoso río grande de las Amazonas. Ed., introd., y notas de Jorge Hernández Millares. México, Fondo de Cultura Económica (Biblioteca americana; Serie de cronistas de Indias, 28), 1955. 157 p., fold. maps.
Useful re-edition of Carvajal's account, presented from the mutilated text of the Colección Muñoz and supplemented by the complete, but probably more recent copy of the Duque de T'Serclaes. The appendix reprints documents published in Medina's rare edition of 1894.

2701. **Castellanos, Juan de.** Elegías de varones ilustres de Indias. Prólogo de Miguel Antonio Cara Bogotá, ABC (Biblioteca de la Presidencia de Colombia, 9-12), 1955. 4 v. 696, 676, 741, 617 p.
Reimpression. An article by Miguel Antonio Caro, published in 1879 is included as a prologue. Without biographical and geographical indices. What we need are critical editions of the chronicles of the Indies to prepare us as well as possible to use them adequately as historical sources.

2702. **Gil Munilla, Ladislao.** Descubrimiento del Marañón. Prólogo de D. Amando Melón. Sevilla, Escuela de Estudios Hispano-Americanos (Publ., 84), 1954. 389 p., illus., maps (part fold.), facsim.
An important contribution to the history of the discovery of the South American continent. The author straightens out geographical confusions, to localize the so-called Marañon with successive expeditions from the Atlantic coast and Andean highland during 1500-1542, and thus links Orellana's journey better to its historical antecedents. Special stress is laid on the commercial interest in discovering the land of cinnamon.

2703. **Giraldo Jaramillo, Gabriel.** Estudios históricos. Bogotá, Ministerio de Educación Nacional, Ediciones de la Revista Bolívar (Biblioteca de autores colombianos, 86), 1954. 387 p.

Contains studies mainly referring to colonial history. The author, e. g., discusses the value of the "Voyages de François Coreal aux Indes Occidentales" as a historical source, especially for the Nuevo Reino de Granada in late 17th century, without being able to throw new light on the enigmatical person of Coreal. Other articles are dedicated to the geographic-historical works of two Italian Jesuits employed in South American missions, Juan Domingo Coleti and F. S. Gilij. The contributions on Manuel de Socorro, founder of the first newspaper in Bogota (1791), and on the introduction of vaccination into the New Kingdom of Granada should be mentioned.

2704. **Levillier, Roberto.** En defensa de Vespucio y de la verdad histórica (R Indias, Madrid, 14:57-58, julio-dic. 1954, p. 455-508).
Reply of the writer to the critics of his thesis on the Vespucci question.

2704a. ————. La escritura de Vespucio de acuerdo con autógrafos nuevamente descubiertos (R Indias, Madrid, 16:64, abril-junio 1956, p. 177-206).
Palaeographic study to define the specific characters of Vespucci's handwriting.

2705. **Merino, Luis.** Las Noticias secretas de América y el clero colonial, 1720-1765 (Miss Hisp, 13:37, 1956, p. 5-82; 13:38, 1956, p. 193-254; 13:39, 1956, p. 385-452).
The author discusses extensively the problem of the veracity of the Noticias secretas de América and the degree to which this famous pamphlet may be used as a reliable historical source. He emphatically states that the observations of Antonio de Ulloa and Jorge Juan refer to the "estado presente de los Reinos del Perú" and predominantly to the region of present Ecuador and are intended to point out the abuses in colonial life and not to draw a comprehensive picture of that life. Then he adduces a vast contemporary documentation which gave evidence of manifest exaggerations in Ulloa's and Juan's statements and hint at preconceived opinions and political ideologies as of these authors. A remarkable advance in the criticism of the Noticias secretas. . . .

2705a. ————. The relation between the Noticias secretas and the Viaje a la América meridional (Americas, Franciscan Hist, 13:2, Oct. 1956, p. 111-125).
A first attempt to examine the trustworthiness of Antonio de Ulloa's Noticias secretas by comparing them with his report in the Viaje . . . and considering the sources of his information.

2706. **Picón-Salas, Mariano.** Suramérica: período colonial. México, Instituto Panamericano de Geografía e Historia (Publ. 160; Comisión de Historia, 58; Programa de historia de América, 2:2), 1953. 52 p.
Brief sketch of historical themes. A more systematically selected and critically commented bibliography seems to be desirable for the pur-

pose of outlining the structure of the history of America.

2706a. Romero, Francisco. Llanto sagrado de la América meridional; lo publica nuevamente, conforme a la edición milanesa de 1693, con una introducción biográfico-crítica, Gabriel Giraldo Jaramillo. Bogotá, ABC, 1955. 138 p., illus., facsim.

Re-edition of a rare and forgotten treatise in defense of the Indians against corrupt colonial authorities and ill-treatment by brutal and greedy colonists. The author, an Augustinian monk, continues Las Casas' struggle for justice in the late 17th century. Interesting observations of aboriginal life in the Colombian region of Neiva and Timana.

2707. Seco, Carlos. Algunos datos definitivos sobre el viaje Hojeda-Vespucio (R Indias, Madrid, 15:59, enero-marzo 1955, p. 89-107).

Concludes from the *Pesquisa contra Alonso de Hojeda* that Vespucci in 1499 sailed, in the company of Hojeda, only along the coasts of Guayana and Venezuela.

NEW GRANADA AND VENEZUELA

2708. Acosta Saignes, Miguel. Vida de negros e indios en las minas de Cocorote, durante el siglo XVII (*in* Estudios . . . Manuel Gamio [see item 21], p. 555-572).

Summary of Negro and Indian labor conditions in the 17th-century Venezuelan copper mine of Cocorote, taken from five manuscript volumes of the Archivo General de la Nación, Caracas. Statistics on numbers and occupations of persons employed, and data on wages, costs, provisions, and living conditions. [C. Gibson]

2708a. Aguado, Pedro de. Recopilación historial. Con introducción, notas y comentarios de Juan Friede. Bogotá, ABC (Biblioteca de la Presidencia de Colombia, 31-34), 1956-1957. 4 v. 672, 585, 526, 452 p.

A revised edition of this basic chronicle first published completely by Jerónimo Becker in 1916-1918. The Colombian historian Friede, who carefully prepared the transcription, decided on "Recopilación historial," among the various titles that have been used to head this chronicle, as most probably intended by the author. He does not mean to produce a critical edition, but his extensive introduction constitutes a learned treatise on life and work of Fray Aguado, indispensable for estimating the reliability of his writing as a historical source.

2709. Arcila Robledo, Gregorio (ed.). Probanza sobre que "los religiosos de San Francisco de dicha nuestra orden fueron los primeros que comenzaron a enseñar la dicha doctrina christiana a los naturales e yndios deste rreino" (Hist, Bogotá, 1:2-4, abril-oct. 1955, p. 101-125).

Documentation on the Franciscan beginnings in colonial New Kingdom of Granada.

2710. Cartagena — ataque francés — 1697 (B Hist Cartagena, 40:121-123, enero-marzo 1955, p. 116-134).

Detailed report of the Santo Oficio de la Inquisición on the occupation and pillage of Cartagena de Indias by French ships.

2711. Elías de Tejada, Francisco. El pensamiento político de los fundadores de Nueva Granada. Sevilla, Escuela de Estudios Hispano-Americanos (Col. Mar Adentro, 9), 1955. 263 p.

The author reviews and evaluates the political institutions and ideas of the 16th-century New Granada from the standpoint of present Spanish *tradicionalismo.* This may be done, but is not a scientific approach to history. Restoration of medieval *fueros* seems to be incompatible with the trends of modern history.

2712. Fals-Borda, Orlando. Fray Pedro de Aguado, the forgotten chronicler of Colombia and Venezuela (Americas, Franciscan Hist, 11:4, Apr. 1955, p. 539-574).

Summary on Fray Pedro's life and writings with some critcal remarks on his historiography.

2712a. ————. Indian congregation in the New Kingdom of Granada: land tenure aspects, 1595-1850 (Americas, Franciscan Hist, 13:4, Apr. 1957, p. 331-351).

How the effort of the colonial government to gather the Indians into *reducciones* and to grant, for their benefit, collective land (*tierras del resguardo*) worked out in practice in the provinces of Tunja and Villa de Leiva, Colombia. The author states that the socializing policies of the civil congregations maintained the continuity of social solidarity throughout the centuries. A model case, based on documentation of the local archives, for the study of Indian land tenure and the application of Spanish colonial legislation.

2712b. ————. Odyssey of a sixteenth-century document: Fray Pedro de Aguado's *Recopilación historial* (HAHR, 35:2, May 1955, p. 203-220).

How the manuscript of Pedro de Aguado's chronicle survived the centuries till its first publication in 1906.

2713. Florez de Ocáriz, Juan. Genealogías del Nuevo Reyno de Granada. T. 3. Bogotá, Kelly, 1955. 290 p.

New edition directed, annotated, and illustrated by Enrique Ortega Ricaurte with collaboration of Carlota Bustos Losada. Re-edition of the original of 1674, with pertinent documents and illustrations. [R. R. Hill]

2714. Friede, Juan. Las ideas geográficas en la Conquista del Nuevo Reino de Granada (R Indias, Madrid, 15:61-62, julio-dic. 1955, p. 523-551).

A valuable study of the Conquest of the Nuevo Reino de Granada, showing the influence of erroneous geographical notions on historical events.

2714a. ————. La muerte de D. Álvaro de Oyón, "el Tirano" (R Indias, Madrid, 14:57-58, julio-dic. 1954, p. 527-538).
Conjectures on the ideological motives of the revolt (1553) of Oyón, who was said to be fighting "por la patria"—the earliest known use of this term with reference to the New World.

2714b. ————. (ed.). Documentos inéditos para la historia de Colombia. Bogotá, Academia Colombiana de Historia, 1955-. 1, 1509-1528, 396 p.; 2, 1528-1532, 417 p.; 3, 1533-1535, 394 p.; 4, 1536-1538, 393 p.
An important collection of documents relating to the history of Colombia from 1509 to 1550, projected in 10 volumes. This publication is the result of the first systematic search for early Colombian material in the Archivo General de Indias, and most of the documents are published here for the first time. Cedulas, provisions, letters, and other documents. A rich source of information about many aspects of early Spanish colonization. Excellent indices of persons, places, and topics.

2715. García Bacca, Juan David (ed.). Antología del pensamiento filosófico en Colombia, de 1647 a 1761. Selección de manuscritos, textos, traducción, introducciones. Bogotá, Imp. Nacional (Biblioteca de la Presidencia de Colombia, 21), 1955. 362 p., facsims.
Selection from the unpublished manuscripts of seven philosophers, with instructive introduction into the philosophical thought of colonial Colombia. Scholarly contribution to the study of the historical development of philosophical speculation in Hispanic America.

2716. Giraldo Jaramillo, Gabriel (ed.). Relaciones de mando de los virreyes de la Nueva Granada. Memorias económicas. Bogotá, Banco de la República (Archivo de la economía nacional), 1954. 283 p.
Re-edition of those parts of the *Relaciones* which refer to financial and economic affairs of New Granada during the 18th century. Useful sourcebook.

2717. Gómez Canedo, Lino. Un intento de evangelizar a los indios aruacas en 1553 (R Hist Am, 40, dic. 1955, p. 575-593).
Refers to an unsuccessful attempt of the bishop of Cartagena to Christianize the Indians of the Guayana coast. Publishes official documents about organization of this mission enterprise.

2717a. Gumilla, Joseph. El Orinoco ilustrado; historia natural, civil y geográfica de este gran río. Bogotá, ABC (Biblioteca de la Presidencia de Colombia, 8), 1955. 427 p., facsims.
Another reprint of this work first published in 1741 and written by a misionary of the Jesuit reducciones in the regions of the upper Orinoco.

2718. Hernández B., Ernesto. Urabá

heróico. Bogotá, ABC (Biblioteca de autores colombianos, 106-107), 1956. 2 v. 316, 386 p.
Extensive narrative of the discovery and conquest of the Darien coast and of the first Spanish town on continental America, Santa Maria la Antigua del Darien. The bibliography of publications used is not exhaustive. For the voyages of Juan de la Cosa it is desirable to refer to Antonio Ballesteros, *La marina cántabra y Juan de la Cosa* (Santander, 1954) and the materials cited in this work.

2719. Hernández de Alba, Guillermo. Regidores de Bogotá en el siglo XVIII (B Hist Antig, 42:487-488, mayo-junio 1955, p. 357-375).
Publishes certified list of 1760 which enumerates all members of the cabildo of Bogota from 1732 to 1759.

2720. Mateos, Francisco. El recuerdo de Claver, 1654-1954 (Razón y Fe, año 53, 149:674, fasc. 3, marzo 1954, p. 221-234).
Brief comments on the apostle of the Negro slaves at Cartagena de Indias with reference to documentation in the Archivo General de Indias.

2721. Morales Padrón, Francisco. Introducción a la nacionalidad venezolana (Estud Am, 11:52, enero 1956, p. 1-18).
Brief survey of the radical transformations which occurred in Venezuelan life during the 18th century.

2721a. ————. Rebelión contra la Compañía de Caracas. Sevilla, Escuela de Estudios Hispano-Americanos (Publ., 100), 1955. 144 p., illus., maps (part fold., part col.), facsims.
Excellent detailed narrative of the revolt (1749-1752) of Juan Francisco de León, motivated by economic interests.

2722. Morón, Guillermo. Una defensa de los encomenderos (R Indias, Madrid, 17:67, enero-marzo 1957, p. 123-134).
Extracts from a report preserved in the Colección Muñoz of Madrid and dated from 1688, relating to the institution of the encomiendas in Venezuela.

2722a. ————. Los orígenes históricos de Venezuela. I. Introducción al siglo XVI. Madrid, Instituto Gonzalo Fernández de Oviedo, 1954. 385 p.
Ambitious aim to write the history of the origins of the Venezuelan nation in several volumes. The result of this first part is an incongruous mixture of bibliographical and documental data ("depósito documental") and narrative text. A systematic treatment of the historical sources including neglected materials such as those from the Archivo de Indias in Seville should have proved more convenient. Nevertheless useful.

2723. Ortega Ricaurte, Enrique (ed.). Historial de Cúcuta: documentos sobre su fundación. Bogotá, Archivo Nacional de Colombia (Publ., 25), 1956, 251 p.

A collection of 18th-century documents dealing with the founding of the city of Cucuta. The documents are from the Archivo Nacional, and have been edited and annotated by Dr. Ortega, assisted by Ana Rueda Briceño. They reveal the steps taken in the foundation and give the names of the individuals who were the first settlers. [R. R. Hill]

2724. Otero D'Costa, Enrique. El Adelantado Pascual de Andagoya (B Hist Antig, 41:481-482, nov.-dic. 1954, p. 634-673).

Defends the hypothesis that the Biru of Andagoya was the present river Baudo and deals extensively with Andagoya's expedition to San Juan.

2724a. ————. Estudio crítico sobre la Relación dirigida al Rey por el Adelantado Pascual de Andagoya (B Hist Antig, 42:487-488, mayo-junio 1955, p. 376-387).

Some critical notes concerning the famous Relación of Andagoya.

2724b. ————. Orígenes de la gobernación de San Juan (B Hist Antig, 42:485-486, marzo-abril 1955, p. 208-251).

Completes preceding article (see item 2724) with a collection of available information about the early organization of the province of San Juan.

2725. Ots Capdequí, José María. El indio en el Nuevo Reino de Granada durante la etapa histórica final de la dominación española (R Indias, Madrid, 17:67, enero-marzo 1957, p. 11-57).

Continuing the utilization of his researches in the National Archives of Colombia, the author surveys of state of Indian affairs during the 18th century as to encomiendas, tributos, mitas, reducciones, misiones, cacicazgos, resguardos, etc., and ascertains the constant endeavor of the government to maintain and defend the established institutions for the benefit of the Indians. Numerous references to supplementary colonial legislation.

2726. Otte, Enrique. La expedición de Gonzalo de Ocampo a Cumaná en 1521 en las cuentas de Tesorería de Santo Domingo (R Indias, Madrid, 16:63, enero-marzo 1956, p. 51-82).

Interesting data from the Archivo General de Indias on an expedition financed by the Crown with the purpose of pearl-fishing and procuring Indian slaves for labor in gold mines and sugar mills of the Isla Española.

2726a. Pardo, Isaac J. Esta tierra de gracia. Imagen de Venezuela en el siglo XVI. Caracas, 1955. 363 p.

A survey history of 16th-century Venezuela, written from standard sources. Lyrical but with a factual base. [C. Gibson]

2727. Porras Troconis, G. Vida de San Pedro Claver, esclavo de los esclavos. Bogotá, Editorial Santafé, 1954. 220 p.

Panegyrical narrative of the life of the Jesuit missionary Pedro Claver, the apostle of the Negroes at Cartagena de Indias. The background of Negro slavery is insufficiently exposed and the Spanish legislation about it mostly ignored. Indian slavery had not been prohibited by the Catholic Kings as the author asserts.

2728. Probanza de servicios de Fray Pedro Aguado (Hist, Bogotá, 1:2-4, abril-oct. 1955, p. 136-166).

"Transcripción de Carlos Restrepo Canal, introducción y notas de Roberto Herrera Sota." Complete edition of important document concerning the first historian of the New Kingdom of Granada.

2729. Ramos, Demetrio. La defensa de la Guayana (R Indias, Madrid, 16:66, oct.-dic. 1956, p. 525-584).

An important study, based on archival materials, on the strategic plans for the defense of the Spanish Empire, especially during the 18th century.

2730. Reichel-Dolmatoff, Gerardo (ed.). Diario de viaje del P. Joseph Palacios de la Vega entre los indios y negros de la provincia de Cartagena en el Nuevo Reino de Granada, 1787-1788. Bogotá, ABC, 1955. 111 p.

First publication of a manuscript from the Archivo Histórico Nacional of Bogota about the congregación of scattered Indians, Negroes, mestizos, and mulattoes near the San Jorge River in southern Cartagena. Interesting observations on the transformation process of aboriginal population.

2731. Restrepo Posada, José. El Ilustrísimo Señor Don Fray de los Barrios (B Hist Antig, 42:489-490, julio-agosto 1955, p. 457-473).

Concerns the translation of the bishopric of Santa Marta to Santa Fe de Bogota in 1553.

2731a. Riascos Grueso, Eduardo. Ciudades colombianas que han cambiado de ubicación (B Ac Hist Valle Cauca, 24:105, sept. 1956, p. 174-183).

Useful list of colonial cities in Colombia which changed their site or name.

2732. Ribero, Juan de. Teatro de el Desengaño. Bogotá (Biblioteca de la Presidencia de Colombia, 26), 1956. 381 p.

Reprint of the very rare and almost unknown edition of a highly appreciated devotional book (1742) whose author served in the Jesuit missions of the Meta Territory of Colombia and distinguished himself as a learned expert on the native languages in this region.

2733. Robledo, Emilio. Bosquejo biográfico del señor oidor Juan Antonio Mon y Velarde, visitador de Antioquia, 1785-

1788. Bogotá, Banco de la República (Archivo de la economía nacional, 11-12), 1954. 2 v. 230, 422 p.
An important source work for the history of Bourbon reforms in the latter part of the 18th century. Reproduces, mostly for the first time, valuable documents concerning the *visita* of the Oidor Juan Antonio Mon y Velarde to the province of Antioquia. Publication is preceded by introductory notes about the history of Antioquia and the life of Mon.

2733a. ————. Introducción de la caña de azúcar en Colombia (B Hist Antig, 41:471-472, enero-feb. 1954, p. 63-70).
Brief notes about sugar plantations in the New Kingdom of Granada—a hitherto unexplored field of studies for that region.

2733b. ————. Vida del Mariscal Jorge Robledo. Bogotá, Ministerio de Educación Nacional. Ediciones de la Revista Bolívar (Biblioteca de autores colombianos, 100), 1955. 508 p.
A valuable contribution to the study of the conquest and colonization of New Granada. The annex publishes many documents from the Archivo General de Indias.

2734. Rojas, Ulises. Fundación de Nuestra Señora de la Concepción de Neiva (B Hist Antig, 42:489-490, julio-agosto, 1955, p. 474-490).
Documents concerning the foundation of the town of Neiva in 1612.

2735. Sánchez Pedrote, Enrique. La idea del poder en dos virreyes neogranadinos (Estud Am, 11:56, mayo 1956, p. 405-416).
Examines the political ideas of two viceroys of the Kingdom of New Granada in relation to the enlightened absolutism of 18th-century Spain, and hints at their modifications by contact with the different colonial environment.

2736. Santa Gertrudis, Juan de. Maravillas de la naturaleza. Bogotá, (Biblioteca de la Presidencia de Colombia 28-29), 1956. 2 v. 423, 460 p., maps.
First printing of a diffuse narrative written by a Franciscan friar about his missionary activities near the river Putumayo in Southern Colombia (1756-1767) and his travels in New Granada and Peru.

2736a. Tejado Fernández, Manuel. Aspectos de la vida social en Cartagena de Indias durante el seiscientos. Sevilla, Escuela de Estudios Hispano-Americanos (Publ., 87), 1954. 345 p.
Monograph on the Inquisition of Cartagena de Indias, supplementing Medina's work. Uses the papers of the Inquisition for a general description of social life.

2737. Valtierra, Ángel. El esclavo de los esclavos: San Pedro Claver. Tercer cen-

tenario de su muerte (1654-1954). Bogotá, 1954. 126 p.
Short summary of the item below.

2737a. ————. El santo que libertó una raza: San Pedro Claver S. J., esclavo de los esclavos negros. Su vida y su época (1580-1654). Bogotá, Antares, 1954. 909 p.
Fundamental work on this Spanish Jesuit and famous missionary to the Negro slaves in Cartagena de Indias, published on the occasion of the 300th anniversary of his death.

QUITO—PERU—UPPER PERU

2738. Arroyo, Luis. Los franciscanos y la fundación de Chiclayo. Con prólogo de Jorge Zevallos Quiñones. Lima, 1956. 91 p., facsims.
Documented notes about the origins of the Peruvian town Chiclayo, founded as a reducción of converted Indians around a Franciscan monastery.

2739. Barriga, Víctor M. (ed.). Los mercedarios en el Perú en el siglo XVI. Documentos inéditos del Archivo de Indias de Sevilla, 1526-1590. V. 4. Arequipa, Perú, Imp. Portugal, 1953. 380 p.
The author continues his publication of documents referring to the history of the Mercedarians in Peru with materials collected in the Archivo General de Indias. Some documents excite more general interest as, e. g., those presented by the mestizos of Cuzco and Lima in 1582 and 1583 in protest against Royal prohibition of their being ordained priests.

2740. Bataillon, Marcel. Les "Douze Questions" peruviennes résolués par Las Casas (*in* Hommage à Lucien Febvre, v. 2, Paris, 1953, p. 221-230).
Concerns the *Doce Dudas* of Las Casas, showing that it grew out of a letter from the Dominican Bartolomé de Vega. [R. D. Hussey]

2740a. Bromley, Juan (ed.). Libros de cabildos de Lima. Libro décimo-octavo (años 1616-1620). Lima, Concejo Provincial de Lima, 1955. 960 p.
Transcription of the Actas de Cabildo of Lima for the period indicated.

2741. Cédulas y provisiones sobre repartimientos de tierras (R Arch Nac Perú, 19:1, 1955, p. 46-61; 19:2, p. 260-266; 20:1, 1956, p. 151-170).
A collection of cedulas and laws issued for the viceroyalty of Peru, with other basic documents, dealing with legal agreements and sale of lands to the Indians. There is an introductory note by Felipe Márquez Abanto. To be continued [R. R. Hill]

2742. Céspedes del Castillo, Guillermo. Datos sobre comercio y finanzas de Lima,

1707-1708 (Mer Per, año 29, 35:333, dic. 1954, p. 937-945).
Refers to the economic situation of Peru during the War of the Spanish Succession.

2742a. ──────. La renta del tabaco en el virreinato del Perú (R Hist, Lima, 21, 1954, p. 138-163).
Instructive study on the history of the tobacco monopoly in colonial Peru, based on documentation from the Archivo General de Indias.

2742b. ──────. Reorganización de la hacienda virreinal peruana en el siglo XVIII (An Hist Der Esp, 23, 1953, p. 329-369).
An important contribution on the financial reforms in Peru, particularly during the years 1773-1785. The author points out the significant fact that in the Spanish Empire all economic reorganization had to be initiated by the government.

2743. Clark, Charles Upson. The treatment of smallpox in Peru in 1589 (J Hist Med Allied Sci, 10:3, July 1955, p. 327-331).
Abstracts and extracts from ms. 3043 of the Biblioteca Nacional, Madrid. It concerns the conference called by Viceroy Don Ferdinando de Torres y Portugal, and the resulting acts, to deal with the *viruelas y saramoion* [or *sarampion* or *alfombrilla*] raging in Quito, coming from New Granada, and already known in Paita and Trujillo. [R. D. Hussey]

2744. Cook, Warren. Fray Buenaventura de Salinas y Córdova: su vida y su obra (R Mus Nac, 24, 1955, p. 19-49).
Valuable notes about life and writings of this Lima-born Franciscan, author of the *Memorial de las historias del Nuevo Mundo Pirú* (1630) which is an important source on political organization and social structure of the viceroyalty of Peru at that time.

2745. Cornejo Bouroncle, Jorge. El sentido libertario de la revolución de Túpac Amaru (R Arch Hist Cuzco, 5:5, 1954, p. 396-411).
The author again expounds his opinion, explained in two earlier books, that the rebellion of Túpac Amaru had further-reaching aims than the mere restoration of social justice.

2746. Crespo R., Alberto. La guerra entre vicuñas y vascongados, Potosí, 1622-1625. Prólogo del doctor Aurelio Miró Quesada S. Lima, Tip. Peruana, 1956. 170 p.
An important study which is not only a detailed and documented narrative of the social struggle in colonial Potosí, but also illustrates the pronounced antagonism between the traditional feudal spirit of ancient Spanish conquistadores and the bourgeois economic mentality of new immigrants from northern Spain and especially Basques. This subject deserves a general treatment and systematic research.

2747. Deustua Pimentel, Carlos. El vi-
rreinato del Perú entre 1777-1786. Estudio de un informe (Mer Per, año 29, 35:324, marzo 1954, p. 106-122).
Critical summary of a manuscript from the end of the 18th century: Mariano de Loredo, *Verdadera situación del reino del Perú.*

2747a. Echánove, Alfonso. Origen y evolución de la idea jesuítica de "reducciones" en las misiones del Perú (Miss Hisp, 12:34, 1955, p. 95-144; 13:39, 1956, p. 497-540).
Documented study in the doctrinal origin and practical elaboration of the Jesuit mission communities, principally a history of the first Jesuit residencia of Juli near the Lake of Titicaca. The reducciones of Indians had their antecedents in Spanish colonial legislation since the Laws of Burgos and the Instructions of Cisneros for the reformation of the Indies.

2748. Egaña, Antonio de. Monumenta peruana, vol. I (1525-1575). Roma (Monumenta Historica Societate Iesu, 75; Monumenta Missionum, 7), 1954. 800 p.
First volume of a documentary publication on the Peruvian Jesuits. Carefully edited, with introduction, notes, and detailed index. Most of the documents are from the Jesuit Archives in Rome and the Archivo General de Indias in Seville, and contain the correspondence between the general of the Order in Rome and the Jesuit missionaries. An important source.

2749. Espejo Núñez, Teófilo. El historiador Enrique Torres Saldamando (1846-1896) (Letras, 50-53, 1.-2. semestre 1954, p. 230-243).
A discussion of the life and work of Torres Saldamando, a student of the Peruvian encomienda and cabildo. [J. L. Helguera]

2750. Garcia, Rozendo Sampaio. A margem de "Comercio e contrabando entre a Bahia e Potosí no século XVI" (R Hist, São Paulo, 6:23, julho-set. 1955, p. 169-176).
Additional remarks to the Marie Helmer article (item 2753) with transcription of an unpublished document from the Archivo de Simancas.

2751. Gento Sanz, Benjamín. Semblanza histórica del cronista peruano Fray Diego de Córdova y Salinas (R Hist Am, 40, dic. 1955, p. 425-486).
Life and writings of this Peruvian Franciscan (1591-1654?) with special valuation of his *Crónica de la religiossisima provincia de los Doce Apóstoles del Perú.*

2752. Guil Blanes, Francisco. La filosofía en el Perú del XVII (Estud Am, 10:47, agosto 1955, p. 167-183).
Outlines the unexplored field of the Peruvian philosophical thought and teaching in the 17th century, especially pointing to Padre Diego de Avendaño.

2752a. **Hanke, Lewis.** The imperial city of Potosí. An unwritten chapter in the history of Spanish America. The Hague, Nijhoff, 1956. 60 p., illus.
English edition of the study reviewed in *HLAS, no. 19,* item 3451a.

2753. **Helmer, Marie.** Un tipo social: el "minero" de Potosí (R Indias, Madrid, 16:63, enero-marzo 1956, p. 85-92).
From her research on the Peruvian *mita,* the author publishes and comments on the private letter of a Basque miner of Potosi which contains interesting details about his social position and mentality.

2754. Informaciones sobre encomenderos y encomiendas (R Arch Nac Perú, 19:1, p. 12-45; 19:2, p. 182-213; 20:1, p. 42-60).
A continuation of documents from the Archive published in v. 1 and 2 of the *Revista.* They contain much detailed information regarding the encomenderos and the encomiendas, affording an analysis and appreciation of the customs, life, economy, and social habits of the indigenous population and indicating the zeal of the superior authorities to remedy abuses and attend to complaints. To be continued. [R. R. Hill]

2755. **Lastres, Juan B.** La medicina en el descubrimiento y conquista del Perú. Lima, PGACE, 1956. 136 p., illus.
Assemblage of data on medical practices of the Peruvian conquest, by a prolific writer on Peru's medical history. Adds little to the author's previous works. [C. Gibson]

2756. Libro de cabildos de la ciudad de Quito, 1610-1616. Versión de Jorge A. Garcés. Prólogo de J. Roberto Páez. Quito, Instituto Municipal de Cultura, Dirección del Museo de Historia (Publ. del Archivo Municipal, 26), 1955. 600 p.
Continues the transcription of the *Actas de Cabildo* by the skilled palaeographer and deserving editor Jorge Garcés, with carefully compiled indices.

2757. **Lohmann Villena, Guillermo.** El gobierno de los naturales en el Perú hasta la creación de los corregidores de indios, 1535-1565 (Estud Am, 12:61, oct. 1956, p. 201-221).
Methodical treatment of the circumstances which affected the status of the Peruvian Indians in the beginning, when Inca sovereignty had collapsed and Spanish political organization was still mostly nonexistent.

2757a. **Loredo, Rafael** (ed.). Nuevos capítulos de la tercera parte de la crónica del Perú de Pedro Cieza de León: El tercer viaje de Pizarro (Mer Per, año 30, 36:340, julio 1955, p. 453-473 and año 31, 37:347, feb. 1956, p. 75-95).
Continues publication initiated in this periodical with año 21, 27:233, agosto 1946, p. 409-440 and año 26, 37:289, abril 1951, p. 144-159. The

last issues contain chapters 26-41 relating the first part of Pizarro's third voyage for the conquest of Peru. The complete edition of this important chronicle at an early date is much to be desired.

2758. **McPheeters, D. W.** The distinguished Peruvian scholar Cosme Bueno, 1711-1798 (HAHR, 35:4, Nov. 1955, p. 484-491).
Some notes about the scientific activites of this learned Aragonese established in Peru. The author did not make use of the archival data on Cosme Bueno published by this reviewer under the title "Las fuentes para la historia demográfica de Hispano-América durante la época colonial" (An Estud Am, 5, 1948, p. 267-323) which give more correct information about the antecedents of Bueno's *Descripciones* and cite the interesting "Censura del libro intitulado *Descripción del Virreinato del Perú,* dada por Juan Bautista Muñoz el 25 de febrero de 1777" (Ms. of the Biblioteca del Palacio, Madrid).

2759. **Mateos, F.** El venerable Padre Diego Martínez en Juli (Miss Hisp, 14:40, 1957, p. 79-104).
Notes about life and activities of one of the first Jesuit missionaries in Peru, and a heretofore unpublished letter of 1581.

2760. **Moore, J. Preston.** The cabildo in Peru under the Habsburgs. A study in the origins and powers of the town council in the viceroyalty of Peru, 1530-1700. Durham, N. C., Duke University Press, 1954. 309 p., illus., map.
Detailed description of facts and functions which characterize the Peruvian town council, similar to the more comprehensive work of Constantine Bayle (1952) not consulted by the author. A useful treatment of the subject, but mainly based on published records of the cabildos without referring to the abundant material in the Archives. Further research on the Hispanic American municipalities should be focussed on exact and special problems of legal, economic, or social history.

2761. **Moreyra y Paz-Soldán, Manuel.** El tribunal del consulado de Lima. Cuaderno de Juntas (1706-1720). Documentos para la historia económica del virreinato peruano. T. I. Lima, Instituto Histórico del Perú, 1956. lxxii, 388 p.
The author, who in 1950 published an important study, *El Tribunal del Consulado de Lima,* now initiates the edition of the Cauderno de Juntas of this merchant guild, preserved since 1706, with the exception of the years from 1749 to 1770 and 1788 to 1791. The first volume contains the proceedings of the Consulado, royal orders, letters of the viceroys, and other documents for the years 1706-1720, and is prefaced by a substantial introduction and commentary. Footnotes and good indices will be much appreciated. Highly interesting source materials for economic and social history of colonial Peru.

2761a. ———, and **Guillermo Céspedes del Castillo** (eds.). Virreinato peruano:

documentos para su historia. Colección de cartas de virreyes. Conde de la Monclova. Lima, Instituto Histórico del Perú. T. 2, 1695-1698, 1954, xlvi, 345 p.; t. 3, 1699-1705, 1955, lxxxvi, 424 p.

Correspondence (345 items) from the Archive of the Indies, of the Conde de Monclova, Viceroy of Peru, 1689-1705, dealing with affairs in the viceroyalty during his administration. In the appendix (v. 3) there are the will of Monclova, a contemporary opinion of his work, and a summary of his residencia taken after his death. The introduction to v. 1 is a study of the viceregal situation and administration of the epoch; that of v. 2 treats of the documents and their classification, with an indication of content; and that of v. 3 is an essay about the man, his family, his experiences before coming to Peru, events in Peru, and his administration and its problems. [R. R. Hill]

2762. Pacheco Vélez, César. Hipólito Unánue y la generación peruana de los precursores (Mer Per, año 30, 36:342, sept. 1955, p. 642-661).

Points out how the Enlightenment and Bourbon reforms constitute the background of Unánue's intellectual and patriotic zeal for progress.

2763. Paz Soldán, Carlos Enrique. Himnos a Hipólito Unanue. Lima, Universidad Nacional Mayor de San Marcos de Lima, Facultad de Medicina, Biblioteca de Cultura Sanitaria del Instituto de Medicina Social, 1955. 337 p., illus.

Speeches collected on occasion of the anniversary of Unánue's birth, in a panegyrical tone but with interesting information on the intellectual culture and especially the progress of medical science in Peru at the eve of Independence.

2764. Puente Candamo, José A. de la. La idea de la Comunidad Peruana y el testimonio de los precursores (R U Cat, Lima, 15:1, 1955, p. 34-72).

2764a. ————. El Perú en el pensamiento de los precursores (Mer Per, año 30, 36:345, dic. 1955, p. 860-878).

The two parts of this essay, on the social problems and on the political problems, are remarkable contributions to the study of the formation of Peruvian nationalism during the colonial period.

2765. Rowe, John Howland. The Incas under Spanish colonial institutions (HAHR, 37:2, May 1957, p. 155-199).

Explains the Inca revolts in the colonial period as consequence of the oppressive character of Spanish colonial institutions which are marked "by economic exploitation and personal degradation of the natives." Irrespective of any apologetics, it may be questioned that this statement comprehends the whole historical reality.

2765a. ————. El movimiento nacional inca del siglo XVIII (R U, Cuzco, 43:107, 2. Semestre 1954, p. 17-47).

References to Inca revolts in the 18th century.

2766. Tibesar, Antonine. The "alternativa": a study in Spanish-Creole relations in seventeenth-century Peru (Americas, Franciscan Hist, 11:3, Jan. 1955, p. 229-283).

First-hand research on the forced alternate election of Spaniards and Creoles to the main offices of the Franciscan Order. An important contribution to the history of the origins of American nationalism. As to the reason for establishing the *alternativa,* this reviewer would stress political considerations of the Crown for settling the perilous contentions between Spaniards and Creoles; for example, the Audiencia of Guadalajara, in 1606, suggests "que V. M. mande a los generales de las órdenes que *en el ínterin que se sosiegan estas revoluciones, tengan alternativa* en los oficios y mitad de ellos, así los nacidos en las Indias, como en la Castilla."

2767. Tribunal mayor del consulado de la Ciudad de los Reyes (R Arch Nac Perú, 20:1, p. 3-41).

Documents respecting the founding, the regulations, and the functioning of the Consulado in Peru, with introductory notes by Oscar Malca Olguín. To be continued. [R. R. Hill]

2768. Valcárcel, Daniel. Carácter fundamental de la rebelión de Túpac Amaru (Mer Per, año 31, 37:348, marzo 1956, p. 141-151).

In this essay and the one below, the author interprets the rebellion of Túpac Amaru as an upheaval to restore justice for the oppressed Indian population and to enforce Spanish laws upon disobedient or remiss colonial authorities. Therefore Túpac Amaru is not to be considered as precursor of the Wars of Independence. Interesting notes about Peruvian social structure in the 18th century.

2768a. ————. Reforma de San Marcos en la época de Amat. Lima, Ediciones de San Marcos (Serie Documentos para la historia de la educación en el Perú, 2), 1955. 54 p., 4 plates.

The author, charged with writing the history of San Marcos University during the 18th century, deals in this monograph with the reorganization of Peruvian education after the expulsion of the Jesuits and comments on and publishes the *constituciones* issued by Viceroy Amat in 1771.

2768b. ————. Sentido social de la rebelión de Túpac Amaru (Letras, 50-53, 1.-2. semestre 1954, p. 161-175).

2769. Vargas, José María. Misiones ecuatorianas en archivos europeos. México, Instituto Panamericano de Geografía e Historia (Publ. 188, Comisión de Historia, 80, Misiones en los archivos europeos, 9), 1956. 192 p.

Brief description of six Ecuadorean missions to European archives, giving an indication of the materials copied and what became of them. 90

percent of the space is devoted to the mission of Father Enrique Vacas Galindo, with a full listing of the transcripts he secured relating to the history of Ecuador. [R. R. Hill]

2770. Vargas Ugarte, Rubén. Concilios limenses, 1551-1772. T. 3. Historia. Lima, Tip. Peruana, 1954. 212 p.

Historical portion of a work for which the documents have been previously published (t. 1-2, Texto de las actas conciliares y documentos aclaratorios), by a major authority on the ecclesiastical history of Peru. The organizations, meetings, and surrounding circumstances of the six councils in Lima, 1551-1772, are thoroughly described. [C. Gibson]

2770a. ————. Historia del Perú. Virreinato, siglo XVII. B. A., Ediciones Studium, 1954. 501 p., illus.

This and the item below are a continuation of Vargas Ugarte's history of Peru reviewed in *HLAS, no. 15, 1949*, item 1580. Detailed narrative of historical events centered in the account of character and government of the Viceroys, with occasional surveys of economic and social life. Abundance of first-hand information.

2770b. ————. Historia del Perú. Virreinato (siglo XVIII), 1700-1790. Lima, Imp. Gil, 1956. 475 p.

See item above.

2770c. ————. Impresos peruanos. Lima, Biblioteca Peruana, 1953-. T. 7, 1584-1650, 1953, 272 p.; t. 8, 1651—1699, 1954, 331 p.; t. 9, 1700-1762, 1956, 366 p.

These volumes initiate a new section in the welcome *Biblioteca Peruana* of R. Vargas Ugarte. They record and describe all books and pamphlets printed in Peru till the year 1829 and include many items not listed by J. T. Medina, *La imprenta en Lima (1584-1824)*. In an introductory study on the printing press in Peru, Vargas Ugarte is able to contribute some new details to the classic work of the Chilean historian. An indispensable bibliographical handbook.

2771. Vázquez - Machicado, Humberto. Los caminos de Santa Cruz de la Sierra en el siglo XVI. México, Editorial Cultura, 1955. 487-551 p.

"Sobretiro del No. 40 de la Revista de Historia de América, dic. 1955." Detailed study of the overland route from Charcas to Santa Cruz de la Sierra and from there to the river Paraguay. Useful to form an idea of the difficulties of travelling and trading in that region. Considering the political and economic importance of the means of communication in colonial Hispanic America, we still need many monographs about the land and water routes of each region and their variations in the course of time.

CHILE

2772. González Echenique, Javier. Los estudios jurídicos y la abogacía en el reino de Chile. Santiago, Universidad Católica de Chile (Estudios de historia del derecho chileno, 2), 1954, 369 p.

A well-constructed study on the lawyer in colonial Chile: intellectual and practical formation, legal and social status, and multiple activities. The author used unpublished documents from Chilean archives, but supplementary materials may be found in the Archivo General de Indias of Sevilla. We need similar monographs on this subject for other regions of the Spanish empire.

2773. Hernández, Roberto. El fundador de Melipilla y el Convento de San Agustín (B Ac Ch Hist, 21:51, 2. semestre 1954, p. 63-76).

Some dates relating to the foundation of Melipilla and its first church by the Capitán General de Chile, J. A. Manso de Velasco, in 1742.

2774. Huneeus Pérez, Andrés. Historia de las polémicas de Indias en Chile durante el siglo XVI (1536-1598). Santiago, Universidad de Chile, Facultad de Ciencias Jurídicas y Sociales, 1955? 152 p.

An informative study of the influence of the juristical mentality of Old Spain upon the practical organization of colonial life in the 16th century. The author examines step by step the conflict between the theologicojuridical doctrine, especially of Vitoria, and the political and economic realities in the conquest and colonization of Chile, and tries to balance the efficiency of one force against the other. Remarkable contribution to the discussions of the application of Spanish colonial law.

2775. Jara, Álvaro. Pineda y Bascuñán, hombre de su tiempo (B Ac Ch Hist, 21:51, 2. semestre 1954, p. 77-85).

Three documents concerning the Chilean antagonist of Indian slavery and author of *El cautiverio feliz*. . . .

2776. Medina, José Toribio. Colección de documentos inéditos para la historia de Chile. 2. serie. T. 1, 1558-1572. Santiago, Fondo Histórico y Bibliográfico J. T. Medina, 1956. 502 p.

The Administrative Commission of the Fondo Histórico y Bibliográfico José Toribio Medina initiates, as a complement of the collection of documents published by Medina (30 v., 1888-1902), a second series of historical sources, chiefly drawn from the manuscript collections of that eminent Chilean historian. Medina had compiled copies of documents from nearly all archives of Spain and left a total of 234 manuscript volumes from which he had published, in his *Colección*, 83 manuscript volumes. Now this work of Medina is to be published posthumously, to include all documents up to the date 1806. The first volume contains 162 letters covering 1558-1572.

2776a. ————. Historia del Tribunal de la Inquisición de Lima (1569-1820). Santiago, Fondo Histórico y Bibliográfico J. T. Medina (1), 1956. 2 v. 333, 530 p.

Another welcome re-impression of a standard work of J. T. Medina first published in 1887, with introductory notes by Marcel Bataillon.

2777. Mellafé, Rolando, and Sergio Villalobos. Diego de Almagro: 1, Descubrimiento del Perú ₍por Rolando Mellafé₎. Diego de Almagro: 2, Descubrimiento de Chile ₍por Sergio Villalobos₎. Prólogo de Guillermo Feliú Cruz. Santiago, Universidad de Chile, Instituto Pedagógico, 1954. 156 p.

These two monographs, resulting from seminar courses at the University of Chile, contribute to the history of the discovery and conquest of Peru and Chile, and to a critical revision of its sources and authorities and some new interpretations of the historical events. Mellafé points out more exactly the economic and social environment at the city of Panama which affected the formation of the companies for the expeditions to Peru. Villalobos throws new light on the departure of Almagro from Cuzco for Chile. Both studies are now indispensable.

2778. Riveaux Villalobos, Sergio. La justicia comercial en el reino de Chile. Santiago, 1955. 97 p.

The author adds a new contribution to the history of the Consulado fundamentally investigated by Robert S. Smith. He shows the Chilean efforts to become disengaged from subordination to the Consulado of Lima and the antecedents to the establishment of a merchant guild at Santiago de Chile (1795), and explains the commercial jurisdiction of this tribunal. Uses principally the papers of the Archive of the Consulado at Santiago.

2778a. Valdivia, Pedro de. Cartas de Pedro de Valdivia que tratan del descubrimiento y conquista de Chile. Ed. facsimilar dispuesta y anotada por José Toribio Medina. Introd. de Jaime Eyzaguirre. Santiago, Fondo Histórico y Bibliográfico José Toribio Medina, 1953, i. e. 1954. xxxiv, 337 p., facsims., coats of arms.

Splendid re-edition of that of 1929, with an introductory note by Jaime Eyzaguirre on the discovery of Valdivia's letters, and bibliographical annotations on Valdivia by Victor M. Chiappa (p. 255-329).

2779. Wolff, Inge. Chilenische Opposition gegen die Wirtschaftspolitik des Vizekönigreiches Peru, 1778-1810. Ein Beitrag zur Geschichte der interkolonialen Wirtschaftsbeziehungen Spanisch-Südamerikas am Vorabend der Unabhängigkeit (Vier Soz Wirt, 43:2, Juni 1956, p. 146-168).

Based on materials of the Archivo General de Indias. Demonstrates the strained commercial relations between Chile and Peru on the eve of Emancipation. Contribution to the history of inter-colonial commerce as recently cultivated by Arcila Farías and Borah.

LA PLATA

2780. Acevedo, Edberto Óscar. Un evangelizador de indios del Chaco. Pequeña biografía del P. Suárez de Cantillana, 1719?-1799 (An Estud Am, 11, 1954, p. 1-59).

An important contribution, based on archival materials, on the Spanish frontier problem in the Chaco. Deals with the endeavor of Colonial authorities to obtain dominion over these regions by missionizing the Indians and settling them in reducciones, and emphasizes the merits of Father (later Bishop) Suárez de Cantillana in these activities.

2781. Canedo, Lino G. Un dictamen franciscano-agustiniano sobre el servicio personal y libertad de los indios del Río de la Plata, Lima, 1598 (Americas, Franciscan Hist, 11:3, Jan. 1955, p. 329-354).

A manuscript, preserved in the Biblioteca Nacional of B. A., concerning the discussions upon the *servicios personales* of the Indians, with comments.

2782. Carilla, Emilio. Rosas de Oquendo y el Tucumán (Mer Per, año 30, 36:336, marzo 1955, p. 182-210).

The author compiles available data about the life of the soldier and poet Mateo Rosas de Oquendo (1559?-1612) who wrote satirical poems on colonial life and a now lost epic of the conquest of Tucuman.

2783. Chaunu, Pierre. Au point d'impact de deux colonisations: l'état jésuite du Paraguay, un empire du maté (A Éc Soc Civ, 10:4, oct.-déc. 1955, p. 559-564).

Interesting observations in connection with the book by Magnus Mörner, *The political and economic activities of the Jesuits in the La Plata region*, 1953 (see HLAS, no. 19, item 3491).

2784. Comadrán Ruiz, Jorge. La Real Ordenanza de Intendentes del Río de la Plata (An Estud Am, 11, 1954, p. 515-559).

Valuable contribution on prerevolutionary reform. Discusses the establishment of the intendency system in the Virreinato de Buenos Aires and the consequences of this administrative innovation of Spanish absolutism in the Age of Enlightenment and hints at monographic studies in preparation on some intendencias of the Rio de la Plata.

2785. Cortesão, Jaime. O território da Colônia do Sacramento e a formação dos estados platinos (R Hist, São Paulo, 5:17, jan.-março 1954, p. 135-165).

Detailed study of Portuguese and Spanish colonization in the Banda Oriental during the 18th century and the origins of independent Uruguay.

2786. Fúrlong Cardiff, Guillermo. Domingo Muriel, S. J., y su *Relación de las misiones* (1766). B. A., Librería del Plata (Escritores coloniales rioplatenses, 7), 1955. 220 p.

Another contribution of this author on Jesuit activities in the La Plata region, including a minute specification of the writings of Muriel, who, as professor of the University of Cordoba, worked to introduce modern European philosophy. First publication of Muriel's *Breve noticia de las misiones vivas de la Compañía de Jesús en la provincia del Paraguay.*

2786a. ————. Francisco J. Iturri y su "Carta crítica," 1797. B. A., Librería del Plata (Escritores coloniales rioplatenses, 6), 1955. 154 p., illus.
Interesting study on the life and writings of the expelled La Plata Jesuit Iturri, whose manuscript "Historia natural, eclesiástica y civil del virreinato del Río de la Plata" remains undiscovered. For this discussion of Iturri's "Carta crítica," Fúrlong has omitted to consult the substantial article of Antonio Ballasteros, "Don Juan Bautista Muñoz, La historia del nuevo mundo" (R Indias, Madrid, 10, 1942, p. 589-660) who criticizes much more favorably the historiography of Muñoz, but conjectures the author-name of the "Carta crítica" to be a pseudonym. This subject should be re-examined as a contribution to the ideological controversies and political intrigues in late 18th-century Spain.

2786b. ————. La hipotecnia de José Sánchez Labrador, S. J., 1749-1766. Una crónica desconocida sobre el caballo criollo (Hist, B. A., 1:1, agosto-oct. 1955, p. 77-88).
Notices of horse- and mule-breeding in the La Plata region during the 18th century.

2786c. ————. Joaquín Camaño, S. J., y su "Noticia del Gran Chaco" (1778). B. A., Librería del Plata (Escritores coloniales rioplatenses, 8), 1955. 182 p.
In the same series Fúrlong publishes Camaño's short survey of the Gran Chaco and extracts of letters from this Creole Jesuit who was an eminent cartographer and ethnologist. All these volumes published by the distinguished Argentine historian unearth and make available rich source material for the history of the La Plata region.

2786d. ————. Tomás Falkner y su "Acerca de los Patagones" (1788). B. A., Librería del Plata. (Escritores coloniales rioplatenses, 5), 1954. 215 p.
Detailed treatise on the English Jesuit who came in 1730 as a surgeon on a slave ship of the South Sea Company to B. A. and converted to Catholicism. The author emphasizes the scientific value of Falkner's "Description of Patagonia" and "Of the Patagonians." Data on the immigration of Englishmen into the La Plata region.

2786e. ———— (and others). Historia y bibliografía de las primeras imprentas rioplatenses, 1700-1850. T. 2. La imprenta en Buenos Aires, 1785-1807. B. A., Librería del Plata, 1955. 596 p.
Father Fúrlong continues the publication of his descriptive catalogue of prints issued at B. A., indispensable in every reference library. This second volume contains 739 items.

2787. García, Flavio A. Rastreos históricos en juicios de residencia rioplatenses (B Hist, 69, 1956, p. 33-52).
Examines the documentation on the residencia enforced upon the first governors of Montevideo.

2788. Levillier, Roberto. New light on Vespucci's third voyage (Im Mundi, 11, 1954, p. 37-46).
Levillier, one of the main defenders of the general authenticity of Vespucci's claimed exploits, discusses the bases for regarding him as the first navigator to survey the River Plate and to travel as far south as Patagonia. [R. D. Hussey]

2789. Luque Colombres, Carlos. Notas a un documento sobre la encomienda de Casavindo y Cochinoca (Hist, B. A., 2:5, julio-sept. 1956, p. 138-152).
Remarkable documentation about suppression of the *encomienda* in Tucuman.

2790. Lynch, John. Intendants and cabildos in the viceroyalty of La Plata, 1782-1810 (HAHR, 35:3, Aug. 1955, p. 337-362).
The author rightly demonstrates that the centralization of authority imposed by the Ordinances of Intendants made the cabildos more active and more sure and conscious of themselves and prepared them for their role in the revolution for independence.

2790a. Mariluz Urquijo, José M. Las ideas religiosas del Marqués de Avilés (Mer Per, año 29, 35:33, dic, 1954, p. 975-985).
Some notes from a book in preparation about the viceroyalty of La Plata in time of the Marqués de Avilés, showing how the sincere religious devotion of this viceroy became reconciled to the jealous care for the royal patronage of the Indies.

2791. Mateos, F. La anulación del tratado de límites con Portugal de 1750 y las misiones del Paraguay (Miss Hisp, 11:33, 1954, p. 523-564).
The reasons the author gives for the revocation of the treaty of 1750 by the Spanish government should be re-examined after consulting the unexplored state papers preserved in the Archivo General de Simancas.

2792. Molina, Raúl Alejandro. La enseñanza porteña en el siglo XVII. Los primeros maestros de Buenos Aires (Hist, B. A., 1:3, enero-marzo 1956, p. 39-78).
Interesting data on elementary teachers and methods of teaching in 17th-century B. A.

2792a. ————. Los estudios superiores porteños en el siglo XVII (Hist, B. A., 2:6, oct.-dic. 1956, p. 38-52).
Beginnings of secondary education in B. A.

2792b. ————. Misiones argentinas en los archivos europeos. México, Instituto

Panamericano de Geografía e Historia (Publ. 167; Comisión de Historia, 65; Misiones americanas en los archivos europeos, 7), 1955. 745 p.
First, a study of Argentine historiography to combat the black legend. Then a survey of the life and writings of those who carried on work in European archives, including official missions dealing with boundaries; representatives of libraries and archives and of the National University; ecclesiastical scholars; and private individuals. The final part lists the transcripts secured, giving their location. [R. R. Hill]

2792c. ————. Primeras crónicas de Buenos Aires. Las dos memorias de los hermanos Massiac (1660-1662) (Hist, B. A., 1:1, agosto-oct. 1955, p. 89-133).
Summary of early descriptions of B. A. and Spanish translation of the two French reports on colonization projects in the La Plata region.

2792d. ————. ¿Quiénes fueron los verdaderos fundadores de Buenos Aires? Una lista desconocida (Hist, B. A., 1:1, agosto-oct. 1955, p. 29-39).
Publishes the hitherto unknown list of passengers who went to the Rio de la Plata in the expedition of Alonso de Vera (1582).

2793. Otruba, Gustav. Der Anteil österreichischer Jesuitenmissionäre am "heiligen Experiment" von Paraguay (Mit Inst Öst Ges, 63, 1955, p. 430-445).
Contributes many unknown data about the presence of German Jesuits in the La Plata province.

2793a. ————. Die Wirtschaftsverfassung des "Jesuitenstaates" in Paraguay nach dem Zwettler Cod. 420 (P. Florian Baucke) (Archiv für Völkerkunde, 11, 1956, p. 116-134, illus., maps).
On the basis of quotations from the valuable manuscript work of P. Florian Baucke, the author comments on the economic activities of the Jesuits in Paraguay without having consulted the more comprehensive treatment of this subject by Magnus Mörner.

2794. Radaelli, Sigfrido Augusto. Blasones de los virreyes del Río de la Plata. Madrid, Ediciones Cultura Hispánica, 1954. 174 p., illus., ports., coats of arms, facsims.
Coats of arms, portraits, and a brief biography of each of the Platine viceroys.

2795. Ribera, Adolfo Luis. La platería en el Río de la Plata. B. A., Instituto de Arte Argentino, 1955. 110 p., illus.
Erudite supplements to the publication of Fernando Márquez Miranda (Ensayo sobre los artífices de la Platería en el Buenos Aires colonial, 1933), with hitherto unknown data on Indian handicraft in the Guarani reducciones.

2796. Rodríguez, Mario. The genesis of economic attitudes in the Río de la Plata (HAHR, 36:2, May 1956, p. 171-189).
This study analyzes the origin of the antagonism between Platine cattlemen and porteño merchants in the 17th century. The settlers of the Rio de la Plata also feared Portuguese competition in the hide trade and united with the mother country in the expulsion of the Portuguese from Colonia do Sacramento.

2797. Service, Elman Rogers. Spanish-Guarani relations in early colonial Paraguay. Ann Arbor, Mich., University of Michigan, Museum of Anthropology (Anthropological papers, 9), 1954. 106 p., map.
Describes and explains the early relations of Spaniards and aborigines in Paraguay and their influence in the process of acculturation. Deserves attention for the study of the general problems of racial and cultural mestizaje.

2798. Universidad de la República. Instituto de Investigaciones Históricas y Laboratorio de Zoología. Documentos para la historia de la República Oriental del Uruguay. T. 2. Relatos de viajes, memorias y autobiografías. Viaje de William Toller a la banda oriental y Río de la Plata en 1715. Montevideo, 1955. 82 p., illus.
Translation of an interesting manuscript originally written in English by William Toller, and describing his voyage from Plymouth to B. A. in 1715. The author was mainly interested in the animals of the places he visited, and the work contains many descriptions and drawings of the birds and quadrupeds of Argentina. [C. Gibson]

2799. Zorraquín Becú, Ricardo. Los cabildos argentinos (R Fac Der Cien Soc, B A, 11:47, enero-marzo 1956, p. 95-156).
Another interesting monograph on colonial municipalities, based mainly on published records of the town councils in the La Plata region.

SPANISH AMERICA AND HAITI:
NINETEENTH AND TWENTIETH CENTURIES

MEXICO
AND CENTRAL AMERICA

WALTER V. SCHOLES

DURING 1955-1956 a number of authors made very important contributions to Mexican history. Not only were excellent books and articles published on political and diplomatic affairs but monumental studies of the economic and social life were produced. In the political realm, Nettie Lee Benson's book on early federalism successfully challenges accepted interpretations of how the federal system developed in Mexico. Stanley R. Ross's biography of Madero will certainly stand for a long time as the best one volume on this major political figure. The diplomacy of the first administration of Díaz is given its first full treatment by Daniel Cosío Villegas (item 2815).

The volumes by Francisco R. Calderón (item 2816) and Luis González y González et al. (item 2817) on economic and social history must be especially singled out as truly major contributions.

MEXICO

2800. Alessio Robles, Vito. El cacique Vidaurri y el presidente Comonfort (Mem Ac Mex Hist, 15:1, enero-marzo 1956, p, 64-86).
Shows Vidaurri's refusal to accept the decisions of the national government of Mexico, 1856-1857, and Vidaurri's relations with Comonfort after the War of Reform.

2801. ————. Los orígenes y las incidencias del Plan de Ayutla (Mem Ac Mex Hist, 14:1, enero-marzo 1955, p. 22-42).
Stresses background of the Gadsden Purchase and the part played by Comonfort in the Plan of Ayutla.

2802. Anaya Ibarra, Pedro María. Precursores de la Revolución Mexicana. México, Secretaría de Educación Pública (Biblioteca enciclopédica popular, nueva época, 227), 1955. 122 p.
Biographical sketches of Ricardo Flores Magón, Camilio Arriaga, and Praxedis G. Guerrero. Appended (p. 113-122) is a brief article on Basilio Vadillo, by Rodolfo Delgado.

2803. Antuñano, Estevan de. La industria del algodón en México, 1833. México, Manuel Porrúa, 1955. 103 p.
Reprint of this 19th-century document calling for the development of the textile industry in Mexico.

2804. Arenas Guzmán, Diego. Del maderismo a los tratados de Teoloyucan. México, Biblioteca del Instituto Nacional de Estudios Históricos de la Revolución Mexicana (2), 1955. 211 p.
This material was first published in *El Universal*, 1932-1933. It is based on correspondence from the archives of Robles Domínguez and covers the period 1911-1914.

2805. Arnáiz y Freg, Arturo. El doctor Mora, teórico de la reforma liberal (Hist Mex, 5:4, abril-junio 1956, p. 549-571).
Essay on the liberal thought of José María Luis Mora.

2806. Ashford, Gerald. Jacksonian liberalism and Spanish law in early Texas (SW Hist Q, 57:1, July 1953, p. 1-37).
Because many Texas laws were taken from Spain and Mexico, the land laws were especially well drawn to fit conditions in the Southwest. The land laws of the U. S., in many important cases, were so drawn that they held Texans back from wanting to become part of the U. S.

2807. Asociacion Cívica Yucatán (ed.). De la guerra de Castas. Causa de Manuel Antonio Ay, el primer indio maya rebelde fusilado en Valladolid el 30 de julio de 1847. México, 1956. 42 p.
Pages 11-42 have the transcription of the manuscript containing the case against the first Maya Indian shot in the civil war of 1847 in Yucatan.

2808. Barrera Fuentes, Florencio. Historia de la Revolución Mexicana. La etapa precursora. México, Biblioteca del Instituto Nacional de Estudios Históricos de la Revolución Mexicana (1), 1955. 339 p.
Covers 1900-1910; the interpretation is favorable to the revolution.

2809. Beauregard, Pierre Gustave Toutant. With Beauregard in Mexico. The Mexican War reminiscences of P. G. T. Beauregard, edited by T. Harry Williams. Baton Rouge, La., Louisiana State University Press, 1956? 115 p., illus., maps.
Reminiscences of Scott's march from Veracruz to Mexico City.

2810. Benson, Nettie Lee. La diputación provincial y el federalismo mexicano. México, El Colegio de México, 1955. 237 p.

This very able study disproves the long held belief that federalism was foreign to Mexican thought. Dr. Benson shows that long before the Constitution of 1824 the Mexicans wanted, and had, federalism.

2811. Berbusse, Edward J. Neutrality diplomacy of the United States and Mexico, 1910-1911 (Americas, Franciscan Hist, 12:3, Jan. 1956, p. 265-283).
This article develops the differences of opinion existing within the government of the U. S. Finally, a strict interpretation of neutrality was used. This interpretation helped the revolutionists against Díaz.

2812. Blaisdell, Lowell L. The consul in a crisis: Lower California, 1911 (Mid Am, 37:3, July 1955, p. 131-139).
Trials and tribulations of a young consul in Ensenada.

2813. Cassaretto, Mary. El movimiento protestante en México, 1940-1955. México, 1956. 181 p.
Feels that increase in the number of Protestants in Mexico is due to (1) greater number of Protestant missionaries in Mexico after World War II, (2) persecution of Catholics in Mexico until 1940, (3) too few priests in Mexico, and (4) increase of the lower middle class in Mexico.

2814. Cole, Merl Burke. Romantic tragedies of Mexico. Boston, Christopher Pub. House, 1956. 311 p., illus.
Gossip concerning the Revolution in Mexico by the wife of a special American envoy. At times it is interesting but not very revealing.

2815. Cosío Villegas, Daniel. Estados Unidos contra Porfirio Díaz. México, Hermes, 1956. 344 p.
Excellent study of the relations between Mexico and the U. S. during the first term of Díaz. Stress is placed on the question of recognition and border troubles with the author pointing out the parts played by Evarts, Foster, and Vallarta.

2816. ————. (ed.). Historia moderna de México. [2]. La República Restaurada. La vida económica, por Francisco R. Calderón. México, Hermes, 1955. 812 p., illus., map.
This is certainly the best study available on the economic life of Mexico, 1867-1876. The author deals with agriculture, tariff, mining, imports and exports, railroad construction, the free zone, local and national finances, public works, and investment schemes of foreigners. It is truly a monumental work and will be used by everyone interested in Mexican history. Excellent bibliography. It constitutes volume 2 of the projected six-volume history prepared under the general direction of Daniel Cosío Villegas (see *HLAS, no. 19*, item 3574). See also following item.

2817. ————. (ed.). Historia moderna de México. [3]. La República Restaurada. La vida social por Luis González y González, Emma Cosío Villegas y Guadalupe Monroy. México, Hermes, 1956. 1011 p., illus., maps.
To date it is impossible to find a better study than this one on the social life of Mexico, 1867-1876. The authors deal with music, theater, art, literature, education, charity, the urban and rural proletariat, religious fiestas, the Indian, and a general description of the population. This volume is a very important contribution to Mexican history. See also preceding item.

2818. Cue Canovas, Agustín. El tratado McLane-Ocampo. Juárez, los Estados Unidos y Europa. Prólogo de Vicente Sáenz. México, América Nueva (Col. Autores contemporáneos, 7), 1956. 248 p.
An attempted apology for the McLane-Ocampo treaty.

2819. Delaney, Robert W. Matamoros, port for Texas during the Civil War (SW Hist Q, 58:4, April 1955, p. 473-487).
Shows the overnight growth of the port with its trade not only with Europe and Texas but also with New Orleans and N. Y.

2820. Díaz, Porfirio. Archivo del general . . . Memorias y documentos. Prólogo y notas de Alberto María Carreño. México, Elede (Col. de obras históricas mexicanas, 3), 1955. T. 19, 317 p., illus.; t. 20, 317 p., illus.
V. 19 covers the period Feb. 26, 1877-Mar. 16, 1877. V. 20 covers Mar. 16, 1877-Apr. 4, 1877. Consists, in general, of letters to Díaz concerning military, financial, and political affairs.

2821. Donoso, Ricardo. Una amitsad mexicano-chileana: Matías Romero y José Alfonso (Hist Mex, 6:2, oct-dic. 1956, p. 294-320).
Letters of Romero to Alfonso, 1890-1898, that cover a number of subjects but especially U. S. relations with Chile.

2822. Dusenberry, William. The Mexican Agricultural Society, 1879-1914 (Americas, Franciscan Hist, 12:4, April 1956, p. 385-389).
Description of the organization and its activities.

2823. Fernández de Córdoba, Joaquín. Nuestros tesoros bibliográficos en los Estados Unidos (Hist Mex, 6:1, julio-sept. 1956, p. 129-160).
Index to Mexican historical documents at Yale, Michigan, Sutro Library, Bancroft Library, and the Huntington Library.

2824. Fuentes Mares, José. Santa Anna. Aurora y ocaso de un comediante. México, Jus, 1956. 391 p. & illus.
A political biography of Santa Anna.

2825. **García Granados, Ricardo.** Historia de México desde la restauración de la república en 1867, hasta la caída de Huerta. 1. edición completa. México, Jus, 1956. 2 v. 538 p.; 482 p.
New edition which, for the first time, includes material on Madero, Huerta, and Carranza.

2826. **González Bustamente, J. J.** Mariano Arista, precursor del Plan de Ayutla (Mem Ac Nac Hist Geog, 2. época, año 11, [special no., "Mariano Arista, precursor del Plan de Ayutla"], p. 5-47).
Entire issue given over to Arista as president. Author claims that although Arista was conservative, he changed while president and that the ideas of revolution to be found in the constitution of 1857 germinated during the term of Arista.

2827. **González Navarro, Moisés.** Las huelgas textiles en el Porfiriato (Hist Mex, 6:2, oct.-dic. 1956, p. 201-216).
Describes the reasons for the textile strikes during the presidency of Díaz.

2828. **González Ramírez, Manuel** (ed.). La caricatura política. México, Fondo de Cultura Económica (Fuentes para la historia de la Revolución Mexicana, 2), 1955. xlii, 143 p. & illus.
These political cartoons cover 1900-1924. They are especially good for the period, 1900-1914, covering Días, Madero and the American intervention. The notes by the editor are excellent.

2829. ———— (ed.). Planes políticos y otros documentos. México, Fondo de Cultura Económica (Fuentes para la historia de la Revolución Mexicana, 1), 1954. lxxiii, 353 p. & illus., ports., facsims.
A very convenient compilation of Mexican revolutionary plans from 1906 down to the Plan Almazanista in 1940.

2830. **González Valadez, Carolina.** Fiestas y paseos en la ciudad de México, 1877-1910. México, 1955. 145 p.
Description of the customs of the people during the presidency of Díaz.

2831. **Graebner, Norman A.** Empire on the Pacific. A study in American continental expansion. N. Y., Ronald Press, 1955. 278 p., maps.
The author has material on how the U. S. acquired the Southwest and California.

2832. **Hall, Martin H.** The Campbell-Sherman diplomatic mission to Mexico (B Hist Phil Ohio, 13:4, Oct. 1955, p. 254-270).
Failure of these two poor souls to carry out their mission to Juárez, 1866-1867, for the simple reason that they could not find him.

2833. **Harrison, John P.** Un análisis nor-teamericano de la Revolución mexicana en 1913 (Hist Mex, 5:4, abril-junio 1956, p. 598-618).
The author attempts to rehabilitate John Lind by publishing, with an introduction and notes, a letter from Lind to William Jennings Bryan (Veracruz, Sept. 19, 1913). The material presented indicates that Lind and Wilson were trying to understand that the 20th century had arrived in Mexico while the old-line diplomats still viewed the revolution with 19th-century ideas.

2834. **Henderson, H. M.** A critical analysis of the San Jacinto campaign (SW Hist Q, 59:3, Jan. 1956, p. 344-361).

2835. **Hutchinson, C. A.** Valentín Gómez Farías and the "Secret Pact of New Orleans" (HAHR, 36:4, Nov. 1956, p. 471-489).
The author points out how Cuevas, in his *Historia,* misused material in order to denounce Gómez Farías. The Mexican patriot was never a "traitor."

2836. **Iturribarría, Jorge Fernando.** Historia de Oaxaca. La restauración de la república y las revueltas de la Noria y Tuxtepec, 1867-1877. T. 4. Oaxaca, México, Publicaciones del Gobierno del Estado de Oaxaca, 1956. 253 p.
A political history which shows the tie between the state and national government.

2837. **Jordán, Fernando.** Crónica de un país bárbaro. México, Ediciones Asociación Mexicana de Periodistas, 1956. 494 p.
A survey history of Chihuahua.

2838. **Knapp, Frank A., Jr.** Edward Lee Plumb, amigo de México (Hist Mex, 6:1, julio-sept. 1956, p. 9-23).
A description of Plumb's activities in Mexico, 1855-1876, as a prospector, investor, associate with American companies in Mexico, and as a diplomat.

2839. **Link, Arthur S.** Wilson; the New Freedom. Princeton, N. J., Princeton University Press, 1956. 504 p.
Chapters 11 and 12 have an excellent account of Wilson's Mexican policy, 1913-1914.

2840. **López-Portillo y Weber, José.** Conspiración de los canales, el ferrocarril de Tehuantepec, el petróleo mexicano (Mem Ac Mex Hist, 14:2, abril-junio 1955, p. 130-167; 14:3, julio-sept. 1955, p. 206-270).
Shows the interest, in the 19th and early 20th century, of foreign nations in building an interoceanic canal or railroad in Central America or Mexico.

2841. McCornack, Richard Blaine. Porfirio Díaz en la frontera texana, 1875-1877 (Hist Mex, 5:3, enero-marzo 1956, p. 373-410).
Based upon manuscript in Washington, the author is able to show, contrary to general belief, that the U. S. did not aid Díaz in his revolt in 1876 against Lerdo.

2842. Magdaleno, Mauricio. Las palabras perdidas. México, Fondo de Cultura Económica, 1956. 225 p. & illus.
Memoirs of the Mexican political campaign of 1929 by the well-known Mexican novelist. As a supporter of Vasconcelos the author has a number of brilliant insights concerning the campaign.

2843. Mancisidor, José. Hidalgo, Morelos, Guerrero. México, Grijalbo (Biografías Gandesa), 1956. 359 p., illus.
Biographical sketches of the three men.

2844. Mena P., Mario A. El Congreso Constituyente restaurado y el federalismo, 1830. México, Manuel Porrúa, 1956. 41 p.
Shows the quarrel between the executive and legislature in the state of Mexico, 1830.

2845. Miquel i Vergés, Josep Maria. La diplomacia española en México, 1822-1823. México, El Colegio de México, 1956. 195 p., facsms.
Based on the reports of Juan Ramón Osés, secretary of the Spanish Mission in Mexico, 1823.

2846. Moreno, Pablo C. Torreón a través de sus presidentes municipales. México, Patria, 1955. 140 p., illus.
Brief biographical sketches of the municipal presidents, 1888-1955.

2847. Moreno M., Rafael. La teología ilustrada de Hidalgo (Hist Mex, 5:3, enero-marzo 1956, p. 321-336).
The author points up the modern aspects of Hidalgo's "Disertación sobre el verdadero método para estudiar teología."

2848. Nunn, William Curtis. Escape from reconstruction. With a foreword by Austin L. Porterfield. Fort Worth, Tex., Texas Christian University, 1956. 140 p., illus.
A description of Confederate settlers in Mexico after 1865.

2849. Ochoa Campos, Moisés. La reforma municipal. Historia municipal de México. México, 1955. 538 p.
Survey history of municipalities based primarily on interpretations taken from Weber. Thesis.

2850. Orozco Muñoz, Julio. La imprenta en San Francisco. Apuntes para su his-

toria. León, Gto., México, Linotip. Lumen, 1955. 70 p.
Survey from 1877.

2851. Palomares, Justino N. Anecdotario de la Revolución. México, 1954. 294 p.
Anecdotes of the revolution in northern Mexico by the poet Palomares.

2852. Plan de Ayutla. Conmemoración de su primer centenario. México, Universidad Nacional Autónoma de México, Ediciones de la Facultad de Derecho, 1954. 374 p.
Eleven articles by various authors dealing with the Santa Anna administration of 1853-1855, the political and constitutional background of the Plan, the military aspects of the revolution, liberals and moderates, and church property. Most of the articles are very good.

2853. Quirk, Robert E. Cómo se salvó Eduardo Iturbide (Hist Mex, 6:1, juliosept. 1956, p. 39-58).
The tale of how American agents got Eduardo Iturbide out of Mexico City in 1914.

2854. Ramos, Roberto. Libros que leyó don Miguel Hidalgo y Costilla. Guanajuato, México, Imp. del Gobierno del Estado, 1953. 25 p.
Catalog of the books in Hidalgo's library.

2855. Ross, Stanley R. Francisco I. Madero, apostle of Mexican democracy. N. Y., Columbia University Press, 1955. 378 p., maps, port.
An excellent biography of Madero. The first 217 pages are devoted to the rise of Madero to power. The last part is given over to revolutions against Madero and U. S.-Mexican relations. The work is based on manuscript sources and to date it probably is the best study of Madero available.

2856. Rouaix, Pastor. Principales pronunciamientos que registra la historia mexicana (Mem Ac Nac Hist Geog, 2. época, 12:1, 1956, p. 5-39).
This is a convenient listing, 1822-1864, of the revolutions in Mexico with a brief statement concerning each one. The author lists 140 revolts.

2857. Saldaña, José P. Episodios contemporáneos. Monterrey, México, 1955. 201 p.
History by anecdotes on 20th-century Nuevo Leon. The author is associated with the Acción Cívica Nacionalista in Monterrey.

2858. Simmons, Merle E. Porfirio Díaz in Mexico's historical ballads (New Mex Hist R, 31:1, Jan. 1956, p. 1-23).
The author shows some anti-Díaz ballads while Díaz was in power. Then came the Revolution. Since 1920 the ballads on Díaz have mellowed.

2859. **Smith. Lois Elwyn.** Mexico and the Spanish Republicans. Berkeley, University of California Press (University of California publications in political science, 4:2), 1955, p. 165-316.
Presents the position taken by Mexico during the Spanish Civil War and how Mexico helped the Republicans.

2860. **Tamayo, Jorge L.** Oaxaca en el siglo XX. Apuntes históricos y análisis político. México, 1956. 87 p.
A brief account of the effect of political revolution on Oaxaca.

2861. **Universidad Michoacana de San Nicolás de Hidalgo.** Hidalgo en el Colegio de San Nicolás. Documentos inéditos. Morelia, México, 1956. 149 p.
Documents concerning Hidalgo's relations with the Colegio especially covering the years 1776-1800.

2862. **University of Texas. Library.** Independent Mexico in documents: Independence, Empire and Republic. A calendar of the Juan E. Hernández y Dávalos manuscript collection, the University of Texas Library. Prepared by Carlos Eduardo Castañeda and Jack Autrey Dabbs. México, Jus, 1954, i. e. 1955. 604 p., port.
Very good guide to the collection which was acquired in 1943. It consists of approximately 3000 items and is especially important for the period 1808-1824. Most of the documents listed are still unpublished. Excellent index at the end of the volume.

2863. **Urquizo, Francisco Luis.** Páginas de la Revolución. México, Biblioteca del Instituto Nacional de Estudios Históricos de la Revolución Mexicana, 1956. 274 p.
Description of the Madero and Carranza revolutions by a participant.

2864. **Velasco Valdés, Miguel.** Historia del periodismo mexicano. Apuntes. México, Manuel Porrúa (Biblioteca mexicana, 14), 1955. 258 p.
This should prove to be a handy reference work for it includes a brief history of Mexican newspapers giving the names of the papers, a statement on the policies of the editors, and a description of whether the paper is liberal or conservative.

2865. **Velázquez, María del Carmen.** Temas políticos a través de proclamas, mensajes y manifiestos (Hist Mex, 5:4, abril-junio 1956, p. 572-595).
Analysis of the outstanding political proclamations of Mexico down to 1917. They reflect actual conditions in Mexico and outside political thought.

2866. **Vidal, Salvador (ed.).** La provincia de Zacatecas en 1803 (Mem Ac Nac Hist Geog, 2. época, 11:6, 1955, p. 5-35).
A document, from the archives in Zacatecas, that deals with the economic conditions in the area in 1803.

2867. **Zarco, Francisco.** Historia del Congreso extraordinario constituyente, 1856-1857. Estudio preliminar de Antonio Martínez Báez. Índices de Manuel Calvillo. México, El Colegio de México, 1956. 1421 p.
A much needed new edition of the debates of the constitutional congress, 1856-1857. Index.

2868. **Zuno, José G.** Don Pedro Moreno, ensayo historico. Guadalajara, México, Editorial Gráfica, 1955. 161 p.
Laudatory biography of a leader in Mexico's move for independence.

CENTRAL AMERICA

2869. **Aizpurua, Armando.** Biografía del General Manuel Quintero V. Panamá, Ministerio de Educación, Departamento de Bellas Artes, 1956. 398 p.
Biography of a popular military and political figure in 20th-century Panama.

2870. **Castillo Pimentel, Ernesto.** Panamá y los Estados Unidos. Panamá, 1953. 336 p.
Survey of U. S.-Panama relations during the past 50 years. It is especially useful for the treaties signed in the period.

2871. **Durón, Rómulo Ernesto.** Historia de Honduras, desde la independencia hasta nuestros días. T. 1. Tegucigalpa, Ministerio de Educación Pública (Col. Rómulo E. Durón, 2), 1956. 270 p.
Political history of Honduras, 1821-1829.

2872. **Herrarte, Alberto.** La Unión de Centroamérica. Tragedia y esperanza. Ensayo político-social sobre la realidad de Centroamérica. Guatemala, Ministerio de Educación Pública (Col. Documentos, 13), 1955. 581 p.
Survey of the people, economy, culture, and history of Central America. The author suggests that the only answer to their problems is federation.

2873. **Iglesias, Luis.** Los misioneros redentoristas y la república de El Salvador, C. A. Apuntes para la historia religiosa de El Salvador. México, Gerardo Mayela, 1956. 147 p. & illus.
List and description of the missions, especially since 1930.

2874. **Instituto Morazánico de Honduras.** Colección de leyes, decretos y órdenes del Gobierno Provisorio del General

Francisco Morazán en el Estado de Costa Rica, 1841 a 1842. Tegucigalpa, 1956. 127 p.

2875. **Mayes, Guillermo.** Honduras en la independencia de Centro América y anexión a México. Tegucigalpa, Tip. Nacional, 1956. 131 p.
A good survey with useful material on the revolutionary movements in Honduras, 1811-1819.

2876. **Molina, Pedro.** Escritos del doctor . . . conteniendo la reproducción íntegra de los escritos . . . del periódico *El editor constitucional* . . . Guatemala, Ministerio de Educación Pública (Col. Documentos, 10-12), 1954. T. 1, 342 p.; t. 2, p. 353-592; t. 3, p. 599-898.
Reproduction of the newspaper. V. 1 covers July 24-Dec. 11, 1820; v. 2, Dec. 18, 1820-May 21, 1821; v. 3, May 28-Aug. 20, 1821, and the new title *El genio de la libertad*, Aug. 27-Dec. 10, 1821. Reproduction is very well done. Gives a good insight into liberal thought of the period. No index.

2877. **Mosk, Sanford A.** The coffee economy of Guatemala, 1850-1918: development and signs of instability (Interam Ec Aff, 9:3, winter 1955, p. 6-20).
Shows the increase of coffee production from mid-19th century to 1897. This period brought a revival and extension of peonage. The first major set-back to coffee earnings took place in 1897. A period of instability continued after that.

2878. **Pérez Valenzuela, Pedro.** Santo Tomás de Castilla. Apuntes para la historia de las colonizaciones en la costa

atlántica. Guatemala, Tip. Nacional, 1956. 259 p.
Description of attempted English and Belgian settlements in Guatemala, 1824-1850.

2879. **Rippy, J. Fred.** State Department operations: the Rama Road (Interam Ec Aff, 9:1, summer 1955, p. 17-32).
This is a discussion of Roosevelt's "commitment" in 1939 to build a road in Nicaragua in order to gain the friendship of Somoza. Rippy is disturbed for he feels that Roosevelt squandered money.

2880. **Rodríguez Cerna, José.** Centroamérica en el Congreso de Bolívar. 2. ed. Guatemala, Ministerio de Relaciones Exteriores, 1956. 338 p.
A collection of documents, 1825-1826, showing Central America's part in the Congress of Panama, 1826.

2881. **Scheips, Paul J.** Gabriel Lafond and Ambrose W. Thompson, neglected Isthmian promoters (HAHR, 36-2, May 1956, p. 211-228).
Attempts by a Frenchman and an American to develop interest in the Chiriqui region.

2882. **Selser, Gregorio.** Sandino, general de hombres libres. B. A., Ediciones Pueblos de América, 1955. 300 p.
Biographical study of Augusto César Sandino. It is pro-Sandino and thus anti-U. S.

2883. **Valdés Oliva, Arturo.** Caminos y luchas por la independencia. Guatemala, Ministerio de Educación Pública, 1956. 482 p.
Political and military history of Central America's movement for independence.

WEST INDIES
ARTURO SANTANA

GENERAL

2901. **Mathews, Thomas.** The project for a confederation of the Greater Antilles (Carib Hist R, 5:2, Oct. 1955, p. 70-107).
Documented article on the origins and development of the confederation idea in the Greater Antilles from the early 19th to the 20th century, emphasizing the activities towards that purpose in the Spanish-speaking islands, especially Cuba and Puerto Rico. Based on some manuscript material from the National Archives in Washington and, mainly, on printed primary and secondary sources.

2902. **Rodríguez Demorizi, Emilio** (ed). Invasiones haitianas de 1801, 1805 y 1822. Ciudad Trujillo, Editorial del Caribe (Academia Dominicana de la Historia, 1), 1955. 371 p.
Relations, documents, and articles dealing with

the Haitian invasions of the Dominican Republic in 1801, 1805, and 1822, together with an introductory study of the events. [R. R. Hill]

CUBA

2903. **Abascal, Horacio.** Historia de la fundación de la Academia de Ciencias de la Habana (U Habana, 19:112-114, enero-junio 1954, p. 168-179).
A short history of the establishment of this institution in 1860, with a preliminary introduction on medical studies in Cuba before that date.

2904. **Amador Sánchez, Luis.** No centenário de José Martí. Função histórica do poeta (R Hist, São Paulo, 5:17, jan.-março 1954, p. 199-209).
Short biographical essay on Martí as the leader of Cuban independence, followed by a brief critical analysis of his poetry in relation to his po-

litical ideas and activities. Contains a bibliography.

2905. Arisa, A. José Martí. Quito, Casa de la Cultura Ecuatoriana, 1954. 45 p.

Extended essay on the life and works of the Cuban Apostle. Appraises Martí within the structure of the history of the Americas.

2906. Baeza Flores, Alberto. Vida de José Martí. El hombre íntimo y el hombre público. Habana, Comisión Nacional Organizadora de los Actos y Ediciones del Centenario y del Monumento de Martí, 1954. 798 p.

This volume received the biography award of the Martí Centennial Committee. Biographical study by a litterateur rather than a historian, the author being a well-known journalist and holder of a number of prizes in poetry and fiction. The volume, in poetic and vivid prose, is mostly an extended essay. There is excess of passion and lack of scholarly apparatus. Historians will lament the absence of all bibliographical data and footnote citations (except for a vague critical essay on bibliography at the end of the volume) since the author had access to what was, at the time, unpublished documentation.

2907. Bueno, Salvador. La crítica finisecular en Cuba (Atenea, año 31, 117:351-352, sept.-oct. 1954, p. 61-68).

Brief biographical essay on three 19th-century Cuban literary critics who also played an important political role in the island's independence movement: Enrique Piñeyro (1839-1911), Rafael María Merchán (1844-1905), and José de Armas y Céspedes (1866-1919).

2907a. ————. Félix Varela en nuestra historia (R Bib Nac, Habana, 2. serie, 5:1, enero-marzo 1954, p. 19-43).

Bibliographical essay on Father Félix Varela (1787-1853), precursor of Cuban independence, containing also a detailed analysis of the many different aspects of his personality. There is neither a bibliography nor footnote citations.

2908. Camacho, Pánfilo D. Aguilera, el precursor sin gloria. Habana, Ministerio de Educación, Dirección de Cultura (Biblioteca Bachiller y Morales, 2), 1951. 195 p.

Undocumented biography of Francisco Vicente Aguilera, Cuban patriot and vice-president of the first Cuban Republic after the Grito de Yara. An "obra de divulgación" in simple, impressionistic style. No bibliography.

2909. Carrillo, José. El verdadero José Martí. Tres ensayos críticos. México, Bayo Libros, 1953. 272 p.

Three different essays on Martí, written from a Marxist-communist viewpoint, on his educational and philosophical ideas and on the present-day value of his ideology for the Spanish American world. All three of them were originally presented as public lectures in Mexico. Bibliographical appendix only for the first and longest essay, the one on Martí's educational ideas.

2910. Una carta de Máximo Gómez (Clío, 23:103, abril-junio 1955, p. 112-113).

Textual transcription of a letter dated Mar. 28, 1899, from Máximo Gómez to some Dominican friends, Cayetano Armando Rodríguez and Ostermán Lamarche, on the possibility of his permanent return to the Dominican Republic in the immediate future.

2911. Castañeda, Orlando. José Güell y Renté, una figura de leyenda de nuestra historia (R Bib Nac, Habana, 2. serie, 6:2, abril-junio 1955, p. 195-207).

Brief biographical essay on José Güell y Renté (1818-1884), Cuban poet and politician, at one time a member of the Spanish Royal Senate. Contains some bibliographical notes.

2912. Collado y López, Olga. Nicolás Heredia, vida y obra (R Bib Nac, Habana, 2. serie, 5:3, julio-sept. 1954, p. 103-197).

Biographical essay and critical study of the life and works of the journalist and writer Nicolás Heredia (1855-1901) who lived a great part of his life in Cuba and played a role in the final stages of the Cuban independence movement. A major part of the article is a critical analysis of Heredia's works. Contains a bibliography.

2913. Conangla Fontanilles, José. Martí y Cataluña. Examen retrospectivo de unos conceptos inverisímiles, atribuídos al gran Apóstol cubano. Habana, Comisión Nacional Organizadora de los Actos y Ediciones del Centenario y del Monumento de Martí, 1954. 218 p.

Through a study of Martí's correspondence and writings, tries to show the Cuban "Maestro" was not the author of a derogatory opinion on Catalonia appearing in two of Martí's newsletters written in N. Y. in 1882 for *La opinión nacional* of Caracas. This serves as a pretext for an extended survey of the commercial and political relations between Cuba and Catalonia during the 18th and 19th centuries. An appendix contains the complete text of the offending newsletters.

2914. Corbitt, Duvon C. Historical publications of the Martí Centennial (HAHR, 34:3, Aug. 1954, p. 399-405).

Report and critical comment on the most important Martiana appearing in 1953, i. e., new editions of Martí's writings, biographies, monographs about him, etc. Brings notice of many other volumes published before that date.

2914a. ————. Historical publications of the Oficina del Historiador de la Ciudad de la Habana (HAHR, 35:4, Nov. 1955, p. 492-498).

Report on the editorial accomplishments, since 1937, of the Oficina. Comments on three different series: the *Actas capitulares del ayuntamiento de la Habana*, the *Colección histórica cubana y americana* and the *Cuadernos de historia habanera*.

2915. Cuba. Archivo Nacional. Inventario general del archivo de la delegación del

Partido Revolucionario Cubano en Nueva York (1892-1898). T. 2. Habana, 1955. 446 p. (Publ., 44).

A continuation of item 3710, *HLAS, no. 19.* Lists 9617 letters to the delegation from individuals, clubs, agencies, and other organizations, as well as the documents accumulated by the delegation. Under each heading the items are entered alphabetically by writer. The date and place are given, but no indication of the subject matter. [R. R. Hill]

2916. Delgado, Miguel. La caída del Titán. San Pedro, diciembre 7 de 1896. Aclaraciones históricas. 2. ed. Habana, 1955. 158 p., illus.

Historical literature of the polemic-apologetic type. The author writes in defense of his brother, Colonel Juan Delgado González, a hero of Cuba's last War of Independence who fought with Maceo at that leader's last stand at San Pedro, performing there the heroic feat of rescuing the leader's body after the latter had been killed by the Spaniards. The author's task is to defend his brother from the accusations hurled at him by General José Miró Argenter, Chief of Staff to Maceo and also a participant at San Pedro, who in his "Crónicas de la guerra," first published at Habana in 1909, made Colonel Delgado chiefly responsible for Maceo's death, due to his not maintaining the proper vigilance around the insurgent camp. In the main, Señor Delgado succeeds in proving his point. The book, a collection of letters and *ponencias* put together by a thin thread of narrative, makes no attempt at presenting a complete panorama of Maceo's last campaign. Based on published memoirs and secondary works. Contains a bibliography, but there are no citations to sources throughout the text.

2917. Entralgo, Elías. Los conceptos libertadores de Enrique José Varona (U Habana, 19:112-114, enero-junio 1954, p. 104-167).

Analytical essay on the political ideology of this Cuban thinker, comparing him with Martí. Detailed discussion of some subjects such as nationalism and *separatismo*. Originally presented as a public lecture.

2918. Fernández-Rúa, José L. 1898: Cuba y Filipinas. Madrid, Publicaciones Españolas (Temas españoles, 98), 1954. 29 p.

A publication for popular consumption, based on Madrid press reports during the year under consideration. Reflects the passionate state of Spanish public opinion on the events that led to the loss in 1898 of the Spanish West Indies and the Philippines.

2919. Gay-Calbó, Enrique. Las "Crónicas de la guerra de Cuba" (R Bib Nac, Habana, 2. serie, 6:2, abril-junio 1955, p. 79-94).

Brief résumé (with commentary) of the first part of the "Crónicas de la guerra de Cuba," originally published by Nicolás Heredia in the Cuban journal *El Fígaro* during the year 1896.

2919a. ————. El Revisor político y literario (R Bib Nac, Habana, 2. serie, 6:4, oct.-dic. 1955, p. 65-94).

Historical study, from its appearance in 1823, of a 19th-century Cuban periodical which the author considers of great importance as a continuator in the island of the ideas of Father Varela. Contains facsimiles of the first number.

2920. Gómez, Juan Gualberto. La cuestión de Cuba en 1884 (R Bib Nac, Habana, 2. serie, 5:1, enero-marzo 1954, p. 9-15).

A reprint of the twelfth and last chapter of the volume by the same title published by Gómez at Madrid in 1885.

2920a. ————. Por Cuba libre. Homenaje de la ciudad de la Habana al gran cubano en el centenario de su nacimiento, 1854-12 de julio-1954. Habana, Oficina del Historiador de la Ciudad, 1954. 453 p.

Divided into two parts: (1) "Juan Gualberto Gómez, paladín de la independencia y de la libertad de Cuba," by Emilio Roig de Leuchsenring, p. 7-136, a detailed study of the political activities and writings of this leader in the Cuban independence movement which points out the continuous intellectual and personal influence of Martí on Juan Gualberto Gómez; and (2) "Trabajos de Juan Gualberto Gómez," p. 137-448, a collection of Gómez's writings divided into three parts: a short unpublished autobiography, writings for his political campaigns for Cuban independence during the Spanish colonial period (1884-1898); and his speeches and writings favoring independence during the first American occupation (1898-1901).

2921. González, Manuel Pedro. José Martí, anticlerical irreductible (Cuad Am, año 13, 73:1, enero-feb. 1954, p. 170-197).

Analytical study of Martí's anticlerical viewpoints, based on many quotations taken from the Maestro's *Obras completas* (Habana, 1936-1953, 74 v.). The author stresses Martí's spiritual conception of life and his deism.

2922. González y Gutiérrez, Diego. La continuidad revolucionaria de Varela en las ideas de Martí. Habana, Academia de la Historia de Cuba, 1953. 25 p.

Originally presented as a lecture before the Academia de la Historia de Cuba. A sketchy comparison of the revolutionary and political ideas of Father Varela and Martí in order to show the existing ideological continuity. Contains ample quotations from both *próceres* on such topics as liberty, democracy, slavery, and the political future of Cuba. There are neither source citations nor bibliography.

2923. Guiral Moreno, Mario. La autenticidad de un grupo histórico (R Bib Nac, Habana, 2. serie, 6:4, oct.-dic. 1955, p. 105-111).

An analysis of the authenticity of a photograph in which José Martí and Máximo Gómez appear together. Brief bibliography and a reproduction of the disputed photograph.

2924. Hurtado Galtés, Félix; Horacio Abascal y Vera; and César Rodríguez Expósito. La obra y la gloria de Finlay reconocidas por el XIV Congreso Internacional de Historia de la Medicina. Habana, Ministerio de Salubridad y Asistencia Social (Cuadernos de historia sanitaria, 7), 1955. 99 p., illus., ports., facsims.
Presented by the Cuban delegation at the XIV International Congress of History of Medicine held at Rome and Salerno in 1954. Short biography of the Cuban physician Dr. Carlos J. Finlay (1833-1915) and a study of his research on yellow fever.

2925. Índice del libro veinte y uno de reales órdenes. Índice o extracto de las reales cédulas, órdenes e instrucciones de este libro correspondiente al año de 1816 (B Arch Nac, Habana, 53-54, enero 1954-dic. 1955, i.e. 1956, p. 328-349).
Index for v. 21 in the "Reales Órdenes" series at the Archivo Nacional in Habana. Covers the "Reales Órdenes," "Cédulas," and "Instrucciones." Continuation of a series intermittently published in the *Boletín*.

2926. José Martí en la Comisión Monetaria Internacional Americana, Washington, 1891. Habana, Banco Nacional de Cuba, 1957. 123 p.
A facsimile edition of the minutes of the International American Monetary Commission and the Spanish translation, with a preface by Emeterio S. Santovenia and an introductory study by Félix Lizaso. [R. R. Hill]

2927. Ldo. D. José Martí y Pérez, solicita habilitación para ejercer su profesión de Abogado a reserva de presentar su título (B Arch Nac, Habana, 51-52, enero 1952-dic. 1953, i.e. 1954, p. 47-52).
Transcription of the text of an expediente, dated in the year 1878, at present preserved in the Archivo Nacional of Cuba.

2928. Lizaso, Félix, and Ernesto Ardura. Personalidad e ideas de José Martí. Habana, Comisión Nacional Organizadora de los Actos y Ediciones del Centenario y del Monumento de Martí, 1954. 73 p.
Essays on Martí's personality and ideas by two Cuban writers already well known for numerous other works on the Apostle.

2929. Lockmiller, David Alexander. Enoch A. Crowder, soldier, lawyer, and statesman. Columbia, Mo., University of Missouri (Studies, 27), 1955. 286 p., illus.
Laudatory biography. More than a third of the volume is devoted to General Crowder's official duties and contributions, primarily in the fields of judicial and electoral reform, in the Philippines and Cuba and later as ambassador to Cuba, up to 1927. There are occasional glimpses of his reactions to outstanding personalities in these republics. Based on Crowder's private papers.

2930. Martínez Bello, Antonio. El temperamento de Martí (R Bib Nac, Habana, 2. serie, 5:1, enero-marzo 1954, p. 61-106).
The author, after a detailed analysis of the life and works of Martí, tries to demonstrate—following Jung's theory on psychological types—that Martí's character was predominantly extroverted, with a balanced mixture of both idealism and realism. Undocumented apologetic essay.

2931. Martínez Fortún, Ortelio. Estudio biográfico del médico español don Claudio Delgado y su aportación al estudio de la fiebre amarilla. Madrid, Dirección General de Sanidad, 1954. 118 p., illus.
Biographical study of a Spanish physician (1843-1916) who lived many years in Cuba and collaborated there with Dr. Carlos J. Finlay in the latter's studies on yellow fever. Extensive bibliographical references.

2932. Martínez-Fortún y Foyo, José A. El diario de la Habana en la mano. Índices y sumarios (años de 1812 a 1848). Habana, 1955. 260 p.
An index of the different subjects covered and the most important news items contained in the *Diario de la Habana* from its first number dated Saturday, Sept. 1, 1810, to the year 1848 when it changed its name to *Gaceta de la Habana*. The summaries are short, mostly mere captions that do not really summarize the news items. News on medical, scientific, and welfare matters are emphasized and covered more extensively than others. Based on collections of the newspaper in the library of the Sociedad Económica de Amigos del País, the Biblioteca Nacional, and the University of Habana. Although not presenting useful synthesis of the news items, it is of great value as a research tool. Mimeographed.

2933. Méndez, Manuel Isidro. Acerca de "La Mejorana" y "Dos Ríos." Habana, Oficina del Historiador de la Ciudad (Cuadernos de historia habanera, 56), 1954. 28 p.
Sketchy analysis of the celebrated interview held at the hacienda La Mejorana between Máximo Gómez, José Martí, and Antonio Maceo, May 5, 1895. It has been asserted by some Cuban historians that this meeting resulted in irreconcilable differences between Maceo and Martí on the supremacy of a civil government over the military leaders, which differences prompted Martí voluntarily to sacrifice his life at Dos Ríos. The author asserts that while there were contending viewpoints at La Mejorana, they never resulted in irreconcilable differences and that "las discrepancias en lo atinente a la lucha, se conciliaron sin imposición de parte, cual procedía entre hombres libres, con los mismos derechos y guiados sólo por el bien patrio, ante el que, los tres, en otras ocasiones, habían sabido

deponerse." Based on published primary and secondary sources.

2934. Mesa Rodríguez, Manuel I. (ed.). Centón epistolario de Domingo del Monte. T. 7, 1823-1843. Habana, Academia de la Historia de Cuba, 1957. 198 p.

This last volume of the Centón Epistolario comprises 194 letters written to Domingo del Monte by Félix Manuel de Jesús Tanco y Bosmeniel between 1823 and 1843. They deal with interesting intimate political and literary questions. Included are poetical and other compositions which serve to reveal much regarding the writer and his friendship with Domingo del Monte. [R. R. Hill]

2935. Montalvo, José R. Disertación acerca de la vida intelectual de la isla de Cuba (R Bib Nac, Habana, 2. serie, 5:4, oct.-dic. 1954, p. 7-19).

Reprint edition of a lecture originally given in 1877 before the Real Academia de Ciencias of Habana. The author (1843-1901) complains about the backward intellectual state of Cuban society at that time and calls for the establishment of scientific and literary institutions which would work for the intellectual advancement of the island.

2936. Nieto y Cortadellas, Rafael. Apuntes genealógicos sobre el habanero don José Alvarez de Toledo: su vida, su familia (R Bib Nac, Habana, 2. serie, 5:2, abril-junio 1954, p. 61-91).

Biographical essay on this early 19th-century Cuban adventurer (1779-1854) who, after having been in the Spanish naval service, became during the second decade of the 19th century a prominent revolutionary filibusterer in northeastern New Spain and southwestern U. S., later deserting the revolutionary cause, and ending his days in the Spanish diplomatic service. Contains a well-documented genealogical study on his ancestry from the 16th century on.

2936a. ————. Una rama cubana de los Roca de Togores (R Bib Nac. Habana, 2. serie, 6:1, enero-marzo 1955, p. 113-145).

Genealogical data on the Cuban branch of this prominent Spanish family that arrived in Habana toward the end of the 18th century. The data, taken from church parochial archives, cover the period 1787-1928.

2937. Pérez, Justo. ¿Se suicidó José Martí en la Boca de Dos Ríos? (R Arch Bib Nac, 33:3-4, sept.-oct. 1954, p. 119-123).

Résumé of the different and opposing viewpoints held by several Cuban historians on Martí's death at Dos Rios: whether it was or was not voluntary and on purpose.

2938. Riera Hernández, Mario. Cuba política, 1899-1955. Habana, Imp. Modelo, 1955. 628 p.

A survey of the origin of Cuban political parties and political campaigns and elections in the first half of the 20th century. Contains lists of winning candidates and the total votes received by them. Also accounts of the civil revolts, major laws and decrees, biographical sketches of presidents, lists of cabinet members and a synthesis of the electoral laws promulgated since 1900. Very useful reference work for students of Cuban government since independence.

2939. Rodríguez Demorizi, Emilio. Papeles dominicanos de Máximo Gómez. Adición y enmiendas (Clío, 22:99, mayo-junio 1954, p. 104-105).

Textual transcription of a letter dated Aug. 29, 1897, by Máximo Gómez, in which he comments on several contemporary Cuban and Spanish events, especially Antonio Cánovas del Castillo's death and his policies toward Cuba. This is a corrected version of the letter which was published originally by Rodríguez Demorizi in his *Papeles dominicanos de Máximo Gómez* (Ciudad Trujillo, Montalvo, 1954, 449 p.).

2940. Rodríguez y Expósito, César. Médicos en la vida de Martí. Prólogo por Armando J. Coro. Habana, Ministerio de Salubridad y Asistencia Social (Cuadernos de historia sanitaria, 8), 1955. 75 p., illus.

A profusely illustrated account of the many physicians connected with Martí throughout his life, both professionally and as his collaborators in Cuba's struggle for independence. Contains some hitherto unknown biographical data on Martí and his views on medical science and medical men. There are bibliographical notes and an appendix with Martí's death certificate.

2941. Santovenia, Emeterio S. Armonías y conflictos en torno a Cuba. México, Fondo de Cultura Económica (Tierra firme, 61), 1956. 318 p.

An extended essay on the diplomatic history of Cuba as a Spanish colony, built around the theme of the Cuban people as passive subjects of international rivalry. Except for a brief introduction covering the early colonial period and a postscript on the Platt amendment, the bulk of the book deals with the 19th century. Dr. Santovenia restricts himself to diplomatic history in the narrow sense; he does provide, however, a well-balanced account of the changing patterns of international policy affecting Cuba on the part of the U. S., the European powers, and the Latin American republics. The material on Latin American attitudes toward Cuban independence is of great importance, being less fully known than the policies of the U. S. and the European powers. Throughout the book the author deals objectively with subjects which are for the Cuban highly charged with emotion. There is an appendix of selected secondary works and source collections for each chapter, but there is no specific documentation throughout the text.

DOMINICAN REPUBLIC

2942. Alfau Durán, Vetilio. En torno a Duarte y su idea de unidad de las razas

(Clío, 22:100, julio-sept. 1954, p. 107-114).

Text of a lecture with some bibliographical notes. Discusses the racial problem and the abolitionists debate in Santo Domingo during the period 1822-1861.

2942a. ————. En torno a la Trinitaria (Clío, 22:99, mayo-junio 1954, p. 97-102).

Some news on this patriotic secret society created by Juan Pablo Duarte in 1838, and on its founding members (the author shows them to have been only nine) and their personalities and achievements. Based on printed primary sources.

2942b. ————. Weyler en Santo Domingo (Clío, 23:104, julio-sept. 1955, p. 138-141).

Data on the activities in the Dominican Republic, during the Spanish reoccupation of her former colony (1861-1865), of the later much discussed Captain General of Cuba, Valeriano Weyler y Nicolau. Based on Weyler's published memoirs, fragments of which are textually reproduced, and on other published sources.

2943. Diario de La Guaira (B Arch Gen, Ciudad Trujillo, año 18:84, enero-marzo 1955, p. 56-65).

Collection of letters commenting on Dominican politics, written, most of them, from La Guaira, Venezuela, 1880-1881, by the Dominican politician Juan Bautista Pradas.

2944. Documentos históricos (Clío, 23:101, oct.-dic. 1954, p. 197-202).

Transcribed text, annotated by Vetilio Alfau Durán, of eight documents, dated between 1819 and 1906, from several Dominican archives, comprising baptismal, marriage, death and other records of members of the Sociedad Trinitaria.

2945. Dominican Republic. Archivo General de la Nación. Fondos de la anexión a España, 1861-1865: Catálogo (B Arch Gen, Ciudad Trujillo, año 19, 19:88-89, enero-junio 1956, p. 162-239; 19:90-91, julio-dic. 1956, p. 260-337).

A chronological listing of the documents in the Archive dealing with the annexation of Santo Domingo by Spain (1861-1865). The date and a brief identification are given for each document, all of which are in Section G of the Archive. [R. R. Hill]

2945a. ————. ————. Obras de Trujillo. Ciudad Trujillo, Montalvo, 1956. 294 p. (Archivo general, 12).

A listing of the articles about General Trujillo which appeared in the *Listín diario*, 1930-1942, *La nación*, 1942-1948, and *El Caribe*, 1948-1955. Arranged chronologically. There is an introduction by Ramón Lugo Lovatón, former director of the Archive. [R. R. Hill]

2946. Galíndez, Jesús de. La era de Trujillo. Un estudio casuistico de dictadura

hispanoamericana. Santiago, Editorial del Pacífico, 1956. 452 p.

Spanish version of Professor Galíndez's much-commented-on doctoral dissertation, presented originally at Columbia University and supposedly responsible for the author's untimely death. Generalissimo Trujillo and his regime are presented as a case study, a typical example of the political and administrative organization created by the Spanish American caudillo, whose main characteristics, according to the author, are lack of a doctrinal basis and subversion of legal and political institutions which are left as formal but empty structures. After sketching the history of the Dominican Republic up to the year 1930 when Trujillo came to power, the first part of the book is devoted to a chronological synopsis of his era up to 1955. The second part is a detailed analysis of different aspects of the regime throughout its evolution during these years: the constitutional farce, controlled elections, widespread terrorism, worker's syndicates, army, press, cultural life, foreign policy, and the dictator's personal life. Towards the end the author objectively renders judgment on the positive and negative aspects of the regime, the conclusion being, however, a sweeping condemnation. Unfortunately, the footnotes and bibliography undoubtedly appended to the original dissertation are not included here, giving us no idea as to the sources (besides the author's own personal experiences and reminiscences) utilized, and diminishing considerably the value to the scholar of this Spanish version.

2947. Índice general de los libros copiadores de la sección de relaciones exteriores (B Arch Gen, Ciudad Trujillo, año 18, 18:84, enero-marzo 1955, p. 84-104).

Index to the correspondence in the foreign affairs section of the Archivo General de la Nación (Ciudad Trujillo), Jan. 27-May 9, 1875. Continuation of a series published intermittently.

2948. Larrazal Blanco, Carlos. Noticias de la Independencia dominicana en Venezuela (Clío, 22:99, mayo-junio 1954, p. 102-103).

Reproduces news items published in the Venezuelan press during the year 1845 on the Dominican revolution for independence which had started the year before.

2949. Mejía Ricart, Gustavo Adolfo. Historia de Santo Domingo. V. 7. Ciudad Trujillo, Pol Hermanos, 1954. 442, xxxv p.

Political, religious, and institutional history of the Spanish colony in Hispaniola during the period of Haitian and French occupation from 1801 to 1809, ending with the reconquest of the territory by Spain in 1809. Most of the printed Spanish and French primary sources have been utilized, as well as some material from the Archivo General de la Nación in Ciudad Trujillo. No mention is made, however, of the most important relevant works by present-day American and European historians, the subject matter being presented, mostly, from a local angle. Eight volumes in total are planned in this national history of the Dominican Republic. For notice of earlier volumes see *HLAS, no. 14, 1948,* item 1848; *no. 15, 1949,* item 1618; *no. 17, 1951,* item 1552, and *no. 18, 1952,* item 1719. Represents a considerable "tour de force" in bibliographical and data compilation as can be appreciated from the bibliography to each chapter and the superabundance of detailed data throughout the text and notes. As in the case of previous volumes, it is an extensive chronicle and storehouse of facts, rather than a historical work in our contemporary sense. Many important documents are included, either in the text, or in the elaborate footnotes.

2949a. ————. Historia de Santo Domingo. V. 8. Ciudad Trujillo, Pol Hermanos, 1956. 453 p.

Continuation of item above. This volume covers the period known as the reincorporation with Spain (1809-1820) and the achievement of independence under Núñez de Cáceres in 1821. There are extensive accounts of the operation of the Spanish regime under the different governors sent from the metropolis and of the events which led up to the final break in 1821. Printed primary sources as well as material from the Archivo General de la Nación in Ciudad Trujillo have been utilized. Important documents are included in the text and the extensive footnotes. This latest addition to the series shares the same virtues and deficiencies of previous volumes.

2950. Peña Batlle, Manuel Arturo. Antecedentes históricos y sociológicos de la anexión a España (Clío, 22:99, mayo-junio 1954, p. 84-91).

Reprint of an undocumented essay originally published as a newspaper article in 1929. A vague discussion of the background, from 1838 to 1844, of the Spanish annexation of the Dominican Republic in 1861.

2951. Polanco Brito, H. E. La parroquia de San José de los Llanos. Breves notas históricas (Clío, 23:104, julio-sept. 1955, p. 125-132).

A discussion of the origins of San José de los Llanos together with data on its ecclesiastical history, 1863-1952. Based on published primary and secondary sources and original research in parochial archives and in the Archivo General de la Nación (Ciudad Trujillo).

2952. Rodríguez Demorizi, Emilio. Antecedentes de la anexión a España. Ciudad Trujillo, Montalvo (Academia Dominicana de la Historia, 4), 1955. 463 p.

Documents and contemporary articles (1860-1864) relating to the annexation of Santo Domingo to Spain and its effect on the former country. There is a study of the causes of the annexation and a bibliography. [R. R. Hill]

2952a. ————. Relaciones dominico-españolas (1844-1859). Ciudad Trujillo, Montalvo (Academia Dominicana de la Historia, 3), 1955. 428 p.

Correspondence of Spanish agents, and other documents from the Archivo Histórico Nacional at Madrid, dealing with the relations between Spain and the Dominican Republic and events in the latter country, 1844-1859, together with a reproduction of the newspaper *La República* for 1856. [R. R. Hill]

2953. Sevez, Francois F. Pedro Alejandrino Pina (Clío, 22:101, oct.-dic. 1954, p. 175-196).

Biographical data on Pedro Alejandrino Pina (1820-1870), especially his activities as a member of the Sociedad Trinitaria and as a leader in the Dominican independence movement. Contains bibliography and some transcribed documents.

HAITI

2954. Baur, John E. The presidency of Nicolas Geffrard of Haiti (Americas, Franciscan Hist, 10:4, Apr. 1954, p. 425-461).

An analysis of Geffrard, who dominated Haitian political life from 1859 until 1867; his role as a leader and the problems he faced during that period. All the many facets of his presidency—economic, military, foreign policy, etc., —are brought under discussion. To the author he was perhaps the ablest Haitian ruler between Boyer and the 20th century. Drawn almost exclusively from printed primary and secondary sources.

2955. Boyd, Willis D. James Redpath and American Negro colonization in Haiti, 1860-1862 (Americas, Franciscan Hist, 12:2, Oct. 1955, p. 169-182).

A study of the movement for Negro colonization in Haiti organized in Boston by James Redpath, Scottish-born printer-journalist and agitator. With Haitian funds, and aided by a decree of Haitian president Nicolas Geffrard, the movement, although doomed to quick failure, succeeded in transporting an indeterminate number of American Negroes to Haiti.

2956. Lugo Lovatón, Ramón. Sentencias penales de la época haitiana, de 1822 a 1831 (B Arch Gen, Ciudad Trujillo, año 16, 16:79, oct.-dic. 1953, p. 329-353; año 17, 17:80, enero-marzo 1954, p. 24-46; 17:81, abril-junio 1954, p. 219-230; 17:82, julio-sept. 1954, p. 327-337; 17:83, oct.-dic. 1954, p. 400-408; año 18, 18:84, enero-marzo 1955, p. 66-79; 18:85, abril-junio 1955, p. 157-165).

Transcribed text of penal decrees handed down by Haitian judicial authorities in occupied Santo Domingo, 1822-1831. They cover a wide variety of subjects: the different conspiracies hatched during that period against the Haitian regime, smuggling, counterfeiting, and common thievery and murder. Of importance for the history of the Dominican Republic during this period, as they show the gradual displacement of Spanish penal law in favor of its Haitian counterpart, which was of French origin, and the beginnings of a growing resistance to Haitian occupation.

2957. **Manigat, Leslie F.** Le délicat problème de la critique historique. Un example: les sentiments de Pétion et de Boyer vis-a-vis de l'Indépendance nationale (R Soc Haitienne Hist Géog, 25-26:95-96, oct. 1954-janv. 1955, p. 19-59).

An analysis of the attitudes of Boyer and Pétion towards the reestablishment of French sovereignty in Haiti. The author's opinion is that both Boyer and Pétion were favorable to such a solution, both of them being mulatto *affranchis*, a social group who often owned land and favored an entente with the whites in order to keep the slave masses under control. He concludes, however, that the pressure of public opinion in Haiti forced both men to reject any other solution but that of independence. Based on printed and manuscript sources, of special value being the testimony of French diplomatic negotiators.

2958. **Nicolas, Hogar.** L'occupation américaine d'Haïti: la revanche de l'histoire. Madrid, Industrias Gráf. España, n. d. 305 p.

Unobjective and passionate account of the American occupation of the island Negro republic. Utilization of archival material has been limited to those in Haiti and the Haitian Embassy in Washington. The results of the occupation are sometimes lauded, but the methods employed are consistently condemned. The author was secretary of the Haitian Embassy in Washington.

PUERTO RICO

2959. **Brau, Salvador.** Disquisiciones sociológicas y otros ensayos. Introducción de Eugenio Fernández Méndez. Río Piedras, Puerto Rico, Universidad de Puerto Rico, Ediciones del Instituto de Literatura, 1956. 409 p. & illus.

A collection of some heretofore dispersed writings by the 19th-century Puerto Rican historian and man of letters, Salvador Brau. Some of them were originally presented as public lectures before Spanish and local learned societies. Although centering on the historical development of Puerto Rican society, they cover a wide variety of subjects: social classes, the rural population, religion, education, agriculture, etc. Of great value for an understanding of social and cultural change up to and through the 19th century in Puerto Rico. The extensive (120 p.) introduction provides not only a biography of Brau but also a panorama of the socio-cultural history of Puerto Rico during his lifetime. Unfortunately, no explanatory annotations have been included throughout the text.

2960. **Carta de Ramón Emeterio Betances al Sr. Julio Henna** (Hist, Río Piedras, 4:1, abril 1954, p. 104-105).

Textual reproduction of a letter dated Paris, July 17, 1897, from Dr. Ramón Emeterio Betances, chief agent of the Cuban and Puerto Rican revolutionists in France, to Dr. Julio Henna, president of the Sección Puerto Rico of the Partido Revolucionario Cubano. Betances sketches a plan for obtaining forced monetary contributions for a coming revolt in Puerto Rico, under menace of destruction to their property, from wealthy Puerto Rican planters residing in Europe. There is no indication as to the location of the original source.

2961. **Carta del señor Charles de Ronceray, cónsul norteamericano en San Juan, al Sr. Lewis Cass, Secretario de Estado de los Estados Unidos** (Hist, Río Piedras, 4:2, oct. 1954, p. 236-239).

Textual transcription of a letter from the U. S. consul at San Juan, Puerto Rico, Charles de Ronceray, to Secretary of State Lewis Cass, dated Jan. 14, 1860, and preserved among the Consular Records at the National Archives in Washington. Consul Ronceray discusses at length the opportunities for American capital in the Puerto Rican import-export business, a field at that time neglected by American entrepreneurs.

2961a. **Circular de don Aurelio Méndez Martínez a varios puertorriqueños, Samaná, 11 de mayo de 1896** (Hist, Río Piedras, 5:1, abril 1955, p. 136-145).

Textual transcription of a letter originally published in the *Memoria de los trabajos realizados por la Sección Puerto Rico del Partido Revolucionario Cubano, 1895-1898* (N. Y., 1898), appendix 6, p. 41-48. It is a circular letter sent by the representative of the Sección Puerto Rico of the Partido Revolucionario Cubano at Samana, Dominican Republic, to several agents and sympathizers of the independentist cause throughout Puerto Rico. In it, Señor Méndez Martínez sketches in detail the steps which the recipients were to undertake as the first stages in an islandwide revolutionary movement.

2962. **Cruz Monclova, Lidio,** and **Antonio J. Colorado.** Noticias y pulso del movimiento político puertorriqueño (1808-1898-1952). México, Orión, 1955. 162 p.

A panorama of the political development of Puerto Rico during the 19th and 20th centuries. The first part describes the development throughout the 19th century of a liberal political movement, favored by a majority of public opinion, and discusses the two tendencies within it, *asimilismo* and *autonomismo*. The second part covers the evolution of the different political parties of the island during the 20th century, together with the socio-economic factors related to this evolution. The book contains neither footnotes nor bibliography. The autonomic charter granted by Spain in 1897 and the present constitution of the Commonwealth of Puerto Rico are reproduced in the appendix.

2963. **Fernández Méndez, Eugenio.** Reflexiones sobre 50 años de cambio cultural en Puerto Rico (Hist, Río Piedras, 5:2, oct. 1955, p. 257-279).

Undocumented essay. Analizes, from a historico-anthropological viewpoint, the socio-economic and technological changes which have transformed Puerto Rican society since the annexation of the island to the U. S. in 1898. In the last part the author describes what have been, to him, the different stages in the islanders' reaction to the impact of American penetration, putting forth his theory that the island is evolving toward a final stage of cultural autonomy from the U. S.

2964. Gautier Dapena, José A. Génesis, fundación y triunfo de la Unión de Puerto Rico (Hist, Río Piedras, 6:1, abril 1956, p. 3-34).

Documented article on the origins and rise of the Unión de Puerto Rico, political party which under the leadership of Luis Muñoz Rivera came to power in Puerto Rico during the first years of the 20th century and continued in control for a long time afterwards. Based on contemporary newspapers and published primary and secondary sources.

2965. Gómez Acevedo, Labor. Sanz, promotor de la conciencia separatista en Puerto Rico. San Juan, Ediciones de la Universidad de Puerto Rico, 1956. 293 p.

Documented monograph on the two terms of General José Laureano Sanz as governor of Puerto Rico, 1868-1870 and 1874-1875. This was a period of the greatest importance in the political history of the island, when the reverberations of the Grito de Yara and the liberal revolution in Spain plus the conspiratorial activities of Puerto Rican revolutionists kept the island in a state of great political unrest. Sanz inaugurated a policy of stern repression and persecution, not only against the "separatistas," but also against those liberal leaders who only advocated reforms by the mother country. At the same time, he subverted for his own ends those liberal institutions granted to the island from Madrid by General Prim's liberal government. It is the author's contention that though the "separatistas" were still a minority in Puerto Rico, Sanz's policies promoted their cause, for it convinced many natives of the island that it was useless to expect any reform from Spain. In the first three chapters an introduction is provided for the main topic, the author sketching the politico-administrative and economic history of Puerto Rico since the beginnings of the 19th century. Originally presented as a doctoral dissertation at the Universidad Central de Madrid. Based on published primary and secondary sources and archival research at the Archivo Histórico Nacional in Madrid.

2966. Lebrón Rodríguez, Ramón. La vida del prócer. San Juan, Imp. Soltero, 1954. 76 p.

Short semi-biographical essay on Luis Muñoz Rivera, the most important Puerto Rican political figure during the last years of the 19th and early years of the 20th century. Written by a man closely associated with the *prócer*, the book is not a biography proper, but a series of unconnected reminiscences. Contains neither footnotes nor bibliography.

2967. Lo de Puerto Rico (Hist, Río Piedras, 5:2, oct. 1955, p. 280-284).

Textual transcription of an article, originally published in the newspaper *El Liberal* of Madrid, and reproduced on Nov. 8, 1887, in *El País* of Habana. Comments on the persecutions suffered during that year by the leaders of the newly-formed autonomist movement in Puerto Rico, criticizing the Madrid authorities for their part in these activities.

2968. Lugo-Silva, Enrique. The Tugwell administration in Puerto Rico, 1941-1946. Río Piedras, Puerto Rico, Editorial Cultura, 1955. 185 p.

Originally presented as a doctoral dissertation. A historical panorama of Rexford G. Tugwell's administration, from 1941 to 1946, as the last American governor of Puerto Rico. The book covers a period of the greatest importance in the history of the island: the impact of a new ideology, a planned economy, and the welfare state. The author does not present his subject, at any time, from an all-encompassing viewpoint, but rather divides his book into chapters and sub-units devoted to the different administrative agencies created by Governor Tugwell. Based mainly on newspaper reports and official printed records.

2969. Rivera, Antonio. Ubicación de un municipio: Lares (Hist, Río Piedras, 5:1, abril 1955, p. 3-61).

Documented essay in Puerto Rican local history. Sketches the history of the town of Lares from its establishment in 1832 up to the end of the Spanish regime during the last decade of the 19th century, covering a wide variety of subjects: its foundation, boundary disputes with other municipalities, urban growth, religious life, cultural and educational development, economic progress, etc. Everything is presented from an exaggeratedly provincial angle, the author never attempting to connect these local developments with the historical evolution of the island. The data presented, nevertheless, help toward a better understanding of many aspects of municipal life in the Spanish West Indies during the 19th century. The author based his research mainly on manuscript material from the Lares municipal archives.

2969a. ———. Viva Puerto Rico li . . . li . . . li . . . (Hist, Río Piedras, 4:1, abril 1954, p. 51-72).

Documented essay on the reformist and revolutionary opposition to the Spanish regime in Puerto Rico from 1869 to 1874 as seen from a local angle: the municipality of Arecibo, in the northern coast of the island. It is Dr. Rivera's aim to see the history of Puerto Rico not through San Juan, traditional capital and link with the mother country, but rather through what he calls an "extra capitalino" angle. The study shows how during these years that run from the overthrow of Isabela II to the restoration of the Bourbons in 1874, the political climate in Puerto Rico was not one of passive acceptance of the Spanish colonial regime but one of constant conspiratorial and opposition political activity, a ferment which took place, however, not so much in the capital as in other important cities and towns of the island. Based upon documentary material from the Municipal Archives at Arecibo and published reminiscences and political literature of the period.

2970. Rivera Rivera, Julio. Orígenes de la organización obrera en Puerto Rico, 1838-1898 (Hist, Río Piedras, 5:1, abril 1955, p. 91-112).

Presents the historical development of the labor movement in Puerto Rico during its early organization days, from the middle until the end of the 19th century, that is, up to the annexation of the island by the U. S. The material offered for the period previous to 1890 is very short and sketchy. Based on printed sources but, even so, much basic relevant published material has not been utilized.

2971. Román Baldorioty de Castro se despide de sus correligionarios (Hist, Río Piedras, 6:1, abril 1956, p. 71-72).

Textual transcription of a letter addressed to the Partido Autonomista Puertorriqueño by its president, the publicist and educator Román Baldorioty de Castro, and dated Ponce, Puerto Rico, Jan. 14, 1888, in which he submits his resignation, pleading, besides ill health, the fact that after the Spanish persecutions and arrests of the year 1887 "un hombre procesado no está en buena situación para servir bien los intereses de un gran partido." There is no indication as to the original source for this document.

2972. Tejada, Francisco Elías de. Puerto Rico y el federalismo en el pensamiento de Hostos (Estud Am, nov.-dic. 1954, p. 451-460).

An analysis of Puerto Rico's place within Eugenio Maria de Hostos' federalist plans. According to the author, the basis of Hostos' ideology was his deep patriotic conviction that only through a West Indian federation could the problems of Puerto Rico be solved. Based on Hostos' published writings.

SOUTH AMERICA (EXCEPT BRAZIL)

CLIFTON B. KROEBER, DAVID BUSHNELL, AND J. LEÓN HELGUERA

GENERAL

2975. Arciniegas, Germán. La Pola y la juventud romántica del historiador Mitre (B Hist Antig, 43:499-500, mayo-junio 1956, p. 296-309).

An essay on continent-wide literary-political romanticism: the story of the Colombian heroine Policarpa Salavarrieta dramatized in Montevideo (1838) by the young Argentine exile Bartolomé Mitre. [D. Bushnell]

2976. Boulton, Alfredo. Los retratos de Bolívar. Caracas, 1956. 176 p., 41 ports. (part col.).

An excellently printed and illustrated study, based on wide and careful research; of value not only for the history of Spanish American portraiture but also for the social and political history of the period. [D. Bushnell]

2977. Causa criminal seguida contra el Coronel Graduado Apolinar Morillo y demás autores y cómplices del asesinato perpetrado en la persona del señor General Antonio José de Sucre (Mus Hist, 7:21, mayo 1955, p. 201-240; 8:22, feb. 1956, p. 176-230; and 8:24, agosto 1956, p. 171-193).

Conclusion of printing of Morillo's testimony in court concerning his part in the assassination of Antonio José de Sucre (1830). This testimony was taken at Bogota (1842), and upon refusal by the president of Nueva Granada to excuse Morillo, he was executed for Sucre's murder (Nov. 30, 1842). He blamed José María Obando for the assassination. [C. B. Kroeber]

2978. Congreso Nacional de Historia del Libertador General San Martín, 1950. Actas. Mendoza, Argentina, Universidad Nacional de Cuyo, 1953-1955. 4 v. 377, 537, 502, 484 p.

A collection of essays and monographs, some broadly descriptive and/or interpretative (e. g., Ricardo Levene, "San Martín en la historia del derecho argentino"), others presenting detailed data on specialized topics (e. g., Francisco Cignoli, "La organización sanitaria en 'Las Campañas' de San Martín"; Humberto F. Burzio, "Numismática sanmartiniana del protectorado del Perú"). The quality varies, but all four volumes will prove useful to students of the Independence period. [D. Bushnell]

2979. Cortés Madariaga, José. El viaje de don José Cortés de Madariaga por el Río Negro, Meta, y Orinoco (Crónica Caracas, 4:17, marzo-abril 1954, p. 250-288).

Report on a journey in 1811: scenery, missions, commerce, and alternative routes of transportation. [D. Bushnell]

2980. Ecuador. Museo de Historia. Museo histórico. Órgano del Museo de Historia, Departamento de Educación y Cultura Popular. Quito. Año 8, no. 23, mayo 1956.

A special issue, featuring a collection of inedited letters from Sucre to the Ecuadorian patriot Vicente Aguirre, written 1923-1930 and referring both to personal affairs and to current happenings in Peru, Bolivia, and Gran Colombia. Also included are a few letters of lesser significance from Bolívar to Aguirre, and others from Sucre to the Cabildo of Quito, mostly written while he was departmental intendant. [D. Bushnell]

2981. Fasolino, Nicolás. Francisco J. Echagüe y Andía; José Bonifacio Redruello. Santa Fe, Argentina, El Litoral, 1955. 171 p.

Two studies by the Archbishop of Santa Fe, concerning priests from Santa Fe who acted on opposing sides in the Independence struggle: the patriot Echagüe in Lima, and the royalist Redruello in Uruguay (with diplomatic sidetrip to Rio). An original and valuable contribution to the history of the period. [D. Bushnell]

2982. Gandía, Enrique de. Las guerras de los absolutistas y liberales en América (R Indias, Madrid, 14:57-58, julio-dic. 1954, p. 407-431).
A stimulating article (like most by Gandía), centering upon the feud between the Spanish absolutist General Pedro Antonio de Olañeta in Alto Peru and "liberal" Viceroy José de Laserna, 1823-1825; but slightly extravagant in arguing that without such disputes Spain could have fought on indefinitely. [D. Bushnell]

2983. ————. Napoleón y la independencia de América. B. A., Ediciones A. Zamora (Col. El Mundo y el hombre, 11), 1955. 285 p.
Related chapters to prove such points as that it was Napoleon's actions, not his example, that influenced the beginnings of South American wars of Independence (likewise, it was the Enlightenment, not the French Revolution, which served to inspire idealists there). Good documentation marred, as always, by his insistence on conclusions that are hobbies of his own rather than crucial aspects of the history (i. e., the French Revolution was not so much a revolution as a return to normalcy). [C. B. Kroeber]

2984. Grisanti, Ángel. El gran mariscal de Ayacucho y su esposa la marquesa de Solanda. La vida matrimonial del general Sucre, expuesta dentro de un plano histórico, sustentado en documentos, inéditos en parte. Caracas, Imp. Nacional, 1955. 255 p., illus.
Takes a dim view of the Marquesa, but mainly for remarrying while the martyred Sucre's bed was "still warm." Also examines Sucre's earlier relations with other women, incorporating Grisanti's *Vida galante del gran mariscal* . . . which had been published separately (Ediciones Edime, Caracas, 1953). [D. Bushnell]

2985. ———— (comp.). El archivo del Libertador. Índice. Caracas, Imp. Nacional, 1956. V. 1, Colección O'Leary, 226 p., illus. V. 2, Colección de documentos obtenidos en el Archivo Nacional y procedentes de otras fuentes, 99 p., illus.
Guide to manuscript material in the Archivo del Libertador, Caracas. Some of the documents have been published but by no means all. [D. Bushnell]

2986. Leturia, Pedro de. Autenticidad e integridad de la Encíclica del Papa León XII sobre la revolución hispanoamericana (R Hist Am, 34, dic. 1952, p. 413-447).
The author's last word on a subject on which he was the acknowledged expert. [D. Bushnell]

2987. López, Manuel Antonio. Recuerdos históricos del coronel Manuel Antonio López, ayudante del Estado Mayor General Libertador. Colombia y Perú, 1819-1826. Bogotá, Imp. Nacional (Biblioteca de la Presidencia de Colombia, 6), 1955. 246 p., ports., fold. maps.

Reissue, after many years, of a useful source on the Independence struggle. [D. Bushnell]

2988. Moliner de Arévalo, Matilde. Ingleses en los ejércitos de Bolívar: el Coronel Enrique Wilson (R Indias, Madrid, 13:51, enero-marzo 1953, p. 89-108).
Proves, with Spanish documents, that Wilson offered his services to Spain *after*, not before, attempting a "revolt" against Bolívar in Apure (1818)—and was scornfully rebuffed. [D. Bushnell]

2989. Muzzio, Rodolfo A. Fragata "Hércules" y bergantín "La Santísima Trinidad." B. A., Instituto Browniano (Serie Hazañas y aventuras de barcos argentinos), 1955. 207 p., illus., port., fold. map.
A solid research monograph, dealing with the exploits of William Brown and his Argentine fleet in the Rio de la Plata and Pacific, 1814-1816, and with the later seizure of the *Hércules* by British authorities. [D. Bushnell]

2990. Pérez, Joaquín. San Martín y José Miguel Carrera. La Plata, Argentina, Universidad Nacional de Eva Perón, Departamento de Historia (Monografías y tesis, 1), 1954. 331 p.
A competent research monograph, describing the role of the Chilean exile Carrera in Argentine civil disturbances (1814-1821) and his simultaneous scheming to wrest Chile first from the Spaniards and then from O'Higgins. San Martín enters the picture somewhat intermittently as a restraining influence. [D. Bushnell]

2991. Rojas Mery, Eulojio. El general Carrera en el exilio. 2. ed., corregida y aumentada con varios e interesantes documentos. Santiago, Instituto de Investigaciones Históricas José Miguel Carrera, 1955. 242 p., illus.
Rejects the usual view of Carrera as a trouble maker and likens him to the Cid Campeador, while vilifying O'Higgins and San Martín who blocked his return to Chile. Interesting, but too passionate to take at face value. [D. Bushnell]

2992. Rumazo González, Alfonso. O'Leary, edecán del Libertador. Biografía. Caracas, Ediciones Edime, 1956. 254 p., illus.
A readable, fairly adequate short life of Daniel F. O'Leary (1802-1854), not overlooking his career in Venezuela and abroad after Bolívar's death; based on standard printed sources. Comparable in style and scope to the same author's recent *Simón Bolívar* (Caracas, Edime, 1955, 403 p.), but more noteworthy since on O'Leary there are few alternatives to choose from. [D. Bushnell]

2993. Tobar Donoso, Julio. El tratado de 1860 (B Ac Nac Hist, Quito, 35:86, julio-dic. 1955, p. 201-248).
Narrative of events (1858-1860) leading to a

treaty between Ecuador and Peru (Jan. 25, 1860) forced by Peruvian military pressure. It remained unratified; this discussion, mainly from printed materials, is informative. [C. B. Kroeber]

ARGENTINA

2994. Acevedo, Edberto Óscar. Situación actual de la historia argentina (Estud Am, 9:43, abril 1955, p. 353-396).
Summary report of articles in eight numbers of *Esto es*, the Argentine periodical, by three groups of Argentine historians ("classic-liberals," "revisionists," and "Marxists") who responded to questions about the present status of Argentine historiography. These writers were, among others, Ricardo Levene, Julio Irazusta, and Rodolfo Puiggrós; Ricardo Zorraquín Becú was added "sin clasificación." This is the clearest statement yet of this important controversy whose roots go down half a century, if not a century and a half. [C. B. Kroeber]

2995. Belgrano, Manuel. Escritos económicos. Introd. por Gregorio Weinberg. B. A., Raigal (Biblioteca Manuel Belgrano, de estudios económicos), 1954. 336 p.
Periodical articles and *memorias* on a wide variety of economic topics, 1796-1811. Significant at times for the descriptive material they contain, but more concerned with interpretation, in a generally physiocratic vein. [D. Bushnell]

2996. Bischoff, Efraín U. Expedición de Bedoya al Chaco. Córdoba, Argentina, Universidad Nacional de Córdoba, Facultad de Filosofía y Humanidades, Instituto de Estudios Americanistas (Cuaderno de historia, 27), 1954. 50 p.
Colonel Francisco de Bedoya's expedition of 1817 into the Gran Chaco illustrates the difficulty of containing Indian raids during the wars of Independence. A documentary account from archives of Cordoba. [C. B. Kroeber]

2997. Chávez, Fermín. Civilización y barbarie en la cultura argentina (Estud Am, 10:49, oct. 1955, p. 409-431).
Intelligent argument against Domingo F. Sarmiento's famous dichotomy (Argentine civilization as city based; barbarism as typical of the countryside and of the Gaucho), thus opposing writings of Ezequiel Martínez Estrada and José Luis Romero among others. This is both a Hispanist and nationalist Argentine argument, carried as far as it can logically be made to go. [C. B. Kroeber]

2998. Cutolo, Vicente Osvaldo. Nuevos datos sobre la enseñanza de la economía política en la Universidad de Buenos Aires, 1829-1831 (R Fac Der Cien Soc, B A, 3. época, 10:43, mayo-junio 1955, p. 465-478).
At a time of political crisis the young University of Buenos Aires did have interesting activity in the legal and social sciences, of some liberal trend. These few data are assembled mostly from printed works, but with thoughtful comments. [C. B. Kroeber]

2999. Dalurzo, Beatriz F. Descentralización administrativa. Concepto, caracteres, elementos constitutivos (R Cien Jur Soc, 3. época, 15:74-75, 1953, p. 491-512).
Useful relating of abstract definitions of various forms of decentralization and delegation of authority (territorially and functionally) with Argentine practice since 1853. Relies in part on Rafael Bielsa's past work; a useful and thoughtful article. [C. B. Kroeber]

3000. Fernández, Ariosto. Manuel Belgrano y la Princesa Carlota Joaquina, 1808 (Hist, B A, 1:3, enero-marzo 1956, p. 79-88; 2:5, julio-sept. 1956, p. 33-46).
Citing documents mainly from Brazilian archives, several of which are printed here, the author underscores both the eagerness of Belgrano *et al.* in 1808-1809 to establish Carlota as Regent at B. A. and their relative disinterest after the May Revolution. [D. Bushnell]

3001. Figueroa Güemes, Martín G. La gloria de Güemes (R Cien Jur Soc, 3. época, 16:78-79, 1954, p. 181-322).
A partial biography of the military hero of northern Argentine Independence, Martín Güemes, based on a few new documents and older histories. [C. B. Kroeber]

3002. Gandía, Enrique de. Vida y muerte de Francisco de Paula Cudina, emisario de Goyeneche (Hist, B A, 2:6, oct.-dic. 1956, p. 155-165).
Comment and documentary excerpts on the trial and execution of a royalist courier in 1812; throws some light, e. g., on the role of Bishop Benito de la Lué y Riego of B. A. [D. Bushnell]

3003. Gargaro, Alfredo. Las joyas de las damas mendocinas no fueron donadas para el Ejército de los Andes (Hist, B A, 2:5, julio-sept. 1956, p. 63-75).
Convincingly disproves a pious legend as indicated in the title, showing that the jewels (etc.) were really given in 1815 for the defense of B. A. against a feared Spanish invasion. A related item by the same author is "Los sueldos de San Martín; espisodio histórico, 1815-1816" (Hist, B A, 2:6, oct.-dic. 1956, p. 166-168). [D. Bushnell]

3004. Giovannoni, G. José. Historia del ilustre restaurador; cronología federal. Mendoza, Argentina, 1954, i. e. 1955. 395 p.
A chronology of facts about the Argentine leader Juan Manuel de Rosas, 1793-1877, drawn from "revisionist" works in his favor; in no way a full history of Rosas. [C. B. Kroeber]

3005. González, Julio César. Un general en jefe desconocido del Ejército Expedicionario del Norte, 1811 (Hist, B A, 1:4, abril-junio 1956, p. 44-60).
An excellent brief article, explaining how and why the B. A. junta named General Francisco del Rivero of Cochabamba to head its forces in Alto Peru following the Huaqui disaster. He surrendered before the appointment took effect. [D. Bushnell]

3006. Ibarguren, Carlos. La historia que he vivido. B. A. Peuser, 1955. 504 p.
An important memoir by the Argentine public figure and historian (1877-), in two parts: a history of his father's life, and then the author's own life and times. Chapters of general Argentine history are mixed with personal observations and sketches of the important figures in the nation over the past half century. In part a basic source, this book is broadly and at times minutely informative on Argentine politics and cultural life as seen from the conservative Right. [C. B. Kroeber]

3007. Irazusta, Julio. Pedro de Ángelis, vocero de Rosas (Estud Am, 9:44, mayo 1955, p. 411-446).
On the Neapolitan publicist (1784-1859) and historian who managed propaganda for Juan Manuel de Rosas in Argentina. Mostly from published data, this intelligent article deals with Angelis as publicist of the dictatorship. [C. B. Kroeber]

3008. Landa, Augusto. San Martín y la contribución extraordinaria impuesta al pueblo de San Juan (San Martín, 10:32, oct.-dic. 1953, p. 7-15).
Brief scholarly item, chiefly concerned with an unsuccessful effort by the clergy to escape emergency taxation. [D. Bushnell]

3009. Lombille, Román J. Eva, la predestinada. Alucinante historia de éxitos y frustraciones. B. A., Gure (Col. de testimonios políticos), 1955. 155 p.
A series of strongly written episodes from the public career of Eva Perón, for a time co-ruler of Argentina with her husband Juan Domingo. The anecdotes and psychological explanations in this book are of unknown derivation but worth reading. [C. B. Kroeber]

3010. Macchi, Manuel E. Urquiza, última etapa. 2. ed., con un estudio preliminar de las primeras actividades comerciales de Urquiza. Santa Fe, Argentina, Castellví, 1955. 197 p.
Short essays accompanied by documents from the Urquiza archive to explain several phases of the Argentine president's early commercial and later political career (1860-1870), and his political thought. Adds a little to the Urquiza we know. [C. B. Kroeber]

3011. Marfany, Roberto H. La semana de mayo; diario de un testigo. B. A., Ángel Domínguez e Hijo, 1955. 62 p., port., facsims.
Critical comments on a brief anonymous diary (printed in full, p. 60-62), seeking to clarify such details of the 1810 Revolution as emblems used and the bishop's stand in *cabildo abierto*. [D. Bushnell]

3012. Martino, Julio Delfín. Vida de Mariano Moreno. Prólogo de Fermín J. Garay. B. A., Tall. Signo, 1954. 210 p.
A popular-style biography, with argumentative footnotes; interesting for its running fire of liberal, anti-"revisionist," and (very slightly veiled) anti-Peronista commentary. [D. Bushnell]

3014. Ortega, Exequiel César. La primera pena de muerte resuelta por la Junta de Mayo; la "tragedia de Cruz Alta" y su problema histórico. B. A., Lumen, 1954. 214 p., illus.
Detailed examination of the execution of Santiago Liniers and other counterrevolutionaries in August 1810, concluding that the deed was highly arbitrary though conceivably useful as an example. Well documented, but burdened with extraneous philosophizing. [D. Bushnell]

3015. Pérez Amuchástegui, Antonio Jorge. San Martín en Inglaterra. Conferencia pronunciada el 19 de junio de 1952 en el Museo Mitre. B. A., 1954. 47 p.
Essay covering the years 1824-1825. Pictures San Martín as leading an active life, working for the recognition of Independence, and maintaining close relations with agents of other Latin American countries. [D. Bushnell]

3016. Piccirilli, Ricardo. San Martín y la desmembración de la Logia de Lautaro (Hist, B A, 1:3, enero-marzo 1956, p. 88-117).
Examines the factionalism of Argentine politics, 1819-1822, and its disruptive influence upon the Lautaro Lodge and its branches. Little specifically on San Martín, and more general history than discussion of lodges as such. [D. Bushnell]

3017. Romaña, José María de. Iglesia y estado en la política peronista (Estud Am, 11:55, abril 1956, p. 377-389).
Strongly anti-President Perón of Argentina, from the Roman Catholic Church point of view, this article does much to set forth the basic issues posed for Argentina by Perón's law of May 20, 1955, which was to end the favored position the Church had held in the country since "established" to an extent in the Constitution of 1853. [C. B. Kroeber]

3018. Soler Cañas, Luis. San Martín, Rosas y la falsificación de la historia; las inexactitudes de Ricardo Rojas. B. A., Latitud 34 (Col. Latitud 34, 1), 1951. 123 p.
A good example of Rosista revisionism, citing San Martín as a warm admirer of the dictator. The theme of San Martín's approval of Rosas is also developed, a bit more calmly and convincingly, in two studies included in the *Actas del Congreso Nacional de Historia ...* (item 2978): Orlando Lázaro, "Corresponsales y Contemporáneos, San Martín y Rosas," and Manuel Somoza, "San Martín y la Política Argentina. ..." [D. Bushnell]

3019. Torre Revello, José. La biblioteca de Hipólito Vieytes (Hist, B A, 2:6, oct.-dic. 1956, p. 72-89).
Valuable data concerning the intellectual interests of an Argentine publicist and patriot (d. 1815), in addition to a list of books. [D. Bushnell]

3020. Zapiola, Federico. Zapiola, soldado de Chacabuco y Maipo. B. A., Prestigio, 1956. 177 p., illus.

Biography of General José Matías Zapiola (1780-1874), Secretary of the Lautaro lodge, companion of San Martín, later in eclipse under Rosas. Written by an admiring descendant, without full scholarly apparatus, but generally sound if not definitive. [D. Bushnell]

BOLIVIA

3021. Documentos para la historia de la Revolución de 1809. Carlos Ponce Sanginés y Raúl Alfonso García (recopiladores). La Paz, Biblioteca Paceña, 1954. V. 2, 750 p.; v. 3, 999 p.; v. 4, 652 p.

These volumes, like v. 1 (*HLAS, no. 19*, item 3861), make an important contribution to the available materials on a neglected aspect of Spanish American Independence. V. 2 contains the "Proceso instaurado contra los gestores de la revolución"; it is preceded by an "Homenaje a Murillo," by Ismael Vásquez, defending the leader of the abortive July 1809 uprising at La Paz, Pedro Domingo Murillo, against the criticism of Alcides Arguedas. V. 3. offers a collection of memoirs, documents, and articles, of varying importance, most of which have been formerly published but hard to find. The study by Valentín Abecía Baldivieso, "La Revolución de 1809," on p. 850-991 of this volume, was issued separately by the same Biblioteca Paceña, also in 1954. V. 4 contains "Expediente del Obispo La Santa y Ortega," papers relating to the royalist bishop of La Paz, 1809-1816, and "Documentos del Archivo del Conde Guaqui," covering various aspects of the 1809 Revolution. [D. Bushnell]

3022. Fellman Velarde, José (ed.). Álbum de la Revolución. 128 años de lucha por la independencia de Bolivia. La Paz, Subsecretaría de Prensa, Informaciones y Cultura, 1955? Unpaged, illus.

A propaganda picture book of the rise of the MNR (Movimiento Nacionalista Revolucionario) party in Bolivia during the past generation, accompanied by a basic propaganda story. The pictures well demonstrate the struggle and the terror of those times. [C. B. Kroeber]

CHILE

3023. Chile, Biblioteca Nacional. Gazeta ministerial de Chile. No. 73-100, 1819. Santiago, 1954. clxviii, 329 p. (Col. de antiguos periódicos chilenos).

Contains the issues from Jan. 2 to July 15, inclusive. These had been reprinted before (*HLAS, no. 19*, item 3868), but the present edition adds a lengthy prologue by Guillermo Feliú Cruz discussing both the political ideas of O'Higgins and the War of Independence in South America. [D. Bushnell]

3024. ———. ———. Viva el Rey, gazeta del Gobierno de Chile. Illustración araucana sacada de los arcanos de la razón. El Augurio feliz. 1813-1817. San-

tiago, 1954. lxxxvii, 401 p. (Col. de antiguos periódicos chilenos).

Contains the official (royalist) gazette, Dec. 16, 1815, to Feb. 11, 1817, with an essay by J. T. Medina on the same; also certain leaflets, etc., dealing mainly with the controversy set off by the Treaty of Lircay (May, 1814) between royalists and patriots. [D. Bushnell]

3025. Wolff, Inge. Algunas consideraciones sobre causas económicas de la emancipación chilena (An Estud Am, 11, 1954, p. 169-196).

Disappointingly brief, but based on archival research and well worth noting. Concludes that Chile's desire for economic independence from viceregal Peru was a significant factor in the revolt against Spain. [D. Bushnell]

COLOMBIA

3026. Bateman, Alfredo D. El Observatorio Astronómico de Bogotá; monografía histórica con ocasión del 150. aniversario de su fundación. 1803-agosto 20-1953. Prólogo de Carlos López Narváez. Bogotá, Universidad Nacional, 1954. 189 p., illus.

Of interest for Colombian intellectual history. Written mainly in the form of sketches of the figures who have headed the observatory, and covering more than just their astronomical activities. [D. Bushnell]

3027. Belmonte, Pedro Luis. Antecedentes históricos de los sucesos del 8 y 9 de junio de 1954. Bogotá, Imp. Nacional, 1954. 184 p., illus.

A bare-faced attempt to link the university students' protests in Bogota, the riot and the bloody reprisals by the Rojas Pinilla regime with a subversive ("Communist") plot. No credible evidence is produced to sustain the author's contention. [J. L. Helguera]

3028. Borrero, Eusebio. Cartas del General . . . al General Pedro Alcántara Herrán (B Ac Hist Valle Cauca, 4. época, 22:97-98, abril 1954, p. 3-75).

A decade (1837-1847) of correspondence which reveals the strong regionalism of southern Colombia and its dissatisfaction with Bogota rule. Original letters are in the Herrán Archive, housed in Academia Colombiana de Historia, Bogota. [J. L. Helguera]

3029. Bushnell, David. Two stages in Colombian tariff policy: the radical era and the return to protection (1861-1885) (Interam Ec Aff, 9:4, spring 1956, p. 3-23).

An interesting and well-executed exploratory essay into an almost untouched aspect of Colombian economic history. Rafael Núñez's protectionism is attributed to political rather than to economic convictions. [J. L. Helguera]

3030. Caro Molina, Fernando (ed.). De Agustín Codazzi a Manuel María Paz.

Cali, Colombia, Editorial La Voz Católica, 1954. 318 p.
Three short biographical sketches of Manuel María Paz (1820-1902) precede a compilation of documents relating to the expeditions of geographic exploration led by Colonel Agustín Codazzi, 1850-1859. Almost all the documents, while interesting and useful, have seen previous publication. Paz served as artist and map-maker with the Codazzi group. [J. L. Helguera]

3032. Garzón Moreno, Ricardo. Apuntes sobre la historia de Túquerres (R Hist, Pasto, 5:32-33, enero-junio 1955, p. 578-593).
An interpretative essay, read as a speech at the 50th anniversary celebration of Nariño department, which, despite its informal documentation, is a successful attempt to place the Tuquerres district in its departmental context. It lists numerous *tuquerreños* who, from 1846-1904, figured in provincial and national life of Colombia. [J. L. Helguera]

3033. Gilmore, Robert Louis. Nueva Granada's socialist mirage (HAHR, 36:2, May 1956, p. 190-210).
This is a trail-blazing essay based on contemporary newspapers, pamphlets, and books, which indicates the impact of French socialist ideas on Colombian thought during the decade of the 1850's. [J. L. Helguera]

3034. Giraldo Jaramillo, Gabriel. Bibliografía histórica de Colombia de 1954 (B Hist Antig, 42:483-484, enero-feb. 1955, p. 40-68).
A critical guide to historical studies published in books, newspapers, and scholarly journals during 1954 in Colombia. Also included are anthropological items. The commentary is valuable. [J. L. Helguera]

3035. Gómez Parra, Aurelio. Biografía del general y doctor Lucas Caballero (Estudio, 25:250, oct. 1956, p. 107-130).
An informative sketch of a *santanderino* politician, industrialist, liberal caudillo, and author (1868-1942). [J. L. Helguera]

3036. Guerra, José Joaquín. Estudios históricos. Bogotá, Ministerio de Educación Nacional, Revista Bolívar (Biblioteca popular de cultura colombiana, 157-160), 1952. 4 v. 330, 322, 319, 433 p.
See item 3038. [D. Bushnell].

3037. Hamilton, J. P. Viajes por el interior de las provincias de Colombia. Bogotá, Banco de la República (Archivo de la economía nacional, 15, 16), 1955. 2 v. 176, 135 p.
One of the better travel accounts, written in the mid-1820's. It had not been translated into Spanish and has been hard to come by in the original English. [D. Bushnell]

3038. Holguín, Carlos. Cartas políticas. Bogotá, Editorial ABC (Biblioteca popular de cultura colombiana, 152), 1951. 255 p.
The Guerra and Holguín items both came to hand late but are still worth noting. Guerra's "studies" (item 3036) were intended as an exposé of all the errors and inconsistencies of Colombian Liberalism in the 19th and early 20th centuries; not profound scholarship, and slightly outdated, they are nevertheless utterly sincere and form a convenient source book for the Conservative interpretation of history. The Holguín item gives a more skillful statement of the same viewpoint; written in 1893 by the first *bona fide* Conservative president of the "Regeneration" era, it discusses Colombian politics chiefly since 1858. [D. Bushnell]

3039. Jiménez Tobón, Gerardo, and Ovidio Rincón. Gobernantes de Caldas; 1905-1955, cincuentenario de Caldas. Manizales, Colombia, Imp. Departamental de Caldas, 1955. 288 p., ports.
Short sketches of the administrations, with brief biographical notes, of the 32 men who have ruled the department of Caldas since its foundation in 1905 up to 1955. No source references are given, but the authors apparently utilized local official reports. A useful chronicle of departmental progress, especially road and school building. The work points up the frequent changes in gubernatorial authority in one of Colombia's more important departments. [J. L. Helguera]

3040. Lemaitre Román, Eduardo. Reyes. Bogotá, Iqueima, 1953. 330 p., illus.
Rafael Reyes (1849-1921), president of Colombia 1904-1909, is sympathetically portrayed in this book. Reyes was unquestionably one of the most important men in Colombian history—a fact which the author does not succeed in conveying. Secondary sources; no scholarly apparatus is found, other than a two-page list of books and newspapers consulted by the author. [J. L. Helguera]

3041. Martínez Delgado, Luis. Comentarios sobre la administración del Doctor Manuel María Mallarino (Bolívar, Bogotá, 37, marzo-abril 1955, p. 369-399).
An interpretative essay on the moderate and conciliatory presidency of Mallarino, 1855-1857. Also a good short biographical sketch. [J. L. Helguera]

3042. Mosquera, Manuel José. Antología del ilustrísimo señor Manuel José Mosquera, arzobispo de Bogotá, y escritos sobre el mismo. Bogotá, Sucre (Biblioteca de historia eclesiástica Fernando Caycedo y Flórez, 1), 1954. 619 p., illus., ports.
Basically a reprint of the most outstanding sermons preached by Manuel José Mosquera during his career as archbishop (previously published by Manual María Mosquera in his *Documentos para la biografía e historia del . . . señor D. Manuel José Mosquera. . . .* 3 v., Paris, 1858). It also contains various memorial and funeral orations preached at the time of Mosquera's death and exile in 1853. The archbishop is revealed as a liberal Roman Catholic prelate who had to contend with a reactionary priesthood and a radical civil government. [J. L. Helguera]

3043. ————. Cartas del Arzobispo Mosquera al Dr. Joaquín Miguel Araujo (B Ac Nac Hist, Quito, 34:83, enero-junio 1954, p. 15-27).

12 letters (three 1825, two 1826, one 1829, one 1835, one 1837, three 1838, one 1839), from Manuel José Mosquera to his former professor Araujo (d. 1841), a Quito theologian of some local prestige who taught at the seminary there. Useful information is found on the state of the Colombian church, both in Popayan, 1825-1829, and in Bogota, 1835-1839, on the reforming ideas of Mosquera, and his comments on early Protestant efforts in Cartagena, 1837. [J. L. Helguera]

3044. **Ospina, Eduardo.** The Protestant denominations in Colombia. A historical sketch with a particular study of the so-called "religious persecution." Bogotá, Imp. Nacional, 1954. 212 p.

Revised version of a work first published in Spanish. An obviously partisan, officially-sponsored study, but significant both for giving the "other side" to balance Protestant complaints of persecution and for its frank statement of the desirability of limiting religious toleration. [D. Bushnell]

3045. **Paz, Clodomiro.** Efemérides payanesas (Popayán, 34:241-250, enero-agosto 1953, p. 867-981).

A labor of love, and a useful collection in a single source of factual data dealing with Popayan from its foundation in 1536 to 1944. It is arranged by day and month, not by year. Much biographical and local information is contained herein. [J. L. Helguera]

3046. **Restrepo, José Manuel.** Autobiografía. Apuntamientos sobre la emigración de 1816, e índices del Diario político. Bogotá, Empresa Nacional de Publicaciones (Biblioteca de la Presidencia de Colombia, 30), 1957. 255 p.

The autobiography (covering the years 1781-1862) is sketchy, but the "Apuntamientos" give some insight into the mechanics of the royalist "Pacification" of 1816, from which Restrepo finally escaped to Jamaica and the U. S. For his Diario político y militar, the index to which is printed here, see HLAS, no. 19, item 3877. [D. Bushnell]

3047. **Restrepo Echavarría, Emiliano.** Una excursión al territorio de San Martín, en diciembre de 1869. Bogotá, Banco de la República (Archivo de la economía nacional, 14), 1955. 357 p.

Detailed economic description of the Colombian llanos in mid-19th century. [D. Bushnell]

3048. **Serna Giraldo, Rubén.** Alcaldes mayores de la ciudad de San Bonifacio de Ibagué 1550-1955 (B Hist Antig, 42:491-492, sept.-oct. 1955, p. 606-618).

Apparently based upon the municipal archives of Ibague, this is merely a list of the alcaldes mayores of the city, with the dates in which their tenures began. The average period in office was about a year. Few repetitions occurred during the colonial period—unlike the national period, in which certain family names occur frequently during a decade. [J. L. Helguera]

3049. **Solano Benítez, Guillermo.** Ramón González Valencia. Puente Nacional, Colombia, Tall. de la Escuela Media de Artes y Oficios de Puente Nacional, 1953. 221 p., illus.

Cover title: El bayardo colombiano, Ramón González Valencia. A hagiography, rather than a biography. The life and career of the conservative warrior Ramon González Valencia (1851-1928) are presented in a mediocre and pedestrian fashion. No new facts and no constructive thesis are advanced. Almost half of the book, p. 39-132, deals with González Valencia's role in the civil war of 1899-1902. [J. L. Helguera]

ECUADOR

3051. **Castillo, Abel Romeo.** La imprenta de Guayaquil independiente, 1821-1822; historia, bibliografía, catálogo, notas, facsímiles. Guayaquil, Ecuador, Casa de la Cultura Ecuatoriana, Núcleo del Guayas, 1956. 204 p., facsims.

An excellent job, with a general discussion followed by full description of all publications known, including individual issues of periodicals. Of interest for more than just its immediate topic. [D. Bushnell]

3052. **Castro, Julio.** Cuaspud. Un diario histórico (B Ac Nac Hist, Quito, 33:81, enero-junio 1953, p. 80-104).

A well-written and colorful contemporary account of the campaign of General Tomás C. de Mosquera in Ecuador (1863) which culminated in the defeat of the Ecuadorian army led by General Juan José Flores at Cuaspud. Castro served as paymaster for the Ecuadorian forces. Begins at Quito, Nov. 1, 1863; ends with the annihilation of Flores' troops at Cuaspud on Dec. 7, 1863. Lack of food rather than lack of valor is held to have been the cause of Ecuadorian defeat. [J. L. Helguera]

3053. ————. Páginas de una cartera de viaje. Un viaje con García Moreno en 1861 (B Ac Nac Hist, Quito, 33:82, julio-dic. 1953, p. 175-219).

Transcription of a dairy kept by Castro, an official, of several trips, steamer and mule-back, made in the month of December 1861, from Guayaquil to Manabi, accompanying García Moreno on an inspection of the Ecuadorean provinces of the coast and Letacunga. The energetic efforts of García Moreno to improve Ecuador's industry and agriculture are well brought out. A useful picture of travel conditions and of the almost unknown hinterlands in the last century. [J. L. Helguera]

3054. **Loor, Wilfrido.** García Moreno y sus asesinos. Quito, La Prensa Católica, 1955. 244 p., illus.

A major contribution to the García Moreno legend, this work is definitive insofar as it is concerned with the mechanics of the assassination plot, its principal protagonists, and its culmination on Aug. 6, 1875, when the clerical president met his Maker. Loor places the blame for the murder on the Masons of Lima and upon the ubiquitous "international Jews." He offers no documentary substantiation for this charge, but does commendably better with all the other aspects of his account. Indeed, the book is weighted down with fresh sources, principally those drawn from the unpublished *sumario* of the crime, the testimony of witnesses, participants, from García Moreno's correspondence now housed with the Jesuits in Quito, and from a number of contemporary newspapers, pamphlets, and broadsides. Despite the metaphysical motif which runs through the book—García Moreno, a saint; his murderers, agents of the devil—it succeeds in establishing the Quito lawyer, Manuel Polanco y Carrión (1832-1877) as the moving spirit of the killing. [J. L. Helguera]

3055. **Magnin, Juan.** Breve descripción de la Provincia de Quito . . . (B Ac Nac Hist, Quito, 25:85, enero-junio 1955, p. 89-115).

Magnin's map of the Quito audiencia is reproduced for the first time, not entirely readable. See also p. 72-89, for Julio Tobar Donoso's "Un nuevo mapa de misiones ecuatorianas," an explanation of Magnin's description here reprinted (having earlier been printed in the *Revista de Indias*, no. 1, 1940). [C. B. Kroeber]

3056. **Reyes, Óscar Efrén.** Breve historia general del Ecuador. 5. ed., ampliada y corregida. Quito, Fray Jodoco Ricke, 1955-1956. 3 v. in 2, 935 p., illus.

A new edition, little changed except for the poorly conceived and worse executed poster-like drawings which detract considerably from the book's appearance. The history of Ecuador, from its earliest Indian origins to 1949, is narrated in a sprightly style. As in the previous editions, the author has devoted scant attention to 17th-century developments, but deals objectively with the stormy 19th century, thus continuing the work's value as the best short general history of Ecuador. [J. L. Helguera]

3057. **Rolando, Carlos A.** Crónica del periodismo en el Ecuador, año 1850 a 1869 (B Cent Inv Hist, 10:23-24, 1955, p. 55-94).

More an annotated bibliography than a discussion of the Ecuadorian press, this article contains significant facts but is vague as to the life-span of most of the journals listed. The press in Quito, Guayaquil, and Cuenca is emphasized, though papers in lesser towns are commented upon as well. The political position of all is noted. [J. L. Helguera]

3058. **Veintemilla, Marieta de.** Páginas de la historia (Mus Hist, 8:24, agosto 1956, p. 141-170; 8:25, dic. 1956, p. 194-228).

The first two chapters of a highly partisan (anti-Flores, anti-García Moreno) defense of the political activities of the author's uncle, General Ignacio de Veintemilla, president of Ecuador 1875-1877 and 1882-1883. Period 1830-1875 covered in the first chapter; the second, stresses the achievements of the first Veintemilla regime, up to 1877. [J. L. Helguera]

PARAGUAY

3058a. **Cardozo, Efraim.** La Princesa Carlota Joaquina y la Independencia del Paraguay (R Indias, Madrid, 14:57-58, julio-dic. 1954, p. 359-383).

An able synthesis of the fruitless negotiations of 1810-1811 involving authorities in Paraguay, Spanish representatives in Rio (including Carlota), and the Portuguese government. All agreed on opposition to B. A., but in Paraguay distrust of Portuguese entanglements helped precipitate full independence. [D. Bushnell]

3059. **Chaves, Julio César.** El Presidente López. Vida y gobierno de don Carlos. B. A., Ayacucho, 1955. 364 p., illus.

Very strong sources and restrained judgment are the virtues of this biography of Carlos Antonio López, dictator of Paraguay, 1841-1862. Adding to previous works by others, and proceeding without the aid of socio-economic histories which have yet to be written for Paraguay, this is an important book. [C. B. Kroeber]

PERU

3060. **Alcalde Mongrut, Arturo.** El *Memorial de ciencias naturales*. Lima 1827-1828. Contribución a la bibliografía de Mariano E. de Rivero y Ustariz. Lima, Editorial San Marcos, 1954. 150 p.

An outstanding bibliographical treatise describing the scientific periodical published in Lima (December 1827-November 1828) by the Peruvian savant, Rivero y Ustariz (1795-1857). The 12 numbers of the *Memorial* are minutely described, and reveal the progress achieved by Peruvian students of metallurgy, chemistry, agriculture, and archaeology by 1828. [J. L. Helguera]

3061. **Barreda, Felipe A.** Elespuru. Lima, Lumen, 1957. 112 p., illus.

A very fine genealogy of the Elespuru family—based on archival sources of both Peru and Spain—showing one relationship of various other politically prominent Peruvians of the 19th century. [J. L. Helguera]

3062. **Basadre y Chocano, Modesto.** Diez años de historia política del Perú, 1834-1844. Prólogo y notas de Félix Denegri Luna. Lima, Huascarán (Biblioteca de la República, 3), 1953. 189 p., illus.

First published as a series of newspaper articles in Lima's *La Patria* (Oct. 9, 1877-Jan. 30, 1878), this account is evidently based on a now-lost diary as well as upon contemporary pamphlets and periodicals. Basadre y Chocano (1816?-1905) was well acquainted with the principal figures and events of which he wrote. Largely concerned with political and military events, the book is nonetheless a major fount of information—especially biographical—and is excellently footnoted, indexed, and edited, which enhances its value even further. [J. L. Helguera]

3063. Cornejo Bouroncle, Jorge. Pumacahua. La revolución del Cuzco de 1814. Estudio documentado. Cuzco, Perú, H. G. Rozas, 1956. 709 p.

Essentially a collection of documents, from regional archives, tied together by snatches of text. Covers in great detail the revolutionary stirrings (real or rumored) in southern Peru from Tupac Amaru to 1814, then takes up the unsuccessful 1814 uprising in which the cacique Mateo García Pumacahua played a leading role. This work is also printed in *Revista del Archivo Histórico del Cuzco*, 6, 1955 and 7, 1956. [D. Bushnell]

3064. Denegri Lunas, Félix. *El Discreto*, periódico de Manuel Lorenzo de Vidaurre (Fénix, 9, 1953, i. e. 1955, p. 352-412).

After a short introduction, reproduces all 10 numbers of a periodical of 1827, concerned almost wholly with juridical and constitutional ideas. [D. Bushnell]

3065. Eguiguren, Luis Antonio (ed.). Guerra separatista del Perú; Unanue, Arequipa y la historia creadora. Lima, Librería e Imp. Gil, 1955. 109 p.

Drawn from the treasure trove of the Archivo General de Indias, Seville, these documents (1815-1818) are further proof of the strong sentiments of class and caste felt by the Creoles of Peru. Hipólito Unánue, as *procurador* of the Royal Province of Arequipa, figures as the spokesman for the region in its demands that it be recognized as most loyal by the Crown, and that Arequipa's city *regidores* be granted the title of *señorías*—due to the fact that more than 300,000 pesos had been donated to the Crown from 1781 to 1815 by the city fathers. [J. L. Helguera]

3066. Estévez, Alfredo, and Óscar Horacio Elía. San Martín Protector del Perú. Anotaciones acerca de algunas cuestiones económico-financieras (Universidad, Santa Fe, 30, mayo 1955, p. 23-83).

Considerable detail (including certain documents) on San Martín's unsuccessful experiment with paper money; otherwise skims the surface. [D. Bushnell]

3067. Humphreys, R. A. Letters of William Miller, Lord Cochrane, and Basil Hall to James Paroissien, 1821-1823 (Fénix, 10, 1954, i.e. 1956, p. 203-234).

Miller and Cochrane describe events and personalities in the liberation of Peru, from an English viewpoint; Hall's one letter is on the merits of San Martín. [D. Bushnell]

3068. Kiernan, V. G. Foreign interests in the War of the Pacific (HAHR, 35:1, Feb. 1955, p. 14-36).

The 1879-1883 war seen from the viewpoint of Britain and France, as revealed by the sources of the Public Record Office, London. British policy, on the whole, favored Chile, while France and the U. S. supported Peru. A solid piece of archival research. [J. L. Helguera]

3069. Lastres, Juan B. La cultura peruana y la obra de los médicos en la emancipación. Lima, Editorial San Marcos, 1954. 494 p.

A study covering the condition of medicine and public health in Peru at the time of Independence, as well as the role of physicians in the struggle—both their political role (e. g., Hipólito Unánue) and their direct concern with military medicine. Offers new data; also, a documentary appendix. [D. Bushnell]

3070. ———. Hipólito Unanue. Lima, 1955. 224 p., illus.

A full-length biography of the Peruvian scientist and patriot, Unánue (1755-1833), emphasizing his importance as one of the fathers of Peruvian preventative medicine. The deep influence that the French Enlightenment exercised on his thinking is well brought out, as is his significant role as a pioneer of scientific and medical education in Peru. The author has made use of all the older printed sources both by and about his subject, and the book has the additional advantage that it is well footnoted and well indexed, though it lacks a formal bibliography. [J. L. Helguera]

3071. León Barandiarán, Augusto D. La guerra de Balta. Lima, Centro de Estudios Histórico Militares, 1955? 54 p.

This is a short monograph based on contemporary newspapers, which narrates the story of the successful revolt led by Colonel José Balta in the city of Chiclayo, against the government of General Mariano Ignacio Prado, Dec. 6, 1867-Jan. 7, 1868. A biographical sketch of Balta (1816-1872), plus the numerous proclamations and *pasacalles* reprinted herein, add further to the value of this interesting little study. [J. L. Helguera]

3072. Odría, Manuel Arturo. Principios y postulados del movimiento restaurador de Arequipa; extracto de discursos y mensajes, 1948-1955. Lima, 1956. 230 p., illus.

Brief selections from speeches and proclamations of the Peruvian president (1948-1956), expressing his domestic and international policies —but always, unfortunately, simply the public-relations statement of the case. [C. B. Kroeber]

3073. Pareja Paz-Soldán, José (ed.). Las constituciones del Perú; exposición, crítica y textos. Recopilación y estudio preliminar de José Pareja Paz-Soldán. Madrid, Ediciones Cultura Hispánica (Las Constituciones hispanoamericanas, 6) 1954. 1076 p.

This work deals with the constitutions and major constitutional amendments that Peru has produced, from 1823 to 1948. The prologue (p. 7-61) is one of the best interpretative sketches of Peruvian national period history and political development in print. It is followed by more than 300 pages of good commentary on each of the Peruvian constitutions (p. 65-398). The complete texts of the basic charters form the bulk of the book. Valuable. [J. L. Helguera]

3074. Raez Patiño, Sara. Ensayo de una

bibliografía castillista (Fénix, 10, 1954, i. e. p. 157-187).

An excellent tool for the study of Ramón Castilla. More than 500 items are listed, including official documents, contemporary pamphlets, newspaper articles, and books. [J. L. Helguera]

3075. Rivera Serna, Raúl. Don Ramón Castilla de 1821 a 1830 (Fénix, 10, 1954, i. e. 1956, p. 3-22).

Text and documents describing the military and political career of young Castilla, later to become president of Peru. [D. Bushnell]

3076. San Cristóval, Evaristo. El Mariscal Castilla y el periodismo de su época (R Mil Perú, 50:602, feb. 1954, p. 43-61).

Really a bibliography of the leading newspapers of Lima which excoriated or lauded Ramón Castilla during his most active role in Peruvian politics, 1845-1862. Selections from editorials are given. Well done, well written. [J. L. Helguera]

3077. Sumario indagatorio del delito de infidencia, actuado por el Tte. Cnel. Castilla (Fénix, 10, 1954, i. e. 1956, p. 23-111).

The complete court file and correspondence relating to subversive movement among certain Peruvian army officers which was designed to join Peru (especially south Peru) to Marshal Andrés Santa Cruz's Bolivia. An early example of Ramón Castilla's unyielding nationalism. [J. L. Helguera]

3078. Testimonio de la causa por conspiración seguida al Coronel Ramón Castilla (Fénix, 10, 1954, i. e. 1956, p. 112-141).

Records of the military trial held in Lima in 1832 in which General Ramón Castilla was falsely accused of conspiring to bring about the overthrow of Marshal Agustín Gamarra. Castilla was accused of being an agent of General Antonio Gutiérrez de la Fuente. The strong character of Castilla is revealed in the testimony. Original 30 manuscript pages are found in Peruvian Biblioteca Nacional. [J. L. Helguera]

3079. Velarde B., César Augusto. La expedición de Castilla al Ecuador (1858-1860). Lima, Imp. del Ministerio de Guerra, 1954. 23 p.

Castilla's daring and successful amphibious expedition to Guayaquil is well studied in this military monograph. In addition, a good operations map and a brief but choice list of authorities are displayed. [J. L. Helguera]

URUGUAY

3080. García, Flavio A. En torno a un despacho de Coronel Español a favor de Artigas (B Hist, 65, abril-junio 1955, p. 89-98).

Concerning Artigas' negotiations in 1814-1815 with both Spanish and Portuguese (motivated chiefly by his dispute with B. A.) and a Spanish effort to win his allegiance. Not especially noteworthy in itself, but one of a series of items by García in this periodical, based on research in Spanish archives and dealing with the Independence era in Uruguay. He has also usefully extracted and published the debates of the Portuguese Cortes referring to Uruguay (B Hist, 68, enero-marzo, 1956, p. 33-64; 69, abril-junio 1956, p. 91-129). [D. Bushnell]

3081. Petit Muñoz, Eugenio. Artigas y su ideario a través de seis series documentales. 1. parte. Montevideo, Universidad de la República, Instituto de Investigaciones Históricas (Ensayos, estudios y monografías, 3; Serie: Cuadernos artiguistas, 1), 1956. 232 p.

A first installment of the "documentary series" promised in the title, each to consist of key documents with extended comment. The three "series" included here illustrate Artigas' democratic federalism, 1811-1814, and follow an interesting introduction on the aims of the May Revolution. Interpretation is able but somewhat involved. [D. Bushnell]

3082. Universidad de la República. Instituto de Investigaciones Históricas. Biblioteca de impresos raros americanos. T. 3. Gazeta de Montevideo, v. 2, 1811, enero-junio. Montevideo, 1954. ccii, 448 p.

In addition to reprinting the royalist *Gazeta de Montevideo*, contains background studies by several historians, e. g., on the propaganda of B. A. patriots that the *Gazeta* was intended to counteract. [D. Bushnell]

3083. Uruguay. Comisión Nacional Archivo Artigas. Archivo Artigas. T. 4. Prólogo de Luis Bonavita. Montevideo, 1953. 550 p.

Documents relating to the Uruguayan patriot uprising of 1811, including some on the antecedents. There is a useful abstract for every item, and the entire volume reflects the highest scholarly standards. The prologue was issued separately as *Escenario y actores de la revolución oriental de 1811* (Montevideo, Monteverde, 1954, 48 p.). [D. Bushnell]

3084. Zina Fernández, Romeo. Historia militar nacional. T. 1. El ejército artiguista. Montevideo, Centro Militar (Biblioteca General Artigas, 26), 1955. 216 p.

Synthesis of data referring to military organization, equipment, etc., in the Independence era, plus background starting with Homer. [D. Bushnell]

VENEZUELA

3085. Alvarado, Lisandro. Obras completas. V. 5. Historia de la revolución federal en Venezuela. Caracas, Ministerio de Educación, Dirección de Cultura y Bellas Artes, 1956. 662 p., illus., port., fold. maps.

The second edition of a work which first appeared in Caracas in 1909. The present version is greatly enhanced by two good indices, one of persons, the other of places. The long and sanguinary course of the Venezuelan civil struggles, known under the collective name of the Federal Revolution (1857-1864), are studied from a political and military standpoint. Despite its faults in organization and emphasis, this work, heavily based on contemporary newspaper accounts and in part on archival materials, remains one of the few important books dealing with the Venezuelan Federal Wars. [J. L. Helguera]

3086. Archila, Ricardo. Historia de la sanidad en Venezuela. Prólogo del doctor Daniel Orellana. Caracas, Imp. Nacional, 1956. 2 v. 399, 455 p., illus.

A solid, well-documented monograph dealing with the history of public health in Venezuela, covering the subject from pre-Conquest days to the present. In view of the number of medical men who have from time to time played important political roles in Venezuelan history, the book, in addition to its primary emphasis, is a useful biographical guide. [J. L. Helguera]

3087. Beltrán Guerrero, Luis. Introducción al positivismo venezolano (R Nac Cult, 18:112-113, sept.-dic. 1955, p. 193-219).

An important contribution to the study of Venezuelan intellectual history, in the period 1830-ca.1930. Shows influence of positivism in the laws, notably during the period 1880-1910. An essay with bibliography attached. [J. L. Helguera]

3088. Blanco Peñalver, P. L. Historia territorial de Venezuela. T. 1. ed. Caracas, Escuelas Gráficas Salesianas, 1954. 174 p.

An historical treatise of Venezuelan political and ecclesiastical divisions, emphasizing the period since 1821. Based on printed sources (decrees, laws, public documents), the work is useful. The author, however, is over-verbose and repetitious, and the book is gravely handicapped by its lack of maps. A planned second volume is to be devoted to the Federal Territories of Amazonas and Amacuro. [J. L. Helguera]

3089. Briceño, Manuel. Los ilustres o la estafa de los Guzmanes. Caracas, Fe y Cultura, 1953? 246 p.

An excoriating biography of the three Guzmáns, Antonio (fl. 1790-1810), Antonio Leocadio (1801-1884), and Antonio Guzmán Blanco (1829-1899). Despite its biting polemic nature, this book, now reprinted for the third time (previous editions: Curaçao, 1883; Bogata, 1884) has long served as an important source for the otherwise obscure early life of Antonio Leocadio Guzmán. [J. L. Helguera]

3090. Depons, François. Informe sobre la cesión de la capitanía general de Caracas a Francia. Causas políticas que hacen indispensable esta cesión. Copia y traducción . . . Martín García Villasmil (Crónica Caracas, 6:28-29, abril-junio 1956, p. 108-118).

Plan of 1806 by the French agent Depons, urging annexation as a benefit to both France and

Spain, forestalling the schemes of England and Miranda. [D. Bushnell]

3091. Fernández, Pablo Emilio. Gómez, el rehabilitador. Caracas, Villegas, 1956. 339 p., illus.

A bitter-sweet interpretation of the life and work of Juan Vicente Gómez (1857-1935), for nearly three decades dictator of Venezuela (1908-1935). The author adds nothing new to the Gómez saga, aside from some anecdotal information evidently gleaned from his own father, General Emilio Fernández (died 1929), who is revealed as one of the more important early Gómez followers. The book contains no scholarly apparatus, other than a short 'bibliografía' on p. 345-346, and is not based on any documentary material. Gómez emerges almost unscathed. Though references are frequent to his cruelty, more attention is given his material achievements. [J. L. Helguera]

3092. García A., Guillermo S. Valores humanos del telégrafo en Venezuela en el primer centenario del telégrafo eléctrico en Venezuela, 1856-1956. Maracay, Venezuela, Nueva Segovia, 1956. 312 p.

Based on secondary sources and on a few mid-19th-century newspapers, this book contains short biographical sketches of 18 men prominent in the development of Venezuelan telegraphy. A highly subjective work, more poetical than factual. [J. L. Helguera]

3093. González, Juan Vicente. Epístolas catilinarias sobre el ocho de julio. Compilación y estudios de Víctor José Cedillo y Virgilio Tosta. Caracas, Ediciones Garrido, 1955. 126 p.

This is the first edition, in book form, of four stinging attacks on the authors of the July 8, 1835, attempt at revolt against the rule of Dr. José María Rojas by some of the leading military figures of Venezuelan Independence. As preventatives for further military-led subversion, González (1808-1866), notable publicist and political writer, offered stern legal measures and increased encouragement to European immigration. Originally printed in 1835 in broadsheet form. The two introductions by Sres. Cedillo and Tosta add value to the book. [J. L. Helguera]

3094. Grases, Pedro. Orígenes de la imprenta en Cumaná. Caracas, 1956. 8 p.

Assembles data from published works and documents to show that the first printing done at Cumana was in 1810 or 1811 rather than in 1812. [C. B. Kroeber]

3095. Guevara, Arturo. Espejo de justicia; esbozo psiquiátrico-social de don Simón Rodríguez. Caracas, Imp. Nacional, 1954. 632 p., illus., ports.

A study of Simón Rodríguez, in which the basic facts are presented together with long extracts from his writings and much rambling interpretation; emphasis is on the "aspecto médico-psicológico." [D. Bushnell]

3096. Hernández Ron, Santiago. Orígenes de las dos primeras emisiones de las estampillas de correo de Venezuela. Caracas, Tip. Eizmendi, 1956. 71 p.

A well-documented study of the development of Venezuelan postage stamps, 1859-1863. Based on archival materials, principally those of the Secretaría de Hacienda, located in the Archivo General de la Nación in Caracas. The first issue was lithographed in the U. S. in 1858. [J. L. Helguera]

3097. **Iribarren-Celis, Lino.** La revolución de 1854. Caracas, Tip. Americana, 1954. 206 p.

A poorly written attempt to portray the combined effort of the Liberal and Páez groups in Barquisimeto to overthrow the José Gregorio Monagas regime in July-August 1854. The revolt failed, as does the author's attempt to convey significant new information. [J. L. Helguera]

3098. **Larrazábal Blanco, Carlos.** La primera gestión de Núñez de Cáceres en Venezuela (Clío, 22:98, enero-abril 1954, p. 17-18).

Consists of a letter from Cáceres to Intendant Carlos Soublette, La Guaira, Apr. 23, 1823, Soublette's formal note of acknowledgment, and a lot of conjecture. [R. D. Hussey]

3099. **Lecuna, Vicente.** Catálogo de errores y calumnias en la historia de Bolívar. T. 1. N. Y., Colonial Press, 1956. 407 p., illus., ports., facsims., plans.

This volume, unfortunately left in semi-finished form at the author's death, offers a miscellany of facts and comment chiefly referring to debated aspects of Bolívar's family, early life, and career to 1815. It is partisan, but less purely polemical than the title suggests. [D. Bushnell]

3100. **Lisboa, Miguel María.** Relación de un viaje a Venezuela, Nueva Granada y Ecuador. Caracas, Ediciones de la Presidencia de la República de Venezuela, 1954. 442 p., illus., maps.

Here, for the first time in Spanish, is an important and well-written travel classic by a Brazilian who travelled in Venezuela, Colombia, and Ecuador during 1852-1853. Lisboa, a man of the world, wrote objectively, but with much sympathy for and perception of the peoples he described. Social life in Caracas, Bogota, Quito, and many of the lesser cities of the Gran Colombian states is thoroughly portrayed, and the author's comments on politics and economic life cannot be ignored by anyone studying the region. The first edition (in Portuguese) appeared in Brussels in 1866. This translation, unfortunately, while adequate, abounds with typographical errors, and lacks most of the good illustrations which adorned the first edition. [J. L. Helguera]

3101. **López, Casto Fulgencio.** Juan Bautista Picornell y la conspiración de Gual y España. Narración documentada de la pre-revolución de Independencia venezolanos. Caracas, Ediciones Nueva Cádiz (Biblioteca de escritores venezolanos, 13),

1955. 440 p., illus. (part col.), ports., facsims., plan.

López has obviously written this rather thick volume for a small professional audience but has refused to make customary concessions to scholarship such as footnoting sources of information. The chief criticism is that this study adds little to existing literature and document collections by Héctor García Chuecos, Pedro Grases, Harris G. Warren, or (even) Blanco and Aspurúa. [J. S. Hanrahan]

3102. **Matos Romero, Manuel.** Perijá: fundación e historia. Caracas, Tip. Matheus, 1956. 206 p., illus.

Perija, a mountainous tropical Venezuelan hinterland which borders on the Colombian department of Magdalena, is still a frontier area—fit for fine cattle and fierce Motilón Indians, both of which have a disproportionately large share of this book devoted to them. The history of the area from its first white settlement in 1722 to the present, based on secondary sources and upon personal observation by the author, is narrated in a sprightly if ethnocentric fashion. A convenient, but hardly scholarly, introduction to the region. [J. L. Helguera]

3103. **Parra-Pérez, Caracciolo.** Mariño y la Independencia de Venezuela. Madrid, Ediciones Cultura Hispánica, 1954-. V. 1, El libertador de Oriente, 1954, 525 p.; v. 2, El disidente, 1954, 619 p.; v. 3, El ilustre general, 1955, 496 p.

These volumes take General Santiago Mariño from a brilliant start in 1813-1814, when as liberator of eastern Venezuela he stood virtually on an equal plane with Bolívar, through his later split with Bolívar, to his emergence, by 1825, as a second to Páez. They are well written though slightly diffuse, defend Mariño rather convincingly against his critics, and incorporate some valuable new material (e. g., British correspondence from Trinidad). Yet there are also places, notably in v. 3, where existing sources do not appear to have been fully exploited. Hence an important work (of which more is to come) but not quite definitive. [D. Bushnell]

3104. ———. Una misión diplomática venezolana ante Napoleón en 1813. Caracas, Secretaría General de la Décima Conferencia Interamericana (Col. Historia, 4), 1953. 89 p., ports., facsim.

Short research monograph on the efforts of Manuel Palacio Fajardo (also representing Cartagena) to obtain French help for Independence, 1813-1814. Napoleon was favorable but busy. [D. Bushnell]

3105. **Pi Sunyer, Carlos.** La goleta "Ramona" (B Ac Nac Hist, Caracas, 39:153, enero-marzo 1956, p. 61-79).

Authoritative study of the policies pursued by British officials on Curaçao toward Venezuelan Independence, 1810-1811. The central theme concerns a royalist vessel whose seizure heartened the patriots and whose ultimate release directly aided Spanish reconquest. [D. Bushnell]

3106. El **Publicista de Venezuela** (B Ac

Nac Hist, Caracas, 38:150, abril-junio 1955, p. 192-204; 38:151, julio-sept. 1955, p. 331-343; 39:153, enero-marzo 1956, p. 26-37; 39:154, abril-junio 1956, p. 169-180).
Each of these installments reprints an issue of the official organ of the Venezuelan patriot Congress: no. 3, July 11, 1811; no. 4, July 25, 1811; no. 5, Aug. 1, 1811; no. 6, Aug. 8, 1811. See *HLAS, no. 19*, item 3916, for earlier issues. [D. Bushnell]

3107. Rodríguez, Simón. Escritos. Compilación y estudio bibliográfico por Pedro Grases. Prólogo por Arturo Uslar Pietri. Edición conmemorativa del centenario de la muerte del maestro del Libertador. Caracas, Sociedad Bolivariana de Venezuela, 1954. 2 v. 365, 376 p., port., facsims.
Contains all the works, including letters, known at the time of compilation; the *Consejos de amigo* (*HLAS, no. 19*, item 3918) was discovered too late. [D. Bushnell]

3108. Uslar Pietri, Juan. Historia de la rebelión popular de 1814. Contribución al estudio de la historia de Venezuela. Paris, Ediciones Soberbia, 1954, 243 p.
Refers to the race-class warfare unleashed by the Spaniard Boves against the Second Venezue-lan Republic in 1814. Little if any new data, but a fairly able synthesis. [D. Bushnell]

3109. Vallenilla Lanz, Laureano. Disgregación e integración. Ensayo sobre la formación de la nacionalidad venezolana. Caracas, Tip. Garrido, 1953, xiii-lxxix, 195 p.
This is the second edition (1st, Caracas, 1930) of a brilliant and well-documented attempt (heavily influenced by the theories of Gustave Lebon) to explain the turbulent Venezuelan 19th-century political and social scene in the light of the Colonial heritage. Federalism is held to be an expression of the anarchical and anti-social tendencies spawned during the latter years of the 18th century. A second volume of this book is still reportedly in manuscript, in the possession of the author's descendants. [J. L. Helguera]

3110. Venezuela. Dirección del Ceremonial y Acervo Histórico de La Nación. Oficina de Compilación, Clasificación y Publicación del Archivo del Libertador. Toma de razón, 1810 a 1812. Registro de nombramientos y actos oficiales emanados de la Primera Junta Patriótica y de la Primera República de Venezuela. Caracas, 1955, 503 p., facsims.
Mostly routine civil and military administration, but a valuable addition to the printed sources. [D. Bushnell]

BRAZIL
GEORGE BOEHRER

Most of the works listed below have followed the patterns established in recent years. A few, however, are worthy of special notice.

The first *As ciências no Brasil* (item 3202), although uneven in quality, marks a great step forward in the development of the history of science in Brazil. For the colonial period, the appearance of the first volume of the catalogue of the manuscripts relating to Brazil (item 3250) in the collections of the dukes of Cadaval is very welcome and will be useful if general access to the collections is permitted.

One volume of letters and two biographies set in the Empire and the Republic are noteworthy. The publication of the correspondence between Dom Pedro II and the Condessa do Barral, published in two editions (items 3266 and 3268), has achieved a certain *succès de scandale*. Historians are divided as to whether the established opinions on the emperor must be severely or only slightly modified. Lauro Roméro's biography of Clóvis Bevilaqua (item 3289), by its competence and understanding of one of the molders of Brazilian legal and philosophical thought in the transitional years of the late Empire and early Republic, fills a long felt vacuum. Affonso de Mello Franco's biography of Afrânio (item 3282) ran the risk of a title evocative of a previous classic. The hazard was almost successfully overcome; the volume fails comparatively only in that neither Mello Franco attained the status of either Nabuco.

GENERAL

3200. Almeida, Antônio Paulino de. Memória histórica de Xiririca (El Dorado Paulista) (B Dept Arq, n. f. 14, 1955, p. 5-168).
A historical account of the region of Xiririca, with geographical, economic, and personal data. Prepared at the time of the centenary of the founding of the town. [R. R. Hill]

3201. Andréa, Júlio. A marinha brasileira.

Florões de glórias e de epopéias memoráveis. Rio, Artes Gráf. C. Mendes Júnior, 1955. 367 p. & illus.
A naval almanac containing much useful information. There are short, usually 2-page, biographies of leading naval personages; lists of shipwrecks, cabinet ministers, commanders-in-chief, etc.

3202. Azevedo, Fernando de (ed). As ciências no Brasil; obra organizada e publicada sob a direcão e com uma introducão de Fernando de Azevedo. São Paulo, Edicões Melhoramentos (Série Cultura e ciência), 1955. 2 v., illus., ports., maps (part fold.), diagrs., facsims. 412, 399 p.
A generally good historical treatment of the development of science in Brazil. Beginning with the excellent introduction by Azevedo, the sections devoted to the individual disciplines are of uneven merit. To be noted from the historian's viewpoint are those on botany (Mário Guimarães Ferri), zoology (Oliveira M. de Pinto), astronomy (Abraão de Morais), political economy (Paul Hugon), anthropology (Azevedo), and geography (J. V. da Costa Pereira). The two volumes mark a great improvement over previous works devoted to the history of science.

3203. Azevedo, Thales de. O catolicismo no Brasil. Um campo para a pesquisa social. Rio, Ministério da Educacão e Cultura, Serviço de Documentação (Os cadernos de cultura, 87), 1955. 70 p.
Substantially the same as his "Catholicism in Brazil: a personal evaluation" (Thought, 28: 109, summer 1953, p. 253-274) but published now with notes. An extremely frank essay which places the present state of Catholicism in stark terms.

3204. Bahia, Renato. O estudante na história nacional. 1. ed. Salvador, Brazil, Progresso, 1954. 217 p.
A history of student life and activities, chiefly literary and political. The earlier chapters concern the Jesuit *Colégios*, the *seminário* of Olinda, and Coimbra. The sections on the 19th century center on São Paulo and Recife. The author correctly acknowledges that his work is not definitive.

3205. Barbosa, Rui. Antología; selección y notas de Luís Viana Filho; traducción de Justo Pastor Benítez. [Revisión y prefacio de Helcio Martins]. Rio, Casa de Rui Barbosa, 1954. 256 p.
A Spanish edition of the Portuguese anthology (see *HLAS, no. 19*, items 4003 and 5231). This edition varies from the original in that some selections have been broken up and a few have been omitted.

3206. Brazil. Biblioteca Nacional. Divisão de Obras Raras e Publicações. Documentos históricos. Revolução de 1817. V. 107. Rio, 1955. 278 p.

The seventh volume on this topic (see also *HLAS, no. 19*, item 4007) is mostly concerned with the revolt in Limoeiro. This is followed by counterrevolutionary testimony. José Honório Rodrigues again discusses the importance of the documents in a preface.

3207. ―――――. Comissão de Estudo dos Textos da História do Brasil. Bibliografia de história do Brasil. 1. e 2. semestres de 1951. Rio, Ministério das Relações Exteriores, Serviço de Publicações, 1956. 147 p.
A continuation of this series. Divided into works published in Brazil and foreign countries; serial and periodical publications, Brazilian and foreign; and articles in periodical publications and newspapers.

3208. ―――――. Serviço de Documentação Geral da Marinha. Subsídios para a história marítima do Brazil. V. 14. Rio, 1955. 352 p., illus.
Two articles are of note in this issue: Levy Scavarda, "A Escola Naval através do tempo," a history of the Naval School; and "Notas sôbre a actuação da Marinha brasileira na revolução de 1930."

3209. ―――――. ―――――. Subsídios para a história marítima do Brasil. V. 15. Rio, 1956. 235 p., illus.
Of interest in this issue are: Levy Scavarda, "O Serviço de Documentação Geral da Marinha," on the libraries, archives, museums, etc. of the Navy; and Antônio Maria Carvalho, "Notas sôbre a ação da Marinha nos acontecimentos revolucionários de 1930 (Depoimento do Exmo. Sr. Almirante de Esquadra Antônio Maria de Carvalho)."

3210. Carneiro, Levi. Dois arautos da democracia: Rui Barbosa e Joaquim Nabuco. Rio, Casa de Rui Barbosa, 1954. 289 p., illus.
A collection of conferences and papers. The bulk of the volume concerns Rui Barbosa. The more significant papers are "Rui Barbosa e a Constituição de 91" and "Rui Barbosa, advogado."

3211. Cascudo, Luís da Câmara. Notas e documentos para a história de Mossoró. Natal, Brazil, Imp. Natal-R. G. do Norte (Col. Mossoroense, série C, 2), 1955. 254 p.
An account of the *povoação*, later city (1852), of Santa Luzia de Mossoro in the state of Rio Grande do Norte. Most of the emphasis is on the 19th century. Included is an interesting account of the abolition movement in Mossoro.

3212. Castro, Óscar Oliveira. Vultos da Paraíba; patronos da Academia. Rio, Imp. Nacional, 1955. 37 p., 2 plates, 30 ports.
Portraits of 30 prominent Paraibanos who are the "patrons" of the Academia Paraibana de Letras, preceded by an introductory essay containing some biographical information. Among

the patrons are Pedro Américo, Inácio Rolim, Coelho Lisboa, and Aristides Lobo.

3213. Cobb, Gwendolin B. Bancroft Library microfilm: Portugal and her empire (HAHR, 34:1, Feb. 1954, p. 114-125).
A description of the microfilming project of the University of California. There are some 100,-000 exposures, mainly covering the period from late 16th century to the early 19th. The Arquivo Histórico Colonial is the principal archive utilized; some use was made of those of Torre do Tombo, Ajuda, Coimbra, and Porto.

3214. Delamare, Alcibíades. Vila Rica. 2. ed. Rio, Livraria Clássica Brasileira, 1955. 280 p., illus.
A historical guidebook with a discussion of Aleijadinho, Marilia, the Inconfidência, etc. The work is not of much worth and the illustrations are very poor.

3215. Dunlop, Charles Julius. Rio antigo. V. 1. Rio, Gráf. Laemmert, 1955. 149 p., illus.
"Uma coletânea de artigos de colaboração de Charles J. Dunlop publicados em diversos jornais e revistas." 70 short descriptions, Rio social history of the latter part of the 19th and the early years of the 20th centuries. Each is preceded by photographs.

3216. Gerson, Brasil. História das ruas do Rio de Janeiro. Rio, Souza, 1954. 350 p., illus.
A very compact and highly informative description, district by district, of the streets and squares of Rio. The volume is marred by the lack of indices, references, and maps.

3217. Gouveia, Maurílio de. História da escravidão. Prefácio de Pedro Calmon. Rio, 1955. 423 p., illus.
A general review of slavery and its Brazilian form in colonial and national times. There is a rather good discussion of the abolition movement in the late Empire. A rather handy manual, slightly documented.

3218. Lacombe, Americo Jacobina. Brasil, período nacional. México, Instituto Panamericano de Geografía e Historia (Publ., 184; Comisión de Historia, 76; Programa de historia de América, 3; Período nacional, 1), 1956. 166 p.
This volume of the project of the History of America is a rapid synthesis of the Empire and Republic. It is especially valuable for the extensive bibliography found in the notes.

3219. Leite, Aureliano. Subsídios para a *História da civilização paulista*. Ed. monumental comemorativa do IV centenário da cidade de São Paulo. Enriquecida de vasta bibliografía sôbre pessoas, coisas, lugares e acontecimentos paulistas. São Paulo, Saraiva, 1954. 599 p., illus. (part col.), ports., maps, facsims.

An enlargement of the author's *História da civilização paulista* (see *HLAS, no. 12, 1946*, item 2183), brought to 1950. The new material is largely concerned with economic and social history. The bibliography has been brought to date.

3220. Lima, Augusto de. História de Nossa Senhora em Minas Gerais. Origens das principais invocações. Belo Horizonte, Brazil, Imp. Oficial, 1956. 291 p., illus.
29 separate invocations of the Virgin venerated in Minas Gerais are treated. Portuguese and European backgrounds are given. The volume is principally based on Frei Agostinho de Santa Maria, Jorge Cardozo, *et al.* Despite the author's demurral "Este livro não se destina à edificação religiosa . . . ," the work is very pietistic.

3221. ————. Pequena história da inconfidência de Minas Gerais. 2. ed. V. 1. Belo Horizonte, Brazil, Imp. Oficial, 1955. 339 p., illus.
A highly enthusiastic and uncritical discussion of Tiradentes and his fellow conspirators. Appendices include a description of the return of the bodies of those exiled to Africa, and "Tiradentes," a lyric drama in four acts.

3222. Manchester, Alan K. Em busca de uma chave para a história do Brasil (Kriterion, 7:29-30, julho-dez. 1954, p. 419-429).
Suggests that the continued union of Brazil is due to three factors: the growth of a socially stable landed aristocracy accustomed to centralized authority, the transference of the court to Rio in 1808, and the retention of a centralized form of government during the first two decades of Independence.

3223. Maranhão, João de Albuquerque. História da casa de Cunhaú. Prefácio de Gilberto Freyre. Recife, Brazil, Arquivo Público Estadual, 1956. 290 p., illus., ports.
A history of the Albuquerque Maranhão family. The name Cunhaú derives from the *sesmaria* given by the founder Jeronimo to his sons Antônio and Matias. Poorly documented and written in a personal style, this work, which leaves much to be desired, is nevertheless useful.

3224. Mendonça, Renato. Fronteira em marcha. Ensaio de uma geopolítica brasileira. Prefácio de José Carlos de Macedo Soares. 2. ed., rev. e aumentada. Rio, Livraria São José, 1956. 199 p., illus.
Concerned briefly with the origins of Brazil's international policies, mainly with Brazil's activities in the La Plata, and finally with Brazil's impingement on the world scene in recent years, this volume mainly strengthens the author's previous works.

3225. Morse, Richard M. São Paulo since Independence: a cultural interpretation (HAHR, 34:4, Nov. 1954, p. 419-444).

An examination of São Paulo city through its cultural activity. Stress is placed on mid-19th-century romanticism and on the *modernista* movement. The author believes that ". . . only with the knowledge and vision acquired through urban institutions may the insistent problems of agrarian Latin America be effectively solved."

3226. Mueller, Bonifácio. Convento de Santo António do Recife, 1606-1956. Esbôço histórico. Recife, Brazil, 1956. 179 p.

A compact, well-documented description of the Franciscan convent founded in 1606 by Marcos André. Contains analyses of the church and convent, their artistic features, courses of studies, income, notable friars, politics, etc. Based on Brazilian and Portuguese archives and on monographic works.

3227. Novaes, Maria Stella de. Relicário de um povo; o Santuário de Nossa Senhora da Penha, no Espírito Santo, Brasil. Vitória, Brazil, Escola Técnica de Vitória, 1954. 203 p., illus.

A generally pious account of the image and cult of the Virgin under this invocation which began in Espírito Santo in 1570 and became the focus for frequent pilkrimages. The second section contains verse in honor of the Virgin. Attached is a list of superiors, guardians, and chaplains stationed at the shrine.

3228. Pacheco, Felipe Conduru. Dom Francisco de Paula e Silva, XXIII Bispo do Maranhão; esboço biográfico. Petrópolis, Brazil, Editôra Vozes, 1955. 106 p., illus.

A topical and eulogistic treatment of Dom Francisco (1866-1916) who entered the Congregation of the Mission and became bishop of Maranhão in 1907. The subject was author of *História ecclesiástica de Maranhão.*

3229. Pereira, Antônio Baptista. Rui Barbosa em Santos, em 1868 e em 1912. Rio, Casa de Rui Barbosa, 1956. 44 p.

Two journalistic articles concerning the arrival of Rui and Castro Alves in Santos on their way to law school in São Paulo, and on Rui's appearance in Santos during the campaign of 1912.

3230. Pessôa, Corina de Abreu. Cartas de Montevidéo sôbre alguns textos da história platina. Rio, Ministério da Guerra (Biblioteca do Exército, 186-187), 1953. 309 p.

A discursive discussion in letter form of the La Plata region, mainly in reference to Brazil. Covering the period through the Paraguayan War, the work, while based on extensive reading, offers little that is new.

3231. Pimenta, José de Melo. Quem fundou São Paulo? Contribuição ao estudo histórico sôbre a fundação de São Paulo. São Paulo, 1954. 220 p., illus.

The author is one of the founders and First Secretary of the "Movimento Pró Nóbrega" whose principal aim was the popular acceptance of Nóbrega as the founder of the city. This volume is chiefly the history of the association and is largely made up of the minutes of its popular conferences. It is interesting as a chronicle of the activities of professional and amateur historians who were eventually crowned with success.

3232. Porto, Carlos Eugênio. Roteiro do Piauí. Rio, Ministério da Educação e Cultura, Serviço de Documentação (Col. Vida brasileira, 4), 1955. 186 p., illus.

An uneven but informative work on the history (through Independence), physical description, stockraising, and epidemics (the author's specialty) of Piauí. Chapter 3 (p. 37-62) discusses the priority of Domingos Afonso Mafrense over Domingos Jorge Velho in colonial Piauí.

3233. Ribeiro, João S. Ordens honoríficas, nacionais e estrangeiras. Rio, Edições O Cruzeiro, 1955. 155 p.

A guide to honorary orders with brief histories of them. Incomplete lists of foreigners decorated by Brazil and Brazilians decorated by other nations are given.

3234. São Paulo (state). Departamento do Arquivo. Relatório das atividades do Departamento do Arquivo do estado durante o ano de 1954 e seu programa para o exercício de 1955. [Por] José Soares de Souza, director (B Dept Arq, n. f., 14, 1955, p. 169-188).

An account of the work and achievements of the Archive in 1954 and its program for 1955. [R. R. Hill]

3235. Silva, Costa e. Santos noutros tempos. Ilustrações de Ribs. São Paulo, Emprésa Gráf. da Revista dos Tribunais, 1953. 658 p., illus.

A number of literary essays originally published in *A Tribuna.* The great majority deal with the 19th century. There are evidences of some research.

3236. Stein, Stanley J. Biblioteca histórica paulista (HAHR, 34:4, Nov. 1954, p. 493-501).

A comprehensive review article analyzing the 10 works reprinted in connection with the IV centenary of São Paulo. Most of the volumes have been noted in *HLAS.*

3237. Taunay, Affonso de Escragnolle. História da cidade de São Paulo. São Paulo, Edições Melhoramentos, 1953. 272 p., illus.

São Paulo's chief historian here presents an extremely convenient summary of his previous monographic works on the city.

3238. ————. Velho São Paulo. São Paulo, Edições Melhoramentos, 1952-1954? 3 v. V. 1, Primeiras plantas, colégio, sé, paço, 78 p.; v. 2, Depoimentos sôbre a cidade através dos séculos, ruas

principais, a abadia de S. Bento . . ., 73 p.; v. 3, Evolução da cidade sob o império, ruas secundárias, o mosteiro de Nossa Senhora da Luz . . ., 85 p.; illus.
A pictorial history of São Paulo. Most of the illustrations date from the 19th and 20th centuries. The volumes are not of great merit.

3239. Valladão, Alfredo. Mathias Valladão, sua figura na medicina brasileira. São Paulo, Empresa Gráf. da Revista dos Tribunais, 1954. 69 p., illus.
"Publicado no 'Jornal de commércio,' edições de 24 de janeiro de 1953 e 7 de fevereiro de 1954." Matias Valladão (1860-1920), after graduating from the Medical School in Rio, practiced in São Paulo where he became a leading physician and the leading clinician. This work is an enlargement upon those pages on the subject in the author's *Campanha da Princeza.*

COLONIAL PERIOD

3240. Abreu, João Capistrano de. Capítulos de história colonial, 1500-1800. 4. ed., rev., anotada e prefaciada por José Honório Rodrigues. Rio, Sociedade Capistrano de Abreu, 1954. 386 p.
The fourth edition of this classic is meticulously edited. There is a fine prefatory article on Capistrano and historiography. The text is followed by notes of Capistrano, of John Casper Branner, of Philip von Leutzelburg, and of the editor.

3241. Antonil, André João [pseud., i. e. João Antonio Andreoni]. Cultura e opulência do Brasil. Salvador, Brazil, Progresso (Col. de estudos brasileiros), 1955. 253 p.
A new and inexpensive edition of this famous work by the 17th-18th century Jesuit whose book was suppressed by Portugal upon publication.

3242. Boxer, C. R. In the time of the Flemings: the Dutch in Brazil, 1624-54 (Hist Today, 4:3, Mar. 1954, p. 159-168).
A general readable and balanced description of the Dutch experiment at a Brazilian empire.

3243. Ferreira, Tito Lívio. Padre Manoel da Nóbrega, fundador de São Paulo. São Paulo, Saraiva, 1957. 261 p.
A highly readable and partially documented study of Nóbrega by one of his more ardent champions. This interesting attempt to combine scientific writing with "romance" is necessarily unsuccessful.

3243a. Van Hoboken, W. J. Witte de With in Brazilië, 1648-1649. Amsterdam, N. V. Noord-Hollandsche Uitgevers Maatschappij, 1955. 324 p.
Admiral Corneliszoon Witte de With was sent to Brazil during the most decisive days of the Dutch occupation. Greatly restricted by the

policies of the Dutch West India Company, he returned to Europe without authorization. This work is principally based on Dutch sources but also on some Portuguese monographic works.

3244. Horch, Rosemarie Erika. Der Pater Viegas de Menezes und die ersten Druckversuche im brasilianischen Staate Minas Gerais (Gutenberg Jahr, 1953, p. 135-138).
José Joaquim Viegas de Menezes, born in Vila Rica do Ouro Preto in 1778, studied in São Paulo, Coimbra, and Lisbon. Returning to Brazil, he published the "Mappa do donativo voluntário. . . ."

3245. Leite, Serafim. Breve itinerário para uma biografia do P. Manuel da Nóbrega, fundador da província do Brasil e da cidade de São Paulo (1517-1570). Rio, Livros de Portugal, 1955. 267 p.
The author states that, because of the absence of complete documentation, it is at present impossible to write the definitive biography of Nóbrega. Nevertheless, until a better work appears, this will serve well.

3246. Lima, Augusto de. Notícias históricas (de norte a sul). Rio, Livros de Portugal, 1954. 351 p., illus.
Short, penetrating literary essays on various little-known aspects of Brazilian history to John VI. The author's stated purpose is to correct history as it is presently taught.

3247. Lins, Ivan Monteiro de Barros. Aspectos do Padre Antônio Vieira. Prefácio de M. Paulo Filho. Rio, Livraria São José, 1956. 390 p., illus.
An episodic but well-digested treatment of Vieira under six main topics. The last, "Philosopher and moralist," seems forced and reflects the author's own philosophical system.

3248. Mello, José Antônio Gonsalves de. Henrique Dias, governador dos pretos, crioulos e mulatos do Estado do Brasil. Recife, Brazil, Universidade do Recife, 1954. 71 p.
Henrique Dias, Pernambucan (d. 1661) played a major role in the fight against and the expulsion of the Dutch. Commander of the "black" troops, he becomes a *mestre do campo* and was honored by the king. This volume is another in the series written by the author for the Recife centenary of 1954 (see *HLAS, no. 19,* items 4050-4053).

3249. Nóbrega, Manuel da. Cartas do Brasil e mais escritos do . . . (Opera omnia). Com introdução e notas históricas e críticas de Serafim Leite. Coimbra, Portugal, Tip. da Atlántida, 1955. 570 p.
A new and complete edition of the letters from Brazil of Manuel da Nóbrega (1545-1568), a pioneer Jesuit in that country, who contributed greatly to the colonization. There are 42 autographs, original translations and copies, together with original text of letters in languages other

than Portuguese and some letters to Nóbrega. There are a scholarly introduction and extensive historical and critical notes. [R. R. Hill]

3250. Rau, Virginia, and Maria Fernanda Gomes da Silva (eds.). Os manuscritos do arquivo da Casa de Cadaval respeitantes ao Brasil. V. 1. Coimbra, Portugal, Atlântida, 1955, i. e. 1956. 540 p. & facsims.

The uncertain knowledge that the manuscript collection of the dukes of Cadaval was extremely rich in Brasiliana is confirmed by the appearance of the first volume of manuscripts relating to Brazil. This volume is divided into the 16th and 17th centuries and "documentos sem data." The first of the former is dated 1542, the last 1699. The documents are both public and private. Where their title does not indicate the contents, the editors give a short description. There is a useful index and a short introduction by Virginia Rau.

3251. Rio-Branco, Miguel Paranhos de. Alexandre de Gusmão e o Tratado de 1750. Rio, Ministério da Educação e Saúde, Serviço de Documentação (Os Cadernos de cultura), 1953. 60 p.

A useful summary of the activities of the Brazilian-born diplomat (1695-1752). Aside from his work in connection with the Treaty of Limits, he was a member of the delegation to the Congress of Cambrai, ambassador to Rome, and a promoter of the development of Rio Grande do Sul.

3252. Rodrigues, Edith Porchat. Informações históricas sôbre São Paulo no século de sua fundação (em ordem alfabética). São Paulo, Martins, 1956. 180 p.

A useful annotated topological, historical, but mainly biographical dictionary of 16th-century São Paulo. There is an extensive bibliography, a glossary of technical, Indian, and African terms, and a chronological index.

3253. Rodrigues, José Honório. Brasil, período colonial. México, Instituto Panamericano de Geografía e Historia, (Publ., 155, Comisión de Historia, 53), 1953. 175 p.

Part of the project of the History of America, this is a good summary of colonial Brazil, valuable for the bibliography.

3253a. São Paulo (state). **Departamento do Arquivo.** Documentos avulsos de interesse para a história e costumes de São Paulo. São Paulo, 1954-1955. V. 4, 1706-1822, 120 p.; v. 5, 1732-1822, 195 p.; v. 6, 1784-1821, 130 p.

A collection of documents from the Archive. Contains letters, orders, and decisions of the captain general; official proclamations and circulars; letters patent and proposals for appointment; testaments; land allotments; and other miscellaneous items dealing with the his-

tory of São Paulo The documents are in chronological order in each volume. [R. R. Hill]

3254. ————. ————. Documentos interessantes para a história e costumes de São Paulo. V. 80-82. Oficios do General Martim Lopes Lobo de Saldanha. 1777-1780. São Paulo, 1955-1956. 3 v. 189, 208, 215 p.

A continuation of item 4061 of *HLAS, no. 19.* Correspondence of the governor of São Paulo for the years indicated, dealing with the activities of the Captaincy. They reveal much regarding the life of 18th-century Brazil. [R. R. Hill]

3255. Silva, Alberto. Dos españoles en la historia del Brasil. Madrid, Ediciones Cultura Hispánica (Santo y seña, 13), 1953. 99 p.

Two short papers on the 16th-century Jesuit misionary, Antônio Blasquez, and on Don Fadrique, who retook Bahia from the Dutch in the 17th century.

3256. Taunay, Affonso de Escragnolle. A grande vida de Fernão Dias Pais. Rio, Olympio (Col. Documentos brasileiros, 83), 1955. 308 p., illus.

The life of the great *bandeirante* (1608-1681) who contributed so greatly to Brazilian and Paulista expansion. This is an extremely careful study which closely examines the legends surrounding Dias Pais' activities and death.

3257. ———— (ed.). Relatos sertanistas. São Paulo, Martins (Biblioteca histórica paulista, 7), 1953. 231 p., illus.

19 documents on the *bandeiras* into Minas Gerais with short notes and bibliographic essays by the editor.

3259. Wiznitzer, Arnold. The records of the earliest Jewish community in the New World. With a foreword by Salo W. Baron. N. Y., American Jewish Historical Society, 1954. 108 p., illus., port., maps, facsims.

The earliest Jewish community in the New World also became the earliest in the present U. S. The records in question are those of the communities of Recife and Mauricia. This edition contains the Minute Book of the Recife community, 1649-1653. It parallels but is more complete than the author's article in *Anais da Biblioteca Nacional*, 74, 1953, p. 213-240. There is a useful glossary.

EMPIRE

3260. Avé-Lallemant, Robert Christian Berthold. Viagem pelo sul do Brasil no ano de 1858. Tradução do Instituto Nacional do Livro [por Teodoro Cabra] da ed. de Leipzig, 1859. Rio, Instituto Nacional do Livro (Col. de obras raras, 4), 1953. 2 v. 398, 360 p., illus., port., facsim.

A good but incomplete edition of the author's *Reise durch Süd-Brasilien.* It is interesting because it presents a nationalistic German's observations on São Paulo, Santa Catarina, and Rio Grande do Sul. It is especially good for scenic description and for the German colonies.

3261. Barbosa, Rui. Obras seletas de . . . VI. Campanhas jornalísticas. Império, 1869-1889. Rio, Casa de Rui Barbosa, 1956. 245 p.

Rui's major articles during the last years of the Empire. Twenty-seven are from *Diario de notícias*, three from *Jornal do commércio*, two from *Diario da Bahia*, and one each from *O Pais* and *Radical paulistano*.

3262. Brazil. Serviço de Documentação Geral da Marinha. Subsídios para a história marítima do Brasil. V. XIII. Rio, 1955. 167 p.

This volume is almost exclusively devoted to a monograph by Lucas Alexandre Boiteux, "A Armada Imperial contraposta à confederação do Equador' " (p. 11-150), based on official documents. There is a bibliography but there are no citations.

3263. Dornas Filho, João. A propaganda republicana em Minas (Kriterion, 9:35-36, jan.-junho 1956, p. 199-233).

This article generally considers the activity of the Republican Party after 1870 and mainly concentrates on the post-1885 and especially post-1888 years when organized republicanism reached its greatest heights. There is much useful information.

3264. Girão, Raimundo. A abolição no Ceará. Fortaleza, Brazil, A. Batista Fentenele, 1956. 269 p.

A thorough description of the abolition movement in Ceara, the first province to liberate its slaves. Discussed are the successive manumission and propaganda societies, beginning in 1878, the propaganda itself, and the public ceremonies attendant to manumission. There are short biographies of the leading abolitionists.

3265. Gonçalves, Roberto Mendes. O Barão Hubner na Côrte de São Critovão. Rio, Ministério da Educação e Cultura, Serviço de Documentação (Os Cadernos de cultura, 75), 1955. 34 p.

Alexander Hübner, an Austrian diplomat, was minister to Argentina. He stopped in Rio in 1822 for a visit. Here are printed extracts from his unedited diary, including one of his interviews with Dom Pedro II.

3266. Magalhães Júnior, Raymundo (ed.). D. Pedro II e a Condessa de Barral, através da correspondência íntima do imperador, anotada e comentada. Rio, Editôra Civilização Brasileira, 1956. 436 p., ports., facsims.

A more than popular edition of the letters of Dom Pedro II to the *aia* of the Princesses Imperial. The countess became the intimate friend and perhaps the mistress of the Emperor. The intimacy of their friendship, while suspected and

a subject of gossip during the Empire, is now revealed. This edition is useful and was published primarily to give further divulgation of the Emperor's thoughts. It should result in a reevaluation of Dom Pedro II.

3267. Peretti, João (comp). Notícia breve do 2. reinado, numa troca de correspondência. Recife, Brazil, 1955. 180 p., ports.

"Separata da Revista do Instituto Arqueológico, Histórico e Geográfico Pernambucano, Vol. XLIII, anos de 1950 a 1953." Political and social life as described in letters to, and a few from, Anselmo Francisco Peretti (1812-1877), a Pernambucan who during his political career was a deputy, provincial president, president of the Tribunal do Comércio and president of the Tribunal da Relação. The letters cover the period April 1838 to December 1849. Among his correspondents were Felipe Lopes Neto, Herculano Alves da Silva, Sousa Franco, Paraná, Sinimbú, Manoel Felizardo Sousa e Mello, and Eusébio de Queiros.

3268. Sodré, Alcindo (ed.). Abrindo um cofre. Cartas de Dom Pedro II à Condessa Barral. Rio, Livros de Portugal, 1956. 331 p.

These are the same letters found in the edition by R. Magalhães Júnior (see item 3266). This edition is more attractively printed, but the former is more critical.

3269. Valladão, Alfredo. Vultos nacionais. Rio, Olympio, 1955. 533 p.

20 short but skillful analysis of various 19th-century figures, including Afonso Celso Júnior, Américo and Fernando Lobo, Nabuco, Lúcio de Mendonça, Eusébio de Queirós. Only rarely is there critical apparatus, but there is evidence of thoughtful penetration. The papers were originally presented in commemorative sessions at the Instituto Histórico and the Instituto dos Advogados, or in two instances as articles in the *Jornal do commércio*.

3270. Woodcock, George. The Brazilian Empire, an experiment in liberal monarchy (Hist Today, 6:6, June 1956, p. 404-413).

A short popular analysis of the role of the Empire, marred by frequent oversimplifications.

REPUBLIC

3271. Alexander, Robert J. Brazilian "Tenentismo" (HAHR, 36:2, May 1956, p. 229-242).

A study of the role the army officers have played in Brazilian politics since 1922-1942. Successful in the revolution of 1930, they were unable to control Getúlio Vargas. Some followed him, others went into the opposition. Revived in 1945, their candidates have been defeated in 1945, 1950, and 1955.

3272. Andrade, Rodrigo Melo Franco de. Rio-Branco e Gastão da Cunha. Rio, Instituto Rio-Branco, 1953. 281 p., illus.

Gastão da Cunha, a member of the Chamber where he first collaborated with Rio Branco, later entered diplomatic service. The treatment is necessarily sporadic but is well done. The study is mainly based on Parliamentary proceedings and on the family archives.

3273. Barbosa, Rui. Obras completas. V. 26, 1899. A imprensa. Rio, Ministério da Educação e Cultura, 1954. T. 3, 392 p.; t. 4, 410 p.

Rui's articles and editorials in the *Imprensa* from January 1 to April 30, 1899. T. 4 contains five appendices commenting on Rui's stand on various issues.

3274. ————. Obras completas. V. 28, 1901. T. 1. Discursos parlamentares. Rio, Ministério da Educação e Cultura, 1955. 240 p.

In appendices are three public letters explaining Rui's role in the Provisional Government and during the Naval Revolt. They were originally written to answer his critics.

3275. ————. Obras completas. V. 30, 1903. T. 1. Discursos parlamentares. Rio, Ministério da Educação e Cultura, 1956. 422 p.

The appendices include material on the election for the senate seat and a speech given to the graduating class of the Colégio Anchieta.

3276. ————. Obras completas. V. 31, 1904. T. 4. Limites entre o Ceará e o Rio Grande do Norte. Rio, Ministério da Educação e Cultura, 1954. 414 p. & map.

Rui was the lawyer for Rio Grande do Norte in the boundary question. His notes have been supplemented by those of José da Câmara, the editor.

3277. ————. Obras completas. V. 32, 1905. T. 1. Discursos parlamentares. Rio, Ministério da Educação e Cultura, 1955. 260 p.

Attached are Rui's political writings and extra-Parliamentary speeches of 1905.

3278. ————. Obras seletas. II-V. Tribuna parlamentar. República. Rio, Casa de Rui Barbosa, 1954-1955. 4 v. 463, 298, 274, 273 p.

Rui's more famous discourses in the Constitutional Convention and in the Senate until 1917, plus his speech on his resumption of the Senate seat in 1921.

3279. ————. Oração aos moços. Prefácio de Edgard Batista Pereira. Rio, Casa de Rui Barbosa, 1956. xxxvii, 100 p., facsims.

Critical edition of Rui's 1920 speech to the *formandi* of the São Paulo law school. The facsimile of the original publication of 1921 in the student journal *Dionysios*, no. 2, is also given.

3280. Brazil. Serviço de Documentação Geral da Marinha. Subsídios para a história marítima do Brasil. V. 12. Rio, 1953. 325 p. & illus.

This volume continues "A Marinha Brasileira e a segunda guerra mundial (1939-1945)," begun in v. 5 (see *HLAS, no. 11, 1945,* item 2652). It contains statistics, orders, communiques, operations, etc.

3281. Ferreira, Barros. Meio século de São Paulo. São Paulo, Edições Melhoramentos, 1954. 95 p., illus.

A commemorative popular guide to the social history of the last 50 years of São Paulo.

3282. Franco, Affonso Arinos de Mello. Um estadista da República: Afrânio de Mello Franco e seu tempo. Rio, Olympio (Col. Documentos brasileiros, 85), 1955. 3 v. V. 1, Fase provincial; v. 2, Fase nacional; v. 3, Fase internacional. 1704 p. & illus.

Afrânio de Mello Franco (1870-1943) achieved international reputation as a diplomat. He was the Permanent Ambassador to the League, and, with the Vargas regime, Minister of Foreign Affairs. He represented Brazil at frequent international conferences. Affonso de Mello Franco has achieved a major work in this biography which at the same time is a history of the epoch.

3283. Gerson, Brasil. Pequena história dos fanáticos do Contestado. Rio, Ministério da Educação e Cultura, Serviço de Documentação (Os Cadernos de cultura, 83), 1955. 59 p.

The Contestado movement in Santa Catarina and Parana, 1912-1916, was similar to that of Canudos. Largely, a blending of folk-catholicism and anti-republicanism, it was sporadic and difficult to overcome.

3284. Lacombe, Américo Jacobina. Rio Branco y Rui Barbosa. Versión castellana de José Alarcón Fernández. Rio de Janeiro, Casa de Rui Barbosa, 1955. 121 p., ports.

Spanish translation of a work originally published in 1948. A study of the relationship between the two men which began in 1889 with Rui's review of *Le Brésil* and continued until Rio Branco's death. Published here are letters and telegrams by both men, and editorials, etc., by Rui.

3285. Lobo, Hélio. Rio-Branco e o arbitramento com a Argentina; a questão do território de Palmas, também chamada das Missões. Rio, Olympio (Col. Documentos brasileiros, 69), 1952. 189 p.

In the first major step in his career, Rio Branco successfully presented Brazil's claim in this dispute which was arbitrated by Cleveland. Rio Branco's life in the U. S. (1893-1895) is fully treated. The work is based on private papers now in Itamaraty.

3286. Nogueira, Rubem. História de Ruy Barbosa. 1. ed. Salvador, Brazil, Progresso (Col. estudos brasileiros), 1954. 222 p., illus.

An introspective, highly sympathetic and episodic biography.

3287. Peregrino, Umberto. "Os sertões" como história militar. Rio, Biblioteca do Exército (Col. Taunay), 1956. 75 p.

Short examination of Euclydes da Cunha's value as a military historian. Quoting heavily from *Os sertões,* the author concludes that Cunha well fulfilled the requirements for a military historian (p. 24, 74).

3288. Rache, Pedro. Homens de Ouro Prêto. Memórias de um estudante. Rio, Coelho Branco, 1954. 182 p., illus.

The nostalgic recollections of a student from Rio Grande do Sul at the School of Mining in Ouro Preto during the years 1896-1900. The professors, fellow students, and student life are recalled. Most of the author's friends were *gaúchos,* among them the Vargas family. Getúlio makes a brief appearance.

3289. Roméro, Lauro. Clóvis Bevilaqua. Rio, Olympio, 1956. 371 p., illus.

Clóvis Bevilaqua was a professor of law, the author of the "Projecto do código civil," which occasioned the *Réplica* of Rui Barbosa, essayist, philosopher, and a member of the Permanent Court of Arbitration. Along with Sílvio Romero and others, he formed the Brazilian mind at the turn of the century. This work, which supersedes all others, is composed of a 109-page biographical sketch, followed by discussions of Bevilaqua as author, philosopher, lawyer, and sociologist. A complete bibliography is attached.

International Relations
Since 1830

BRYCE WOOD

ORGANIZATION OF AMERICAN STATES: GENERAL

3400. Barrera Reyes, Arturo. O. E. A., la Organización de Estados Americanos; medios pacíficos para la solución de conflictos interamericanos. México, Universidad Nacional Autónoma de México, Escuela Nacional de Jurisprudencia, 1955. 94 p.
A thesis for the law school of the Universidad Nacional Autónoma de México, dealing with procedures used by the OAS for pacific settlement.

3401. Canyes, Manuel. The Organization of American States and the United Nations. 3rd ed. Washington, Pan American Union, Division of Law and Treaties, 1955. 37 p.
Revision of a legal analysis of formal relationships between the OAS and the UN.

3402. Colombia. Ministerio de Relaciones Exteriores. Nota del gobierno de Colombia ante la Comisión Interamericana de Paz sobre el asilo de Víctor Raúl Haya de la Torre, presentada en Wáshington el día 18 de noviembre de 1953. Bogotá, Imp. Nacional, 1953. 33 p.
Besides the text of the title document, this collection contains the text of a Colombian note to Peru, July 7, 1953, and to the diplomatic representatives of the American states in Bogota of the same date; the reply of the Peruvian government, dated July 18, 1953, and text of a speech by the Colombian foreign minister to the OAS council, Nov. 16, 1953. All of these documents refer to the Haya de la Torre asylum case.

3403. Guerra Íñiguez, Daniel. El arbitraje de las disputas internacionales en América, según las previsiones de los tratados; estudio comparativo. Caracas, Colegio de Abogados del Distrito Federal (Publ., 2), 1956. 54 p.

An introductory review of the history of arbitration in the Americas, written from a legal point of view.

3404. Pan American Union. Division of Laws and Treaties. Applications of the Inter-American Treaty of Reciprocal Assistance, 1948-1956. Washington, 1957. 247 p.
Also in Spanish: *Aplicaciones del Tratado Internacional de Asistencia Recíproca, 1948-1955.* Official summary of the action of the OAS in the following cases: Costa Rica-Nicaragua, 1948-1949; request by Haiti, 1949; situation in the Caribbean, 1950; situation in Guatemala, 1954; Costa Rica and Nicaragua, 1955; request by Ecuador, 1955; This useful reference work contains many documents and a commentary on the Rio treaty.

3405. ————. ————. Las reuniones de consulta: origen, desarrollo y papel que desempeñan en las relaciones interamericanas, [por] Manuel Canyes. Washington, 1955. 17 p.
Official account of the history and procedural aspects of meetings of consultation of foreign ministers.

ORGANIZATION OF AMERICAN STATES: INTER-AMERICAN COUNCIL OF JURISTS

3406. Inter-American Council of Jurists. Inter-American Juridical Committee. Comparative study of the Bustamante code, the Montevideo treaties, and the restatement of the law of conflict of laws. Washington, Pan American Union, Department of International Law, 1954. 182 p. (CIJ, 21, Eng.)
A preliminary contribution to studies of the codification of international private law in the Americas.

3407. Inter-American Council of Jurists, III, Mexico, Jan. 17-Feb. 4, 1956. [Actas].

México, Secretaría de Relaciones Exteriores, 1956. 316 p.
Report of the Mexican delegation to the meeting, with short commentary and 300 pages of documents.

3408. ————. Mexico, Jan. 17-Feb. 4, 1956. Actas y documentos. V. 1. Actas de las sesiones de la Comisión I. Informes y proyectos. Washington, Unión Panamericana, 1956. 276 p.
This volume contains records of Commission I of the Council, which considered questions of territorial waters, and those relating to multilateral treaties. V. 2 is to include the final act and minutes of Commissions 2 and 3.

3409. Zorrilla de San Martín, Juan. Discursos, artículos y notas de derecho internacional público. Edición de homenaje a don Juan Zorrilla de San Martín en el centenario de su nacimiento. Montevideo, Universidad de Montevideo, Facultad de Derecho (Biblioteca de publ. oficiales, sección 3, 82), 1955. 228 p., illus.
The main body of this book, published in honor of Zorrilla de San Martín, consists of his newspaper articles on various legal and political topics. The last 23 pages contain notes for lectures on international law; the first part of the book contains appreciative essays of Zorrilla de San Martín's work.

ORGANIZATION OF CENTRAL AMERICAN STATES

3410. Reunión de Ministros de Relaciones Exteriores de las Repúblicas Centroamericanas. I, Antigua, agosto 1955. Actas taquigráficas de las sesiones plenarias de la primera reunión . . . Guatemala, 1955. 171 p.
This verbatim record of the meeting is of some interest because it includes texts of speeches; unfortunately, however, most of the text is unintelligible because it records discussions about articles of documents whose text is not in this volume.

PAN AMERICANISM

3411. Costa Rica. Ministerio de Relaciones Exteriores. Siglas internacionales. Trabajo de la Sección Centro América, Panamá, el Caribe y de Estudios Internacionales. San José, Imp. Nacional, 1954. 23 p.
A list of abbreviations of the Spanish names of some 500 public and private organizations and business firms, selected presumably for the Costa Rican newspaper reader, and organized more or less alphabetically. The list has possible reference value, but the defenders of older linguistic forms will no doubt hope its use need not become widespread.

3412. Cuevas Cancino, Francisco M. Del Congreso de Panamá a la Conferencia de Caracas 1826-1954. El genio de Bolívar a través de la historia de las relaciones interamericanas. Caracas, Ragon, 1955. 2 v. 300, 312 p.
See note to item 3419.

3413. Discursos pronunciados por los señores Presidentes de México y los Estados Unidos de América, el 19 de octubre de 1953, al inaugurar la Presa Falcón, obra de los dos países. México, Secretaría de Gobernación, 1953. 15 p.
Text of speeches at the dedication of the Falcon Dam.

3414. Mello, Affonso de Toledo Bandeira de. O espírito do Pan-Americanismo. Rio, Ministério das Relações Exteriores, Secção de Publicações, 1956. 91 p.
An essay on the origins and development of the spirit of Pan Americanism.

3415. Nabuco, Mauricio. Algumas reflexões sôbre diplomacia. Rio, Irmãos Pongetti, 1955. 101 p.
An admirable essay on the nature of the diplomatic career and the functions of diplomats, with observations on many topics such as the role of face saving among states.

3416. Panamá. Ministerio de Relaciones Exteriores. El libro de oro de la Reunión de Panamá. Panamá, 1956. 494 p., illus.
Official complete record of the meeting of the presidents of the American states in Panama on the occasion of the 130th anniversary of the Congress of Panama.

3417. Planas Suárez, Simón. La reunión de Panamá, juntamente la O. E. A. y los presidentes de las Repúblicas Americanas, cónclave misterioso y patente finalidad, notable comunicado de la Cancillería venezolana. Caracas, Tip. Garrido, 1956. 39 p.
This is a curious pamphlet, heavy with sarcasm, written shortly before the 1956 meeting of American presidents in Panama, and warning that the meeting would be the occasion for putting an end to the independence of the Latin American states.

3418. Valois Arce, Daniel. Realidad y teoría de la cooperación americanista en Bolívar. Bogotá, Imp. Municipal (Col. La cruz y la espada, 1), 1954. 36 p.
An essay in appreciation of Bolívar's contributions to Pan Americanism.

3419. Yepes, Jesús María. Del Congreso de Panamá a la Conferencia de Caracas, 1826-1954. El genio de Bolívar a través de la historia de las relaciones interamericanas. Caracas, Cromotip, 1955. 2 v. 263, 322 p.

This work gained first prize in an international competition organized by the Venezuelan government in 1952, as a feature of the preparation for the Caracas conference. The title of this work, like that of the accompanying study by Cuevas Cancino (see item 3412) which gained the second prize, is the theme of the competition in which 43 manuscripts were entered. Yepes' book is the more traditional, the more historical, and gives almost exclusive attention to Latin American interests in and influences upon the growth of Pan Americanism. The work by Cuevas Cancino, author of a recent study of the good neighbor policy, is analytical, rather than traditionally historical, and devotes one whole chapter to "The Good Neighborhood." Both works are worthy of study by scholars in the U. S. concerned with the history of ideas and institutions that share in the growth of inter-American collaboration.

POLICY OF THE UNITED STATES

3420. **Arévalo, Juan José.** Fábula del tiburón y las sardinas. América Latina estrangulada. B. A., Meridión (Col. América una, 1), 1956. 215 p.

The author, ex-president of Guatemala, attacks the U. S. and U. S. business enterprise in frenzied prose: "The press of the entire world, in all languages . . . is in the hands of the multimillionaires of New York" (p. 193). Dr. Arévalo, an ex-professor, presumably has calculated the propaganda value of such distortions.

3421. —————. Guatemala, la democracia y el imperio. 2. ed. Prólogo de Vicente Sáenz. México, América Nueva (Col. Autores contemporáneos, 1), 1954. 144 p.

This tract by the former Guatemalan president was written between June 20 and June 27, 1954, during the revolution against the government of President Arbenz. The book's theme is denunciation of the policy of the U. S. toward Guatemala as imperialistic and as desiring the maintenance of the "Balkanization" of Central America.

3422. **Bingham, Jonathan B.** Shirt-sleeve diplomacy; Point 4 in action. N. Y., Day, 1954. 303 p., illus.

A breezy, entertaining, and optimistic account of activities undertaken by the U. S. government in the field of technical assistance in Latin America and elsewhere.

3423. **Brown, William Adams, Jr.,** and **Redvers Opie.** American foreign assistance. Washington, Brookings Institution, 1953. 615 p.

A scholarly history of economic and military assistance by the U. S. in World War II and after, with several references to Latin America.

3424. **Carnero Checa, Genaro.** El águila rampante; el imperialismo yanqui sobre

América Latina. México, Ediciones Semanario Peruano, 1956. 366 p.

A survey, country by country, intended to demonstrate the need for "the second war of independence, against Yankee imperialism." Is Colombia in a fratricidal civil war? The allegation is that it is because Washington controls the Colombian army, etc. The exaggerations in this and similar works may affront the intelligence of some readers; at the same time the exaggeration represents an intensity of anti-U. S. feeling that should be examined and understood by scholars and others in the U. S.

3425. **Galich, Manuel.** Por qué lucha Guatemala. Arévalo y Arbenz: dos hombres contra un imperio. B. A., Elmer, 1956. 374 p.

A former foreign minister of Guatemala in the Arbenz administration reviews the history of Guatemala since 1944 and attacks the alleged intervention of the U. S. in the revolution against Arbenz in 1954. This is a more responsible work than some of those written on this subject. There is an interesting list (p. 234) of Latin American diplomats who in Galich's opinion have not been "lobbyists" for the U. S. at inter-American conferences.

3426. **Hanson, Simon G.** The end of the good-neighbor policy (Interam Ec Aff, 7:2, autumn 1953, p. 3-49).

A well-informed commentator on Latin American affairs charges that the foundations of the good-neighbor policy are in danger of destruction principally as a result of economic policies adopted after 1952.

3427. —————. The good-partner policy (Interam Ec Aff, 10:2, autumn 1956, p. 45-96).

A bitingly critical review of the "good partner" policy as applied since 1952 and an unfavorable comparison of this policy with that of the "good neighbor." Especial attention is given to recent policies in economic relations with Bolivia and Brazil.

3428. **Leopold, Richard William.** Elihu Root and the conservative tradition. Boston, Little, Brown (The Library of American biography), 1954. 222 p.

The author, a professor of history at Northwestern University, devotes several pages to Root's "trail-blazing role as the twentieth century's first good neighbor."

3429. **National Planning Association.** Technical cooperation in Latin America—recommendations for the future, by the NPA Special Policy Committee on Technical Cooperation. Washington, 1956. 192 p., tables. (NPA reports on technical cooperation in Latin America).

Based on other studies by the association, this volume surveys economic development and cultural change in Latin America, the nature of technical cooperation, and programs of technical cooperation operating in Latin America. Recommendations for improvement of programs are given in some 70 pages, and 55 pages are devoted to statistical tables of funds expended, by country and by field.

3430. Peña Batlle, Manuel Arturo. Política de Trujillo. Prefacio de E. Rodríguez Demorizi. Ciudad Trujillo, Impresora Dominicana, 1954. 204 p., illus.
Collection of essays and articles by former Dominican diplomat, described in the preface by E. Rodríguez Demorizi as a "perfect expositor" of the thought of Trujillo. Among articles with such titles as "Exaltation of the era of Trujillo," is one on alleged interventionist activities of Ellis O. Briggs and Spruille Braden in refusing a Dominican request to buy arms in the U. S.

3431. Ramírez Novoa, Ezequiel. La farsa del panamericanismo y la unidad indoamericana. B. A., Indoamérica, 1955. 215 p.
The author is described on this book's jacket as a Peruvian lawyer and a young Aprista. Panamericanism is regarded as a policy of the U. S. aimed at the promotion of "painless imperialism" in Latin America; the good neighbor policy is said to be no more than Washington's adaptation to the depression and the anticipated World War II.

3432. Taylor, Philip B., Jr. The Guatemalan affair: a critique of United States foreign policy (Am Pol Sci R, 50:3, Sept. 1956, p. 787-807).
The author disapproves of the policy of the U. S. in Guatemala and in the United Nations in 1954; he charges the U. S. government with "intervention," and states that "Guatemala's geographic position relative to the United States and to the Panama Canal renders rather unreasonable a statement that even a thoroughgoing Communist government could have been a substantial threat to the security of the United States" (p. 804). On the latter point, many may well disagree; on the former, no evidence is offered that the Castillo forces were armed by the U. S. government, and of course no U. S. military personnel took part in the fighting. Is it not time that scholars in the U. S. give a more discriminating definition to "intervention" than one which includes the varied forms of influence short of the use of force?

3433. United States. Department of State. Military assistance to Latin America. Washington, 1953. 7 p. (Publ., 4917; Inter-American series, 44; Background).
An official explanation and defense of the military assistance policies of the U. S.

3434. Warren, Harris G. Diplomatic relations between the United States and Argentina (Interam Ec Aff, 8:3, winter 1954, p. 63-83).
A review of Argentine-U. S. relations in the post-World War II period, spiced with some critical comments on the policy of the U. S. Department of State.

POLICY OF OTHER COUNTRIES

3435. Castañeda, Jorge. México y el orden internacional. México, Colegio de México, 1956. 245 p.
This book is an important statement of the views of a group of Mexican teachers, officials, and diplomats on the general features of Mexican foreign policy, particularly as related to the issues presented by membership in the UN and the OAS. This is the Spanish version of a book to be published in English by the Carnegie Endowment for International Peace. Of special interest here is the critical view taken of recent policies of the U. S. in inter-American affairs. The conclusion is reached that if the Rio treaty of 1947 were used "contrary to its purpose, as a means of intervening in the internal affairs of the American states," Mexico should seriously consider denouncing the Rio treaty. The presumed reference here is to possible use of the treaty to prevent a communist regime from gaining power in an American state.

3436. Galíndez, Jesús de. La era de Trujillo. Un estudio casuístico de dictadura hispanoamericana. Santiago, Editorial del Pacífico, 1956. 452 p.
The author of this book has disappeared, and public suspicion that he was kidnapped in N. Y. on orders of the Dominican government has been expressed in the press and the House of Representatives of the U. S. Congress. The preface to this work states that the writing of it cost Galíndez his life. The first 200 pages contain a history of the era of Trujillo, 1930-1955. The second part of the book is an analysis of the Trujillo regime and includes chapters on "A parody of constitutionalism," elections, social organization, "Personal style of the tyrant," international relations, and chapters on both the positive achievements of the regime and domestic and foreign criticism of it.
This book does not contain the documentation which presumably accompanied the manuscript when it was presented as a thesis for the degree of doctor of philosophy at Columbia University, nor does it have an index. This latter omission is particularly unfortunate in a work of great specificity as to names of persons and organizations, and as to dates and places of incidents.
Galíndez' work is of value, not only to those who wish to understand what the Trujillo dictatorship is like, but also to those who wish to understand the phenomenon of Latin American dictatorships in general, for there is much here on the techniques of tyranny. After a perusal of this book, one hopes that the preface is in error in stating that the Trujillo dictatorship "is not unique in America, but it is the most typical."

3437. Magnet, Alejandro. Nuestros vecinos argentinos. Santiago, Editorial del Pacífico (Col. América), 1956. 427 p.
A serious and critical study of the Perón regime by a Chilean commentator, with particular reference to Argentine-Chilean relations.

3438. Menezes, Adolpho Justo Bezerra de. O Brasil e o mundo ásio-africano. Prefácio de João Neves da Fontoura. Rio, Irmãos Pongetti, 1956. 400 p., illus.

The author, a Brazilian diplomat, discusses problems of colonialism and East-West relations. The chief interest of the book is in its exposition of an anticipated place for Brazil as a mediator between white and colored peoples, the developer of a new man, "homo brasiliensis," whose virtues may in time become those of men in countries far from Brazil. India is compared unfavorably to Brazil as the great mediating nation.

3439. Planas Suárez, Simón. Venezuela soberana: panamericanista no regionalista. Caracas, Tip. Americana, 1954. 456 p.

A collection of articles attacking bitterly all manifestations of a regional grouping of northwestern South American states, including the Flota Mercante Grancolombiana, and demanding the maintenance of the complete independence of Venezuela within the confines, if such they be, of the Pan American system.

3440. Rodríguez Demorizi, Emilio. Trujillo y Cordell Hull: un ejemplo de política panamericanista. Ciudad Trujillo, Editora del Caribe, 1956. 33 p.

A collection of statements by Trujillo, and accounts of his visits to the U. S. between 1939 and 1956; included are a few notes of thanks from Hull in response, for example, to Trujillo's message on Hull's retirement. This is a curious study in diplomatic psychology.

3441. Suárez, Marco Fidel. El derecho internacional en los "sueños de Luciano Pulgar." Doctrinas internacionales. Bogotá, Biblioteca Marco Fidel Suárez (2), 1955. 275 p.

This book consists of 10 chapters concerned with various phases of international law and politics. The chapters are in the form of conversations between unknown diplomats and this form allows the author, formerly foreign minister of Colombia, considerable freedom to express his opinions of the policies of other countries, and their policies. Most of these conversation pieces appear to have been written between 1910 and 1920.

TERRITORIAL QUESTIONS

3442. Cabeza de Vaca, Manuel. Aspectos históricos y jurídicos de la cuestión limítrofe. Las negociaciones en Washington y los desenvolvimientos posteriores. Quito, Tall. Gráf. Nacionales, 1956. 151 p.

A serious, pro-Ecuadoran account of the boundary conflict with Peru, containing many documents of interest to scholars, particularly on the 1940-1941 period. On the question of the time for cessation of hostilities scheduled for July 26, 1941, the author states that the Argentine, Brazilian, and U. S. ministers in Quito "insisted" that the Ecuadoran government revoke its mobilization decree as demanded by Peru. It is unfortunate that the author gives no citations whatever for the quoted documents, although he says all of them have been previously made public.

3443. Carbajal, Carlos. La plataforma sub-marina del Uruguay. Montevideo, El Siglo Ilustrado, 1956. 78 p., illus.

An Uruguayan admiral describes the Uruguayan continental shelf as including an area of about 50,000 km. sq., and recommends that Uruguay make formal claim to control its continental shelf and the resources it may contain.

3444. Diez de Medina, Eduardo. De un siglo al otro. Memorias de un hombre público. La Paz, Don Bosco, 1955. 466 p., illus.

Memoirs of a noted Bolivian diplomat and minister of foreign affairs. He states his case for having opposed the Chaco War. There is more emphasis given here to formal ceremonies, banquets, and *homenajes* than to the fundamental problems of policy with which the author was connected.

3445. Fronteras y demarcación política del Perú. Chorrillos, Perú, Librería del Centro de Instrucción Militar del Perú, 1953. 62 p.

The Peruvian frontiers described in terms of the names of geographical points; there are no maps or even sketches in this pamphlet.

3446. Moreno, Juan Carlos. Nuestras Malvinas. La Antártida. 7. ed., aumentada y actualizada. B. A., El Ateneo (Col. Cultura universal), 1956. 282 p., illus.

The first edition of this work appeared in 1938, and its use as a text in Argentine schools has been authorized. It combines history, geography, accounts of travels, and reflections to the effect that Great Britain must recognize the Argentine sovereignty over the Falklands.

3447. Whitaker, Arthur P. Anticolonialism in Latin America (Orbis, 1:1, Apr. 1957, p. 51-76).

A review of attitudes prevalent in Latin America that oppose political, military, and economic colonialism, and that identify the chief exponent of such colonialism as the U. S. The author raises some disturbing issues as to the state of inter-American solidarity.

TREATY COLLECTIONS

3448. Carnegie Endowment for International Peace. Division of International Law. Conferencias internacionales americanas. Segundo suplemento, 1945-1954. Washington, Unión Panamericana, Departamento Jurídico, 1956. 451 p.

Continuing its useful documentary work, the Endowment here publishes, for the conferences of Chapultepec, Rio (1947), Bogota, Washington (1951), and Caracas, the agendas, rules of procedure, personnel of delegations and secretariats, and texts of resolutions, conventions, treaties, etc.

3449. El Salvador. Ministerio de Relaciones Exteriores. Tratados centroamericanos de libre comercio suscritos por El Salvador, Honduras, Nicaragua, Gua-

temala, Costa Rica. San Salvador, 1953. 123 p.
Texts of trade treaties from 1918-1953.

3450. Honduras. Secretaría de Relaciones Exteriores. Tratados internacionales. T. 1. Período colonial, República Federal de Centro América y tratados bilaterales con Costa Rica. Tegucigalpa, 1954. 515 p.
The first volume of a series intended to provide a full record of Honduran adhesion to bilateral and multilateral treaties and international acts. The present volume includes texts of treaties and other documents from 1493 to 1843, and texts of treaties with Costa Rica from 1839 to 1904.

3451. Organization of American States. Inter-American treaties and conferences. Firmas, ratificaciones y depósitos con notas explicativas. Washington, Pan American Union (Serie sobre derecho y tratados), 1954. 100 p.
This publication provides detailed information including dates of ratification, and supplements the tables given in item below.

3452. Pan American Union. Division of Law and Treaties. Status of the Pan American treaties and conventions. Washington, 1954. 31 p., tables. (Law and treaty series).
Reissue of this useful reference pamphlet.

3453. Venezuela. Ministerio de Relaciones Exteriores. Libro amarillo de la república de Venezuela presentado al Congreso Nacional en sus sesiones ordinarias de 1956 por el Ministro de Relaciones Exteriores. Caracas, 1956. cxcvi, 515 p.
Report of the Minister of Foreign Affairs for the calendar year 1954. There are some 200 pages of general description of the work of the ministry, and 500 pages of texts of speeches, treaties, and other documents. It is of interest to observe that this ministry appears to have very little to do with petroleum problems.

3454. ————. Tratados públicos y acuerdos internacionales de Venezuela. V. 8. 1944-1947. Caracas, Ragon, 1955. 702 p.
Texts of bilateral and multilateral treaties to which Venezuela is a party; this is the first of four volumes planned to include treaties in the period 1944-1955.

3455. ————. Tratados públicos y acuerdos internacionales de Venezuela. V. 9. 1947-1952. Caracas, 1956. 870 p., illus.
Ninth volume in a series containing unannotated texts of bilateral and multilateral treaties.

Labor and Social Welfare

LABOR

THOMAS F. MOSIMANN

3500. Abello Roca, Carlos Daniel. Inspecciones de trabajo. Barranquilla, Colombia, Editora Barranquilla, 1955. 222 p.
Thesis, Xaverian University, Bogota. The functions of the labor inspection offices of Colombia. No index is provided.

3501. Alba, Víctor. Esquema histórico del movimiento obrero en América Latina. México, Costa-Amic (Col. Panoramas, 8), 1957. 155 p.
The preface states that this small book was a preparatory essay for the author's recent and more extensive work on Latin American labor (see *HLAS, no. 19*, item 4300). Alba's flair for condensing and summarizing the activities of complex groups of individuals and organizations over long periods gets free rein. Will be found informative and useful even by those who do not accept all the analyses and conclusions of this well-known Socialist writer.

3502. Ángel, Ángel de. Contabilidad para sindicatos de obreros. Río Piedras, Puerto Rico, Universidad de Puerto Rico, Instituto de Relaciones del Trabajo, 1956. 104 p.
The author, a lecturer in accounting at the University of Puerto Rico, has prepared a book, admirably planned and presented, to convey the practical principles of simple accounting procedures for the use of labor unions. An excellent book which deserves wide circulation among those it is designed to serve.

3503. Angulo A., Jorge M. Manual de legislación del trabajo y previsión social. Trujillo, Perú, Universidad Nacional de Trujillo (Biblioteca Carlos Pedemonte y Talavera, 5, Textos universitarios, 1), 1954. 262 p.
Another addition to the number of excellent books presenting and interpreting Peruvian labor law. Intended as a text and manual, its presentation is logically and systematically developed. Chapters relate to the labor contract; matters relating to work; matters relating to remuneration: matters affecting "empleados," matters affecting "obreros," indemnification; women and children;

the victim of accident and disease; safety and social security; and state intervention. A subject index is provided.

3504. Argentina. Ministerio de Trabajo y Previsión. Anuario de legislación social argentina. B. A., 1955? 1021 p.
Texts of the laws, decrees, and decisions of government agencies promulgated in 1951 relating to labor and social legislation. Indexes are provided for the years 1943-1950 which give, by number of the law or decree, references to the issue of *Revista de trabajo y previsión* in which they have been published.

3505. La Confederación de Trabajadores de América Latina (C. T. A. L.) y la Federación Sindical Mundial. Estudio sobre la explotación comunista. 2. ed. México, Ediciones Occidentales, 1955? 45 p.
Detailed study of Communist influence in the CTAL and FSM (WFTU).

3506. Dominican Republic. Departamento de Trabajo. Revista del trabajo. Ciudad Trujillo. 2. época, año 1, no. 1, enero-marzo 1956-.
Articles on labor philosophy and current events. Contains a section on recent labor legislation.

3507. El Salvador. Ministerio de Trabajo y Previsión Social. Recopilación de leyes de trabajo promulgadas hasta marzo de 1952. No. 2. San Salvador, 1953? 60 p.

3509. Galarza, Ernesto. Strangers in our fields. Washington, U. S. Section, Joint United States — Mexico Trade Union Committee, 1956. 80 p., illus.
A description of the Mexican contract labor program primarily from the viewpoint of the worker himself. Chapters are included on housing, earnings, food, and other items covered by the general contract specified under the international executive agreement between the U. S. and Mexico. Various instances of violation of the contract terms are cited. The pamphlet

pleads for full recognition by employers of the workers' rights and more effective compliance inspection.

3510. Guatemala. Ministerio de Gobernación. Código de trabajo. Decreto no. 330 del Congreso y sus reformas contenidas en decreto no. 570 del Presidente de la República. Guatemala, 1956. 245 p.

The labor code of Guatemala as revised in February 1956.

3511. International Labour Office. Minimum wages in Latin America. Geneva, 1954. 184 p. (Studies and reports, n. s., 34).

This 1954 study will remain an essential reference work for the study of minimum wage systems in Latin America. The introduction states: "Legislation providing for the regulation of minimum wages now exists in almost all of the Latin American countries, and some machinery designed to carry out the provisions of such legislation is in operation in the majority of them. The present volume gives, in part 1, a comparative survey of these systems of wage regulation and, in part 2, a series of short studies on the systems in existence in the various individual countries." Part 2 includes sections on all Latin American countries except Honduras.

3512. Lacerda Filho, Nobre de. Homens, saúde e trabalho. Rio, Organização Simões, 1956. 166 p.

In this little book the author approaches, in rather popular style but with serious analysis, the problem of industrial safety. Discusses some causes of accidents, various standards for factory inspection, how statistics of accidents should be compiled, and even gives some interesting examples of the use of Brazilian folklore in safety propaganda. Readable and instructive.

3513. Landerreche Obregón, Juan. Participación de los trabajadores en las utilidades de las empresas. México, Jus, 1956. 257 p.

This excellent book discusses the principles behind profit-sharing plans and describes briefly recent profit-sharing plans in Latin America, Eastern Europe, the U. S. and Canada. The author, having established that "profit-sharing has not always failed in practice," devotes the second half of his book to a study of the principles and problems involved in setting up such plans in Mexico in the light of current institutions and attitudes.

3514. México. Instituto Técnico Administrativo del Trabajo. Boletín del . . . México. 1. época, no. 1, 1956-.

Bulletin commemorating the opening of the Instituto Técnico Administrativo del Trabajo (ITAT) under the auspices of the ILO and the government of Mexico. Description and functions of the Institute. Articles on labor law, safety, labor administration, and the history of labor inspection in Mexico.

3515. México. Secretaría del Trabajo y Previsión Social. Memoria de labores, enero a diciembre de 1956. México, 1957. 137 p. & tables.

A yearbook of the Secretaría. Statistical data presented in the annexed tables include: estimates of total national income and total wages and salaries through 1955, indexes of wages in industries under Federal jurisdiction through 1956, cost-of-living indexes for 18 areas, data on wages and wage changes in establishments which revised their contracts with the intervention of the Secretaría during 1956, industrial accidents statistics, strike statistics and related data, comprehensive data on establishments under Federal jurisdiction, weekly earnings 1952-1956 for certain industries, statistics of labor inspection, and other administrative statistics. The labor statistics, in particular, are accompanied by explanatory and useful footnotes.

3516. Ortega Ramos, Virginia. Protección a la mujer en el derecho del trabajo. México, Tip. Ortega, 1955. 120 p.

Thesis, University of Mexico.

3517. Ortiz de la Roche, Mario. Derecho laboral colombiano. 1. parte. El contrato de trabajo. Medellín, Colombia, Editorial Universidad de Antioquia, 1955. 464 p.

The labor code of Colombia is discussed in detail in this exhaustive work. The major part of the book is devoted to the labor contract, its concepts, and interpretation. The exegesis includes comments on the philosophical and historical developments of the concepts and opinions from other legal authorities. In addition to the treatise on the labor contract, separate chapters relate to social benefits to the worker, obligatory rest periods, paid vacations, benefits paid by employers, industrial accidents and diseases, and the management of a corporation in relation to Colombian labor law.

3518. Pla Rodríguez, Américo. El salario en el Uruguay; su régimen jurídico. Montevideo, Universidad de Montevideo, Facultad de Derecho y Ciencias Sociales (Biblioteca de publ. oficiales, Sección 3, 83), 1956. 2 v. 693, 684 p.

Submitted as a thesis to the Faculty of Law and Social Sciences of the University of Montevideo. The first volume outlines the historical development of the juridical aspects of wage problems in Uruguay. The second adopts an impressive systematic development of the basic concepts, definitions, and applications. The discussion cites legislation, jurisprudential decisions and commentary by the author. An extensive work of more than 1200 pages that should have great value for legal reference. Three indexes are included: an index of authors, an analytic index by subject, and a "general index" or outline of the book by titles of sections.

3519. Poblete Troncoso, Moisés. La economía agraria de América Latina y el trabajador campesino. Santiago, Universidad de Chile, 1953. 314 p.

This most recent work of the author draws to some extent upon his earlier works. In scope this book covers three broad phases of its topic:

(1) agriculture and the economic structure of Latin America; (2) the agricultural laborer from pre-Conquest days to the present; (3) modern problems of the agricultural worker. Such breadth of theme carries with it its own difficulties. The author, however, has included an impressive amount of background information and analytical comment. The statistical data included obviously have been selected with some care and from comparatively reliable sources, such as censuses and special economic studies, although at the time of writing data from the censuses of 1950 were not available.

3520. Pontes, Ribeiro. Acidentes do trabalho. Comentarios. Rio? Livraria Freitas Bastos, 1955. 230 p.

Authoritative detailed commentary on the legislation concerning industrial accidents in Brazil.

3521. Revista jurídica del trabajo. Folleto jurídico. 1956 ed. Santiago, 1957. 190 p.

Current issue of an established publication summarizing Chilean labor law, jurisprudence, and opinions of various state agencies in the field of labor for 1956.

3522. Salazar, Rosendo. Historia de las luchas proletarias de México. 1930-1936. México, Tall. Gráf. de la Nación, 1956. 272 p.

In an earlier work of the same title, published 1938, the author established the form which is followed also in this volume, that of a day-by-day chronology. Under each date he describes and comments upon important labor events, such as strikes, legal rulings, acts of prominent labor officials and organizations. The earlier volume covered the period 1923-1929. The present volumn covers the years 1930-1936.

3523. Stern, Bernardo; Camilo Almarza; José Domenech; and **Roberto Testa.** Prescindencia. Economía y política en el movimiento obrero. B. A., Ateneo Democrático de Trabajadores, 1956. 46 p.

A brochure, somewhat in the form of an open letter to the president of Argentina, analyzing the economic problems facing the workers, particularly the problem of inflation. In view of the scarcity of published expressions of trade union

opinion since the fall of Perón, this booklet is timely and interesting. The author speaks against "monetary inflation" caused by the excessive issuance of paper money, and does not concede that there is an "inflation of wages and salaries." He speaks principally for higher productivity in the broad sense which takes into account all factors of production, and advocates also a reduction in the number of government employees. Since the authors are themselves members of the railway union and are connected with an industry which itself in recent years has acquired an excessive number of workers, the publication represents a courageous attempt at objective analysis.

3524. United States. Bureau of Labor Statistics. Labor in Chile. Washington, 1956. 18 p. & tables. (Foreign labor information).

3525. ————. ————. Labor in Cuba. Washington, 1957. 26 p. (Foreign labor information).

3526. ————. Department of Labor. Latin American labor legislation; comparative studies of selected provisions. Washington, 1956. 60 p. (Foreign labor information).

The U. S. Department of Labor publishes at intervals bulletins describing labor organization, legislation, and practice in other countries of the world.

3527. Universidad Central del Ecuador. Revista de derecho social ecuatoriano. Quito. Año 4, no. 12-15, 1955. 245 p.

Quarterly. Two articles are of special interest. One of these, "A half-century of labor law in Ecuador," by Hugo Valencia, is the first chapter of a forthcoming work on labor law (available also as a reprint). The other, entitled "Juridical labor dictionary and alphabetical index," is the first section (A-E) of a glossary of labor terms with jurisprudential references. The author states his hope that the book, of which this is a part, will be a manual for interested persons, including workers who wish to understand the labor code of Ecuador.

SOCIAL WELFARE
CARL H. FARMAN

GENERAL

3551. Comité Interamericano de Seguridad Social. Estudio preliminar de un plan común de trabajo para el servicio estadístico del seguro social del continente americano (Estadística, 13:47, junio 1955, p. 291-307).

"The first part of the study deals with general and economic statistics relating to social insurance as a whole; the second, with the principal aspects of particular insurance statistics, classified according to risk; and the third, with the

possible relation between social insurance statistics and other general national statistics." The III Inter-American Statistical Conference sent copies of a preprint of this to the governments and social security agencies of the hemisphere for review and comment. The report was originally presented at Rio in 1947.

3552. Congreso Iberoamericano de Seguridad Social, II. Actas y trabajos. Lima, Comisión Iberoamericana de Seguridad Social, 1954. 3 v. 289, 397, 221 p.

This encyclopedic compilation contains significant information on social security in many countries of Latin America (as well as Portugal and Spain), including Argentina, Bolivia, Chile, Costa Rica, Cuba, the Dominican Republic, Ecuador, Honduras, Paraguay, Peru, and Venezuela. In v. 1, the treatment is expository and general; in v. 2, the programs are considered in relation to the subject matter of technical committees: social insurance in agriculture, financial issues, conservation of the rights of migratory workers, and educational aspects of social security.

3553. Cordero, Armando. La reunión internacional de seguridad social celebrada en Guatemala (Seg Soc, Ciudad Trujillo, 8:52, nov.-dic. 1956, p. 9-12).
See also item 3584.

3554. Cubas, Emilio. Desarrollos recientes en el campo de la seguridad social (1953-1955). V. 2. América. México, Conferencia Interamericana de Seguridad Social, 1956. 202 p. (XII Asamblea General de la Asociación Internacional de la Seguridad Social, México, nov.-dic. de 1955).
Outlines for each American nation the main provisions of social insurance legislation in 1953, and follows this with a chapter on 1953-1955 developments. Each country's programs are thus reviewed in two places, with a division in time dictated largely by the fact that the ISSA emphasizes periodic reports. The author is director of the Instituto de Previsión Social, Paraguay, and his work is a valuable reference volume.

3555. El curso iberoamericano de racionalización y mecanización de los servicios administrativos de la seguridad social (R Iberoam Seg Soc, 5:3, mayo-junio 1956, p. 563-668).
This course was held in Bogota in June 1956 with the aim of promoting interchange of ideas and expert advice on this phase of social security administration. 25 administrative agencies from 11 Latin American countries and Spain were represented by 48 experts. The account gives the reports (and reporting individuals and committee members) on registration of employers and workers, contributions, benefits, accounting, fiscal control, and statistics.

3556. La XII asamblea general y las reuniones de la A. I. S. S. en México (Seg Soc, México, 5:19, enero-feb. 1956, p. 5-19).
Briefly summarizes the character and results of the first meeting in the Western Hemisphere of the International Social Security Association, whose headquarters are in Geneva, and which has close links with the International Labour Office and the Inter-American Social Security Conference. Other articles in this issue are from the sessions; they include a brief review of recent developments in social security in the countries of America by Emilio Cubas, notes on Mexican hospitality by Lucien Van Maele, and the text of the resolutions adopted by the Twelfth General Meeting. (See also item 3554). Photographic illustrations.

3557. Farman, Carl H. World trends in social security benefits, 1935-55 (Soc Sec B, 19:5 May 1956, p. 18-22).
Tables show for all countries the kinds of social security programs operating in 1935 and 1955, with dates of the first laws in each case. The text traces new developments over this relatively recent period, and because the nations of the Americas were exceptionally active in that time they are well represented in this concise world survey.

3558. Güell P., Cipriano. Importancia socio-económica de la seguridad social en los países de Centroamerica, México y el Caribe (Seg Soc, México, 5:24, nov.-dic. 1956, p. 23-29).
Based chiefly on data for Costa Rica, of whose Social Security Fund the author is manager, this paper notes the social significance as found chiefly in the medical and rehabilitation services provided by social security, and the economic services in the cash benefits for both short-term risks and for pensions, as well as in the investments made possible by utilizing the reserves accumulated under old-age, invalidity, and survivor's insurance.

3559. Inter-American Conference on Social Security, V, Caracas, 1955. Memoria de labor. Caracas, 1955.

3559a. Marti Bufill, Carlos. Crónica de la Reunion de Organismos de Seguridad Social de Centroamérica, México y el Caribe (R Iberoam Seg Soc, 5:6, nov.-dic. 1956, p. 1405-1423).
Notes the composition, topics studied, and conclusions of this conference, called at the invitation of Guatemala and attended by the representatives of 11 nations and Puerto Rico. The two main themes were the economic and social importance of social security and, secondly, health insurance. See also item 3563.

3560. Miró, Carmen A. Estatísticas da previdência social: objetivos, âmbito e programa mínimo. Washington, Instituto Interamericano de Estatística (Documento de trabalho, grupo II, Social: (4a) Estatísticas da previdência social; III Conferência Interamericana de Estatística, Quintandinha, Petrópolis, Brasil, junho 9-22, 1955), 1955. 19 p.
A technical paper by the director general of Panamanian statistics giving minimum standards of social insurance reporting for each type of benefit. Includes a bibliography and a list of social insurance institutions in the countries of North and South America.

3561. Oficina Iberoamericana de Seguridad Social. Primer ciclo de conferencias de intercambio técnico. Madrid, Instituto de Cultura Hispánica, 1956. 145 p.
Contains six papers, one in the field of medical social work, the others on social security. They are: "Biblioterapia en las instituciones hospi-

talarias," by Natalia Miranda (Spain); "El seguro social obrero en Chile," by Fernando Toro Garland (Chile); "Cooperativismo y seguridad social," by Eduardo Bel Escalona (Chile); "La seguridad social, de Versailles a Filadelfia," by Julio Lozano Hurtado (Colombia); "La seguridad social en el Perú," by Carlos Manuel Chávez Gutiérrez (Peru); and "Los infortunios laborales en la legislación chilena," by Rubén Mera Manzano (Chile).

3562. Organización Iberoamericana de Seguridad Social. Conclusiones y recomendaciones del curso de cooperación técnica actuarial celebrado en Madrid del 20 de octubre al 20 de diciembre de 1955 (R Iberoam Seg Soc, 5:1, enero-feb. 1956, p. 111-116).

World trends that affect social security institutions include inflation, population growth, and greater longevity. Each of these issues is the subject of several recommendations, the text of which is here given. The participants also offered a group of general suggestions on matters of administration, work injury insurance, extension of coverage to agriculture, benefits for dependents, and related matters.

3563. Reunión de organismos de seguridad social de Centro América, México y el Caribe (Seg Soc, México, 5:24, nov.-dic. 1956, p. 3-22, 131).

This entire issue is devoted to the Guatemalan meeting of October 1956, which included presentation of several papers that are noted elsewhere under the authors. The basic information here cited notes membership, has some general speeches, and contains the text of the conclusions of the conference. See also item 3550.

3564. Seminario Americano de Actuarios de Seguridad Social, I, Asunción, abril-mayo 1957. Estadísticas y bases actuariales de la seguridad social. (Informe sobre el Tema "A"). México, Conferencia Interamericana de Seguridad Social, Secretaría General (Cuaderno, 1), 1957. 56 p.

Contains recommendations on statistics for each type of social insurance program, including the basic data considered necessary and likewise the method of collecting and presenting the information and analyzing the costs of operations. Also gives the text of the resolutions adopted at the meeting.

3565. Sixth Conference of American States Members of the International Labour Organisation (Ind Lab, 16:12, Dec. 15, 1956, p. 486-502).

Summarizes the half-dozen talks at the opening of the Conference, notes the admission of Paraguay to the ILO, and gives the conclusions of the meetings in considerable detail. Principal topics under review were labor-management issues, productivity, and cooperatives.

3566. Ugarte, Luis Ángel. Evolución de los conceptos de salud y enfermedad (Inf Soc, 11:2, abril-junio 1956, p. 3-34; 11:3, julio-sept. 1956, p. 3-42).

This work—encyclopedic in plan and systematic in treatment—traces development of health and sickness concepts from the stone age to the present day. It includes a review of the primitive ideas of Peruvian and other Indian groups, a summary of Inca views in the chapter on ancient historic civilizations, and information on the National Institute of Hygiene and Public Health of Peru.

3567. Valcárcel, Jorge A. El seguro de vejez (Inf Soc, 10:4, oct.-dic. 1955, p. 33-44).

Also, reprinted in *Revista iberoamericana de seguridad social*, 5:3, mayo-junio 1956, p. 786-796. Analyzes factors affecting old-age insurance costs, with various international and American comparisons of life-expectancy benefit formulas, administrative structure, and other factors. A thought-provoking critique of some of the weaknesses in Latin American retirement legislation.

ARGENTINA

3568. Argentina; beneficios, obligaciones y derechos para el personal que presta servicios en casas de familia. Decreto-ley núm. 326, Buenos Aires, 14-1-56 (R Iberoam Seg Soc, 5:2, marzo-abril 1956, p. 468-475).

This protective law gives domestic servants such basic guarantees as a minimum of 9 consecutive hours of rest nightly, 24 hours or two half-days off each week, and paid annual vacations. Sick pay and the extension of retirement coverage to domestics are likewise among the provisions.

3569. Argentina. Comisión Nacional de la Vivienda. Plan de emergencia. Informe elevado al Ministerio de Trabajo y Previsión. B. A., 1956. 281 p., illus., plans, diagrs., forms.

The Commission, created December 1955 to draft an emergency program on short notice, visited all parts of the country, including slum housing areas, and presented its recommendations. These center mainly on eliminating the "Villas Miseria" ("agrupaciones de viviendas rudimentarias e improvisadas") and stimulating new construction. Contains material on cost and financing and on the planning and construction of dwellings.

3570. Establishment of a national sickness insurance committee in Argentina (Ind Lab, 16:3, Aug. 1, 1956, p. 138-139).

3571. Ossorio y Florit, Manuel. La reforma de la ley de reparación de accidentes del trabajo (R Iberoam Seg Soc, 5:2, marzo-abril 1956, p. 504-509).

Reprinted from *Gaceta del trabajo*, B. A., 1. quincena de diciembre 1955. Far-reaching liberalizations in the Argentine law on work injuries are critically examined in the light of their effect on the costs of production, incentives to stop work, the insurance contract, and other phases of labor jurisprudence and national and international experience in the field of accident compensation. See also item 3573.

3572. **Problemas actuales del régimen obligatorio** (R Iberoam Seg Soc, 5:6, nov.-dic. 1956, p. 1439-1441).
Summarizes findings of an official commission concerning obstacles facing the Argentine retirement programs in 1956. The difficulty in investing satisfactorily the 5 billion pesos of annual income is noted, as are the general effect of inflation and the persisting actuarial deficit. An impressive if brief analysis of the dangers consequent to the way in which the great expansion of Argentina's old-age and survivor programs was carried out in the years after 1945.

3573. **Rivas, José M.** Algo más sobre el decreto-ley 650/55 de reformas a la ley 9.688 (R Iberoam Seg Soc, 5:2, marzo-abril 1956, p. 477-482; review of a study in *Gaceta del trabajo*, B. A., 211, 1. quincena de 1956).
Argentina's 1955 amendments to its work-accident legislation expanded coverage to include all persons who work for others, instead of specifying certain industries to which the program should apply, as was formerly the case. It also liberalized benefits and the conditions for receiving them. The author analyzes and defends these changes with special reference to criticisms made by other Argentinian authorities on labor law. See also item 3571.

BRAZIL

3574. **Iório, Oswaldo.** Inversões do I. A. P. I. e sua taxa de rentabilidade (Industriários, 48, dez. 1955, p. 5-15).
Shows in considerable detail the kinds of investments—real estate, mortgage loans, inventories, etc.—made by the largest Brazilian social insurance institute, that for industrial workers. Also notes the yield from each kind of investment, and the trend in interest rates, 1951-1954 inclusive.

3575. ————. Mostra gráfica de alguns aspectos do I. A. P. I. (Industriários, 50, abril 1956, p. 6-14).
Charts and tables show concisely a number of interesting and provocative facts about the Brazilian social insurance institute for industrial workers as of 1955. Assets receivable are more than twice those in fact realized because of nonpayment by the government and employers. Benefits were 96 percent of contributions in 1955 (up from 49 percent in 1949), and total expenses exceeded income substantially in 1954 and 1955. The method is something of a model for graphic presentation, as is the subject matter.

3576. **Rural Welfare Service in Brazil** (Ind Lab, 15:10, May 15, 1956, p. 426-427).
Objectives, administrative structure, financial resources, and general aspects of the Rural Welfare Service established in September 1955 to improve living conditions in outlying areas. The ministries of agriculture, of labor, industry and commerce, of education and culture, and of health are represented on its Board of Directors. Financing includes an annual federal grant of 100 million cruzeiros and from one to three percent of the payroll of rural undertakings.

3577. **Torres, João Camillo de Oliveira.** A crise da previdência social no Brasil. Belo Horizonte, Brazil, Edições Diálogo, 1954. 92 p.
By use of economic, demographic, and other social data, the author documents his case that the Brazilian retirement systems operate under a number of unfavorable conditions, including inflation, low industrialization, and a legal structure which the author feels is unsuited to the country. He makes several suggestions looking toward a better balanced system, among them lower reserve funds and more unification in the administration of medical services.

3578. **Vaz, Vasco.** Considerações em torno dos problemas dos menores transviados (B Inst Intl Am Prot Infan, 30:2 (117), junio 1956, p. 118-128).
Three out of every ten children aided in 1956 by the Brazilian Serviço de Assistencia de Menores were delinquents. The author, psychiatrist of the Serviço, makes a statistical analysis by sex, race, place of residence, form of misconduct, and other factors bearing on these individuals and their behavior. A definite addition to the factual information in the field.

CHILE

3579. **Chile: la actividad del Servicio de Seguridad Social en 1955** (Seg Soc, México, 6:21, mayo-junio 1956, p. 66-68).
Includes data on number of persons covered, income for various forms of social security, number of pensions and expenditure, and number of beneficiaries under the family allowance program.

3580. **Chile: Decreto núm. 402, aprobando el reglamento de subsidios de enfermedad y maternidad y auxilio de lactancia** (R Iberoam Seg Soc, 5:1, enero-feb. 1956, p. 157-166).
An important measure setting out the conditions under which cash benefits are payable for sickness, maternity, and nursing in the Chilean social security system.

CUBA

3581. **Raggi Ageo, Carlos M.** Importancia socio-económica de la seguridad social (Seg Soc, México, 5:24, nov.-dic. 1956, p. 31-37).
General considerations of some of the results of social security in any country where it operates are followed by significant and welcome data on the Cuban retirement systems, their general nature and specific accomplishments. The facts are selective and scattered rather than systematic, and statistical information is not included.

3582. **Reglamento del seguro social del ingeniero civil de la república de Cuba** (Seg

Soc, México, 5:20, marzo-abril 1956, p. 42-89).

Text of a decree making detailed provision for the administrative organization and procedure of another of the many Cuban retirement funds, that for civil engineers, which operates under the law of November 1955, as amended.

DOMINICAN REPUBLIC

3583. Celebraron el Día Iberoamericano de la Seguridad Social (Seg Soc, Ciudad Trujillo, 8:48, marzo-abril 1956, p. 10-18).

"Spanish-American Social Security Day," established by decree in the Dominican Republic, coincided with the ninth anniversary of the founding of the national social insurance system. Here are brief addresses on accomplishments in the country, by Dr. Luis Escoto Gómez, Dr. José G. Soba, and Dr. Ramón Baez (hijo).

3584. Datos sobre el funcionamiento del seguro social en la República Dominicana se dieron a conocer (Seg Soc, Ciudad Trujillo, 8:52, nov.-dic. 1956, p. 21-24).

A journalistic comment on the social insurance program of the country as portrayed at the Guatemalan conference (from *Nuestro Diario,* oct. 31, 1956). See also item 3553.

3585. Información básica presentada por la Caja Dominicana de Seguros Sociales para el estudio de la seguridad social agrícola (Seg Soc, México, 5:23, sept.-oct. 1956, p. 24-41).

Presents general information on agriculture in the Dominican Republic and notes the position of employees, tenant farmers, and independent farmers on their own land. The concluding section is a review of the rural social security benefits, which protect against the risks of sickness, maternity, work injuries, old age, and death.

3586. El seguro social dominicano (Seg Soc, México, 5:22, julio-agosto 1956, p. 5-42).

This adaptation of the longer study by Dr. Armando Cordero is a systematic review of the background, present development, legal provisions, and statistics of health, pension, and accident insurance in the Dominican Republic. The system has developed rapidly and has attained relatively large coverage since its establishment in 1947.

3587. Velázquez, Juan O. El partido dominicano, génesis de la política social de Trujillo (Seg Soc, Ciudad Trujillo, 8:50, julio-agosto 1956, p. 10-21).

Includes useful information on the development of welfare, particularly child welfare institutions, in the Dominican Republic.

EL SALVADOR

3588. El Salvador: reglamento para afiliación, inspección y estadística del Instituto Salvadoreño del Seguro Social (Seg Soc, México, 5:23, sept.-oct. 1956, p. 42-46).

The text of decree 53, June 11, 1956, concerning employer and worker registration and related matters, under which the social insurance program advanced its operations in the *municipio* of San Salvador.

3589. New employment office in El Salvador (Ind Lab, 15:6, Mar. 15, 1956, p. 239-240).

GUATEMALA

3590. Desarrollo y proyecciones del régimen guatemalteco de seguridad social (Seg Soc, México, 5:24, nov.-dic. 1956, p. 69-125).

Presented at the 1956 social security meeting for which Guatemala was the host country, this account of the interesting if somewhat limited social security programs of the nation is systematic and detailed. Although limited to providing benefits for work accidents, general accidents, and maternity for selected groups and areas only, the quality and scope of the services provided make Guatemalan benefit expenditure as large as in comparable countries that undertake to offer health and pensions insurance also.

3591. Seguro de enfermedad; consideraciones generales, consideraciones médicosociales sobre Guatemala y proyecto en estudio del Instituto Guatemalteco de Seguridad Social (R Iberoam Seg Soc, 5:6, nov.-dic. 1956, p. 1337-1401).

Presents medical and social information on Guatemala (which is 70 percent rural and 72 percent illiterate), including hospital studies, and gives details of the plan to introduce health insurance when practicable. Valuable for its data on Guatemala and for its relevance to the problems facing the establishments of such services in a country that is in many respects underdeveloped. Presented at the meeting in Guatemala of the social security agencies of Central America, Mexico, and the Caribbean, 1956.

HAITI

3592. Haïti. Département du Travail. Deuxième Séminaire Haïtien de l'Enfance, du 2 au 9 mai 1956. Avec la collaboration de l'Institut Interaméricain pour la Protection de l'Enfance. Port-au-Prince, Imp. de l'État, 1956. 145 p., illus., ports.

Various aspects of Haitian childhood were discussed in the proceedings of this second conference, which, like the first, was a cooperative undertaking between Haiti and the Inter-American Institute for the Protection of Childhood. 24 speakers discussed themes relating to the legal, moral, and economic welfare of the child. Photographic illustrations.

3593. Haïti. Institut d'Assurances Sociales. Loi organique et réglements généraux avec les dernières modifications. Port-au-Prince, Département du Travail, 1956. 76 p.

Has the text of the 1951 law, as amended in

1955, providing for work accident insurance and also for a program of health and maternity insurance that has not yet been put into effect. Also contains the 1952 regulation of social insurance administration, as amended in June 1956. Besides its significance for Haiti, the carefully worked out legislation is an interesting example of how beginning social insurance laws may be introduced in an agricultural country with very modest per capita income.

MEXICO

3594. Huerta, Miguel. La distribución de los médicos en la República Mexicana (Seg Soc, México, 5:20, marzo-abril 1956, p. 97-100).
Presents highly significant information on the "superconcentration" in urban areas of Mexico's physicians, dentists, and other medical personnel whose more general distribution is needed if the social insurance program is to cover the whole nation. Also presents data on ages and incomes of physicians in Mexico.

3595. México. Secretaría del Trabajo y Previsión Social. Memoria de labores, enero a diciembre de 1955. México, 1956. 127 p., tables.
Emphasis in the report is on mediation and conciliation functions performed by the ministry, as well as on labor inspection services. Attention is also given to work in industrial safety, hygiene, and social work as related to these functions. Tables give much information on collective bargaining, wages, and work injuries as well as on the work of the ministry.

3596. Ortiz Mena, Antonio. Los desarrollos recientes en el campo de la seguridad social en México (Seg Soc, México, 5:19, enero-feb. 1956, p. 63-98).
Summarizes benefits under each branch of Mexican social insurance, traces historical and legislative backgrounds of the law, and discusses problems of providing medical care and protecting the rural population. An informative study by the director of the Mexican Social Insurance Institute, presented before the sessions of the Twelfth General Assembly of the International Social Security Association.

3597. El seguro social mexicano para los trabajadores del campo (Seg Soc, México, 5:23, sept.-oct. 1956, p. 5-23).
Background data, including demographic and economic information, are followed by accounts of the areas considered and a general statement of the medical organization best suited to bring the social security services to the rural population. A practical and important study.

NICARAGUA

3598. Ley orgánica de seguridad social. Administración Somoza. Managua, Tall. Nacionales, 1956. 113 p.
This decree of December 1955 is one of the very few in Latin America to provide for both insurance and assistance within the same framework. The insurance benefits include pensions, health

insurance, and workmen's compensation, though in first application the last-named was temporarily left to former work accident legislation. This booklet has 40 pages of background information. The decree also appears in the *Revista iberoamericana de seguridad social*, 5:2, marzo-abril 1956, and in English translation in the *Legislative series* of the International Labour Office (1955-Nic. 2, Geneva, 1956, 24 p.).

3599. Ley orgánica de seguridad social en Nicaragua (Seg Soc, México, 5:20, marzo-abril 1956, p. 27-40).
Systematically reviews the principal administrative and benefit provisions of decree no. 161, December 1955, making provision for a general social security system. An extended summary in English appears in *Industry and labour*, 15:10, May 15, 1956, p. 427-434. See also item above.

3600. Nicaragua. Ministerio de Salubridad Pública. Reglamento general de la ley orgánica de seguridad social (R Iberoam Seg Soc, 5:6, nov.-dic. 1956, p. 1487-1528).
By this measure of October 1956, Nicaragua fixed the contributions rate for retirement and health insurance at 12 percent of wages—paid half by the employer and a fourth each by the worker and the government—and determined on early January 1957 for the beginning of registration and benefit operations in Managua. The promptness with which the Nicaraguan law was drafted and put into effect—even on a limited scale—was exceptional.

PANAMA

3601. Falk, Isidore Sydney. Health in Panama; a survey and a program. Prepared for the government of the republic of Panama. Stonington, Conn., 1957. 460 p., maps, diagrs., tables.
Reviews in detail the health situation in Panama: organization of services, finance, personnel, health centers, and hospitals. Part 2, "A development program for the department of public health" (chapters 12-22, inclusive), makes specific recommendations that broadly parallel the topics treated in part 1. An outstanding study from the factual and normative standpoints; the conclusions were largely accepted, with corresponding budgetary planning, by the government that came into office while the study was still in progress.

3602. Ferrer Valdés, Manuel. El seguro de enfermedad en Panamá (Seg Soc, México, 5:24, nov.-dic. 1956, p. 44-48).
Clearly explains the operations of a program that has consistently provided over a 15-year period a larger benefit outlay than has the old-age and invalidity insurance for which the greater part of Panamanian social insurance contributions are intended.

PARAGUAY

3603. Lettich, Lidia. Informe de la Sección de Servicio Social, ejercicio de 1955 (R

Iberoam Seg Soc, 5:3, mayo-junio 1956, p. 763-768).

Reprinted from *Revista del Instituto de Previsión Social*, Paraguay, feb. 1956. The Sección de Servicio Social carries out a wide variety of services, among them work in children's clinics and mothers' clubs, workers' housing, maternity insurance, and various clinics, hospitals, and sanatoria. Interviews with 6000 persons—mainly the sick—in the first 11 months of 1955 led to detailed follow-up work where needed. Shows clearly the importance of the Section in informing Paraguayan workers of their rights, privileges, and duties under the social insurance program.

3604. Odriosola, Ricardo. El niño y la seguridad social (R Iberoam Seg Soc, 5:4, julio-agosto 1956, p. 1005-1014).

Reprinted from *Revista de Instituto de Previsión Social*. Includes a review of Paraguayan developments for child care under the social insurance program as part of a broad statement of the needs of children in the Western Hemisphere. Also contains statements of the rights and needs of children as developed in several American conferences and congresses.

PERU

3605. Ferrero, Rómulo A. La renta nacional (Inf Soc, 12:2, abril-junio 1957, p. 3-32).

Analyzes the nature and composition of national income, and the statistical and other information needed to determine it. Discusses the Peruvian national income including its composition, geographical distribution, and the means for increasing it. The per capita income in 1954 was estimated at 2185 gold soles (about $115), an increase of some 26 percent since 1945.

3606. Perú. Caja Nacional de Seguro Social. Décimacuarta memoria . . . año 1955. Lima, 1956. 13 p., plus tables.

Two thirds of Peru's benefit outgo went for health services during 1955, 28 percent for short-term cash benefits, and another 5 percent for funeral costs and the long-term pension payments. A total of 396,000 wage earners were affiliated with the Fund, and income mounted to 196 million soles. These and other points, including a section on hospital statistics, are included in the 14th report of the National Social Insurance Fund.

URUGUAY

3607. Application of international labour standards in Uruguay (Ind Lab, 15:3, Feb. 1, 1956, p. 91-92).

Uruguay has adopted the unusual step of providing legal penalties for violations of the ILO conventions which the country ratified in 1933. It has since held conferences and taken other measures, which are here described, to promote effective standards, whether or not the country has ratified conventions in that field. Areas of activity include unemployment insurance, health insurance, old-age security in industry and agriculture, and various others in the social security field.

3608. Marco, Hugo A. de. Parafiscalidad social y profesional en la República Oriental del Uruguay. Montevideo, Universidad de la República, Instituto de Finanzas (Cuaderno, 4), 1954. 36 p.

Uruguay's pension programs, family allowances, and unemployment compensation are items outside the regular budget that have great economic as well as social significance. Their income, assets, and related financial aspects are here explained, and their relative importance shown in tables for the period 1945-1950. The result is a useful factual review of a significant phase of Uruguayan welfare laws in the national economy.

3609. Seminario de Trabajo sobre Administración de Servicios de Protección a la Infancia, 2a. etapa, 2a. parte, 1956 (B Inst Intl Am Prot Infan, 30:3 (118), sept. 1956, p. 242-255; 30:4 (119), dic. 1956, p. 295-380).

A general summary of the course in Montevideo, Aug. 1-Sept. 10, 1956, that constituted the second stage, continued from 1955, of social work training. This is followed in the second issue by the text of 12 papers from the seminar, some on Uruguayan institutions and others on the general themes of legal, moral, economic, social, educational, and health protection of the child and the family. Illustrated.

OTHER COUNTRIES

3610. Costa Rica. Ministerio de Salubridad Pública. Breve informe de la labor de salubridad pública en el año 1953. San José, 1954. 119 p., tables.

Portrays through text and tables the work of each of the divisions of the Ministry of Public Health, including mother and child protection, school health, nutrition, health centers, bio-statistics, the General Office of Medico-Social Assistance, and many others. Contains concise information on social insurance, hospital care, workmen's compensation, and the contributory health program of the Compañía Bananera de Costa Rica.

3611. Ecuador. Instituto Nacional de Previsión. Informe de labores (B Inf Estud Soc Ec, 18:68-69, enero-junio 1955, p. 3-18).

Traces legislative changes in Ecuadorian social insurance, gives the budget for 1955, considers investment policy, and presents financial statements for the Caja de Pensiones (white-collar and government workers) and the Caja del Seguro (for wage earners). Shows particularly the wide scope of investments of the social insurance reserves, which are an important source of capital funds.

3612. Rengifo, Jesús María. Seguridad social militar (R Iberoam Seg Soc, 5:6, nov.-dic. 1956, p. 1533-1544).

Reprinted from *Universitas*, Bogota, 1956. Relatively few sources deal with the military pension systems of Latin America, so that this rather full account of such programs in Colombia fills a need. It traces legislative developments over more than 50 years and explains in detail the existing benefit structure.

3613. **Sahagún Torres, Jesús.** Estado actual de la protección materno-infantil en Venezuela (B Inst Intl Am Prot Infan, 30:2 (117), junio 1956, p. 80-110).

Venezuelan expenditures for public health went up from four bolivars per capita in 1936-1937 to 31.50 bolivars in the fiscal year 1955-1956. This account of child health services includes information on urban and rural care, training of doctors and others, prenatal, obstetrical, and postnatal services, nursing care, and related activities. An authoritative review of one of the most highly developed services of its kind in the Americas.

Language and Literature

SPANISH AMERICAN LANGUAGE

DANIEL S. WOGAN

THE LISTINGS in this section of *HLAS No. 20* extend our knowledge of American Spanish in several areas. Various problems relating to terms of address and the *voseo* are ably treated by Silva Fuenzalida, Sologuren, Kiddle, and Flórez, while Corominas, Morínigo, and Sandman discuss questions of etymology. The formation of hypocoristics is investigated in detail by Peter Boyd-Bowman. The latter is also the author of a basic study, which will be broadened to include later periods, on the regional origins of the Spanish colonists who settled the Antilles between 1493 and 1519. Malaret, Becerra, Rodríguez Herrera, Boggs, and Padrón contribute valuable lexical material. Berta Vidal de Battini, the distinguished Argentine philologist, in her fine monograph, *El español en la Argentina*, makes available a wealth of original data on the pronunciation, intonation patterns, geography, and other aspects of Argentine language. Notable likewise are the facsimile edition of Rufino José Cuervo's *Diccionario de construcción y régimen de la lengua castellana*, vol. 2, published in handsome format by the Instituto Caro y Cuervo, and the sixth volume of Andrés Bello's *Obras completas,* issued under the auspices of the Ministerio de Educación at Caracas.

The training in linguistics young scholars receive in North American universities is put to good use by Olmsted, Ringo, Murphy, Hyman, and McWilliams. Their work clearly indicates a growing trend toward the application of the methods of linguistic science to the study of American Spanish.

3625. **Academia Colombiana.** Nuevas normas de ortografía. Bogotá, 1956. 16 p.
Lists points of disagreement with the *Nuevas normas de prosodia y ortografía* issued by the Royal Spanish Academy in 1952. Curiously, the Colombian Academy is in general more conservative than its parent body in Spain.

3626. **Álvarez, María Edmée.** Estudio de la lengua española a través de autores hispanoamericanos. México, Universidad Nacional Autónoma de México, Facultad de Filosofía y Letras, 1954. 393 p.
Merely a hodgepodge of Spanish American prose and poetry fitted out with notes and exercises for use as a textbook.

3627. **Arriola, Jorge Luis.** Pequeño diccionario etimológico de voces guatemaltecas. Guatemala, Ministerio de Educación Pública (Biblioteca de cultura popular, 50), 1954. 199 p.

A new edition of this useful but not always reliable work, somewhat enlarged. First edition, Guatemala, 1941.

3628. **Badía Margarit, A. M.** Hispanoamericano *ojalá* "aunque" (R Filol Esp, 38:1-4, enero-dic. 1955, p. 223-228).
On the theoretical development of *ojalá* and the subjunctive to express concession.

3629. **Becerra, Marcos E.** Rectificaciones i adiciones al diccionario de la Real Academia Española. México, 1954. 832 p.
The fruit of pertinacious dissatisfaction with the *DRAE* over a period of 20 years, classified as follows: Voces comunes y cultas varias; Animales; Plantas; Biología.

3630. **Bello, Andrés.** Obras completas de . . . 6. Estudios filológicos, 1. Caracas, Ministerio de Educación, Biblioteca Nacional, 1954. cxii, 601 p., illus.

The sixth volume of this fine edition of Bello's works is devoted largely to orthoëpy and metrics.

3631. Boggs, Ralph S. Términos del lenguaje popular y caló de la capital de Méjico (B Filol, 8, 1954-1955, p. 35-43).
Notes on some 66 terms collected by the author from an underworld acquaintance in 1938. A number of them, e. g. *chamaco, cacle, cuate, esquincle,* have been satisfactorily studied before.

3632. Boyd-Bowman, Peter. Cómo obra la fonética infantil en la formación de los hipocorísticos (Nueva R Filol Hisp, 9:4, oct.-dic. 1955, p. 337-366).
Thorough investigation of the phonetics and morphology of Spanish hypocoristics, with abundant examples taken predominantly from American Spanish.

3633. ————. The regional origins of the earliest Spanish colonists of America (PMLA, 71:5, Dec. 1956, p. 1152-1172).
A very thorough study, with elaborate statistical tables, of the regional origins of 5481 colonists during the years 1493-1519. The author's figures show that the primitive, or Antillean period, of Spanish settlement in America "is clearly dominated in number, unity and prestige of colonists by the Andalusian provinces of Sevilla and Huelva." Basic investigation in an important area not heretofore systematically explored.

3634. ————. Sobre la pronunciación del español en el Ecuador (Nueva R Filol Hisp, 7:1-2, enero-junio 1953, p. 221-233).
Supplies data on Ecuadoran phonetics and linguistic geography, particularly with respect to the variants of *ll, s, r, j, f,* and *y.*

3635. Cadavid Uribe, Gonzalo. Oyendo conversar al pueblo (U Antioquia, 28:110, enero-feb. 1953, p. 365-369).
Notes on Colombian folk speech compared with usage in other areas of Spanish America.

3636. Cárdenas, Daniel N. Nasal variants after final "s" in the Spanish of Jalisco (PMLA, 70:3, June 1955, p. 556-561).
The author holds that the nasal resonance in forms such as *pazn, puesn,* is a physiological phenomenon independent of indigenous substratum. Hardly one third of his informants in Jalisco, Mexico, exhibited it.

3637. Cela, Camilo José. Historias de Venezuela: La catira. Barcelona, Noguer, 1955. 405 p.
In this violent tale Spain's foremost contemporary novelist uses Venezuelanisms to the point of saturation. It should be considered an artistic tour de force rather than an authentic reflection of Venezuelan folk speech. The author has supplied an extensive glossary, p. 361-402.

3638. Charnley, M. Bertens. Situatives in colloquial Chilean (Rom Philol, 9:1, Aug. 1955, p. 26-30).

Unique topography combines with local traditions to lend special meanings to *arriba, abajo, adentro, alto,* etc., in many parts of Chile.

3639. Corominas, Juan. Diccionario crítico etimológico de la lengua castellana. V. 3, L-RE. Madrid, Gredos (Biblioteca románica hispánica. Diccionarios etimológicos, 5), 1956? 1117 p.
See *HLAS, no. 19,* item 4518a.

3640. ————. Falsos occidentalismos americanos (B Filol, Santiago, 8, 1954-1955, p. 65-70).
Argues for the American origin of several words of debatable provenance, among them *batea, cancha, caracha, chigrero, opa,* and *tusa.*

3641. Cortichs de Mora, Estrella. Aspectos del habla de Tepotzotlán, México (Nueva R Filol Hisp, 8:2, abril-junio 1954, p. 137-155).
Highly readable study of numerous terms used by agricultural workers in this ancient municipality. Contains data of interest to folklorists, anthropologists, and sociologists.

3642. Cowles, Ella N. Lexical characteristics of American Spanish observed in regional literary works (Hispania, AATSP, 37:1, Mar. 1954, p. 39-43).
Observation on the internal and external sources of American Spanish based on a study of 108 regional works.

3643. Cuervo, Rufino José. Diccionario de construcción y régimen de la lengua castellana. T. 2. C-D. Bogotá, Instituto Caro y Cuervo, 1954. 1348 p.
The second volume of this facsimile edition of Cuervo's unfinished dictionary. See *HLAS, no. 19,* item 4520.

3644. Echeverría, Aquileo J. Concherías. Romances, epigramas y otros poemas. San José, Trejos, 1953. 318 p.
Contains a glossary of regionalisms used by the poet, p. 292-314.

3645. Fein, Delia. Semántica y estilística. Montevideo, Letras, 1955. 337 p.
18 essays on literary and linguistic topics by a member of the Instituto de Estudios Superiores de Montevideo. Those concerned with folk speech, verbal categories in *Martín Fierro,* gestures, and diminutives are especially interesting.

3647. Flórez, Luis. *Vos* y la segunda persona verbal en Antioquia (Thesaurus, 9:1-3, 1953, p. 280-286).
Detailed notes on the verbal forms used with the archaic pronoun *vos* in the Department of Antioquia, Colombia, where the *voseo* has taken root in the familiar speech of all social classes.

3648. Herrero Mayor, Avelino. Lengua y gramática. Reflexiones sobre el bien hablar y el mal decir. B. A., Fides, 1955. 126 p.

Eight rather unsubstantial essays on grammar, points of usage, language growth, etc., with occasional reference to Argentine speech.

3649. Hyman, Ruth L. [n] as an allophane denoting open juncture in several Spanish American dialects (Hispania, AATSP, 39:3, Sept. 1956, p. 293-299).

An analysis of the tendency to velarize final /n/ in the speech of informants from Costa Rica, Cuba, Honduras, Mexico, Nicaragua, Panama, Peru, Spain, and Venezuela. Makes a strong case for considering [n] as a junctural allophone of /n/.

3650. Kahane, Henry R., and Angelina Pietrangeli (eds.). Descriptive studies in Spanish grammar. Urbana, Ill., University of Illinois Press (Illinois studies in language and literature, 38), 1954. 241 p.

See items 3654, 3662, and 3672.

3651. Kiddle, Lawrence B. Some social implications of the voseo (Mod Lang For, 38:3-4, Sept.-Dec. 1953, p. 50-54).

Classifies the opinions of 39 informants representing all Spanish America on the social status of *vos* plus archaic verb forms in their respective regions.

3652. Lacayo, Heberto. Apuntes sobre la pronunciación del español de Nicaragua (Hispania, AATSP, 37:3, Sept. 1954, p. 267-268).

Notes on the language of 90 working class individuals from all departments of Nicaragua. The phenomena observed are in general found in the folk speech of other Spanish American areas.

3653. León Rey, José Antonio. El lenguaje popular del oriente de Cundinamarca. Bogotá, Imp. del Banco de la República, 1955? 100 p.

A highly rhetorical, academic discourse on the Spanish language with passing reference to popular usage in the author's native region of Colombia.

3654. McWilliams, Ralph Dale. The adverb in colloquial Spanish (*in* Descriptive studies in Spanish grammar [see item 3650], p. 73-137).

Analyzes adverbial functions in 20 modern Mexican plays, checked with informants to establish patterns of form and position. A fresh approach to the problem, but unfortunately nothing very concrete or useful emerges.

3655. Malaret, Augusto. Lexicón de fauna y flora, continuación (Thesaurus, 9:1-3, 1953, p. 264-279).

Ñandubay to *papita*. See HLAS, no. 18, 1952, item 2347.

3656. ————. Vocabulario de Puerto

Rico. N. Y., Las Américas Publishing Co., 1955. 293 p.

A reprint of this extensive collection of archaisms, neologisms, and aboriginal words gathered by Malaret from the literature and spoken language of Puerto Rico, first published in 1937 (San Juan, Puerto Rico).

3657. Menton, Seymour. Mexican baseball terminology: an example of linguistic growth (Hispania, AATSP, 37:4, Dec. 1954, p. 478-481).

Adduces evidence that the vocabulary of baseball in Mexico, drawn mainly from American English, is still in a developmental stage.

3658. Miller, Elizabeth Helen. "La rumba" de Ángel de Campo y su valor literario. México, 1953. 89 p.

Hasty comments on the language of an obscure Mexican novel, published serially in 1890-1891, are provided on pages 26-33 of this Master's thesis.

3659. Moldenhauer, Gerardo. Filología y lingüística. Esencia, problemas actuales y tareas en la Argentina. Santa Fe, Argentina, Universidad Nacional del Litoral, Instituto de Filología, 1952. 74 p.

Calls attention to the need for a critical bibliography of Argentine Spanish, investigation of substratum languages, regional lexicography, bilingualism, topography, and other linguistic areas the author believes have not been sufficiently explored.

3660. Morales R., Raimundo. Crítica de lenguaje. Santiago, Editorial Universitaria, 1953. 313 p.

Sundry grammatical matters discussed from a perceptive viewpoint with occasional reference to Chilean usage.

3661. Morínigo, Marcos A. Para la etimología de *poncho* (Nueva R Filol Hisp, 9:1, enero-marzo 1955, p. 33-35).

Argues against a possible New World origin of the word.

3662. Murphy, Spencer L., Jr. A description of noun suffixes in colloquial Spanish (*in* Descriptive studies in Spanish grammar [see item 3650], p. 1-48).

Affords an interesting approach to the classification of Mexican Spanish suffixes. The source materials are literary but informants were used to determine semantically related words.

3663. ————. Notes on *anglicismos* in American Spanish (Hispania, AATSP, 37:4, Dec. 1954, p. 457-459).

An analysis, with examples, of the phonemic, morphemic and sememic patterns of adaptation shown by English words on passing into Spanish.

3664. Olivera, Miguel Alfredo. El habla de Buenos Aires (Cursos Conf, año 22,

44:262-264, enero-marzo 1954, p. 433-454).

Mostly the usual generalizations about *porteño* speech, including the idea that "el plebeyismo lingüístico" was implanted by the Rosas dictatorship.

3665. Olmsted, David L. A note on the dialect of Regla, Cuba (Hispania, AATSP, 37:3, Sept. 1954, p. 293-294).

Brief remarks on some phonetic and phonemic features of Spanish spoken in Regla, a suburb of Habana.

3666. Padrón, Francisco. El médico y el folklore. San Luis Potosí, México, Tall. Gráf. de la Editorial Universitaria, 1956. 342 p.

Popular Mexican medical terminology collected and explained by a practicing physician, with interesting chapters on witchcraft, food customs, nicknames, and folk medicine.

3667. Peralta Lagos, José María ("T. P. Mechín," pseud.). Burla burlando. San Salvador, Ministerio de Cultura, Departamento Editorial, 1955. 262 p.

Contains a glossary of Salvadorean idioms and provincialisms, p. 249-262.

3668. Pichardo, Esteban. Pichardo novísimo; o diccionario provincial casi razonado de vozes y frases cubanas. Novísima edición, corregida y ampliamente anotada por Esteban Rodríguez Herrera. Habana, Selecta, 1953. lxiii, 716 p., port., facsms.

This, the fifth edition of Pichardo's famous work, retains the title of the fourth edition (1875). The editor has added an essay on Pichardo's life and lexicographical labors, abundant notes, and illustrative citations from Cuban authors, but has not attempted to bring the dictionary up to date as the title might suggest.

3669. Rabanales O., Ambrosio. Introducción al estudio del español de Chile. Santiago, Universidad de Chile, Instituto de Filología (Anexo no. 1 del Boletín de Filología), 1953. 142 p.

A *chilenismo*, according to the author, is "toda expresión oral, escrita o sematolálica originada en Chile desde cualquier punto de vista gramatical, por los chilenos que hablan el español como lengua propia o por los extranjeros residentes que han asimilado el español de Chile." A detailed, analytical exposition of this concept constitutes this highly original and informative monograph.

3670. Ransom, Helen M. Diminutivos, aumentativos, despectivos (Hispania, AATSP, 37:4, Dec. 1954, p. 406-408).

On the widespread use of such devices in Mexico, with numerous examples.

3671. ————. Viles pochismos (Hispania, AATSP, 37:3, Sept. 1954, p. 285-287).

Scattered, occasionally humorous remarks on Mexican borrowings from American English.

3672. Ringo, Albert Winfred. The position of the noun modifier in colloquial Spanish (*in* Descriptive studies in Spanish grammar [see item 3650], p. 49-72).

A discussion of the position of adjectives in 49 20th-century Mexican plays. The problem, stated in descriptivist terms, becomes excessively complex, for, as the author summarizes it, "the position of the noun modifier in colloquial Spanish depends on, or is connected with, certain linguistic phenomena of a very diverse nature, which, to be sure, overlap partly."

3673. Rodríguez Demorizi, Silveria R. de. Arcaísmos en Santo Domingo (B Ac Dom Lengua, 14:45, agosto 1954, p. 18-28).

Offers some 82 obsolete or obsolescent expressions preserved in the spoken Spanish of Santo Domingo, with citations of their use by Golden Age writers. Few novelties.

3674. Rodríguez Herrera, Esteban. El plebeyismo en Cuba (B Filol, Santiago, 8, 1954-1955, p. 407-438).

Extensive list of words and idiomatic expressions current in popular Cuban speech. Many of these terms have worked their way up from *germanía* and *ñáñigo* circles.

3675. Rosario, Rubén del. La lengua de Puerto Rico. Ensayos. San Juan, Imp. Soltero, 1955. 32 p.

Miscellaneous comments on Puerto Rican pronunciation, Anglicisms, archaisms, language and national feeling, etc., reprinted from *Asomante* (1946) and *El imparcial* (1955).

3676. Sandmann, M. Un problema de geografía lingüística antillana (Nueva R Filol Hisp, 9:4, oct-dic. 1955, p. 383-385).

Proposes *champignon* as the parent of *yonyón* and related forms in the Antilles.

3677. Silva Fuenzalida, Ismael. El uso de los morfemas 'formales' y 'familiares' en el español de Chile: un estudio etnolingüístico (B Filol, Santiago, 8, 1954-1955, p. 439-455).

Analysis of numerous non-verbal situations associated with the use of formal and informal pronouns of address in Chile.

3678. Smither, William J. Dissertations in the Hispanic languages and literatures, 1954 (Hispania, AATSP, 38:2, May 1955, p. 182-186). Dissertations in the hispanic languages and literatures, 1955 (*Ibid.*, 39:3, Sept. 1956, p. 320-324).

Dissertations in American Spanish listed as accepted by universities in the U. S. during the period covered are: R. A. Galván, *El dialecto español de San Antonio, Tejas;* S. L. Murphy, *A description of noun suffixes in colloquial Mexican Spanish;* E. W. Ringo, *The position of the noun modifier in colloquial Mexican Spanish;* L. Gurren, *A comparison on a phonetic basis of the two chief languages of the Americas,*

English and Spanish; S. Soporta, Morpheme alternants in Spanish.

3679. Sologuren, Javier. Fórmulas de tratamiento en el Perú (Nueva R Filol Hisp, 8:3, julio-sept. 1954, p. 241-267).
A thorough study of terms of address based on written and spoken Peruvian Spanish.

3679a. Suárez, Marco Fidel. El castellano en mi tierra (B Ac Ven, 22:82-84, abril-dic. 1954, p. 23-53).
A somewhat perfervid discourse on the Spanish language that refers occasionally to the Spanish of Colombia, the author's native land.

3680. Valle, Rafael Heliodoro. Bibliografía hispanoamericana del español (Hispania, AATSP, 37:3, Sept. 1954, p. 274-284).
Valuable principally for references to linguistic notes published in inaccessible newspapers and journals of Spanish America.

3681. ————. El español de la América Española (Hispania, AATSP, 36:1, Feb. 1953, p. 52-57).
Scattered but graceful comments on the diversity of terms for similar things in Spanish America.

3682. Vargas Ugarte, Rubén. Glosario de peruanismos. Lima, Universidad Nacional Mayor de San Marcos, 1953. 74 p.
Approximately 290 words from written and oral sources. The author, a Peruvian historian, is unaware that many of these terms have been studied before or that most of them are not limited to Peru, as he seems to believe.

3683. Vidal de Battini, Berta Elena. El español de la Argentina. Estudio destinado a los maestros de las escuelas primarias. B. A., Ministerio de Educación de la Nación, Dirección General de Enseñanza Primaria, 1954. 89 p.
Though normative in purpose, a richly rewarding study of Argentine Spanish from the standpoint of pronunciation, morphology, syntax, vocabulary, and linguistic geography. The result of researches begun in 1945 which took the author to all points of the national territory, this monograph, within its self-imposed limits, is the most skillfully organized, comprehensive investigation yet undertaken in its field. Outstanding are the maps providing totally new information on the pronunciation in Argentina of y, ll, rr, s, and fixing clearly the regional diversity in intonation patterns. An extremely satisfactory study in all respects.

3684. Villegas, Francisco. El argot costarricense (Hispania, AATSP, 38:1, Mar. 1955, p. 27-30).
Notes on words and idioms current in popular Costa Rican Spanish.

3685. Villone, Vicente Atilio. Martí, un glosario de voces americanas (Humanitas, 2:4, 1954, p. 315-325).
Reproduces the list of Americanisms compiled by Martí and published for the first time in the Lex edition of his Obras completas (Habana, 1946). Noteworthy for the light it sheds on Martí's endless preoccupation with language.

3686. Woodbridge, Hensley C. Spanish in the American South and Southwest: a bibliographical survey for 1940-1953 (Orbis, 3:1, 1954, p. 236-244).
Lists and annotates some 23 studies, mostly lexical, and points to the need for further investigation in the areas of syntax, slang, and the effect of English on Spanish phonology in the U. S.

3687. Zamora, Antonio. Diccionario de sinónimos españoles. B. A., Claridad (Col. Diccionarios, 2), 1954. 393 p.
This handy, inexpensive work does not overlook such Americanisms as atorrante, galpón, garúa, changüí, and macana.

SPANISH AMERICAN LITERATURE: THE COLONIAL PERIOD

IRVING A. LEONARD

Major figures of colonial literature more or less symbolic of their respective periods are: El Inca Garcilaso de la Vega, Sor Juana Inés de la Cruz, and Joaquín Fernández de Lizardi. Over the years they and their writings have stimulated many of the significant contributions to the study of pre-Independence letters of Spanish America. Since the tricentennial in 1951 of the birth of the Mexican nun-poetess, she has inspired a voluminous output of essays, texts, and criticism, but more recently this production has tapered off; the items reported below are relatively few and unimportant. That other significant figure of early Mexican letters, Fernández de Lizardi, who of late has received far less notice, now rivals her in the number and quality of studies devoted to them. Especially valuable are J. R. Spell's articles on the intellectual and social background of El Periquillo Sarniento (items 3716, 3717).

The Peruvian mestizo chronicler, Inca Garcilaso, continues to claim increasing attention. The 350th anniversary of the publication of his *La Florida* was the occasion of an extended celebration and symposium in Lima in 1955 (items 3702, 3718). More important still, 1956 marked the first modern printing since 1829 of this novelesque narrative of the De Soto expedition. More like a novel than his better known masterpiece. *Los Comentarios Reales,* this new edition (item 3724) was published in pleasing format and typography by the Fondo de Cultura Económica of Mexico City, and thus is accessible for courses in colonial letters; a most readable work.

The lively chronicle of the conquest of Mexico by that salty veteran, Bernal Díaz del Castillo, surely belongs to literature as well as history. A convincing symptom of its perennial interest, outside as well as within the Spanish-speaking world, is offered by the appearance of *two* English versions in 1956. One was the first American edition of the Maudslay translation (item 3732), and the other a newer rendition of portions of this narrative (item 3731). Even more significant, perhaps, is the fact that the first of these English versions, published in an attractive format, was distributed as a "dividend" by the Book-of-the-Month Club in the summer of 1956, and hence was printed in tens of thousands of copies. It was also featured by the History Book Club.

Besides the long-needed text of the Inca Garcilaso's *La Florida*, a four-volume edition of Juan de Castellanos' colossal, versified chronicle, *Elegías de varones ilustres de Indias*, appeared in Bogotá in 1955 (item 3722), the first complete reprinting, apparently since the mid-19th century. Thus a wider opportunity for perusal of this gigantic poem is available.

A book-length contribution deserving special commendation is the admirable synthesis by J. J. Arrom of the colonial theater throughout Spanish America (item 3729). Its treatment of the Baroque drama is especially interesting.

Miscellaneous figures and aspects of literary culture are, as usual, subjects of numerous articles, essays, and books, and they introduce some little-known writers and writings of the colonial centuries. The matter of the relatively free circulation of printed works in the former colonies, which certainly stimulated colonial letters, continues to receive documentary support (item 3745), though one writer strives to revive the myth of Spanish repression and obscurantism in this respect (item 3728).

INDIVIDUAL FIGURES

3700. Aporte para la biografía de don Pedro de Oña (R Arch Nac Perú, 19:1, 1955, p. 62-88; 19:2, 1955, p. 243-259; 20:1, 1956, p. 85-100).
A series of documents relating to the Chilean poet (1570-1643?), including his *Juicio de residencia* of 1610, sale of a Negro slave girl, *el Libro manual de Real Caja del Cuzco* (1616-1617), last will of Doña Juliana de Oña, reproductions of the poet's signature, etc. To be continued.

3701. Carilla, Emilio. Rosas de Oquendo y el Tucumán (Mer per, año 30, 36:336, marzo 1955, p. 182-210).
A sketch of Mateo Rosas de Oquendo, Spanish soldier and poet of the 16th century during his residence in Tucuman. His poetry is analyzed as a reflection of the period, and two fragments of autobiographical interest are reproduced in an appendix.

3702. Centro de Estudios Histórico-Militares. Nuevos estudios sobre el Inca Garcilaso de la Vega. Actas del symposium realizado en Lima del 17 al 28 de junio de 1955. Edición auspiciada por el Banco de Crédito del Perú. Lima, 1955 [i. e. 1956]. 331 p.
Contains 11 papers read at the Symposium held at Lima, June 17-28, 1955, by such authorities as Porras Barrenechea, Durand, Miró Quesada, Valcárcel, Jiménez Borja, etc., on literary, historical, ethnological, psychological, etc., aspects of the Peruvian chronicler (1539-1616) and his works. (See also item 3718.)

3703. Doctor Don Diego Esquivel y Navia (R Arch Hist Cuzco, 5:5, 1954, p. 329-345).
Text of two powers of attorney and a property inventory of the author of the *Anales del Cuzco.*

3704. Espinosa Pólit, Aurelio. El primer poeta ecuatoriano de la colonia, padre Antonio Bastidas (B Ac Nac Hist, Quito, 36:87, enero-junio 1956, p. 5-19).
A lecture on a Jesuit poet (1615-1681) born in

Guayaquil and allegedly the first to write poetry in Quito.

3705. Gustafson, Donna. Un díptico barroco: Calderón y Sor Juana (U México, 11:12, agosto 1955, p. 17, 26).
A comparison of the Mexican nun's play *Los empeños de una casa*, and the *Casa con dos puertas mala es de guardar* of the great Spanish playwright, indicating similarities and differences.

3706. Jara, Álvaro. Pineda de Bascuñán, hombre de su tiempo (B Ac Ch Hist, 21:51, 2. semestre 1954, p. 77-85).
Text of three documents pertaining to the author of the curious 17th-century narrative, *El cautiverio feliz.* These are certificates of sales of slaves (one of an Indian war captive in 1674) and of lands.

3707. Larroyo, Francisco. Sor Juana Inés de la Cruz y la defensa de la educación femenina superior (Fil Let, México, 28:55-56, julio-dic. 1954, p. 197-202).
A very thin essay based mainly on a paragraph of Sor Juana's well-known biographical *Respuesta a Sor Filotea.* The author scouts any belief in traces of Descartes in her writing or thinking.

3708. Latcham, Ricardo A. Un clásico colonial: el padre Alonso de Ovalle (Bolívar, Bogotá, 45, nov.-dic. 1955, p. 853-864).
Biographical sketch and brief critical study of a Chilean Jesuit (1601-1651), author of the *Histórica relación del reino de Chile.*

3709. List Arzubide, Germán. Gutierre de Cetina y su tiempo (Lib Pue, 17:13, enero 1955, p. 14-39).
A retelling, with considerable historical padding, of the few details known of the Spanish poet (1520-1557?), famous for the verses beginning "ojos claros, serenos," who was gravely wounded in Puebla, Mexico, in 1554 while courting a lady.

3710. Lozano, Carlos. El Periquillo Sarniento y la Histoire de Gil Blas de Santillane (R Iberoam, 20:40, sept. 1955, p. 263-274).
Asserts that Lizardi develops personality more slowly and soundly and his canvas is broader than LeSage's. *Gil Blas* is, allegedly, a criticism of the *petit monde* aristocrats, its language is more *altisonante*, and its composition more synthetic than *El Periquillo.* Similar episodes in both are pointed out, but Lizardi develops psychology better and creates an authentic Mexican type.

3711. McPheeters, D. W. The distinguished Peruvian scholar Cosme Bueno, 1711-1798 (HAHR, 35:4, Nov. 1955, p. 484-491).
A biographical sketch of the 18th-century scholar renowned for his *Descripciones de provincias* and other writings which influenced Humboldt and were borrowed by Concolorcorvo in *Lazarillo de ciegos caminantes* and by other writers.

3712. Moldenhauer, Gerardo. Observaciones críticas para una edición definitiva del Sueño de Sor Juana Inés de la Cruz (B Filol, Santiago, 8, 1954-1955, p. 293-306).
On the *Primer sueño* of the Mexican nun-poetess.

3713. Morgan, Patricia. Sor Juana Inés de la Cruz (Atenea, año 33, 124:369, marzo-abril 1956, p. 256-288).
Brief essay on life and work of the Mexican nun-poetess (1651-1695), analyzing her work in relation to her time and place, with a bibliography.

3714. Ortiz D., H. Bernal Díaz ante el indígena (Hist Mex, 5:2, oct. 1955, p. 233-239).
The conquistador-chronicler speaks very favorably, in general, of the courage, crafts, wealth, and intelligence of the native civilization, while repelled by their bloody religious cult and ceremonies.

3715. Porras Barrenechea, Raúl. Una joya bibliográfica peruana: *La historia de las Indias* de Gómara, con anotaciones marginales manuscritas del Inca Garcilaso (*in* Perú. Biblioteca Nacional. Memoria que el Director . . . presenta al Sr. Ministro de Educación Pública, 1955, p. 65-75).
Reprinting of article published in *El Comercio* at Lima in 1948, studying marginal notes of a Zaragoza 1555 edition of Gómara's work. These notes appear by two hands, one of the Inca Garcilaso and the other of an anonymous soldier identified as the conquistador Gonzalo Silvestre who provided much of the data for the Inca Garcilaso's *La Florida.*

3716. Spell, Jefferson Rea. The historical and social background of *El Periquillo Sarniento* (HAHR, 36:4, Nov. 1956, p. 447-470).
A very useful and heavily documented article identifying names and places mentioned in Fernández de Lizardi's best novel. It is accompanied by a very adequate map of Mexico City in that author's time, which greatly facilitates locating the streets and buildings referred to in the text.

3717. ————. The intellectual background of Fernández de Lizardi as reflected in *El Periquillo Sarniento* (PMLA, 71:3, June 1956, p. 414-432).
An illuminating study of the works utilized by El Pensador Mexicano (1776-1827) in his best novel. The ideas diffused in his writings were derived from a wide reading of 18th-century French and Italian didactic works available in Spanish, as well as the older and contemporary products of Castilian literature.

3718. Symposium sobre el Inca Garcilaso de la Vega (R Cent Estud Hist Mil, 8:10, julio-agosto 1954, p. 172-193).

Brief digests of papers read on occasion of the 350th anniversary of the publication of *La Florida*, including: A. Miró Quesada, "Creación y elaboración de la Florida"; José del C. Marín, "El arte militar en la obra del Inca"; Luis E. Valcárcel, "Garcilaso y la etnografía del Perú"; Carlos D. Valcárcel, "Concepto de la historia en los Comentarios Reales y las fuentes históricas usadas por el Inca"; R. Porras Barrenechea, "Nuevos fondos documentales sobre el Inca"; José Jiménez Borja, "El valor educativo de los Comentarios Reales"; Narciso Yepes Miranda, "Garcilaso: símbolo del americanismo"; Vladimiro Bermejo, "Algunos estudios críticos sobre Garcilaso"; José Durand, "Garcilaso y la cultura de su época."

3719. **Valcárcel, Daniel.** Ignacio de Castro, humanista tacneño y gran cusqueñista (1732-1792). Lima, Biblioteca de la Sociedad Peruana de Historia (Serie 1, Monografía, 4), 1955. 152 p.

A study of the life and works of an 18th century Peruvian figure of encyclopedic attainments; of illegitimate origin, he was a writer for the *Mercurio peruano*. His liberal tendencies made him a sympathizer of the Tupac Amaru rebellion, and rate him a precursor of independence.

TEXTS

3720. **Abad, Diego José.** Poesías castellanas. San Luis Potosí, Bolivia, Estilo, 1956.

Poems by a Mexican Jesuit (1729-1779), expelled with his Order in 1767, who wrote a Latin poem *De Deo Deoque Homini heroice*, a sort of *suma teologica*. Edited by Joaquín A. Peñalosa.

3721. **Balbuena, Bernardo de.** Grandeza mexicana. México, Imp. Universitaria (Biblioteca del estudiante universitario, 23), 1954. 208 p.

A re-issue of the 1941 edition, with fragments of the *Siglo de oro* and of *El Bernardo* included. Edited by Francisco Monterde.

3722. **Castellanos, Juan de.** Elegías de varones ilustres de Indias. Prólogo de Miguel Antonio Caro. Bogotá, ABC (Biblioteca de la Presidencia de Colombia, 9-12), 1955, 4 v. 696, 676, 617 p.

First new and complete edition of this long poem since that of the Biblioteca de Autores Españoles published in Madrid in 1847. This colossal poem of over 100,000 verses is a rhymed chronicle by a conquistador of Nueva Granada, and its value is more historical than literary. It is presented with a sketch of its author and his works, and his last will, but without critical apparatus.

3723. **Domínguez Camargo, Hernando.** San Ignacio de Loyola, fundador de la

Compañía de Jesús. Poema heróico. Síguenle las poesías del "Ramillete de varias flores poéticas" y la "Invectiva apologética." Bogotá, ABC (Biblioteca de la Presidencia de Colombia, 25), 1956. 446 p., illus.

Reprinting of posthumous, incomplete poem of five Books, 24 cantos, and 1200 octaves by a fervent adherent of the Cordoban poet, Luis de Góngora. He was ranked by some critics with Sor Juana Inés, Balbuena and other such New World figures. Born in Bogota, much of his life was spent as a clergyman in Tunja where he worked on his long poem on St. Ignatius. In a somewhat rambling introduction the editor characterizes him as "el primer aristócrata de las letras americanas," though admitting that his octaves are monotonous and dull, relieved now and then by flashes of gongoristic genius. Miscellaneous shorter poems of Domínguez Carmargo are included with this reprinting, the original of which was published in Madrid in 1666. It is a work for specialized tastes.

3724. **Garcilaso de la Vega, Inca.** La Florida del Inca. Historia del adelantado Hernando de Soto. Prólogo de Aurelio Miró Quesada. Estudio bibliográfico de José Durand. México, Fondo de Cultura Económica, 1956. xcii, 471 p., illus.

The first modern edition since 1829 of this important work of colonial literature. Its composition was influenced by the romances of chivalry and Italian narratives of the sixteenth century, and is much more novelesque in character than the *Comentarios reales*. The prologue is an extensive study of the Inca Garcilaso and his work, utilizing the most recently discovered materials. Format and printing are admirable. Edited by Emma S. Speratti Pinero.

3725. **Sigüenza y Góngora, Carlos de.** Relaciones históricas. Selección, prólogo y notas de M. Romero de Terreros. México, Imp. Universitaria (Biblioteca del estudiante universitario, 13), 1954. xxix, 185 p.

A new edition of the 1940 collection of historical writings by the 17th-century Mexican savant (1645-1700), including the picaresque narrative *Infortunios de Alonso Ramírez*, the *Relación de lo sucedido a la Armada de Barlovento*, and the *Alboroto y motín de los indios de México el 8 de junio de 1692.*

3726. El testamento de Potosí. Romance anónimo. Notas y comentarios de José Enrique Viaña R. Potosí, Bolivia, Editorial Potosí (Col. de la cultura boliviana, Cuad. 2), 1954. 77 p.

ESSAYS, TRANSLATIONS, AND MISCELLANY

3727. **Alatorre, Antonio.** Breve historia de un problema: la mexicanidad de Ruiz de Alarcón (*in* Anthology, Mexico City College, 1956, p. 27-46).

English version of the same article on p. 241-260. A review of the fruitless efforts of critics, from Hartzenbusch to the present day, to identify the Mexican-born dramatist of Spain's Golden Age theater with Mexican literature. Alarcón's one clear reference to his native land in his play *El semejante a sí mismo* and the fancied Mexican origin of the *mesura y cortesía* noted in his writings are tenuous strands by which to attach him to Mexican letters, and recent studies tend to destroy a lingering illusion.

3728. Arciniega, Rosa. La prohibición de libros en América (Cuad Am, año 14, 84:6, nov.-dic. 1955, 197-204).
Apparently an effort to revive the disproven conviction that official repression prevented the comparatively free circulation of books in colonial Spanish America. The author repeats the error of drawing conclusions from extant legislation rather than from an investigation of its effectiveness, and ignores available studies in Spanish clearly refuting her contentions.

3729. Arrom, José Juan. El teatro de Hispanoamérica en la época colonial. Habana, Anuario Bibliográfico Cubano, 1956. 233 p., 12 illus.
A welcome synthesis in five chapters, from pre-Hispanic beginnings to the end of the 18th century, with extensive bibliography and index. The theater as literature is described, with half the volume devoted to the Baroque period which is divided into two parts: *la alborada*, 1600-1681, and the *apogeo y ocaso*, 1681-1750.

3730. Bognoli, José Clemente. Cronistas españoles de la conquista americana (Mus Hist, 8:22, feb. 1956, p. 49-62).
Offers a "profile" of Alonso Enríquez de Guzmán, a *sevillano* who took part in the civil wars in Peru and wrote a fairly entertaining account of his career.

3731. Díaz del Castillo, Bernal. The Bernal Díaz chronicles; the true story of the conquest of Mexico. Translated and edited by Albert Idell. Garden City, N. Y., Doubleday, 1956. 414 p., maps.
A new translation of portions of the Bernal Díaz classic; the first since A. P. Maudslay's of a half century ago, and a much freer rendition though not more accurate.

3732. ————. The discovery and conquest of Mexico. Edited from the only exact copy of the original ms. (and published in Mexico) by Genaro García. Translated with an introduction and notes by A. P. Maudslay. Introd. to the American ed. by Irving A. Leonard. N. Y., Farrar, Straus, and Cudahy, 1956. 478 p., illus., maps.
The first American edition of the Maudslay translation with intercalated excerpts from Cortés' *Cartas relaciones;* introduction by Irving A. Leonard (p. xi-xviii) and extracts from introduction of the Genaro García Spanish edition of 1904-1905 (p. xix-xxxi).

3733. Fals-Borda, Orlando. Odyssey of a sixteenth-century document — Fray Pedro de Aguado's *Recopilación historial* (HAHR, 35:2, May 1955, p. 203-220).
The history of the manuscript of an early chronicle, *Relación historial resolutoria de Santa María y Nuevo Reino de Granada,* which was based on first hand contact with the conquerors and first settlers of present-day Colombia, and which remained unpublished until the 20th century.

3734. García Icazbalceta, Joaquín. Las "bibliotecas" de Eguiara y Beristáin (B Bibl S Hac Cr Púb, 37, junio 15, 1955, p. 4, 6; 39, julio 15, 1955, p. 4; 41, agosto 15, 1955, p. 5-6).
Reprinting of the distinguished 19th-century Mexican bibliophile's article (1878) concerning the 18th-century Mexican bibliophiles.

3735. Grases, Pedro. La imprenta y la cultura en la Primera República, 1810-1812. Caracas, Universidad Central de Venezuela, Instituto de Filosofía, 1956. 24 p., illus.
A discussion of the early press in Venezuela and its publications such as the first review *El lucero,* the *Calendario manual y guía universal de forasteros, Derechos del hombre, La lógica* of Condillac, etc. Facsimile illustrations.

3736. ————. Orígenes de la imprenta en Cumaná (El Farol, 17:164, junio 1956).
Pamphlets of 1810 are traced to a press established in Cumana and indicate the beginning of printing that year in that locality. Cumana was thus the second city after Caracas to publish periodical imprints.

3737. Jackson, William Richard. Early Florida through Spanish eyes. Edited by R. S. Boggs. Miami, Florida, University of Miami Press (Hispanic American studies, 12), 1954. 179 p.
A doctoral dissertation examining the impressions of Florida recorded by early Spanish chroniclers and explorers beginning with Ponce de León.

3738. Lohmann Villena, Guillermo. Poesías vascas en Lima en el siglo XVIII. San Sebastián, Spain, Real Sociedad Vascongada de Amigos del País, 1957. 6 p.
Verses in multiple languages were frequently inscribed on funeral monuments, and one in Lima in 1761 included stanzas in the Basque speech which are here reproduced with a Spanish translation. This brief essay offers a curious sidelight on colonial literary customs.

3739. López Estrada, Francisco. La literatura contemporánea considerada desde Lima por Rodrigo de Carvajal (1627-1631). Primeras jornadas de lengua y literatura hispanoamericana. Comunicaciones y ponencias. Salamanca, Spain, Actas salamanticencia (Serie de filosofía y letras, 10:1-2), 1956. 2 v. 509, 346 p.

Rodrigo de Carvajal y Robles was a very learned and competent poet of Lima who wrote on Castilian as well as local themes, including his worthy *La conquista de Antequera* (Lima, 1627) celebrating the victory of the Infante, Don Fernando, in 1410.

3740. Mariluz Urquijo, José María. La biblioteca de un Oidor de la Real Audiencia de Buenos Aires (R Fac Der Cien Soc, B A, 10:44, julio-agosto 1955, p. 808-814).

Text of an inventory of books belonging to the Oidor Francisco de Ansotegui (1812), with commentary.

3741. Márquez Abanto, Alberto. Don Antonio Ricardo, introductor de la imprenta en Lima: su testamento y codicilo. Poder: don Toribio Alfonso de Mogrovejo, Arzobispo de Lima, y demás obispos a favor de don Juan López de Baides y otro, para que gestione ante su Majestad licencia para el funcionamiento de la imprenta de Lima (R Arch Nac Perú, 19:2, 1955, p. 290-305).

Biographical data on the first printer in Peru, and text of documents dated 1584 and 1586.

3742. Núñez, Enrique Bernardo. El teatro del Coliseo (Crónica Caracas, año 4, 4:19, agosto-dic. 1954, p. 588-605).

A history of the first theater built in Caracas (1784), with a contemporary plan of the structure.

3743. Pedro, Valentín de. América en las letras españolas del Siglo de Oro. B. A., Editorial Sudamericana (Historia y crítica literarias), 1954. 365 p., illus.

The author, a South American of long residence in Spain, systematically searches the writings of major and minor figures of the golden age of Peninsula literature for indications of their interest in the New World, but with meager results. It is clear that the trans-Atlantic domains of the Spanish crown offered little inspiration to the artistic endeavors of the Spaniards.

3744. Rojas, Arístides. Orígens del teatro en Caracas (Crónica Caracas, año 4, 4:19, agosto-dic. 1954, p. 575-587).

The first license to perform a play was granted by the Cabildo, June 28, 1600, and the first theater built was in 1784, a gift of Manuel González Torres Navarro to the city. The first play definitely known by title was the *Auto a Nuestra Señora del Rosario,* written between 1766 and 1769.

3745. Torre Revello, José. La biblioteca que poseía en Potosí don Pedro de Altolaguirre, 1799 (Hist, B. A., 1:4, abril-junio 1956, p. 153-162).

The 87 titles of the personal library of the treasurer of the mint in the famous mining town of Peru include fictional works of Cervantes, Zayas, Quevedo, LeSage, and even a romance of chivalry; also historical writings of Herrera, Inca Garcilaso, Ulloa, Mariana, Saavedra y Fajardo; essays of Feijóo, and works of French writers such as Buffon, Rollin, and Butel-Dumont. This list is convincing evidence of the unhampered circulation of books when the French Revolution had tightened censorship. Appendix reproduces complete inventory.

3746. Tudisco, Anthony. The land, people, and problems of America in eighteenth-century Spanish literature (Americas, Franciscan Hist, 12:4, Apr. 1956, p. 363-384).

The vision of America contained in the works of 18th-century Spanish writers, and the importance of their writings for an understanding of the history of the period in Spanish America.

3747. Valdés, Octaviano. El barroco, espíritu y forma del arte de México (Ábside, 20:4, oct.-dic. 1956, p. 380-409).

This "discurso de recepción" in the Mexican Academy devotes much of its space to Sor Juana Inés de la Cruz' enigmatic *Primer sueño.* "De aquí que este *Sueño,* por su forma y contenido, sea, no barroco, sino ultrabarroca . . ." The author stresses a comparison with the *Muerte sin fin* of José Gorostiza.

BIBLIOGRAPHICAL WORKS

3748. Beltrán Martínez, Román. Bibliógrafos mexicanos. Obras de don Carlos de Sigüenza y Góngora (B Bibl S Hac Cr Púb, 41, agosto 15, 1955, p. 3, 5).

Detailed description of the *Piedad heróica de Fernando Cortés,* followed by a list of other works of the Creole savant (1645-1700).

3749. Grases, Pedro. La fecha de impresión del libro de Quintana (R Nac Cult, 18:115, marzo-abril 1956, p. 39-44).

One of the first products of the press in Venezuela, Juan Nepomuceno Quintana's *La intolerancia político-religiosa,* a polemical tract, allegedly published in 1811, is proven to have appeared in August 1812.

3750. Lohmann Villena, Guillermo. Fuentes bibliográficas del Epítome de Pinelo (RIB, 5:3, julio-sept. 1955, p. 153-162).

Brief notes on the private book collections and catalogues utilized by León Pinelo, the 16th-century bibliographer, in his important *Epítome de la biblioteca oriental, occidental, naútica y geográfica* (Madrid, 1629), with facsimiles of the *portada* and sample pages.

3751. Torre Revello, José. Tratados de arquitectura utilizados en Hispano-América, siglos XVI a XVIII (RIB, 6:1, enero-marzo 1956, p. 3-23).

From colonial shipping manifests, book-dealers' inventories, and records of private libraries, the author singles out architectural treatises of Spanish and Italian authorities published from 1526 to 1715, including Sagredo, Cataneo, Gamucci, Alberti, Vitruvio, Arfe de Villafañe, Vignola, Palladio, Carducho, San Nicolás, Pacheco, and Torija which are listed in the appendix of this article.

SPANISH AMERICAN LITERATURE: NINETEENTH AND TWENTIETH CENTURIES

GENERAL

ÁNGEL FLORES

3800. Anderson Imbert, Enrique. Historia de la literatura hispanoamericana. México, Fondo de Cultura Económica (Breviarios, 89), 1954. 430 p.
Excellent survey of Latin American literature: succinct yet thorough and dependable, the work of a writer of taste and critical acumen.

3801. Arrieta, Rafael Alberto. Introducción al modernismo literario. B. A., Columba (Col. Esquemas, 24), 1956. 63 p.
Brief exposition on the French sources of Modernism, its precursors, influential journals, and leading representatives.

3802. Barrera, Isaac J. Historia de la literatura ecuatoriana. Quito, Casa de la Cultura Ecuatoriana, 1944-1955. 4 v. V. 3, Siglo XIX, 1954, 589 p.; v. 4, Registro de la producción literaria hasta nuestros días, 1955, 233 p.
V. 1 and 2 were published by Editorial Ecuatoriana. V. 3 of this over-written history of Ecuadorean literature deals with the 19th century and its crowning figures: Olmedo, Montalvo, Mera. V. 4 is focused on the 20th century, but fails utterly to illuminate the more exciting figures of today: the author seems full of reservations and prejudices.

3803. Baudrit González, Fabio. Cifra antológica de Fabio Baudrit González. San José, Editorial Universitaria (Sección Antologías; Autores costarricenses, 1), 1956. 341 p.
Short stories, sketches, legends, and articles by a Costa Rican humanist.

3804. Borges, Jorge Luis. Leopoldo Lugones. B. A., Troquel (Diálogos del presente, 5), 1955. 99 p.
Written with the collaboration of Betina Edelberg. Perceptive introduction to Modernism and especially to one of its seminal figures, the Argentine Lugones. Borges points out his successes and failures as poet and writer of prose fiction.

3805. Cardona Peña, Alfredo. Crónica de México. México, Antigua Librería Robredo (México y lo mexicano, 23), 1955 [i. e. 1956]. 115 p.
A poet's picturesque and anecdotical vision of Mexico.

3806. Carella, Tulio. El tango: mito y e- sencia. B. A. Ediciones Doble P (Grandes escritores argentinos; Ensayos, 2), 1956. 127 p.
Repository and chrestomathy of tango lore: its origin, development, and influences. Poet Carella, displaying humorous erudition, retranslates into Spanish the English versions of the Spanish lyrics of several Argentine tangos.

3807. Carilla, Emilio. Lengua y estilo en el "Facundo." Tucumán, Argentina, Universidad Nacional de Tucumán, Departamento de Extensión Universitaria (Cuadernos de extensión universitaria, 4), 1955? 31 p.
The old truism that "the style is the man" seems to find eloquent corroboration in the case of Sarmiento whose *Facundo* reflects his militant psychology.

3808. Carrera, Julieta. La mujer en América escribe . . . Semblanzas. 1. ed. México, Ediciones Alonso, 1956. 332 p.
50-odd gossipy sketches of women writers, good, bad, or indifferent. Among the best are those dealing with Claudia Lars, Marta Brunet, Alfonsina Storni, Teresa de la Parra, Juana Ibarbourou, and Gabriela Mistral.

3809. Carsuzán, María Emma. La creación en la prosa de España e Hispanoamérica. B. A., Raigal, 1955. 200 p.
After surveying the development of prose from Quevedo to Bécquer, the author centers her analysis on the precursors of modern Latin American prose (Martí, Lugones, etc.) and on the cultivators of Argentine fiction (Payró, Cambaceres, etc.).

3810. Ciudad. B. A. No. 1, primer trimestre 1955-.
Excellent magazine of the Argentine literary vanguard, strong in its critical material. The first issue emphasized the work of Ezequiel Martínez Estrada; the second, no. 2-3, that of Jorge Luis Borges.

3811. Colegio Nacional. El Colegio Nacional a Alfonso Reyes, uno de sus miembros fundadores, en su cincuentenario de escritor. México, 1956. 254 p., illus., music. (Biblioteca, 13).
Contributions on scientific and literary subjects presented as tribute to Alfonso Reyes. Interesting essays by Silvio Zavala on the influence of the geographical milieu on the various European colonies in America, and by Castro Leal on Díaz Mirón.

3812. Comisión Popular Ejecutiva de Homenaje a Ricardo Rojas. Homenaje a Ricardo Rojas. Tucumán, Argentina, La Raza, 1955. 79 p.
Report on the placing of a plaque on the house where Rojas was born. October 1954 marked the 50th year of the publication of Rojas' first book, *La victoria del hombre.*

3813. Crema, Edoardo. Interpretaciones críticas de literatura venezolana. Caracas, Universidad Central de Venezuela, Facultad de Humanidades y Educación, Instituto de Estudios Hispanoamericanos (Estudios hispanoamericanos, 1), 1954? 390 p.
Authoritative studies of Venezuelan writers: among others, Juan Vicente González, Daniel Mendoza, Romero García, Uslar Pietri, and Arráiz.

3814. Cuesta Gonsenheim, Sylvia. Literatura y periodismo en José Martí. México, Universidad Femenina de México, 1953. 61 p.
Repertorial survey of Martí's periodical contribution. Thesis.

3815. Cúneo, Dardo. El romanticismo político: Leopoldo Lugones, Roberto J. Payró, José Ingenieros, Macedonio Fernández, Manuel Ugarte, Alberto Gerchunoff. B. A., Ediciones Transición, 1955. 139 p.
Impact of Argentine political strife on the writings of leading modern writers. Dispassionate analysis, often sound.

3816. Díaz-Plaja, Guillermo, and Francisco Monterde. Historia de la literatura española, [por] Guillermo Díaz-Plaja. Historia de la literatura mexicana, [por] Francisco Monterde. México, Porrúa, 1955. 625 p., illus.
An expensive exposition of banalities and commonplace generalizations.

3817. Domínguez, Luis Arturo. Antología de escritores del estado Falcón. Coro, Venezuela, Centro de Historia del Estado Falcón, 1955. 431 p.
66 literary creators from Falcon State, Venezuela, who, except for Ángel Miguel Queremel (1899-1939), are probably known only to specialists.

3818. Dromundo, Baltasar. Mi calle de San Ildefonso. México, Guaranía, 1956. 263 p.
Mexico City at the beginning of the century as remembered by a gifted newspaperman.

3819. Durand, Luis. Gente de mi tiempo. Santiago, Nascimento, 1953. 227 p., illus.
Amusing remembrances of the late Durand's friends: Neruda, Subercaseaux, Latorre, and other Chilean intellectuals.

3820. Dussuel, Francisco. Historia de la literatura chilena. Santiago, Ediciones Paulinas, 1954. 248 p.
Orthodox yet undogmatic survey of Chilean letters; in systematic arrangement and intelligent flexibility surpasses most manuals extant.

3821. Ferrer Canales, José. Varona, escritor. México, Universidad Nacional Autónoma de México, Facultad de Filosofía y Letras, 1952. 394 p.
A pedestrian account of Varona's formative period: his readings, his writings on foreign literature and translations, his contributions to esthetics and education. Thesis.

3822. Finot, Enrique. Historia de la literatura boliviana. 2. ed., complementada. La Paz, Gisbert, 1955. 621 p. & illus.
New edition of Finot's survey, supplemented by an appendix on the literature of the colonial period by José de Mesa and Teresa Gisbert, and another on the contemporary period by Luis Felipe Vilela, both schematic, desultory, and helping but little the late Finot.

3823. García Blanco, Manuel. El escritor mexicano Alfonso Reyes y Unamuno. México, Graf. Panamericana, Archivo de Alfonso Reyes, Serie F, Documentos, 1), 1956. 51 p.
Archivistic trivia.

3824. Ghiano, Juan Carlos. Lugones, escritor. Notas para un análisis estilístico. B. A., Raigal (Biblioteca Juan María Gutiérrez), 1955. 177 p.
Random notes on Lugones and his influence.

3825. González Vargas, Enrique. El Instituto Literario del Estado de México en la época de Ignacio Manuel Altamirano. Toluca, México, Agrícola Mexicana (Cuadernos del estado de México), 1956. 75 p.
Mid-19th-century literary life in Toluca, Mexico.

3826. González Vera, José Santos. Cuando era muchacho. Santiago, Nascimento, 1956. 273 p.
Delightful remembrances of things past by a Chilean virtuoso. Originally published in 1951.

3827. Grossmann, Rodolfo, and Luis Arturo Castellanos. El autor y el público hispano-americano: esbozo de una sociología literaria, por Rodolfo Grossmann. Aporte escénico de novelistas españoles, por Luis Arturo Castellanos. Rosario, Argentina, Universidad Nacional del Litoral, Instituto de Letras, 1952? 60 p.
Professor Grossman's 1952 lecture on the sociology of taste, followed by Dr. Castellanos' exposition on the theatre and Spanish novelists Azorín, Valle Inclán, Unamuno.

3828. Gutiérrez Nájera, Manuel. Manuel

Gutiérrez Nájera; estudio y escritos inéditos, por Boyd G. Carter. México, Ediciones de Andrea (Col. Studium, 2. serie, 12), 1956. 160 p.
Footnoting Gutiérrez Nájera's periodical contributions, especially to *El correo germánico*.

3829. Hernández, José. Las Islas Malvinas. Compilación, sumarios y notas de Joaquín Gil Guiñón. B. A., Joaquín Gil, 1952. 63 p.
Some brief travel notes on a trip to the Falkland Islands by the author of *Martín Fierro*, and correspondence concerning them. [B. Wood]

3830. Holguín y Caro, Margarita (ed.). Los Caros en Colombia. Su fe, su patriotismo, su amor. 2. ed. Bogotá, Instituto Caro y Cuervo, 1953. 334 p., illus.
First edition, 1942. One Caro about other Caros; family papers.

3831. Ibarra de Anda, Fortino. 20 años de libros. Ensayos de crítica. México, Juventa, 1956. 103 p.
Random comments on book publishing in Mexico, by a bibliographer and a lover of books.

3832. Iraizoz, Antonio. Libros y autores cubanos. Santa María del Rosario, Cuba, Editorial Rosareña, 1956. 178 p.
Miscellaneous essays: the French Heredia, Espronceda in Cuba, a grandson of Voltaire born in Cuba, Martí, Marxism, cats and poetry.

3833. Key-Ayala, Santiago. Obras selectas. Madrid, Edime (Clásicos y modernos hispanoamericanos), 1955. 1245 p.
Omnibook containing paramount contributions by the biographer of Bolívar and Miranda, who is also interested in linguistics and folklore.

3834. León, Trigueros de. Perfil en el aire. San Salvador, Ministerio de Cultura, Departamento Editorial (Col. Contemporáneos, 5), 1955. 260 p., illus.
Garrulous presentation of a score of Spanish and Latin American writers, including Alfonso Reyes, Maples Arce, Labrador Ruiz, Moreno Villa, and Rafael Alberti.

3835. López Bermúdez, José. Teoría de la palabra. México, Editorial Mar, 1954. 233 p.
Dithyrambic mouthings on Claudel, Bécquer, Neruda, López Velarde, García Lorca, and the rest.

3836. López Villarino, María del Socorro. Luis G. Urbina, el poeta y el prosista. México, Imp. Mexicana, 1956. 93 p. & illus.
Thesis for a Master's in Spanish literature, contributing little toward the understanding of the Mexican poet Urbina.

3837. Magdaleno, Mauricio. Ritual del año. México, Los Presentes (14), 1955. 151 p.
Evocations of old towns and landscape.

3838. Martínez, José Luis. La emancipación literaria de México. México, Antigua Librería Robredo (México y lo mexicano, 21), 1955. 88 p.
On getting away from Spanish models in Latin American literature, and, more specifically, on the mental "emancipation" of Mexico.

3839. ————. La expresión nacional. Letras mexicanas del siglo XIX. México, Imp. Universitaria (Serie Letras, 20), 1955. 306 p.
Reprint of book reviews and articles on 19th-century Mexican writers from Lizardi to Rabasa.

3840. Mead, Robert G., Jr. Breve historia del ensayo hispanoamericano. México, Ediciones de Andrea (Manuales Studium, 3), 1956. 142 p.
Pithy summary of the development of essay writing in Latin America.

3841. Medina, José Ramón. Examen de la poesía venezolana contemporánea. Caracas, Ministerio de Educación, Dirección de Cultura y Bellas Artes (Col. Letras venezolanas, 4), 1956. 55 p.
A young poet examines the poetry of Venezuela of the last 20 years.

3842. Morón, Guillermo. El libro de la fe. Madrid, Ediciones Rialp, 1955. 255 p.
Religious approach to culture, followed by laudatory essays on Uslar Pietri and Picón Salas.

3843. Pultera (hijo), Raúl. Lugones. Elementos cardinales destinados a determinar una biografía. B. A., 1956. 522 p.
Notes and newspaper clippings concerning Lugones' activities.

3844. Ramírez y Astier, Aniceto. Galería de escritores zulianos. Contribución al estudio de las letras venezolanas. T. 2. Maracaibo, Venezuela, Universidad Nacional del Zulia, 1952. 237 p.
A rather dull anthological presentation of 32 writers from Zulia State, Venezuela.

3845. René-Moreno, Gabriel. Estudios de literatura boliviana. Prólogo de Humberto Vásquez-Machicado. Potosí, Bolivia, Editorial Potosí (Col. de la cultura boliviana, 5-6; Col. 2, Los escritores del siglo XIX, 2-3), 1955-1956. 2 v. Parte 1, 265 p.; parte 2, 377 p.
René-Moreno's contributions to Chilean periodicals (1856-1864) on Bolivian cultural figures of the 19th century, including Manuel José Tovar, Mariano Ramallo, Nestor Galíndez, etc.

3846. **Reyes, Alfonso.** Obras completas. I. Cuestiones estéticas. Capítulos de literatura mexicana. Varia. México, Fondo de Cultura Económica (Letras mexicanas), 1955. 369 p.
Containing Reyes' writings for 1903-1913: *Visión de Anáhuac, Las vísperas de España,* and *Calendario.*

3847. ————. Parentalia. Primer capítulo de mis recuerdos. México, Los Presentes, 1954. 74 p.
Reyes on Reyes' relatives. Mildly amusing.

3848. **Samper, José María.** Selección de estudios. Bogotá, Ministerio de Educación Nacional, Ediciones de la Revista Bolívar (Biblioteca de autores colombianos, 38), 1953. 305 p.
14 pieces: on Bolívar the Liberator; Bolívar the poet; on Julio Arboleda, José María Vergara y Vergara, Joaquín Acosta, and other Colombian writers.

3849. **Sánchez, Luis Alberto.** ¿Tuvimos maestros en nuestra América? Balance y liquidación del novecientos. B. A., Raigal (Biblioteca Nuestra América, 3), 1956. 192 p.
The reaction of the 1920 generation of Latin American writers to the "masters" of the *fin du siécle,* especially Rodó. First published in 1941 under title *Balance y liquidación del novecientos.*

3850. **Sarmiento, Domingo Faustino.** Polémica literaria. B. A., Cartago, 1955. 203 p.
Articles dealing with literature as expression and vehicle of popular culture.

3851. **Semprum, Jesús.** Crítica literaria. Selección y notas de Pedro Díaz Seijas y Luis Semprum. Caracas, Ediciones Villegas, 1956. 411 p.
Some 40 essays on Latin American literature, principally Venezuelan, by the late Jesús Semprum (1882-1931).

3852. **Tamayo Vargas, Augusto.** Literatura peruana. T. 2. Lima, Imp. Domingo Miranda, 1954. 359 p.
The author brings down to 1940 his survey of Peruvian literature, elucidating, often felicitously, the main currents of the 18th and 19th centuries.

3853. **Torres, Edelberto.** Enrique Gómez Carrillo, el cronista errante. Guatemala, Librería Escolar, 1956. 384 p. & illus.
Exhaustive biography of the journalist Gómez Carrillo. Torres emphasizes Gómez Carrillo's erotic life comparing him to Casanova.

3854. **Torres Ríoseco, Arturo.** Breve historia de la literatura chilena. México, Ediciones de Andrea (Manuales Studium, 1), 1956. 175 p.

A hasty by-product of an industrious literary historian.

3855. **Uruguay. Instituto Nacional de Investigaciones y Archivos Literarios.** En el centenario de Zorrilla de San Martín. Zorrilla de San Martín y Tabaré, conferencia de Charles V. Aubrun. Más sobre Unamuno y Zorrilla, carta de Raúl Montero Bustamante. Montevideo, 1955. 39 p. (Série 2, estudios y testimonios).
Ecstasy over *Tabaré*—insincere, shallow.

3856. **Uslar-Pietri, Arturo.** Pizarrón. Caracas, Edime (Autores venezolanos), 1955. 338 p.
Journalistic utterances on international cultural trends.

3857. **Visca, Arturo Sergio** (ed.). Correspondencia de Zorrilla de San Martín y Unamuno. Montevideo, Instituto Nacional de Investigaciones y Archivos Literarios (Serie 1, Epistolarios), 1955. 66 p., facsims.
An exchange of letters, 1906-1911.

3858. **Von Bertrab, Hermann.** Un humanista moderno (Gabriel Méndez Plancarte). México, Universidad Iberoamericana, 1956. 181 p.
Thesis for the Master's degree in "Castilian letters" from the University of Chihuahua, on the great Mexican humanist Gabriel Méndez Plancarte (1905-1949), editor, poet, and translator of Ovid's *Metamorphosis.*

3859. **Zorrilla, José.** México y los mexicanos (1855-1857). Prólogo, notas y bibliografía de Andrés Henestrosa. México, Ediciones de Andrea (Col. Studium, 9), 1955. 158 p.
Travel and descriptions of 19th-century Mexico by the Spanish Romantic poet Zorrilla.

PROSE FICTION
EDUARDO NEALE-SILVA

DIGNAS DE mención especial, en el campo del relato psicológico, son la novela corta *Teléfono ocupado,* de Silvina Bullrich, y *Los Ingar,* de C. E. Zavaleta. Entre las narraciones indigenistas quizás la mejor sea *La bruma lo vuelve azul* de Ramón Rubín.

Considerada en su totalidad, la producción novelística verdaderamente notable de estos últimos años no es abundante. El tema indigenista parece ir cediendo el paso al relato socio-psicológico; el tema político, en cambio, sigue siendo de interés, pero ninguna de las obras de asunto político aquí incluidas logra descollar, unas por falta de estructuración artística, otras por exceso de vehemencia y otras, en fin, por su obsesivo afán delator.

En el campo del cuento, por el contrario, es posible señalar varias colecciones que sobresalen por su calidad artística. Es motivo de especial regocijo que Ezequiel Martínez Estrada vuelva al campo novelístico después de un largo e involuntario silencio: *Tres cuentos sin amor* y el volumen *Marta Riquelme; Examen sin conciencia* son bellos exponentes de los dones creativos de este hombre singular. Novedosos e impresionantes son los relatos de Virgilio Rodríguez Macal (*Sangre y clorofila*), en los cuales se revela un escritor de gran sentido dramático y voluntad de forma. Dignas también de mención especial son las narraciones nativistas de Hugo Lindo (*Guaro y champaña*) y dos colecciones argentinas: *Caballos,* de Luis Gudiño Kramer y *Cenizas,* de Diego R. Oxley. Entre los estudios de personajes y de un ambiente social conviene recordar el volumen de Gastón García Cantú (*Los falsos rumores*) y las conmovedoras narraciones recogidas en el volumen *De sol a sol,* por Julio C. da Rosa.

En estos últimos años han venido apareciendo varias ediciones nuevas de autores conocidos, tales como las *Obras completas* de Eugenio Cambaceres y de José S Álvarez ("Fray Mocho"), dos volúmenes que serán de positiva utilidad a todos los interesados en las letras americanas. En el grupo de las antologías se destacan la de Salvador Bueno (*Antología del cuento en Cuba*) y la de E. M. S. Danero (*Antología gaucha*).

En el campo de la críticas se hallan dos estudios que llaman la atención a pesar de su brevedad, el de Ramón Díaz Sánchez sobre Teresa de la Para, de especial interés por contarse entre los pocos trabajos interpretativos de cierta envergadura sobre la escritora venezolana, y el Gervasio Guillot Muñoz sobre Carlos Reyles, por referirse a algunos aspectos no bien conocidos de la personalidad del autor de *El embrujo de Sevilla*. Dos

estudios meritorios de carácter global son el volumen de Enrique Williams Alzaga sobre el tema de la pampa en la novela argentina y la monografía de J.S. Brushwood sobre la novela romántica mexicana.

Y antes de terminar, una breve alusión al volumen de Aristóbulo Echegaray sobre *Don Segundo Sombra.* Esta pequeña obra es sintomática de un intento de volaración negativa de la novela de Güiraldes. A pesar de las muchas observaciones acertadas que en ella se presentan, es de lamentar que el autor, llevado muchas veces de su punto de vista socio-económico, no vea lo que se debiera ver en una obra de imaginación (véase *HLAS, no. 19*, párrafo 4969).*

---

*Saúl Sibirsky (Cornell College, Mount Vernon, Iowa) consented, at the invitation of Dr. Neale-Silva, to contribute a substantial number of items to this section. Each of them is followed by Sr. Sibirsky's name. (Editor's note.)

NOVELS AND SHORT STORIES

3900. Aguilar, Octavio. El juez Olaverri y Juan Canastuj. Historias policíacas. Guatemala, Landívar, 1956. 91 p.
13 situaciones en que un perspicaz vagabundo, convertido en ayudante del juez, encuentra la solución de distintos crímenes. Libro de pocos méritos.

3901. Aguilera Malta, Demetrio. La isla virgen. Con un estudio preliminar por Ángel F. Rojas. Quito, Casa de la Cultura Ecuatoriana (Biblioteca de relatistas ecuatorianos), 1954. xxiii, 404 p.
La lucha de clases en tierra montuvia, presentada a través de múltiples escenas unificadas por un ambiente de pasión, desesperanza y tragedia y por la presencia constante de la naturaleza. Primera edición, con idéntico prólogo, 1942.

3902. Álvarez, José Sixto ("Fray Mocho," pseud.). Obras completas. Prólogo y notas por F. J. Solero. B. A., Schapire, 1954. 618 p.
Contiene: *Esmeraldas, Salero criollo, Memorias de un vigilante, Un viaje al país de los matreros, En el mar austral* y *Cuentos.*

3903. Amorim, Enrique. Corral abierto. B. A., Losada, 1956. 203 p.
Extraña mezcla de novela detectivesca (hasta la p. 112) con un relato sobre la vida peripatética del héroe y una visión sombría de las miserias de un villorrio llamado "Campo abierto." A pesar de los excelentes retratos de personajes—algunos de ellos sin ninguna relación directa con la vida del héroe—y de la variedad de escenas en distintos ámbitos sociales, este libro deja un poco defraudado al lector.

3904. ————. Todo puede suceder. Montevideo, Vir, 1955. 118 p.
Después de un largo y lento comienzo de valor puramente ambiental, se entra en la acción misma de esta novela, en la cual aparecen dos mujeres hechizadas por la personalidad misteriosa de un celador extranjero. Trama sencilla, a veces desmedida e inexplicable.

3905. Andreu Iglesias, César. Los derrotados, México, Los Presentes, 1956. 310 p.
En un estilo escueto y preciso el autor hilvana los esfuerzos de diversos personajes idealistas que persiguen la ilusión de un Puerto Rico independiente. La trama está enmarcada en la historia de la isla y el desenlace, a primera vista trágico, se transforma en esperanza nacionalista. Se malogra un tanto el fin de la novela al prolongarse en demasía después de presentarse los sucesos culminantes de la obra, pero el tema y la trama despiertan sumo interés. [S. Sibirsky]

3906. Araya, Enrique. La jaula por dentro. Santiago, Artes y Letras, 1955. 180 p.
Relato epistolar de un burócrata paupérrimo que se desahoga escribiendo. Obra de poca profundidad, en que se contradicen a menudo los conocimientos del personaje y su preparación, su pobreza y sus peripecias. Revela la obra cierta agudeza social y psicológica, aunque no siempre quede logrado el efecto humorístico. [S. Sibirsky]

3907. Asturias, Miguel Ángel. El Papa Verde. Novela. B. A., Losada, 1954. 319 p.
Apasionado memorial de agravios en contra de la United Fruit Co., y sus métodos de penetración económica: maquinaciones políticas, despojo de campesinos indefensos, propaganda internacional, etc. La intención delatora, obvia desde el comienzo, reduce en parte la eficacia de la novela como representación de la realidad. Lenguaje altamente poético e imaginería audaz, no siempre consonante con el asunto del libro. Vocabulario, p. 313-318. Traducción francesa de Francis de Miomandre, Le Pape Vert (Paris, Éditions Albin Michel, 1956).

3908. Ayala Gauna, Velmiro. Los casos de don Frutos Gómez. Cuentos correntinos. Santa Fe, Argentina, Castellví, 1955. 174 p.
Pesquisas del comisario don Frutos Gómez. Colección de 14 cuentos (tres de los cuales habían ya aparecido en Nuevos cuentos correntinos) en los cuales hay una evidente intención detectivesca que obliga al autor a seguir un patrón determinado de exposición, investigación y pruebas, menoscabando con ello la naturalidad y frescura de la narración.

3909. Barros Ortiz, Diego. Kronios. La rebelión de los Atlantes. Santiago, Zig-Zag (Biblioteca americana), 1954. 227 p.
Novela imaginaria en que se recrea con delicadeza el mundo misterioso de la famosa isla Atlántida, relacionándose a los dioses de la mitología griega con las divinidades indias americanas. [S. Sibirsky]

3910. Bilbao La Vieja, Genaro. Pueblo chico. La Paz, Don Bosco, 1955. 159 p.
Novela corta, de escaso valor literario por versar sobre un tema muy trillado—amores contrariados y rcnconciliación final de dos familias a través del nieto. Personajes convencionales, técnica defectuosa, lenguaje académico.

3911. Bioy Casares, Adolfo. Historia prodigiosa. México, Obregón (Col. literaria, 4), 1956. 151 p.
Cuentos psicológicos que revelan las preocupaciones intelectuales del autor y su predilección por la mitología y elementos kafkianos. Tienen más relieve los comentarios y meditaciones que la acción misma. [S. Sibirsky]

3912. Borges, Jorge Luis. Ficciones. B. A., Emecé (Obras completas de Jorge Luis Borges, 5), 1956. 197 p.
Nueva edición de las ocho piezas de El jardín de los senderos ocultos, publicadas por primera vez en 1942, y de los seis cuentos de la serie Artificios, más tres narraciones nuevas, entre las cuales descuella "El sur," uno de los mejores cuentos de Borges.

3913. Bosch, Juan. La muchacha de la Guaira. Santiago, Nascimento, 1955. 197 p.
Perito en la técnica del cuento, el autor presenta varias narraciones que difieren en su argumento pero que muestran idéntico desarrollo. A una corta exposición de datos importantes sigue una larga descripción del ambiente, entrelazándose los personajes y su psicología con la trama, para desembocar súbitamente en el desenlace final. El estilo cambia continuamente para amoldarse a la complejidad de los protagonistas. Éstos se ven obligados inesperadamente a utilizar toda la gama de sus sentimientos y recursos mentales. Sitúa el autor sus relatos en diversas regiones americanas, creando bellos cuadros de costumbres, en especial de indios montañeses. [S. Sibirsky]

3914. Bueno, Salvador (ed.). Antología del cuento en Cuba, 1902-1952. Habana, Ministerio de Educación, Dirección de Cultura, 1953. 399 p.
Excelente colección, con prólogo de Salvador Bueno. Dice el prologuista: "El objetivo de esta antología consiste en cernir, estructurar y organizar la producción cuentística cubana en este medio siglo de república independiente, entre 1902 y 1952 . . . No he desdeñado ninguna tendencia de calidad en las letras cubanas contemporáneas."

3915. Bullrich, Silvina. Teléfono ocupado. B. A., Goyanarte, 1955. 108 p.
Otra excelente novela de la autora de Bodas de cristal. Sobre un fondo de aparentes trivialidades telefónicas, diseña la protagonista la psicología de sus interlocutores, reconstruyendo a la vez su propio pasado amoroso bajo el apremio de un posible chantage. Hay en este libro un magnífico sondeo del alma humana y muy acertadas observaciones sobre la vida contemporánea.

3916. Cambaceres, Eugenio. Obras completas. Observaciones y notas por E. M. S. Danero. Santa Fe, Argentina, Castellví (Clásicos argentinos), 1956. 263 p.

Excelente volumen a doble columna en que se reúnen *Pot pourri, Música sentimental, Sin rumbo* y *En la sangre.*

3917. Cané, Miguel. Juvenilia. Santa Fe, Argentina, Castellví (Clásicos argentinos), 1954. 293 p.

Edición aumentada con un capítulo inédito, ilustraciones documentales, un apéndice, profusas notas y una biografía del autor por E. M. S. Danero.

3918. Carballido, Emilio. La veleta oxidada. México, Los Presentes (50), 1956. 93 p.

Incomprensión conyugal, bajezas morales, adulterio—he aquí los temas de esta ágil y escueta novela corta. Más que el argumento mismo o la psicología de los personajes, lo que llama la atención aquí es la extraña mezcla de libidinosidad y exquisitez en el personaje central.

3919. Carpena, Elías. El cuatrero Montenegro. B. A., Ciordia & Rodríguez (Col. Ceibo, 28), 1955. 138 p.

Narraciones de la vida rural uruguaya que se destacan por su estilo denso y dramático y el rítmico avance de la narración, aunque se note por lo general poca originalidad en los desenlaces y en los temas. Presentan estos relatos una naturaleza majestuosa y salvaje que se posesiona de las almas de los personajes, llevándoles a soñar pesadillas que luego creen reales. [S. Sibirsky]

3920. Carrasquilla, Tomás. Cuentos de . . . Edición ilustrada con base en las príncipes. Medellín, Colombia, B. A. Gutiérrez (Col. popular de clásicos maiceros, 4), 1956. 510 p., illus., ports., facsms.

Pulcra edición ilustrada de una buena porción de los cuentos del maestro Carrasquilla, hecha por don Benigno A. Gutiérrez, prestigioso compilador antioqueño.

3921. Correa, Miguel Ángel ("Mateo Booz," pseud.). Aleluyas del brigadier. Santa Fe, Argentina, Castellví (El Litoral), 1955. 179 p.

Colección de viñetas sobre la vida en Santa Fe durante las años que siguieron a la independencia. En esta recreación histórico-artística la acumulación de minucia entorpece, en algunas ocasiones, el desarrollo del relato. El libro está concebido como superposición de escenas, cada una de ellas con sus propios fines y contornos.

3922. Cox, Patricia. Alconedo. Biografía novelada. México, Unidad Mexicana de Escritores (Col. Tehutli, 3), 1955. 114 p.

Historia de una juventud frustrada por las desgracias. La obra se desarrolla en el México colonial dieciochesco. Con ritmo pausado y denso, el autor presenta incidentes en la vida del niño José Luis que reflejan nítidamente el ambiente de la época. El libro es en realidad una biografía novelada que el autor promete continuar. [S. Sibirsky]

3923. Danero, Eduardo M. S. (ed.). Antología gaucha. Cuentos. Santa Fe, Argentina, Castellví, 1956. 236 p.

Cuentos, narraciones, relatos y anécdotas de 73 autores diferentes, entre los cuales figuran notables escritores y un considerable número de cuentistas menos conocidos, algunos de los cuales pudieron haberse eliminado.

3924. Díaz Lozano, Argentina. Peregrinaje. Novela. 2. ed. en español. Guatemala, Ministerio de Educación Pública (Col. Contemporáneos, 43), 1955. 286 p., illus.

Obra premiada en 1943 en el concurso patrocinado por Farrar and Rinehart y traducida al inglés por Harriet de Onís con el título de *Enriqueta and I* (1944). En ella se cuenta la vida de una maestra de instrucción primaria a través de las experiencias de su hija. Libro sencillo, de agradable lectura, pero de poca trascendencia por quedar apenas insinuados los problemas fundamentales de Honduras. Primera edición en español, Santiago, Zig-Zag, 1944.

3925. Domínguez, Berta C. de (ed.). Narraciones panameñas. Tradiciones, leyendas, cuentos, relatos. 1. selección. México, Selecta (Col. Castilla del Oro, 1), 1954. 203 p.

15 narraciones de autores panameños contemporáneos, adaptados de acuerdo con los requisitos del programa oficial de segunda enseñanza.

3926. Donoso, José. Veraneo y otros cuentos. Santiago, Editorial Universitaria, 1955. 115 p.

Siete narraciones sobre personajes "raros"; en casi todas hay escenas superfluas sobre aspectos poco interesantes de la vida diaria. Quizás la mejor de todas sea la última ("Dinamarquero") en que la acción tiene por escenario las soledades de Tierra del Fuego.

3927. Donoso, Juan. Las leyendas del hombre. Santiago, Zig-Zag (Biblioteca de escritores chilenos), 1954. 302 p.

Colección de cuentos notables por su pureza de expresión y acierto descriptivo, en que se tratan los eternos problemas del ser humano y sus ilusiones en una atmósfera de bella y suave melancolía. Ahonda el autor en la psicología de personajes por lo general solitarios y doblegados por mil vicisitudes. [S. Sibirsky]

3928. Edwards Bello, Joaquín. Valparaíso. Fantasmas. Santiago, Nascimento, 1955. 413 p.

Ameno libro de recuerdos y aventuras contados con la gracia, penetración y desparpajo característicos del autor. Sobresale por sobre los demás personajes la noble figura de Perpetua, representación del sentido común y abnegación de la mujer chilena de la clase baja.

3929. Felere, Rosa María. La aldea sin luz. Santiago, Nascimento (Col. Araucaria), 1954. 197 p.

Historia de un doctor que trae la comprensión y el amor a un grupo de almas sin luz. Tema sentimental y sencillísimo, caracteres de una sola dimensión, mensaje noble pero ingenuo.

3930. Gaillardou, José Adolfo. Pampa de furias. B. A., Zamba, 1955. 274 p.

Visión pesimista del agro argentino: los sufrimientos del campesino ante la maldad humana y las calamidades de los malos tiempos. Incidentes triviales, escenas dramáticas forzadas, estilo inartístico.

3931. García Cantú, Gastón. Los falsos rumores. México, Fondo de Cultura Económica (Letras mexicanas, 22), 1955. 150 p.

Breves narraciones, escritas con indudable maestría, en que se presentan, con preferencia, personajes típicos de las provincias mexicanas, especialmente burócratas y déspotas municipales, que personifican el machismo, la brutalidad y la ambición. La sencillez del estilo y la buena estructuración de los diálogos sirven admirablemente para destacar los múltiples motivos y sucesos de cada cuento. [S. Sibirsky]

3932. García Delepiani, Antonio. El dolor de la tierra. Caracas, Impresiones Guía, 1956. 258 p. & illus.

Noveliza esta obra los intentos de consorcios ingleses de adquirir concesiones en la Guayana venezolana. Tema de gran interés que revela la sinceridad del autor. Al final del libro se añaden documentos comprobantes acerca de los alegatos del autor. Estéticamente, el valor de este libro es menoscabado por la idealización exagerada de ciertos personajes nacionales y las múltiples exclamaciones patrióticas del autor. [S. Sibirsky]

3933. Giaconi, Claudio. La difícil juventud. Santiago, Renovación, 1954. 180 p.

Colección de amenos cuentos sobre la desconcertante intimidad de personajes que a primera vista no parecen ofrecer material creativo: niños, un viejo jubilado, etc. El pesimismo, la incomprensión y la soledad son las notas características de estas narraciones. [S. Sibirsky]

3934. González Campo, Federico. Frutos de sombra. Guatemala, Ministerio de Educación Pública (Col. Contemporáneos, 44), 1955. 92 p.

Proyección espiritual en el misterio del más allá, expresada en lenguaje altamente poético. Acompañan a esta obrita dos apreciaciones impresionistas, una de Manuel José Arce H., y otra de Efraín de los Ríos.

3935. González Zenteno, Luis. Caliche. Santiago, Nascimento, 1954. 310 p.

Novela en que el autor maneja con maestría el diálogo para crear notables escenas y cuadros de costumbres de la región nortina chilena. Trata la novela en especial los esfuerzos de anarquistas y comunistas en los campamentos salitreros. Decepciona el fácil simbolismo de la escena final. [S. Sibirsky]

3936. Goyanarte, Juan. Tres mujeres. B. A., Goyanarte, 1956. 140 p.

El caos nacional en los últimos días del régimen peronista. Novela política de escaso valor artístico.

3937. Gramcko, Luis. Cuentos de mi tierra. Caracas, Imp. López, 1955. 129 p.

Narraciones breves y graciosos cuadros ambientales sobre personajes de diversa índole dominados por la maldad. Acaban siempre en un tono humorístico o irónico, pocas veces bien logrado. [S. Sibirsky]

3938. Gravina, Alfredo D. Fronteras al viento. B. A., Platina, 1955. 317 p.

Novela de trascendencia social y obvio propósito educativo en que se analizan los cambios histórico-económicos del Uruguay y los primeros intentos de asociación peonal en la búsqueda de una mejora de salarios y de condiciones de vida. Se describen aquí con sentido humanitario, la pobreza, aislamiento y trabajo agobiador del hombre de campo. A pesar de las continuas intromisiones del autor y su falta de concisión, crea gran interés la detallada recreación de la vida campesina actual. [S. Sibirsky]

3939. Guidiño Kramer, Luis. Caballos. Santa Fe, Argentina, El Litoral, 1956. 142 p., illus.

15 narraciones sobre caballos. Excelentes algunas por la honda comprensión de bestias y "cristianos" que en ellas se encierra. Otras son apenas divagaciones de la imaginación o simples recuerdos. Entre las mejores está la titulada "Un potrillo."

3940. Guerrero, Manuel. Tierra fugitiva. Novela. 2. ed. Santiago, Austral, 1954. 309 p.

Obra de propósito netamente social, por responder a una teoría sobre el mejoramiento de la vida de campesinos y obreros industriales. Pocas veces da planos inconexos y solamente en raras ocasiones hay deslices que entorpecen el natural desenlace de la trama. Muchas de las escenas quedan grabadas en la mente del lector por su fuerte emotividad o excelencias descriptivas. Podría objetarse la falta de mayor complejidad en muchos de los personajes, que dejan la impresión de estar recargados de bondad o de maldad. [S. Sibirsky]

3941. Guevara, Mireya. En la cuerda floja. Caracas, Jaime Villegas, 1954. 198 p.

Esta novela interesa especialmente por su estilo epigramático, el cual deja a menudo la sensación de vacío: la rapidez de la narración no le permite al lector ni concentrarse en la psicología de los personajes ni en el argumento. Aunque la obra logra transmitir en sus trozos decisivos la angustia de los protagonistas, carece de verdadera originalidad. [S. Sibirsky]

3942. Guido, Beatriz. La caída. B. A., Losada (Novelistas de España y América), 1956. 140 p.

Intento de estudio psicológico de una joven provinciana que va a Buenos Aires a hacer estudios universitarios. Trama pobre y mal hilvanada, personajes poco convincentes, minucia de escaso interés.

3943. ————. La casa del ángel. B. A., Emecé, 1954. 174 p.

Preocupaciones, sueños y rebeldías de una muchacha, relatados en primera persona, con el encanto de las confesiones ingenuas. Aunque hecha de fruslerías intrascendentes, la trama tiene interés como expresión de los problemas de la adolescencia femenina.

3944. Hidalgo, Baltasar. Metamorfilia. México, Los Presentes (21), 1955. 108 p.

Cuatro narraciones en que se destaca siempre algo extraordinario en la conducta humana a través de aventuras poco verosímiles, presentadas unas con morosa elaboración y otras dentro de una cadena de elementos sorpresivos.

3945. Lafourcade, Enrique (ed.). Antología del nuevo cuento chileno. Santiago, Zig-Zag (Biblioteca de escritores chilenos), 1954. 338 p., illus.

24 cuentistas de la última generación. Obra variada, pero desigual. En el prólogo se reúnen datos tomados de manuales y diccionarios.

3946. Lillo, Baldomero. Antología de . . . por Nicomedes Guzmán. Santiago, Zig-Zag (Biblioteca de novelistas), 1955. 301 p., port.

Trabajo de divulgación, con un prefacio en que se examinan los juicios de varios críticos y se encuadra la figura de Lillo en la generación de 1900. Colección útil, impresa en papel de baja calidad.

3947. Lindo, Hugo. Guaro y champaña. San Salvador, Ministerio de Cultura, Departamento Editorial (Col. Contemporáneos, 2), 1955. 151 p.

11 amenos cuentos sobre la vida del pueblo bajo y del sector citadino, agrupados en dos secciones bajo sus respectivos símbolos: guaro y champaña. Abundancia de color local, sentido dramático, destreza artística. En todos ellos el interés está centrado en la peripecia de los personajes.

3948. Lozzia, Luis Mario. Domingo sin fútbol. Novela. B. A., Editorial Sudamericana, 1956. 202 p.

Vida de personajes típicos bonaerenses, entrelazados por accidentes fortuitos y no por una ilación detallada de la acción. Se estudian aquí los esfuerzos del ser por merecer el elogio que acarrea una obra creativa, la rebeldía frente a toda autoridad incomprensible y la tristeza que los años y desengaños traen. Las complejas y concisas observaciones del autor ante sus personajes producen gran deleite intelectual. [S. Sibirsky]

3949. Luján, Mónica. "Tipuani," el camino del infierno. La Paz, Impresora Boliviana, 1954. 112 p.

Deshilvanado relato sobre la vida de un grupo de mineros bolivianos, hecho a base de simple acumulación de episodios. Técnica elementalísima.

3950. Manauta, Juan José. Las tierras blancas. Novela. B. A., Ediciones Doble P (Grandes escritores argentinos; Novelas, 8), 1956. 245 p.

Trozos de la vida de unos cuantos personajes— la madre, el hijo, el muchachón pendenciero, Angélica, etc.—entretejidos en una urdimbre de desgracias, hambres y miserias. A pesar de su novedosa configuración novelística, este relato no logra despertar verdadero interés por la ordinariez de los hechos que presenta.

3951. Mancisidor, José. El alba en las simas. Novela. México, América Nueva (Colección Autores contemporáneos, 2), 1955. 259 p.

Las maquinaciones políticas e internacionales que culminaron en la expropiación de los intereses petroleros en México. Galería de capitalistas explotadores, políticos y militares de manga ancha, periodistas sobornados y mujeres envilecidas. Aunque inspirado en un sincero amor a lo nacional, este libro no satisface del todo porque sus personajes se mueven, no por determinantes propios, sino a voluntad de la intención delatora del autor.

3952. ————. Me lo dijo María Kaimlová. México, Impresora Juan Pablos (Los Presentes, 35), 1955. 125 p.

Libro de impresiones varias, en que se recrean las experiencias del escritor con seres humanos conocidos por los caminos de la vida y que personifican los tristes resultados de las guerras de nuestro siglo. Presentados en estilo sobrio y acompasado, los hechos hablan por sí. [S. Sibirsky]

3953. Márquez Salas, Antonio. Las hormigas viajan de noche. Cuentos. Caracas, Asociación de Escritores Venezolanos (Cuadernos literarios, 90), 1956. 74 p.

Cuentos alucinantes, de marcado sentido onírico, más notables por sus múltiples sugerencias, símbolos e imágenes que por la trama misma. En todos predomina una nota insistente de irrealidad, de zozobra y de misterio. Hay que poner estas narraciones dentro de la corriente de novelística última.

3954. Martínez Estrada, Ezequiel. Marta Riquelme. Examen sin conciencia. B. A., Nova (Col. Imaginación; Novela), 1956. 99 p.

La primera de estas dos novelas cortas es una interesante narración escrita en forma de exégesis de un manuscrito perdido; en ella se diseña, por medio de múltiples recursos técnicos, la personalidad de una mujer extraordinaria, mitad ángel, mitad demonio. La segunda es un divertimiento literario, entre humorístico e irónico, en que la insuficiencia de los practicantes de medicina resulta ser tan grande como la bellaquería de quienes los examinan. En suma, dos excelentes narraciones.

3955. ————. Tres cuentos sin amor. B. A., Goyanarte, 1956. 138 p.

Intensos relatos de resonancias kafkianas. En los dos primeros se dramatiza la pequeñez del esfuerzo humano ante las fuerzas arrolladoras de la adversidad; el tercero es una patética recreación de un ambiente de desesperanza y muerte que recuerda las mejores páginas de Horacio Quiroga.

3956. Massís, Mahfúd. Los sueños de Caín. Cuentos. Santiago, Arvas, 1953. 102 p.

Cuentos espeluznantes sobre temas que parecen productos de un desequilibrio mental. A veces asoma el tono burlón; frecuentemente el autor se aprovecha de motivos que la sociedad por lo general elude. La imaginación fértil del escritor y el caudal de símbolos e imágenes son sorprendentes. [S. Sibirsky]

3957. Medeiros, María Paulina. Un jardín para la muerte. Santiago, Zig-Zag (Biblioteca americana), 1954. 139 p.

Delicada narración puesta en boca de una muchacha en que se mezclan la fantasía de una adolescente y las sospechas y celos de una persona mayor. Libro poético, cargado de delirante dramatismo. Es de especial valor la recreación del ambiente fronterizo de un pueblo uruguayo que mira hacia el Brasil. Primera edición, B. A., S. Rueda, 1951 (See *HLAS, no. 17, 1951*, item 2394).

3958. Medinaceli, Carlos. La Chaskañawi. Novela de costumbres bolivianas. 2. ed. La Paz, Juventud, 1955. 246 p.

Intento de interpretación costumbrista de la vida boliviana en un pueblo chico. Trama insuficiente; falta de lógica en la justificación de los acontecimientos; personajes indefinidos o mal estudiados, con excepción de la chola Claudina (la Chaskañawi). Confusionismo de ideas sobre el alma del paisaje, concepción pueril de la moral social. Único mérito de este libro: abundancia de detalles folklóricos.

3959. Meléndez, Luis. Isabel Talbot. Santiago, Zig-Zag (Biblioteca de novelistas), 1955. 268 p.

A pesar del título de la novela, el personaje central es William Talbot, cuya narración autobiográfica sirve al autor para captar el mundo psicológico y social de la burguesía de Valparaíso. Las meditaciones de William resultan en ocasiones inverosímiles a causa de su edad y educación, y menoscaban con frecuencia el interés que suscita el estudio de la familia Talbot y los cambios sufridos por el puerto. [S. Sibirsky]

3960. Mendirichaga, Rodrigo. Un alto en el desierto. México, Los Presentes (48), 1956. 161 p.

13 cuentos sobre distintos aspectos de la vida mexicana. Estilo natural, buen diálogo, interés dramático en la mayoría de ellos. En algunos—los menos—la trama es excesivamente melodramática o sentimental.

3961. Merino Reyes, Luis. Regazo amargo. Santiago, Zig-Zag (Biblioteca de novelistas, 1955. 140 p.

Novela que trata un momento en la vida de un personaje abúlico y desapegado de su ambiente. No siempre se justifica la inclusión de personajes que desaparecen de la trama al capricho del autor, pero interesan varios tipos chilenos captados en su significación social y psicológica. [S. Sibirsky]

3962. Montaine, Eliseo. El viaje. B. A., Emecé (Novelistas argentinos contemporáneos), 1956. 183 p.

Novela de marcado tono sentimental en que la vida interna de los personajes está pintada grosso modo. Basada en las relaciones entre los pasajeros de una diligencia de fines de siglo. Trama organizada a base de recursos fáciles que chocan al lector. [S. Sibirsky]

3963. Moreno Heredia, Cornelio. Viaje en mí mismo. Cuentos. Cuenca, Ecuador, 1953. 108 p.

15 cuentos variadísimos acerca de individuos estrafalarios, acontecimientos misteriosos, casos de perturbación mental y también simples estados de alma. En algunos cuentos el final queda un poco en el aire; en otros se insiste demasiado en detalles efectivistas. En todos ellos hay, sin embargo, interés, economía de medios y una nota de singularidad.

3964. Muñoz Rueda, Enrique. Beatriz Palma. Caracas, Edime, 1956. 207 p.

Panorama de la vida caraqueña durante la época del gomecismo. La novela presenta una sociedad abúlica y corrupta y acaba en una confesión desesperada de una delación al régimen imperante. [S. Sibirsky]

3965. Noguera, Guadalupe. Voûs. México, Impresiones Modernas (Lince, cuadernos literarios, 3), 1956. 67 p.

Aberraciones de erotómanos y lesbianas en contraste con la limpieza de alma de una joven sana e ingenua. En el prólogo de Guillermo Rousse declara la autora: "He querido mostrar hasta dónde pueden conducir el desenfreno y el vicio . . . Me ha parecido necesario hacerlo absteniéndome de formular consideraciones éticas." Relato descoyuntado, personajes borrosos de tipo seudointelectual, diálogo a veces confuso.

3966. Orphée, Elvira. Dos veranos. B. A., Editorial Sudamericana, 1956. 189 p.

Novela incoherente en que se enlazan dos asuntos distintos—la vida de Sixto, el huérfano, y las aventuras amorosas de un almacenero, en cuya casa sirve aquél. Sobran no pocos incidentes triviales o superfluos.

3967. Otero Silva, Miguel. Casas muertas. B. A., Losada, 1955. 181 p.

Vida cuotidiana de un poblachón venezolano diezmado por el paludismo. Aunque la trama es de escaso interés y está pobremente estructurada, esta novela llama la atención como recreación de un ambiente. Segunda edición, Caracas, 1956.

3968. ————. Fiebre. Novela de la revolución venezolana. 3. ed. Caracas, Ediciones Pasa, 1956. 262 p.

Las zozobras, miserias y horrores de la lucha por la libertad en días de Juan Vicente Gómez. Véase *HLAS, no. 5, 1939,* item 3759.

3969. Oxley, Diego R. Cenizas. Cuentos. Santa Fe, Argentina, Casteliví (El Litoral), 1955. 171 p.

Vida de peones, capataces y aventureros del norte argentino. En la mayoría de estas narraciones se crea un ambiente con gran pericia artística. A veces la técnica recuerda páginas de Horacio Quiroga y de Benito Lynch.

3970. ————. Tierra arisca. B. A., Ediciones Doble P (Grandes escritores argentinos; Novelas, 3), 1955. 194 p.

Más que novela este libro es una acumulación de escenas unificadas por el ambiente de pobreza y primitivismo en que se mueven los pobladores del noroeste santafesino—la tierra arisca. Son dignas de encomio algunas escenas dramáticas y varias descripciones paisajistas.

3971. Peltzer, Federico J. Tierra de nadie. B. A., Emecé (Novelistas argentinos contemporáneos), 1955. 198 p.

Trágicos amores de un muchacho huérfano con una beldad rústica del interior argentino. Tema de escasa novedad, manejado con poca destreza. Fuera de los detalles sobre el ambiente, poco hay de verdadero interés en este libro.

3972. Pfänder, Bruno. La noche es de piedra. Mendoza, Argentina, D'Accurzio, 1955. 170 p.

Obra compleja, en especial por su novedad, y que se desentiende en gran parte de las unidades tradicionales de la novela al conducir al personaje central a una mayor comprensión de su ser a través de recuerdos suscitados por los acaeceres de la vida común. Siguiendo la ruta de James Joyce, el autor recrea con variado éxito los diferentes y simultáneos planos del pensar, expresándose por medio de imágenes y símbolos que con frecuencia asombran por su eficacia creadora. [S. Sibirsky]

3973. Piazza, Luis Guillermo. La siesta. México, Obregón (Col. Ahuizote, 4), 1956. 74 p.

Minúsculo relato sobre el tema de la pubertad. Esquema de inocencias, ingenuidades, torpezas y perversión.

3974. Pla, Roger. Paño verde. B. A., Instituto Amigos del Libro Argentino (Biblioteca de novelistas argentinos), 1955. 159 p.

Burda imitación de las novelas sobre gangsters: desplantes matonescos, peleas, robos, tiroteos, muertes. Tema vulgar; personajes de película.

3975. Portugal Catacora, José (ed.). El cuento puneño. Puno, Perú, 1955. 496 p.

Recopilación de "lo que en materia de relato han producido a la fecha los escritores del departamento de Puno." Como ocurre muchas veces en colecciones inspiradas por el orgullo de provincia, falta aquí un riguroso sentido de selección.

3976. Prieto, Raúl. Hueso y carne. México, Fondo de Cultura Económica (Letras mexicanas, 28), 1956. 283 p.

60 cuentos de temática variadísima. Junto al intenso realismo que los informa se advierte a veces una nota irónica. Características comunes de estos relatos son la brevedad de medios y el poder sugestivo de lo que queda implícito entre líneas.

3977. Puga, Mario. Puerto cholo. México, Los Presentes (26), 1955. 257 p.

Vida de un ex-pescador y marino que regresa a su pueblo donde se identifica con los trabajadores. La intención partidarista falsea la idiosincrasia de los personajes y destruye la unidad de ambiente.

3978. Reyes, Salvador. Valparaíso, puerto de nostalgia. Santiago, Zig-Zag (Biblioteca de novelistas), 1955. 205 p.

Vida tumultuosa de un grupo juvenil ansioso de aventuras y placeres. Escenas barojianas en casas de pensión, bares y prostíbulos. Abundancia de detalles sobre la vida bohemia de Valparaíso. Estilo periodístico; pobreza de análisis anímico.

3979. Ribeyro, Julio Ramón. Los gallinazos sin plumas. Lima, Círculo de Novelistas Peruanos, 1955. 135 p.

Violencias, dolores y miseria de los de abajo. Cuentos de fuerte realismo y muy buena factura, en que sobran, a veces, algunos detalles nauseabundos.

3980. Robleto, Hernán. Cárcel criolla. San José, 1955. 304 p.

Visión caleidoscópica de los horrores de la tiranía en Nicaragua. La trama de este libro es una elemental superposición de episodios escalofriantes y de comentarios periodísticos. La veracidad histórica de varios pasajes la corrobora el autor por medio de notas al pie de la página. Lengua descuidada; falta de calidad estética.

3981. Rodríguez Macal, Virgilio. Sangre y clorofila. Cuentos. Guatemala, Ministerio de Educación Pública (Segundo Festival de Arte y Cultura), 1956. 157 p.

Impresionantes escenas de sangre, vida y muerte asociadas a esplendorosos paisajes tropicales. Excelentes caracterizaciones, intensidad dramática y sentido artístico. Una de las mejores colecciones del año.

3982. Rosa, Julio C. da. De sol a sol. Montevideo, Ediciones Asir, 1955. 168 p.

Narraciones sobre campesinos uruguayos del departamento de Treinta y Tres en que se recrean con acierto el habla y los dichos de los personajes de la campaña y se intercalan imágenes de la naturaleza que resultan ser verdaderas evocaciones poéticas. La mayor parte de los personajes son víctimas de la mala suerte y se defienden instintivamente. Su desolación, sencillez y bondad conmueven al lector. [S. Sibirsky]

3983. Rosa, Marco Antonio. Tío Margarito. Historia novelada folklórica. 2. ed. Tegucigalpa, 1954. 184 p.

Mezcolanza de escenas truculentas, anécdotas sentimentales, bocetos paisajistas y detalles folklóricos, con un fondo de nimiedades didácticas sobre el arte de vivir.

3984. Rubín, Ramón. La bruma lo vuelve azul. México, Fondo de Cultura Económica (Letras mexicanas, 16), 1954. 116 p.

Recreación de la vida huichole y sondeo del alma india. A pesar de tener los personajes principales muy pocas posibilidades de desarrollo, el autor logra crear una novela corta en que se funden armoniosamente lo antropológico y lo folklórico con el drama familiar.

3985. ————. La sombra del techincuagüe. Guadalajara, México, Ediciones Altiplano, 1955. 281 p.

En este libro hay materiales más que suficientes para una excelente novela: variedad de personajes, incidentes fuera de lo común, transfondos psicológicos, etc. Por desgracia, llevado de la peripecia y de una especie de prurito sensacionalista, el autor cae a veces en lo melodramático, en lo truculento o en lo absurdo. Así y con todo, Ramón Rubín da pruebas de ser un autor de indudables dotes narrativas.

3986. Ruiz Guiñazú, Alejandro. La deuda. B. A., Kraft (América en la novela), 1955. 151 p.

Novela de asunto trivial y de poco interés, en la que sobran las disquisiciones ensayísticas y los rellenos melodramáticos.

3987. St. Loup B., Enrique. Charlas de café. Cuentos. La Paz, 1955. 217 p.

Historietas varias sobre flaquezas y perversiones humanas. Abundancia de aventuras y sorpresas. Estilo pobre, a veces francamente pedestre.

3888. Salazar Arrué, Salvador ("Salarrué," pseud.). Trasmallo. San Salvador, Ministerio de Cultura, Dirección General de Bellas Artes, 1954. 163 p., illus.

20 relatos sobre aspectos varios de la vida salvadoreña. Algunos son apenas escenas de interés folklórico. Otros intentan revelar al alma del pueblo a través de pequeños incidentes, peculiaridades del habla popular y un turbio fondo de primitivismo, ignorancia y superstición. El defecto principal de la mayoría de ellos es el no tener una trama propriamente tal.

3989. Silberstein, Enrique. El asalto. Novela. B. A., La Reja (Prosistas de América y España), 1956. 145 p.

Preparativos de un robo, meticulosa ejecución de éste y fracaso final, todo mezclado con escenas de la vida noctámbula de Buenos Aires y retratos de personajes pintorescos. Regocijado relato sin grandes pretensiones ni mayores méritos.

3990. Solero, Francisco Jorge. La culpa. B. A., Ediciones Doble P (Grandes escritores argentinos; Novelas, 7), 1956. 244 p.

Mezcla de novela psicológica (con manifiestas influencias de Faulkner) y un vulgar relato de aventuras, en el cual se detallan las actividades, engaños y atrocidades de un grupo de traficantes en morfina. Trama de muy desigual interés, alargada por medio de intercalaciones, ya sobre la vida psicológica de uno de los personajes o sobre la intimidad de varios personajes secundarios, especialmente mujeres.

3991. Tamayo, Marcial. Cuentos de . . . Pedro Miedo. Concepción, Chile, Ediciones Surazo, 1953, i.e. 1954. 79 p.

Diez cuentos de un autor novel. Audacias imaginistas de baja ley, excesiva frondosidad, temas de poco interés. Lo mejor de algunas narraciones es la intensidad de las escenas finales.

3992. Trueba, Eugenio. Antesala. México, Los Presentes (40), 1956. 125 p.

Cuentos conmovedores en que se presenta al minero atribulado por la miseria o al indio que ignora la complejidad y la maldad de la vida moderna. La comprensión del autor le lleva a animar a animales que también sufren a causa de la bestialidad humana. Impresiona la excelente presentación del ambiente y la buena estructuración de la narración. [S. Sibirsky]

3993. Ugarte R., Miguel Ángel de. Cuentos y leyendas de mi tierra y otros lares. La Paz, Letras, 1954. 168 p., illus.

15 relatos folletinescos sobre sucesos extraordinarios o espeluznantes. El segundo—premiado por un periódico boliviano—es una obvia imitación de don Ricardo Palma; en otros se emplean recursos melodramáticos. Lengua descuidada, estilo discursivo.

3994. Valadés, Edmundo. La muerte tiene permiso. México, Fondo de Cultura Económica (Letras mexicanas, 20), 1955. 100 p.

14 cuentos de gran penetración en el alma humana. Entre los mejores está el primero, que da título a la colección.

3995. Vegas Seminario, Francisco. Entre algarrobos. Lima, Círculo de Novelistas Peruanos, 1955? 163 p.

Colección de cuentos novedosos en la trama y sorprendentes en su desenlace. Desgracias y vida azarosa del indio piurano. Notas sobresalientes son la violencia y el drama, desvirtuadas a veces por la preponderancia de la parte narrativa. Se centra el interés del autor en el argumento, sin que por eso carezcan de valor estético las descripciones. [S. Sibirsky]

3996. Verbitsky, Bernardo. Un noviazgo. B. A., Goyanarte, 1956. 243 p.

El tema central de este libro no es precisamente el noviazgo de Carmen y el periodista Quirós sino más bien la vida de éste y de sus compañeros de trabajo. La inclusión de asuntos apenas relacionados con el tema central, la falta de ritmo interior entre capítulos y el escaso interés de la trama misma explican por qué esta novela deja la impresión de ser obra hecha con poco sentido de forma y de selección.

3997. Villarreal, Juan Manuel. Mi propia horca. B. A., Kraft (América en la novela), 1956. 226 p.

Desavenencias de un matrimonio joven que terminan con la acomodación final de la esposa a la vida campesina. Es éste un intento de estudio psicológico. Descontando una que otra escena bien lograda, la mayor parte de este relato carece de verdadera calidad artística.

3998. Vita y Lacerra, Armando de. Orilla y centro de la vida. B. A., Francisco A. Colombo, 1955, 154 p.

Desahogos emocionales de seres que pretenden escapar de sus angustias o que llegan a una resignación final que les dulcifica brevemente la vida. Lenguaje preciso y escogido. [S. Sibirsky]

3999. Wagner de Reyna, Alberto. La fuga. Santiago, Zig-Zag (Biblioteca de novelistas), 1955. 252 p.

Primera novela del conocido pensador peruano. Aun cuando hay en ella pasajes bien logrados y una buena recreación del ambiente estudiantil limeño de hace 20 años, el libro parece ser una obra mixta: detrás del novelista se adivina a un ensayista.

4000. Wernicke, Enrique. La ribera. B. A., Jacobo Muchnik, 1955. 238 p.

Novela de marcado tinte melancólico que narra en forma autobiográfica la vida malograda de un personaje argentino típico: su soledad, su incapacidad de lograr algún asidero y las infiltraciones de la vida social en su refugio bonaerense. [S. Sibirsky]

4001. Zavaleta, Carlos Eduardo. El Cristo Villenas. México, Los Presentes (46), 1956. 117 p.

Siete cuentos, de los cuales seis fueron tomados del libro *La batalla*, del mismo autor. En todos ellos hay falta de cohesión por añadirse al tema central demasiados asuntos secundarios.

4002. ————. Los Ingar. Novela. Lima, Juan Mejía Baca & P. L. Villanueva, 1955. 120 p.

Relato de las peripecias de un joven peruano, en que se trazan, eficazmente, dentro de una sencilla trama, las maniobras oportunistas de los gobernantes de un pequeño pueblo y los recursos defensivos de una familia ignorante e instintiva, pero honrada. Llama la atención en especial la agudeza psicológica en la pintura de los personajes. [S. Sibirsky]

STUDIES

4003. Barnola, Pedro Pablo. Eduardo Blanco, creador de la novela venezolana. Estudio crítico de su novela *Zárate*. Bogotá, Pontificia Universidad Católica Javeriana (Tesis, 59), 1954. 199 p.

Documentada y encomiástica valoración en 11 capítulos. En uno de ellos se examinan las opiniones de los críticos y en otros el valor de la novela como expresión criollista. Hay, sin embargo, algunos aspectos negativos del novelista que están tratados muy someramente.

4004. Brushwood, John Stubbs. The romantic novel in Mexico. Columbia, Mo., The University of Missouri Studies (26: 4), 1954. 98 p., illus., ports.

Estudio del género, seguido de un comentario breve de las obras de 31 autores. Véase la reseña de Renato Rosaldo (RIB, 5:3, julio-sept. 1955, p. 194-197).

4005. Cruz, Salvador de la. La novela iberoamericana actual. México, Departamento de Divulgación de la Secretaría de Educación Pública, 1956. 98 p., illus.

Brevísimos datos y comentarios impresionistas—a veces superficiales o equivocados—sobre novelistas, en la mayoría hispanoamericanos. Se incluyen cinco novelistas españoles.

4006. Díaz Sánchez, Ramón. Teresa de la Parra. Clave para una interpretación. Caracas, Garrido, 1954. 201 p., illus.

Interesantísimo libro de glosas interpretativas sobre la personalidad y obra de Teresa de la Parra. Trabajo hecho a base del epistolario y parte del diario de la gran escritora venezolana (1895-1936).

4007. Echegaray, Aristóbulo. Don Segundo Sombra. Reminiscencia infantil de Ricardo Güiraldes. B. A., Ediciones Doble P (Grandes escritores argentinos; Ensayos, 1), 1954. 105 p.

En este ensayo se juzga la novela de Güiraldes como documento socio-histórico más que como poetización de un mito. Apoyándose en las afirmaciones del novelista sobre su intención artística, señala el crítico varias deficiencias lingüísticas y algunas fallas en la concepción de los personajes. La aspereza de los comentarios podría resumirse en esta cita: "De ahí que todo el relato sea un puro friso de lo espectacular, de lo deportivo y no de lo substancial intrínseco."

4008. Guillot Muñoz, Gervasio. La conversación de Carlos Reyles. Montevideo, Instituto Nacional de Investigaciones y Archivos Literarios (Serie 2, Estudios y testimonios, 2), 1955. 54 p., ports.

Nutrido ensayo sobre la personalidad del escritor uruguayo vista a través de su conversación: gustos personales, predilecciones literarias, ocurrencias, equivocaciones, ideas filosóficas y convicciones socio-económicas.

4009. Orgambide, Pedro G. Horacio Quiroga. El hombre y su obra. B. A., Stilcograf, 1954. 170 p.

Amena e instructiva recapitulación de datos sobre la vida y obra del gran cuentista uruguayo, basada en la biografía de Brignole y Delgado, el diario del viaje a París y numerosos estudios parciales.

4010. Perera, Hilda. Aspectos de *La vorá-*

gine de José Eustasio Rivera . . . con la colaboración de Marcela Serrallach, Daphnis Loppe y George Meldelson. Santiago, Cuba, Manigua, 1956. 80 p.
Buen estudio sobre el sentido y forma de *La vorágine,* seguido de cinco trabajos breves por tres diferentes colaboradores, quienes discutieron con la autora el contenido total del libro.

4011. Santovenia, Emeterio S. Personajes y paisajes de Villaverde. Discurso de contestación [por] Juan J. Remos. Habana, Sección de Literatura de la Academia Nacional de Artes y Letras, 1955. 135 p., illus.
Ensayo informativo más que apreciación crítica del tema.

4012. Vila Selma, José. Rómulo Gallegos. Sevilla, Escuela de Estudios Hispano-Americanos (Publicaciones, no. general 86; Col. Mar adentro, 5), 1954. 194 p.
Análisis de temas, procedimientos y rutas intelectuales en la obra de Gallegos. Trabajo útil y sugerente, aunque no definitivo—como lo dice el propio autor en una breve introducción.

4013. Williams Alzaga, Enrique. La pampa en la novela argentina. B. A., Ángel Estrada (Ediciones argentinas de cultura), 1955. 382 p., illus.
Estudio del tema gauchesco desde los comienzos hasta Mallea, pasando por las obras de viajeros, por Echeverría, Sarmiento, Payró, Güiraldes, Lynch y numerosos novelistas menores y cuentistas. Valiosos datos para la historia literaria, excelentes ilustraciones. Apreciación crítica un tanto difusa. Exceso de citas y de detalles sobre la trama de las obras estudiadas.

POETRY

ARNOLD CHAPMAN

The books here surveyed for the period 1954-1956 prove that Spanish American poetry shows no sign of flagging. Not only is the quantity impressive but also the wide range of thematic and stylistic choice underscores the lack of regimentation. Thus we encounter extremes: from "social" poetry to pure poetry; from free verse to sonnet (the latter displaying a surprising vigor); from simplicity to the neo-Baroque; from the conventional to the wildly experimental (less of this than might have been anticipated).

A noteworthy trend is the continued development of regional foci. In our purview are collections centered about Cuenca, Cuzco, Arequipa, Valparaiso, and Rio de la Plata (in the outstanding *Cien poesías rioplatenses* of Roy Bartholomew), as well as the more familiar national anthologies. In this respect it becomes clear that Mexico is maintaining its lead in the formation of strong poetical tradition, through the advanced work of its poets, beautifully evidenced by the *Anuario* put out by the Instituto Nacional de Bellas Artes in Mexico City; and the labor of critics in buildings its standards: in, for instance, Xirau's *Tres poetas de la soledad* and Dauster's *Breve historia de la poesía mexicana.* Historical perspective is enhanced by revaluating poets of the past. Díaz Mirón is the object of three studies, of which Monterde's is by far the best.

The period contains several collections by elderly or recently deceased poets, whose verses are a record of changing tastes. Egas, Fernández Ríos, Mata, Olivari, and Rega Molina appear in this light. The leaders continue to set the pace; Neruda, Parra, Florit, Paz, Torres-Ríoseco, Vitier, Molinari, Nandino, Fernández Retamar—all make the contributions expected of them. Among the younger poets of promise, Claribel Alegría, Manuel José Arce the younger, and Francisco Salazar Martínez are the most outstanding.

In criticism the careful analytical method finds more and more practitioners, especially in studies on the creative process of single poets. Such is Evangelina Bergadá on Mastronardi, María Hortensia Palisa Mujica de Lacau on Nalé Roxlo, Bernardo Gicovate on Herrera y Reissig, and César Fernández Moreno on Baldomero Fernández Moreno, his father; all superior work.

VERSE

4050. Aguayo Spencer, Rafael (ed.). Flor de moderna poesía mexicana. México, Libro-Mex (Biblioteca mínima mexicana, 9), 1955. 143 p.
A brief selection, 41 poets in all, arranged, except for the first three, in strictly chronological order according to date of birth, from Gutiérrez Nájera (1859)—taken by the editor as the first modern poet—to Ramón Mendoza Montes (1925). The "Bibliografía de autores incluídos" gives the barest biographical jottings and a mention of most important works.

4051. Alegría, Claribel. Acuario. Santiago, Editorial Universitaria, 1955. 62 p.
Engaging, diaphonous verses in whose warm lyricism the poetess gathers about her the things of her personal universe: love, maternity, home. Although few in quantity, these poems are quintessential, refined of all dross. The last previous collection by this Salvadorian poetess was *Vigilias* (1953).

4052. Amor, Guadalupe. Otro libro de amor. México, Tezontle, 1955. 45 p.
A series of assertions about a certain kind of love: furious, passionate, volcanic, obsessive, explicit, loud.

4053. Amorim, Enrique. Sonetos del amor en octubre. B. A., Botella al Mar, 1954. 31 p.
A versatile Uruguayan writer puts his hand to poetry once more. These 23 sonnets are a personal history of a love, from springtime adolescence to the backward glance of maturity. The prevailing note is wonder at the miracle of love itself. Amorim's expression, always engaging, here goes from sensuous to abstract, from representational to hermetic.

4054. Arce (hijo), Manuel José. En el nombre del Padre. Guatemala, Ministerio de Educación Pública (Col. Contemporáneos, 45), 1955. 154 p., illus.
50 poems by a very young poet give ample evidence of a talent from which a great deal can be expected. His self-assurance, versatility, and grace are meanwhile such as to make these verses well worth while. Foreword by Claudia Lars.

4055. Arvelo, Rafael, and **Francisco Pimentel.** Poesías escogidas. Caracas, Villegas (Col. Maracapana), 1954. 194 p.
An unusual occurrence in Spanish-American letters: humorous verse. Although two generations apart, Arvelo and Pimentel were both born in 19th-century Venezuela, both involved to a certain extent in politics—Pimentel imprisoned for nine years under Gómez. Beyond these similarities are considerable differences: Arvelo is the facile improviser and epigrammatist; Pimentel the kindly, delightful humorist. Although by no means great poetry, it is highly entertaining. Foreword by J. A. de Armas Chitty.

4056. Ascasubi, Hilario. Poesías para el pronunciamiento de Urquiza. Compilación y prólogo: Manuel E. Macchi. Santa Fe, Argentina, Castellví, 1956. 204 p., illus.
Despite the title, this anthology contains not only the verses indicated but also the entire 1851 edition of Ascasubi's work, plus one poem dated 1852. The prologue is done with a historian's flair for detail, and helps greatly to situate these occasional poems within their epoch. Some notes are provided, besides Ascasubi's own.

4057. Asturias, Miguel Ángel. Bolívar. San Salvador, Ministerio de Cultura, 1955. Unpaged, illus.
A minor production of a major writer. Sumptuously gotten up as a book, this short (14-page) poem is a paean of praise to the Liberator, in his meaning as a man and as a patriotic myth. There are no surprises here.

4058. Barquero. Efraín. La piedra del pueblo, 1951-1953. Santiago, Alfa, 1954. 127 p.
A perfect example of "proletarian" poetry, from the aggressively red letters of the title, through the introduction by Neruda, to the last poem of the collection. Anyone who has read examples of this kind of writing, especially of Nicomedes Guzmán, will recognize the attitudes, tags, and clichés.

4059. Barrenechea, Julio. Diario morir. Santiago, Nascimento, 1954. 116 p.
This well-known Chilean poet lays aside the concerns of politics to write his first book of poetry in six years. In a variety of meters, and with graceful skill, the poet turns a retrospective eye upon his past. Apparently accepting Heidegger's belief, Barrenechea takes the recognition of death as an essential of being. Limpid and lyrical style tempers the seriousness of his theme.

4060. Barrios Cruz, Luis. La sombra del avión. Prólogo de Pedro Sotillo, Caracas, Tip. Garrido, 1954. 105 p.
The central idea is that the poet wishes to glide across the face of Venezuela like the shadow of an airplane. Fervent, solemn, patriotic, but minor poems.

4061. Bartholomew, Roy (ed.). Cien poesías rioplatenses, 1800-1950. Apéndice con los poemas de William Henry Hudson. B. A., Raigal, 1954. liii, 398 p.
Despite his youth, being only 24 when this book appeared, Bartholomew has succeeded in producing an almost definitive work. Not only does it present in handy form the poetry of a whole region (he is to be congratulated on not limiting himself to Argentina) but also because it gives a perspective through the poems themselves, the short biobibliographical notes, and the thoughtful "Nota sobre la poesía en el Río de la Plata." Of slow genesis, this compilation shows effects of the author's study under Pedro Henríquez Ureña, Alfonso Reyes, and Raimundo Lida. The scope (why exactly 100 poems?) is from Lavardén to Sara de Ibáñez.

4062. Beltrán Mago, Luis. Sonetos a la isla. Caracas, Ediciones Cosmos, 1956. 118 p.
Setting aside the free verse of his earlier two volumes, Beltrán Mago here writes 49 sonnets, which have as their twin motifs love and the sea. The patterns are mainly acoustical, nonrepresentational.

4063. Benavides Vega, Carlos (and others). Club 7. Guayaquil, Ecuador, Casa de la Cultura Ecuatoriana, Núcleo del Guayas, 1954. 96 p.
"La presente selección . . . obedece al particular criterio de cada uno de sus miembros. Somos sólo cinco jóvenes unidos por la amistad y por esta unánime devoción al arte." Poets representend: Benavides Vega, Ileana Espinel Cedeño, Gastón Hidalgo Ortega, David Ledesma Vázquez, Sergio Román Armendáriz. There is a certain family resemblance, consisting of shared vocabulary, themes, and seriousness. Influences of García Lorca and Neruda are not infrequent in these promising young poets.

4064. Bernárdez Jacques, Elbio. El arquetipo. B. A., 1955. 60 p.
Homage to the Gaucho as phenomenon and as symbol. Though fervent, it adds little to the oft-told tale of what the "archetype" means to Argentina.

4065. Bustamante, Cecilia (and others). Tres poetas. Lima, Ediciones Pro-Hombre, 1956. 60 p., illus.
An attractive anthology, with poems of Cecilia Bustamante, Jorge Bacacorzo, and Arturo Corcuera. It promises a cross section of Peruvian poetry, since each poet comes from a different area of the country where he is actively writing. The general approach is avant-garde.

4066. Campos, Daniel. Celichá. Páginas del Gran Chaco boliviano. Nota biográfica por Armando Alba. Potosí, Bolivia, Editorial Potosí (Cuadernos de la Colección de la cultura boliviana, 1), 1954. 141 p., port.
A literary curiosity; a reprint of a late 19th-century ultra-Romantic poetic legend in the style of Tabaré. First published in 1897, it won first prize in a contest commemorating the founding of the Bolivian Republic; based on the poet's first-hand observations during a trip to the Gran Chaco.

4067. Cartagena Portalatín, Aída. Una mujer está sola. Ciudad Trujillo, La Española (Col. La isla necesaria, 9), 1955. 48 p.
Locally acclaimed as a leading exponent of feminine verse in the Antilles—a movement indeed active—the poetess here continues her cultivation of pure poetry, complete with personal symbols. Her last previous volume was Mi mundo el mar (1953). For remarks on the series to which this belongs, see item 4094.

4068. Cifuentes, José Luis (ed.). Algunos poetas contemporáneos de Guatemala. Guatemala, Ministerio de Educación Pública (Segundo Festival de Arte y Cultura), 1956. 110 p.
A collection by Olga Martínez Torres, Augusto Meneses, Roberto Zúñiga Vega, Miguel Marsicovétere y Durán, Antonio Morales Nadler, Neri González, José Luis Cifuentes. A rambling prologue by Cifuentes ends thus: "La poetisa de Guatemala es Olga Martínez Torres . . . Este volumen, no es sino un desfile encabezado por ella." The poems are in a variety of meters and themes, but are chiefly amatory.

4069. Cordero Espinosa, Jacinto. Despojamiento. Cuenca, Ecuador, Casa de la Cultura Ecuatoriana, Núcleo del Azuay, 1956. 205 p., illus.
13 poems giving a vision of bewildered, suffering humanity. In dense, sonorous language the poet tells that all men are his brothers, though they be poor and humble. One poem is also given in Quechua translation.

4070. Cunha, Juan. Triple tentativa. Montevideo, Ediciones Número, 1954. 95 p.
A solid collection of verses by a Uruguayan poet actively writing since the late twenties. The title indicates the tripartite distribution: "Otra canción otra," short, aphoristic pieces with the lilt of the Gaucho guitar; "Biografía poesía," more sophisticated verses using the amorphous flow of the interior monologue; "Escritura sobre la piedra," miscellaneous in technique, some narrative, some funambulatory. Over all is the earthy savor of the poet's province, giving continuity to otherwise detached impressions. An important book.

4071. Darío (nieto), Rubén. Tránsito del recuerdo. B. A., Sacdic, 1954. 159 p.
A poet well in command of his instrument, with a tendency toward excessive fluency. Inevitably there are echoes of his illustrious grandfather, and, now and then, a reminder of Chocano. The favorite motifs: the seasons, death.

4072. Egas M., José María. Unción, El milagro y otros poemas. Guayaquil, Ecuador, Imp. Municipal, 1954. 187 p.
Except for six poems, this edition is a reprinting of earlier editions of Egas' work. Unción appeared in 1923, Unción y otros poemas, 1941, El milagro, 1951. Commentary on this poet, often compared with Amado Nervo, is given by César E. Arroyo, César Andrade y Cordero, Aurelio Espinosa Pólit, and others.

4073. Estrella Gutiérrez, Fermín. La niña de la rosa. B. A., Emecé, 1955. 71 p.
Musical verses by a veteran Argentine writer. Although he is best known, outside his own country, at least, as a literary historian, he has nine books of poetry to his name, beginning in 1924. This slim volume of 30 stanzas evokes the image of a love, seen in dreaming retrospect.

4074. Falco, Líber. Tiempo y tiempo. Montevideo, Asir, 1956. 128 p., illus.
A collection of nearly all the poems of this recently deceased writer, including many hitherto unpublished. For the most part these are brief, lyrical notes on people, moments, and places.

4075. Fasejo, Nicol. El surtidor armónico. Guayaquil, Ecuador, Casa de la Cultura Ecuatoriana, Núcleo del Guayas, 1956. 216 p.
In spite of the poet's spirited foreword, lashing out at the followers of Breton, Reverdy, and Cocteau, as well as "social" poets, the verses that follow are singularly lacking in originality. Perhaps their main value is that as imitations they display, as in a museum, relics of literary vogues of the past 40 years.

4076. Félix, Eduardo. El moscardón. Madrid, Afrodisio Aguado, 1955. 135 p.
This work by an Ecuadorian poet is a survival of Symbolist-Decadent writing, more perhaps reminiscent of Herrera y Reissig than of Lautréamont. Although in dialogue, it is "teatro inmóvil," wherein various unusual characters— Moscardón, Gato Sonámbulo, Pájaro Ciego, Reloj, Muñeco—deliver themselves of cryptic remarks, and are echoed by choruses.

4077. Fernández Retamar, Roberto. Ala-

banzas, conversaciones, 1951-1955. México, El Colegio de México, 1955. 100 p.
The latest verse from a rising protagonist of Cuban letters. In a de luxe edition, the poet displays versatility in ranging from cabalistic imagery, in which Surrealism has left its mark, to a cultivation of pictorial color that reminds one of Julián del Casal's Habana scenes. The 48 poems give evidence of wide reading and intellectual elaboration.

4078. **Fernández Ríos, Ovidio.** Cofre de sándalo. Poesías completas. Montevideo, Mentor, 1955. 246 p., illus.
An omnibus, literally hundreds of poems by a patriarch of Uruguayan letters. In a dignified, self-respecting way the poet ranges across a panorama of 50 years' writing. Now and then a title like "Elevación" or a line like "Rosas, rosas, muchas rosas!" reminds one how deep was the influence of Nervo at one time.

4079. **Florit, Eugenio.** Asonante final y otros poemas (1946-1955). Habana, Orígenes, 1955, i. e. 1956. 81 p.
Florit's seventh book of verses, it brings together pieces originally published in periodicals and anthologies of many nations. He here strives for an incisive attack on reality; earnestness and ingeniousness counterbalance a lack of music and color.

4080. **Gabaldón Márquez, Joaquín.** El poeta desaparecido y sus poemas. Caracas, Edime, 1954. 142 p.
The curious story of a man who in his youth was known as "the poet of the Generation of '28" in Caracas, but who, like Rimbaud, stopped writing verse abruptly, never to resume it. In this case imprisonment for political reasons was the immediate cause; and Gabaldón Márquez diverted his energies to the study of history. In a humorous essay, he writes of himself as a twin brother, a war casualty, and sets the stage for the exhumation of his scattered literary remains.

4081. **García Prada, Carlos** (ed.). Poetas modernistas hispanoamericanos. Antología. Introducción, selecciones y notas críticas y bibliográficas. . . . Madrid, Ediciones Cultura Hispánica (La encina y el mar, Poesía de España y América, 22), 1956. 355 p.
An excellent anthology which amply realizes its purpose of making these poets available to students, presenting once more those verses which have best stood the test of time, and taking advantage of the most recent results of scholarship. There are few surprises here, with the possible exception of the inclusion of Porfirio Barba Jacob; but with the brief introductions and the section "Obras de consulta" (p. 339-347), the further study of the standard Modernist poets is greatly facilitated.

4082. **González Carbalho, José.** Libro de canciones para Rosalía de Castro. B. A., Ediciones Galicia, 1954. 96 p.
In a 22-page foreword, the poet explains how Rosalía de Castro sums up for him his own childhood, when his father, a Galician immigrant to Argentina, would speak to him in the dialect of his native region. The poems that follow are a versified unfolding of the prose statement, wherein Rosalía de Castro communicates long-forgotten sights and sounds—the ticking of a clock, his father's hands on a book, the *saudades* of his friends—and the poet composes glosses on her life. Edition sponsored by the Centro Gallego, B. A.

4083. **Guido y Spano, Carlos.** Poesías escogidas. Autobiografía. Con una semblanza y notas por E. M. S. Danero. Santa Fe, Argentina, Castellví, 1955. 185 p.
A good looking edition of this traditional poet; one that no doubt fills an existing need for a new edition of his works, besides suggesting a revaluation. However, both "semblanza" and notes are exceedingly sketchy, hardly worthy of the subject. Nor is it possible to tell whether the notes are the author's or the editor's. The *Autobiografía* consists of a prose selection titled "Carta confidencial a un amigo que comete la indiscreción de publicarla."

4084. **Heredia, José Ramón.** Círculo poético. B. A., Losada (Poetas de España y América), 1956. 136 p., illus.
Fine paper and typography lend dignity to still another in this outstanding Losada series. This volume brings the Venezuelan poet up to date; with one exception, the poems here have all appeared previously in books and periodicals in Caracas. The characteristic of these verses is an atmosphere of ritual, whose verbalization is prophetic. "Saludo a Vicente Huidobro" shows a strong bond of admiration, but Heredia has not yet ridded himself of some Romantic platitudes.

4085. **Johnson, Mildred Edith** (ed. and tr.). Swan, cygnets, and owl. An anthology of Modernist poetry in Spanish America. With an introductory essay by J. S. Brushwood. Columbia, Mo., The University of Missouri (Studies, 29), 1956. 199 p.
In her preface Miss Johnson states, "In my translations I have attempted to reproduce the ideas and imagery expressed in the original without omitting any or adding any of my own. A freer translation would probably be more artistic but would lack fidelity." This program has been followed honestly. One might raise questions about the selection of poems, however. It is surprising to find Valencia omitted entirely, and Neruda included among the post-Modernists. Why Darío should ocupy only three pages, while González Martínez has five and a half, is not explained. Brushwood's 33-page essay is on an elementary level, and sometimes opinionated. There is no table of contents or index. Spanish and English.

4086. **Kósice, Gyula** (ed.). Antología de la poesía madí. B. A., Madí, 1955. 138 p., illus.
The sampler of an avant-garde sect, interesting as much for what it professes to do as for what it actually accomplishes, which is an open ques-

tion. Displaying a strong desire for newness—it is printed on brown wrapping paper, with split leaves, large blank pages, and a horror of punctuation—it nevertheless strikes one as standardized within a pattern of novelty. A prologue by Kósice endeavors to explain the cult of "Madí," a type of poetry that banishes all representational forms, reduces all to the image, and breaks language down into the smallest component part. Includes 13 poets; the youngest was born in 1936.

4087. Leiva, Raúl. Danza para Cuauhtémoc. México, Los Presentes, 1955. 82 p., illus.

An attempt on the part of a Guatemalan poet to utilize the barbaric rhythms of Aztec ritual dances to a message of American solidarity. War and poetry are blended in the insistence of the drum. Although the conception is most fascinating, and the verses enthralling at first, it is not possible to remain at fever pitch until the end of the book.

4088. Lizalde, Eduardo. La mala hora. México, Los Presentes, 1956. 55 p., illus.

Socially-conscious verses, setting forth in prosaically denuded language the plight of the poor, their resistance to suffering; and making the anti-imperialist complaint: i. e., predictable themes of the left-wing writer, with earnestness but little grace save an occasional flash of sardonic humor. An epigraph from Neruda suggests Lizalde's affiliations.

4089. Mata, Andrés A. Poesías completas. Prólogo de Arturo Uslar Pietri; epílogo, revisión y cuidado de los poemas a cargo de José Ramón Medina. Caracas, Edime, 1956. 250 p., illus.

The first nearly complete edition of a poet partly attached to the Modernist movement in Venezuela, though maintaining a strong Romantic allegiance. Poems of his earliest book, *El decálogo* (1884), are not included, in spite of the title. Uslar Pietri's prologue is informative, if guarded in tone. Useful to complete the literary history of Hispanic America toward the end of the last century.

4090. Mata, Gonzalo Humberto. Funeral de mi sangre. Cuenca, Ecuador, Tall. de la Universidad, 1954. 62 p.

A psychiatrist would find much interesting material in this tearful tribute to the poet's dead mother. As he pictures the Mother as Saint, the poet goes back over the events of his life, from conception onward. The style is largely bombastic.

4091. Matos Romero, Manuel. Improvisadores populares del Zulia. . . . Supersticiones. Prólogo de Héctor Guillermo Villalobos. Caracas, 1956. 121 p., illus.

A collection of improvised verses by celebrated local masters of the art, with a thumbnail sketch of each. At the end, a few scattered remarks on the superstitions of the Zulia region. This is raw material for the study of Latin American folklore, but must be taken with caution, for the author, although he gives transcriptions of *con-*

trapunteos, parrandas, cantaurías, and other like occasions, fails to identify his immediate sources.

4092. Mejía, Gustavo Adolfo (ed.). Antología de poetas dominicanos. V. 1. Ciudad Trujillo, La Palabra de Santo Domingo, 1954. 202 p.

A not entirely successful attempt to present an orderly historical picture. There are two main divisions: "Los poetas de la Colonia"; "La generación de la Guerra." With more method this would have been less a maze of type and more a useful research tool.

4093. México. Instituto Nacional de Bellas Artes. Anuario de la poesía mexicana, 1954. México, 1955. 253 p.

One of the most important books in the period under review. Not only does it bring a rich harvest of 101 poets, an amazingly thorough sifting of contemporary verse both in the provinces and in the capital, thus giving an unsurpassed view of the year's work, but also it contains a lucid *"Advertencia"* by Andrés Henestroza that surveys poetic movements in Mexico after Modernism. The reader who combines this volume with that of Dauster (item 4125), will be extraordinarily well informed in this area. It is to be hoped that after reviving a custom fallen into disuse, this *Anuario* will be followed regularly by others.

4094. Mieses Burgos, Franklin. El héroe. Poema con intención escénica en dos sueños. Ciudad Trujillo, La Española (Col. La isla necesaria, 7), 1954. 58 p., illus.

A pretentious pseudo-Greek production. It unfortunately invites comparison with Sophocles. Matters are made more difficult by the format of the book, set by the *Isla necesaria* series, which suffers from gigantism in page and type face.

4095. Molinari, Ricardo E. Días donde la tarde es un pájaro. B. A., Emecé, 1954. 102 p.

Haunting poems by a well-educated writer. Taking elemental things like flowers, time, water, sky, light, and wind, the poet searches the repertory of their associations. These pieces remind one of Yeats, with their metaphysical direction and their stately music. Although difficult, they are extremely rewarding. Poems written 1950-1954.

4096. Nandino, Elías. Nocturna suma. México, Tezontle, 1955. 86 p.

The thoughtful voice of a believer, singing a message of calm strength, avoiding strong effects that would clash with the Nervo-like tranquility of the prevailing mood. The epigraph is from Emerson: "God is; and God is in me."

4097. Neruda, Pablo. Nuevas odas elementales. B. A., Losada (Poetas de España y América), 1956. 184 p.

A profitable return to a poetic project begun in 1954. Obviously Neruda did not then deliver himself of all he had to say of interest. He begins with a declaration of principles, in the first poem: "Yo destroné la negra monarquía, la cabellera inútil de los sueños, pisé la cola del reptil mental." He maintains his ability to see mystery, meaning, and excitement in things that non-poets pass by without comment. Appropriately, the last of these 50 poems is a tribute to Whitman. "Oda a la tipografía," separately published by Nascimento, is here, p. 159-168.

4098. ————. Odas elementales. B. A., Losada (Poetas de España y América), 1954. 235 p.

A book that makes an epoch in Neruda's production. Following up a line opened by the "Tres cantos materiales" of *Residencia en la tierra* (1944), he considers discrete subjects and unfolds his lyrical associations from them. The 67 "Odas" are arranged alphabetically according to topic, a varied catalogue. The elements of the ancients are here, with the exception of water; fruits, vegetables, seasons; persons; places; qualities. The more truly elemental is the theme, the greater the force of the poem, in general.

4099. **Novo, Salvador.** Poesía, 1915-1955. México, Impresiones Modernas (Col. Lince, 1), 1955. 341 p., port.

A thoroughly complete collection of Novo's poetry, beginning with some he wrote at the age of eleven. While the earliest have only biographical interest, the efforts of maturity, in many manners and moods, record the attempts at self-expression by a bright, talented, inquiring mind.

4099a. **Ocho poetas mexicanos:** Alejandro Avilés, Roberto Cabral del Hoyo, Rosario Castellanos, Dolores Castro, Efrén Hernández, Honorato Ignacio Magaloni, Octavio Novaro, Javier Peñalosa. México, Ábside, 1955. 181 p.

This anthology contains 50 pages originally printed in the review *Ábside* (18:4, oct.-dic. 1954). A good sampling of the more conservative of contemporary Mexican poetry, it would have been improved by the addition of notes to guide the reader.

4100. **Olivari, Nicolás.** La musa de la mala pata. Prólogo de González Carbalho. B. A., Deucalión (Col. Boedo y Florida), 1956. 140 p.

A reprinting of selected verse. The title poems, first published in 1926, had a *succès de scandale* because of the way in which they twitted the bourgeoisie. Today their Banvillesque cleverness is quite dated, a somewhat painful reminder of the Jazz Age with its pathetic iconoclasm. The volume also presents a handful of Olivari's other poetry.

4101. **O'Neill de Milán, Luis.** Arca de recuerdos. San Juan, Biblioteca de Autores Puertorriqueños, 1955. 129 p.

A collection of benevolent verses dedicated to family and friends. Lack of originality is the chief problem here. Titles such as "Visión doliente" give evidence of a retarded Romanticism.

4102. **Parra, Nicanor.** Poemas y antipoemas. Santiago, Nascimento, 1954. 158 p.

A significant volume by one of Chile's best-known poets. "Poemas" are stanzas regularly constructed, with rhyme or assonance, and a more or less standard diction; "antipoemas" are free verse of very irregular appearance couched in colloquial, relaxed language. In all there is a remarkable sprightliness which, creating an acidly ironical effect, comments on the small incidents that befall city-dwelling man. "Premio del Concurso Nacional de Poesía, patrocinado por el Sindicato de Escritores de Chile."

4103. **Paz, Octavio.** Semillas para un himno. México, Tezontle, 1954. 59 p.

A leader of contemporary Mexican literature in a group of intensely lyrical moments. According to the poet, there are "infrequent, instantaneous" messages that come from somewhere, and which must be seized at once, no matter if they are without beginning or end. Thus the statements of this book are made without benefit of punctuation, and are apparently isolated one from the other. Each line has the possibility of being a timeless aphorism. The second part of the book consists of versions of a poem by Andrew Marvell, and of four sonnets by Gérard de Nerval.

4104. **Portogalo, José.** Poemas con habitantes, 1950-1954. B. A., Sophos (Biblioteca nueva), 1955. 125 p.

One more evidence of the astounding power Whitman still exerts in Spanish American poetry. In this instance Portogalo, a self-professed poet of the people, seeks out humanity as his subject ("La multitud me llega / cada día en las luces de la aurora"), and this fact explains the title.

4105. **Rega Molina, Horacio.** Antología poética. B. A., Espasa-Calpe (Col. Austral, 1186), 1954. 146 p.

A selection by the poet himself from several books, from *Poema de la lluvia* (1922) to *Sonetos de mi sangre* (1951). All texts are the same as at first publication, except the "Oda provincial" whose original 1940 reading has been slightly revised.

4106. **Ribera Chevremont, Evaristo.** La llama pensativa. Los sonetos de Dios, del amor y de la muerte. San Juan, Imp. Venezuela, 1955. 67 p.

A cycle of 50 sonnets in which shallowness of thought is scarcely noticed because of a remarkable richness of melody. The sounds intertwine interestingly through rhyme, alliteration, repetition, and other devices.

4107. **Rivera, José Eustasio.** Tierra de promisión. Bogotá, Imp. Nacional, 1955. 76 p.

A de luxe reprinting, "bajo el cuidado de la Dirección de Información y Propaganda del Estado para conmemorar el cincuentenario de la fundación del Departamento del Huila." For each poem there is a handsome woodcut by Sergio Trujillo Magnenat, tending to emphasize the Parnassianism of Rivera's themes and treatment. A valuable preface by Rafael Maya tells of the poet's recognition by his contemporaries, describes his attitude, and attempts to classify the sonnets.

4108. Salazar Martínez, Francisco. El mendigo del sol. Caracas, Tip. Garrido, 1956. 61 p.

The work of a gifted poet. Each poem shows a firm grasp of the thematic problem; perception is converted into canticle and thus elevated far above the prosaic. Only when the ritualistic begins to grow self-conscious do the dangers of this approach become apparent. At other times the poet is capable of charming humor applied to serious topics.

4109. Sánchez Sorondo, Matías Guillermo. La tragedia del hombre. B. A., Editorial Suramericana, 1956. 190 p.

Rhymed reflections, mostly sonnets of varying line-length, meagerly furnished with imagery or other powers of evocation. There are many reminiscences of the writer's readings, particularly in the classics.

4110. Sociedad de Escritores de Valparaíso. Veinte poetas de Valparaíso. Valparaíso? Chile, Ediciones Océano, 1955. 88 p.

"La Sociedad de Escritores de Valparaíso, fundada en el pasado año, ha querido presentar a un grupo de poetas que forman parte de esta institución." This heterogeneous assemblage of poets cannot be called a movement or a school, but only proves that versification is an exercise attractive to many persons in Valparaiso.

4111. Torres Bodet, Jaime. Fronteras. México, Tezontle, 1954. 143 p.

Poetry as solace. The themes here are elemental —seasons, hours of the day, small familiar thoughts—and the style is calm, cerebral, sedate. Charming for entertainment, not calculated to arouse the passions.

4112. Torres Ríoseco, Arturo. Cautiverio. Antología poética, 1940-1955. Prólogo de Gabriela Mistral. México, Ediciones de Andrea (Antologías Studium, 1), 1955. 183 p.

Once more Torres-Ríoseco proves he has so mastered the art of song that he can control it, shape it, and place in it the essence of his being. "Homenaje en forma de sonetos" is a cycle of 18 pieces modelled in classic form and infused with humble pride in the possession of love, the summum bonum. "Sonetos y saludos" is the title of the last and largest section, whose main themes are observations on people (containing a delightful "Saludo a Ernesto Montenegro," in Gauchesque sextains); more love poems; and elegies, sensitive reflections on human mortality.

4113. Townsend, Francis Edward (ed. and tr.). Quisqueya. A panoramic anthology of Dominican verse. Ciudad Trujillo, Editora del Caribe, 1954. 101 p.

First printed in 1947, the present edition has a new preface by Otto Vega. Selection largely by Armando Óscar Pacheco. The translator is described as "formerly an Honorary Vice-Consul of the Dominican Republic in the U. S. and currently the Public Affairs Officer at the U. S. Embassy in Ciudad Trujillo." The translations are shrewdly done, but all sound as though they were originally written by Townsend. Among the 41 poets represented, very few are of major calibre.

4114. Vázquez Cey, Arturo. Alas en el ciprés. B. A., Librería Perlado, 1955. 157 p.

The theme is human mourning. The poet, in verses whose angularity at times betrays the violence of his feeling, struggles to understand mortality, to reconcile it with God's providence. The first part, "Candelabros invasores," stands in the presence of the corpse; "Vacíos los espacios" concentrates on the sense of loss.

4115. Villalobos, Héctor Guillermo. En soledad y en vela. Poemas (saldo romántico). Caracas, Edime (Autores venezolanos), 1954. 149 p.

Good-humored, contemplative, placid, friendly compositions in a thoroughly traditional, Hispanic vein. Now and then an overtone of Amado Nervo or of Azorín. 59 poems in all.

4116. Vitier, Cynthio. Canto llano, 1954-1955. Habana, Orígenes, 1956. 62 p.

The latest book of a very active poet and scholar: 50 short poems mostly in *verso de romance* and related quatrains. Finely compressed verses, impeccable and rounded, tell of an anguished attempt to find the answer to the riddle of existence, whose conditions are Time and Word. A Biblical atmosphere pervades the plain song. An outstanding volume by an authentic poet.

4117. Zorrilla de San Martín, Juan. Tabaré; an Indian legend of Uruguay. Translated into English verse by Walter Owen. Revised by Frank P. Hebblethwaite. Washington, Pan American Union, 1956. xliii, 366 p.

The last major translation of the late distinguished translator of *La Araucana, Fausto,* and *Martín Fierro;* and worthy to stand next to the earlier successes. It is not entirely Owen's version, however, since the revisor (Frank P. Hebblethwaite) has replaced some passages omitted. The translation is poetic, rich (except for occasional cacophonies), accurate, and with an air of inevitability that every good translation must have. One might wish Owen had, however, carried over Zorrilla's variety in the metres, instead of putting all into iambic pentameter quatrains. A UNESCO project, it is heavily laden with contributions, the best of which is Enrique Anderson-Imbert's workmanlike introduction. Spanish and English.

STUDIES

4118. Ara, Guillermo. Leopoldo Lugones, la etapa modernista. B. A., 1955. 75 p.

A study undertaken with reluctance by a critic who feels that Lugones was untrue to himself during his Modernist phase. *Las montañas del oro, Los crepúsculos del jardín,* and the *Lunario sentimental* are rapidly treated. A bibliography of Lugoniana is provocative but incomplete.

4119. Ayala, Juan Antonio. Lydia Noga-

les, un suceso en la historia literaria de El Salvador. San Salvador, Ministerio de Cultura, 1956. 299 p., illus.

Recapitulates the story of a furor in Salvadorian literary circles 10 years ago. Possibly a hoax, the poems of this "poetisa duende" suddenly began to appear, but "she" was never publicly seen before "she" fell silent. Meanwhile the country was divided between "nogalistas" and "antinogalistas." All this is told with tongue in cheek by a resident Spanish writer, complete with the poems involved, and many testimonials. The reader is left in doubt at the end, but will probably find the suspense bearable.

4120. Bergadá, Evangelina. La obra poética de Carlos Mastronardi. La Plata, Argentina, 1955. 81 p., illus.

A study of the themes and creative process of a poet identified with his native province of Entre Rios, particularly through a discussion of "Luz de provincia." In the process, the history of various post-Modernist movements in Argentina is traced. Although not profound or erudite, it is nevertheless suggestive and free from distracting critical mannerisms.

4121. Caffarel Peralta, Pedro. Díaz Mirón en su obra. México, Porrúa, 1956. 179 p.

Aspects of the poet selected as being representative and at the same time little explored. While conducted in a way that is excessively nervous, scrappy, and journalistic, this study does provide a series of flash-photos of Salvador Díaz Miron's choice and treatment of themes.

4122. Carrillo, José. Radiografía y disección de Salvador Díaz Mirón. México, Bayo, 1954. 137 p.

An untidy re-examination of the famed Mexican poet, professedly using concepts of "historical materialism" to defend Díaz Mirón from friends and enemies alike. More is learned of Carrillo, however, than of Díaz Mirón; encyclopedic literary knowledge, often superficial, is needlessly displayed.

4123. Castillo, Homero. Caupolicán en el modernismo de Darío (Atenea, año 32, 120:357, marzo 1955, p. 267-275).

Darío's interest in American themes was constant throughout his production, even in Azul . . ., where least expected. In the sonnet to Caupolicán, Darío improves on Ercilla, while using La Araucana as a source. The text of the sonnet is analyzed for expressive devices.

4124. Concha, Edmundo. Pedro Antonio González, poeta precursor (Atenea, año 33, 125:371, julio-agosto 1956, p. 99-107).

The purpose here is the placing of the poet (1863-1903) within his epoch as a forerunner of Modernism, and the comprehension of both.

4125. Dauster, Frank. Breve historia de la poesía mexicana. México, Ediciones de Andrea (Manuales Studium, 4), 1956. 198 p.

Successful as a quick survey of the subject, essential for students. It satisfies a long-standing

need for a synthesis of Mexico's poetry, and will be welcomed by all in the field. The organization is systematic, as befits such a work, setting up the categories necessary to the assimilation of diverse materials. Value judgments in the form of asterisks before the names of certain poets, a common feature in this series of manuals, are occasionally unorthodox.

4126. Etchebarne, Miguel D. La influencia del arrabal en la poesía argentina culta. B. A., Kraft (Col. Cúpula), 1955. 194 p.

A conscientious, scholarly examination of a phase of Argentine culture which, although its influence on the novel is well documented, had heretofore not been related to poetry. The author begins by defining his central term (arrabal: "cualquiera de los sitios extremos de una población") and its associated concepts, suburbio and bajo fondo. The study goes beyond the stated theme, and takes in aspects of sociology, anthropology, folk literature, dialectology, general literary theory. An excellent bibliograpy is appended.

4127. Fernández Moreno, César. Introducción a Fernández Moreno. B. A., Emecé, 1956. 275 p., illus.

A conscientious, densely written book with an unusual feeling of intimacy as the son, himself a writer, examines with admiration every important aspect of the father's life and work. Although it does not claim to be impartial, it so carefully documents judgments that it would be easy to consider this more than an introduction to this noted Argentine poet who died in 1950. There is an extensive bibliography of works by and about Baldomero Fernández Moreno.

4128. Fernández Retamar, Roberto. La poesía contemporánea en Cuba, 1927-1953. Habana, Orígenes, 1954. 130 p.

A poet studies the poetry of his country with notable success. Written as a doctoral thesis, it avoids excesses of pedantry (although the author apologizes for its didactic tone and scholarly apparatus) while retaining the advantage of careful organization. Generations of poets are subdivided into tendencies, somewhat incautiously termed "schools." An impressive "Bibliografía general" rounds out a study that becomes an indispensable tool.

4129. Florit, Eugenio. Alfonso Reyes: la obra poética (R Hisp Mod, 22:3-4, julio-oct. 1956, p. 224-247).

The illustrious Mexican writer is considered under two main headings: "Formas y orientaciones," and "Temas." Reyes is allowed to speak for himself, in numerous quotations.

4130. Garet Más, Julio. La cigarra de Eunomo. Montevideo, Ediciones de "Numen," 1954. 141 p.

A collection of short, impressionistic articles on 34 Uruguayan poetesses, from María Eugenia Vaz Ferreira to Marosa di Giorgio. They were first read over a radio station in Salto, then published in Central American and Uruguayan journals. The focus is entirely on the poetry, generally with an appreciative approach. Of unequal worth, but at best these pieces give one poet's judgment of another's, with an insight perhaps denied to those outside the art.

4131. Gicovate, Bernardo. Julio Herrera y Reissig and the Symbolists. Berkeley, Calif., University of California Press, 1957. 106 p.

An excellent presentation, in non-regional terms, of a poet who deserves to be better known outside Spanish America. Controversial, his work "offers an opportunity for the study of the strange quickening produced in an alert mind when it comes in contact with a foreign culture." Chapter headings: *Modernismo* and its relation to French poetry; Influences in the works of Herrera y Reissig; From image to myth: the impasse of Symbolism; The early poems of Herrera y Reissig; A private diction; Experiments in the structure. According to Gicovate, the poet largely failed in his attempt to utilize the resources of Symbolism and discover an "all-inclusive pattern" in which to situate himself.

4132. Gómez de Fernández, Dora. La poética de Franz Tamayo. La Paz, Departamento de Publicaciones y Difusión Cultural del Ministerio de Educación (Col. Cuadernos juveniles, 1), 1956. 106 p.

The tone is set by the first sentence of the book: "Franz Tamayo es el más grande poeta que Bolivia ha producido en toda su historia. Esperamos probar que es uno de los mejores poetas de América." The authoress, a teacher, goes about her work in a businesslike way, but is limited by having under consideration only one work of Tamayo's, *La Prometheida.* The first of a projected series of critical studies by Bolivian writers.

4133. Gonzáles, Manuel Pedro. José María Heredia, primogénito del romanticismo hispano. Ensayo de rectificación histórica. México, El Colegio de México, 1955. 158 p.

Although the mainstay of the thesis—that Heredia was the first to write authentically Romantic verses in the Spanish language—had been placed some years before by another scholar, this study makes a large contribution by advocating and practising a close scrutiny of texts. Through it we come once more to the conclusion that it is often impossible to apply, on this side of the Atlantic, traditional European literary categories in pure form.

4134. Hamilton, Carlos D. Itinerario de Pablo Neruda (R Hisp Mod, 22:3-4, julio-oct. 1956, p. 286-297).

Raises and attempts to answer certain questions about the later Neruda, after "conversion," particularly after the *Residencias.* In the Chilean poet, Communism is "social romanticism," not Marxism. Some defects show up in the *Odas elementales;* but in any case Neruda is the second moment of realization in Hispanic American poetry, Darío being the first.

4135. Leiva, Raúl. La poesía de Bernardo

Ortiz de Montellano (Cuad Am, año 16, 92:2, marzo-abril 1957, p. 201-213).

On the one-time director of the review *Contemporáneos* in Mexico. An analysis of his lyrical development, from *El trompo de siete colores* onward, and a description of his particular contribution: a Freudian advance into the world of dreams.

4136. Lens y de Vera, Eduardo Félix. Heredia y Martí. Dos grandes figuras de la lírica cubana. Habana, Editorial Selecta, 1954. 43 p.

Little if any new light is shed on these consecrated poets. 20 pages of this pamphlet are anthology. It was presented as a lecture to a chapter meeting of the AATSP in Florida.

4137. Monterde García Icazbalceta, Francisco. Díaz Mirón. El hombre, la obra. México, Ediciones de Andrea, 1956. 106 p.

Three years after the centenary of Salvador Díaz Mirón's death, studies about him continue to appear, of which the present is certainly one of the best. Monterde's meticulous scholarship is once more in evidence in this pleasing, reliable book. If at first it seems brief, it is because it is designed to fill in, with the results of 15 years' investigations, the gaps left by others. Monterde's purpose is to trace the poet's development through his successive stages of Romanticism, Modernism, and after, evaluating each tendency as it appears. Bibliography.

4138. Nieto, Luis Carlos. Poesía cuzqueña. Derrotero para una ubicación de la poesía cuzqueña contemporánea. V. 1. 2. ed., revisada, corregida y ampliada. Cuzco, Perú, Ediciones Sol y Piedra, 1956. 185 p.

Claiming to be the first such work on the poetry of Cuzco, this goes back 35 years to trace the background development since *Colónida* and Modernism to the present. Three distinct periods are found: 1920-1927, 1927-1940, 1940-1955. The bias of the writer, himself a poet, is evident through his praise of Ilya Ehrenburg and the later Neruda and his detestation of "pure" poetry.

4139. Orrego, Antenor. César Vallejo, el poeta del solecismo (Cuad Am, año 16, 91:1, enero-feb. 1957, p. 209-216).

With some heat the author asserts that despite laudatory appreciations of Vallejo in recent years, he is still misunderstood—his *indigenismo,* his *mestizaje,* his use of free verse. Revaluation is much needed, keeping in mind a genuine artist's need to deviate.

4140. Palisa Mujica de Lacau, María Hortensia. El mundo poético de Conrado Nalé Roxlo. Poesía y estilo. B. A., Raigal (Biblioteca Juan María Gutiérrez), 1954. 321 p.

A solid contribution to stylistics by a pupil of Amado Alonso. Following Alonso's analytical method, the authoress marshals an array of data that is, in the long run, likely to overwhelm a poet of modest stature. In any event, a virtuoso performance which informs as it dazzles.

4141. Peñuelas, Marcelino C. Whitman y Chocano: unas notas (Cuad Am, año 15, 89:5, sept.-oct. 1956, p. 223-231).

Although Chocano himself suggested the comparison, the two poets have absolutely nothing in common.

4142. Plá y Beltrán, Pascual. Tres poetas venezolanos en su ardiente dimensión (Cuad Am, año 15, 90:6, nov.-dic. 1956, p. 220-237).

What Luis Barrios Cruz, Vicente Gerbasi, and Ida Gramcko have in common is success in giving deeper meaning to *nativismo*.

4143. Sánchez, Luis Alberto. Gabriela Mistral (Asomante, año 12, 12:2, abriljunio 1956, p. 39-47).

The real sources of knowledge about Gabriela Mistral are literary. These are scattered notes about the poetess, informative but disconnected.

4144. Schulman, Ivan. Función y sentido del color en la poesía de Manuel Gutiérrez Nájera (R Hisp Mod, 23:1 enero 1957, p. 1-13).

On the basis of a single text it is asserted that Modernism began in 1881-1882, and not with *Azul* . . . Gutiérrez Nájera's system of color values is that of the Modernist in general; it corresponds to three movements, Romantic, Parnassian, Symbolist. An elementary analysis of poems according to colors.

4145. Torrealba Lossi, Mario. Los poetas venezolanos de 1918. Caracas, Editorial Simón Rodríguez (Colegio de Profesores de Venezuela), 1955. 116 p., illus.

Projected apparently as a text book, it enters a field much in need of clarification but does not shed as much light as it might because of digressions and because of the evident haste of its writing. Nevertheless, it affords information difficult to obtain elsewhere, and the opinions of its knowledgeable author give a hurried cross-section of modern literary criticism.

4146. Torres Ríoseco, Arturo. *A rebours* and two sonnets of Julián del Casal (Hisp R, 23:4, Oct. 1955, p. 295-297).

Manuel de la Cruz was right in saying that Casal had never seen in any form the paintings of Moreau, but that he relied on the brief descriptions of the canvases given by Huysmans. Comparison of Casal's two sonnets on Salome with the French text supports this view.

4147. Xirau, Ramón. Tres poetas de la soledad. México, Antigua Librería Robredo (México y lo mexicano, 19), 1955. 73 p.

On three Mexican poets: José Gorostiza, Xavier Villaurrutia, and Octavio Paz. A serious although very brief consideration of one aspect of Mexico's poetic production in this century. By far the greatest emphasis is on ideas; hence it is a thematic essay whose chief method is careful analysis. Octavio Paz, with 32 pages, is given the lion's share of the attention. Together, these three poets are placed within the *Contemporáneos* generation.

DRAMA

FRANK DAUSTER

THE PERIOD 1953-1956 continued the trend noted in the preceding volume, a trend which may without undue optimism be interpreted as pointing toward a firmly established Spanish American theater. This can be seen in the quantities of hopeful articles published in Spanish America, in the continued, if tenuous, existence of independent movements in nations virtually barren of organized theater, and in the clear indications of a renaissance in Mexico.

The millennium has not yet arrived. The hopeful predictions are frequently based on quantitative results in *concurosos*, rather than on solid quality. Much Spanish American theater still suffers from the grossest kind of romantic zeal, expressing itself in works which suffer from a complete lack of technical skill. This period saw the publication of the usual number of political attacks, and the usual quantity of praise of political leaders. Whatever the virtues of the latter, the plays themselves are insignificant.

But the fact remains that there is a ferment. Mexico has clearly taken the lead as a theatrical center, closely followed by Buenos Aires. But plays are being produced and published in virtually every Spanish American nation, and enough of them are dramatically significant to outweigh the rubbish which accompanies them.

Among the more interesting developments during this period is the tendency toward integration of dramatic and dance elements, a tendency shared by young and established writers alike. The most significant new theatrical group is *Poesía en voz alta*, in Mexico, whose literary director is Octavio Paz and whose theater director is Héctor Mendoza. Devoted to the best in theater they have not neglected the works of promising Mexican playwrights.

Although no new plays appeared of the stature of some in recent years, there are several which deserve special mention. The young Chilean Jaime Silva has produced a delightful reinterpretation of Plautine comedy, and the outstanding Mexican poet Octavio Paz has begun to write for the theater. There have appeared editions of the work of Roberto Payró and Julio Sánchez Gardel, and a second edition of Carlos Gorostiza's El puente. Salvador Bueno and José Marial have produced critical studies of note. Special mention should be made of Carlos Ancira's drama, Después nada, a tour de force, which, despite major weaknesses, contains a leading role of unusual power and depth.

Among periodicals, we register regret at the disappearance of Panorama del teatro en México. During its two years of existence, it established a pattern which, it is hoped, will soon be followed. Finally, and perhaps most significant, is the publication of the three volumes of the Fondo de Cultura Económica's Teatro mexicano del siglo XX (item 4234), a work whose importance cannot be overestimated.

PLAYS

4200. Alfonso, Paco. Yari-yari, Mamá Olúa y Cañaveral. Teatro. Prólogo de Luis A. Baralt. Habana, La Milagrosa, 1956. 230 p.

Cañaveral is propaganda for the guajiros mistreated by company officials, and is of no dramatic interest. Yari yari, Mamá Olúa oscillates between conscious Afro-Cubanism after the fashion of Nicolás Guillén and strained poetic dialogue. Uncomfortably reminiscent of Uncle Tom's Cabin in certain respects (dialogue, theme, sentimentality), this lyrical folk drama with music has moments of promise. The three acts correspond to the capture of an African village, the passage on a slave ship, and slavery in Cuba.

4201. Alpern, Hymen, and José Martel (eds.). Teatro hispanoamericano. N. Y., Odyssey Press, 1956. 412 p.

A text edition whose value is vitiated by a dubious choice of plays and some misleading critical commentary. Omission of Villaurrutia, Nalé Roxlo, Díaz Díaz and others in the "Breve reseña del teatro hispanoamericano," inclusion of the sesentón Eichelbaum among "los dramaturgos jóvenes," and similar errata present a distorted picture. Contents: Alsina's La marca de fuego; Sánchez' Los derechos de la salud; Eichelbaum's Divorcio nuptial; Moock's La serpiente;

Rojas' Ollantay (which is not adapted from "el antiguo clásico peruano," but based on folk sources); Ascensio Segura's Ña Catita.

4202. Ancira, Carlos. Después nada. Pieza en 3 actos (Panor Teat Méx, 1:5, dic. 1954, p. 19-46).

A harrowing drama of a great actor's return to the stage and recognition that the spark is gone. The supporting characters are not clearly defined, but the lead role is strong enough to hold the play together.

4203. Arreola, Juan José. La hora de todos. Juguete cómico en un acto. México, Los Presentes, 1954. 69 p.

An imaginative and technically advanced work whose content is ridden with all the cliches of the social theater. The villainous captain of industry is so thoroughly evil that the effect is lost.

4204. Arriví, Francisco. Medusas en la bahía. Drama en un acto (Asomante, año 10, 11:2, abril-junio 1955, p. 88-105).

A suspenseful study of a Puerto Rican caught in the racial intolerance of his own family. Tasteful use of stage devices and thoughtful dialogue lead to an excellent climatic scene. Part of the trilogy Bolero y plena.

4205. ————. El murciélago. Drama en un acto (Asomante, año 11, 12:1, enero-marzo 1956, p. 71-85).

A superior play, whose effective use of flashback forcefully contrasts life in Puerto Rico with life in New York. Minor key drama of frustration and loneliness.

4206. Basurto, Luis G. Toda una dama. Pieza en 3 actos (Panor Teat Méx, 1:7, feb. 1955, p. 19-57).

A plausible but loosely constructed study of a woman's realization that her marital problems are of her own making. The resolution is too abrupt and the first act weak.

4207. Belaval, Emilio S. La muerte. Comedia de delirantes en 3 actos y en prosa. San Juan, Biblioteca de Autores Puertorriqueños, 1953. 114 p.

Sarcastic satire on the state of civilization, as exemplified by the staff and guests of a luxury hotel. Their transformation into human beings when faced by death, and subsequent return to a dehumanized state are expressed amusingly and theatrically, although a striving for poetic expression occasionally leads the author into forced dialogue.

4208. Béneke, Walter. El paraíso de los imprudentes. Pieza en 3 actos. San Salvador, Departamento Editorial del Ministerio de Cultura (Col. Teatro), 1956. 119 p.

The confused and rootless youth of today's Paris seen with compassion and portrayed with taste. Despite the theme, the dialogue never becomes vulgar or sentimental. The theme of lost youth is somewhat overplayed, to the detriment of clear characterization, but the characters are sympathetic and understandable.

4209. Bruno, Jorge. El cuarto de Anatol. Montevideo, El Tinglado, 1956. 77 p.

An absorbing but obscure experimental treatment of man's frustration in society, making enormous demands on the protagonist, who is on stage almost continuously throughout a play which is really one extended act. Undeniable technical virtuosity and a flair for incisive dialogue do not avoid the pitfalls of obscurity, leading into extended possible interpretations.

4210. Cantón, Wilberto. Escuela de cortesanos. Comedia-ballet en 3 actos. México, Helio-México (Col. Teatro mexicano), 1956. 77 p.

Comedy intrigue during the Viceregency in Mexico, done with spirit and flair. The mixture of elements, ranging from farce through high comedy, is handled with tact, and demonstrates an interesting aspect of the talents of the author, previously known for the semi-existentialist *Saber morir.* First published in a periodical (Panor Teat Méx, 1:3, sept. 1954, p. 35-66).

4211. Carballido, Emilio. Rosalba y los llaveros. Comedia en 3 actos (Panor Teat Méx, 1:9, mayo-junio 1955, p. 21-67).

A sophisticated city girl brings air, light, and a considerable measure of havoc into the stuffy existence of some provincial cousins. Straight commercial theater, with quick dialogue and sophisticated wit to prevent the underlying good-humored sentiment from degenerating into sentimentality.

4212. Carlino, Carlos. La Biunda. Tierra del destino. B. A., Ediciones del Instituto Amigos del Libro Argentino (Col. Teatro, 1), 1955. 152 p.

In the tradition of the *criollo* theater, these dramas suffer from a lack of convincing protagonists. The protagonist of *La Biunda* is so spiritless that her suicide is more shocking than dramatic. *Tierra del destino,* with fewer pretensions, is more successful.

4213. Díaz Sánchez, Ramón. Debajo de estos aleros. Comedia dramática en 3 actos (Teatro, Madrid, 16, mayo-agosto 1955, p. 55-77).

Under its original title of *La casa,* won the Premio Nacional de Literatura de Venezuela. Demonstrates a sense of dramatic effect and a feeling for movement. The melodramatic aspects do not detract from the play until the overdone declamatory ending.

4214. Dragún, Osvaldo. La peste viene de Melos. Pieza en 3 actos y 6 cuadros. B. A., Ariadna (Col. Coral, 7), 1956. 78 p.

The heroic resistance of the Melians against Athenian aggression and their betrayal because of low economic motives, placed in the framework of poetic drama. Very uneven, with some scenes, particularly the early ones, having a moving dialogue. The characters are paper.

4215. Estrada, hijo, Ricardo. Ella y él. Teatro pequeño. Guatemala, Imp. Universitaria, 1956. 19 p.

A brief and pleasant one-act play of a love haunted by memories of previous affairs. Interesting without being really dramatic.

4216. Fabregat Cuneo, Roberto. El pinar de Tierras Altas. Tres actos y un intermedio (R Nac, año 16, 15:179, nov. 1953, p. 181-229).

Witty comedy whose charm becomes almost pompous in the third act. The *intermedio* is structurally unnecessary and adds little to the play proper.

4217. García, Juan Agustín. Obras completas. B. A., Zamora (Col. Argentoria, 5), 1955. T. 2, p. 770-1472.

The Argentinian sociologist's writings for and about the theater, characterized chiefly by a total lack of understanding. The plays are *Del uno al otro, El mundo de los snobs, Un episodio bajo el terror,* all too dull to be readable, and *La cuarterona,* a satire on the rigid repressions of the colonial period, including some moments of real freshness.

4218. González Paredes, Ramón. El personaje rival. Drama en un acto (Cult U, 54, marzo-abril 1956, p. 41-60).

The old plot of a suspicious fiancé who invents an imaginary person in order to test his fiancée's love. Before the obvious happens, excessive use of monologue and explanations cannot remove all the amusement. Particular virtues are an agile dialogue and a marvelous 13-year-old.

4219. Gorostiza, Carlos. El puente. B. A., Losange (Publ. teatral periódica, 8), 1954. 124 p.

Second edition of the drama originally published in 1949. See *HLAS, no. 15, 1949,* item 2440.

4220. ————. El reloj de Baltasar. Comedia en 3 actos. B. A., Losange (Publ. teatral periódica, 24), 1955. 79 p.

Fantasy-drama of a man who has the secret of perpetual life, by a craftsman who makes the problem plausible and dramatic. Underlying Baltasar's search for a normal existence is a concept of time as the expression of life's fruition. The somewhat intellectualized atmosphere is relieved by carefully integrated comic themes and a romantic triangle.

4221. Gramcko, Ida. María Lionza. 3 actos. Barquisimeto, Venezuela, Editorial Nueva Segovia, 1955. 60 p.

A verse dramatization of folk myth whose elements of spectacle and dance could be theatrically effective, but whose verse frequently degenerates into inferior rhyming.

4222. Magaña, Sergio. Moctezuma II. Tragedia en 3 actos y un prólogo (Panor Teat Méx, 1:1, julio 1954, p. 35-82).

An attempt at revindication of Moctezuma which suffers from the author's insistence on placing it in the framework of classical tragedy; a theatrical but dramatically unjustified chorus muddies the action. The vain, frivolous Moctezuma of Act I does not prepare the audience for the tragic figure of Acts II and III, defeated by treachery but clinging to his advanced ideas. A provocative but only moderately successful attempt.

4223. Orosa Díaz, Jaime. Se vende un hombre. Farsa en 3 cuadros. Mérida, México, Universidad Nacional del Sureste, 1956. 92 p.

Based on incidents leading to the death of the Mexican patriot, Felipe Carrillo Puerto, and published in his honor, this is a study of brutality rather than a comedy. All characters are stylized except the general commissioned to kill Carrillo Puerto, and the focus is on his degeneration from an apparently normal being to a drunken assassin.

4224. Payró, Roberto J. Teatro completo. Estudio preliminar de Roberto F. Giusti. B. A., Librería Hachette (Col. El pasado argentino), 1956. 587 p.

The excellent study by Giusti divides Payró's theater into two major periods, the socially oriented and the moral. He underlines Payró's importance in the transition from the "dramón circense" and the ingenuous melodrama to a more cosmopolitan theater, which retains certain characteristics visible in the earlier periods.

4225. Paz, Octavio. La hija de Rappaccini. Pieza en un acto (R Mex Lit, 1:7, sept.-oct. 1956, p. 3-26).

One of Mexico's most distinguished and influential poets, and presently literary director of *Poesía en voz alta*, here turns to the theater. The result is an exquisitely written fable of the dance of life, the eternal struggle between life and death. The play's only defect is its literary excellence, which might detract from its effectiveness on stage.

4226. Pereña, Alfredo. La escoba verde. Cuento de brujas. Comedia en 3 actos. México, Compañía Mexicana Impresora, 1954. 128 p.

A pleasant fable of three young and ineffectual witches. Occasionally self-conscious cuteness does not detract from the dance of color and word.

4227. Plaza, Angélica. La tierra ilimitada. Montevideo, Letras, 1954. 187 p.

Includes three plays, *Vencedor del fuego, Dioses y lianas,* and *Coyote hambriento,* based on Indian legend and related themes. Only the first achieves dramatic effect; all are primarily spectacle and hampered by verbosity. Also included is an essay, "Lo telúrico abstracto en el indio," which makes some telling points about Indian psychology but lacks focus.

4228. Rapoport, Nicolás. Teatro. Prólogo de Álvaro Yunque. B. A., Losange, 1955. 125 p.

Four plays chiefly remarkable for their sentimentality and false dialogue. They are pervaded by the theme of honest love redeeming all. Contains: *Porque soy una mujer, La intrusa, Otoñal, El manantial.*

4229. Ríos, Juan. Ayar Manko. 3 actos (Mer Per, año 29, 35:326, mayo 1954, p. 265-308).

A poetic drama of a struggle for power among Inca princes, marred by verbose philosophizing. The attempt to create dialogue similar in structure to pre-Conquest poetry leads to rhetorical repetitiousness. Another example of the trend toward mixture of dramatic and dance elements.

4230. Salazar Bondy, Sebastián. No hay isla feliz. Drama en 3 actos. Prólogo de Jorge Basadre. Lima, Ediciones Club de Teatro, 1954. 110 p.

A melodrama of disillusionment and negation which has provoked controversy between nationalist and internationalist wings of the Peruvian theater.

4231. Sánchez Gardel, Julio. Teatro. Estudio preliminar de Juan Carlos Ghiano. B. A., Hachette (Col. El pasado argentino), 1955. 253 p.

Contains *Noche de luna, Las campanas, Los mirasoles,* and his best work, the violent and poetic *La montaña de las brujas.* The preliminary study is extensive and intelligent, commenting on background, the *rioplatense* theater, the author's life and works, and his dramatic language.

4232. Silva, Jaime. El otro avaro. Santiago? Ediciones del Joven Laurel, 1954. 120 p.

A lighthearted adaptation of Plautus' *Aulularia,* patterned closely after the conventional structure, but with the addition of a god who takes a casual but decisive interest in the hectic goings-on. Skillful use of modern staging techniques add a new dimension to the comedy, which is heightened by sharp and vivid dialogue. The author, only 20 at the time of publication, is definitely a promise for the future.

4233. Solana, Rafael. La ilustre cuna. Comedia en 3 actos (Panor Teat Méx, 1:6, enero 1955, p. 19-46).

Satire of well-known personalities hung on a loose framework. More akin to the sketch than to his other works, this play suffers from the author's belief that one learns to write only by writing. Serious revision would have prevented the third act from turning into a conglomeration of poorly unified scenes; it would, as a consistent practice, turn a prolific and interesting playwright into a serious and important dramatist.

4234. Teatro mexicano del siglo XX. México, Fondo de Cultura Económica (Letras mexicanas, 25, 26, 27), 1956. V. 1, Francisco Monterde (ed.), xxviii, 608 p. V. 2, Antonio Magaña Esquivel (ed.), xxxv,

701 p. V. 3, Celestino Gorostiza (ed.), xxvii, 741 p.

An anthology of Mexican theater covering the last 56 years, with excellent prologues by three of Mexico's most outstanding students of the theater. Included in the 32 plays presented are many important works which have become unavailable, and 11 previously unpublished. Notable among these are Carballido's *La danza que sueña la tortuga,* Schroeder Inclán's *Hoy invita la güera,* Solana's *Debiera haber obispas,* and Retes' *Una ciudad para vivir.* The first is a comic but sympathetic study of a Don Juan accidentally trapped by a confirmed old maid; the second is comedy of manners cloaking satire; the third is vitriolic lampooning of provincial hyprocrisy; and the fourth a drama of small people caught in a materialistic world which does not understand them. Although the overall quality is somewhat uneven, and a few of the plays are valueless, this anthology remains an invaluable aid to the study of Mexican theater. Vol. 1: Manuel José Othón, *El último capítulo;* Marcelino Dávalos, *Así pasan . . . ;* Federico Gamboa, *La venganza de la gleba;* José Joaquín Gamboa, *Via crucis;* Carlos Noriega Hope, *La señorita Voluntad;* Víctor Manuel Díez Barroso, *Véncete a ti mismo;* Ricardo Parada León, *Hacia la meta;* Lázaro and Carlos Lozano García, *Al fin mujer;* María Luisa Ocampo, *Al otro día;* Julio Jiménez Rueda, *La silueta de humo;* Carlos Díaz Dufóo, *Padre mercader.* Vol. 2: Francisco Monterde, *Proteo;* Juan Bustillo Oro, *San Miguel de las Espinas;* Mauricio Magdaleno, *Pánuco 137;* Celestino Gorostiza, *El color de nuestra piel;* Xavier Villaurrutia, *El yerro candente;* Alfonso Reyes, *Ifigenia cruel;* Rodolfo Usigli, *El gesticulador;* Concepción Sada, *Un mundo para mí;* Miguel N. Lira, *Vuelta a la tierra;* Luis G. Basurto, *Cada quien su vida;* Edmundo Báez, *Un alfiler en los ojos.* Vol. 3: Salvador Novo, *La culta dama;* Agustín Lazo, *El caso de don Juan Manuel;* Emilio Carballido, *La Danza que sueña la tortuga;* Sergio Magaña, *Los signos del zodíaco;* Federico Schroeder Inclán, *Hoy invita la güera;* Luisa Josefina Hernández, *Los frutos caídos;* Rafael Solana, *Debiera haber obispas;* Héctor Mendoza, *Las cosas simples;* Ignacio Retes, *Una ciudad para vivir;* Jorge Ibargüengoitia, *Clotilde en su casa.*

4235. Usigli, Rodolfo. Mientras amemos. Pieza en 3 actos (Panoramas, 1, primavera 1956, 81 p.).

Written between 1937 and 1948, *Mientras amemos* gives the impression that it was written as an exercise in overcoming the basically visual nature of the theater. For reasons not entirely clear, a man hires a double to replace him; eventually, the double and his employer's wife elope. Since one or another of the characters is partially blind throughout, the first and last acts take place in virtual darkness. The motivations are ignored, and the play raises a series of esthetic questions left unanswered. Not Usigli at his best.

4236. Zavattini, Cesare, and Luis García Berlanga. Soldado y criada. Libreto cinematográfico (Número, 6:27, dic. 1955, p. 160-175).

Simple, unpretentious and effective script for a film episode, demonstrating the peculiar advantages and disadvantages of the camera as a dramatic medium.

STUDIES

4237. Abascal Brunet, Manuel, and Eugenio Pereira Salas. Pepe Vila. La zarzuela chica en Chile. Santiago, Imp. Universitaria, 1955. 225 p., illus.

Biography of a leading actor of the "género chico", with considerable information on casts, titles, etc.

4238. Babín, María Teresa. Apuntes sobre *La carreta* (Asomante, 9:4, oct.-dic. 1953, p. 63-79).

A detailed analysis and attempt at evaluation of one of the most important works of the Puerto Rican theater. See *HLAS, no. 18, 1952,* item 2692.

4239. Braschi, Wilfredo. Treinta años de teatro en Puerto Rico (Asomante, 11:1, enero-marzo 1955, p. 95-101).

A useful but uncritical summary, of service to specialists and those who wish a handy introduction to the area.

4240. Bueno, Salvador. Medio siglo de literatura cubana, 1902-1952. Habana, Comisión Nacional Cubana de la Unesco, 1953. 234 p.

The chapter entitled "Itinerario del teatro" (p. 119-138) is a complement to J. J. Arrom's *Historia de la literatura dramática cubana,* covering the new generation, to which he assigns 1937 as a starting point. He believes that in spite of the divorce between the commercial and "art" theaters, "los últimos 15 años han demostrado plenamente la existencia de un teatro cubano."

4241. Cantón, Wilberto. Balance teatral 1954 (Panor Teat Méx, 1:6, enero 1955, p. 5-13, 50-54).

A summation of the year's activity in the Mexican theater, with discussion of the most important plays and the productions staged by individual theaters. "Se aceleró el movimiento ascendente que desde hace dos o tres años se nota: se estrenaron más obras nacionales, se abrieron nuevos teatros y se rompieron récords de duración."

4242. Cuadernos de arte dramático. B. A. Año 2, no. 7-8-9, agosto 1953.

Devoted to the history of the Argentine theater, this number includes several articles previously published in *Cuadernos de cultura teatral*: Pedro Henríquez Ureña's classic study, "El teatro en la América Española en la época colonial"; José Luis Lanuza, "La historia como tema de teatro"; Ernesto Morales, "1810-1830: Panorama del teatro", a detailed study of the drama of the period and its relation to politics; Pablo Acchiardi, "Juan Aurelio Casacuberta y el arte del actor". Others are "Cinco años en Buenos Aires: El teatro de 1820 a 1825", a detailed study by an unknown theater lover of the period, and "El circo y la representación gaucha," by Antonio Cunill Carbanella, an outline of the development from circus acrobat to dramatic personage.

4243. Dauster, Frank. The contemporary Mexican theater (Hispania, AATSP, 38:1, Mar. 1955, p. 31-34).
A brief discussion of the years 1928-1953, stressing the importance of *Ulises* and *Orientación* in the development of the present theater renaissance in Mexico.

4244. Franck, Frederick W. La vida y obra de Víctor Manuel Díez Barroso, dramaturgo mexicano. México, 1954. Various pagings.
A review of Díez Barroso's work consisting almost entirely of periodical articles quoted in large part or in entirety, quantities of Díez Barroso's periodistic writing, and two previously unpublished plays, *Las pasiones mandan* and *¡Adiós manito!* Valuable because it brings together material not otherwise easily available. Thesis, Universidad Nacional Autónoma de México.

4245. Giusti, Roberto F. El teatro rioplatense. Del circo a las modernas expresiones de vanguardia (Cuad Am, año 13, 77:5, sept.-oct. 1954, p. 198-212).
A very good résumé of the development from *Juan Moreira* to Conrado Nalé Roxlo. The critical appreciations are intelligent and appreciative, the background is brief but adequate.

4246. Imbert, Julio. Crédito, credencial y credo de Gregorio de Laferrere (Comentario, 3:10, enero-marzo 1956, p. 77-82).
Underlines the skill and detachment of Laferrere's approach to drama, and the lack of heroism, the "averageness", of his characters. Attributes this to Laferrere's conviction of the mediocrity of his society.

4247. Jones, Willis Knapp. Breve historia del teatro latinoamericano. México, Ediciones de Andrea (Manuales Studium, 5), 1956. 239 p.
An uncritical compilation whose value is mitigated by frequently faulty bibliographical data.

4248. ————. El teatro de Martí (*in* Congreso de Escritores Martianos, I, Habana, 1953. Memoria. Habana, 1953, p. 718-728).
An appreciation of Martí as playwright, an aspect which never matured because of other demands on him and external situations which led him to consider the stage as a pulpit.

4249. Magaña Esquivel, Antonio. Manuel Eduardo de Gorostiza y su obra dramática (Estaciones, 1:1, primavera 1956, p. 85-91).
A lucid sketch of Gorostiza's work, including summaries and discussion of outstanding characteristics. An enthusiastic appreciation.

4250. Marial, José. El teatro independiente. B. A., Alpe, 1955. 260 p.
A study of the experimental theater in B. A., stressing particularly the importance of *Teatro del Pueblo* under Leónidas Barletta in the late 1930's and early 1940's. Includes discussions of the most important groups, leading authors and directors, and a review of the movement, giving repertories, casts, and other information. Ends with an analysis of the problems of the movement and a plea for solidarity and intergroup cooperation.

4251. Mendoza López, Margarita. El grupo de los siete autores dramáticos (Teat, México, 11-12, oct. 1955, p. 1-20).
Includes, in addition to the above article, the "Manifiesto de los siete", "El grupo de los siete" by Celestino Gorostiza, a bibliography of the group, and articles on José Joaquín Gamboa (by Ricardo Parada León), Carlos Noriega Hope (by Carlos and Lázaro Lozano García), and Víctor Manuel Díez Barroso (by Francisco Monterde). An important contribution to the study of a group influential in the birth of the modern Mexican theater.

4252. Montoya, María Tereza. El teatro en mi vida. México, Ediciones Botas, 1956. 365 p., illus.
Chatty and enthusiastic memoirs of the grande dame of Mexico's theater. Although addicted to exclamation marks and coy commentary, she has written a mine of information on Mexican theater. Valuable for the factual data included.

4253. Pineda, Rafael. Pasado y presente del teatro en Venezuela (El Farol, 15:150, feb. 1954, p. 32-33).
An outline of the debility of the Venezuelan theater and an analysis of the causes, emphasizing the transitory and amateur nature of those groups which do exist.

4254. Rose, Gonzalo. Teatro contemporáneo del Perú (Humanismo, 3:17-18, feb. 1954, p. 83-87).
Avant-garde discussion of the period 1946-1951, singling out the foundation of the Compañía Nacional de Comedias in 1946 as the beginning of a new epoch.

4255. Sorenson, Thora. Recent developments in the Argentine theatre (Hispania, AATSP, 39:4, Dec. 1956, p. 446-449).
Enthusiastic and grandiloquent praise of Nalé Roxlo, Yunque, Tálice, Suárez de Deza, and Carlos Gorostiza. Generally reasonable, but Nalé Roxlo's *Una viuda difícil* is "realistic" only in a very limited sense, and attributing realistic, romantic, classic and ultramodern characteristics to Rojas' *Ollantay* would seem to be stretching a point.

4256. Spell, Jefferson Rea. Gorostiza and England (Atlante, 3:1, Jan. 1951, p. 15-31).
An account of the activities of Manuel Eduardo de Gorostiza as Mexican representative in Europe, including a summary account of his activities in the theater.

ESSAYS

ROBERT G. MEAD, JR.

4257. Bernárdez Jacques, Elbio. La cultura argentina a través de un pensamiento socrático. B. A., 1956. 84 p.
Interesting reflections, mostly iconoclastic, on the last half-century of Argentina's life and culture and its intellectuals, which end with a plea for a return to autochthonous *argentinismo* as a cultural foundation.

4258. Blanco, Tomás. Los cinco sentidos. Cuaderno suelto de un inventario de cosas nuestras. Con decoraciones de Irene Delano. San Juan, Pan American Book Co., 1955. 56 p., illus.
Short pieces in poetic prose evoking the sights, sounds, fruits, and other aspects of nature in Puerto Rican life.

4259. Brughetti, Romualdo. Prometeo. El espíritu que no cesa. B. A., La Mandrágora (Escritores del siglo XX, 1), 1956. 159 p.
The author, a well-known art critic and essayist, has Prometheus retell his story in the first person and then survey human culture from the beginning to the present. For Brughetti, Prometheus is no longer a symbol but is to be found in every human, great or small, who believes in love and moral advancement and defends the other noble aspects of existence: liberty, justice, intelligence, culture, and brotherhood.

4260. Düring, Ingemar. Alfonso Reyes helenista. Madrid, Ínsula (Instituto Ibero-Americano, Gotemburgo, Suecia), 1955. 87 p.
A succinct consideration of Reyes as a student and talented *divulgador* of Greek thought and literature who refuses to dwell in the lonely ivory tower of the professional Hellenist.

4261. Martínez Estrada, Ezequiel. Cuadrante del pampero. B. A., Deucalión (Col. Ahora y aquí, 1), 1956. 303 p.
A collection of essays on national and foreign topics by Argentina's foremost cultural analyst, these writings attest Martínez Estrada's love of liberty, his balanced, incisive mind, his wide range of interests, and his deep, long-standing efforts to dissect Argentine culture. More heterogenous than either of his earlier volumes on the subject (*Radiografía de la pampa*, 1933; *Cabeza de Goliat*, 1940), the book is a valuable addition to the works of an author who is far from prolific.

4262. Masferrer, Alberto. Estudios y figuraciones sobre la vida de Jesús. San Salvador, Ministerio de Cultura (Biblioteca popular, 14), 1956. 163 p.
A reprint of a book first published in 1927. Short chapters on various incidents in the life of Christ which skillfully humanize the divine aspects of Jesus.

4263. Olguín, Manuel. Alfonso Reyes, ensayista. Vida y pensamiento. México,

Ediciones de Andrea (Col. Studium, 11), 1956. 228 p.
The first effort to analyze succinctly the entire body of the noted Mexican writer's prose works and to relate them to the four stages the author distinguishes in Reyes' life. The book is penetrating in its criticism and contains a bibliography of Reyes' works as well as a comprehensive critical bibliography. Indispensable to all future students of Mexico's leading literary figure.

4264. Reyes, Alfonso. Obras completas. Visión de Anáhuac. Las vísperas de España. Calendario. México, Fondo de Cultura Económica (Letras mexicanas, 2), 1956. 374 p.
This second volume of the complete works of the Mexican *maestro* contains some of his best-known essays, written in Spain between 1914 and 1924. *Visión de Anáhuac* is a lyrical evocation of the land, sky, and eventful history of the Valley of Mexico; *Las vísperas de España,* is a collection of interpretive *crónicas*, and *Calendario* contains sketches ranging from epigrams to prose poems.

4265. ————. Marginalia. 2. serie, 1909-1954. México, Tezontle, 1954. 212 p.
Minor prose: essays, letters, comments on varied themes in literature, philosophy, and history which exhibit the customary charm and wit of the author as well as his ability to penetrate almost instantly to the heart of the matter.

4266. Romero, José Luis. Argentina: imágenes y perspectivas. B. A., Raigal (Problemas de la cultura en América, 4), 1956. 159 p.
11 essays, all written during the last decade, on themes and figures of Argentine history, past and present, spiritual and social. Giving internal unity to Romero's analytical meditations is his constant, deep preoccupation with the men and institutions which have stood in the way of the development of Argentine democracy.

4267. Sánchez, Luis Alberto. La libertad de la cultura en la América Latina (Cuad Am, año 16, 91:1, enero-feb. 1957, p. 14-24).
A brief consideration of the barriers to the effective freedom of thought in the Latin American nations to be found in the press, the university, the school, belles-lettres, science, arts, social institutions, and public opinion. Sánchez concludes that to insure intellectual liberty Latin American leaders of thought must face the problems of the area with an attitude based upon freedom of inquiry, tolerance, dignity, and mutual cooperation.

4268. Santovenia, Emeterio S. Vidas humanas. Habana, Librería Martí, 1956. 648 p.
A collection of over 100 short critical essays on great leaders, authors, humanists and teachers of the Americas, with special emphasis on Martí and other notable Cubans. In each piece

the author seeks to explain the moral forces and the ethical and intellectual values which characterizes his subject.

4269. Torre, Guillermo de. Las metamorfosis de Proteo. B. A., Losada, 1956. 334 p.

De Torre's penetrating, balanced and original mind is at its best in this collection of essays and studies (mostly from the last decade) on writers, intellectual freedom and other important issues of our time. The book is notable for its felicitous prose style and the critic's efforts to remain "siempre en el fiel de la balanza" in his judgments.

4270. Torres-Rioseco, Arturo. La hora del panamericanismo (Cuad, 23, marzo-abril 1957, p. 91-94).

Brief, pointed analysis of the factors which obstruct inter-American understanding, an appreciation of those institutions in the U. S. which contribute to improving this understanding, and an expression of faith in the ability of the U. S. to achieve an understanding of the cultural values of the other American nations.

4271. Zea, Leopoldo. Hispanoamérica y el mundo occidental (Torre, 4:14, abril-junio 1956, p. 145-157).

A Mexican historian of ideas examines the obstacles, some deriving from the Spanish heritage, others from the policies of such nations as England, France, and the U. S., which have impeded the full incorporation of Spanish America into the western world. He concludes that such an incorporation can occur only when the leading western nations establish an "empire" where such values as spiritual liberty and material well-being will be available to all on a truly equal basis.

BRAZILIAN LANGUAGE AND LITERATURE

RALPH EDWARD DIMMICK

Prose fiction accounted for the most widely discussed works of 1956. João Guimarães Rosa's novel *Grande sertão: veredas* and his collection of tales *Corpo de baile* excited controversy chiefly because of their style. Though this manner of writing was hailed by some critics as the essence of everything Brazilian, there is room for doubt whether a majority of readers may not have found it as exotic and difficult of comprehension as any foreign importation. Ciro dos Anjos' *Montanha** and Mário Palmério's *Vila dos Confins* both took politics as their theme. The former aroused curiosity because of its references to recent events of Brazilian history; the latter was generally held to mark the most distinguished literary debut of the year.

Other novels of note included in the bibliography, some dating from former years, are Orígenes Lessa's *Rua do Sol,* Rui Mourão's *As raízes,* Ernâni Satyro's *O quadro negro,* and Godofredo Rangel's posthumous *Falange gloriosa* and *Os bem casados.* In the field of the short story attention may be called to Luiz Canabrava's *Sangue de Rosaura* and to Otto Lara Resende's *Bôca do Inferno.*

No significant new voice has appeared in poetry. Carlos Drummond de Andrade, Ascenso Ferreira, and João Cabral de Melo Neto brought out single-volume editions of their previous collections; Cecília Meireles, Antônio Rangel Bandeira, and Cassiano Ricardo (*O arranha-céu de vidro,** *João Torto e a fábula**) produced new volumes which rank with their best.

A field which has been cultivated with particularly fruitful results in recent years is that of the memoir. In 1956 Gilberto Amado brought out an additional volume of his reminiscences, *Mocidade no Rio e primeira viagem à Europa;* in *Meus verdes anos* José Lins do Rêgo recalled his childhood; and Limeira Tejo, with *Enéias,* initiated what he termed "the memoirs of a resentful generation."

Interest in the theater continues high. Antônio Callado's *Frankel* is not entirely successful, but Jorge Andrade's *A moratória* is the best writing for the stage to come out of Brazil in recent years. Décio de Almeida Prado's published criticism, *Apresentacão do teatro brasileiro,* gives valuable information on the current renaissance in the dramatic art.

A number of useful contributions to literary scholarship are included in the bibliography. *A literatura no Brasil,* under the general editorship of Afrânio Coutinho,

---

* These works, widely praised in Brazil, were not available for consultation by the editor and do not appear in the bibliography. It is hoped that they may figure in future volumes of the *Handbook.*

was brought nearer completion by the publication of volumes on the colonial and Romantic periods; and Alceu Amoroso Lima, in his *Quadro sintético da literatura brasileira*, provided a thoughtful essay on the most recent generation of Brazilian writers. Sérgio Milliet brought out another volume of his *Diário crítico*; M. Cavalcânti Proença analyzed Mário de Andrade's *Macunaíma*; Monteiro Lobato found a biographer in his friend Edgard Cavalheiro; and Raymond S. Sayers produced a study on the Negro in Brazilian literature.

Half a century after his death, Machado de Assis continues to excite interest. The bibliography registers new translations of his novels into English and French; Octavio Mangabeira reproduced the plots of his narratives in outline form; Raimundo Magalhães Júnior extracted from his writings a collection of maxims; and the last-mentioned enthusiast and J. Galante de Sousa brought out editions of works which had been "lost" in the files of the periodicals in which they originally appeared.

Four figures of note died during 1955: Amadeu de Queiroz, Jaime Ovalle, Atílio Milano, and Ataúlfo de Paiva. José Lins do Rêgo replaced the last-mentioned in the Brazilian Academy of Letters, and his departure from convention in the speech he made upon his reception caused the greatest scandal in that august body since Graça Aranha's attack upon its conservatism in 1923.

GENERAL

4275. BIL. Bibliografia e informações para leitores. Rio. Ano 1, no. 2, out. 1956. 8 p.

New literary review giving news of happenings in the world of letters, but no critical articles.

4276. Brandão, Théo. O reisado alagoano (R Arq Mun, 19:155, jan.-março 1953, p. 11-225, illus.).

Well-documented study of the popular celebration of the Epiphany, including verses and music. Won first prize in the folklore contest sponsored by the Discoteca Pública Municipal of the municipality of São Paulo in 1949.

4277. O Estado de São Paulo: suplemento literário. São Paulo. Ano 1, no. 1, out. 6, 1956-.

An outstanding Brazilian newspaper has initiated a weekly magazine section, covering literature and the arts, of exceptional interest.

4278. Lins, Álvaro, and Aurélio Buarque de Hollanda. Roteiro literário do Brasil e de Portugal. Antologia da língua portuguêsa. Rio, Olympio, 1956. V. 1, Portuguêses, 369 p.; v. 2, Brasileiros, p. 374-882.

Generally good choice of authors (86 Brazilians, all deceased), the most surprising omission being Coelho Neto. Selections aim to present various facets of major writers and to avoid the "usual" anthology pieces. Biographical and critical notes brief but helpful; some errors in dates.

4279. Magalhães Júnior, R. Idéias e imagens de Machado de Assis. Dicionário antológico, com mil verbêtes, abrangendo tôda a obra machadiana, desde a colaboração em *A marmota* até o *Memorial de*

Aires. Rio, Editôra Civilização Brasileira, 1956. 220 p.

The aphorisms and maxims of Machado have long been the delight of readers who would doubtless welcome an anthology thereof. This volume, however, mixes sententious sayings with descriptions and sketches.

4280. Para todos. Quinzenário da cultura brasileira. Rio, São Paulo. Ano 1, no. 1, 10-23 maio 1956-.

New fortnightly with broad coverage of cultural events, including articles by many leading contemporary writers.

4281. Revista do teatro amador. São Paulo. Ano 1, no. 2, set. 1955. 24 p.

New magazine reflecting the greatly increased interest in the theater in Brazil.

4282. Romero, Sílvio. Folclore brasileiro: 1) Cantos populares do Brasil; 2) Contos populares do Brasil. Edição anotada por Luís da Câmara Cascudo. Rio, Olympio (Col. Documentos brasileiros, 75-75B), 1954. 3 v.

The first great collections of Brazilian folklore, annotated by the leading specialist in the subject today.

4283. Sociedade Cultural Nova Crítica. Diálogo. Revista de cultura. São Paulo. No. 1, set. 1955-.

Quarterly cultural review of high quality.

4284. Spinelli, Raffaele (ed. and trans.). Croce del sud. Antologia di poeti brasiliani. Milan, Fratelli Bocca Editori, 1954. 254 p.

Outline of the history of Brazilian poetry followed by an anthology. Two-thirds of the selections are verse written since 1920. The Italian translations are only fair, but evidence a growing interest in Brazilian literature in Europe.

BIBLIOGRAPHY AND LANGUAGE

4285. Arnulfo, Irmão. Guia ortográfica. Sistematização prática e didática das normas ortográficas vigentes, com riqueza de exemplificação e copioso vocabulário. Pôrto Alegre, Brazil, Globo, 1954. 133 p.
Useful elucidation of difficult points of spelling, capitalization, etc., according to official usage.

4286. Fernandes, Francisco, and F. Marques Guimarães (comps.). Dicionário brasileiro contemporâneo. Pôrto Alegre, Brazil, Globo, 1953. 1143 p., illus.
The best features of this dictionary are the wealth of popular expressions and others peculiar to Brazil and the fact that it is illustrated.

4287. Fortes, Herbert Parentes. Uma interpretação da crase portuguêsa. Rio, Ministério da Educação e Cultura, Serviço de Documentação, 1954. 99 p.
Crase is a "problem" in Brazil because, contrary to the case in Portugal, it does not correspond to any phonetic reality. Acute observations despite poor presentation.

4288. Instituto Brasileiro de Bibliografia e Documentação. Periódicos brasileiros de cultura. Ed. preliminar. Rio, 1956. 182 p.
Selective inventory of current Brazilian periodical publications in all fields of knowledge, classified by topic. Literature, p. 152-154. Useful bibliographical information, but no indication of the nature of the journal or of the standard of its contents.

4289. Klinger, Bertholdo. Ano XVI da ortografia simplificada brazileira. Opusculo 8. 3, ed. da "Cartilha Osbriana." Outras re-edisões. Algums es-inéditos. Rio, Editôra Gráfica Laemmert, 1956. 130 p.
Those who have been confused by changes in the official spelling of Portuguese in recent years will perhaps wish to see an attempt at a thoroughgoing simplification of the orthography.

4290. Leão, Múcio. João Ribeiro. Ensaio biobibliográfico. Rio, Academia Brasileira de Letras, 1954. 89 p., illus.
Brief biography of an important critic of the early years of this century. Bibliography far from complete.

4291. ————. José de Alencar. Ensaio bio-bibliográfico. Rio, Academia Brasileira de Letras, 1955. 71 p., illus.
The biography runs to anecdotes; the bibliography is described as "tentativa" and is not without errors.

4292. Nascentes, Antenor. O linguajar carioca. 2. ed., completamente refundida.

Rio, Organização Simões (Col. Rex, 7), 1953. 217 p.
Observations on the Portuguese spoken in Rio. Presentation lacks clarity; no good distinction is made between what is common in Brazil and that which is peculiar to the capital.

4293. Peixoto, Almir Câmara de Matos. Sistematização da acentuação gráfica oficial. Rio, Organização Simões (Col. Padre Nóbrega, 6), 1954. 70 p.
Clarification of the use of written accents.

4292. Silva, António de Morais e. Grande dicionário da língua portuguêsa. 10. ed., revista, corrigida, muito aumentada e actualizada por Augusto Moreno, Cardoso Júnior e José Pedro Machado. Lisboa, Editorial Confluência, 1949-. V. 5, 1953, 1045 p.; v. 6, 1954, 955 p.; v. 7, 1954, 955 p.; v. 8, 1955, 897 p.; v. 9, 1956, 1003 p.
This monumental dictionary, of exceptional value for its examples of usage, has now reached the word "seival."

4295. Soares, Antônio Joaquim de Macedo, and Julião Rangel de Macedo Soares. Dicionário brasileiro da língua portuguêsa. Elucidário etimológico crítico das palavras e frases que, originárias do Brasil, ou aquí populares, se não encontram nos dicionários da língua portuguêsa, ou nêles vêm com forma ou significação diferente (1875-1888). Rio, Instituto Nacional do Livro, 1954-1955. 2 v. 275, 207 p.
Though dating from the 19th century, still a recommendable source of information on matters of Brazilian dialectology.

CRITICISM, BIOGRAPHY, ESSAYS

4296. Amado, Gilberto. Mocidade no Rio e primeira viagem à Europa. Rio, Olympio, 1956. 447 p.
Less personal than preceding installments of Amado's memoirs, this volume is concerned chiefly with his contemporaries in the years 1910-1914. Sharply etched portraits of leading journalists, literary figures, and politicians, especially Pinheiro Machado, accompany a vivid evocation of the intellectual life of Rio at that time. Amado's main preoccupation abroad appears to have been with European attitudes towards Brazil: episodes recounted in this regard are as revealing of his spirit as of the mentality of his foreign acquaintances. Despite the author's irritating air of self-satisfaction, his book is witty and makes delightfully enjoyable reading.

4297. Assis, Joaquim Maria Machado de. Diálogos e reflexões de um relojoeiro. Escritos de 1886 ("A+B"), de 1888 e

1889 ("Bons Dias"), recolhidos da "Gazeta de Notícias." Organização, prefácio e notas de R. Magalhães Júnior. Rio, Editôra Civilização Brasileira, 1956. 277 p.
If all these newspaper articles published under pseudonyms are really by Machado, they evidence a greater interest on his part in events of the day—especially politics—than has previously been claimed.

4298. Athayde, Tristão de [pseud.; i. e., Alceu Amoroso Lima]. Pela América do Norte. Rio, Ministério da Educação e Cultura, Serviço de Documentação (Os cadernos de cultura, 88, 89), 1955. 2 v. 115, 109 p.
Reprint of articles written for Brazilian newspapers while Lima was in the U. S., Canada, and Mexico, giving his reactions to those countries. Interesting chiefly for the light thrown on his thinking in matters of politics and religion.

4299. Bandeira, Antônio Rangel. Da liberdade de criação artística. Rio, Instituto Nacional do Livro (Biblioteca de divulgação cultural, 3), 1956. 103 p.
"Os caminhos da arte devem ser livres, múltiplos e imprevisíveis. Para o artista deve ser concedida até a liberdade de falhar. Arte e liberdade, arte e povo e arte e cultura—não são expressões contraditórias. São faces duplas de uma só realidade."

4300. Bandeira, Manuel. Noções de história das literaturas. [4. ed.] São Paulo, Companhia Editôra Nacional (Biblioteca do espírito moderno, série 4, Literatura, 4, 4a), 1954. 2 v. 277, 353 p.
Fourth edition. The section on Brazilian literature (v. 2, p. 50-140) is generally considered one of the best short treatments of the subject.

4301. Barreira, Dolor. História da literatura cearense. T. 3. Fortaleza, Brazil, Instituto do Ceará (História do Ceará, monografia, 18, t. 3), 1954. 674 p.
The only writers of importance treated in this volume (which covers the years 1911-1914) are José Albano, Antônio Sales, and Papi Júnior. For previous volumes of this work see HLAS, no. 14, 1948, item 3005, and HLAS, no. 17, 1951, item 2579.

4302. Batchelor, C. Malcolm. Álvares de Azevedo, a transitional figure in Brazilian literature (Hispania, AATSP, 39:2, May 1956, p. 149-156).
"Beneath the aura of bas romantisme which surrounds Noite na taverna and Macário, there is a brutal realism, an interest in the clinical details of physical love, violent death, and abnormal psychology, which sets Azevedo apart . . . from the Lamartines and Shelleys. . . . It is Azevedo's interest in the nature of reality, his search for truth and his belief that the theater should be an honest representation of life . . . which definitely establish his position as a transitional figure in Brazilian literature."

4303. Bizzarri, Edoardo. Graciliano Ramos, romancista (Diálogo, 1, set. 1955, p. 43-54; 2, dez. 1955, p. 43-60).
Good study of "um dos mais angustiados, perplexos e púdicos autores com que conta a literatura." Emphasizes Graciliano's evolution with regard to characterization; views Vidas sêcas as the culmination of his art.

4304. Brandão, Octavio. Os intelectuais progressistas: Tavares Bastos, Tobias Barreto, Sílvio Romero, Euclides da Cunha, Lima Barreto. Rio, Organização Simões (Col. Rex, 8), 1956. 164 p.
Somewhat elementary analysis of the ideology of prominent literary figures of the turn of the century, by a Communist intellectual.

4305. Broca, Brito. Raul Pompéia. São Paulo, Melhoramentos (Grandes vultos das letras, 21), 1956? 80 p.
Superficial, but readable, biography of the author of O Ateneu.

4306. Cannabrava, Euryalo. A cultura brasileira e seus equívocos. Discursos de posse e recepção na Cátedra de Filosofia do Colégio Pedro II, pronunciados por Euryalo Cannabrava e Cândido Jucá (filho) 22 de abril de 1953. Rio, Imp. Nacional, 1955. 57 p.
Cannabrava gives a thoughtful analysis of the Brazilian tendency to substitute stylistic brilliance for logic in argumentation, with suggestions as to the place of philosophy in secondary education. Jucá provides information on Cannabrava.

4307. Casasanta, Mário. Machado de Assis e os pronomes (R U Minas Gerais, 10, maio 1953, p. 185-195).
"Fácil seria acumular a lista de elementos comprobatórios de que Machado de Assis foi dos que menos cochilaram na matéria e, em especial, de que a sua boa mulher não exerceu em sua linguagem a influência que se lhe atribui."

4308. Cavalheiro, Edgard. Monteiro Lobato. Vida e obra. 2. ed., revista e aumentada. São Paulo, Companhia Editôra Nacional, 1956. 2 v. 375, 375 p., illus.
The subtitle of this work should be "o homem e a obra," since emphasis is upon the personality and thought of Lobato, relatively little information being given on the events of his existence. Based on the author's personal acquaintance with the subject, and the latter's extensive archives, this is a sympathetic and impressive portrait of one of the most important and controversial figures in modern Brazilian literature. The extended analyses of Lobato's writing and the bibliographies and other appended material make this a work of prime value to all future students of the man. First edition published 1955.

4309. César, Guilhermino. História da literatura do Rio Grande do Sul (1737-

1902). Pôrto Alegre, Brazil, Globo (Col. Província, 10), 1956. 414 p.
Superior to the usual run of regional literary histories, this work reveals extensive research and a good sense of aesthetic values; it attempts to indicate features which give gaúcho literature a character of its own and to show the place of letters in the development of Rio Grande do Sul; it keeps in mind the broad panorama of Brazilian literature in general. There are errors of detail, but despite the lack of intrinsic importance of the writers treated, the book makes interesting reading.

4310. Coaracy, Vivaldo. Catavento. Crônicas. Rio, Olympio, 1956. 310 p.
The four points of V. Cy's compass are life on the island of Paqueta, man's relation with animals, philosophical considerations, and Brazilian manners. Writing with gentle humor or biting satire, with deep compassion for the suffering of others or poetic feeling for the beauties of nature, he has as usual produced a collection of essays of great charm.

4311. Coutinho, Afrânio. Correntes cruzadas. (Questões de literatura). Rio, A Noite, 1953, 383 p.
The most important part of this volume is the introduction, in which Coutinho proclaims the need in Brazilian letters for the creation of a "consciência crítica," based on the systematic study of literature on the university level, with emphasis on aesthetic values rather than on literary history. The text, a sort of critic's diary, contains interesting pronouncements and evidences wide reading, but is unduly fragmentary.

4312. ————. (ed.). A literatura no Brasil. V. 1. T. 1 e 2. Direção de . . . com a assistência de Eugênio Gomes e Barreto Filho. Rio, Editorial Sul Americana, 1956. 2 v. 1020 p., illus.
Covering the colonial and Romantic periods, this two-tome "volume" contains essays by Hernâni Cidade (Renaissance background), Matoso Câmara Jr. (literary vocabulary, Romantic verse), Luís da Câmara Cascudo (folklore), Fernando de Azevedo (education and literature), Antônio Cândido de Melo e Sousa (the writer and his public), Wílson Martins (literature and the land), Afránio Coutinho (transition from Baroque to Rococo; origin, definition, chronology, and characteristics of Brazilian Romanticism), Domingos Carvalho da Silva (origins of poetry), Armando de Carvalho (Jesuit literature), Eugênio Gomes (Antônio Vieira, Botelho de Oliveira, Nuno Marques Pereira, Alvares de Azevedo, Junqueira Freire), Segismundo Spina (Gregório de Matos). Cândido Jucá Filho (Relação do Naufrágio, neo-classic prose writers), C. Burlamáqui Kopke (sermons), José Aderaldo Castelo (academies, the pre-Romantics), A. Soares Amora (literature in the 17th century), Waltensir Dutra (Arcadianism, Casimiro de Abreu, Fagundes Varela), Cassiano Ricardo Leite (Gonçalves Dias), Fausto Cunha (Castro Alves), Heron de Alencar (José de Alencar and Romantic fiction), an extended general introduction by Afrânio Coutinho, and bibliographies by Xavier Placer. The sections vary greatly in approach and value; those by Coutinho, Azevedo,

Antônio Cândido, and Castelo are most rewarding; those by Cassiano Ricardo and Fausto Cunha, disappointing. The bibliographies cover a large amount of source material but are not easily manageable; there are a number of minor errors and inconsistencies. Like v. 2, issued in 1955, this is a definitely useful reference work despite unevenness.

4313. ————. Por uma crítica estética. Rio, Ministério da Educação e Cultura, Serviço de Documentação (Os cadernos de cultura, 70), 1954. 48 p.
A leading contemporary literary scholar "acredita que em Aristóteles estão os fundamentos da renovação da crítica segundo a perspectiva verdadeiramente poética ou literária."

4314. Donato, Hernâni. Vicente de Carvalho, o poeta do mar. São Paulo, Melhoramentos (Grandes vultos das letras, 14), 1955? 57 p., illus.
Brief, popular-style biography, and study of an outstanding Parnassian poet.

4315. Elton, Elmo. O noivado de Bilac. Com a correspondência inédita do poeta à sua noiva—D. Amélia de Oliveira. Rio, Organização Simões (Col. Rex, 6), 1954. 142 p.
Information concerning Bilac's ill-starred engagement to a sister of Alberto de Oliveira.

4316. Eneida [pseud., i. e. **Eneida de Morais].** Alguns personagens. Rio, Ministério da Educação e Cultura, Serviço de Documentação, 1954. 71 p.
Although this collection includes portraits of such well-known figures as Di Cavalcanti, Murilo Mendes, Carlos Ribeiro, and J. M. Cardoso de Oliveira, the most delightful is that of Eneida's maid, Clocló.

4317. Fagundes, Morivalde Calvet. Lobo da Costa. Ascensão e declínio de um poeta. Pôrto Alegre, Brazil, Edição Sulina (Col. Meridional, 3), 1954. 218 p.
Biography of a minor poet of the 19th century, with selections from his works.

4318. Fernández, Oscar. The contemporary theatre in Rio de Janero and in São Paulo, 1953-55 (Hispania, AATSP, 39:4, Dec. 1956, p. 423-432).
General survey of the theatrical scene: plays, native and foreign; troupes; schools of drama; criticism, etc. With regard to plays by Brazilian authors, Fernández observes: "The fault which more than any other seems to underlie these national works is an evident lack of good dramatic technique in conjunction with the failure to achieve a unity of plot to direct and control the play . . . Their authors . . . focus their objective almost exclusively on the element of entertainment and concern themselves very little with composition." Of criticism, he notes: "One can say that Brazilian criticism is more condescending than objective, and that it tends to be unduly laudatory."

4319. Frieiro, Eduardo. Páginas de crítica e outros escritos. Belo Horizonte, Brazil, Itatiaia, 1955. 443 p.
Criticism dating chiefly from 1938 to 1944. Frieiro's technique is to give a résumé of the book under review.

4320. Garcia, Othon Moacyr. Esfinge Clara. Palavra-puxa-palavra em Carlos Drummond de Andrade. Rio, Livraria São José, 1955. 78 p.
"Um dos processos poéticos de que mais freqüentemente se serve Carlos Drummond de Andrade em sua obra é o que podemos chamar de *associação semântica* e *paronomástica* ou jôgo de *palavra-puxa-palavra* . . . O sistema consiste . . . no encadeamento de palavras, quer pela afinidade ou parentesco semântico, quer pela semelhança fônica . . . quer, ainda, pela evocação de fatos estranhos à atmosfera do poema pròpriamente dito (frases-feitas, elementos folclóricos, reminiscências infantis, circunstâncias de fato, resíduos de leitura)."

4321. ————. Luz e fogo no lirismo de Gonçalves Dias. Rio, Livraria São José, 1956. 98 p.
A study of Gonçalves Dias' comparisons and metaphors reveals a surprising lack of variety, with a great concentration on images relating to light and fire.

4322. Jansen, José. Apolônia Pinto e seu tempo. Rio, Serviço Nacional de Teatro (Col. Dionysos), 1953. 198 p., illus.
Biography of a celebrated actress, active 1870-1925.

4323. Jurema, Aderbal. Poetas e romancistas de nosso tempo. Recife, Brazil, Editôra Nordeste (Provincianas, 2. série), 1953. 204 p.
In these articles of criticism, covering approximately the years 1949-1952, the author exhibits good judgment and common sense and avoids intellectual pretentiousness.

4324. Lapa, Manuel Rodrigues. Figuras da Inconfidência (Anhembi, ano 6, 21:62, jan. 1956, p. 241-259).
Excellent study of the rôle of the poets Tomás Antônio Gonzaga, Cláudio Manuel da Costa, and Alvarenga Peixoto in the Minas conspiracy of 1789.

4325. Lessa, Clado Ribeiro de. Vida e obra de Varnhagen (R Inst Hist Geog Br, 223, abril-junio 1954, p. 82-297; 224, julho-set. 1954, p. 109-315; 225, out.-dez. 1954, p. 120-293; 226, jan.-março 1955, p. 3-168; 227, abril-junho 1955, p. 85-236).
Careful, extensive study of a leading historian and literary scholar.

4326. Lima, Alceu Amoroso. Quadro sintético da literatura brasileira. Rio, Agir, 1956. 168 p.

The value of this work lies in its final third, devoted to a penetrating analysis of current tendencies in Brazilian literature. For lack of a better name, Lima terms the trend *neomodernismo*. According to him, the movement is one of evolution rather than revolution; concern is with eternal values rather than mere modernity; emphasis is on discipline rather than liberty; and, contrary to the aristocratic trend of Modernism, writers now seek to make themselves understood by the public. In poetry, emphasis is on versification rather than on poetic content; in the novel, stress is on external reality rather than on the life of the soul; impressionism and expressionism no longer hold sway in criticism, which is conceived as scientific and objective; in spiritual matters what is to be noted is a lack of religious disquietude. Finally, one can note for the first time an impressive number of women writers and a greatly increased interest in the theater.

4327. Machado Filho, Aires da Mata. Crítica de estilos. Rio, Agir, 1956. 245 p.
Observations on the style of classics and contemporaries. The best section is that devoted to Gonçalves Dias' "Canção do Exílio."

4328. Mangabeira, Octavio. Cinqüentenário do falecimento de Francisco Mangabeira. Rio, Academia de Letras da Bahia, 1954. 49 p.
Information on a minor poet of the turn of the century by his distinguished brother.

4329. Melo Filho, Osvaldo F. de. Introdução à história da literatura catarinense (Sul, 9:27, maio 1956, p. 7-18).
First chapter of a projected book. Particularly interesting for the discussion of literature written in German in Santa Catarina.

4330. Mendes, Oscar. Nabuco, Mauriac e Baudelaire. Rio, Ministério da Educação e Cultura (Os cadernos de cultura, 85), 1955. 96 p.
The essay on Nabuco is more panegyrical than critical.

4331. Menezes, Djacir. Evolução do pensamento literário no Brasil. Rio, Organização Simões (Col. Rex, 4), 1954. 396 p.
The substance of a series of lectures delivered at the Argentine-Brazilian cultural institute in B. A., these essays possess the virtue of presenting a highly personal approach to Brazilian literature. Even allowing for the negative qualities this necessarily implies, it is difficult to see how one can justify treating Castro Alves without discussing "Os escravos," devote more space to Galeão Coutinho than Graciliano Ramos, and refer to the author of *Memórias de um sargento de milícias* as Manual Antônio de Macedo.

4332. Menezes, Raimundo de. Guimarães Passos e sua época boêmia. São Paulo, Martins, 1953. 272 p., illus.
Anecdotic, popular-style biography of a poet and Bohemian of the latter part of the 19th century.

4333. Milliet, Sérgio. Diário crítico. V. 8, 1951-1952. São Paulo, Martins, 1955. 306 p.

"Meu intuito é apenas o de manter o leitor a par do que se publica entre nós—e por vêzes no estrangeiro. Minha ambição é chamar a atenção para alguns aspectos dessa produção, convocando e comentando. Não emito juízos; digo o que sinto e penso . . . Na medida do possível tento de compreender o objetivo do autor e procuro verificar se o atingiu . . . Mais importante do que condenar se me afigura encorajar."

4334. Montello, Josué. Artur Azevedo e a arte do conto. Rio, Livraria São José, 1956. 70 p.

Best known in his own day as a writer of comedies, Azevedo now lives as a short story writer. "Artur Azevedo, esquivando-se às modernas orientações literárias de seu tempo, preferia obedecer às inclinações do próprio temperamento, a acomodar-se, numa passividade de ocasião e circunstâncias, aos modelos externos, que não condiziam com o feitio natural de sua literatura."

4335. Montenegro, Olívio. O romance brasileiro. Prefácio de Gilberto Freyre. 2. ed., revista e aumentada. Rio, Olympio (Col. Documentos brasileiros, 10), 1953. 310 p.

This is not a history of the Brazilian novel: the author's stated purpose was "fixar uma impressão do romance brasileiro desde que êle surgiu na nossa literatura, e o real das suas tendências." A valuable work of impressionistic criticism, the new edition has been considerably enlarged, with chapters on Lima Barreto, Mário de Andrade, Otávio de Faria, Cornélio Pena, Lúcia Miguel Pereira, Luís Inácio de Miranda Jardim, and a new essay on Manuel Antônio de Almeida. Other chapters, such as that on Érico Veríssimo, have likewise been brought up to date.

4336. Moraes, Carlos Dante de. Condições histórico-sociais da literatura riograndense (Prov São Pedro, 19, 1954, p. 7-18).

The historical and sociological background of literary production in Rio Grande do Sul.

4337. ————. Itinerário de Jorge de Lima (Ordem, 55:2, fev. 1956, p. 93-108; 55:3, março 1956, p. 188-203).

While recognizing the importance of Lima's poems on Negro themes, the author concentrates his analysis upon the mystical verse of the later years.

4338. Moreyra, Alvaro. As amargas, não . . . (Lembranças). Rio, Lux, 1954. 330 p.

Not organized memoirs, but rather a potpourri of random thoughts and recollections, some humorous, some poetic, some personal, some general in nature. Pleasant occasional reading.

4339. ————. O dia nos olhos. Rio, Lux, 1955? 240 p.

Random thoughts of a poet, occasionally evidencing a delightful sense of humor.

4340. Moser, Gerald M. A sensibilidade brasileira de Manuel Bandeira (R Iberoam, 20:40, sept. 1955, p. 323-336).

"Antes que as alusões a determinadas cidades ou tipos populares, o que aparece na poesia de Bandeira é a alma do Brasil, vista à luz da emoção." As for the country as it appears in his verse, "Bandeira foi inventando um Brasil para uso pessoal, intuitivamente, feito da experiência de todos os dias."

4341. Orico, Osvaldo. Da forja à Academia. (Memórias dum filho de Ferreiro). Rio, Olympio, 1954. 290 p.

Some measure of the author's character may be had from his statement: "Sou hoje um homem sem vaidades, um indivíduo que se desprendeu dos falsos européis que nos deixam as gloríolas literárias," followed by a series of flattering quotations from others in his regard. When not engaged in calling attention to his own merits, however, Orico manages to present some very entertaining episodes of his school days in Belém and behind-the-scenes glimpses of literary life in Rio.

4342. Peregrino, Umberto. Vocação de Euclides da Cunha. Interpretação das suas experiências na carreira militar. Rio, Ministério da Educação e Cultura, Serviço de Documentação, 1955. 41 p.

"Os Sertões seriam . . . obra diferente, se o seu autor fôsse de todo em todo estranho à ciência militar."

4343. Piazza, Walter F. Aspectos folclóricos catarinenses. Florianópolis, Brazil, Comissão Catarinense de Folclore (Col. Folclore), 1953. 138 p., illus.

Includes a section on Italian contributions to the folklore of Santa Catarina, but says nothing of possible Germanic influences.

4344. Prado, Décio de Almeida. Apresentação do teatro brasileiro. Crítica teatral, 1947-1955. São Paulo, Martins, 1956. 484 p.

This criticism, written for Brazil's leading newspaper at the time of a great dramatic renaissance, possesses considerable historic value. Of national authors, Prado says: "Em relação aos autores nacionais, cometo a heresia de pensar que, considerados em bloco, alguma coisa ainda os separa do nível já alcançado pelos nossos melhores atores, cenógrafos e encenadores . . . Para se escrever bom teatro, é necessário nascer e crescer dentro do bom teatro, recebendo as primeiras lições . . . na adolescência . . . O instrumento já existe: precisa surgir quem saiba manejá-lo com técnica e originalidade. Então existirá, na verdade, um teatro brasileiro."

4345. Proença, M. Cavalcanti. Roteiro de Macunaíma. São Paulo, Anhembi, 1955. 355 p.

This extended commentary on the outstanding prose work of Brazilian Modernism, Mário de Andrade's Macunaíma, does much to clarify obscure elements of folklore and language which make the novel difficult reading. A chapter-by-chapter exegesis of the text is accompanied by a section on popular usage as exemplified therein, a lengthy glossary, a study of the work's evolution, and essays on the biographical element and other aspects of the novel. One may disagree with some of Proença's findings, but the net value of his work is not to be denied.

4346. Rêgo, José Lins do. Meus verdes anos. Memórias. Rio, Olympio, 1956. 351 p.

These childhood memoirs might well be considered a rewrite of the first volume of the author's Sugar Cane Cycle, *Menino de engenho*. Episodes and characters are repeated throughout, the latter often with the same names, in a clear demonstration of the autobiographical nature of the earlier work. As José Lins' talent lies mainly in the evocation of his own past experience, his reminiscences make good reading and form a social document of unquestionable value.

4347. Rosa, Júlio Oliveira. Paulo Setúbal. São Paulo, Melhoramentos (Grandes vultos das letras, 6), 1954? 54 p.

Popular-style biography of a popular novelist of the twenties.

4348. Sayers, Raymond S. The Negro in Brazilian literature. N. Y., Hispanic Institute in the United States, 1956. 240 p.

Objective, manifesting extensive research, this is a study of the personality assigned to the Negro in Brazilian literature from the Discovery to the end of the 19th century—as a comic figure, the object of compassion, or a symbol of sensuality; as the melancholy slave, the faithful servant, or the noble rebel. One wonders whether a treatment by themes such as these might not have produced clearer conclusions than those resulting from Mr. Sayers' development by genres; however, as a source for future students, this is a work of incontestable value.

4349. Schade, George D. Three contemporary Brazilian novels; some comparisons and contrasts (Hispania, AATSP, 39:4, Dec. 1956, p. 391-396).

Discussion of Graciliano Ramos' *Angustia,* Rachel de Queiroz' *As três Marias,* and Jorge Amado's *Terras do sem fim.* Schade prefers the sobriety of style and emphasis on characterization of the first two to Amado's rhapsodic approach.

4350. Silveira, Junot. O romance de Tobias Barreto. Salvador, Brazil, Caderno da Bahia, 1953. 218 p.

A *vie romancée* of a prominent late Romantic.

4351. Souza, Lincoln de. O condor sergipano. Síntese bio-bibliográfica de Tobias Barreto de Menezes. Rio, Ministério da Educação e Cultura, Serviço de Documentação, 1954. 27 p.

Factual information on a prominent late-Romantic poet and essayist.

4352. Tejo, Limeira. Enéias. Memórias de

uma geração ressentida. Pôrto Alegre, Brazil, Globo, 1956. 260 p.

Less a personal memoir than a picture of the patriarchal society of the Northeast into which the author was born, this book covers the years up to the revolution of 1930, which marked the final downfall of that society. Town, country, and school life, political struggles, religious ceremonies, banditry, horse racing, droughts, all are brilliantly described, producing a work of great artistic merit as well as a valuable social document.

4353. Ulles, Mário. A vida íntima do teatro brasileiro. Memórias. De 1903 a 1953. São Paulo, Emprêsa Gráf. da Revista dos Tribunais, 1954. 161 p., illus.

Behind-the-scenes picture of the Brazilian theater in the first half of the century, by an actor and prompter.

4354. Val, Waldir Ribeiro do. Raimundo Correia, estudante. Rio, Ministério da Educação e Cultura, Serviço de Documentação, 1955. 114 p.

The most interesting feature of this essay on Correia's student days in São Paulo is the bibliography of criticism concerning him.

4355. Wey, Walter. Manual de literatura brasileira. Montevideo, Instituto de Cultura Uruguaio-Brasileiro, 1955? 286 p.

Manual for secondary school use, including brief selections from principal authors studied. Interesting for up-to-dateness, catholicity of taste, and generally sound judgment.

4356. Wolf, Ferdinand. O Brasil literário. História da literatura brasileira. Tradução, prefácio e notas de Jamil Almansur Haddad. São Paulo, Companhia Editôra Nacional (Biblioteca pedagógica brasileira, série 5, Brasiliana, 278), 1955. 329 p.

Published in French by an Austrian in 1863, this was the first independent history of Brazilian literature and is not without interest today.

4357. Woodbridge, Benjamin Mather, Jr. Mestre Machado revê uma poesia (Anhembi, ano 7, 25:74, jan. 1957, p. 245-248).

Interesting example of how Machado de Assis reworked an early composition for a later republication.

PROSE FICTION

4358. Accioly, Breno. Dunas. Rio, O Cruzeiro (Col. Contemporânea, 10), 1955. 209 p.

An air of hallucination pervades this first-person novel telling the story of a degenerate who serves for a time as assistant to a jockey, inherits a fortune from him, and drives out the mother of his equally degenerate daughter on mere suspicion. Less successful than the author's previously published short stories.

4359. Accioly Netto, A. A vida não é nossa. Rio, O Cruzeiro, 1954. 214 p.
These tales of people to whom life did not bring what they had planned show a commendable degree of variety, but none are truly successful.

4360. Aranha, Graça. Canaán. Introducción, traducción y notas de Antonio Alatorre. México, Fondo de Cultura Económica (Biblioteca americana, 26; Serie de literatura moderna: Vida y ficción), 1954. 255 p.
Spanish translation of one of the most important novels of the turn of the century. Good introductory study.

4361. Assis, Joaquim Maria Machado de. Dom Casmurro. Traduit du portugais par Francis de Miomandre. Paris, Éditions Albin Michel, 1956. 334 p.
The success of this French translation is perhaps due in part to the Gallic qualities of Machado's style—simplicity, clarity, and somewhat cynical wit.

4362. ———. A idéia do Ezequiel Maia. Notas e introdução de J. Galante de Sousa. Rio, Organização Simões, 1954. 52 p.
With this volume, Galante de Sousa initiates issuance of authoritative editions of works by Machado de Assis previously unpublished in book form and declares his intention of re-editing volumes whose current text cannot be held reliable.

4363. ———. Posthumous reminiscences of Braz Cubas. Translated from the Portuguese by E. Percy Ellis. Rio, Instituto Nacional do Livro (Col. de traduções de grandes autores brasileiros, 1), 1955. 304 p.
It is difficult to see why the Instituto Nacional do Livro should have chosen to begin its program of publication of great works of Brazilian literature in translation with this pedestrian effort, when the excellent Grossman version had already appeared in two editions.

4364. Barbosa, Rolmes. Réquiem para os vivos. Romance. Pôrto Alegre, Brazil, Globo, 1956. 316 p.
Chronicle of a Paulista family, covering the period 1580-1755. Better-than-average writing; good historical atmosphere; characterization too elementary to be convincing.

4365. Canabrava, Luiz. Sangue de Rosaura. (Contos). Rio, Olympio, 1954. 132 p.
Tales of the mentally abnormal, with emphasis on atmosphere. Won the Fábio Prado prize for 1953.

4366. Carneiro, Jorge. A visão dos quatro séculos. São Paulo, Martins, 1954. 330 p.
Historical novel of the founding of São Paulo, centering on the figure of Anchieta. Alencar did this sort of thing with much more art a century ago.

4367. Carvalho, Campos de. A lua vem da Ásia. Rio, Olympio, 1956. 191 p.
Purporting to be the work of a madman, this is certainly one of the strangest novels ever written. Without plot or logical thought, it nevertheless possesses humor and is not uninteresting.

4368. Castro, Luiz Cláudio de. Igarités. Contos. Rio, Ministério da Educação e Cultura, Serviço de Documentação, 1955. 67 p.
Emotional crises, as seen in the mind of the protagonists. Author shows promise.

4369. Cruls, Gastão. De pai a filho. Rio, Olympio, 1954. 523 p.
Story of a family in which the father dies of paresis and the son commits suicide because of inhibitions which prevent his having sexual relations. The two episodes are not closely linked; otherwise the narration is well managed. The chief defect is a lack of psychological depth: the inner drama of the wife is little more than suggested.

4370. Delouche, Ângela. Boneca partida e outros contos. Recife, Brazil, Secretaria de Educação e Cultura de Pernambuco, 1955. 66 p.
These short stories display considerable understanding of human nature and the presentation shows much promise.

4371. Dourado, Waldomiro Autran. Três histórias na praia. Rio, Ministério da Educação e Cultura, Serviço de Documentação, 1955. 50 p.
Interrelated stories of a lonely man, a neurotic, and a Lesbian, well presented from the standpoint of mood.

4372. Dupré, Sra. Leandro [i. e. Maria José Dupré]. Angélica. São Paulo, Saraiva, 1955. 192 p.
A childless couple adopts a girl who proves unworthy of them. Sra. Dupré keeps the reader's interest but fails to rise to the level of literature.

4373. Ferreira, Jurandir. Telêmaco. São Paulo, Saraiva (Col. Romances do Brasil, 6), 1954. 237 p.
This novel of a social outcast—a habitual drunkard and ne'er-do-well—suffers from a confused presentation. Certain sections, especially in the long episode of Virginia's ill-fated romance, suggest that Ferreira's real talent may lie in the field of satire.

4374. Jobim, Rubens Mário. Vento leste nos Compos Gerais. Romance histórico. Rio, Gráf. Laemmert, 1952, i. e. 1953. 167 p.
More *história romanceada* than *romance histórico*, this is an essentially factual account of the siege of Lapa during the revolution of 1894.

4375. Lessa, Orígenes. Rua do Sol. Rio, Olympio, 1955. 261 p.

Loosely knit episodes of childhood 50 years ago, related with keen insight, sly humor, and at times profound emotion. A work of unusual interest and charm.

4376. Machado-Florence, Antônio Benedicto. O desembargador Ruival. São Paulo, Martins, 1954. 655 p.

Several of the characters—the judge whose ignorance of the law forced him to rely on a bohemian friend, the anti-social "colonel" who rose to meet a civic crisis—had great possibilities; unfortunately the author depicted them only from the outside. Interesting accounts of political life in a small town and the great influenza epidemic.

4377. Mangabeira, Octavio. Machado de Assis. (Seus contos e romances em ponto pequeno, precedidos de introdução, traços biográficos e uma exposição intitulada "Como foi elaborado e a que se destina êste livro"). Rio, Editôra Civilização Brasileira, 1954. 651 p.

Résumés of the plots of Machado's novels and short stories. Perhaps useful as a reference work; hardly a substitute for reading the original, however, since the value of Machado's work lies not in the stories he tells but in the way he tells them.

4378. Monteiro, José Ortiz. Eles possuirão a terra. São Paulo, Edigraf, 1955. 213 p.

Left-wing novel depicting the plight of the rural lower classes, monotonously written in the briefest of sentences and paragraphs.

4379. Mourão, Rui. As raízes. Rio, Olympio, 1956. 143 p.

Well-done psychological study of a barber whose obsession for a gold-digger leads him to the abandonment of his family, crime, and the partial loss of his reason.

4380. Palmério, Mário. Vila dos Confins. Rio, Olympio, 1956. 407 p.

Written by a man who is himself a member of the Chamber of Deputies, this first novel presents a remarkably vivid picture of the machinations connected with a municipal election in a small town, presumably in Minas Gerais, and of Brazilian rural life in general. Local vocabulary and popular turns of expression are employed both for the sake of authenticity and for artistic effect, without the excesses of a Guimarães Rosa.

4381. Pereira, Armindo. Açoite. Rio, O' Cruzeiro (Col. Contemporânea, 12), 1956. 160 p.

The universal theme of the wicked stepmother is here combined with the Brazilian motif of the cruelty of a white mistress to a suspected favorite of her husband among the Negroes of his fazenda. Treated as a folk tale, rather than from the point of view of realism, this is a narrative of genuine merit.

4382. Rangel, Godofredo. Os bem casados.

São Paulo, Melhoramentos (Ficção nacional, 2), n. d. 215 p.

First-rate satire of a weak-willed young man trapped into marriage and totally absorbed by his wife's family. Keen observation of small-town life and superior writing distinguish this posthumous work.

4383. ————. Falange gloriosa. São Paulo, Melhoramentos (Ficção nacional, 1), n. d. 275 p.

In this novel of academic life at a pair of provincial secondary schools, Rangel's concern is not with the pupils but with the downtrodden faculty—their professional incompetence, their precarious economic situation, their petty intrigues—and with the domineering figure of the principal, part huckster, part politician, part businessman, and in no respect an educator. The satire too often becomes mere caricature, but one cannot fail to recognize the underlying truth of the picture and the vastly amusing character of the narrative.

4384. Resende, Otto Lara. Bôca do Inferno. Rio, Olympio, 1957. 139 p.

Delving into the morbid aspects of child psychology in a small back-country town, and writing with genuine talent, Resende has produced a collection of short stories of unusual interest.

4385. Rocha, Beatriz. O parque de diversões. Rio, Ministério da Educação e Cultura, Serviço de Documentação (Os novos), 1955. 60 p.

Descriptions of moods, rather than short stories.

4386. Rocha, Jones. A décima praga. Rio, Ministério da Educação e Cultura, Serviço de Documentação, 1955. 147 p.

These short stories, concerned chiefly with psychological problems, show a promise which the author's death at the age of 24 has prevented from being realized.

4387. Rodrigues, Francisco Pereira. Memórias dum vereador. Pôrto Alegre, Brazil, Livraria Sulina, 1955. 182 p.

Novel of municipal politics and sex in southern Brazil.

4388. Rosa, João Guimarães. Corpo de baile. Rio, Olympio, 1956. 2 v. 822 p.

Presented throughout in the language and mode of thought of the uncultivated rural inhabitants of Minas Gerais, the seven narratives of this collection represent a stylistic tour de force. Highly poetic at times, in other passages the expression is so local as to be obscure or even incomprehensible. Despite its savor of the land and its interest for the philologically inclined, in the end the style is monotonous, especially as the tales are built on the most tenuous of narrative threads. Nevertheless, this is undoubtedly one of the most original works in recent Brazilian fiction.

4389. ————. Grande sertão: veredas. Rio, Olympio, 1956. 594 p.

First-person tale of a bandit of the backlands and his apparently misdirected affection for one of his comrades. There is no precise characterization; the narration is far from clear; and, while the reproduction of popular turns of expression is not without its picturesque—and even poetic—side, unrelieved for 600 closely packed pages it is wearisome. The strongly autochthonous character of the work has caused some to consider it "the great Brazilian novel," however.

4390. Satyro, Ernâni. O quadro-negro. Rio, Olympio, 1954. 339 p.
Although presenting a vivid picture of small-town aspects, this is not so much a regionalist as a psychological novel, with emphasis upon the introspective, indecisive character of the narrator-protagonist and his attempt to adjust to the soil whence he had sprung after an extended absence—the clash between his ideas and practical reality. Well-written; of much more than average interest.

4391. Veríssimo, Érico. Night. Translated by L. L. Barrett. N. Y., Macmillan, 1956. 166 p.
English version of *Noite*. See *HLAS, no. 19*, item 5328.

VERSE

4392. Andrade, Carlos Drummond de. 50 poemas escolhidos pelo autor. Rio. Ministério da Educação e Cultura, Serviço de Documentação (Os cadernos de cultura, 100), 1956. 98 p.
Interesting as the personal choices of an outstanding contemporary poet.

4393. ————. Fazendeiro do ar & poesia até agora. Rio, Olympio, 1955. 561 p.
Includes all of the author's previously published collections (except for the *vers de circonstance* of *Viola de Bôlso*), plus a new section, "Fazendeiro do ar." After the frankly Modernistic verse of his early days and the poems of social content of later years, Andrade has returned in some measure to the past, drawing themes from his memories and adopting forms such as the sonnet. Of his evolution he observes: "A publicação de 'obras completas' não implica a aceitação, pelo autor, de tudo quanto êle já compôs. Há partes que o tempo tornou peremptas, mas que não podem ser riscadas do conjunto, como a vida não pode ser passada a limpo. O autor não se arrepende nem se orgulha de haver mudado. Reconhece, apenas, que mudou."

4394. Bandeira, Antônio Rangel. A forma nascente. São Paulo, Clube de Poesia do Brasil (Col. IV Centenário, 4), 1956. 56 p.
In philosophic verse, frequently of great beauty, Bandeira attempts to capture and define the moment at which form (a shape, a motion) comes into being.

4395. Bandeira, Manuel. 50 poemas escolhidos pelo autor. Rio, Ministério da Educação e Cultura, Serviço de Documentação (Os cadernos de cultura, 77), 1955. 86 p.
It is interesting to note the poet's own preferences in his work: all compositions of his maturity, with emphasis upon the more recent.

4396. Brasil, Geraldino. Coração. Maceió, Brazil, Universidade do Recife, 1956. 62 p.
Parallelism and other repetitious devices are the most obvious stylistic characteristics of these lyrics voicing the author's emotions and reactions to people and events of the day.

4397. Carneiro, Dulce G. Além da palavra. São Paulo, Clube de Poesia (Col. Novíssimos, 9), 1953. 54 p.
While some of these verses seem uninspired exercises, a poem such as "Gato" is a brilliant achievement in observation, condensation of thought, and metaphor.

4398. Downes, Leonard S. (trans.). An introduction to modern Brazilian poetry. Rio, Clube de Poesia do Brasil, 1954. 86 p., illus.
While it is useful to have English versions of Brazilian poetry, these translations have two disadvantages: a sameness of style (despite the variety in the originals) and an overly "poetic" manner, ill-suited to the simplicity and directness of Modernism.

4399. Ferreira, Ascenso. Poemas (1922-1953). Recife, Brazil, Nery da Fonseca, 1955. 212 p., illus., music.
Of this important Modernist poet, Roger Bastide wrote: "Aliando a intuição à ciência, êle realizou algo muito difícil, a poesia popular. . . . O povo não faz poesia popular. . . . O povo renega o que faz exatamente o seu valor lírico, as palavras de sua gíria, a construção de suas frases. . . . . Seria preciso, para arrancar ao seu lirismo e transpô-lo ainda com todo o seu frescor e seu encantamento, um homem que estivesse em contato direto com êle . . . mas que . . . por sua cultura se isolasse o suficiente dêle para extrair do "folk" essa poesia de que êle é portador sem ter consciência. Era preciso escolher os têrmos que, no vocabulário, possuiam mais fôrca de sugestão, ou mais riqueza de sensualidade; era preciso tirar na linguagem os torneios de frase que tinham uma significação poética, enfim era preciso possuir, no mais alto grau, como Ascenso Ferreira, o senso do ritmo . . . e saber achar de novo o ritmo folclórico, enriquecendo-o."

4400. Guimaraens Filho, Alphonsus de. Sonetos com dedicatória. Rio, Ministério da Educação e Cultura, Serviço de Documentação (Os cadernos de cultura, 101), 1956. 54 p.
In these tributes to other poets (chiefly Brazilian), the author is singularly successful in re-creating the essential atmosphere of their work.

4401. Haddad, Jamil Almansur (ed.). As obras-primas da poesia religiosa brasileira. Prefácio, seleção e notas de Jamil Alman-

sur Haddad. São Paulo, Martins, 1954. 395 p.

In a country characterized by religious indifference, it is not surprising that verse of Christian inspiration is low in both quantity and quality. Save in the case of Alphonsus de Guimaraens, it is either the product of minor poets, or second-rate work by major ones.

4402. Ivo, Lêdo. Acontecimento do soneto. Ode à noite. Rio, Orfeu, n. d. 45 p.

"Serei, mergulhado no passado, cada vez mais moderno e mais antigo," says the poet explaining his return to classic forms. The expression borders on the gongoristic.

4403. Kopke, Carlos Burlamaque (ed.). Antologia da poesia brasileira moderna (1922-1947). São Paulo, Clube de Poesia de São Paulo (Col. Documentos, 1), 1953. 324 p., illus.

Selections generally good, but the arrangement, which scatters work by the same poet throughout the book, is confusing.

4404. Leão, Carlos. Poesias, 1855-1919. Rio, Pongetti, 1955. 98 p.

Works of a minor Romantic.

4405. Machado, Aníbal M. Poemas em prosa. Rio, Editôra Civilização Brasileira (Col. Maldoror), 1955. 65 p.

The most interesting poems in this collection are those of a philosophic nature, on man's attempt to build a façade to present to the world, the transitory existence of a bubble, the difficulty of bringing into harmony the variety of thoughts and feelings that assault one at night, etc.

4406. Marques, Oswaldino. Usina do sonho. Rio, Livros de Portugal, 1953. 154 p.

In his enthusiasm for unusual vocabulary, the poet forgets that the principal purpose of words is to convey meaning.

4407. Meireles, Cecília. Canções. Rio, Livros de Portugal (Poesia sempre, 3), 1956. 112 p.

Short lyrics, notably musical in effect, but vague in meaning, as if belonging to a dream world. "Assim moro em meu sonho: como um peixe no mar. O que sou é o que vejo. Vejo e sou meu olhar. . . . E meu corpo é minha alma, e o que sinto é o que penso."

4408. Melo Neto, João Cabral de. Duas águas. Rio, Olympio, 1956. 270 p.

Collected works (including several previously unpublished) of an outstanding poet of the younger generation. The division implied by the title is between verse to be studied in solitude and verse to be read to a listening audience. The order is the reverse of composition, with a resulting effect of anti-climax: the difference between the deeply personal feeling and expression of "Uma faca só lâmina" and the rather conventional items of "Pedra do sono" is striking evidence of the remarkable progress the poet has made in the last 15 years.

4409. Menezes, Berredo de. Catedral dos vácuos. Poesias. Rio, Ministério da Educação e Cultura, Serviço de Documentação, 1955. 42 p.

The vacuity of these surrealistic poems is of truly cathedral-like proportions.

4410. Moura, Isnar de. Poesia de três idades. Recife, Brazil, Editôra Nordeste, 1953. Unpaged.

Despite the statement: "nunca houve intensão [sic] literário nos meus versos," the author has written verse of considerable charm, the best of which is perhaps that concerned with the sea.

4411. Napoleão, Martins. Opus 7. Rio, Editôra Coelho Branco, 1953. 164 p.

Verse largely religious in inspiration.

4412. Olinto, Antônio. Nagasaki. Rio, Olympio, 1956. 76 p.

The most interesting poems in this collection are those concerning the atomic bombing of Nagasaki.

4413. Pena Filho, Carlos. Memórias do boi Serapião. Recife, Brazil, Gráf. Amador, 1955. 19 p., illus.

Notable rather for the handsome graphic presentation than for the text of the poem, in which an ox regrets man's increasing indifference to animals.

4414. Pinheiro, Fred. Prisma. Rio, Ministério da Educação e Cultura, Serviço de Documentação, 1955. 63 p.

Sr. Pinheiro describes the poetic art as "esgrimir palavras . . . que o domar nos custa." Too often it would seem that he is dominated by words, however. His less pretentious efforts are the most pleasing, suggestive of the earliest Portuguese lyric tradition.

4415. Quintanilha, Dirceu. A outra face do tempo. Rio, Pongetti, 1953. 46 p.

A sense of regret for what might have been characterizes these short lyrics.

4416. Schmidt, Augusto Frederico. 50 poemas escolhidos pelo autor. Rio, Ministério da Educação e Cultura, Serviço de Documentação (Os cadernos de cultura, 98), 1957. 102 p.

Schmidt's work is highly uneven. This collection represents his personal preferences.

4417. Sousa, Milton de Lima. Érmo de pupila. São Paulo, Empresa Gráf. da Revista dos Tribunais, 1955. 70 p.

The author is strongly conscious of the musical value of words but not of their meanings: it is impossible to discover any line of thought in these poems.

DRAMA

4418. Accioly Netto, A. Três máscaras. Rio, O Cruzeiro, 1956. 214 p.

Of the three plays in this volume (*Helena fechou a porta, A vida não é nossa, A mentira de cada dia*), the first won notoriety in 1950 as a parody of the Perón regime with a plot imitated from *Lysistrata*. All are mediocre at best.

4419. Andrade, Jorge. A moratória (Teat Br, 9, agôsto-set. 1956. p. 13-35).

Drama of a family that lost its fazenda in the coffee crisis of 1929. Action on two planes—past and present—skillfully intertwined. Outstanding among recent Brazilian writings for the theater.

4420. Azevedo, Arthur. Uma véspera de Reis (Teat Br, 2, dez. 1955, p. 11-19).

Though Azevedo was the most popular writer of light comedy at the end of the last century, little of his dramatic production was ever published. This matrimonial farce was one of his early successes.

4421. Callado, Antônio. Frankel (Teat Br, 7, maio-junho 1956, p. 15-33).

A lack of truly dramatic qualities makes this an argument over the problem of how far a scientist may go in his experiments on human beings rather than a play.

4422. Sampaio, Silveira. Triângulo escaleno (Teat Br, 6, abril 1956, p. 21-27).

Farce involving a husband and wife and the latter's lover, with unusually sprightly dialogue.

4423. Vianna, Renato. Obras completas. 1. Sexo. Deus. Rio, A Noite, 1954. 221 p.

First volume of the collected works of the man who strove hardest to create an interest in good theater in Brazil in the 1920's and 1930's. A comparison with other plays of the period shows these to be far more serious in intent; one has but to read *A moratória* (see item 4419), however, to realize how much they still leave to be desired.

HAITIAN LANGUAGE AND LITERATURE

MERCER COOK

On page 368 of his *Haití; pueblo afroantillano*, Richard Pattee wisely observes: "La literatura haitiana es el triunfo de la voluntad humana sobre el medio." The struggle for existence, or, in its most acute form, the struggle for political power, in Haiti leaves little time for the cultivation of poetry, drama, or fiction. This is especially true in an election year. Thus, it is not surprising that, in the months preceding and following the dramatic conclusion of President Magloire's term, politics reduced poetry to its lowest common denominator.

Nevertheless, there have been a few oases on the political desert. One of these is the publication of the Lubin anthology, *Poésies haïtiennes*, in Rio. Another is the widespread interest taken by intellectuals in the celebration of the 80th birthday of Dr. Price-Mars. According to *Conjonction* (no. 63-64, juillet 1956) there was published in October 1956 a volume in which some 60 Haitians and foreigners paid tribute to the distinguished author of *Ainsi parla l'oncle*. Apparently no public celebration is planned for Dantès Bellegarde, whose brilliant and honorable career reached its 80th milestone on May 15, 1957.

Haitians played a prominent rôle in the first congress of Negro authors and artists held at the University of Paris in September 1956. Sponsored by the magazine *Présence africaine*, this meeting attracted a large Haitian delegation, headed by Dr. Price-Mars, who served as chairman of the congress. Other Haitian authors who attended included poet René Dépestre, critic René Piquion, and novelist Jacques Alexis. Some of their contributions, along with a communication by Maurice Lubin on Haitian poetry, are scheduled for publication in a special issue of *Présence africaine*.

4450. Desroussels, Félix [pseud., i. e. Jean Baptiste Dorismond]. L'île d'amour. À la recherche des lumières du monde. Poèmes caraïbes. Préface de Jean Baptiste Dorismond. Port-au-Prince, Imp. de l'État, 1954. 156 p.

Poems written between 1948 and 1954 on a variety of subjects, ranging from religion to hurri-

cane Hazel. In his preface the author refers to his courageous use of a journalistic style. The result is often more prosaic than poetic.

4451. Duplessis Louverture, Louis, and Antoine Dodard. Face à face, par Louis Duplessis Louverture. Tambour, par Antoine Dodard. Gonaïves, Haïti, Presses Artibonitiennes (Coll. du centcinquantenaire de l'indépendance), 1953. Un-paged.

Poems by two poets of the Artibonite, with an intelligent preface by Hébert Magloire. The violent verses of Antoine Dodard seem considerably inferior to the more finished efforts of Louis Duplessis Louverture.

4452. Fouchard, Jean. Artistes et répertoire des scènes de Saint-Domingue. Port-au-Prince, Imp. de l'État, 1955. 271 p.

Actors, playwrights, and plays presented on the St. Domingue stages are listed in this dictionary. Bibliographical references accompany each entry.

4453. ————. Le théâtre à Saint-Domingue. Port-au-Prince, Imp. de l'État, 1955. 353 p.

A study of the theatre in colonial St. Domingue, based on Moreau de St. Méry, old newspapers, and unpublished archives or relatively unknown published accounts. The theaters, authors, composers, plays, and actors—including Negro performers—are discussed.

4454. Lubin, J. Dieudonné. Le sens d'une mystique. Questions politico-sociales. Port-au-Prince, Imp. V. Valcin, 1955. 67 p.

With a preface by Edner St. Victor, the author here reprints a series of articles first published in *Le matin.* Evaluating the Haitian contribution to the arts and sciences, he pleads for greater originality and increased diligence. In general, the work is more impassioned than enlightening, most of the ideas being no more original than the usual flattery of the now-discredited former president.

4455. Lubin, Maurice A. (ed.). Poésies haïtiennes. Rio, Casa do Estudante do Brasil, 1956. 147 p., photos.

55 poets of the 19th and 20th centuries are represented here by one or a few more poems each. The compiler does not claim it is a definitive selection, but an "ébauche d'une Anthologie de la Poésie Haïtienne." In collaboration with Carlos St. Louis, M. Lubin issued a 635-page *Panorama de la poésie haïtienne* in 1950 (see *HLAS, no. 16, 1950,* item 2945). [Ed.]

4456. Minuty, Julien V. Orchidées. Poè-

mes. Port-au-Prince, Imp. de l'État (Coll. du sesquicentenaire de l'indépendance d'Haïti), 1953. 49 p.

Almost half of these 18 poems are patriotic and rather trite. Occasionally, however, there are passages that make one want to see more of his work.

4457. Pattee, Ricardo. Haití; pueblo afroantillano. Madrid, Ediciones Cultura Hispánica (Col. Pueblos hispánicos; sangre de Hispania fecunda, 3), 1956. 446 p.

This interesting general study of Haiti in Spanish surveys Haitian literature in chapter 14, p. 363-394. The volume contains a useful 25-page bibliography.

4458. Paultre, Émile. Le sel de la terre. Poèmes. Port-au-Prince, Imp. N. A. Théodore, 1956. 30 p.

Quatrains and Alexandrines by the gifted author of an *Essai sur M. Price-Mars* (Port-au-Prince, 1933). To appreciate this poet's talent, one need only compare his "Détresse au littoral" with Dorismond's prosaic treatment of hurricane Hazel.

4459. Salgado, Antoine. La rivière rouge. Pièce en trois actes. Préface de Colbert Bonhomme. Port-au-Prince, Imp. La Gazette du Palais, 1953? 91 p.

A three-act play, first presented on Oct. 30, 1953. Superficially reminiscent of Roumain's *Gouverneurs de la rosée,* it lacks the artistry of that popular peasant novel. The language is stilted and declamatory, the action unconvincing. If this play was an "astonishing success," as claimed in the preface, its weaknesses were no doubt obscured by its rhetorical verbiage.

4460. Wilson, Ruth Danenhower. Here is Haiti. N. Y., Philosophical Library, 1957. 204 p.

These are the impressions of a sympathetic observer who has made three visits to Haiti since 1950. Chapter 6, "Poets, painters, and drummers," touches briefly on Haitian literature. Referring to the map of Haitian poetry, which accompanied the Lubin-St. Louis *Panorama,* Mrs. Wilson asks: "But is a land not truly civilized whose poetry is so known and loved that her poets can literally put it on the map?" (p. 38).

Law

HELEN L. CLAGETT

COLLECTIONS OF LAWS AND BIBLIOGRAPHIES

4475. Bayitch, S. A. Guide to inter-American legal studies; a selective bibliography of works in English. Coral Gables, Fla., University of Miami Law Library, 1957. 297 p.

Exhaustive guide which points up the need for more publication in this field. The items are arranged first by subject matter and then by country in two separate bibliographies.

4476. Estrada y Zayas, Edmundo. Leyes-decretos. V. 1. Habana, Lex, 1956. 1971 p.

Compilation of the so-called "law-decrees" enacted by the Batista government, which is to cover from Mar. 10, 1952, to Jan. 27, 1955. This first volume covers only through December 1953. Unfortunately, only a chronological index has been included, not entirely necessary since the material itself is also arranged chronologically. It is hoped that the second volume will contain a subject index.

4477. Inter-American Bar Association, Conference, IX, Dallas. Proceedings. Dallas, Texas, 1956. 303 p.

The meeting held in Dallas, at Southwestern Legal Center, April 1956, was the second in the U. S., the other having been held in Detroit, Michigan, in 1949. The addresses, resolutions, and the principal papers read at the meeting have been translated into English in this volume.

4478. López de Goicoechea, and Segismundo Pares Valdés. Legislación del transporte terrestre, marítimo, aéreo. Habana, Isidro, 1954. 750 p.

Commencing with the laws of 1902 and proceeding through June 1954, the joint authors comment on provisions governing all types of transportation—land, sea, and air.

4479. Núnes, Pedro. Dicionário de tecnologia jurídica. 3. ed. Rio, Freitas Bastos, 1956. 2 v.

Enlarged edition which makes laudable attempt to cover in the Portuguese language the technical terms in a wide range of fields, including forensic medicine, civil, commercial, criminal, fiscal, parliamentary, administrative, international, and constitutional law, among others.

PHILOSOPHY OF LAW, HISTORY OF LAW, JURISPRUDENCE

4480. Arístegui, Abel J. (and others). Del actual pensamiento jurídico argentino. B. A., Ediciones Arayú (Col. mayor de la teoría general del derecho), 1955. 363 p.

Ten authors have collaborated in this collection of essays on aspects of the theory of law, particularly as developed in Argentina, although some are general in nature.

4481. Bielsa, Rafael. Los conceptos jurídicos y su terminología. 2. ed. aumentada. B. A., Depalma, 1954. 210 p.

An orderly compilation of various articles and pamphlets formerly published on use of legal terminology, the origin of certain phrases used in law, the shades of difference in certain concepts—such as between competence and jurisdiction, expropriation and confiscation, etc.—and suggestions for legal authors and writers of doctoral dissertations and theses in compiling their publications.

4482. Bonilla, Evangelio. Historia del derecho romano. Montevideo, Casa del Estudiante, 1954. 301 p.

There can be little novelty in a history of Roman law, a field which has been covered in every language, in every country, and on all possible aspects. This work is no exception, as it follows the general outlines used in textbooks of this type.

4483. Bonilla Armado, José. Jerga del hampa. Lima, Nuevos Rumbos, 1956. 119 p.

Glossary of slang and typical terms used by delinquents in Peru attempting to prove definite connection between juvenile crime and jargon.

4484. Botas Arredondo, Andrés. Algunos problemas de la aplicación del derecho. México, Universidad Nacional Autónoma de México, 1954. 142 p.

Discusses the sources, methods, and bases for application of law in time and space as well as in theory and in practice.

4485. Cova García, Luis. Fundamento jurídico del nuevo ideal nacional. Caracas, Villegas, 1955. 222 p.

Rose-colored discussion of the policy and program of President Pérez Jiménez, emphasizing the economic, legal, and social protection of the Venezuelan national based on the rule of law —a new deal program.

4486. David, René. L'originalité des droits de l'Amérique latine. Paris, Centre de Documentation Universitaire, 1956? 19 p.

4488. Gusmáo, Paulo Dourado de. O pensamento jurídico contemporâneo. São Paulo, Saraiva (Col. Direito e cultura, 3), 1955. 198 p.

General text on legal philosophy by a professor of the subject.

4489. Lima, Mário Franzen de. Da interpretação jurídica. 2. ed. Rio, Revista Forense, 1955. 296 p.

Subject is analyzed from various viewpoints, including the logical, sociological, scientific, historical, and "free" methods of interpretation. New trends and concepts are pointed out, and chapters are devoted to the duties of the legislator and judge in connection with this topic.

4490. Pizani, Rafael. Introducción al derecho. Caracas, Pensamiento Vivo, 1956. 405 p.

The professor's lectures on general principles of law have been transcribed from phonographic recordings. This method is probably replacing the former method of having students take stenographic notes of lectures, and then having them published with the professor's corrections and editorial assistance.

4491. Recaséns Siches, Luis. Nueva filosofía de la interpretación del derecho. México, Fondo de Cultura Económica (Publ. Diánoia), 1956. 304 p.

Distinguished scholar seeks new angles for discussion in the field of legal philosophy. As an acknowledged expert and author, he has already covered practically every aspect of the subject in his numerous teachings and writings.

ADMINISTRATIVE LAW (EXCLUSIVE OF TAXATION)

4492. Chandías, Mario E. Tasación de inmuebles urbanos. B. A., Alsina, 1954. 242 p.

Originally intended only for the author's use as an engineer called on to evaluate and assess real property, this useful handbook evolved for use of technical and legal personnel. Tables used in other countries, tables worked out for home consumption, depreciation tables, and other materials of this type are found at the back of the volume. Legal angles include rental laws, leases, joint ownership, tax provisions applicable to real property, and others.

4493. Fabal, Gustavo. La fiscalización del presupuesto a la luz del derecho comparado. Habana, Imp. Lanuza, 1955. 166 p.

Concrete result of United Nations cooperation in the field of finance and economics. As a recipient of a grant from this organization, the author was able to study at first hand the systems employed in the Latin American countries for preparation and expenditures of the budget.

4494. Fraga, Gabino. Derecho administrativo. 6. ed. México, Porrúa, 1955. 617 p.

The only authoritative Mexican commentator on administrative law has had to enlarge and republish his basic work repeatedly since 1934.

4495. Perdomo, Julio M. Proceso del gasto en la ejecución presupuestal. Montevideo, A. M. Fernández, 1956. 368 p.

The author is an accountant, but combines both the technical and legal aspects of budget control in this repertorial work on official income and expenditures.

4496. Urzúa Macías, Efraín. Teoría general del derecho administrativo. Guadalajara, México, Imp. Universitaria, 1955. 143 p.

Theoretical discussion with little practical application to domestic law except where examples are given to illustrate some point or aspect of the subject.

CONSTITUTIONAL LAW

4497. Benson, Nettie Lee. La diputación provincial y el federalismo mexicano. México, Colegio de México, 1955. 237 p.

Historico-legal analysis of the early development of the federal system of government in Mexico from the local provincial organization prior to 1821.

4498. Campos, Francisco. Direito constitucional. Rio, Freitas Bastos, 1956. 2 v. 460, 526 p.

Fine analytical study of constitutional precepts, approached from a comparative viewpoint. This departs from the usual "commentary on the constitution," in that it interprets and discusses underlying theory, and not merely the actual law and practice.

4499. Constitución de la República de Guatemala, decretada por la Asamblea Nacional Constituyente en 2 de febrero de 1956. Guatemala, Ministerio de Gobernación, 1956. 136 p.

4500. Falcão, Alcino Pinto. Da imunidade parlamentar; informe de direito constitucional comparado e particular brasileiro. Rio, Revista Forense, 1955. 120 p.

Professional report on privileges and immunities of legislators in many nations.

4501. González Calderón, Juan Antonio.

No hay justicia sin libertad. B. A., Zavalía, 1956. 219 p.

Long an expert and champion of constitutional law, the author states that he commenced writing this work in 1951, hiding the manuscript from President Peron's police who visited unannounced at night, but waited until Peron's downfall before he could have it published. He uses the pertinent subtitle "judicial power and prejudicial power," and deals with violations of individual rights and constitutional powers in the past decade.

4502. Lancis y Sánchez, Antonio. El proceso electoral de 1954. Habana, Lex, 1955. 150 p.

Critical of the Batista regime and the electoral code of 1952, as well as of the actual electoral process which was finally permitted to take place in 1954 after much postponement. The author is professor of constitutional law. An unusual addition to the work is a transcription of a TV program, similar to our "Meet the Press" program, in which the author was quizzed on these topics by a group of journalists.

4503. Peniche López, Juan José. De la libertad de prensa. México, Cultura, 1955. 110 p.

Comparative in character.

4504. Rabasa, Emilio. El artículo 14 y el juicio constitucional. México, Porrúa, 1955. 353 p.

Although continuously paged, there are two separate works of the eminent constitutional lawyer included in this volume, the first analyzing the "due process" clause of the Mexican constitution, and the second the unique constitutional suit known as the "amparo." The expansion and recognition of the *amparo* in the past decade is of great interest in the international field.

4505. ————. La constitución y la dictadura. México, Porrúa, 1956. 246 p.

Third edition of a thoughtful study on the political organization of Mexico, first published in Madrid in 1917 by this eminent constitutional lawyer.

4506. Rodríguez Araya, Agustín. Nuevas bases. B. A., Raigal, 1956. 153 p.

Stimulating discussion of what elements should be considered important in the revision of the constitution now under consideration in Argentina. The author, apparently an exile for many years, makes a number of recommendations, including separation of Church and State, public education on a compulsory basis, autonomy of the university, less centralization in government, more power to states and local government, particularly in financial matters, and thoughtful consideration of labor and family rights.

CIVIL LAW

4507. Agüero Aguirre, Mario. El fideicomiso sobre fraccionamientos de terrenos. México, Gena, 1954. 141 p.

Thesis of interest, comparing the Anglo-American trust and the fídeicommissum, as developed in Mexico, with special application to purchase of tracts of land for subdivision purposes. All aspects are thoroughly covered on the last point.

4508. Bonazzola, Julio César. Fuentes de las obligaciones. B. A., Perrot, 1955. 105 p.

Sources of obligations deal principally with problems of unjust enrichment and those arising out of operation of law situations.

4509. Borda, Guillermo A. Tratado de derecho civil argentino. B. A., Perrot, 1955. 4 v.

Following the organization of the "books" of the civil code, the author has produced two volumes on the general introductory part of the code and two on family law, expecting to continue with contracts, property and successions. These are extensively annotated with case law, comparative legislation, and illustrative cross references. This will constitute an exhaustive treatise on the subject when completed.

4510. Bugeda Lanzas, Jesús. La propiedad horizontal. Habana, Cultural, 1954. 236 p.

Primarily an analytical study of a 1952 law enacted in Cuba, but treats the development of this type of co-ownership in Spain and Cuba, as well as in other countries. The financing of this type of cooperative housing in Cuba is under FHA, but the initials do not stand for "Federal Housing Administration." The Cubans refer to Fomento de Hipotecas Aseguradas, or Secured Mortgage Development. A number of forms are incorporated at the end.

4511. Gajardo, Samuel. Protección de menores. Santiago, Editorial Jurídica de Chile (Cartillas del Instituto Histórico y Bibliográfico de Ciencias Jurídicas y Sociales, 9), 1955. 124 p.

A small auxiliary text to be used in the law classes of the University of Chile. The Institute is an organization of the law school professors, but includes as honorary members the president of the bar association and the Chief Justice.

4512. Gamarra, Jorge. Estudios sobre obligaciones. Montevideo, Medina, 1956. 185 p.

Text on obligations, which bear some resemblance to common law concepts of quasi-contracts and torts. As a former judge, the author analyzes judicially and comparatively various aspects of this legal institution.

4513. Gatti, Hugo E. Albaceas. Montevideo, Universidad de Montevideo, Facultad de Derecho y Ciencias Sociales (Biblioteca de publ. oficiales, sección 3, 90), 1956. 380 p.

Well-documented study on the rights and duties of executors and administrators. The discussion is comparative in nature, with excerpts and citations to European authors.

4514. Grandoli, Mariano J. Algunos aspectos de la ley de adopción. B. A., Guadalupe, 1955. 31 p.

Critical analysis of the Argentine adoption law, an aspect of family law which has become more fully developed only in recent years in connection with pension and labor legislation, in addition to inheritance law. The author, however, urges an emphasis on the protection of the legitimate family first.

4515. Larraín Eyzaguirre, Iván. La parroquia ante el derecho civil chileno; o, Estatuto jurídico de la parroquia. Santiago, Editorial Jurídica, 1956. 428 p.

The relations of parochial law to other fields, such as the labor, domestic relations, economic and financial, educational, etc., are discussed. Substantive civil as well as canon law is commented upon in this connection.

4516. Molina Pasquel, Roberto. Evolución del pensamiento jurídico mexicano en materia de trust y de fideicomiso. México, Academia Mexicana de Jurisprudencia y Legislación Correspondiente de la de España, 1955. 37 p.

Legal dissertation delivered orally by an incoming member of the Academy. The author is a known authority on common law trusts and their adaptation to civil law jurisdictions. This pamphlet contains in addition an address made in reply by Miguel Macedo, already a member of the association.

4517. Paolillo, Alfredo. Las fundaciones en el derecho uruguayo. Montevideo, Universidad de Montevideo, Facultad de Derecho y Ciencias Sociales (Biblioteca de publ. oficiales, 86), 1956. 414 p.

4518. Pierre, Juan Carlos. El desalojo; su régimen actual. B. A., Arayú, 1955. 142 p.

Recent legislation on landlord-tenant relations and the power of eviction are discussed exhaustively in this monograph, including the working of these laws in actual practice. Cases in the local courts are incorporated.

4519. Ravelo Nariño, Agustín. El contrato de arrendamiento de finca rústica en la legislación cubana. Santiago de Cuba, Universidad del Oriente, Facultad de Derecho y Ciencias Sociales, 1956. 548 p.

The University, upon selecting prize-winning doctoral dissertations, gives the students the option of cash prizes or having their work published. In this case the latter choice was made by the author. The lease contracts, particularly in relation to the sugar industry, have been carefully analyzed and compiled in this fine scholarly work.

4520. Sidjanski, Dusan. Droit d'auteur; ou Copyright. Les rapports entre les différents systèmes en vigueur. Lausanne, Switzerland, F. Rouge (Lettres sciences techniques, 114), 1954. 133 p.

The author has assembled much informative data on copyright of all the principal nations for use in his comparative analysis. This is a subject of growing importance internationally.

4521. Silverio Amallo, Horacio. El divorcio. B. A., 1955. 105 p.

Commentary on recent attempt under Perón administration to permit absolute divorce. This was promptly repealed following his deposition from power. The work also covers other domestic relation problems on minors, family property, marriageable age set by law, absence and presumption of death, and others.

4522. Somarriva Undurraga, Manuel. Evolución del código civil chileno. Santiago, Nascimento, 1955. 564 p.

The Chilean civil code was promulgated just a century ago, as the work of Andrés Bello. Its history and development is traced by the eminent professor of civil law, for the centennial celebration.

4523. ————. Indivisión y partición. Santiago, Universidad de Chile, Facultad de Derecho (Col. de estudios jurídicos y sociales, 5-6), 1956. 2 v.

Concise, searching study of aspects of property rights where joint or common ownership is involved, whether by inheritance, community property law, or other methods of possession and ownership.

4524. Uzcátegui, Emilio. El niño en la legislación ecuatoriana. 2. ed. Quito, Casa de la Cultura Ecuatoriana, 1955. 240 p.

Much progress in this field has encouraged the author to bring out a current edition on all aspects of legislation touching on the subject of children, including the administrative, civil, criminal, and labor law fields.

CRIMINAL LAW

4525. Aftalión, Enrique R. Derecho penal administrativo. B. A., Arayú, 1955. 377 p.

Although admittedly limited to sanctions such as fines, expropriation of property, attachment of salary, and similar penalties, the penal aspects of administrative law have become more important in recent years. Collaborators in the present work with chapters on various aspects of the subject are Laureano Landaburu, Julio Cueto Rúa and Carlos Jáuregui. Worthwhile acquisition for reference collections.

4526. Arocha Morton, Carlos A. Crítica a la dogmática jurídico-penal. México, Porrúa, 1955. 100 p.

General monograph, analyzing various schools of thought in the penal field.

4527. Arriaga Pina, Fernando. La necesidad de un código protector del menor. México, Escuela Nacional de Jurisprudencia, 1955. 52 p.

A thesis constituting a compact analysis of existing legislation and recommendations for future law on child welfare and juvenile delinquency problems.

4528. Brouder, Carlos. La delincuencia en el deporte; estudio para una ley sobre delitos deportivos. B. A., Roque Depalma, 1956. 201 p.

In view of recent tort legislation in the field of sports, the author gives a fully rounded discussion of the subject, and recommends enactment of a broader criminal statute in the field.

4529. Carrancá y Trujillo, Raúl. Derecho penal mexicano. Parte general. T. 1. 4. ed. México, Robredo, 1955. 301 p.

A current edition of a law school textbook. An important chapter deals with the penal legislation in force as of 1955 in the individual states of Mexico.

4530. ————. Principios de sociología criminal y de derecho penal. México, Escuela Nacional de Ciencias Políticas y Sociales, 1955. 247 p.

Writing in textbook style with numbered paragraphs, the professor of criminal law presents a comprehensive comparative treatise for his students.

4531. Código penal e lei das contravenções penais anotados. . . . Vieira Ferreira Neto. Rio, Aurora, 1956. 411 p.

Systematically annoted by a judge, showing previous legislation and amendatory or deleted provisions for comparative purposes. An appendix contains report of the code commission giving underlying bases for recommended changes in the penal code as well as law on misdemeanors.

4532. Cuevas del Cid C., Rafael. Introducción al estudio del derecho penal. Guatemala, Imp. Universitaria, 1954. 309 p.

Unusually fine and scholarly work for a thesis. The author has apparently done much research in both domestic and foreign works, and presents an excellent analytical study on criminal law in general.

4533. Flores Díaz, José Tomás. La sentencia penal. Caracas, Pensamiento Vivo, 1955. 149 p.

General treatise comparing types of sentences rendered in criminal cases, with special reference to Venezuelan practice.

4534. García, Basileu. Instituições de direito penal. São Paulo, Limonad, 1954-. V. 1, pts. 1-2. 806 p.

In his treatment of criminal law and criminology, the professor attempts to make his work more interesting and worthwhile than the usual academic approach. In the second volume are found excellent bibliographies of national and foreign authors, and also fine subject and legislative indexes. No further volumes have been received since 1954.

4535. Labatut Glena, Gustavo. Derecho penal. 2. ed. Santiago, Universidad de

Chile, Facultad de Derecho (Col. de estudios jurídicos y sociales, 15, 28), 1954-1955. 2 v. 460, 373 p.

Although the first edition appeared only in 1951, so many amendments have been made in criminal legislation in Chile that a new textbook became mandatory for use in the law courses of the author.

4536. Marques, José Frederico. Curso de direito penal. São Paulo, Saraiva, 1954-1956. 3 v.

General history and development of criminal law, and particularly in Brazil, are found in the first volume, while practically every other aspect of crimes, misdemeanors, violations, and punishment are covered in the next two volumes of this comprehensive school textbook.

4537. Morães, Oswaldo da Costa. Dicionário de jurisprudencia penal e processual militar. Pôrto Alegre, Brazil, Livr. Sulina (Estante Revista jurídica, 5), 1955. 268 p.

Using a brief line or two to explain the holdings of the court in each case, the digests are arranged alphabetically by topic.

4538. Ramírez Sánchez, Alfredo. Etiologie de la délinquance juvénile; le status des mineurs au Venezuela. Paris, Cujas, 1955. 183 p.

One of a number of recent contributions in France to Latin American legal literature. The 1949 Venezuelan law on juvenile delinquency is thoughtfully analyzed and compared.

4539. Rivanera, José J. Código de honor comentado; el duelo en la historia, el derecho y la institución castrense. B. A., Arayú, 1954. 330 p.

Of interest purely for legal history scholars.

4540. Stefanelli, Luis María A. La injuria como causal de rescisión del contrato de trabajo. B. A., Librería Jurídica, 1955. 157 p.

Libel and slander analyzed as grounds for rescision of labor contracts, whether on part of employer or employee.

4541. Vetencourt, Roberto. Defensorios penales. Caracas, Bellas Artes, 1954. 136 p.

Interpretation of defense pleas in criminal law, following the Italian school of criminology.

COURTS AND JUDICIAL PROCEDURE (CIVIL AND CRIMINAL)

4542. Álvarez Tabío, Fernando. El proceso contencioso-administrativo. Habana, Martí, 1954. 607 p.

Claiming that the subject of administrative litigation has been neglected in Cuba because it falls in between ordinary procedure and administrative law, the author attempts to show that there is growing importance and interest in it in other countries as well as in Cuba. He annotates legal provisions with comments, case law, and legislative history. Forms are given, together with excellent indices.

4543. Arcaya, Pedro Manuel. Estudio crítico de las excepciones de inadmisibilidad y otras previas del derecho . . . del título I del libro 2 del Código de procedimiento civil. Caracas, Garrido, 1955. 229 p.

Former diplomat, known as an outstanding bibliophile, turns his attention here to procedural topics.

4544. Barrios de Ángelis, Dante, El Juicio arbitral. Montevideo, Universidad de Montevideo, Facultad de Derecho y Ciencias Sociales (Biblioteca de publ. oficiales, sección 3, 91), 1956. 433 p.

One of the valuable series of legal treatises being issued by the law school. Physically, these works are beautifully published on good paper, with clear print, and with indexes and bibliographies. The present work exhausts the subject of arbitration in Uruguay, with comparative views.

4545. Bielsa, Rafael. Cuestiones de jurisdicción, acciones y recursos. B. A., 1956. 300 p.

Top authority in Argentina on administrative and civil law, particularly as to procedural aspects.

4546. Blonval López, Adolfo. Código de enjuiciamiento criminal de Venezuela. San Juan de los Morros, Venezuela, Caja de Trabajo Penitenciario, 1956. 530 p.

Much-needed annotated text of the code.

4547. Bremauntz, Alberto. Por una justicia al servicio del pueblo. México, Casa de Michoacán, 1955. 289 p.

Excellent study of the theory and practice in the administration of justice in the Federal District, with references also to federal justice. Recommendations for improvement are incorporated, and are well documented.

4548. Briseño Sierra, Humberto. Categorías institucionales del proceso. Puebla, México, Cajica, 1956. 423 p.

Approached from various viewpoints, including the philosophical, theoretical, and practical. Analyzes also theories of distinguished foreign proceduralists.

4549. Código de procedimientos en lo criminal para la justicia federal y los tribunales de la Capital y territorios nacionales. Con las leyes complementarias y el régimen penitenciario nacional. B. A., Lajouane (Códigos y leyes usuales de la República Argentina), 1955. 148 p.

4550. Dias, Mario. Ministério público brasileiro: instituição, atribuições, pro-

cesso. 2. ed. Rio, Konfino, 1955. 2 v. 1314 p.

The enthusiastic reception of the first edition in 1942 and the need for a more current and comprehensive work has led the author to issue this much enlarged edition. The office of public or government attorney, on federal and local levels, is analyzed and detailed in every respect. This covers organization, duties, rights, procedures, internal regulation, forms, and other details in its 970 sections.

4551. Estellita, Guilherme. Do litisconsórcio no direito brasileiro. Rio, Ofic. Gráf. da Universidade do Brasil, 1955. 525 p.

A dissertation presented by the author in a contest for a vacancy on the legal teaching staff of the University. The author is a Federal District judge and free-lance professor.

4552. Loreto, Luis. Estudios de derecho procesal civil. Caracas, Universidad Central de Venezuela, Facultad de Derecho, 1956. 336 p.

One of the leading proceduralists of the hemisphere presents a comparative picture of civil procedure in the leading countries of the world. Various studies made and published previously as essays and articles have been woven into the work.

4553. Oliveira e Cruz, João Claudino de. Dos recursos no código de processo civil. Rio, Revista Forense, 1954. 499 p.

A textbook with numbered paragraphs containing commentaries and excerpts from law and cases on all phases of appeals under Brazilian procedure.

4554. Rodríguez y Rodríguez, Jorge. La administración de justicia en México. México, Universidad Nacional Autónoma de México, 1955. 194 p.

Thesis of interest because of few contributions made on the subject. It is to be deplored, however, that the Spanish refugee professor emphasizes ties with Europe to the absolute exclusion of Anglo-American influence, which history has proved existed without doubt at least as to the organization of the federal and state system of courts in Mexico in the 1820's, if in no other field. The professor is well known as an avowed Hispanist, and a bitter critic of the U. S. The judicial systems of other "great countries" are described in this thesis for purposes of comparison, including Great Britain, Germany, Spain, France, and Italy, absolutely no mention being made of the U. S. in the entire work. In connection with the English system, entire emphasis is placed on critical remarks on the "judge made" law, and the fact that all British judges are completely influenced in their decisions by public opinion and the press, but that they had a weapon of defense in the "contempt of court," which they could exercise at their discretion to penalize any critics of themselves as persons or of the court.

COMMERCIAL LAW

4555. Acevedo Amaya, Valmore. Los depósitos bancarios. Caracas, Universidad Central de Venezuela, Facultad de Derecho, Sección de Publicaciones (Publ., 3), 1955. 118 p.
Instructive examination of an important aspect of banking law. Contains comparative notes to practice and law of other jurisdictions.

4556. Amador Navarro, Esteban. Leyes mercantiles y tributarias de la República del Ecuador. 3 ed. con reformas hasta noviembre de 1956. Guayaquil, Ecuador, Reed & Reed, 1956. 423 p.
Substantial changes having been made in the tax and commercial field, a new edition of this compilation was needed. Valuable case notes have been inserted where applicable.

4557. Bertora, Héctor Raúl. Llave de negocio. 2. ed. B. A., Oresme, 1956. 246 p.
The so-called "key to business" is better known to us as "good will." The legal and financial aspects of good will under the business, corporation, and tax laws are discussed, and especially the methods for its evaluation. A number of North American and Argentine cases are summarized, and practical exercises and tables are to be found in a valuable appendix to the work.

4558. Cámara, Héctor. Disolución de la sociedad anónima por retiro de la autorización gubernativa. B. A., Arayú, 1954. 69 p.
Discusses circumstances under which government authorization to operate can be withdrawn from business organizations, and the effect on business of such withdrawal. A number of Supreme Court decisions dealing with withdrawal of permission to function which amounts to an expropriation of property, as in the case of the Bemberg estates, are commented upon.

4559. Canellas, Marcelo G. Cambios internacionales. B. A., Ciencias Económicas, 1954. 186 p.
Based on class lectures given in the Facultad de Ciencias Económicas of the Universidad de Buenos Aires, the discussion deals principally with technical and economic aspects of international exchange, but touches also on legal and political phases.

4560. Código de comercio de Venezuela, según el texto oficial. Notas de jurisprudencia y repertorio alfabético por Luis Loreto, Francisco Carsi Zamarés y Julio Vázquez. Caracas, Bello, 1956. 383 p.

4561. Corrêa, Celso A. de A. Noções de prática jurídica para o curso técnico de contabilidade. Rio, Aurora (Contabilidade e administração, 23), 1955. 100 p.
Principles of business law useful to accountants are incorporated in this official textbook.

4562. Cruz Ortiz, Neftalí. Prontuario jurídico bancario. Santiago, Editorial Jurídica de Chile, 1956. 484 p.
The title is somewhat misleading, since this is a handbook for use of bankers rather than one on banking law. Contains numbered paragraphs covering all types of legal and judicial documents relating to title of real and personal property of all kinds. Deeds, sales contracts, certificates of co-ownership, expropriation and forced sales, mortgages and other liens, ship mortgages, etc. Also includes international conferences of interest, as well as entire texts of some laws and decrees.

4563. Fernandes, Adaucto. Câmbio marítimo (foenus nauticum). Rio, Coelho Branco, 1955. 279 p.
Comparative study of the development, from Roman and Greek roots, of bottomry in maritime law in various groups of countries. In the bibliography covering the sources consulted for the Anglo-American history, no treatise later than 1907 was listed, but since the basic interest of the author, insofar as foreign countries are concerned, was the early history of this type of maritime risks, these works may have been adequate.

4564. Frangipani, Alfonso U. Seguros de vida. B. A., Prometeo, 1956. 389 p.
Contains both legal and financial aspects of life insurance business, which has still much growth to attain in Latin America in general.

4565. Garo, Francisco J. Derecho comercial. Compraventas. B. A., Depalma, 1956. 2 v. 949 p.
The first volume is devoted to sales within jurisdiction of the territory of the nation, and the second to maritime sales. Commercial aspects, including contracts, documents, rights and duties of vendor and purchaser, etc., are commented on at length and extensively footnoted.

4566. Hernández, Octavio A. Derecho bancario mexicano. México, Jus, 1956. 2 v. 495, 612 p.
Much-needed professional work on banking law and practice. Consists of assembly of much informative data and detailed analysis of this specialized field.

4567. Ley de marcas, nombres y avisos comerciales: su reglamento y clasificación marcaria. Guatemala, Ministerio de Economía y Trabajo, 1955. 40 p.

4568. Malvagni, Atilio. Derecho marítimo; contratos de transporte por agua. B. A., Depalma, 1956. 890 p.
Exhaustive treatise on admiralty law, with particular reference to details on freight and charter parties, insurance, damage or destruction of goods, liability, and other aspects of maritime contracts.

4569. Montanelli, Armando. El martillero público en la República Argentina. B. A., Librería Jurídica, 1954. 293 p.

Covers in great detail all aspects of public auctions and forced sales, including the duties, fees, commissions, and practices in Argentina, as well as the law and cases in this connection.

4570. Morales Paúl, Isidoro. El contrato de fletamento en el derecho venezolano. Caracas, Universidad Central de Venezuela, Facultad de Derecho (Publ., 9), 1956. 130 p.

Repertorial work covering all aspects of freight and charter parties as governed by the commercial code provisions and special maritime law.

4571. Pereira, Aristeu, and Bernardo Timm. Falências e concordatas. Rio, Konfino, 1954. 3 v. 1001 p.

The joint authors have taken the text of the law and inserted commentaries, learned doctrine, related legislation, forms and jurisprudence in point.

4572. Rodríguez Altunaga, Rafael (comp.). Código de comercio vigente en la República de Cuba, seguido de veinticuatro apéndices contentivos de la legislación complementaria. Revisado y concordado por. . . . 2. ed. notablemente aumentada. Habana, Montero (Col. legislativa de bolsillo, 7), 1955. 659 p.

4573. Segura, Luis G. La fiscalización de la sociedad anónima. B. A., Librería Jurídica, 1955. 127 p.

Discussion of an aspect of corporation law practiced in the majority of civil law countries, and one which might be considered in Anglo-American jurisdictions. This provides for supervision and control over corporations in matters of special interest to stockholders, protective of their rights.

4574. Vásquez del Mercado, Óscar. Asambleas de sociedades anónimas. México, Porrúa, 1955. 254 p.

Authoritative and comprehensive discussion of stockholder rights in the business organizations which most closely resemble the Anglo-American corporation.

TAXATION

4575. British Chamber of Commerce in Brazil. The Brazilian income tax regulations, embodying all income tax legislation up to and including law no. 2354 of 29th November 1954. Rio, 1954. 149 p.

Contains both Portuguese and English texts.

4576. Codificação do direito tributário; contribuição do Instituto Brasileiro de Direito Financeiro ao estudo do projeto de código tributário nacional. Rio. Edições Financeiras, 1955. 366 p.

Analysis by a commission of tax experts of a preliminary draft for a new tax code. The draft was compiled by Rubén Gomes de Sousa. At the end of the work is found the approved text following changes made upon recommendation of the commission.

4577. Codificación de disposiciones legales y reglamentarias vigentes de carácter fiscal. Bogotá, Consejo Técnico de la Contraloría, 1956. 4 v.

Codified by José Vicente Muñoz. Very useful compilation of laws and decrees, together with administrative circulars and regulations of the Office of Comptroller General. Contains excellent indexes, both chronological and subject.

4578. Ferrero, Rómulo A. Comentarios acerca de los impuestos en el Perú. Lima, Tip. Peruana, 1955. 35 p.

A series of articles originally appearing in the newspapers is of interest mainly because of the paucity of comment or analysis of tax legislation in Peru. The survey of existing tax legislation was encouraged by the Klein Mission (Economic and Financial) from the U. S.

4579. O impôsto sôbre vendas e consignações no sistema tributário brasileiro. Rio, Edições Financeiras (Série prática fiscal, 1), 1956. 424 p.

The two general introductory chapters and each of the following ones relating to the tax system of the individual states of Brazil is contributed by a different author.

4580. Jiménez Z., Pío S. Régimen impositivo de sucesiones y donaciones. Bogotá, Temis, 1956. 429 p.

The only known up-to-date source for consultation of the gift and transfer tax system and legislation in Colombia.

4581. Mandêtta, Saverio. Impostos, taxas e contribuições: resenha histórica do regime fiscal no Brasil. São Paulo, Colébras (Coletânea da legislação brasileira), 1954. 629 p.

Comprehensive treatise on tax system of Brazil, analyzing the principal types of taxes and imposts in force.

4582. Martínez, Máximo R. Impuesto extraordinario a las ganancias elevadas e impuestos a las ganancias eventuales de capital y a las transferencias de empresas. Montevideo, Tall. Gráf. Donostia, 1956. 160 p.

The texts of the tax laws are compiled in an orderly fashion, and alphabetically arranged by subject matter, under topical subdivisions.

4583. Pereira, Moacir Araujo. Questões fiscais; prática-teoria. Rio, Delta, 1955. 493 p.

Covers financial matters in general, but deals most particularly with tax matters and banking operations. This field is becoming of utmost importance because of foreign trade and potential investment from abroad.

4584. Santos Rowe, Manuel (comp.), In-

dice de legislación fiscal, 1939-1956. México, Jus (Ediciones de la Asociación Mexicana de Investigaciones Administrativas, serie 2, 1), 1956. 191 p.
Well-edited index of all legal and administrative provisions on fiscal relations between the state and the individual. There is no attempt to show relation between earlier and later laws, but all are listed chronologically under an alphabetical subject matter arrangement. For income tax alone, there are about 23 pages of legal provisions.

4585. Tinoco, Pedro R. Comentarios a la ley de impuesto sobre la renta de Venezuela. Madrid, Halar, 1955. 2 v. 774 p.
New income tax law receives an exegetic analysis at the hands of a fiscal expert. General introductory chapters deal with definitions, outline of the tax system and general principles of taxation. Contains an unusually fine subject index, as well as detailed tables of contents.

4586. Wallace, Donald O. (ed.). Dominican Republic income tax service. Centerport, N. Y., Foreign Tax Law Association, 1955. 1 v. (loose-leaf).
One of the series of loose-leaf services in English. The translation as well as the system used to keep the service current leave much to be desired for an efficient and accurate work. This is true in general of the series. See also items 4587-4590.

4587. ————. Ecuador income tax service. Centerport, N. Y., Foreign Tax Law Association, 1955. 1 v. (loose-leaf).
See item 4586.

4588. ————. Mexican income tax service. A digest of the income tax laws of Mexico. By Jorge Flores Meza. Hempstead, N. Y., Foreign Tax Law Association, 1954. 3 v. (loose-leaf).
See item 4586.

4589. ————. Nicaraguan income tax service. Centerport, N. Y., Foreign Tax Law Association, 1956. 1 v. (loose-leaf).
See item 4586.

4590. ————. Panamerican income tax service. Centerport, N. Y., Foreign Tax Law Association, 1954. 1 v. (loose-leaf).
See item 4586.

INTERNATIONAL LAW, PUBLIC

4591. Barros Jarpa, Ernesto. Derecho internacional público. Santiago, Editorial Jurídica de Chile (Manuales jurídicos, 56), 1955. 602 p.
One of a series of textbooks for use in the law schools.

4592. Sierra, Manuel J. Tratado de derecho internacional público. México, Porrúa, 1955. 646 p.
The author is an eminent professor and member of the Permanent Court of Arbitration at The Hague. The usual contents of treatises on public international law are found herein, but an appendix of approximately 125 pages deals with the recent growth in this hemisphere of international law, and with international organizations such as the United Nations, International Court, the Pan American Union as recently reorganized in Bogotá, and other topics.

4593. Sokola, Tadeo. La Organización del Tratado del Atlántico Norte frente al derecho internacional. B. A., Arayú, 1955. 142 p.
Except for an occasional periodical article or chapter in a general text on international law, NATO has rarely been chosen as a subject of literature in Latin America.

4594. Zorrilla de San Martín, Juan. Discusos, artículos y notas de derecho internacional público. Montevideo, Universidad de Montevideo, Facultad de Derecho y Ciencias Sociales (Biblioteca de publicaciones oficiales, sección 3, 82), 1955. 228 p.
On the occasion of the centenary of Dr. Zorrilla's birth, a compilation of his writings and addresses on all aspects of international law was published as an homage to him. The author was statesman and diplomat who took active part in the formation of public law in his country's history.

INTERNATIONAL LAW, PRIVATE

4595. Gallardo, Ricardo. La solution des conflits de lois dans les pays de l'Amérique latine; divorce, separation de corps et nullité du mariage. Paris, Librairie Générale de Droit et de Jurisprudence, 1956. 316 p.
General commentary on treaty provisions dealing with aspects of domestic relations in the field of private international law. Chapters on the conflicts-of-law rules in the individual countries are found in the second half.

MISCELLANEOUS

MINING LAW

4596. Código de minería de la República Argentina. Con un apéndice que contiene la ley de reformas no. 10.273 (sobre condiciones de la concesión de minas), y ley no. 12.161 (sobre régimen legal de las minas de petróleo e hidrocarburos flúidos). B. A., Lajouane (Códigos y leyes usuales de la República Argentina), 1955. 110 p.

4597. Código de petróleo de la República de Guatemala. Decreto 345 del 7 de julio de 1955. Guatemala, Tip. Nacional, 1955. 221 p.

Contains official Spanish text and English translation on opposite pages, but with continuous pagination.

4598. Código del petróleo, y su reglamento. Ed. oficial. La Paz, Yacimientos Petrolíferos Fiscales Bolivianos, 1956. 118 p.

A new oil law in Bolivia frankly designed to attract foreign investment and earn dollar exchange for the government. It was based partially on the Venezuelan and Peruvian petroleum laws, but seems even more favorable to foreign capital.

4599. Rodríguez Escobedo, Carlos. Código de minería; concordancias. Arequipa, Perú, Editorial Universitaria, 1955. 280 p.

Annotations consist of references to provisions of the constitution and other codes, regulatory legislation, financial and tax legislation in point, as well as excerpts from judicial interpretation.

AGRICULTURE

4600. Flores Moncayo, José. Derecho agrario boliviano. La Paz, Don Bosco, 1956. 399 p.

Fundamental treatise on comparative law problems which are of the greatest importance to many Latin American and other countries. Development from the days of ancient Greece to modern times, on such aspects as community ownership, expropriation, and cooperatives, are discussed herein. Procedures followed in attempts at agrarian reforms are analyzed for Bolivia and other countries.

4601. Uzcátegui Urdaneta, Mariano. Aspectos económicos jurídicos del agro venezolano. Caracas, Samán, 1956. 163 p.

Presented as a thesis in political science. The author traces the development of agriculture in Venezuela from colonial times to the present, both as to the economic and the legal bases.

TRANSPORTATION

4602. Bauza Araujo, Álvaro. El helicóptero y su régimen jurídico. Montevideo, Bianchi, 1956. 143 p.

Most interesting monograph on place of the helicopter within the air legislation. Its use in transportation and agricultural fields is, of course, important to Uruguay. Very little has been written on this subject in Latin America, and as far as is known by this editor, the present work is the only one dedicated solely to the subject.

4603. Código del tránsito. Comentarios a su articulado . . . por Eduardo de Acha. Habana, Montero (Biblioteca jurídica de autores cubanos y extranjeros, 170), 1955. 270 p.

The code provisions are followed by case law, legislative history, and cross references. An appendix of related laws on traffic judges, tort liability of third parties, and traffic accidents is found in this work.

4604. Huerta Palau, Pedro. Régimen del transporte automotor de cargas. V. 1. Córdoba, Argentina, Apolo, 1954. 97 p.

The first small volume deals with jurisdiction, and is written from a comparative viewpoint, although the sources consulted are very meager.

EDUCATION

4605. Neves, Carlos de Souza. Ensino superior no Brasil. Rio, Gráf. Olímpica, 1954-. V. 1, 702 p.; v. 2, 599 p.

A compilation of all laws, administrative orders, and internal regulations on all aspects and types of education and instruction. The first volume contains materials on topics lettered from A to D, and the second from D to H.

4606. Varas Contreras, Guillermo. La enseñanza particular ante el derecho. Santiago, Editorial del Pacífico, 1956. 124 p.

Private schools under the educational program and laws are commented on particularly as to legislative history. The author makes recommendations for a new law to govern these institutions.

Music

RICHARD A. WATERMAN

Six new Latin American serial publications dealing wholly or in part with music appeared in 1955, in addition to those listed in *HLAS, no. 19*. These are: *CBM*, Avenida Graça Aranha 57, Rio, October-December 1955. *INC*, Boletín informativo del Instituto Nacional de Cultura, Ministerio de Educación, Habana, November-December 1955. *Luz y sombra*, Teatro 382, Cuzco, Perú, October 1955. *Revista del Instituto Nacional de Cultura*, Palacio de Bellas Artes, Habana, December 1955. *Revista musical de la Orquesta Sinfónica*, Teatro Nacional, San José, December 1955. *S.A.D.E.M.*, Paraguay 1162, B. A., March-June 1955.

An indication of the vigor of musical life in Latin America during recent years is given by the *Buenos Aires musical* tabulation of concert activities in that city during 1955. Under the batons of 35 directors, 120 symphonic concerts were given by eight orchestras, and there were 86 concerts with soloists, instrumental and vocal, and with choral groups. In all, 351 symphonic works by 146 composers were performed. More recently, during 1956, the same publication carried a spirited debate, participated in by many of Argentina's best-known musicians, concerning the wisdom of the 1952 presidential decree requiring that some work by an Argentine composer be included in each public concert of any kind; according to the most recent information the decree is still in force.

During the early part of 1957 two important musical festivals occurred. The first, between March 19 and April 10, was the Second Festival of Latin American Music, organized by the José Ángel Lamas Institution and held in Caracas. The program consisted of nine symphony concerts held in the Auditorio de Bello Monte; during the three-week period Caracas once again acted as the musical capital of the Americas. Then, for two weeks during April, Puerto Rico held the Casals Festival sponsored in the main by the University of Puerto Rico. Alexander Schneider, of the Budapest Quartet, formed the orchestra. Performers of international reputation who participated included Rudolf Serkin, Maria Stader, Joseph Szigeti, Miecyslav Horsovski, Jesús María Sanromá, Isaac Stern, Eugene Istomin, Gerard Souzay, and the Budapest Quartet. Pablo Casals himself, unfortunately, was able to appear as conductor for only a part of one performance.

The *Boletín de música y artes visuales,* long published by the Pan American Union, suspended publication in the middle of 1956. The last issue was no. 74-76 for April-June 1956. It has been replaced by the *Boletín interamericana de música,* initiated with no. 1 for September 1957, by the same organization.

GENERAL

4700. Boggs, Ralph Steele. Folklore bibliography for 1956 (South Folk Q, 21:1, Mar. 1957).

Ballad, song, dance, game, verse, as related to Latin America, p. 34-39.

4701. Guatemala. Ministerio de Educación Pública. Himnos de Centroamérica; septiembre de 1953, 132. aniversario de la Independencia. Guatemala, 1953. 30 p.

Voice and piano arrangements of the "Himno de Centroamérica" and the national anthems of Guatemala, El Salvador, Nicaragua, Honduras,

Costa Rica, and Panama, with texts also printed separately.

4702. Pan American Union. Music Division. Directorio musical de la América Latina: conservatorios, academias y escuelas de música, y orquestas sinfónicas. Musical directory of Latin America: conservatories, academies and music schools, and symphony orchestras. Washington, 1954. 27 p.
A valuable directory of musical institutions in Latin America.

ARGENTINA

4703. Campo, Isabel María del. Retrato de un ídolo; vida y obras de Carlos Gardel. B. A., Albores, 1955. 214 p., illus.
The life story of Carlos Gardel, 1890-1935, "the most famous, beloved, and genuine of the popular singers of Río de la Plata," with an appendix listing his compositions, phonograph records, and films.

4704. Lange, Francisco Curt. La música religiosa en el área de Rosario de Santa Fé y en el Convento San Carlos de San Lorenzo, durante el período aproximado de 1770 a 1820. Rosario, Argentina, Cursos Libres de Portugués y Estudios Brasileños (Ciclo de conferencias de 1955, 4), 1956. 62 p., facsims.
Results of Curt Lange's musicological research in archives of the Cathedral of Rosario and in the Colegio San Carlos in San Lorenzo, with inventory lists of 18th-century musical holdings in both. Includes short histories of musical activities in each place.

4705. Schiuma, Oreste. Poemas musicales argentinos. Prólogo del Prof. Pedro Sofía. B. A., Tall. Gráf. Salvia, 1954. 121 p.
A series of short essays interpreting 32 tone poems by Argentine composers.

BRAZIL

4706. Conservatorio Brasileiro de Música. Revista C. B. M. Órgão oficial do. . . . Rio. Ano 1, no. 1, trimestre out., nov., dez. de 1955—.
First number of the official organ of the Brazilian Conservatory of Music, edited by the director of the Conservatory, Antonietta de Souza, who contributes an article on North American music. Among the articles are Renato Almeida's "Brazilian folkmusic" and Virgil Thomson's "Americanism in music."

4707. França, Eurico Nogueira. A música no Brasil. Rio, Ministério da Educação e Saúde, Serviço de Documentação (Os Cadernos de cultura, 54), 1953. 69 p.
A handbook of Brazilian music. Contains brief treatments of the history of musical performance and composition in Brazil, and biographical sketches of the popular composers Chiquinha

Gonzaga and Ernesto Nazareth, as well as the contemporary composers Villa-Lobos, Camargo Guarnieri, Francisco Mignone, Lorenzo Fernández, Radamés Gnattali, Fructuoso Vianna, Brasílio Itiberê, Luiz Cosme, Cláudio Santoro, and Guerra Peixe.

4708. Giffoni, Maria Amalia Corrêa. Danças folclóricas brasileiras: sistematização pedagógica. São Paulo, Martins, 1955. 355 p., illus., diagrs.
A systematic teacher's manual, concise and complete. The first 70 pages form a treatise on the use of the folk dance in physical education; the remainder of the book gives information, directions, and choreography for 26 Brazilian folk dances.

4709. Lange, Francisco Curt. A música em Minas Gerais durante o século XVIII (Mús Sac, 16:1, jan.-fev. 1957, p. 1-7).
First installment of Portuguese translation of item below.

4710. ————. La música en Minas Gerais durante el siglo XVIII (Estud Am, 12:57-58, junio-julio 1956, p. 1-26).
An account of "one of the most unusual phenomena of the history of music in the Americas," the fantastic efflorescence of all phases of musical art in the wealthy frontier state of Minas Gerais during the 18th century.

4711. Melo, Veríssimo de. Rondas infantis brasileiras (R Arq Mun, 19:155, jan.-março 1953, p. 227-356).
Study of children's round dances (texts and music), objective, well documented, with some attempt to indicate the origin and distribution of the material gathered by the author. [R. E. Dimmick]

4712. Rezende, Carlos Penteado de. Fragmentos para uma história da música em São Paulo. São Paulo, Gráf. Municipal, 1954. 195-224 p., illus.
"Separata do volume 'IV Centenario da fundação da cidade de São Paulo.' " Brief chronologically arranged list of happenings in the musical history of São Paulo between 1500 and 1800. Compare with item 5632, *HLAS, no. 19,* where the same kind of treatment is applied to musical events from 1800 to 1870.

4713. Siqueira, José de Lima. Música para a juventude. Rio, 1953. 3. série, Rudimentos de teoria musical; A música, sua origem e evolução, 240 p.; 4. série, Técnica, estética e pedagogia, 240 p. & 62 songs (unpaged), musical examples.
The third and fourth series of lessons of a course in music for Brazilian secondary schools. Many charts and explanatory diagrams. Each lesson concludes with a series of questions to be answered by the student.

4714. Souza, Affonso Ruy de. Bôemios e seresteiros bahianos do passado. Salvador, Brazil, Progresso (Ensaios; Série miniatura, 17), 1954. 53 p.

Story of the wandering troubadours in 19th-century Brazilian culture. Second part is a biography of one of the most famous of these, Xisto Bahia, 1841-1894.

4715. Universidade do Brasil. Escola Nacional de Música. Relação dos discos gravados no estado de Minas Gerais (fevereiro de 1944). Rio, 1956. 100 p., illus., musical examples.
Catalog of folk-music recordings made in Minas Gerais during February 1944, now in the archives of the Centro de Pesquisas Folclóricas, with analyses and discussions, mostly by Dulce Martins Lamas, of the various types of songs encountered and of the instruments used by the musicians.

MEXICO

4716. Contreras, Guillermo. Silvestre Revueltas, genio atormentado. México, Tall. de Manuel Casas, 1954. 192 p., illus., ports.
Mainly a study of the relationship between abnormality and genius, as illustrated by the life of Revueltas. Contains a short biography of the composer, followed by his classification according to constitutional typology, endocrinology, psychiatry, character, and anthropometry, with some psychological and psychoanalytic documentation.

4717. Martí, Samuel. Instrumentos musicales precortesianos. México, Instituto Nacional de Antropología, 1955. 227 p., illus. (part col.), map, diagrs., music.
Archaeological finds of actual instruments and of figurines of musicians playing instruments, wall paintings, codices, and writings of early chroniclers, give considerable information about the musical instruments of pre-Spanish Middle America. Martí has drawn together as much of this material as possible, along with excellent illustrations, into what must now be considered the standard reference work on the subject. There is also a discussion of modern instruments of pre-Spanish origin.

4718. Pan American Union. Music Division. Composers of the Americas. Biographical data and catalogs of their works. Washington, 1955-1957. 3 v. 98, 155, 128 p.
Valuable compilation of information, familiar

to readers of the *Boletín de música y artes visuales*, where the items have been published in serial form. (See, for example, *HLAS, no. 19*, items 5608-5610).

4719. ————. ————. Musical directory of Latin America: Mexico. Washington, 1956. 69 p.
Factual information concerning most phases of music in Mexico. A valuable reference work.

OTHER COUNTRIES

4720. Macía de Casteleiro, María. La música religiosa en Cuba. Habana, Úcar, García, 1956. 137 p., illus.
An expansion of the essay that won the María Teresa García-Montes de Giberga prize in the contest sponsored in 1956 by the review *Pro-arte musical* on the theme of religious music in Cuba. The first part is largely a résumé of Carpentier's *La música en Cuba*, insofar as it touches on religious music of the 16th, 17th, and 18th centuries. The original essay follows. It includes a directory of religious musicians and composers in Cuba, arranged more or less chronologically, and a serviceable history of Church policy in regard to ecclesiastical music.

4721. Nicaragua. Ministerio de Relaciones Exteriores. Música nicaragüense. Managua, 1953. Unpaged.
28 Nicaraguan tunes, arranged for piano or voice and piano. Includes folk music, dance music, concert waltzes, "classical" music, and the national anthem.

4722. Pan American Union. Music Division. Musical directory of Latin America: Chile. Washington, 1954. 44 p.
Factual information concerning most phases of music in Chile. A valuable reference work.

4723. Raygada, Carlos. Historia crítica del himno nacional. Prólogo de Jorge Basadre. Lima, Mejía Baca & Villanueva, 1954. 2 v. 221, 223 p.
Copiously documented history of the national anthem of Peru, with discussion of its possible influence on subsequent pieces of music. The second volume contains biographies of José de la Torre Ugarte, who wrote the words, José Bernardo Alcedo, who wrote the music, and Claudio Rebagliati, who arranged the definitive version.

Philosophy

ANÍBAL SÁNCHEZ REULET

La presente bibliografía abarca libros y artículos aparecidos durante 1954, 1955 y 1956. El número de entradas es, por lo tanto, mayor que en años anteriores, aunque se ha procurado mantenerlo dentro de límites razonables mediante una selección más rigurosa. No se incluyen, sin embargo, algunas obras de los años 1955 y 1956 que no pudieron ser examinadas a tiempo. Aparecerán registradas en el volumen próximo junto con la producción de 1957.

Gran actividad bibliográfica se ha registrado en los tres años transcurridos. Han aparecido nuevas revistas. En 1955, empezó a publicarse en México con el título de *Diánoia*, el anuario del Centro de Estudios Filosóficos de la Universidad Nacional Autónoma de México. Se propone dar a conocer, no sólo los trabajos de los investigadores de esa institución, sino estudios originales de autores de otros países. El primer número fue preparado bajo la dirección del profesor Eduardo Nicol. En 1956, apareció el primer número de la *Revista dominicana de filosofía*, órgano de la Facultad de Filosofía de la Universidad de Santo Domingo, bajo la dirección de Waldo Ross.

El XVI centenario del nacimiento de San Agustín, que se cumplió en 1954, y el primer centenario de la muerte de Kierkegaard, en 1955, han dado lugar a la publicación de numerosos estudios. La *Revista brasileira de filosofia* dedicó un número de homenaje a Kierkegaard (6:1, jan.-março 1956). La muerte del filósofo español José Ortega y Gasset, acaecida en 1955, dió motivo también a la aparición de artículos y ensayos sobre su personalidad y su obra. Revistas especializadas, como la *Revista cubana de filosofía* (4:13, enero-junio 1956), y otras de carácter general, como *Sur* (241, julio-agosto 1956), le dedicaron números especiales.

Aparte de la producción bibliográfica, hubo otras importantes manifestaciones en el campo de la filosofía americana. Del 9 al 15 de agosto de 1954, se efectuó en San Pablo, como parte de la celebración del IV centenario de la fundación de esa ciudad, un Congreso Internacional de Filosofía organizado por el Instituto Brasileño de Filosofía (véase párrafo 4758). A este Congreso asistieron, además de una numerosa delegación brasileña, representantes de Argentina, Alemania, Chile, Colombia, Cuba, España, Estados Unidos, Francia, Italia, México, Perú, Portugal y Uruguay. En la última sesión plenaria quedó constituída la Sociedad Interamericana de Filosofía bajo la presidencia del Dr. Miguel Reale quien fue, asimismo, presidente del Congreso. Una de las tareas inmediatas de la nueva Sociedad fue la de convocar el IV Congreso Interamericano de Filosofía que se reunió en Santiago de Chile entre el 8 y el 15 de julio de 1956, bajo la presidencia de Jorge Millas. La organización del Congreso estuvo a cargo de la Sociedad Chilena de Filosofía bajo los auspicios del gobierno y las universidades de Chile. Concurrieron a este Congreso delegados de la mayoría de los países latinoamericanos. Contó, también, con la presencia de filósofos de Estados Unidos y Europa.

De acuerdo con el criterio que se ha adoptado para la preparación de esta bibliografía, figuran en ella obras y artículos escogidos de autores latinoamericanos, cualquiera que sea el asunto de que se ocupen, y de autores no latinoamericanos, siempre que traten temas relacionados con el pensamiento y la filosofía de América Latina. Todos los trabajos referentes a la filosofía latinoamericana se agrupan en un apartado especial de la subsección de "Estudios críticos." Las reediciones de obras clásicas del pensamiento latinoamericano figuran en la subsección de "Obras generales." Los estudios que se refieren a aspectos no estrictamente filosóficos del pensamiento latinoamericano, aparecen bajo el título "Historia de las ideas." Con el propósito de dar una visión más completa de lo que se está publicando en América Latina se incluye, bajo el título "Traducciones," una lista mínima de nuevas traducciones de obras clásicas y contemporáneas importantes.

OBRAS GENERALES

4750. Alembert, Jean Lerond d'. Discurso preliminar a la Enciclopedia. A dos siglos de su publicación; estudios pos Francisco Romero; José A. Oría; José Babini; Roberto F. Giusti; y Luis Reissig. B. A., Losada, 1954. 237 p., facsim.

La primera parte contiene el "Discurso preliminar" de la *Enciclopedia*. La traducción ha sido hecha por Aída A. Barbagelata, utilizando el texto de la primera edición (1751). La segunda parte reune estudios de Francisco Romero, sobre los antecedentes del espíritu enciclopédico desde el Renacimiento; de José A. Oría, sobre las relaciones entre la *Enciclopedia* y la Revolución Francesa; de José Babini, sobre la inspiración y contenido científicos del "Discurso preliminar"; de Roberto F. Giusti, sobre la actuación de Diderot en la elaboración de la *Enciclopedia;* y de Luis Reissig, sobre el valor educativo y social de la misma obra.

4751. Benz, Ernst. Zur gegenwärtigen lage der philosophie in Lateinamerika, vor allem Brasilien (Jahr Ak Wis Lit, 1954, p. 267-279).

Informe sobre la situación de la filosofía en América Latina, y especialmente en el Brasil, escrito con motivo del Congreso Internacional de Filosofía realizado en San Pablo en 1954 al cual asistió el autor. Despues de considerar, en general, el papel que la filosofía ha tenido en el desarrollo de la enseñanza universitaria, se analizan algunos de los trabajos presentados al mencionado Congreso y se señalan las influencias de la filosofía alemana en los países latinoamericanos. La información que maneja el autor es fragmentaria y superficial, y sus conclusiones demasiado apresuradas, para poder ofrecer un panorama claro y coherente de la situación actual de la filosofía en América Latina.

4752. Briceño, Alfonso. Disputaciones metafísicas (1638). Texto traducido del original latino con una introducción por Juan David García Bacca. Caracas, Universidad Central de Venezuela, Instituto de Filosofía (Filosofía, 2), 1955. 206 p.

Primera edición en castellano. No reproduce íntegro el texto original, sino sólo una selección. La obra de la que han sido tomadas estas disputaciones metafísicas se publicó en Madrid en 1638, en dos volúmenes, con el título de *Celebriorum controversiarum in primum sententiarum Johannis Scoti doctoris subtilis theologorum facile principis*. Es una importante contribución al conocimiento de la filosofía colonial. Briceño, de la orden franciscana, nació en Santiago de Chile en 1590 y murió en Trujillo en 1668.

4753. Campo, Pedro A. O ensino da filosofia no Brasil (Latinoamérica, 6:62, feb. 1954, p. 75-77).

4754. Casas, Manuel Gonzalo. Introducción a la filosofía. Tucumán, Argentina, Universidad Nacional de Tucumán, Instituto de Filosofía, 1954. 358 p.

Apuntes del curso dictado en la Facultad de Filosofía y Letras de Tucumán. El último capítulo trata de la filosofía en la Argentina. Incluye bibliografía.

4755. Caso, Antonio. El problema de México y la ideología nacional. Prólogo de Leopoldo Zea. México, Libro-Mex (Biblioteca mínima mexicana, 22), 1955. 98 p.

La primera edición de esta obra se publicó en México en 1924.

4756. Coloquio sobre la Federación Internacional de Sociedades de Filosofía. Informe final, Coloquio . . . organizado por la Sociedad Cubana de Filosofía con la colaboración del Centro Regional de la UNESCO en el Hemisferio Occidental. Habana, 1955. 21 p.

Contiene los trabajos, los resúmenes de los debates y las recomendaciones de la reunión celebrada en la ciudad de La Habana del 20 al 22 de octubre de 1955 para discutir la labor realizada por la Federación Internacional de Sociedades de Filosofía y sus proyecciones futuras.

4757. Congreso Latinoamericano de Filosofía y Filosofía de la Educación, I, Quito, abril 10-15, 1953. Primer Congreso Latinoamericano de Filosofía y Filosofía de la Educación . . . convocado por la Facultad de Filosofía, Letras y Ciencias de la Educación de la Universidad Central. Quito, Casa de la Cultura Ecuatoriana, 1954. 391 p., illus.

Contiene los antecedentes, lista de participantes, discursos, trabajos presentados y otros documentos. Las ponencias versaron sobre cuatro temas principales: corrientes de la filosofía contemporánea; la filosofía en la América Latina; la enseñanza y la función de la filosofía en los

PHILOSOPHY

colegios y universidades de la América Latina; y la filosofía y sus relaciones con la educación.

4758. Congresso Internacional de Filosofia, agôsto, 9-15, 1954. Anais. Promovido pelo Instituto Brasileiro de Filosofia. . . . São Paulo, 1956. 3 v. 345, 350-758, 762-1185 p.

El primer volumen contiene, en su primera parte, los discursos protocolares de inauguración del Congreso y las conferencias pronunciadas en celebración del 1. centenario de la muerte de Schelling y del 16. centenario del nacimiento de San Agustín. La segunda parte, recoge las ponencias sobre "Filosofía de la religión y metafísica." En el segundo volumen, formando secciones separadas, figuran los trabajos sobre "Axiología y ética" y sobre "Filosofía jurídica y social." El tercer volumen, dividido a su vez en tres partes, reune los estudios de "Lógica y filosofía de la ciencia," de "Arte y estética," y de Filosofía en América e historia de la filosofía." En una especie de apéndice, se incluyen el reglamento del Congreso y el estatuto de la Sociedad Interamericana de Filosofía, aprobado en la última sesión plenaria. El volumen se cierra con una lista de los asistentes. Los trabajos se publican en el idioma original en que fueron presentados (portugués, castellano, francés, inglés italiano o alemán). Las contribuciones suman, en total, 138. El mayor número corresponde, por supuesto, a los filósofos brasileños entre los que se destacan los trabajos de Leonardo Van Acker, "Philosophie et réligion d'après le Blondélisme"; Vicente Ferreira da Silva, "História e meta-história"; Alexandre Augusto Corrêa, "Jurisprudência e filosofia do direito"; Miguel Reale, "Direito abstracto e dialética da positividade na doutrina de Hegel"; y Euryalo Cannabrava, "Estrutura e teoría científica." Entre los hispanoamericanos, cabe mencionar las contribuciones de los argentinos Ismael Quiles, S. J., "Ser, in-sistencia e historia"; Octavio Nicolás Derisi, "Verdad y libertad"; y Rafael Virasoro, "Libertad y valor"; de los peruanos Luis Felipe Alarco, "Hombre y mundo"; Francisco Miró Quesada, "Sentido ontológico del conocimiento físico"; y Alberto Wagner de Reyna, "La palabra como analogía"; del cubano Humberto Piñera Llera, "Nicolás Hartmann y su crítica del formalismo ético de Kant"; del chileno Jorge Millas, "El problema de la forma en la proposición jurídica"; del uruguayo Juan Llambías de Azevedo, "Platón y el significado del Politikos"; y del mexicano Eduardo García Maynez, "Estructura relacional de la regulación jurídica." En la sección "Filosofía de América" se incluyen, entre otros, un estudio sobre "La filosofía latinoamericana como exponente de una cultura autónoma" de Carlos Astrada, otro sobre "La filosofía de Alejandro Korn" de Eugenio Pucciarelli.

4759. Costa, João Cruz. Um aspecto da filosofia na América (Kriterion, 9:37-38, julho-dez. 1956, p. 289-296).

Señala que uno de los rasgos característicos que ha tenido la filosofía, tanto en los Estados Unidos como en América Latina, es su orientación pragmática.

4760. Derisi, Octavio Nicolás. Filosofía

y vida. B. A., Sapientia (Col. Homo viator), 1955. 62 p.

Colección de cuatro ensayos que tratan de las relaciones y de la unidad que existen, o deben existir, entre filosofía y vida.

4761. ————. Tratado de existencialismo y tomismo. B. A., Emecé, 1956. 501 p.

En la primera parte, se exponen las ideas de Heidegger, Sartre, Jaspers y Marcel. La nota común, esencial a todos, es que parten de una fenomenología irracionalista. La segunda parte está dedicada a hacer una valoración del existencialismo. Como contribución positiva, señala el autor el redescubrimiento del individuo de la finitud y de la contingencia. Como aspecto negativo, la afirmación de una existencia sin esencia. Critica este aspecto dsede la posición tomista tradicional. La tercera parte de la obra busca una solución positiva a los problemas planteados por el existencialismo. El verdadero humanismo tiene que ser de inspiración cristiana: apuntar a la suprema perfección de Dios.

4762. Descartes, René. Discurso del método. Ed. bilingüe; traducción, estudio preliminar y notas de Risieri Frondizi. Río Piedras, Puerto Rico, Universidad de Puerto Rico (Biblioteca de cultura básica), 1954. xc, 236 p., illus., ports., facsims.

El texto francés es reproducido de la edición de Adam-Tannevy. El estudio preliminar (que comprende 77 páginas), y las notas, convierten a esta edición en un instrumento utilísimo y necesario para el estudio y la enseñanza de Descartes en las universidades de Hispanoamérica.

4763. Ferrater Mora, José. Cuatro visiones de la historia universal. B. A., Sudamericana (Ensayos breves), 1955. 155 p.

Presenta cuatro visiones fundamentales de la historia: la visión cristiana, en San Agustín; la visión renacentista, en Vico; la visión racionalista en Voltaire; la visión absoluta en Hegel. En el fondo, existe una unidad de todas ellas: son formas de consolación por la historia. La primera edición de esta obra es de 1945.

4764. García Bacca, Juan David. Antología del pensamiento filosófico venezolano (siglos XVII-XVIII). Introducciones sistemáticas y prólogos históricos, selección de textos y traducción del latín al castellano. Caracas, Dirección de Cultura y Bellas Artes (Biblioteca venezolana de cultura; col. Andrés Bello), 1954. 522 p.

Comprende las "Disputaciones metafísicas" de Alfonso Briceño (1590-1668); los "Tratados filosóficos" de Agustín de Quevedo y Villegas (h. 1660); las "Disputaciones filosóficas" de Tomás Valero (h. 1755); y diversos textos de Juan Antonio de Navarrete (h. 1780) y Salvador José y Mañer (1676-1751). Todos ellos estuvieron o enseñaron en Venezuela.

4765. ———— (ed.). Fragmentos filosóficos de los presocráticos. Caracas, Universidad Central de Venezuela, Instituto

de Filosofía (Filosofía, 1), 1956? 359 p.
Obra para uso de los estudiantes del bachillerato y del primer año de la universidad. Contiene los textos principales, en castellano, con notas aclaratorias al final de cada sección.

4766. Gómez Robledo, Antonio. Filosofía y lenguaje. México, Imp. Universitaria, 1956. 116 p.
Discurso de recepción en la Academia Mexicana (de la lengua) pronunciado el 14 de deciembre de 1955. Plantea el problema del lenguaje filosófico que, a juicio del autor, debe ser rigurosamente conceptual.

4767. León Portilla, Miguel. La filosofía nahuatl. México, Instituto Indigenista Interamericano, 1956. 344 p.
Intenta reconstruir la "Weltanschauung" de los pueblos nahuas, en el período inmediatamente anterior a la Conquista, utilizando fuentes literarias y testimonios de cronistas, especialmente de Sahagún.

4768. Lima, Alceu Amoroso. O existencialismo e outros mitos de nosso tempo. Rio, Agir (Obras completas de Alceu Amoroso Lima; Problemas sociais, 18), 1956. 329 p.
Se reunen en este volumen dos obras publicadas con anterioridad: *Mitos de nosso tempo* publicado en 1943 (ver *HLAS, no. 10, 1944,* párrafo 4555), y *O existencialismo,* de 1951 (ver *HLAS, no. 17, 1951,* item 2910). Aunque no hay cambios en el texto, el autor ha agregado numerosas notas aclaratorias y rectificatorias.

4769. Mahieu, Jaime María de. La naturaleza del hombre. B. A., Ediciones Arayú, 1955. 176 p.
Ensayo de psicología antropológica.

4770. Massera, José Pedro. Estudios filosóficos. Prólogo de Arturo Ardao. Montevideo, Imp. Uruguaya (Biblioteca Artigas; Col. de clásicos uruguayos, 12), 1954. 276 p.
Este volumen reune, por primera vez, los escritos filosóficos del pensador uruguayo José P. Massera (1866-1942). Arturo Ardao, en el prólogo estudia la personalidad y la obra del autor.

4771. Massuh, Víctor. El diálogo de las culturas. Tucumán, Argentina, Universidad Nacional de Tucumán, Instituto de Filosofía (Cuadernos de filosofía, 9), 1956. 84 p.
Estudio comparativo de las culturas de oriente y occidente, desde el punto de vista de la filosofía de la historia. El último capítulo considera el problema de América como cultura naciente con rasgos distintivos propios y posibilidades creadoras para el futuro. El genio de América—especialmente el de la América Hispánica—puede ser, quizás, el de la comunidad y unión de las culturas opuestas.

4772. Piñera Llera, Humberto. La enseñanza de la filosofía en Cuba. Una encuesta internacional organizada por la UNESCO. Habana, Comisión Nacional Cubana de la UNESCO (Cuadernos de divulgación cultural, 12), 1954. 38 p.
Este informe se publicó anteriormente en inglés (véase *HLAS no. 19, 1953,* párrafo 5713).

4773. ————. Sobre la posibilidad real de la filosofía (Diánoia, 1:1, 1955, p. 292-311).
Apoyándose en textos de Husserl y Heidegger, llega a la conclusión de que la realidad de la filosofía es y deberá ser siempre una pura posibilidad.

4774. Romero, Francisco. Ubicación del hombre. Introducción a la antropología filosófica. B. A., Columba (Col. Esquemas, 15), 1954. 71 p., illus.
Breve panorama de las principales direcciones de la antropología filosófica contemporánea, escrito con propósitos de vulgarización. Incluye una bibliografía sobre el tema.

4775. Sociedad Cubana de Filosofía. Idea de la historia de la filosofía. Sociedad Cubana de Filosofía (Instituto de Filosofía) con la colaboración de la Comisión Nacional Cubana de la UNESCO. Habana, Hércules, 1954. 1 v. (unpaged).
Reune la serie de conferencias que, sobre la "Idea de la historia de la filosofía, de su eficacia didáctica y de su importancia actual," se pronunciaron en el ciclo organizado por la Sociedad Cubana de Filosofía, durante el año académico 1953-1954.

4776. Torchia Estrada, Juan Carlos. La filosofía del siglo XX. 1. ed. B. A., Atlántida (Col. Oro de cultura general, 153), 1955. 346 p., illus.
Panorama de la filosofía contemporánea, elaborado con criterio amplio y objetivo, aunque se da especial preferencia a las corrientes alemanas y francesas. El último capítulo está dedicado a la filosofía hispanoamericana. El libro incluye retratos de los pensadores más notables y un apéndice con indicaciones bibliográficas.

4777. Virasoro, Rafael. Ensayos sobre el hombre y sus problemas. Santa Fe, Argentina, Castellví (El Litoral), 1955. 131 p.
Colección de ensayos aparecidos con anterioridad en publicaciones periódicas.

ESTUDIOS CRÍTICOS

Filosofía Latinoamericana

4778. Ardao, Arturo. La filosofía en el Uruguay en el siglo XX. México, Fondo de Cultura Económica (Col. Tierra firme; Historia de las ideas en América, 1), 1956. 193 p.
Estudio de caracter predominantemente informativo sobre las figuras y tendencias principales

de la filosofía uruguaya en el presente siglo. Llega hasta las promociones más recientes.

4779. ———. Tendencias filosofícas en el Uruguay en el siglo XX (Cursos Conf, año 25, 48:272, marzo 1956, p. 27-38).
Catálogo razonado de las figuras que, dentro y fuera de los círculos puramente académicos, han hecho en el Uruguay contribuciones apreciables en el campo de la filosofía. Señala tres direcciones dominantes hasta 1930: una corriente empirista, que también puede ser denominada "filosofía de la experiencia," y en la que coloca a Rodó y a Vaz Ferreira; una corriente materialista, a la que pertenecen figuras tan dispares como Pedro Figari y Emilio Frugoni; y una corriente espiritualista como Fernando Beltsamo y Emilio Oribe. Desde 1930, se inician nuevas tendencias, consonantes con el desarrollo de la filosofía en los otros países de lengua española.

4780. Bazán, Armando. Vida y obra del maestro Enrique Molina. Santiago, Nascimento, 1954. 160 p.
Estudio sobre la personalidad y las ideas del conocido pensador y filósofo chileno.

4781. Cordero, Armando. Estudios para la historia de la filosofía en Santo Domingo. Ciudad Trujillo, Imp. Arte y Cine, 1956. 195 p.
Panorama de las corrientas filosóficas en Santo Domingo desde el siglo XVI hasta nuestros días.

4782. Costa, João Cruz. O positivismo no Brasil (R Br, 5, maio-junho 1956, p. 12-21).

4783. Gaos, José. Filosofía mexicana de nuestros días. México, Imp. Universitaria (Col. Cultura mexicana, 10), 1954. 357 p.
Recoge estudios, conferencias y artículos aparecidos con anterioridad en diferentes publicaciones periódicas. De los quince trabajos incluídos, cuatro están dedicados a estudiar a Antonio Caso. De particular interés son los estudios sobre "Los 'transterrados' españoles de la filosofía en México" y sobre "Lo mexicano en filosofía" con que se cierra el volumen.

4784. García Bacca, Juan David. La filosofía en Venezuela desde el siglo XVII al XIX. Caracas, Universidad Central de Venezuela (Historia de la cultura en Venezuela, 1; Filosofía, 3), 1955, p. 69-84.
Notas sobre algunas de las tendencias dominantes en Venezuela en los siglos XVII y XVIII.

4785. García Tudurí, Mercedes. Ideas pedagógicas de San Agustín (Noverim, 1:1, 1954, p. 55-64).

4786. García Tudurí, Rosaura. La influencia de Descartes en Varela (R Cub Fil, 3:11, enero-abril 1955, p. 28-35).
Sobre la influencia de Descartes en la obra del pensador cubano Félix Varela (1788-1853).

4787. Hernández Luna, Juan. La filosofía contemporánea en México (Cursos Conf, año 25, 48:272, marzo 1956, p. 3-26).
Breve panorama informativo de las principales tendencias filosóficas en México desde principios del siglo. Faltan, sin embargo, algunos nombres significativos, especialmente los de las promociones más recientes. Se publicó originalmente en Filosofía y letras, México, 27, julio-sept. 1947, p. 89-113.

4788. Menezes, Djacir. A filosofia no Brasil no século XX (R Br Fil, 6:2(22), abril-junho 1956, p. 192-212).

4789. Navarro, Bernabé. La filosofía en el México de la colonia (Cuadrante, 3:1-2, verano-otoño 1954, p. 27-44).
Señala las etapas principales del pensamiento y de la enseñanza filosófica en México desde principios del siglo XVI hasta fines del XVIII.

4790. Peñalver Simó, Patricio. Presente y futuro de la filosofía hispanoamericana (Estud Am, 10:50-51, nov.-dic. 1955, p. 575-589).
Después de considerar las diferentes tendencias que hoy dominan en el campo de la filosofía hispanoamericana, concluye que ésta debe orientarse y buscar su unidad en la filosofía cristiana tradicional. El artículo contiene muchas imprecisiones e inexactitudes en la caracterización de tendencias y autores.

4791. Pescador, Augusto. La filosofía en Bolivia en el siglo XX (Cursos Conf, año 25, 48:272, marzo 1956, p. 61-80).
Aunque el trabajo está dedicado principalmente a estudiar autores y tendencias contemporáneas, se ocupa en la primera parte de exponer las ideas de Mamerto Oyola Cuéllar (1838-1902), autor de una obra titulada La razón universal.

4792. Piérola, Raúl Alberto. Alejandro Korn and contemporary philosophy (Phil Phen Re, 14:3, Mar. 1954, p .354-364).

4793. Pucciarelli, Eugenio. La filosofía de Alejandro Korn (in Congresso Internacional de Filosofia. Anais. São Paulo, 1956. V. 3, p. 1137-1145).
Expone las ideas centrales de la concepción filosófica de Korn y, especialmente, su posición frente a la metafísica.

4794. Rodríguez-Alcalá, Hugo. Francisco Romero: vida y obra; bibliografía; antología. N. Y., Columbia University, Hispanic Institute, 1954. 58 p.
Estudio muy documentado de la personalidad y la obra del filósofo argentino.

4795. ———. El socratismo de Alejandro Korn (Re Stud, Dec. 1954, p. 228-245).
Sobre el espíritu socrático del filósofo argentino. Contiene interesantes datos y referencias biográficas.

4796. **Romanell, Patrick.** La formación de la mentalidad mexicana; panorama actual de la filosofía en México, 1910-1950. Presentación de José Gaos. México, Colegio de México, 1954. 238 p.

Traducción de Edmundo O'Gorman, de *Making of the Mexican mind*, publicado en 1952 (véase *HLAS, no. 18, 1952*, párrafo 3101).

4797. **Romero, Francisco.** Alejandro Korn, filósofo de la libertad. B. A., Reconstruir (Col. Radar, 9), 1956. 57 p.

Recoge páginas escritas en distintas ocasiones sobre la personalidad moral y filosófica de Korn. En conjunto, ofrece una fiel semblanza del gran pensador argentino.

4798. **Salazar Bondy, Augusto.** La filosofía en el Perú, panorama histórico. Philosophy in Peru, a historical study. Washington, Unión Panamericana (Pensamiento de América), 1954. 98 p.

Estudio histórico de las ideas e influencias filosóficas en el Perú. En sucesivos capítulos considera la Escolástica, la Ilustración, el Romanticismo y el Eclecticismo, el Positivismo, la vocación espiritualista y la filosofía actual. El volumen contiene, además del original castellano, una tradución inglesa hecha por la profesora Elizabeth Flower de la Universidad de Filadelfia. Incluye una bibliografía selecta.

4799. ————. La filosofía peruana contemporánea (Cursos Conf, año 25, 48:272, marzo 1956, p. 81-95).

Fragmento de un estudio más amplio titulado *La filosofía en el Perú; panorama histórico* (véase párrafo 4798).

4800. **Vidal Muñoz, Santiago.** Apuntes sobre le filosofía en Chile (Cursos Conf, año 25, 48:272, marzo 1956, p. 39-60).

Útil esquema del desarrollo de las influencias y doctrinas filosóficas en Chile. Se inicia con una rápida ojeada del pasado filosófico desde la época colonial, pero da especial preferencia a las figuras contemporáneas, a partir de Enrique Molina (n. 1871).

4801. **Vitier, Medardo.** Cincuenta años de estudio de la filosofía en Cuba (Cursos Conf, año 25, 48:272, marzo 1956, p. 120-132).

Artículo informativo acerca de la producción y actividades filosóficas en Cuba desde principios del siglo.

4802. **Wagner de Reyna, Alberto.** En torno a la filosofía en Hispanoamérica (Finis Terrae, 1:3, 3. trimestre 1954, p. 3-14).

Plantea el problema de las posibilidades, características y porvenir de la filosofía hispanoamericana.

4803. ————. La filosofía en el Perú contemporáneo (R Ed, Santiago, 14:63, nov. 1954, p. 17-24).

Breve estudio de las tendencias y pensadores más importantes del Perú en los últimos cincuenta años.

4804. **Zea, Leopoldo.** La filosofía en México. México, Ediciones Libro-Mex (Biblioteca mínima mexicana, 17, 18), 1955. 2 v. 129, 137-261 p.

Colección de artículos y ensayos. Después de trazar un esquema general de la historia de la filosofía en México, estudia las figuras y tendencias principales del siglo XX.

FILOSOFÍA ANTIGUA Y MEDIEVAL

4805. **Acker, Leonardo van.** Influência e metamorfoses da "Cidade de Deus" de Aurélio Agostinho (R Br Fil, 4:4(16), out.-dez. 1954, p. 501-519).

4806. **Acoglia, Rodolfo M., and Francisco E. Maffei.** Ciencia y metafísica en Aristóteles (Humanidades, La Plata, 34, Sección Filosofía, 1954, p. 31-48).

4807. **Caturelli, Alberto.** La doctrina agustiniana sobre el Maestro y su desarrollo en Santo Tomás de Aquino. Córdoba, Argentina, Universidad Nacional de Córdoba, Instituto de Metafísica, 1954. 17 p.

La primera parte estudia la doctrina del "Maestro interior" en San Agustín. La segunda, el desarrollo de la doctrina en Santo Tomás.

4808. **Correia, Alexandre.** O natural e o sobrenatural en S. Agostinho (R Br Fil, 4:4(16), out.-dez. 1954, p. 484-490).

4809. **Derisi, Octavio N.** Determinación de la influencia neoplatónica en la formación del pensamiento de San Agustín (Sapientia, 10:34, oct.-dic. 1954, p. 272-287).

4810. **Frankl, Víctor.** El descubrimiento de la nada por la filosofía medieval y la ontología existencial de Santo Tomás (Bolívar, Bogotá, 27, marzo 1954, p. 181-218).

Persigue el concepto de la "nada" en la filosofía de San Agustín y en el agustinismo medieval, donde dicho concepto alcanza su máxima expresión. En cambio, con Santo Tomás se inicia, según el autor, la declinación y progresiva eliminación de la idea de la "nada" del horizonte filosófico y cultural de Occidente.

4811. **García Díaz, Adolfo.** La metafísica de Empédocles (Diánoia, 2:2, 1956, p. 167-180).

4812. ————. La noción del no ente en la filosofía de Parménides (Diánoia, 1:1, 1955, p. 104-134).

4813. García Tudurí, Rosaura. La estética en la filosofía de San Agustín (Noverim, 1:1, 1954, p. 11-21).

4814. Gómez Robledo, Antonio. La ciencia como virtud intelectual (Diánoia, 2:2, 1956, p. 55-75).
Sobre el concepto de ciencia en la filosofía aristotélica.

4815. ————. Ensayo sobre las virtudes intelectuales (Diánoia, 1:1, 1955, p. 24-45).
Sobre la teoría de las virtudes intelectuales en Aristóteles.

4816. ————. La ética de San Agustín (Diánoia, 1:1, 1955, p. 236-260).

4817. ————. Filosofía aristotélica del arte (Fil Let, México, 57-59, enero-dic. 1955, p. 13-42).

4818. Mondolfo, Rodolfo. La conciencia moral en Sócrates, Platón y Aristóteles (Humanidades, La Plata, 34, Sección Filosofía, 1954, p. 7-29).

4819. Pita, Enrique B. La causalidad poética en la filosofía de Santo Tomás de Aquino (Cien Fe, 10:39, julio-sept. 1954, p. 7-13).

FILOSOFÍA MODERNA

4820. Batllori, Miguel. Bello y Balmes (R Nac Cult, 16:105, julio-agosto 1954, p. 96-101).
Comenta dos artículos críticos de Bello sobre Balmes.

4821. Czerna, Renato Cirell. A experiência romântica en Kierkegaard e Hegel (R Br Fil, 6:1(21), jan.-março 1956, p. 38-58).

4822. ————. Sôbre o conceito de Logos em Schelling e Rosmini (R Br Fil, 5:4 (20), out.-dez. 1955, p. 579-592).

4823. Mondolfo, Rodolfo. Figuras e ideas de la filosofía del Renacimiento. B. A., Losada (Biblioteca filosófica), 1954. 284 p.
Estudia a Leonardo, Giordano Bruno, Galileo, Campanella. En la segunda parte señala algunas orientaciones del pensamiento renacentista.

4824. Piñera Llera, Humberto. El escepticismo en el Renacimiento (R Br Fil, 4:3(15), julho-set. 1954, p. 349-358).

4825. Queiroz, Amaro Xisto de. A posição da história no criticismo kantiano (Kriterion, 27-28, jan.-junho 1954, p. 32-37).

4826. Reale, Miguel. Direito abstrato e dialética da positividade na doutrina de Hegel (R Br Fil, 4:4(16), out.-dez. 1954, p. 491-500).

4827. ————. Kierkegaard, o seu e o nosso tempo (R Br Fil, 6:2(22), abril-junho 1956, p. 181-191).

4828. Silva, Vicente Ferreira da. Kierkegaard e o problema da subjetividade (R Br Fil, 6:1(21), jan.-março 1956, p. 70-76).

4829. Valentie, María Eugenia. Una metafísica del hombre. Ensayo sobre la filosofía de Leibniz. Tucumán, Argentina, Universidad Nacional de Tucumán, Instituto de Filosofía (Cuadernos de filosofía, 8), 1956. 88 p.
Después de estudiar el pensamiento de Leibniz en función de su época y de las tradiciones culturales de occidente, expone las líneas principales de su metafísica. Las ideas fundamentales de esa metafísica son: unidad, armonía e individualidad. Incluye la bibliografía consultada.

4830. Velloso, Arthur Versiani. A propósito do sesquicentenário de Kant (Kriterion, 27-28, jan.-junho 1954, p. 18-24).

4831. Vianna, Sylvio Barata. Dificuldades relativas ao problema da "coisa em si" na crítica kantiana da razão pura (Kriterion, 27-28, jan.-junho 1954, p. 25-31).

4832. Vita, Luís Washington. Vida, obra e mensagem de Kierkegaard (R Br Fil, 6:1(21), jan.-março 1956, p. 3-21).

FILOSOFÍA CONTEMPORÁNEA

4833. Castro Turbiano, Máximo. Ortega y Gasset y el tema de la razón (R Cub Fil, 4:13, enero-junio 1956, p. 72-85).

4834. Czerna, Renato. A filosofia de Benedetto Croce (A Pernam Fil, 2:2, 1954, p. 11-33).

4835. Derisi, Octavio Nicolás. Las notas fundamentales del existencialismo (R Fil, Eva Perón, 6, 1953, p. 13 ff.).

4836. Ferrater Mora, José. De la filosofía a la "filosofía" (Sur, 241, julio-agosto 1956, p. 21-24).
Sobre el sentido de la tarea filosófica en Ortega y Gasset.

4837. ————. Ortega y la idea de la sociedad (Humanitas, 3:7, 1956, p. 13-20).

4838. García Astrada, Arturo. Aspectos

metafísicos en el pensamiento de Unamuno (Humanitas, 3:7, 1956, p. 37-47).

4839. García Tudurí, Mercedes. Valor de la circunstancia en la filosofía de Ortega y Gasset (R Cub Fil, 4:13, enero-junio 1956, p. 7-14).

4840. García Tudurí, Rosaura. Ideas estéticas de Ortega y Gasset (R Cub Fil, 4:13, enero-junio 1956, p. 26-33).

4841. Granell, Manuel. Ortega y Gasset, el filósofo (Cult U, 51, sept.-oct 1955, p. 5-16).

4842. Herrán, Carlos M. Sobre algunos problemas religiosos en el existencialismo (Humanidades, La Plata, 34, Sección Filosofía, 1954, p. 77-97).
Analiza las implicaciones religiosas del pensamiento de Kierkegaard, Chestov, Karl Barth, Jaspers y Réné Le Senne.

4843. Lizaso, Félix. José Ortega y Gasset (R Cub Fil, 4:13, enero-junio 1956, p. 45-51).

4844. Mañach, Jorge. Imagen de Ortega y Gasset (R Cub Fil, 4:13, enero-junio 1956, p. 104-125).
Ofrece una imagen coherente de la personalidad y del pensamiento del filósofo español.

4845. Mayz Vallenilla, Ernesto. Fenomenología del conocimiento. El problema de la constitución del objeto en la filosofía de Husserl. Caracas, Universidad Central de Venezuela, Instituto de Filosofía (Col. de tesis doctorales, 1), 1956. 372 p.
Tesis doctoral. Investiga la teoría del conocimiento de Husserl centrándola en el problema de la "constitución del objeto." El autor sigue de cerca, y paso a paso, los textos de Husserl, especialmente el libro primero de las *Ideen*, único que tuvo oportunidad de consultar el autor, por estar inéditos los otros dos al momento de redactar su trabajo. El capítulo 1 estudia el método fenomenológico y los principios que lo hacen posible; el capítulo 2 trata de los elementos constituyentes del objeto intencional, y el capítulo 3 de la constitución del objeto "real."

4846. Paita, Jorge A. Dos aspectos en la filosofía de Ortega y Gasset (Sur, 241, julio-agosto 1956, p. 49-57).

4847. Piñera Llera, Humberto. Ortega y la idea de la vida (R Cub Fil, 4:13, enero-junio 1956, p. 15-25).

4848. Quiles, Ismael. Las ideas antirreligiosas de Marx (Estudios, B. A., 88:467, abril 1955, p. 91-98).

4849. Romero, Francisco. Las corrientes filosóficas en el siglo XX (Cuadernos, 19, julio-agosto 1956, p. 11-17).
Sobre las tendencias filosóficas dominantes en los países hispanoamericanos en el presente siglo.

4849a. ————. Ortega y el ausentismo filosófico español (Sur, 241, julio-agosto 1956, p. 24-29).
Señala la falta de una tradición filosófica organizada en España. El destierro de Ortega y Gasset en los últimos veinte años de su vida tiene un relieve simbólico y ejemplifica el triste destino de la filosofía española desde León Hebreo, Vives y Francisco Sánchez.

4850. Sepich, Juan R. La filosofía de ser y tiempo de M. Heidegger. B. A., Editorial Nuestro Tiempo, 1954. 527 p.
Exposición del pensamiento de Heidegger teniendo como base la primera parte de *Sein und Zeit* y *Vom Wesen der Wahrheit*.

4851. Torres Llosa, Enrique. Consideraciones sobre la filosofía de Gabriel Marcel (B Inst Riva-Agüero, 2, 1953-1955, p. 47-68).

4852. Vázquez, Juan Adolfo. Ortega como circunstancia (Sur, 241, julio-agosto 1956, p. 29-32).
Sobre la influencia de Ortega y Gasset en los países hispánicos.

4853. Velloso, Arthur Versiani. O positivismo lógico do grupo de Viena (Kriterion, 9:37-38, julho-dez. 1956, p. 297-327).

4854. Zucchi, Hernán. Teoría y praxis en Ortega y Gasset (Notas Estud Fil, 5:17, enero-marzo 1954, p. 11-18).

HISTORIA DE LAS IDEAS

4855. Ardao, Arturo. Orígenes de la influencia de Renan en el Uruguay. Montevideo, Instituto Nacional de Investigaciones y Archivos Literarios (Serie 2, Estudios y testimonios, 1), 1955. 33 p., ports., facsims.
Estudio bien documentado sobre la influencia de Renán sobre pensadores y escritores uruguayos, como Rodó y Vaz Ferreira, y en el desarrollo del movimiento anticlerical. El introductor de Renán en el Uruguay parece haber sido el periodista y escritor francés Adolfo Vaillant que residió en aquel país desde 1840 hasta su muerte en 1881.

4856. Beltrán Guerrero, Luis. Introducción al positivismo venezolano. Caracas, 1956. 31 p.
"Separata de la Revista Nacional de Cultura, nos. 112-113, sept.-dic. 1955." Apuntes sobre la influencia y desarrollo de las ideas positivistas en Venezuela. Incluye bibliografía.

4857. Cárdenas, Horacio. Resonancias de

la filosofía europea en Venezuela. Caracas, Universidad Central de Venezuela, Instituto de Filosofía, 1957? 24 p.
Rápido panorama de las influencias filosóficas europeas en Venezuela desde la época colonial hasta fines del siglo XIX.

4858. Caturelli, Alberto. El pensamiento de Mamerto Esquiú, O. F. M. Con un apéndice sobre el tomismo en Córdoba. Córdoba, Argentina, Universidad de Córdoba, Instituto de Metafísica, 1954. 246 p.
Estudio sobre la vida y obra del influyente predicador argentino Fr. Mamerto Esquiú (1826-1883). En apéndice, una breve historia de la filosofía y la enseñanza tomista en la Universidad de Córdoba. Incluye bibliografía sobre Esquiú.

4859. Costa, João Cruz. Contribuição à história das idéias no Brasil, o desenvolvimento da filosofia no Brasil e a evolução histórica nacional. Rio, Olympio (Col. Documentos brasileiros, 86), 1956. 484 p.
Reedición de una obra publicada en 1950 (Véase *HLAS, no. 16, 1953*, parágrafo 3271). Contiene un capítulo nuevo sobre las ideas en el siglo XX. El autor ha introducido, además, algunas modificaciones en el texto de la primera edición.

4859a. ————. O positivismo na República. Notas sôbre a história do positivismo no Brasil (R Hist, São Paulo, 7:15, julho-set. 1953, p. 97-131).
Analiza la actitud de los positivistas, y especialmente de Teixeira Mendes, respecto de diferentes problemas políticos, jurídicos y sociales suscitados por el advenimiento del régimen republicano.

4860. Entralgo, Elías. Los conceptos libertadores de Enrique José Varona (U Habana, 19:112-114, enero-junio 1954, p. 104-167).
Sobre el pensamiento político y social de Varona y su reflejo en la historia cubana.

4861. Francovich, Guillermo. El pensamiento boliviano en el siglo XX. México, Fondo de Cultura Económica (Col. Tierra firme; Historia de las ideas en América, 2), 1956. 170 p.
La primera parte estudia el desarrollo y apogeo del liberalismo, el positivismo y el modernismo a principios del siglo. La segunda parte considera la crisis de estos movimientos, a través de la obra de autores tan representativos como Arguedas y Tamayo. La parte tercera presenta las tendencias nacionalistas, socialistas e indigenistas. En la última sección dedica sendos capítulos a los estudios filosóficos y de historia de las ideas en Bolivia.

4862. García Bacca, Juan David. Datos para la historia de las ideas filosóficas en Venezuela durante los siglos XVII y

XVIII (R Nac Cult, 14:100, sept.-oct. 1953, p. 124-127).
Breve estudio sobre el teólogo y filósofo Fray Alfonso Briceño (1590-1668). Nacido en Chile, Briceño enseñó en la Universidad de San Marcos y fue posteriormente obispo de Santiago de León en Venezuela. Murió en Caracas. Es una de las figuras más notables del escotismo del siglo XVII.

4863. Grases, Pedro. La edición de Caracas del *Arte de escribir* de Condillac (R Nac Cult, 17:106-107, sept.-dic. 1954, p. 57-61).
Presenta nueva documentación que prueba que Andrés Bello fue el autor de la traducción, aunque en el texto definitivo intervinieron otras manos.

4864. Jaramillo Uribe, Jaime. Tradición y problemas de la filosofía en Colombia (Ideas Val, año 3, 3:9-10, marzo-mayo 1954, p. 58-82).
Útil para el conocimiento de las ideas filosóficas de algunas figuras colombianas del siglo XIX, como José María Samper y Miguel Antonio Caro. Este artículo ha sido reproducido en *Cursos y conferencias*, B. A., año 25, 48:272, marzo 1956, p. 96-119.

4865. López, Matilde Elena. Masferrer, alto pensador de Centroamérica; ensayo biográfico. Guatemala, Editorial del Ministerio de Educación Pública (Col. Contemporáneos, 42), 1954. 299 p., illus.
Estudia la vida y el pensamiento político y social de Alberto Masferrer (1868-1932). Incluye un ideario y una breve antología.

4866. Luzuriaga, Lorenzo. Origen de las ideas educativas de Bolívar y Simón Rodríguez. Caracas, Universidad Central de Venezuela (Historia de la cultura en Venezuela, 1; Filosofía, 3), 1955, p. 205-225.
Señala tres influencias principales: la filosofía de la Ilustración, Rousseau y las ideas político-educativas de la Revolución Francesa.

4867. Mijares, Augusto. Ideología de la Revolución Emancipadora. Caracas, Universidad Central de Venezuela (Historia de la cultura en Venezuela, 1; Filosofía, 3), 1955, p. 111-124.
Ensayo sobre las ideas políticas y sociales de Simón Rodríguez y de Bolívar.

4868. Monti, Daniel P. La religión de Francisco Ramos Mejía (Nueva Dem, 36:3, julio 1956, p. 48-56).
Sobre el curioso movimiento religioso, de corte protestante, iniciado por Francisco Ramos Mejía (1773-1828) en la Argentina en la primera mitad del siglo XIX.

4869. Pastor Benítez, Justo. Diagrama de las ideas en el Paraguay (R Dom Fil, 2, 1956, p. 58-62).

Esquema de las ideas e influencias filosóficas en el Paraguay desde fines del siglo XIX.

4870. Popescu, Oreste. El pensamiento social y económico de Esteban Echeverría. B. A., Editorial Americana (Col. Historia y tradición argentinas), 1954. 259 p.

En el primer capítulo estudia, en conjunto, la vida y la obra social-económica de Echeverría. Los restantes capítulos están dedicados al análisis de la filosofía política y social, de la doctrina económica, y de la proyección de sus ideas. Incluye amplia bibliografía.

4870a. Sánchez, Juan Francisco. El pensamiento filosófico en Santo Domingo (siglo XVIII). Antonio Sánchez Valverde. Ciudad Trujillo, Arte y Cine, 1955. 118 p.

Reproduce y analiza la "Carta de Valverde al Conde de San Xavier," sobre la filosofía aristotélica, fechada en 1770, cuyo texto fue publicado originariamente en el Archivo Miranda. El autor identifica a Valverde, a quien hasta ahora se había considerado venezolano, con el dominicano Antonio Sánchez Valverde (1729-1790). La "Carta" es un documento interesante para el estudio de las ideas de la Ilustración en Hispanoamérica.

4870b. Soler, Ricaurte. Pensamiento panameño y concepción de la nacionalidad durante el siglo XIX. (Para la historia de las ideas en el Istmo). Prólogo de Rodrigo Miro. Panamá, Imp. Nacional, 1954. 137 p.

Estudia las ideas filosóficas y políticas de Justo Arosemena (1817-1898) y su influencia en la formación de la conciencia nacional del Istmo. Contiene información útil para la historia de las ideas en Panamá y Colombia.

4870c. Tosta, Virgilio. Ideario educativo de don Simón Rodríguez (Cult U, 41, enero-feb. 1954, p. 5-18).

Notas sobre las ideas pedagógicas del educador venezolano, maestro de Simón Bolívar.

4870d. Troncoso Sánchez, Pedro. Espiritualidad y cultura del pueblo dominicano (R Dom Fil, 1, enero-junio 1956, p. 5-29).

Breve historia intelectual de Santo Domingo desde los tiempos coloniales al presente.

4870e. Zea, Leopoldo. Catolicismo y modernismo en la conciencia iberoamericana (Diánoia, 2:2, 1956, p. 76-108).

Ensayo sobre el conflicto entre la concepción tradicional derivada de España y el espíritu moderno que llevó a la emancipación de las naciones hispanoamericanas.

4870f. ———. El puritanismo en la conciencia norteamericana (Diánoia, 1:1, 1955, p. 46-68).

Estudia la influencia de la concepción puritana en la formación de la conciencia del pueblo norteamericano. En el último parágrafo discute el problema de las relaciones entre la América sajona y la hispánica.

GNOSEOLOGÍA Y METAFÍSICA

4871. Cannabrava, Euryalo. Lógica modal e dedução (R Br Fil, 5:1(17), jan.-março 1955, p. 60-68).

4871a. Estrada, José María de. Filosofía del tiempo. B. A., ENE (Col. Temas y valores), 1955. 78 p.

Ensayo sobre el problema del tiempo. Parte de la concepción agustiniana para mostrar las implicaciones de la cuestión en otros pensadores. El volumen incluye, además, un estudio sobre el principio de identidad.

4871b. Frankl, Víctor. El problema de las esencias históricas a la luz de la tradición tomista (Ideas Val, año 3, 3:9-10, marzo-mayo 1954, p. 30-57).

4872. García Bacca, Juan David. Sobre el conocimiento y sus clases: ensayo fenomenológico-matemático (Ideas Val, año 3, 3:9-10, marzo-mayo 1954, p. 7-29).

4872a. García Bárcena, Rafael. Redescubrimiento de Dios (U Habana, 20:124-129, enero-dic. 1956, p. 7-45).

Fragmento de un libro de próxima publicación que llevará el mismo título.

4872b. Gortari, Eli de. Introducción a la lógica dialéctica. México, Fondo de Cultura Económica (Publ. de Diánoia), 1956. 291 p.

Intento de desarrollar una lógica dialéctica, sistemática y rigurosa, que tenga en cuenta y, al mismo tiempo, aclare los problemas que plantea la investigación científica.

4873. Jasinowski, Bogumil. Naturaleza e historia (R Fil, 3:3, dic. 1956, p. 3-17).

Afirma el carácter complementario de la naturaleza y la historia. Son dos órdenes interdependientes y no antagónicos.

4873a. Quiles, Ismael. Clasificación y coordinación de las ciencias (Cien Fe, 10:37-38, enero-junio 1954, p. 11-30).

4873b. ———. Psicología, fenomenología y ontología (Cien Fe, 10:39, julio-sept. 1954, p. 87-96).

4874. Ramos, Samuel. Relación entre la filosofía y la ciencia. México, Universidad Nacional Autónoma de México (Seminario de problemas científicos y filosóficos, Cuaderno, 1), 1955. 8 p.

4874a. Schwartzmann, Félix. Sistema cerrado y leyes de la naturaleza (R Fil, 3:3, dic. 1956, p 28-40).

La existencia de sistemas cerrados en física no implica la existencia de límites cognoscitivos absolutos. Eso sería atribuir a las leyes y principios gnoseológicos un valor ontológico.

4874b. Vázquez, Juan Adolfo. Metafísica y cultura. B. A., Editorial Sudamericana, 1954. 138 p.

Colección de ensayos y artículos sobre diferentes temas y autores. De entre ellos, el más personal es el titulado "La historia de la filosofía y la metafísica," con que se inicia el volumen. El autor considera que la actitud imperante hoy en la historia de la filosofía permite entrever la superación del historicismo, o de las seudometafísicas históricas, al mostrar "la unidad fundamental del conocimiento metafísico en las diversas épocas de la historia occidental y su fundamental concordancia con las intuiciones metafísico-religiosas de los pensadores orientales."

ESTÉTICA Y FILOSOFÍA DEL ARTE

4875. Estiú, Emilio A. Arte y liberación (Humanidades, La Plata, 34, Sección Filosofía, 1954, p. 49-58).

Considera el arte como una forma de liberación. El hombre consigue en el arte lo que no puede lograr consigo mismo: "una *necesaria* liberación de lo que impide su plena libertad en la vida real."

4875a. Fatone, Vicente. Filosofía y poesía. B. A., Emecé (Cuadernos de ensayos, 18), 1954. 138 p.

Examina las relaciones entre la filosofía y la poesía. Intenta mostrar, a través del análisis de doctrinas y problemas, que esas relaciones son más íntimas y esenciales de lo que se supone. Filosofía y poesía cumplen, por lo menos, una misma función liberadora: la de enseñarnos a sospechar que este mundo no se limita a ser lo que es: que es otra cosa.

4875b. Guerrero, Luis Juan. Qué es la belleza. B. A., Columba (Col. Esquemas, 12), 1954. 76 p.

Breviario de estética escrito con propósitos de divulgación. Incluye bibliografía.

4875c. Oyarzún Peña, Luis. La experiencia estética como expresión y creación de formas (R Fil, 3:3, dic. 1956, p. 54-57).

4875d. Piñera Llera, Humberto. Algunas interpretaciones psicoanalíticas del arte (R Cub Fil, 3:12, mayo-dic. 1955, p. 5-12).

Resume las opiniones de Freud, Baudouin y Rauk acerca del arte como producto de una personalidad psicopática.

ÉTICA Y FILOSOFÍA JURÍDICA Y POLÍTICA

4876. García Máynez, Eduardo. Clasificación de los conceptos jurídicos (Diánoia, 2:2, 1956, p. 3-23).

4876a. ————. Lógica del juicio jurídico (Diánoia, 1:1, 1955, p. 3-23).

4876b. Herrera Figueroa, Miguel. Justicia y sentido. Prólogo de Werner Goldschmidt. Tucumán, Argentina, Universidad Nacional de Tucumán, Facultad de Derecho y Ciencias Sociales, 1955. 154 p.

Después de exponer el concepto de justicia en Platón, Aristóteles, San Agustín y Santo Tomás, considera el valor de la justicia en relación con los otros valores jurídicos y con la conducta jurídica.

4876c. Hübner Gallo, Jorge I. Manual de filosofía del derecho. Santiago, Editorial Jurídica de Chile (Manuales jurídicos, 54), 1954. 277 p.

Texto universitario. Resume las clases dictadas por el autor en la Universidad de Chile.

4877. Miró Quesada, Francisco. El normalismo y las ciencias normativas (Diánoia, 2:2, 1956, p. 270-281).

4877a. ————. Teoría de la deducción jurídica (Diánoia, 1:1, 1955, p. 261-291).

4877b. Recaséns Siches, Luis. El logos de "lo razonable" como base para la interpretación jurídica (Diánoia, 1:2, 1956, p. 24-54).

TRADUCCIONES

4878. Abbagnano, Nicola. Introducción al existencialismo. Traducción de José de Gaos. México, Fondo de Cultura Económica, 1955. 179 p.

4878a. Aristoteles. Ética nicomaquea. Traducción y prólogo de Antonio Gómez Robledo. México, Universidad Nacional Autónoma de México, 1954.

4878b. Augustine, Saint. De la vida feliz. Tr. de Ángel Herrera Bienes. B. A., Aguilar, 1955. 92 p.

Título del original latino: *De beata vita.*

4878c. Baumgarten, Alexander Gottlieb. Reflexiones filosóficas acerca de la poesía. Tr. de José A. Míguez. B. A., Aguilar, 1955. 88 p.

4879. Bobbio, Norberto. El existencialismo. Tr. de Lore Terracini. México, Fondo de Cultura Económica, 1954. 96 p. 2. edición.

4879a. Boethius, Ancius Manlius. La consolación de la filosofía. Tr. de Pablo Masa. B. A., Aguilar, 1955. 197 p.

4879b. Brunschvicg, León. Las edades de la inteligencia. Tr. de Amparo Albájar. B. A., Hachette, 1955. 138 p.

4879c. Cresson, André. A filosofia antiga.

Tr. de Beatriz Moura. São Paulo, Difusão Européia do Livro, 1954. 118 p.

4879d. ————. A filosofia francesa. Tr. de Pérola de Carvalho. São Paulo, Difusão Européia do Livro, 1955. 131 p.

4880. Descartes, René. Discurso del método. Tr. de Antonio Rodríguez Huéscar. B. A., Aguilar, 1954. 126 p.

4880a. Duns, Joannes, Scotus. Tratado del primer principio. Tr. de Alfonso Castaño Piñán. B. A., Aguilar, 1955. 11 p.

4880b. Eckart, Meister. El libro del consuelo divino. Tr. de Alfonso Castaño Piñán. B. A., Aguilar, 1955. 91 p.

4880c. Hartmann, Nicolai. La nueva ontología. Traducción e introducción de Emilio Estiú. B. A., Editorial Sudamericana, 1954. 259 p.

4880d. ————. Ontología. I. Fundamentos. Tr. de José Gaos. México, Fondo de Cultura Económica, 1955. 384 p.

4881. Hegel, Georg Wilhelm Friedrich. Lecciones sobre la historia de la filosofía. Tr. de Wenceslao Roces. México, Fondo de Cultura Económica, 1955. 3 v.

4882. Heidegger, Martin. Doctrina de la verdad según Platón y Carta sobre el humanismo. Santiago, Universidad de Chile, Instituto de Investigaciones Histórico-Culturales, Centro de Estudios Humanísticos y Filosóficos (Col. Tradición y tarea; Contemporáneos), 1954? 234 p.

4882a. ————. Introducción a la metafísica. Tr. de Emilio Estiú. B. A., Ed. Nova, 1956.

4882b. ————. Kant y el problema de la metafísica. México, Fondo de Cultura Económica, 1954. 210 p.
Traducción de Greb Ibscher Roth, revisada por Elsa Cecilia Frost.

4883. James, William. Pragmatismo. Tr. de Luis Rodríguez Aranda. B. A., Aguilar, 1954. 248 p.

4883a. Jaspers, Karl. La fe filosófica. Tr. de J. Rovira Armengol. B. A., Losada, 1954. 139 p.

4883b. Jolivet, Régis. Vocabulario de filosofía. Tr. de Leandro de Sesma. B. A., Desclée de Brouwer, 1954. 206 p.

4884. Lavelle, Louis. Las potencias del

yo. Tr. de Julia S. de Parpagnoli. B. A., Editorial Sudamericana, 1954. 304 p.

4884a. Leibniz, Gottfried Wilhelm. Discurso de metafísica. Tr. de Alfonso Castaño Piñán. B. A., Aguilar, 1955. 102 p.

4885. Marcel, Gabriel. Decadencia de la sabiduría. Tr. de Beatriz Guido. B. A., Emecé, 1955. 111 p.

4885a. ————. Posiciones y aproximaciones concretas al misterio ontológico. Tr. de Luis Villoro. México, Imp. Universitaria, 1955. 86 p.

4885b. ————. Prolegómenos para una metafísica de la esperanza. Tr. de Ely Zanetti y Vicente P. Quintero. B. A., Nova (Col. La vida del espíritu), 1954. 280 p.

4886. Mill, John Stuart. Sobre la libertad. Tr. de Josefa Sáinz Pulido. B. A., Aguilar, 1954. 205 p.

4886a. ————. El utilitarismo. Tr. de Ramón Castilla. B. A., Aguilar, 1955. 123 p.

4887. Ogden, Charles Key (and others). El significado del significado. Tr. de Eduardo Prieto. B. A., Paidos (Col. Temas del siglo XX), 1954.

4888. Plato. Alcibíades, o De la naturaleza del hombre. Tr. de José A. Míguez. B. A., Aguilar, 1955. 138 p.

4888a. ————. Diálogo: Fédon, Sofista, Político. Tr. de Jorge Paleikat y Cruz Costa. Pôrto Alegre, Globo, 1955. 2 v.

4889. Plotinus. Eneada primera. Tr. de José A. Míguez. B. A. Aguilar, 1955. 136 p.

4889a. Radbruch, Gustav. Introducción a la filosofía del derecho. México, Fondo de Cultura Económica (Breviarios, 42), 1955. 192 p.
1. ed., traducción de Wenceslao Roces.

4889b. Radhakrishnan, Sarvepalli. Religión y sociedad. Tr. de Josefa Sastre de Cabot. B. A., Editorial Sudamericana, 1955. 346 p.

4890. Russell, Bertrand. Delineamentos da filosofia. Tr. de Brenno Silveira. São Paulo, Ed. Nacional, 1954. 376 p.

4891. Santayana, George. Dominaciones y potestades. Tr. de Guido F. P. Parpagnoli. B. A., 1954. 685 p.

4891a. Schleiermacher, Friedrich Ernst Daniel. Monólogos. Tr. de Ramón Castilla. B. A., Aguilar, 1955. 110 p.

4892. Seneca, Lucius Annaeus. De la brevedad de la vida. Prólogo de José Antonio Míguez. Tr. de Lorenzo Riber. B. A., 1954. 60 p.

4892a. Senne, René le. Introducción a la filosofía. Tr. de Eustasio de Amilibia. B. A., Ateneo (Col. Cultura universal), 1954. 450 p.

4893. Spinoza, Benedictus de. Obras escogidas: Tratado teológico-político; Tratado de la reforma del entendimiento; Ética. Tr. de E. Reus y Bahamonde, M. H. Alberti, Manuel Machado. B. A., Ateneo, 1954. 722 p.

4893a. ————. La reforma del entendimiento. Tr. de Alfonso Castaño Piñán. B. A., Aguilar, 1954. 85 p.

4894. Suárez, Francisco. De las propiedades del ente en general y de sus principios. Tr. de Manuel Fuentes Benot. B. A., Aguilar, 1955. 81 p.

4895. Thomas Aquinas, Saint. De los principios de la naturaleza. Tr. de José A. Míguez. B. A., Aguilar, 1955. 54 p.

4896. Thyssen, Johannes. Historia de la filosofía de la historia. Tr. de Federico Korrell. B. A., Espasa-Calpe (Col. Historia y filosofía de la ciencia), 1954.

4897. Vives, Juan Luis. Introducción a la sabiduría. Tr. de Lorenzo Riber. B. A., Aguilar, 1955. 108 p.

4898. Whitehead, Alfred North. Proceso y realidad. Tr. de Rovira Armengol. B. A., Losada (Biblioteca filosófica, dirigida por Francisco Romero), 1956.

4899. Windelband, Wilhelm. Historia de la filosofía antigua. Tr. de J. Rovira Armengol. B. A., Nova, 1955. 423 p.

Sociology

T. LYNN SMITH

The year 1956 and the opening half of 1957 were ones of rapid development in sociological studies throughout the Latin American area. A considerable number of unusually important books appeared, of which it suffices to mention *Mutirão* by Clovis Caldeira, *Tratado general de sociología* by Luis Recaséns Siches, *Religião e relações raciais* by René Ribeiro, and *Estudios sociológicos (Sociología rural)*. The last of these contains the proceeding of the Sexto Congreso Nacional de Sociología, one of the most important sociological gatherings ever to take place in the Americas, held in Morelia, Mexico, late in 1955. The rapidly increasing number of articles and monographs by the younger generation of sociologists, those working in the various Latin American countries and a few in the U. S., is one of the most significant of recent developments.

Professional gatherings of sociologists are doing much to add to the quality as well as to the quantity of sociological research and writing throughout Latin America. They must be given considerable credit for the recent trend towards a more empirical and pragmatic approach in Latin American sociological studies. Important in this connection was the participation of Latin American sociologists, including Lucio Mendieta y Núñez of Mexico and José Arthur Rios of Brazil, in the Third World Congress of Sociology in 1956. Also highly significant was the Seventh National Congress of Sociology held at Monterrey, Mexico, in December 1956, a meeting devoted entirely to urban sociology. Finally, the six weeks' training seminar in rural sociology organized by the Office of the Northern Zone of the Inter-American Institute of Agricultural Sciences deserves special mention. This seminar, which was held in Habana, attracted agricultural leaders from throughout the Caribbean area for a period of intensive training in some of the most empirical and applied phases of sociology.

GENERAL

4900. Agramonte, Roberto. El mundo rural y sus procesos sociológicos (Cong Nac Soc, VI, 1955, Estud Soc, v. 1, p. 191-229).

This ample and masterly exposition was presented to Mexico's sixth national sociological congress by the representative from Cuba. Aspects singled out for special attention include: the characteristics of the rural social world, competition and conflict, cooperation, rural social organization, leadership, social mobility and social change, and rural progress as an ideal of a democratic system.

4901. Blow, Richard Marco. Obras sociológicas traducidas al español y portugués (Cien Soc, 4:20, abril 1953, p. 63-72).

Util recopilación bibliográfica de las obras sociológicas más importantes traducidas de alguna lengua extranjera y publicadas en español o en portugués. [A. Palerm]

4902. Brazil. Comissão Nacional de Política Agrária. Aspectos rurais brasileiros. Resultados numéricos do inquérito municipal realizado em colaboração com o I. B. G. E. Rio, Ministério da Agricultura, 1955. 168 p.

A tabular presentation of the data secured in 1952 by a question submitted by the National Commission on Agrarian Policy to the representatives of the Instituto Brasileiro de Geografia e Estatística in all of the *municípios* throughout the country. The materials are classified under six large headings; the general level of living; internal migrations and wages in agriculture; the small, the medium, and the large landed properties; agricultural credit; techniques of production; and renting and sharecropping. See also items 4929, 4930, and 4946.

4903. Centro Brasileiro de Pesquisas Educacionais. Educação e ciências sociais. Boletim do . . . Rio. Ano 1, v. 1, no. 1, março 1956-.
The first issue of this new journal is made up as follows: the text of an address given at the inauguration of the Centro Regional de Pesquisas Educacionais de São Paulo, by Fernando de Azevedo; "Barriers to education in the Americas," by Charles Wagley; "Hierarchy of prestige among occupations . . . ," by Bertram Hutchinson; "Occupational preferences and social origins of secondary school students in São Paulo," by Juarez Rubens Brandão Lopes; "Cultural aspects of the Recife area," by J. Roberto Moreira; "Education in community studies in Brazil," by Josildeth Gomes; "The structure of the school," by Antônio Cândido; "A study of the primary school in Blumenau," by Orlando Ferreira de Melo; and "The social sciences in South America," by L. A. Costa Pinto.

4904. Crónica del Sexto Congreso Nacional de Sociología (Cong Nac Soc, VI, 1955, Estud Soc, v. 1, p. 13-64).
A statement relative to the organization and work of Mexico's Sixth National Sociological Congress, devoted to rural sociology, and held at Morelia, Michoacan, Nov. 28-Dec. 2, 1956. A selected bibliography is given on p. 45-55.

4905. Freyre, Gilberto. The masters and the slaves. A study in the development of Brazilian civilization. Translated from the Portuguese by Samuel Putnam. 2d English-language ed., revised. N. Y., Knopf, 1956. lxxi, 537, xliv p.
The lengthy "Preface to the second English-language edition of *The Masters and the slaves*" which Freyre prepared by fusing the introductions to the various Brazilian editions is the principal addition to this edition of one of Brazil's great sociological classics.

4906. Germani, Gino. Estudios de psicología social. México, Instituto de Investigaciones Sociales (Cuadernos de sociología), 1956? 112 p.
This outline of social psychology is divided into two parts. The first, on social psychology for an epoch of crisis, emphasizes the ideas of Harold Laski on the objective conditions of liberty and those of Erich Fromm relative to the subjective conditions of liberty. Part 2, on contributions to contemporary social psychology, includes general treatments of biology and society in social psychology, and the concept of attitudes, along with considerable attention to the contributions of George H. Mead and Bronislaw Malinowski.

4907. ————. La sociología científica. (Apuntes para su fundamentación). México, Instituto de Investigaciones Sociales (Cuadernos de sociología), 1956? 156 p.

A brief theoretical introduction to the theory and method of sociology, the techniques of social investigation, and the relation of sociology to social action or planning.

4908. Inter-American Indian Conference, III, La Paz, Aug. 2-12, 1954. Final act. Washington, Pan American Union (Conferences and organizations series, 38), 1955. 35 p.
This summary report of findings and recommendations includes chapters on sociographic and socioeconomic questions; juridical and political questions, educational questions; questions related to anthropology, demography, and the home; linguistic, literary, and artistic questions; and questions relating to biology and public health.

4909. Linhares, Temístocles. Paraná vivo. Um retrato sem retoques. Rio, Olympio (Col. Documentos brasileiros, 78), 1953. 360 p., illus. & 33 photos.
A series of 15 essays on social, economic, and political problems and changes in the state of Parana.

4910. Maldonado, Adolfo. Sociología. 2. ed. México, Antigua Librería Robredo, 1955. 188 p.
An outline of the author's philosophical and theoretical system of general sociology. Short chapters are devoted to each of the following topics: history and scientific classification of sociology, characteristics of human life, significant factors in the constitution of personality, internal structure of human groups, historical solidarity, natural communities, the race, social dynamics, valorization, and normativity.

4911. Mendieta y Núñez, Lucio. Importancia de la sociología rural (Cong Nac Soc, VI, 1955, Estud Soc, v. 1, p. 65-72).
An able statement of the importance of the field of rural sociology by the director of Mexico's Instituto de Investigaciones Sociales and president of the annual national sociological congresses.

4912. ————. ¿Qué es la sociología rural? (Cong Nac Soc, VI, 1955, Estud Soc, v. 1, p. 77-88).
An excellent summary of the nature, history, methods, objectives, and importance of rural sociology.

4913. Otero, Mariano. Ensayo sobre el verdadero estado de la cuestión social y política que se agita en la República Mexicana. Guadalajara, México, I. T. G. (Biblioteca jalisciense, 1), 1952. 161 p.
The original edition of this book was published in 1842. This new edition is accompanied by a short introduction by Arnulfo Villaseñor Saavedra, a biographical sketch of the author by Marcos Arróniz, and a bibliography of Otero's works by Villa Villaseñor y Villaseñor.

4914. Poviña, Alfredo. La sociología con-

temporánea. B. A., Arayú, 1955. 135 p.
Brief sketches of the development and current
status of sociology in France, England, the U. S.,
Germany, Italy, Spain, and Latin America. For
each country or area, paragraphs on the precursors and founders are followed by others on
systematizers and contemporary currents. Each
treatment concludes with a sketch of the life and
work of a contemporary representative. The representatives chosen are as follows: France, Gur-
vitch; England, Ginsberg; the U. S., Sorokin;
Germany, Freyer; Italy, Gini; Spain, Ortega y
Gasset; and Latin America, Fernando Azevedo.

4915. Recaséns Siches, Luis. Tratado
general de sociología. México, Porrúa,
1956. 636 p.
This admirable text, along with those by Roberto
Agramonte, Francisco Ayala, Raúl Orgaz, and
Alfredo Poviña, ranks among the best comprehensive and systematic treatments of the general
field of sociology. Its publication is a landmark
in sociology in Mexico. Like Agramonte, Recaséns Siches has included much material from
his own studies of Latin American societies, and
those from other competent observers, in the
volume, a feature that makes it especially valuable to sociologists in other countries. The frame
of reference employed is excellent, the coverage
is adequate, and the style of presentation commendable.

4916. Reis, Arthur Cezar Ferreira. O
seringal e o seringueiro. Rio, Ministério
da Agricultura, Serviço de Informação
Agrícola (Documentário da vida rural,
5), 1953. 149 p. & illus.
In this substantial monograph one of Brazil's
greatest authorities on the Amazon region has
contributed an over-all view of rural society in
the area. The subjects of the six principal parts
into which the volume is divided are as follows:
the geographic setting; man and his behavior; the
economic structure; the social process; and the
cultural structure (i.e., linguistic, religious, and
civic affairs).

4917. Silva, Zedar Perfeito da. O vale do
Itajaí. Rio, Ministério da Agricultura,
Serviço de Informação Agrícola (Documentário da vida rural, 6), 1954. 183 p.,
tables, & illus., maps.
The Itajai valley in the state of Santa Catarina
may be regarded as the "heartland" of the German colonies in southern Brazil, and this rural
sociological monograph is among the most fundamental studies of the area done to date. In
the seven chapters into which the author divided
his work, the following subjects are treated: the
location of the colonies and their geographic setting; the human elements and their development
—agricultural techniques, housing, diet, clothing,
and sanitation; economic geography; the *venda*
(trading post), transportation and communication, credit industry, and leadership; groups and
institutions—marriage and the family, education
and the school, religion and the church, competition and conflict, cooperation and neighborhood relations, and political institutions and
government; traditionalism; and generalities.

**4918. Sociedade Brasileira de Socio-
logia.** Seccão de Pernambuco. Revista
pernambucana de sociologia. Recife, Brazil, Universidade do Recife. Ano 1, no. 1,
1954?-.
This new sociological periodical was established
by the Pernambuco Section of the Sociedade
Brasileira de Sociologia. Ano 1, no. 1, has not
been seen. Ano 2, no. 2, 1955, contains contributions by Joaquim Amazonas, Pinto Ferreira,
José Maria Aragão, Nelson Nogueira Saldanha,
Glaucio Veiga, Sílvio Romero, Joaquim Pimenta,
and Antônio Carlos Cintra do Amaral; and ano
3, no. 3, 1956, a translation of a paper, "Que é
sociologia rural," which Dr. Lucio Mendieta y
Núñez presented to the VI Congreso Nacional
de Sociología of Mexico in 1955, along with
other articles by Mário Lins, Pinto Ferreira,
Abelardo Montenegro, Nelson Nogueira Saldanha, Cláudio Souto, Antônio Carlos Cintra do
Amaral, and Frederico Rocha.

4919. Torres, Vasconcelos. Oliveira Viana. Sua vida e sua posição nos estudos
brasileiros de sociologia. Rio, Freitas Bastos, 1956. 203 p.
A sympathetic biography of one of Brazil's
greatest sociologists by one of his former students and protégés. The details supplied give
additional bases for appreciation of the fundamental contributions made by the author of
*O povo brasileiro e sua evolução, Populações
meridionais do Brasil, Instituições políticas brasileiras,* and a lengthy list of other important
works.

4920. Uribe Villegas, Óscar. Relaciones
entre la sociología rural y otras ramas de
la sociología, especialmente la sociología
económica (Cong Nac Soc, VI, 1955, Estud Soc, v. 1, p. 107-111).
A penetrating discussion of the relationship between rural sociology and other branches of
general sociology.

**4921. Venezuela. Consejo de Bienestar
Rural.** Problemas económicos y sociales
de los Andes venezolanos. Parte 2. Caracas, 1956? 136 p.
This elaborate study of social and economic
problems of the Venezuelan Andes was done by
a team of social science specialists, including
geographers, economists, sociologists, and anthropologists. Part 2 is largely sociological in
nature, with chapters on the Andean cultural
zone, the agricultural family, rural communities,
human resources, and changes in Andean society. Bertram Ellenbogen of Cornell University
was the sociologist actively participating in the
project, and George W. Hill, formerly of the
University of Wisconsin, also assisted to some
extent. For reference to part 1, see *HLAS, no.
19,* item 1462.

COMMUNITY

4922. Garmendia, Dionisio Jorge. Una
metodología y su correspondiente técnica
para el estudio de las comunidades rurales

(Cong Nac Soc, VI, 1955, Estud Soc, v. 1, p. 113-118).
A brief summary of methods of rural community analysis used in Uruguay, as presented to the Mexican sociological congress by the delegate from Uruguay.

4923. Moreno, Antonio de P. Grupos y cuasi-grupos sociales de la comunidad rural (Cong Nac Soc, VI, 1955, Estud Soc, v. 1, p. 249-281).
The campesino family, rural social classes, the campesino's political groups, rural unions and cooperatives, and the participation of the rural population in the formation of the national conscience are among the matters treated in this important contribution to Mexico's Sixth National Sociological Congress.

4924. Pi Hugarte, Renzo, and Germán Wettstein. Rasgos actuales de un rancherío uruguayo. Montevideo, Universidad de Montevideo, Facultad de Derecho y Ciencias Sociales (Biblioteca de publ. oficiales, Sección 3, 83), 1955. 190 p.
A study of the problems of housing, education, hygiene and sanitation, economic development, and so forth, in one small Uruguayan rural community.

4924a. Smith, Michael G. Community organization in rural Jamaica (Soc Ec Stud, 5:3, Sept. 1956, p. 295-312). [S. W. Mintz]

4925. Smith, T. Lynn. Algunas observaciones relacionadas con la comunidad rural, referidas especialmente a la América Latina (Cong Nac Soc, VI, Estud Soc, v. 1, p. 231-245).
The nature of the rural community, indicators of its strength or weakness, some causes of weak community organization, and measures for strengthening rural communities are the points developed in this contribution to Mexico's Sixth National Sociological Congress by the participant from the U. S.

4926. Yepes del Pozo, Juan. Grupos y cuasi-grupos sociales de la comunidad rural (Cong Nac Soc, VI, 1955, Estud Soc, v. 1, p. 297-320).
The data in this paper by the Ecuadorian delegate to Mexico's Sixth National Sociological Congress were drawn largely from his own country. The rural family, social classes in rural areas, unions and cooperatives, and the role of the campesinos in national life are all treated with insight and objectivity.

LEVELS OF LIVING

4927. Fals Borda, Orlando. Aspectos psico-sociológicos de la vivienda rural colombiana (R Psicol, 1:2, 1956, p. 1-24).
A psycho-social study of rural housing in Colombia based to a considerable extent upon the results of the 1951 census of housing.

4928. Hoyt, Elizabeth E. The Indian laborer on Guatemalan coffee fincas (Interam Ec Aff, 9:1, summer 1955, p. 33-46).
A study made in 1946-1947 of 50 fincas. Living conditions, food, recreation, religion, education, and use made of money income are described. [W. V. Scholes]

4929. Raposo, Ben-Hur. Condições da vida na agricultura. Rio, Comissão Nacional de Política Agrária, 1955. 68 p.
This study of housing, diet, health, dress, and incomes in rural Brazil is based upon a questionnaire sent in 1952 to the statistical representative in each of Brazil's *municípios* or counties. See also items 4902, 4930, and 4946.

MAN-LAND RELATIONS

4930. Caldeira, Clovis. Arrendamento e parceria no Brasil. Rio, Comissão Nacional de Política Agrária, 1955. 65 p.
This study of renting and sharecropping in Brazil is based upon a questionnaire sent in 1952 to the statistical representative in each of Brazil's *municípios* or counties. See also items 4902, 4929, and 4946.

4931. Diegues Junior, M. O banguê em Pernambuco no século XIX (R Arq Púb, 9-10, 1953, p. 5-20).
A social and economic study of life on the old-fashioned sugar plantation in northeastern Brazil during the 19th century.

4932. Fals-Borda, Orlando. Fragmentation of holdings in Boyacá, Colombia (Rural Soc, 21:2, June 1956, p. 158-163).
Evidence gathered in the Department of Boyacá, Colombia, indicates a considerable degree of fragmentation of holdings in an area in which the scattered-farmsteads pattern of settlement prevails. In the rugged terrain of this part of the Andes, this is said to have some economic advantages.

4933. Heysen, Luis E. Acerca de la reforma agraria (R Mex Soc, 18:1, enero-abril 1956, p. 97-111).
Brief notes upon the need for agrarian reform throughout Latin America, followed by summaries of the statements relating to agrarian reform throughout the world prepared by various agencies of the United Nations.

4934. ————. Procesos de colonización rural en Argentina (Cong Nac Soc, VI, 1955, Estud Soc, v. 1, p. 379-411).
A summary of Argentina's experience in establishing small farmers on the land, with special emphasis on the legal and technical aspects of the subject.

4935. Loomis, Charles P., and John C. McKinney. Systematic differences between Latin-American communities of family farms and large estates (Am J Sociol, 61:5, Mar. 1956, p. 404-412).

A comparison of two communities located in the canton of Turrialba, Costa Rica, which brings out sharply the significant social contrasts between a social system in an area dominated by the large landed estate and one in which family-sized farms are the rule.

4936. Martins, Renato Gonçalves. A questão agrária e o problema do camponês. Rio, Casa do Estudante do Brasil, 1955. 116 p.

This volume contains one of the most comprehensive studies of colonization in Brazil done to date. Following chapters devoted to general official actions and policies, details are given concerning attempts at colonization in the Amazon, the Northeast, along the São Francisco river, in southern Bahia, in Piaui and Maranhão, and in the lowlands of the state of Rio de Janeiro. The appendix contains most of the official decrees and orders issued between 1952 and 1955.

4937. Mendieta y Núñez, Lucio. La reforma agraria de Bolivia (Khana, 4:13-14, dic. 1955, p. 74-80).

A study of the backgrounds and provisions of Bolivia's Ley de Reforma Agraria, and a comparison of the attempts in Bolivia with those of Mexico.

4938. Pérez Guerrero, Edmundo. Colonización e inmigración en el Ecuador. Quito, Casa de la Cultura Ecuatoriana, 1954. 259 p.

Largely an historical study of the movements of various peoples into the territory now encompassed within the boundaries of Ecuador, followed by brief considerations of the problems and possibilities of new settlements in the unoccupied portions of the republic.

4939. Schulman, Sam. Land tenure among the aborigines of Latin America (Americas, Franciscan Hist, 13:1, July 1956, p. 43-67).

This is by far the most comprehensive and understanding study of the subject of land tenure among the aborigines of the Latin American countries that has ever been done. The ample footnote references are a guide to the most important literature on the subject.

4940. ―――. A proposed schema of Latin-American tenure classes (SW Soc Sci Q, 37:2, Sept. 1956, p. 122-136).

A significant contribution to the understanding of the nature of tenure classes in the rural portions of Latin America. Specifically, the author considers the various kinds of farm laborers and farm tenants throughout the Latin American countries and indicates how they should be classified in any thoroughgoing census of agriculture.

4941. Sicard, Émile (and others). Análisis de los grupos rurales en dos sub-divisiones divergentes en el tiempo y en el espacio: Colombia (1950) Hungría (1930) (R Mex Soc, 18:1, enero-abril 1956, p. 51-63).

A study by Sicard and his associates at the International Institute for Diplomatic Studies and Investigations of Paris. Attention was centered upon man-land relationships in Colombia in 1950 in comparison with those prevailing in Hungary in the interim between the two world wars.

4942. Smith, T. Lynn. Reforma agrária (Lavoura, 59, set.-out. 1956, p. 5 ff.).

The text of a lecture given in Rio, 1956, under the auspices of the Confederação Rural Brasileira, the Sociedade Nacional de Agricultura, the Serviço Social Rural, the Comissão Nacional de Política Agrária, and the Fundação Getúlio Vargas, along with a transcript of the ensuing discussion. Indicators of the need for agrarian reform, the objectives of agrarian reform, and measures and techniques for use in agrarian reform are the specific topics considered.

4943. Urquidi, Arturo. Consideraciones de orden doctrinal sobre la reforma agraria en Bolivia (R Mex Soc, 18:1, enero-abril 1956, p. 65-95).

An informative survey of the development of the ideology of agrarian reform in Bolivia from the publication of the program of principles of the Federación Universitaria Boliviana in 1928 to the decree of Aug. 2, 1953, instituting the reform measures.

POPULATION

4944. Argentina. Ministerio de Asuntos Técnicos. Dirección Nacional de Investigaciones Científicas y Técnicas. Boletín del Instituto Étnico Nacional. B. A. Año 1, no. 1, marzo 1954-.

The first issue of this new periodical is devoted entirely to demographic materials, with a short discussion of the demographic problems of Perón's second five-year plan and a more lengthy study of the changes in the age-sex pyramid of Argentina's population taking most of the space.

4945. Báez, Mauricio. Algunas características de la población de Venezuela. Caracas, Ediciones M. A. C. (Col. Planificación agropecuaria, 4), 1956. 79 p., illus.

The changes in the agricultural economy, internal migrations, and rural-urban differences in the composition of the population are the topics treated in this brief study.

4946. Borges, T. Pompeu Accioly. Migrações internas no Brasil. Rio, Comissão Nacional de Política Agrária, 1955. 42 p.

This important study contains an analysis of internal movements of population in Brazil based upon the 1950 census and also the results of a questionnaire sent to 1874 agents of the national statistical organization located in the various *municípios* into which the Brazilian states are divided. Returns received from 1445 *municípios* indicated that the rural exodus was causing serious shortages of agricultural labor within their confines, or in 76 per cent of the nation's *municípios*. The destinies of the migrants and the causes of the migrations are analyzed briefly. See also items 4902, 4929, and 4930.

4947. Burnight, Robert G.; Nathan L. Whetten; and Bruce D. Waxman. Differential rural-urban fertility in Mexico (Am Sociol R, 21:1, Feb. 1956, p. 3-18).
Correlation analysis shows an inverse relationship between the fertility ratio and size of population center, similar to that noted in other Western countries. Proximity to urban centers also reduces the rate of reproduction in the more rural areas.

4948. Cabello, Octavio. The demography of Chile (Popul Stud, 9:3, Mar. 1956, p. 237-250).
A competent study of the current population situation in Chile with special attention given to growth, rural-urban distribution, age and sex structure, educational status, occupations, and the vital processes.

4949. Cumpston, I. M. A survey of Indian immigration to British tropical colonies to 1910 (Popul Stud, 10:2, Nov. 1956, p. 158-165).
This paper is primarily demograpic, and deals with the movement of East Indians to Jamaica, Trinidad, and British Guiana, as well as to other areas. [S. W. Mintz]

4950. Dotson, Floyd, and Lillian Ota Dotson. Urban centralization and decentralization in Mexico (Rural Soc, 21:1, Mar. 1956, p. 41-49).
Data from the censuses of population and field observation indicate that rates of population increase in general have varied directly with the size of the city. An exception is among the satellites surrounding Mexico City.

4951. Inter-American Economic and Social Council. Las inmigraciones en Venezuela. Sus efectos económicos y sociales. Washington, Unión Panamericana, Departamento de Asuntos Económicos y Sociales, 1956. 113 p., tables.
Results of interviews with 524 recent immigrants to Venezuela are presented in this important study. The bulk of the space is used to present the materials on the characteristics of the immigrants (country of origin, age, type of visa, reasons for choosing Venezuela, family status, etc.) but there also is some analysis of the social and economic effect of immigration.

4952. ————. Migraciones internas en Costa Rica. Washington, Unión Panamericana, Sección de Trabajo, Migración y Seguridad Social, 1956. 163 p., graphs, tables.
This is one of the more significant studies of internal migration in Latin America. Historical materials, census data showing province of birth in cross tabulation with province of residence, and the vital statistics were all utilized to determine the direction and volume of the principal currents of migration within Costa Rica. In addition, a survey of 458 heads of households moving to the district of Mansion in the canton of Nicoya supplied important facts relative to the factors and forces responsible for the movements.

4953. Mintz, Sidney W. Puerto Rican emigration: a threefold comparison (Soc Ec Stud, 4:4, Dec. 1955, p. 311-325).

4954. Montesino Samperio, José V. Demografía venezolana. La población del área metropolitana de Caracas. Factores de crecimiento y tendencia futura. Caracas, Corporación Venezolana de Fomento, 1956. 86 p., tables.
A basic study of the growth and development of the Caracas metropolitan area is reported upon in this monograph. The topics discussed include the growth of the population, the factors responsible for the increase (natural increase, migration to the area from other parts of Venezuela, and immigration), and the outlook for the future. Reprint from *Cuadernos de información económica*, 7:6, nov.-dic. 1955, p. 23-65, and 8:7, enero-feb. 1956, p. 29-77.

4955. Smith, T. Lynn. Current population trends in Latin America (Am J Sociol, 62:4, Jan. 1957, p. 399-406).
Since 1900 the proportion of Latin Americans in the total population of the world has risen from 2.7 to 6.5 per cent. A fundamental redistribution in population is under way, featured by a strong tendency to concentrate in towns and cities and a rapid extension of the frontier in southern Brazil and along the eastern front of the Andes. The whiter elements in the population are increasing more rapidly than the darker, and larger proportions of the adults are contracting formal marriage obligations.

4956. Whetten, Nathan L., and Robert G. Burnight. Internal migration in Mexico (Rural Soc, 21:2, June 1956, p. 140-151).
A study based on 1950 census materials showing the state of residence in cross-tabulation with the state of birth. Two major currents of migration are indicated: (1) to the Federal District, and (2) to the tier of states along the northern border of the nation.

RACE

4957. Azevedo, Thales de. Comportamento verbal e efectivo para com os pretos na Bahia (Arq U Bahia, 4, 1955, p. 47-58).
An important study, based on questionnaires submitted to high school and college students and to government functionaries, of the stereotypes of Negroes in the city of Salvador, Bahia.

4958. ————. As elites de côr. Um estudo de ascensão social. Prefácio . . . Charles Wagley. São Paulo, Companhia Editora Nacional (Biblioteca pedagógica brasileira, série 5, Brasiliana, 282), 1955. 203 p.
This is a highly significant study of the process

by which colored persons in the city of Bahia have ascended into the class of the socially elite. Direct observation of the numbers and proportions of Negroes and mulattoes playing important roles in significant social functions was supplemented by personal interviews with 56 colored persons who had ascended to upper-class positions. All in all, this is probably the most fundamental study completed to date of vertical social mobility and race relations in the community which is widely considered as the prototype of complete racial integration.

4959. Betancourt, Juan René. Doctrina negra. La única teoría certera contra la discriminación racial en Cuba. Habana, P. Fernández, 1955. 80 p.

This small volume is dedicated to the author's Negress mother. In it he attempts to set forth the facts relative to racial prejudice and discrimination in Cuba, the positions of the various political parties with respect to racial discrimination, the doctrine or ideology of racial equality. In chapter 2 there is a short section, p. 28-34, on the work of Negro organizations, and a lengthy one, p. 35-46, on the doctrine, promises, and actual behavior with respect to the struggle for racial equality.

4960. Blair, Thomas L. The Negro worker in urban Brazil (Crisis, 61:10, whole no. 518, Dec. 1954, p. 592-599).

A penetrating analysis based on keen observation of how Brazilian Negroes are kept in lower-class positions in Brazilian urban society.

4961. Ortiz, Fernando. Los negros y la transculturación (Khana, 4:7-8, marzo 1955, p. 115-118).

Observations, based upon a lifetime of work, on the contact of races and cultures in Cuba. The term "transculturación" is defined and employed.

4962. Ribeiro, René. Religião e relações raciais. Rio, Ministério da Educação e Cultura, 1956. 241 p.

This volume represents the cooperation of the Instituto Joaquim Nabuco, Recife, Pernambuco, in UNESCO's program of studies of race relations in Brazil. It sought to determine the role of religion in the present state of race relations in the northeastern region. The city of Recife was taken as the site of the study, and the first phase of the investigation was a thorough study of the literature dealing with the historical aspects of the problem. Next the contacts of persons of different racial origins, as they take place in contemporary Recife, were observed and recorded. Finally the Bogardus social distance scale, as modified by Martuscelli, was administered to students in Catholic and Protestant academies, and also to students in the seminaries of the principal religious denominations. All in all, this is one of the most ambitious and significant studies of race relations undertaken in Brazil.

SOCIAL INSTITUTIONS

4963. Araújo, Alceu Maynard. A família numa comunidade alagoana (Sociologia, 17:2, maio 1955, p. 113-131).

A report, based on field work done in 1952-1953, of family organization and relationships in a small rural community in the rice-producing section of Alagoas, Brazil.

4964. Cornejo V., Justino. Meditaciones sobre el caudillismo. Guayaquil, Ecuador, Imp. Guayaquil, 1956. 20 p.

The present social and political situation in Ecuador viewed against the country's history of *caudillismo*. "Communism and socialism here resemble coaches without a locomotive." The caudillo supplies this motive power. The backgrounds and roles of contemporary leaders are described briefly.

4965. Costa, Esdras Borges. Relações de família em Cerrado e Retiro (Sociologia, 17:2, maio 1955, p. 132-146).

An analysis of family organization and relationships in two small centers in Minas Gerais, Brazil.

4966. Ferrari, Alfonso Trujillo. A família em Potengi (Sociologia, 17:2, maio 1955, p. 147-162).

A study of family structure and relationships in a small rural community in the state of Alagoas. The population of the community is largely of mixed white and Negro descent and is highly migratory.

4967. Hill, Reuben. Courtship in Puerto Rico: an institution in transition (Marr Fam Liv, 17:1, Feb. 1955, p. 26-35). [S. W. Mintz]

4968. Sayres, William C. Ritual kinship and negative affect (Am Sociol R, 21:3, June 1956, p. 348-352).

A study of *compadrazgo* in two small villages, Coconuco and Zarzal, near Popayan in the department of Cauca, Colombia.

4969. Willems, Emílio. Intermarriage among German Brazilians (Migr N, 5:2, Mar.-Apr. 1956, p. 10-18).

A study of intermarriage on the part of German settlers and their descendants in south Brazil and especially in the state of Santa Catarina.

4970. Yepes del Pozo, Juan. Sociología económica: la educación y la economía (R Fo, época 2, 42:4, dic. 1955, p. 95-118).

A fundamental study of educational institutions in Ecuador, with emphasis upon the economic factor, education in relation to social stratification, education for work and education for idleness, the social and technical education of the laborer, and the economic education of the public.

SOCIAL PROCESSES

4971. Caldeira, Clovis. Mutirão: formas de ajuda mútua no meio rural. São Paulo, Companhia Editora Nacional (Biblioteca pedagógica brasileira, serie 5, Brasiliana, 289), 1956. 222 p.

This is a thoroughgoing study of mutual aid in Brazil. Chapters on origins, synonyms, the characteristics of mutual aid in Brazil, and the backgrounds among the Portuguese, American Indians, and African Negroes make up part 1. Part 2, the body of the work, deals with the present situation in Brazil as a whole, followed by a lengthy analyses of mutual aid in agriculture in various regions of Brazil, a briefer description of mutual aid in pastoral activities, and concludes with a study of mutual aid among the settlers of European origins in south Brazil.

4972. Diégues Junior, Manuel. La asimilación del inmigrante en el medio rural brasileño (Cong Nac Soc, VI, 1955, Estud Soc, v. 1, p. 413-419).

A brief résumé of the distribution of immigrants in rural Brazil, followed by some keen observations on the nature of the acculturation process in areas with heavy concentrations of immigrants and in areas in which the immigrants are widely dispersed.

4973. Martins, Wilson. Um Brasil diferente. Ensaio sôbre fenômenos de aculturação no Paraná. São Paulo, Anhembi, 1955. 506 p., illus.

This volume is an important contribution to the study of immigration and the assimilation of immigrants in Brazil. This is especially true of the chapter entitled "Homem" which occupies pages 71-288 and contains a wealth of detail relative to the various nationality groups entering Parana, the experiences of each in the state, and the process of acculturation that is going on. Other chapters are devoted to the landscape, the house, food, clothing, technical knowledge, and the "ideas" of the colonists.

4974. Powrie, Barbara E. The changing attitude of the coloured middle class towards carnival (Carib Q, 4:3-4, Mar.-June 1956, p. 224-232). [S. W. Mintz]

4975. Recaséns Siches, Luis. El problema de la adaptación de las gentes de origen rural que migran en las grandes ciudades o centros industriales (Cong Nac Soc, VI, 1955, Estud Soc, v. 1, p. 361-377).

An able exposition of the problems faced by migrants from rural areas in large industrial cities, followed by eight suggestions for alleviating the problems in Mexico.

4976. Tumin, Melvin M., and Arnold S. Feldman. The miracle at Sabana Grande (POQ, 19:2, summer 1955, p. 125-139).

An attempt at a sociological analysis of events following the miraculous appearance of the Virgin in a Puerto Rican country village. [S. W. Mintz]

SOCIAL STRATIFICATION

4977. Bazzanella, W. Estratificação e mobilidade social no Brasil. Fontes biblio-

gráficas. Rio, Centro Brasileiro de Pesquisas Educacionais, 1956. 116 p.

A total of 304 items are included in this annotated bibliography on social stratification and social mobility in Brazil.

4978. Bonilla, Frank. Comentarios sobre la estructura de clase en América Latina (Cien Soc, 7:40, dic. 1956, p. 263-276).

An appraisal of the various contributions published as *Materiales para el estudio de la clase media en la América Latina* (see *HLAS, no. 16, 1950*, item 3347; *no. 17, 1951*, item 3014) with special attention to general frames of reference, and the roles of the family, economic factors, political factors, religious institutions, and the military.

4979. Ellis, Robert A. Social status and social distance (Sociol Soc Re, 40:4, Mar.-Apr. 1956, p. 240-246).

Social status is conceived to have a social distance component, as validated by sociological data collected in the town of Christiana, Jamaica, B. W. I. [S. W. Mintz]

4980. Solari, Aldo. Las clases sociales y su gravitación en la estructura política y social del Uruguay (R Mex Soc, 18:2, mayo-agosto 1956, p. 257-266).

The author estimates that 20 percent of the Uruguayan population belong to the proletarian classes, and about 5 percent to the upper classes. This is followed by a discussion of the connections and relationships of the classes to other aspects of Uruguayan life, and particularly to politics and government.

OTHER

4981. Agramonte, Roberto. La ecología humana y su importancia sociológica (U Habana, 19:115-117, julio-dic. 1954, p. 63-86).

This excellent orientation to the study of human ecology was presented to the V Congreso Nacional de Sociología in Guanajuato, Mexico, in 1954 (see *HLAS, no. 19*, item 6094).

4982. Beals, Ralph L. The Mexican student views the United States (A Am Ac Pol Soc Sci, 295, Sept. 1954, p. 108-115).

Parte de un proyecto de estudio de la actitud de los estudiantes de origen extranjero en los Estados Unidos. [A. Palerm]

4983. Carvajal, René. Vida y tipología rurales (Cong Nac Soc, VI, 1955, Estud Soc, v. 1, p. 181-189).

A thoughtful consideration of the traditions, folklore, social relationships, occupational callings, etc., which distinguish rural life from urban.

4984. Fals-Borda, Orlando. El campesino cundi-boyacense: conceptos sobre su pasividad (R Psicol, 1:1, 1956, p. 1-10).

A psycho-social analysis of the materials, largely historical, relative to the asserted passivity of the campesinos who inhabit the Andean highlands in the departments of Cundinamarca and Boyaca in Colombia.

4985. Herrera Figueroa, Miguel. Anotaciones para una sociología de Tucumán, República Argentina (Cong Nac Soc, VI, 1955, Estud Soc, v. 1, p. 323-329).
Brief notes on rural social life in the province of Tucuman, with special emphasis upon the role of the culture of sugar cane.

4986. Hopper, Rex D. Aspectos ideológicos y de jefatura de la Revolución Mexicana (R Mex Soc, 18:1, enero-abril 1956, p. 19-36).
A study of the ideological conflict which preceded the Mexican Revolution.

4987. Mendieta y Núñez, Lucio. Sociología del arte (R Mex Soc, 18:1, enero-abril 1956, p. 9-18).
Chapters 15 and 16 of a general work that is being published serially, this portion is devoted to a general theoretical orientation to "art and styles" and "art and politics."

4988. Pierson, Donald. Sickness and its cure in a Brazilian rural community (A XXXI Cong Intl Am, p. 281-291).
Folk beliefs, practices, and remedies as observed in one small rural community, near São Paulo, which the author believes is fairly representative of rural Brazil in general.

4989. Reis, Arthur Cezar Ferreira. Aspectos sociais da valorização da Amazônia. Prefácio de Gilberto Freyre. Recife, Brazil, Instituto Joaquim Nabuco de Pesquisas Sociais (Publ. avulsas, 1), 1955. 22 p.

A brief, but important, discussion of some of the social problems involved in attempts to improve the lot of the inhabitants of the great Amazon region, and of some of the measures that offer most promise.

4990. Smith, T. Lynn. Values held by people in Latin America which affect technical cooperation (Rural Soc, 21:1, Mar. 1956, p. 68-75).
The text of an address prepared for the sixth annual Conference for Agricultural Services in Foreign Areas, Washington, D. C., 1955. Points stressed include the great variation in value systems, values associated with the class system, the disrepute of manual labor, the lavish use of labor in the production process, the pressures which are forcing large numbers of those born to upper-class status down the social scale, Latin Americans as generalists, and the widespread belief in the futility of long-range plans.

4991. Unda Briceño, Hugo, and Domingo Ricovery López. Bases para un estudio criminógeno del departamento Libertador del Distrito Federal, años 1951-1953. Caracas, Ministerio de Justicia, 1955. 85 p., graphs, tables.
This study contains important data, and some analysis, relating to the crimes against the person in Venezuela's capital during a three-year period.

4992. Uribe Villegas, Óscar. Requerimientos intrínsecos de la pesquisa social y responsabilidad del investigador (R Mex Soc, 18:1, enero-abril 1956, p. 125-144).
An able exposition of the nature of sociology as a science and of the scientific attitude that must dominate those who undertake sociological research.

General

STATISTICS

PHYLLIS G. CARTER

This year this section lists the official general statistical bulletins of Latin America—that is, the bulletins issued by the national statistical office for the purpose of providing a summary of all the important available recent statistics in their countries.

Statistical bulletins on a single special subject, such as vital statistics or agriculture, are not included here. It should be noted, that three countries, Costa Rica, Honduras, and Uruguay, do not issue a "general" statistical bulletin, so that for even the most summary data it is necessary to go either to their statistical yearbooks or their special subject statistical bulletins.

5000. **Argentina. Dirección Nacional de Estadística y Censos.** Boletín mensual de estadística. B. A. Año 1, no. 1, 1956.
Continuation of *Síntesis estadística mensual de la República Argentina*, published 1947-1955. Demographic, social, and economic data.

5001. **Bolivia. Dirección General de Estadística y Censos.** Boletín estadístico. La Paz. No. 1, julio 1945-.
Title, no. 1 through no. 74, sept.-dic. 1954, was *Revista mensual*. Demographic and economic data.

5002. **Brazil. Instituto Brasileiro de Geografia e Estatística. Conselho Nacional de Estatística.** Boletim estatístico. Rio. Ano 1, no. 1-2, jan.-junho 1943-.
Each issue contains special studies as well as current statistical series, annual summary data, summary results of recent censuses, etc.

5003. **Chile. Servicio Nacional de Estadística y Censos.** Estadística chilena. Santiago. Año 1, no. 1, 1928-.
More or less monthly. Current statistical series,

but not all appearing in every issue, on demography and other social statistics and economic statistics. Other data, including results from latest censuses, from time to time.

5004. **Colombia. Departamento Administrativo Nacional de Estadística.** Boletín mensual de estadística. Bogotá. No. 1, mayo 1951-.
Some notes and comments, but principally data, varying from issue to issue, on demography and other social statistics and economic statistics.

5005. **Cuba. Dirección General de Estadística.** Boletín de estadísticas. Habana. V. 1, no. 1, 1945-.
Quarterly. Title at first was *Boletín mensual*. Notes on the economic situation, and current statistical series on demography (passengers entering and leaving the country—series beginning in issue for July-December 1951), social statistics (total wages paid in the country), and economic statistics. Data for each month of the quarter indicated on the cover, and for several previous months.

5006. **Dominican Republic. Dirección General de Estadísticas.** Informaciones estadísticas dominicanas. Ciudad Trujillo. Vol. 1, no. 1, nov. 1951-.
Special notes from time to time, and current statistical series on demography (births, deaths, marriages, divorces) and economic statistics. In addition there are special tables, varying from issue to issue, on a variety of subjects.

5007. **Ecuador. Dirección General de Estadística y Censos.** Boletín estadístico. Quito. Año 1, no. 1, dic. 1954-enero 1955-.
Contents vary from issue to issue. Replaces *El trimestre estadístico del Ecuador*, published 1945-1947.

5008. **El Salvador. Dirección General de Estadística y Censos.** Boletín estadístico. San Salvador. 2. época, no. 1, enero-feb. 1952-.
Bimonthly. Continues both *Censos*, published from September to December 1951, *and Boletín estadístico*, published from 1933 to December 1949. Includes special studies and comments, and special tables on a variety of subjects including results of recent censuses, as well as current statistical series on climatology, demography, social statistics, and economic statistics.

5009. Guatemala. Dirección General de Estadística. Boletín. Guatemala. No. 1, mayo 1946-.
Bimonthly. Most issues contain reports on the activities of the agency, statistical conferences, programs, etc. Each issue devoted to one or more special subjects.

5010. Haiti. Institut Haïtien de Statistique. Bulletin trimestriel de statistique. Port-au-Prince. No. 1, juillet 1951-.
Each issue contains special studies as well as current statistical series on climatology, demography, social and economic statistics.

5011. Jamaica. Central Bureau of Statistics. Quarterly digest of statistics. Kingston. No. 1, Oct.-Dec. 1947-.
A commentary on the tables appears in most issues. Summary census data, and current statistical series on demography, social statistics, and economic statistics.

5012. México. Dirección General de Estadística. Revista de estadística. México. V. 1, no. 1, enero 1938-.
Bimonthly. Principally economic data, but also current statistical series on demography.

5013. Nicaragua. Dirección General de Estadística y Censos. Boletín de estadística. 3. época, no. 1, 1956-.
Continues the *Boletín de estadística* published 1907-1940, and the bulletin published under various similar titles 1944-1947. Contains summary results of recent censuses and periodic demographic and economic statistics.

5014. Panamá. Dirección de Estadística y Censo. Estadística panameña. Panamá. V. 1, no. 1, oct. 1941-.
Monthly. Contents vary from issue to issue; together, they supply very complete data on a wide range of subjects.

5015. Paraguay. Dirección General de Estadística y Censos. Boletín estadístico del Paraguay. Asunción. V. 1, no. 1, enero-marzo 1957-.
General summary data on all aspects of the life of the country.

5016. Perú. Dirección Nacional de Estadística. Boletín de estadística peruana. Lima. Año 1, no. 1, 1928-.
Semiannual since 1950. Includes notes on the work of the agency, and current statistical series (not all appearing in every issue) on demography and other social statistics and on economic characteristics. From time to time annual data covering several years appear on certain subjects.

5017. Puerto Rico. Bureau of the Budget. Division of Statistics. Puerto Rico monthly statistical report. San Juan. V. 1, no. 1, July 1943- v. 9, no. 10-12, Oct-Dec. 1951.

Apparently no longer published. Had current statistical series on climatology, demography, social statistics, and economic statistics.

5018. Trinidad and Tobago. Central Statistical Office. Quarterly economic report. Trinidad. Jan.-Mar. 1951-.
Includes demographic and social as well as economic statistics.

5019. Venezuela. Dirección General de Estadística. Boletín mensual de estadística. Caracas. Año 1, mes 1, no. 1, enero 1941-.
Current statistical series and some special tables from time to time on demography and other social statistics and economic characteristics.

BIBLIOGRAPHIES

5020. Alfau Durán, Vetilio. Apuntes de bibliografía dominicana en torno a las rectificaciones hechas a la obra del Prof. Waxman. Ciudad Trujillo, Imp. Librería Dominicana, 1956. 8 p.

5021. Brazil. Instituto Nacional do Livro. Editoras e livrarias. Rio, 1953. 863-872 p.

5022. ————. ————. Guia das bibliotecas brasileiras, registadas até 31 de dezembro de 1952. 3. ed. Rio, 1955. 678 p.
"Organizado por Hélio Gomes Machado, com a colaboração de Humberto Soares da Costa e Elza Fontoura de Andrade."

5023. Carvalho, Oswaldo de. Bibliografia de censura intelectual. São Paulo, 1956. 32 p.

5024. ————. Bibliografias paulistas. São Paulo, 1957. 46 p.

5025. Coelho Netto, Paulo. Bibliografia de Coelho Netto. Rio, Borsoi, 1956. 34 p.

5026. Costa, Humberto Soares da. Bibliotecas do centro-oeste do Brasil. Rio, Instituto Nacional do Livro (Col. B 2; Biblioteconomia, 9), 1953. 130 p.

5027. United States. Library of Congress. Union Catalog Division. Newspapers on microfilm. Compiled under the direction of George A. Schwegman, Jr., chief, 2d. ed. Washington, 1953. 126 p.

5028. Universidad Central de Venezuela. Facultad de Humanidades y Educación. Documentos para la historia de la cultura en Venezuela: La guirnalda. Índices analíticos por María Marotta. Caracas, 1956. 20 p. (Serie Monografías bibliográficas, 5).

5029. ————. ————. Documentos para la historia de la cultura en Venezuela: El liceo venezolano. Índices analíticos por Carmen Luisa Escalante. Caracas, 1956. 32 p. (Serie Monografías bibliográficas, 1).

5030. ————. ————. Documentos para la historia de la cultura en Venezuela: La Oliva. Índices analíticos por Alida Castellanos de Goa. Caracas, 1956. 22 p. (Serie Monografías bibliográficas, 4).

5031. ————. ————. Documentos para la historia de la cultura en Venezuela: Revista literaria por Juan Vicente González. Índices analíticos por Aminta Castrillo C. Caracas, 1956. 22 p. (Serie Monografías bibliográficas, 2).

5032. ————. ————. Documentos para la historia de la cultura en Venezuela: *Vargasia*. Índices analíticos por Olga de Giorgi. Caracas, 1956. 20 p. (Serie Monografías bibliográficas, 3).

5033. **Venezuela. Biblioteca Nacional.** Índice bibliográfico de la Biblioteca Nacional. Caracas. No. 1, enero-junio 1956-.

BIOGRAPHY

CHARLES C. GRIFFIN

5034. Diccionario biográfico de Chile. 8. ed., 1950-1952. Santiago, Empresa Periodística Chile, 1952. 1403 p.

5035. **González Arrili, Bernardo.** Vida de Ameghino. Santa Fe, Argentina, Castellví, 1954. 132 p., illus.
A brief popular biographical study of the celebrated Argentine scientist.

5036. ————. Vida y milagros de Mister Morris. B. A., La Aurora, 1955. 121 p., illus.
Pious and eulogistic, but valuable, study of a Protestant missionary-educator in Argentina. Throws light on the religious problem in Argentine education. Chiefly relates to the late 19th and early 20th centuries.

5037. **Grases, Pedro.** Cuatro varones venezolanos. Valentín Espinal, Arístides Rojas, Manuel Segundo Sánchez, Vicente Lecuna. Caracas, Asociación de Escritores Venezolanos (Cuadernos literarios, 79), 1953. 80 p.
Brief essays on first rank figures in Venezuelan intellectual history by a highly qualified expert.

5038. **Hostos, Eugenio Carlos de (ed.).** Hostos, peregrino del ideal; idario y trabajos acerca de Eugenio María de Hostos y apéndice, recogidos y publicados por Eugenio Carlos de Hostos. Paris, Ediciones Literarias y Artísticas, 1954. 461 p., port.
Part of the monumental edition of works by Hostos and about him which is being brought out by his son.

5039. **Peraza Sarausa, Fermín.** Diccionario biográfico cubano. Habana, Ediciones Anuario Bibliográfico Cubano (Biblioteca del bibliotecario, 36, 38, 40, 43-44, 48-49), 1951-1956. 7 v.

5040. Quien es quien en la Argentina. Biografías contemporáneas. 6. ed. B. A., Kraft, 1955. 674 p.

5041. **Tarnói, Ladislao T.** El nuevo ideal nacional de Venezuela; vida y obra de Marcos Pérez Jiménez. Madrid, Ediciones Verdad, 1954. 341 p., illus.
Eulogy.

5042. **Valldeperes, Manuel.** Acción y pensamiento de Trujillo. Introducción de R. Emilio Jiménez. Ciudad Trujillo, Editora del Caribe, 1955. 206 p., illus.
Trujillo as seen by Trujillo.

5043. **Vásquez, José V.** Album cívico hondureño. Ciudad Progreso, Honduras, Tip. Atenea, 1952. 177 p., illus., ports.
Brief biographical data on a large number of Hondurans.

5044. **Villanueva, Laureano.** Biografía del doctor José Vargas. Edición del Concejo Municipal del Distrito Federal. Caracas, Imp. Nacional, 1954. 372 p.
A rather full study of the celebrated physician, educator, and president of Venezuela. Contains some documents.

DESCRIPTION AND TRAVEL

CHARLES C. GRIFFIN

5045. **Almada, Francisco R.** Diccionario de historia, geografía y biografía sonorenses. Chihuahua, México, 1952. 860 p.

5046. **Biesanz, John Berry, and Mavis Biesanz.** The people of Panama. N. Y., Columbia University Press, 1955. 418 p., illus.
A well-informed descriptive survey by authors sympathetic to Panama and hopeful for harmonious future evolution of social relations.

5047. **Cavero, Luis E.** Monografía de la provincia de Huanta. T. 1. Lima, Rimac, 1953. 270 p.
Of possible use to those working in the area. Primarily ephemeral.

5048. Chávez Cisneros, Esteban. Quitupan; ensayo histórico y estadístico. Morelia, México, Fímax Publicistas, 1954. 297 p., illus., ports., maps (part fold.).
A local monograph which should be of interest to students of the evolution of rural Mexico and of the impact of the Revolution in a small west coast area.

5049. Coronado P., J. Adrián. Monografía del departamento de Sacatepéquez. Con diez y seis ilustraciones. Guatemala, Ministerio de Educación Pública (Col. Monografías, 1), 1953. 226 p.
Of interest to the geographer or other social scientist working in this area.

5050. Fergusson, Erna. Mexico revisited. N. Y., Knopf, 1955. 346 p., illus.
A worthwhile study by a veteran writer of popular books of this genre.

5051. Haigh, Samuel; Alejandro Caldcleugh; and Max Radiguet. Viajeros en Chile, 1817-1847. Santiago, Editorial del Pacífico, 1955. 254 p.
Contents: "Viaje a Chile en la época de la independencia, 1817," por S. Haigh; "Viaje a Chile en 1819, 20 y 21," por A. Caldcleugh; "Valparaíso y la sociedad chilena en 1847," por M. Radiguet. Reprint of well-known 19th-century books of travel insofar as they relate to Chile.

5052. Inchauspe, Pedro. Más voces y costumbres del campo argentino. Segunda parte de Voces y costumbres del campo argentino, 1942. 1. ed. Santa Fe, Argentina, Ediciones Colmegna, 1953. 350 p., illus.
Interesting listing and comment on rural Argentine vocabulary.

5053. Montoya Velásquez, Jorge. Pereira en marcha, año de 1953; datos fidedignos ceñidos rigurosamente a la historia de la ciudad. Prólogo a cargo de José Domingo Escobar D. Pereira, Colombia, 1953. 155 p., illus.

5054. Onís, José de. Los Estados Unidos vistos por escritores hispanoamericanos. Madrid, Ediciones Cultura Hispánica, 1956. 376 p.
A Spanish edition of a work published earlier in the U. S., The United States as seen by Spanish American writers, 1776-1890 (see HLAS, no. 18, 1952, item 3361).

5055. Pendle, George. Paraguay, a riverside nation. 2d ed. London, Royal Institute of International Affairs, 1956. 120 p., illus.
A respectable volume in a useful series of brief country handbooks. 1st ed. published 1954.

5056. Perú. Oficina Nacional de Planeamiento y Urbanismo. Guía de ciudades del Perú. Contiene los principales datos físicos, sociales y económicos de las capitales de provincias del país. Lima, 1955. 1 v. (unpaged, chiefly tables).

5057. Recinos, Adrián. Monografía del departamento de Huehuetenango. 2. ed., corr. Guatemala, Ministerio de Educación Pública (Col. Monografías, 2), 1954. 518 p., illus., 2 maps (1 fold.).
An important local study.

5058. Riva Agüero, José de la. Paisajes peruanos. Con un estudio preliminar de Raúl Porras Barrenechea. Lima, Imp. Santa María, 1955. 202 p., illus.
A reprint of an early study by the celebrated Peruvian scholar. Product of the anniversary celebration.

5059. Serstevens, Albert t'. Mexique, pays à trois étages. Grenoble, France, Arthaud, 1955. 434 p., illus., ports., maps (1 fold.).
Interesting general interpretation. Perhaps too rigid a conceptual framework.

5060. Zuluaga Aristizabal, Célimo. Monografía del municipio de Marsella. Bogotá, Ediciones Bodha, 1954. 224 p., illus.

OTHER TOPICS

CHARLES C. GRIFFIN

5061. Cova, Jesús Antonio. Bocetos de hoy para retratos de mañana. Caracas, Villegas, 1953. 235 p.
Brief essays by a veteran journalist who represents the political right.

5062. Encina, Francisco A. Nuestra inferioridad económica: sus causas, sus consecuencias. Nueva ed. Prólogo de Eduardo Moore. Santiago, Editorial Universitaria (Col. América nuestra), 1955. 170 p.
Reprint of a highly personal, but important, interpretation of Chilean economic development to the end of the 19th century.

5063. Encyclopédie de l'Amérique latine: politique, économique, culturelle. Préf. d'Édouard Bonnefous. Paris, Presses Universitaires de France, 1954. 628 p.

5064. Grases, Pedro. En torno a la obra de Bello. Caracas, Tip. Vargas, 1953. 198 p.
An important study by the editor of the definitive edition of Bello's works and foremost modern student of the Venezuelan man of letters and patriot.

5065. Hostos, Eugenio María de. Obras completas. V. 21. España y América.

Prólogo por Francisco Elías de Tejada. Recopilación y arreglo por Eugenio Carlos de Hostos. Paris, Ediciones Literarias y Artísicas, 1954. 627 p.
Another volume in the complete edition of Hostos in progress.

5066. Marasciulo, Edward (comp.). Survey of research and investigations in progress and contemplated in the field of Latin America subjects in colleges and universities in the United States and Canada during the school year 1952-1953. Gainesville, Fla., School of Inter-American Studies, University of Florida, 1953. 24 p.
Tabulates responses to questionnaire. Possibly useful to those engaged in research, but now out of date.

5067. Montenegro, Carlos. Nacionalismo y coloniaje; su expresión histórica en la prensa de Bolivia. 3. ed. La Paz, Alcaldía Municipal (Biblioteca paceña), 1953. 213 p., illus.
An important study of the press in Bolivia.

5068. Pan American Institute of Geography and History. The Pan American Institute of Geography and History, its creation, development and current program, 1929-1954; a quarter century of service to its member governments. Mexico, 1954. 62, xliv p., illus., map (PAIGH publ., 180).
A summary report which provides the best and most authoritative brief view of the activities of this subsidiary organization of the OAS.

5069. Proudfoot, Mary. Britain and the United States in the Caribbean; a comparative study in methods of development. With an introd. by Margery Perham. N. Y., Praeger (Colonial and comparaive studies), 1954. 434 p., fold. map, tables.

Apart from the value of the comparative approach, this work is valuable for those interested in the modern development of the British islands in the Caribbean.

5070. Revista dominicana de cultura. Editor: Emilio Rodríguez Demorizi. Ciudad Trujillo. V. 1, no. 1, nov. 1955-.
A newly established review containing a variety of articles dealing with Dominican cultural subjects. [R. R. Hill]

5071. Silva Castro, Raúl (ed.). Cartas chilenas (siglos XVIII y XIX). Recopiladas con introducción y notas de Raúl Silva Castro. Santiago, Academia Chilena de la Historia (Publ.), 1954. 151 p.
A brief but delightful and instructive popular anthology of letters by Chileans. Illuminating on social history.

5072. Siso, Carlos. La formación del pueblo venezolano; estudios sociológicos. Madrid, García Enciso, 1953. 2 v. 542, 480 p., illus., ports., fold. maps, plan.
Important for the study of Venezuelan social evolution, chiefly in early times.

5073. Universidad de Puerto Rico. Colegio de Ciencias Sociales. Revista de ciencias sociales. Río Piedras, Puerto Rico. V. 1, no. 1, marzo 1957-.
First issue (225 p.) of a quarterly edited by Raúl Serrano Geyls. Spanish text followed by English abstract. Most of the authors in the first number are or have been connected with the University of Puerto Rico. Some of the contributions: Pedro Muñoz Amato, "Las bases políticas del servicio civil"; Reuben Hill, Kurt W. Back, and J. Mayone Stycos, "La estructura de la familia y la fertilidad en Puerto Rico"; Beate R. Salz, "Algunos aspectos psicológicos de la industrialización"; Henry Wells, "La reorganización administrativa en Puerto Rico"; Gordon K. Lewis, "La federación británica del Caribe." There are also book reviews and a review of periodicals. [Ed.]

Key to Periodical
and Other Title Abbreviations

A Am Ac Pol Soc Sci...The Annals of the American Academy of Political and Social
         Science. Philadelphia, Pa.
A Arqueol Etnol........Anales de Arqueología y Etnología. Universidad de Cuyo. Facul-
         tad de Filosofía y Letras. Mendoza, Argentina.
A Assoc Geóg Br.......Anais da Associação dos Geógrafos Brasileiros. São Paulo, Brazil.
A Éc Soc Civ...........Annales, Économies, Sociétés, Civilisations. Paris, France.
A Inst Arte Am.........Anales del Instituto de Arte Americano e Investigaciones Estéticas.
         Universidad de Buenos Aires. Buenos Aires, Argentina.
A Inst Inv Estét........Anales del Instituto de Investigaciones Estéticas. Universidad
         Nacional Autónoma de México. México, D. F., México.
A Inst Nac Antr Hist....Anales del Instituto Nacional de Antropología e Historia. México,
         D. F., México.
A IV Cong Hist Nac....Anais do Quarto Congresso de História Nacional. Instituto His-
         tórico e Geográfico Brasileiro. Rio de Janeiro, Brazil.
A IV Cong Nac Odon...Anales del IV Congreso Nacional de Odontología. Lima, Perú.
A Mus C Eva Perón....Anales del Museo de la Ciudad Eva Perón, nueva serie, Antro-
         pología. Ciudad Eva Perón, Argentina.
A Mus Hist Nat........Anales del Museo de Historia Natural. Montevideo, Uruguay.
A Soc Geog Hist Guat..Anales de la Sociedad de Geografía e Historia de Guatemala.
         Guatemala, Guatemala.
A U Ch................Anales de la Universidad de Chile. Santiago, Chile.
A U Hispalense.........Anales de la Universidad Hispalense. Sevilla, Spain.
A XXXI Cong Intl Am..Anais do XXXI Congresso Internacional de Americanistas. São
         Paulo, 1954. 2 v. 1955.
Ábside ....Ábside. México, D. F., México.
Acta Anthr.............Acta Anthropologica. Sociedad de Alumnos de la Escuela Nacional
         de Antropología. México, D. F., México.
Acta Cien Ven.........Acta Científica Venezolana. Asociación Venezolana para el Avance
         de la Ciencia. Caracas, Venezuela.
Acta Ethn Ac Sci Hung..Acta Ethnographica Academiae Scientiarum Hungariacae. Buda-
         pest, Hungary.
Acta Geog.............Acta Geographica. Societas Geographica Fenniae. Helsinki, Fin-
         land.
Agr Hist...............Agricultural History. Agricultural History Society. Washington,
         D. C.
Aguas En El...........Aguas e Energia Elétrica. Conselho Nacional de Aguas e Energia
         Elétrica. Rio de Janeiro, Brazil.
Am Anthr.............American Anthropologist. Central States Branch of the American
         Anthropological Association and other societies. New York,
         N. Y.
Am Antiq.............American Antiquity. The Society for American Archaeology.
         Menasha, Wis.
Am Indíg.............América Indígena. Instituto Indigenista Interamericano. México,
         D. F., México.
Am J Sociol...........The American Journal of Sociology. The University of Chicago
         Press. Chicago, Ill.
Am Nept ....American Neptune. Salem, Mass.

Am Phil Soc Year Book.American Philosophical Society Year Book. American Philosophical Society. Philadelphia, Pa.

Am Pol Sci R..........American Political Science Review. American Political Science Association. Madison, Wis.

Am Sociol R...........American Sociological Review. American Sociological Society. Pittsburg, Pa.

Amaz Colomb Am......Amazonia Colombiana Americanista. Centro de Investigaciones Lingüísticas y Etnográficas de la Amazonia Colombiana. Sibundoy (Putumayo), Colombia.

Americas, Franciscan
Hist ....The Americas. Academy of American Franciscan History. Washington, D. C.

Américas, PAU.........Américas. Pan American Union. Washington, D. C.

An Est Dist Fed, Rio....Anuario Estatístico do Distrito Federal. Secretaria Geral do Interior e Segurança. Departamento de Geografia e Estatística. Rio de Janeiro, Brazil.

An Estud Am...........Anuario de Estudios Americanos. Escuela de Estudios Hispano-Americanos de la Universidad de Sevilla. Sevilla, Spain.

An Fac Fil, São Paulo...Anuário. Universidade Católica de São Paulo. Facultade de Filosofia do Instituto Sedes Sapientiae. São Paulo, Brazil.

An Hist Der Esp.......Anuario de Historia del Derecho Español. Madrid, Spain.

Anaqueles ....Anaqueles. Biblioteca Nacional. San Salvador, El Salvador.

Anda Mios............Anda Mios. Escuela de Pintura y Escultura del Instituto Juárez. Durango, México.

Anhembi ....Anhembi. São Paulo, Brazil.

Anthr Q...............Anthropological Quarterly. Publication of the Catholic Anthropological Conference. Catholic University of America. Washington, D. C.

Anthropos ....Anthropos. Fribourg, Switzerland.

Antiq Sur.............Antiquity and Survival. The Hague, Netherlands.

Antr Etnol.............Antropología y Etnología. Consejo Superior de Investigaciones Científicas. Instituto Bernardino de Sahagún. Madrid, Spain.

Antr Hist Guat........Antropología e Historia de Guatemala. Instituto de Antropología e Historia de Guatemala. Guatemala, Guatemala.

Antropologica ....Antropologica. Sociedad de Ciencias Naturales La Salle. Caracas, Venezuela.

Arch, Brit Rec Assoc...Archives. British Records Association. London, England.

Arch Hispalense........Archivo Hispalense. Patronato de Cultura de la Excma. Diputación Provincial. Sevilla, Spain.

Arch Hist Soc Iesu......Archivum Historicum Societatis Iesu. Roma, Italy.

Arch Ib Am............Archivo Ibero-Americano. Madrid, Spain.

Arch Per Folk.........Archivos Peruanos de Folklore. Cuzco, Perú.

Archaeology ....Archaeology. Archaeological Institute of America. Cambridge, Mass.

Archit Aujourd'hui......L'Architecture d'Aujourd'hui. Boulogne, France.

Archit R...............Architectural Review. London, England.

Archit Rec.............Architectural Record. New York, N. Y.

Archiv für Völkerkunde.Archiv für Völkerkunde. Museum für Völkerkunde. Wien, Austria.

Ariz Q................Arizona Quarterly. University of Arizona. Tucson, Ariz.

Arq Br Psico..........Arquivos Brasileiros de Psicotécnica. Rio de Janeiro, Brazil.

Arq U Bahia...........Arquivos da Universidade da Bahia. Faculdade de Filosofia. Salvador, Brazil.

Arquit, Habana........Arquitectura. Colegio Nacional de Arquitectos. Habana, Cuba.

Arquitectura ....Arquitectura. México, D. F., México.

Arquivos, Manaus......Arquivos. Associação Comercial do Amazonas. Manaus, Brazil.

Årstryck ....Årstryck 1953-1955. Etnografiska Museet. Göteborg, Sweden.

Art B.................Art Bulletin. The College of Art Association of America. New York, N. Y.

Arte ....Arte. Cochabamba, Bolivia.

Arts Archit............Arts and Architecture. Los Angeles, Calif.

Arts Trad Pop.........Arts et Traditions Populaires. Société d'Ethnographie Française. Paris, France.

Asomante ....Asomante. Asociación de Graduadas de la Universidad de Puerto Rico. San Juan, Puerto Rico.

Atenea ....Atenea. Universidad de Concepción. Concepción, Chile.
Ateneo, Chiapas........Ateneo. Ateneo de Ciencias y Artes de Chiapas. Tuxtla Gutiérrez, México.
Atl Month..............Atlantic Monthly. Boston, Mass.
Atlante ....Atlante. Hispanic and Luso-Brazilian Councils. London, England.

B Ac Ch Hist...........Boletín de la Academia Chilena de la Historia. Santiago, Chile.
B Ac Dom Lengua......Boletín de la Academia Dominicana de la Lengua. Ciudad Trujillo, Dominican Republic.
B Ac Hist Valle Cauca..Boletín de la Academia de Historia del Valle de Cauca. Cali, Colombia.
B Ac Nac Hist, Caracas.Boletín de la Academia Nacional de la Historia. Caracas, Venezuela.
B Ac Nac Hist, Quito...Boletín de la Academia Nacional de Historia. Quito, Ecuador.
B Ac Ven...............Boletín de la Academia Venezolana correspondiente de la Española. Caracas, Venezuela.
B Arch Gen, Ciudad
    Trujillo ....Boletín del Archivo General de la Nación. Ciudad Trujillo, Dominican Republic.
B Arch Gen Chiapas....Boletín. Archivo General de Chiapas. Tuxla Gutiérrez, México.
B Arch Nac, Habana....Boletín del Archivo Nacional. Habana, Cuba.
B Azuc Mex............Boletín Azucarero Mexicano. Unión Nacional de Productores de Azúcar. México, D. F., México.
BBAA ....Boletín Bibliográfico de Antropología Americana. Instituto Panamericano de Geografía e Historia. México, D. F., México.
B Bib Nac, México......Boletín de la Biblioteca Nacional. Universidad Nacional Autónoma de México. México, D. F., México.
B Bibl S Hac Cr Púb....Boletín Bibliográfico de la Secretaría de Hacienda y Crédito Público. México, D. F., México.
B Bur Ethn.............Bulletin du Bureau d'Ethnologie. Port-au-Prince, Haiti.
B CBAI ....Boletim da C. B. A. I. Comissão Brasileiro-Americana de Educação Industrial. Rio de Janeiro, Brazil.
B Cent Estud Roberto
    Mange ....Boletim do Centro de Estudos Roberto Mange. São Paulo, Brazil.
B Cent Inv Antr Méx...Boletín del Centro de Investigaciones Antropológicas de México. México, D. F., México.
B Cent Inv Hist........Boletín del Centro de Investigaciones Históricas. Universidad de Guayaquil. Guayaquil, Ecuador.
B Cleveland Mus Art...Bulletin of the Cleveland Museum of Art. Cleveland, Ohio.
B Dept Arq.............Boletim do Departamento do Arquivo do Estado de São Paulo. São Paulo, Brazil.
B Estud Espec..........Boletín de Estudios Especiales. Banco Nacional de Crédito Ejidal, S. A. México, D. F., México.
B Filol, Santiago.......Boletín de Filología. Universidad de Chile. Instituto de Investigaciones Histórico-Culturales. Santiago, Chile.
B Geog, Rio............Boletim Geográfico. Instituto Brasileiro de Geografia e Estatística. Conselho Nacional de Geografia. Rio de Janeiro, Brazil.
B Geog Rio Grande
    do Sul ....Boletim Geográfico do Estado do Rio Grande do Sul. Pôrto Alegre, Brazil.
B Geol Soc Am.........Bulletin of the Geological Society of America. New York, N. Y.
B Hisp.................Bulletin Hispanique. Annales de la Faculté des Lettres de Bordeaux. Bordeaux, France.
B Hist.................Boletín Histórico. Estado Mayor General del Ejército. Sección Historia y Archivo. Montevideo, Uruguay.
B Hist Antig...........Boletín de Historia y Antigüedades. Academia Colombiana de Historia. Bogotá, Colombia.
B Hist Cartagena.......Boletín Historial Cartagena de Indias. Academia de la Historia de Cartagena de Indias. Cartagena, Colombia.
B Hist Med............Bulletin of the History of Medicine. American Association of the History of Medicine and the Johns Hopkins Institute of the History of Medicine. The Johns Hopkins Press. Baltimore, Md.

B Hist Phil Ohio........Bulletin of the Historical and Philosophical Society of Ohio. Cincinnati, Ohio.
B Indig Ven............Boletín Indigenista Venezolano. Ministerio de Justicia. Comisión Indigenista. Caracas, Venezuela.
B Inf CAPES...........Boletim Informativo CAPES. Campanha Nacional de Aperfeiçoamento do Pessoal de Nivel Superior. Rio de Janeiro, Brazil.
B Inf Cient Nac........Boletín de Informaciones Científicas Nacionales. Casa de la Cultura Ecuatoriana. Quito, Ecuador.
B Inf Estud Soc Ec.....Boletín de Informaciones y de Estudios Sociales y Económicos. Departamento de Investigación Social y Propaganda. Instituto Nacional de Previsión. Quito, Ecuador.
B Inst Am Estud Vas....Boletín del Instituto Americano de Estudios Vascos. Buenos Aires, Argentina.
B Inst Caro Cuervo.....Boletín del Instituto Caro y Cuervo. Ministerio de Educación Nacional. Bogotá, Colombia. (*See:* Thesaurus).
B Inst Intl Am Prot
Infan ....Boletín del Instituto Internacional Americano de Protección a la Infancia. Montevideo, Uruguay.
B Inst Nabuco..........Boletim do Instituto Joaquim Nabuco. Ministério da Educação e Saúde. Recife, Brazil.
B Inst Pesq Ed.........Boletim do Instituto de Pesquisas Educacionais. Secretario General de Educação e Cultura. Rio de Janeiro, Brazil.
B Inst Riva Agüero.....Boletín del Instituto Riva-Agüero. Pontificia Universidad Católica del Perú. Lima, Perú.
B Mém Soc Anthr.......Bulletins et Mémoires de la Société d'Anthropologie de Paris. Paris, France.
B Minneapolis Inst Arts.Bulletin. The Minneapolis Institute of Arts. Minneapolis, Minn.
B Mus Cien Nat........Boletín del Museo de Ciencias Naturales. Caracas, Venezuela.
B Mus Nac Hist Nat....Boletín del Museo Nacional de Historia Natural. Santiago, Chile.
B NY Pub Lib..........Bulletin, New York Public Library. New York, N. Y.
B Paulista Geog........Boletim Paulista de Geografia. Associação dos Geógrafos Brasileiros. São Paulo, Brazil.
B Phila Anthr Soc......Bulletin of the Philadelphia Anthropological Society. Philadelphia, Pa.
B Psico................Boletim de Psicologia. São Paulo, Brazil.
B Soc Chihua Estud Hist.Boletín de la Sociedad Chihuahuense de Estudios Históricos. Chihuahua, México.
B Soc Geog It..........Bollettino della Società Geografica Italiana. Roma, Italy.
B Soc Geog La Paz.....Boletín de la Sociedad Geográfica de La Paz. La Paz, Bolivia.
B Soc Geog Lima.......Boletín de la Sociedad Geográfica de Lima. Lima, Perú.
B Soc Neu Géo.........Bulletin de la Société Neuchâteloise de Géographie. Neuchâtel, Switzerland.
B Soc Suisse Am........Société Suisse des Américanistes. Bulletin. Genève, Switzerland.
B Soc Ven Cien Nat....Boletín de la Sociedad Venezolana de Ciencias Naturales. Caracas, Venezuela.
Baessler Arch..........Baessler-Archiv. Baessler Institut, Staatliche Museum. Leipzig, Berlin, Germany.
Bij Taal Land Volk.....Bijdragen tot de Taal-, Land- en Volkenkunde. 's Gravenhage, Netherlands.
Bolívar, Bogotá.........Bolívar. Ministerio de Educación Nacional de Colombia. Bogotá, Colombia.
Bonn Geog Abhand.....Bonner Geographische Abhandlungen. Bonn Universitat. Geographisches Institut. Bonn, Germany.
Boston Pub Libr Q.....Boston Public Library Quarterly. Boston, Mass.
Bot Mus Leaflets.......Botanical Museum Leaflets. Harvard University. Botanical Museum. Cambridge, Mass.
Brooklyn Mus B........The Brooklyn Museum Bulletin. The Brooklyn Institute of Arts and Sciences. Brooklyn, N. Y.

Cahiers d'Hist Mond....Cahiers d'Histoire Mondiale. Journal of World History. Cuadernos de Historia Mundial. Paris, France.
Cahiers d'Outre-Mer....Les Cahiers d'Outre-Mer. Institut de la France d'Outre-Mer. Bordeaux, France.

Can Geog J............Canadian Geographical Journal. Canadian Geographical Society. Montreal, Canada.
Carib ....The Caribbean [formerly Monthly Information Bulletin]. Port-of-Spain, Trinidad.
Carib For..............The Caribbean Forester. Forest Service. United States Department of Agriculture. Tropical Forest Experimental Station. Río Piedras, Puerto Rico.
Carib Hist R...........Caribbean Historical Review. Historical Society of Trinidad and Tobago. Port-of-Spain, Trinidad.
Carib Q................Caribbean Quarterly. Port-of-Spain, Trinidad.
Chimor ....Chimor. Museo de Arqueología de la Universidad Nacional de Trujillo. Trujillo, Perú.
Chris ....Christoffel. Algemeen Sociaal-Cultureel Maandblad Voor de Nederlandse Antillen. Willemstad, Curaçao.
Cien Art...............Ciencias y Arte. Cuzco, Perú.
Cien Fe...............Ciencia y Fe. Colegio Máximo de San José. Buenos Aires, Argentina.
Cien Soc...............Ciencias Sociales. Pan American Union. Washington, D. C.
Clío ....Clío. Academia Dominicana de la Historia. Ciudad Trujillo, Dominican Republic.
College Art J...........College Art Journal. New York, N. Y.
Com Ext, México.......Comercio Exterior. Banco Nacional de Comercio Exterior. México, D. F., México.
Comentario ....Comentario. Instituto Judío-Argentino de Cultura e Información. Buenos Aires, Argentina.
Cong Nac Soc, VI......Congreso Nacional de Sociología, VI, 1955. Estudios Sociológicos (Sociología rural). México, Universidad Nacional Autónoma de México, Instituto de Investigaciones Sociales, 1956, v. 1.
Conjunt Ec.............Conjuntura Econômica. Fundação Getúlio Vargas. Rio de Janeira, Brazil.
Connoisseur ....The Connoisseur, with which is incorporated International Studio. London, England.
Context ....Context. Yale Divinity School. New Haven, Conn.
Contrib Am Anthr Hist..Contributions to American Anthropology and History. Carnegie Institution of Washington. Washington, D. C.
Crisis ....The Crisis. National Association for the Advancement of Colored People. New York, N. Y.
Crónica, Caracas.......Crónica de Caracas. Concejo Municipal del Distrito Federal, Caracas, Venezuela.
Crónica, Lima.........La Crónica. Lima, Perú. [newspaper].
Cuad ....Cuadernos. Congreso por la Libertad de la Cultura. Paris, France.
Cuad Am..............Cuadernos Americanos. México, D. F., México.
Cuad Hist Arqueol......Cuadernos de Historia y Arqueología. Casa de la Cultura Ecuatoriana. Guayaquil, Ecuador.
Cuad Inst Interam Hist
  Mun Inst.............Cuadernos del Instituto Interamericano de Historia Municipal e Institucional. Habana, Cuba.
Cuad Or Pol...........Cuadernos de Orientación Política. PRI. México, D. F., México.
Cuadrante ....Cuadrante, Revista de Cultura. Universidad Autónoma de San Luis Potosí, México.
Cult U................Cultura Universitaria. Dirección de Cultura de la Universidad Central de Venezuela. Caracas, Venezuela.
Cultura, Lima.........Cultura. Direccíon de Cultura, Arqueología e Historia. Lima, Perú.
Cultura, Rio..........Cultura. Ministerio da Educação e Saúde. Serviço de Documentação. Rio de Janeiro, Brazil.
Cur Rept..............Current Reports. Carnegie Institution of Washington. Department of Archaeology. Washington, D. C.
Cursos Conf...........Cursos y Conferencias. Colegio Libre de Estudios Superiores. Buenos Aires, Argentina.

Diálogo ....Diálogo. Sociedade Cultural Nova Crítica. São Paulo, Brazil.
Diánoia ....Diánoia. Universidad Nacional Autónoma de México. Centro de Estudios Filosóficos. México, D. F., México.

Diário Cong Nac.......Diário do Congresso Nacional. Rio de Janeiro, Brazil.
Dig Ec.................Digesto Econômico. Associação Comercial de São Paulo e da Federação do Comércio do Estado de São Paulo. São Paulo, Brazil.
Diogène ....Diogène. Conseil International de la Philosophie et des Sciences Humaines. Paris, France.
Div Coop..............Divulgação Cooperativista. Niterói, Brazil.
Div Etn...............Divulgaciones Etnológicas. Universidad del Atlántico, Instituto de Investigación Etnológica. Barranquilla, Colombia.

EBSA ....Editóra do Brasil, S. A. Rio de Janeiro, Brazil.
Ec Est................Economía y Estadística. Departamento Administrativo Nacional de Estadística. Bogotá, Colombia.
Economist ....The Economist. London, England.
Ed Ciên Soc...........Educação e Ciências Sociais. Centro Brasileiro de Pesquisas Educacionais. Rio de Janeiro, Brazil.
El Farol..............El Farol. Creole Petroleum Corp. Caracas, Venezuela.
Engenh Min Met........Engenharia, Mineração e Metalurgia. Rio de Janeiro, Brazil.
Estaciones ....Estaciones. México, D. F., México.
Estadística ....Estadística. Journal of the Inter American Statistical Institute. Washington, D. C.
Estud Am..............Estudios Americanos. Escuela de Estudios Hispano-Americanos. Sevilla, Spain.
Estud Hist Am.........Estudios Históricos Americanos. Homenaje a Silvio Zavala. Salutación de Alfonso Reyes. México, El Colegio de México, 1953. 786 p., illus.
Estudio ....Estudio. Academia de Historia de Santander. Bucaramanga, Colombia.
Estudios, B A.........Estudios. Academia Literaria del Plata. Buenos Aires, Argentina.
Et Caetera............Et Caetera. Guadalajara, México.
Ethnohistory ....Ethnohistory. Indiana University. Bloomington, Indiana.
Ethnomus NL...........Ethnomusicology Newsletter. Society for Ethnomusicology. Middletown, Conn.
Ethnos ....Ethnos. Statens Etnografiska Museet. Stockholm, Sweden.
Etn Stud..............Etnologiska Studier. Etnografiska Museet. Göteborg, Sweden.
Étud Da...............Études Dahoméennes. Institut Français d'Afrique Noire. Centre IFAN. Porto-Novo, Dahomey.
Examen Sit Ec México..Examen de la Situación Económica de México. Departamento de Estudios Económicos del Banco Nacional de México. México, D. F., México.

Fanal ....Fanal. International Petroleum Co., Inc. Lima, Perú.
Fénix ....Fénix. Biblioteca Nacional. Lima, Perú.
Fil Let, México.......Filosofía y Letras. Universidad Nacional Autónoma de México. Facultad de Filosofía y Letras. México, D. F., México.
Finis Terrae..........Finis Terrae. Universidad Católica de Chile. Departamento de Extensión Cultural. Santiago, Chile.
Fla Anthr.............The Florida Anthropologist. University of Florida. Florida Anthropological Society. Gainesville, Fla.
Focus ....Focus. American Geographical Society. New York, N. Y.
Fol Ling Am...........Folia Linguistica Americana. Buenos Aires, Argentina.
Formes Coul...........Formes et Couleurs. Lausanne, France.

G Beaux Arts..........Gazette des Beaux-Arts. New York, N. Y.
G Méd, Guayaquil......Gaceta Médica. Servicio San Gabriel, Hospital Luis Vernaza. Guayaquil, Ecuador.
G Méd Méx.............Gaceta Médica de México. Academia Nacional de Medicina. México, D. F., México.
Geog R................The Geographic Review. American Geographical Society of New York. New York, N. Y.
Gutenberg Jahr........Gutenberg Jahrbuch. Gutenberg Gesellschaft. Mainz, Germany.

Habitat ....Habitat. São Paulo, Brazil.
HAHR ....Hispanic American Historical Review. Duke University Press. Durham, N. C.
Hanover F............Hanover Forum. Hanover College. Hanover, Indiana.
Hisp R..............Hispanic Review. University of Pennsylvania Press. Philadelphia, Pa.
Hispania, AATSP......Hispania. American Association of Teachers of Spanish and Portuguese. Wallingford, Conn.
Hist, B A............Historia. Buenos Aires, Argentina.
Hist, Bogotá..........Historia. Instituto Colombiano de Estudios Históricos. Bogotá, Colombia.
Hist, Río Piedras......Historia. Universidad de Puerto Rico. Capítulo Beta Delta de la Sociedad Nacional Honoraria de Historia Phi Alpha Theta. Río Piedras, Puerto, Rico.
Hist Mex..............Historia Mexicana. El Colegio de México. México, D. F., México.
Hist Today............History Today. London, England.
Hum Org..............Human Organization. Society for Applied Anthropology. New York, N. Y.
Humanidades ....Humanidades. Universidad de San Carlos. Facultad de Humanidades. Guatemala, Guatemala.
Humanidades, La Plata..Humanidades. Universidad Nacional de La Plata. Facultad de Humanidades y Ciencias de la Educación. La Plata, Argentina.
Humanismo ....Humanismo. México, D. F., México.
Humanitas ....Humanitas. Universidad Nacional de Tucumán. Facultad de Filosofía y Letras. Tucumán, Argentina.

Ideas Val.............Ideas y Valores. Universidad Nacional. Instituto de Filosofía y Letras. Bogotá, Colombia.
Im Mundi.............Imago Mundi. Leiden, Netherlands.
Ind Lab..............Industry and Labour. International Labour Office. Geneva, Switzerland.
Industriários ....Industriários. Instituto de Aposentadoria e Pensões dos Industriários. Rio de Janeiro, Brazil.
Inf Soc..............Informaciones Sociales. Caja Nacional de Seguro Social. Lima, Perú.
Interam Ec Aff........Inter-American Economic Affairs. Institute of Inter-American Studies. Washington, D. C.
Inti Karka.............Inti Karka. La Paz, Bolivia.
Intl Conc.............International Conciliation. Carnegie Endowment for International Peace. New York, N. Y.
Intl J Am Ling.........International Journal of American Liguistics. Indiana University. Bloomington, Indiana.
Inv Ec................Investigación Económica. Universidad Nacional Autónoma de México. Escuela Nacional de Economía. México, D. F., México.

J Am Folk.............Journal of American Folklore. Philadelphia, Pa.
J Am Inst Archit.......Journal of the American Institute of Architects. Washington, D. C.
J Filol.................Jornal de Filologia. Universidade de São Paulo. Facultade de Filosofia, Ciências e Letras. São Paulo, Brazil.
J Geog................The Journal of Geography. National Council of Geography Teachers. Menasha, Wis.
J Hist Id..............Journal of the History of Ideas. Lancaster, Pa.
J Hist Med Allied Sci...Journal of the History of Medicine and Allied Sciences. Yale University. Department of the History of Medicine. New Haven, Conn.
J Proj Tech...........Journal of Projective Techniques. Society for Projective Techniques and Rorschach Institute. Glendale, Calif.
J Soc Am..............Journal de la Société des Américanistes, publié avec le concours du Centre National de la Recherche Scientifique et du Viking Fund. Paris, France.
J Soc Archit Hist.......Journal of the Society of Architectural Historians. Louisville, Ky.
Jahr Ak Wis Lit........Jahrbuch. Akademie des Wissenschaften und der Literatur. Mainz, Germany.

Johns Hopkins Mag.....Johns Hopkins Magazine. Johns Hopkins University. Baltimore, Md.

Khana ....Khana. La Paz, Bolivia.
Kollasuyo ....Kollasuyo. Universidad Mayor de San Andrés. Escuela de Filosofía y Letras. La Paz, Bolivia.
Kosmos ....Kosmos. Gesellschaft der Naturfreunde. Stuttgart, Germany.
Kriterion ....Kriterion. Faculdade de Filosofia da Universidade de Minas Gerais. Belo Horizonte, Brazil.
Kroeber Anthr Soc Pap..Kroeber Anthropological Society Papers. Berkeley, Calif.

Language ....Language. Journal of the Linguistic Society of America. Baltimore, Md.
Latinoamérica ....Latinoamérica. México, D. F., México.
Lavoura ....A Lavoura. Sociedade Nacional de Agricultura e Confederação Rural Brasileira (1897). Rio de Janeiro, Brazil.
Letras ....Letras. Universidad Nacional Mayor de San Marcos. Facultad de Letras. Lima, Perú.
Lib Pue ....El Libro y el Pueblo. México, D. F., México.
Ling Posnaniensis.......Lingua Posnaniensis. Poznań, Poland.
Lingua ....Lingua. Haarlem, Holland.
Lloydia ....Lloydia. Lloyd Library and Museum. Cincinnati, Ohio.

Mag Art...............Magazine of Art. The American Federation of Art. Washington, D. C.
Man ....The Royal Anthropological Institute. London, England.
Marr Fam Liv.........Marriage and Family Living. National Council on Family Living. Chicago, Ill.
Masterkey ....The Masterkey. Southwest Museum. Los Angeles, Calif.
Mem Ac Mex Hist......Memorias de la Academia Mexicana de la Historia. México, D. F., México.
Mem Ac Nac Hist Geog.Memorias de la Academia Nacional de Historia y Geografía. México, D. F., México.
Mem Col Nac..........Memoria de El Colegio Nacional. México, D. F., México.
Mém IFAN.............Mémoire de l'Institut Français de l'Afrique Noire. Dakar, French West Africa.
Mem R Ac Nac Cien....Memorias y Revista de la Academia Nacional de Ciencias. México, D. F., México.
Mem Soc Cien Nat
La Salle ....Memoria de la Sociedad de Ciencias Naturales La Salle. Caracas, Venezuela.
Mer Per...............Mercurio Peruano. Lima, Perú.
Merc Val..............El Mercado de Valores. Nacional Financiera, S. A. México, D. F., México.
Méx Antig.............El México Antiguo. Sociedad Alemana Mexicanista. México, D. F,. México.
Mid Am...............Mid America. Loyola University. Institute of Jesuit History. Chicago, Ill.
Migr Dig..............Migration Digest. International Catholic Migration Commission. Geneva, Switzerland.
Migr N................Migration News. International Catholic Migration Commission. Geneva, Switzerland.
Mis Dom Perú.........Misiones Dominicanas del Perú. Lima, Perú.
Miss Hisp.............Missionalia Hispanica. Consejo Superior de Investigaciones Científicas. Instituto Santo Toribio de Mogrovejo. Madrid, Spain.
Mit Inst Öst Ges.......Mitteilungen des Instituts für Österreichische Geschichtsforschung. Vienna, Austria.
Mod Lang For.........Modern Language Forum. Los Angeles, Calif.
Mundo Hisp...........Mundo Hispánico. Ediciones Iberoamericanas. Madrid, Spain.
Münster ....Das Münster. Munich, Germany.
Mus Hist..............Museo Histórico. Museo de Historia de la Ciudad de Quito. Quito, Ecuador.
Mús Sac..............Música Sacra. Petropolis, Brazil.

Museum ....Museum. United Nations Educational, Scientific and Cultural Organization. Paris, France.

N Geog Mag............National Geographic Magazine. National Geographic Society. Washington, D. C.
Nat Hist...............Natural History. American Museum of Natural History. New York, N. Y.
Nature ....Nature. London, England.
New Mex Hist R........New Mexico Historical Review. Historical Society of New Mexico and University of New Mexico. Albuquerque, N. Mex.
Newberry Lib B........The Newberry Library Bulletin. Chicago, Ill.
Notas Mus Eva Perón,
   Antropología ....Notas del Museo Eva Perón, Antropología. Universidad Nacional de Eva Perón. La Plata, Argentina.
Notes Mid Am
   Archaeol Ethn ....Notes on Middle American Archaeology and Ethnology. Carnegie Institution of Washington. Washington, D. C.
Noverim ....Noverim. Universidad de Santo Tomás de Villanueva. Departamento de Relaciones Culturas. Habana, Cuba.
Nueva Dem............La Nueva Democracia. Comité de Cooperación en la América Latina. New York, N. Y.
Nueva R Filol Hisp.....Nueva Revista de Filología Hispánica. El Colegio de México. México, D. F., México.
Número ....Número. Montevideo, Uruguay.

Obs Ec Fin.............O Observador Econômico e Financeiro. Rio de Janeiro, Brazil.
Orbis ....Orbis. Bulletin International de Documentation Linguistique. Université Catholique de Louvain. Centre International de Dialectologie Générale. Louvain, Belgium.
Ordem ....A Ordem. Rio de Janeiro, Brazil.

Palacio ....El Palacio. School of American Research, Museum of New Mexico, and Archaeological Society of New Mexico. Santa Fe, N. Mex.
Panor Teat Méx........Panorama del Teatro en México. México, D. F., México.
Panorama ....Panorama. Pan American Union. Washington, D. C.
Panoramas ....Panoramas. México, D. F., México.
Pediatrics ....Pediatrics. American Academy of Pediatrics. Springfield, Ill.
Perú Indíg.............Perú Indígena. Instituto Indigenista Peruano. Lima, Perú.
Petermanns Geog
   Mitteilungen ....Petermanns Geographische Mitteilungen. Veb Geographisch-Kartographische Anstalt. Gotha, Germany.
PH ....La Palabra y el Hombre. Universidad Veracruzana. Xalapa, México.
Phil Phen Re..........Philosophical and Phenomenological Research. Buffalo, N. Y.
PMLA ....PMLA. Publications of the Modern Language Association of America. New York, N. Y.
Pol Agr...............Política Agrícola. Asociación Nacional de Cosecheros. México, D. F., México.
Pol Mex..............La Política Mexicana. Buró de Investigación Política. México, D. F., México.
Popayán ....Popayán. Centro Departamental de Historia. Popayán, Colombia.
Popul Stud............Population Studies. London School of Economics and Political Science. Population Investigation Committee. London, England.
POQ ....Public Opinion Quarterly. Princeton University. School of Public Affairs. Princeton, N. J.
Prés Afr ....Présence Africaine. Paris, France.
Prim Rec Cult Pers.....Primary Records in Culture and Personality. The Microcard Foundation. Madison, Wis.
Pro Am Phil Soc........Proceedings, American Philosophical Society. Philadelphia, Pa.
Pro XXX Intl Cong Am.Proceedings of the XXX International Congress of Americanists, Cambridge, England, 1952. 1954.
Prov São Pedro........Provincia de São Pedro. Pôrto Alegre, Brazil.

Publ Mus Soc Arqueol
   La Serena B ....Publicaciones del Museo y de la Sociedad Arqueológica de la Serena—Boletín. La Serena, Chile.

R Antr, Roma..........Rivista di Antropologia. Societá Romana di Antropologia. Roma, Italy.
R Arch Bib Mus........Revista de Archivos, Bibliotecas y Museos. Consejo Superior de Investigaciones Científicas. Instituto Nicolás Antonio. Madrid, Spain.
R Arch Bib Nac.........Revista del Archivo y Biblioteca Nacionales. Sociedad de Geografía e Historia de Honduras. Tegucigalpa, Honduras. (See: R Soc Geog Hist Hond).
R Arch Hist Cuzco......Revista del Archivo Histórico del Cuzco. Universidad Nacional del Cuzco. Cuzco, Perú.
R Arch Nac Perú.......Revista del Archivo Nacional del Perú. Lima, Perú.
R Arq Mun.............Revista do Arquivo Municipal. Secretaria de Educação e Cultura. São Paulo, Brazil.
R Arq Púb..............Revista do Arquivo Público. Secretaria do Interior e Justícia. Recife, Brazil.
R Banc.................Revista Bancaria. Asociación de Banqueros de México. México, D. F., México.
R Bib Nac, Habana.....Revista de la Biblioteca Nacional. Habana, Cuba.
R Br...................Revista Brasiliense. São Paulo, Brazil.
R Br Ec...............Revista Brasileira de Economia. Fundação Getúlio Vargas. Rio de Janeiro, Brazil.
R Br Est...............Revista Brasileira de Estatística. Instituto Brasileiro de Geografia e Estatística. Instituto Barsileiro de Geografia e Estatística. Rio de Janeiro, Brazil.
R Br Estud Ped........Revista Brasileira de Estudos Pedagógicos. Instituto Nacional de Estudos Pedagógicos. Rio de Janeiro, Brazil.
R Br Fil...............Revista Brasileira de Filosofia. Instituto Brasileiro de Filosofia. São Paulo, Brazil.
R Br Geog.............Revista Brasileira de Geografia. Instituto Brasileiro de Geografia e Estatística. Conselho Nacional de Geografia. Rio de Janeiro, Brazil.
R Br Mun.............Revista Brasileira dos Municípios. Conselho Nacional de Estatística e Associação Brasileira de Municípios. Rio de Janeiro, Brazil.
R Camp Nac Ed Rur....Revista da Campanha Nacional de Educação Rural. Rio de Janeiro, Brazil.
R Can Géog...........Revue Canadienne de Géographie. Société de Géographie de Montréal. Montréal, Canada.
R Cent Estud Hist Mil...Revista del Centro de Estudios Histórico-Militares del Perú. Lima, Perú.
R Cien Ec.............Revista de Ciencias Económicas. Colegio de Doctores en Ciencias Económicas y Contadores Públicos Nacionales y Centro de Estudiantes de Ciencias Económicas. Buenos Aires, Argentina.
R Cien Jur Soc........Revista de Ciencias Jurídicas y Sociales. Facultad de Ciencias Jurídicas y Sociales de la Universidad Nacional del Litoral. Santa Fe, Argentina.
R Col Méd Guat........Revista del Colegio Médico de Guatemala. Guatemala, Guatemala
R Colomb Antr........Revista Colombiana de Antropología. Instituto Colombiano de Antropología. Bogotá, Colombia.
R Colomb Folk........Revista Colombiana de Folklore. Instituto Colombiano de Antropología. Bogotá, Colombia.
R Cub Fil.............Revista Cubana de Filosofía. Dirección de Cultura del Ministerio de Educación. Habana, Cuba.
R Cult.................Revista de Cultura. Universidad Mayor de San Simón. Cochabamba, Bolivia.
R Der Soc Ecuat.......Revista de Derecho Social Ecuatoriano. Universidad Central del Ecuador. Quito, Ecuador.
R Dom Fil.............Revista Dominicana de Filosofía. Universidad de Santo Domingo. Facultad de Filosofía. Ciudad Trujillo, Dominican Republic.
R Ec, México..........Revista de Economía. México, D. F., México.

R Ed, Santiago.........Revista de Educación. Ministerio de Educación Pública de Chile. Santiago, Chile.
R Ens.................Revista do Ensino. Pôrto Alegre, Brazil.
R Esc Cont............Revista de la Escuela de Contabilidad, Economía y Administración. Instituto Tecnológico y de Estudios Superiores de Monterrey. Monterrey, México.
R Estud Pol...........Revista de Estudios Políticos. Instituto de Estudios Políticos. Madrid, Spain.
R F Arm..............Revista de las Fuerzas Armadas. Ministerio de la Defensa de Venezuela. Caracas, Venezuela.
R Fac Der Cien Soc,
   B A ....Revista de la Facultad de Derecho y Ciencias Sociales. Universidad de Buenos Aires. Buenos Aires, Argentina.
R Fac Dir..............Revista da Faculdade de Direito. Universidade de São Paulo, Brazil.
R Fac Hum Cien........Revista de la Facultad de Humanidades y Ciencias. Universidad de la República. Montevideo, Uruguay.
R Fil.................Revista de Filosofía. Universidad de Chile. Santiago, Chile.
R Fil, Eva Perón........Revista de Filosofía. Universidad Nacional de la Ciudad Eva Perón. Instituto de Filosofía. Ciudad Eva Perón, Argentina.
R Filol Esp.............Revista de Filología Española. Consejo Superior de Investigaciones Científicas. Instituto Miguel de Cervantes. Madrid, Spain.
R Fisc Fin..............Revista Fiscal y Financiera. Instituto Mexicano de Técnicos Fiscales. México, D. F., México.
R Fo..................Revista Forense. Colegio de Abogados de Quito. Quito, Ecuador.
R Gen Marina, Madrid..Revista General de Marina. Ministerio de Marina. Madrid, Spain.
R Geog, Barranquilla...Revista Geográfica. Universidad del Atlántico. Instituto de Investigación Etnológica. Barranquilla, Colombia.
R Géog Alp............Revue de Géographie Alpine. Université de Grenoble. Institut de Géographie Alpine. Grenoble, Frances.
R Geog Am............Revista Geográfica Americana. Sociedad Geográfica Americana. Buenos Aires, Argentina.
R Geog Inst Pan Am...Revista Geográfica do Instituto Pan-Americano de Geografia e História. Rio de Janeiro, Brazil.
R Hisp Mod...........Revista Hispánica Moderna. Hispanic Institute in the United States, Columbia University, New York, N. Y., and Departamento de Estudios Hispánicos, Universidad de Puerto Rico, Río Piedras, Puerto Rico.
R Hist, Lima...........Revista Histórica. Instituto Histórico del Perú. Lima, Perú.
R Hist, Pasto...........Revista de Historia. Centro de Historia de Pasto. Pasto, Colombia.
R Hist, São Paulo.......Revista de História. São Paulo, Brazil.
R Hist Am.............Revista de Historia de América. Instituto Panamericano de Geografía e História. México, D. F., México.
R Hist Colonies........Revue d'Histoire des Colonies. Paris, France.
R Iberoam.............Revista Iberoamericana. Instituto Internacional de Literatura Iberoamericana. México, D. F., México.
R Iberoam Seg Soc.....Revista Iberoamericana de Seguridad Social. Ministerio de Trabajo. Instituto Nacional de Previsión. Madrid, Spain.
R Indias, Madrid.......Revista de Indias. Consejo Superior de Investigaciones Científicas. Instituto Gonzalo Fernández, de Oviedo. Madrid, Spain.
R Inst Am Arte........Revista del Instituto Americano de Arte. Cuzco, Perú.
R Inst Hist Geog Br....Revista do Instituto Histórico e Geográfico Brasileiro. Rio de Janeiro, Brazil.
R Inst Nac Cult........Revista del Instituto Nacional de Cultura. Habana, Cuba.
R Inst Soc Solvay.......Revue de l'Institut de Sociologie Solvay. Université Libre de Bruxelles. Institut de Sociologie Solvay. Bruxelles, Belgium.
R Javeriana............Revista Javeriana. Pontificia Universidad Católica Javeriana. Bogotá, Colombia.
R Mex Construc........Revista Mexicana de Construcción. Cámara Nacional de la Industria de la Construcción. México, D. F., México.
R Mex Estud Antr......Revista Mexicana de Estudios Antropológicos. Sociedad Mexicana de Antropología. México, D. F., México.
R Mex Lit.............Revista Mexicana de Literatura. México, D. F., México.

R Mex Soc............Revista Mexicana de Sociología. Universidad Nacional Autónoma. Instituto de Investigaciones Sociales. México, D. F., México.
R Mil Perú............Revista Militar del Perú. Lima, Perú.
R Mus Inst Arqueol.....Revista del Museo e Instituto Arqueológico. Universidad Nacional del Cuzco. Cuzco, Perú.
R Mus Nac............Revista del Museo Nacional. Lima, Perú.
R Nac................Revista Nacional. Ministerio de Instrucción Pública. Montevideo, Uruguay.
R Nac Cult............Revista Nacional de Cultura. Ministerio de Educación Nacional. Dirección de Cultura. Caracas, Venezuela.
R Paris................La Revue de Paris. Paris, France.
R Pat Hist Art Nac.....Revista do Patrimônio Histórico e Artístico Nacional. Ministério de Educação e Saúde. Diretoria do Patrimônio Histórico e Artístico Nacional. Rio de Janeiro, Brazil.
R Ped................Revista de Pedagogia. Rio de Janeiro (?), Brazil.
R Pernam Fil..........Revista Pernambucana de Filosofia. Instituto Brasileiro de Filosofia. Secção de Pernambuco. Recife (?), Brazil.
R Prof................Revista do Professor. São Paulo, Brazil.
R Psicol..............Revista de Psicología. Bogotá, Colombia.
R Ser Púb............Revista do Serviço Público. Departamento Administrativo do Serviço Público. Rio de Janeiro, Brazil.
R Soc Ami Arqueol.....Revista de la Sociedad Amigos de Arqueología. Montevideo, Uruguay.
R Soc Geog Hist Hond..Revista de la Sociedad de Geografía e Historia de Honduras. Tegucigalpa, Honduras. (*Formerly* Revista del Archivo y Biblioteca Nacionales).
R Soc Haïtienne Hist
  Geog ....Revue de la Société Haïtienne d'Histoire et de Géographie. Port-au-Prince, Haïti.
R U, Chile............Revista Universitaria. Universidad Católica de Chile. Santiago, Chile.
R U, Cuzco............Revista Universitaria. Universidad Nacional del Cuzco. Cuzco, Perú.
R U Campinas........Revista da Universidade das Campinas. Campinas, Brazil.
R U Cat, Lima.........Revista Universitaria Católica. Lima, Perú.
R U Minas Gerais......Revista da Universidade de Minas Gerais. Universidade de Minas Gerais. Belo Horizonte, Brazil.
R U Nac, Córdoba.....Revista de la Universidad Nacional de Córdoba. Córdoba, Argentina.
Razón y Fe............Razón y Fe. Madrid, Spain.
Re Stud...............Research Studies of the State College of Washington. Pullman, Wash.
Rend Cl Sci Mor St Fil..Rendiconti della Classe di Scienzi Morali, Storiche e Filogiche. Accademia Nazionale dei Lincei. Roma, Italy.
RIB ....Revista Interamericana de Bibliografía (Inter-American Review of Bibliography). Unión Panamericana. Washington, D. C.
Rom Philol............Romance Philology. University of California Press. Berkeley and Los Angeles, Calif.
Runa ....Runa. Universidad de Buenos Aires. Instituto de Antropología. Buenos Aires, Argentina.
Rural Soc.............Rural Sociology. Rural Sociological Society. North Carolina State College of Agriculture and Engineering. Raleigh, N. C.

Samiska ....Samiska. Indian Psycho-Analytical Society. Calcutta, India.
San Martín............San Martín. Ministerio de Educación de la Nación. Instituto Nacional Sanmartiniano. Buenos Aires, Argentina.
Sapientia ....Sapientia. La Plata, Argentina.
Sci Am...............Scientific American. New York, N. Y.
Sci Pap Jap Antiq Art...Scientific Papers on Japanese Antiquities and Art Crafts. Tokyo, Japan.
Science ....Science. American Association for the Advancement of Science. Washington, D. C.
Seg Soc, Ciudad Trujillo.Seguridad Social. Caja Dominicana de Seguros Sociales. Ciudad Trujillo, Dominican Republic.

Seg Soc, México........Seguro Social. Asociación Internacional de la Seguridad Social de la Conferencia Interamericana de Seguridad Social. Oficina Internacional del Trabajo. México, D. F., México.
Soc Ec Stud.............Social and Economic Studies. University College of the West Indies. Institute of Social and Economic Research. Mona, St. Andrew, Jamaica.
Soc Forces.............Social Forces. University of North Carolina Press. Chapel Hill, N. C.
Sociol Soc Re...........Sociology and Social Research. University of Southern California Press. Los Angeles, Calif.
Sociologia ....Sociologia. Revista Didática e Científica. Publicação da Escola de Sociologia e Política de São Paulo. São Paulo, Brazil.
South Atl Q...........South Atlantic Quarterly. Duke University Press. Durham, N. C.
South Folk Q..........Southern Folklore Quarterly. The University of Florida in cooperation with the Southeastern Folklore Society. Gainesville, Fla.
Staden-Jahrbuch ....Staden-Jahrbuch, Beiträge zur Brasilkunde. Instituto Hans Staden. São Paulo, Brazil.
Stud Ling.............Studies in Linguistics. University of Oklahoma. Norman, Okla.
Stud Philol............Studies in Philology. University of North Carolina Press. Chapel Hill, N. C.
Studio ....Studio. London, England; New York, N. Y.
Südamerika ....Südamerika. Buenos Aires, Argentina.
Sul ....Sul. Florianopolis, Brazil.
Sur ....Sur. Buenos Aires, Argentina.
SW Hist Q............Southwestern Historical Quarterly. Austin, Tex.
SW J Anthr...........Southwestern Journal of Anthropology. University of New Mexico and Laboratory of Anthropology, Santa Fe. Albuquerque, N. Mex.
SW Soc Sci Q..........Southwestern Social Science Quarterly. University of Oklahoma. Southwestern Social Science Association. Norman, Okla.

Teat, Madrid..........Teatro. Madrid, Spain.
Teat, México..........Teatro. México, D. F., México.
Teat Br...............Teatro Brasileiro. São Paulo, Brazil.
Tenn Archaeol.........Tennessee Archaeologist. Tennessee Archaeological Society. Nashville, Tenn.
Terre Vie.............La Terre et la Vie. Société National d'Acclimation et de Protection de la Nature. Paris, France.
Thesaurus ....Thesaurus. Ministerio de Educación Nacional. Instituto Caro y Cuervo. Bogotá, Colombia. (Formerly Boletín del Instituto Caro y Cuervo).
Tierra Firme..........Tierra Firme. Caracas, Venezuela.
Tijd Ec Soc Geog......Tijdschrist voor Economische en Sociale Geografie. Nederlandsche Vereeniging voor Economische Geografie. s'Gravenhage, Netherlands.
Tlatoani ....Tlatoani. Sociedad de Alumnos de la Escuela Nacional de Antropología e Historia. México, D. F., México.
Torre ....La Torre. Universidad de Puerto Rico. Río Piedras, Puerto Rico.
Trab Conf.............Trabajos y Conferencias. Universidad de Madrid. Seminario de Estudios Americanistas. Madrid, Spain.
Tradición ....Tradición. Cuzco, Perú.
Trans Am Philos Soc....Transactions of the American Philosophical Society. Philadelphia, Pa.
Trav Étud And........Travaux de l'Institut Français d'Études Andines. Paris, France; Lima, Perú.
Trim Ec...............El Trimestre Económico. Fondo de Cultura Económica. México, D. F., México.

U Antioquia...........Universidad de Antioquia. Medellín, Colombia.
U Calif Publ Am
  Archaeol Ethn ....University of California Publications in American Archaeology and Ethnology. Berkeley, Calif.
U Habana..............Universidad de la Habana. Habana, Cuba.

U México..............Universidad de México. Universidad Nacional Autónoma. México, D. F., México.
Übersee Rund...........Übersee Rundschau. Ibero-Amerikanischer Verein. Hamburg, Germany.
Universidad, Monterrey.Universidad. Universidad de Nuevo León. Monterrey, México.
Universidad, Santa Fe...Universidad. Universidad Nacional del Litoral. Santa Fe, Argentina.
Universitas, Cien Jur....Universitas: Ciencias Jurídico-Sociales y Letras. Pontificia Universidad Católica Javeriana. Bogotá, Colombia.
USSR ....Union of Soviet Socialist Republics Embassy in the U. S. A. Washington, D. C.

Vie Lang...............Vie et Langage. Paris, France.
Vier Soz Wirt..........Vierteljahrschrift für Sozial- und Wirtschaftsgeschichte. Wiesbaden, Germany.
Visão ....Visão. Rio de Janeiro, Brazil.
VOKS B...............VOKS Bulletin. The Soviet Union Society for Cultural Relations with Foreign Countries. Moscow, USSR.

Water Power...........Water Power. London, England.
West Indische Gids......De West-Indische Gids. s'Gravenhage, Netherlands.
West Pol Q.............Western Political Quarterly. University of Utah. Western Political Association; Pacific Northwest Political Science Association. Salt Lake City, Utah.
Wm Mary Q............The William and Mary Quarterly. Institute of Early American History and Culture. Williamsburg, Va.
Word ....Word. Linguistic Circle of New York. New York, N. Y.

Y Assn Pac Coast Geog.Yearbook of the Association of Pacific Coast Geographers. Cheney, Wash.
Yale U Lib G...........Yale University Library Gazette. New Haven, Conn.
Yan ....Yan. Centro de Investigaciones Antropológicas de México. México, D. F., México.
Yikal ....Yikal Mayathan. Mérida, México.

Zeit Ethn..............Zeitschrift für Ethnologie. Berlin, Germany.
Zeit Morph Anthr.......Zeitschrift für Morphologie und Antropologie. E. Schweizerhart'sche Verlagsbuchhandlung. Stuttgart, Germany.

Index I: Author

Abad, Diego José, 3720
Abascal, Horacio, 2903
Abascal Brunet, Manuel, 4237
Abascal y Vera, Horacio, 2924
Abbagnano, Nicola, 4878
Abecía Baldivieso, Valentín, 3021
Abello Roca, Carlos Daniel, 3500
Abreu, João Capistrano de, 3240
Abreu, Sílvio Fróes, 2083
Ab'Sáber, Aziz Nacib, 2050–2050e, 2122, 2123
Academia Colombiana, 3625
Academia de la Historia. Biblioteca, 2400
Acchiardi, Pablo, 4242
Accioly, Breno, 4358
Accioly Netto, A., 4359, 4418
Acevedo, Edberto Óscar, 2780, 2994
Acevedo Amaya, Valmore, 4555
Acevedo Díaz, Eduardo, 2004
Acevedo Escobedo, Antonio, 1450
Acevedo Latorre, Eduardo, 1973
Acha, Eduardo de, 4603
Acker, Leonardo van, 4805
Acoglia, Rodolfo M., 4806
Acosta, Jorge R., 86
Acosta, Roberto, 2300
Acosta Saignes, Miguel, 268, 275, 2708
Acosta Solís, Misael, 2034
Acosta y Lara, Eduardo F., 382
Acquarone, Ignacio, 1018
Adams, Richard N., 400
Aftalión, Enrique R., 4525
Aga-Oglu, Kamer, 284
Agnew, Arlene, 650
Agramonte, Roberto, 4900, 4981
Agranovsky, Anatoli, 189
Agreda y Sánchez, José María, 2517
Aguado, Pedro de, 2708a
Aguayo Spencer, Rafael, 4050
Agüero Aguirre, Mario, 4507
Agüero Sole, Omar, 1320
Aguilar, Octavio, 3900
Aguilar Pinel, Carlos, 1950
Aguilera, Emiliano M., 2520
Aguilera Malta, Demetrio, 3901
Aguirre Beltrán, Gonzalo, 460–462
Aizpurua, Armando, 2869
Akin, John, 1262
Alambert, Silvia B., 1792
Alanís Patiño, Emilio, 1451, 1452
Alarco, Luis Felipe, 4758

Alarcón Fernández, José, 3284
Alatorre, Antonio, 3727, 4360
Alayza y Paz Soldán, Luis, 2038
Alba, Armando, 4066
Alba, Víctor, 1250, 3501
Albájar, Amparo, 4879b
Albareda, José Daniel, 1453
Alberti, M. H., 4893
Albisetti, César, 650a
Alcalde Mongrut, Arturo, 3060
Alcedo, José Bernardo, 4723
Alegría, Claribel, 4051
Alegría, Ricardo E., 251, 484
Alembert, Jean Lerond d', 4750
Alencar, Heron de, 4312
Alencastre G., Andrés, 651
Alende, Oscar E., 1300
Alessio Robles, Vito, 2800, 2801
Alexander, Robert J., 3271
Alfau Durán, Vetilio, 2579, 2942–2942b, 2944, 5020
Alfonso, Paco, 4200
Allan, P., 340
Almacenes Nacionales de Depósito. Departamento Técnico, 1454–1462
Almada, Francisco R., 5045
Almarza, Camilo, 3523
Almeida, Antônio Paulino de, 3200
Almeida, Fernando Flávio Marques de, 2051, 2124
Almeida, Renato, 4706
Almeida Júnior, A., 1767
Alpern, Hymen, 4201
Alsina, José Arturo, 4201
Altamira, Luis Roberto, 918
Alva Martínez, Carlos, 1463
Alvarado, Lisandro, 3085
Álvarez, José, 651a
Álvarez, José Sixto, 3902
Álvarez, María Edmée, 3626
Álvarez Conde, José, 252
Álvarez Mejía, Juan, 2401
Álvarez Tabío, Fernando, 4542
Alves, Francisco M. Rodrigues, 2245, 2245a
Amábilis Domínguez, Manuel, 40
Amado, Gilberto, 4296
Amado, Jorge, 4349
Amador Navarro, Estéban, 4556
Amador Sánchez, Luis, 2904
Amaral, Antônio Carlos Cintra do, 4918
Amazonas, Joaquim, 4918

Nacional Financiera, 1518-1540
Nájera Farfán, Mario Efraín, 2275
Nandino, Elías, 4096
Napoleão, Martins, 4411
Nascentes, Antenor, 4292
Nash, Manning, 489, 490
National Geographic Society, 17
National Planning Association, 3429
Navarrete, Alfredo, Jr., 1541-1544
Navarrete, Ifigenia M. de, 1545
Navarrete, Juan Antonio de, 4764
Navarro, Barnabé, 4789
Naveda, Bolívar H., 2035
Neder, Matilde, 1793
Neguera, Guadalupe, 3965
Neruda, Pablo, 4097, 4098
Nerval, Gérard de, 4103
Nett, Emily W., 437
Neves, Carlos de Souza, 4605
Newcomb, William W., 491
Nicaragua
    Consejo Nacional de Economia, 1344
    Dirección General de Estadística y Censos, 5013
    Instituto de Fomento Nacional, 1345
    Ministerio de Relaciones Exteriores, 4721
    Ministerio de Salubridad Pública, 3600
Nicholson, Carlos, 2044a
Nicholson, H. B., 147
Nicolas, Hogar, 2958
Nida, E. A., 717a
Nieto, Luis Carlos, 4138
Nieto y Cortadellas, Rafael, 2337, 2936, 2936a
Nigra, Clemente Maria da Silva, 1167
Nimuendajú, Curt, 702a
Nóbrega, Manuel da, 3249
Nogami, Toshiichi, 366
Nogueira, Rubem, 3286
Noguera, Eduardo, 148-150
Noguera, Manuel G., 62
Noriega, Raúl, 233-233c
Noriega Hope, Carlos, 4234
Norton, E. A., 1262
Novaes, Maria Stella de, 3227
Novaro, Octavio, 4099a
Novo, Salvador, 4099, 4234
Novoa, Emilio, 2466
Nowotny, Karl Anton, 234
Noyes, Ernest, 703
Noyola Vázquez, Juan, 1546
Núnes, Pedro, 4479
Núñez, Enrique Bernardo, 3742
Núñez, Mier y Terán, Sebastián, 799
Nunn, William Curtis, 2848

Obando V., Marcelo A., 791
Oblitas Poblete, Enrique, 703a
Obregón, Gonzalo, 979
Obregón Loría, Rafael, 1705
Ocampo, María Luisa, 4234
Ochoa Campos, Moisés, 2849
Odría, Manuel Arturo, 3072
Odriosola, Ricardo, 3604
Oficina Iberoamericana de Seguridad Social, 3561

Ogden, Charles Key, 4887
O'Gorman, Edmundo, 2409, 2411, 2467, 4796
Olderogge, D. A., 235
Olguín, Manuel, 4263
Olinto, António, 4412
Olivari, Nicolás, 4100
Oliveira, Avelino Ignacio de, 2072
Oliveira, Clovis de, 1430
Oliveira, Juscelino Kubitschek, 1763
Oliveira, Paulo Erichsen de, 2073
Oliveira e Cruz, João Claudino de, 4553
Oliveira Júnior, Ernesto Luis de, 1779, 1788
Olivera, Miguel Alfredo, 3664
Olivera Sedano, Alicia, 236
Olivetti, Benedicto, 2257
Olmsted, David L., 3665
Olwer, L. Nicalau d', 2540
O'Neill de Milán, Luis, 4101
Onís, Harriet de, 3924
Onís, José de, 5054
Onody, Oliver, 1431
Opie, Redvers, 3423
Orbegoso Rodrígues, Efraín, 2045
Orellana, Daniel, 3086
Orellana Tapia, Rafael, 151, 152
Orendain, Leopoldo I., 980
Orgambide, Pedro G., 4009
Organización Iberoamericana de Seguridad Social, 3562
Organization of American States, 3451
Oría, José A., 4750
Orico, Osvaldo, 4341
Orosa Díaz, Jaime, 4223
Orozco, José Clemente, 1062, 1063
Orozco Muñoz, Julio, 2850
Orphée, Elvira, 3966
Orrego, Antenor, 4139
Orssich, Adam, 320
Orssich, Elfriede Stadler, 320
Ortega, Exequiel César, 3014
Oretga Flores, Salvador, 1064
Ortega Ramos, Virginia, 3516
Ortega Ricuarte, Enrique, 2713, 2723
Ortiz, Fernando, 4961
Ortiz, Sergio E., 704
Ortiz D., H., 3714
Ortiz de la Roche, Mario, 3517
Ortiz Fernández, Fernando, 2468
Ortiz Mena, Antonio, 3596
Ortiz Mena, Raúl, 1262
Ortiz Oderigo, Néstor R., 480, 563
Ospina, Eduardo, 3044
Ossorio y Florit, Manuel, 3571
Ostrowski, Wiktor, 2016
Otero, Mariano, 4913
Otero D'Costa, Enrique, 2724-2724b
Otero Silva, Miguel, 3967, 3968
Othón, Manuel José, 4234
Otruba, Gustav, 2793, 2793a
Ots Capdequí, José María, 2725
Otte, Enrique, 2726
Outwater, J. Ogden, Jr., 63
Owen, Walter, 4117
Oxley, Diego R., 3969, 3970

Pfänder, Bruno, 3972
Phelan, John Leddy, 2344, 2541a
Philipson, J., 706
Pi Hugarte, Renzo, 4924
Pi Sunyer, Carlos, 3105
Piazza, Luis Guillermo, 3973
Piazza, Walter F., 4343
Piccirrilli, Ricardo, 3016
Pichardo, Esteban, 3668
Pichardo Moya, Felipe, 263
Pickett, Velma, 706a
Picón-Salas, Mariano, 1073, 1074, 2706
Piérola, Raúl Alberto, 1702, 4792
Pierre, Juan Carlos, 4518
Pierson, Donald, 4988
Pierson, Esther, 707
Pierson, William Whatley, 2204
Pietrangeli, Angelina, 3650
Pike, Eunice V., 707a
Pike, Evelyn G., 650
Pimenta, Joaquim, 4918
Pimenta, José de Melo, 3231
Pimentel, Francisco, 4055
Piña Chan, Román, 64
Pinacoteca do Estado de S. Paulo, 1153
Pineda, Rafael, 4253
Pinedo, Federico, 2227
Piñera Llera, Humberto, 4758, 4772, 4773,
  4824, 4847, 4875d
Pinheiro, Fred, 4414
Pinto, Estevão, 708, 708a
Pinto, L. A. Costa, 4903
Pinto, Maria Magdalena Vieira, 2096
Pinto, Oliveira M. de, 3202
Pintores argentinos, 1029
Pires, Heliodoro, 1154
Pita, Enrique B., 4819
Pittman, Marvin S., 1706
Pittman, Richard Saunders, 709
Pizani, Rafael, 4490
Pla, Guí, 2018
Pla, Roger, 3974
Pla Rodríguez, Américo, 3518
Plá y Beltrán, Pascual, 4142
Placer, Xavier, 4312
Plan de Ayutla, 2852
Planas Suárez, Simón, 3417, 3439
Planchart, Enrique, 1075
Plato, 4888, 4888a
Platt, Raye Roberts, 2035a
Plaza, Angélica, 4227
Pleasants, F. R., 981
Plotinus, 4889
Poblete Troncoso, Moisés, 3519
Polanco Brito, H. E., 2951
Pollock, H. E. D., 65, 156
Pompa y Pompa, Antonio, 768
Pompeu Sobrinho, Thomaz, 321, 709a
Ponce, Aníbal, 2232
Ponce Sanginés, Carlos, 3021
Pontes, Ribeiro, 3520
Popescu, Oreste, 4870
Porras Barrenechea, Raúl, 710, 3702, 3715,
  3718, 5058
Porras Troconis, G., 2727
Porta F., Enrique, 941

Porter, Muriel Noé., 157
Porterfield, Austin L., 2848
Porto, Carlos Eugênio, 3232
Portogalo, José, 4104
Portugal Catacorca, José, 3975
Portuondo, José Antonio, 426
Potsch, Waldemiro, 1433
Pouesselle, Lucien, 2137
Pourchet, Maria Júlia, 781, 782
Poviña, Alfredo, 4914
Powell, Jack Richard, 1550
Powrie, Barbara E., 4974
Prado, Décio de Almeida, 4344
Prebisch, Raúl, 1308
Pressoir, Catts, 2345
Price, Thomas J., Jr., 573
Prieto, Eduardo, 4887
Prieto, Raúl, 3976
Procope, Bruce, 482
Proença, M. Cavalcânti, 4345
Proskouriakoff, Tatiana, 66, 72, 158
Proudfoot, Mary, 5069
Prudencio, Roberto, 2244
Prunes, Lourenço Mario, 2069
Public Administration Clearing House, 2205
Pucciarelli, Eugenio, 4758, 4793
Puente Candamo, José A. de la, 2764, 2764a
Puerto Rico. Bureau of the Budget. Division
  of Statistics, 5017
Puga, Mario, 3977
Puig, Pilar, 67
Puiggrós, Rodolfo, 2228, 2994
Pultera (hijo), Raúl, 3843
Pupiales, Mateo de, 710a
Putnam, Samuel, 4905

Queiroz, Amaro Xisto de, 4825
Queiroz, Rachel de, 4349
Quesada, Alejandro, 2042
Quevedo y Villegas, Agustín de, 4764
Quigley, Carroll, 411
Quiles, Ismael, 4758, 4848, 4873a, 4873b
V Salão Nacional de Arte Moderna, 1187
V Salão Paulista de Arte Moderna, 1188
Quintana, Jorge, 2346
Quintanilha, Dirceu, 4415
Quintero, Vicente P., 4885b
Quintero Rivera, Nazario, 1551
Quirk, Robert E., 2853

Rabanales O., Ambrosio, 3669
Rabasa, Emilio, 4504, 4505
Rache, Pedro, 3288
Radaelli, Sigfrido Augusto, 2794
Radbruch, Gustav, 4889a
Radhakrishnan, Sarvepalli, 4889b
Radiguet, Max, 5051
Raez Patiño, Sara, 3074
Raggi Ageo, Carlos M., 3581
Raine, Philip, 2037, 2286
Ramírez, Esteban, 2542a, 2543
Ramírez, Félix C., 159
Ramírez Bonilla, Blanca Gloria, 1552
Ramírez Corría, Filiberto, 2578
Ramírez Novoa, Ezequiel, 3431
Ramírez Sánchez, Alfredo, 4538

Index II: Subject

95, 179, 194. Panama, 267. Peru, 344a, 346a, 347, 350a, 379. St. Lucia, 260. U. S., 284–286. Uruguay, 383. Venezuela, 269, 271, 272.

ANTHROPOLOGY, PHYSICAL
General—Latin America, 792. Brazil, 313b, 321.
Anthropometry—Living, 758, 762, 767, 770, 771, 781, 782, 784, 793, 799. Skeletal, 761, 769, 773, 775, 778, 783, 785, 787, 791, 802, 803.
Deformity, trephining, mutilation—763, 773, 775, 794, 795, 796.
Early man, 759, 775.
Physiological observations—General, 777, 789, 790, 797, 798, 799. Blood groups, 750, 756, 774, 779, 780, 804. Hair, 800. Palm and finger prints, 801.
Population—Mexico, 766. *See also* Population.
Racial groups—755, 757, 764, 772, 775, 781, 782.
Technique—757, 758, 776, 784.
Antonelli, Juan Bautista, 2430
Apodaca, Juan de, 2452
Arango y Parreño, Francisco de, 2583
Araujo, Joaquín Miguel, 3043
Arbenz Guzmán, Jacobo, 1341, 2269, 2271, 2276, 3421
Arboleda, Julio, 3848
ARCHAEOLOGY. *See appropriate sub-headings under* Anthropology, cultural.
ARCHITECTURE
General, 3751. Latin America, 906, 928, 1021a. Argentina, 912, 920, 927, 931, 1022, 1028. Arizona, 1014. Bolivia, 932–934, 936–938. Brazil, 1152, 1156, 1157, 1159, 1161, 1164, 1166, 1168, 1169, 1178, 1179, 1180, 1182–1186, 1189, 3226. Chile, 941-943, 1038, 1039. Cuba, 1013, 1041, 2351. Dominican Republic, 1015. Guatemala, 953-956. Honduras, 1016, 1017. Mexico, 908, 909, 957–962, 965, 966, 971–972, 973, 974, 976, 979, 983, 984, 986–990, 1056, 1067, 2327. Paraguay, 912. Peru, 992, 998, 999, 1002, 1004–1008. Puerto Rico, 1009, 1010. Uruguay, 1011, 1012. *See also* Anthropology, cultural—Art and architecture.
ARCHIVES
Latin America, 2335, 2339. Argentina, 2792b. Brazil, 3206, 3234, 3250. Chile, 2776, 2778. Costa Rica, 2311. Colombia, 3028. Cuba, 2313, 2314, 2316, 2587, 2915, 2925. Dominican Republic, 2328, 2581, 2587, 2944, 2945, 2947. Ecuador, 2769. Haiti, 2583. Italy, 2482. Mexico, 2332, 2506, 2506a, 2553, 2555, 2556. Nicaragua, 2563, 2569. Peru, 2342, 2343. Philippines, 2370. Spain, 2400, 2421. Trinidad and Tobago, 2307. U. S., 2823, 2862. Uruguay, 3083. Venezuela, 2366, 3110.
Arcila Farías, Eduardo, 2414
Arciniega, Claudio de, 987

Arévalo, Juan José, 2275, 2276
ARGENTINA
General, 2017, 3446. Anthropology, 303–310, 688, 717, 720, 720a, 775, 783. Art and architecture, 308, 900, 912, 918–931, 1018–1034. Description and travel, 5052. Economics, 1300–1310, 2226, 3523, 3571, 4557–4559, 4569, 4573, 4583, 4604. Education, 1652, 1700–1702. Geography, 2004–2020a, 2049. Government and politics, 2210–2236. History, 2217, 2228, 2780–2799, 2978, 2981, 2989, 2990, 2994–3020, 3080, 3082, 3807, 3815, 3921, 3936, 4242. International relations, 3434, 3437, 3446. Labor, 3504, 3523. Language, 688, 717, 720, 720a, 3659, 3664, 3683, 5052. Law, 2978, 3504, 4480, 4501, 4506, 4509, 4514, 4518, 4521, 4525, 4545, 4549, 4557–4559, 4569, 4573, 4583, 4596. Literature, 2782, 3701, 3740, 3804, 3806, 3807, 3809, 3810, 3812, 3815, 3824, 3829, 3843, 3902, 3908, 3911, 3912, 3915, 3916, 3917, 3921, 3923, 3930, 3936, 3939, 3942, 3943, 3948, 3950, 3954, 3955, 3962, 3966, 3969, 3970, 3971, 3972–3974, 3986, 3989, 3990, 3996–3998, 4000, 4007, 4013, 4056, 4061, 4064, 4071, 4073, 4082, 4083, 4086, 4095, 4100, 4104, 4105, 4109, 4114, 4118, 4120, 4126, 4127, 4140, 4212, 4214, 4217, 4219, 4220, 4224, 4228, 4231, 4242, 4245, 4246, 4250, 4255, 4257, 4259, 4261, 4266, 4269. Music and dance, 4703–4705. Philosophy, 4750, 4754, 4760, 4761, 4763, 4769, 4771, 4774, 4776, 4777, 4785, 4792–4795, 4797, 4858, 4868, 4870. Social welfare, 3504, 3568–3573. Sociology, 4934, 4944, 4985.
Argüedas, Alcides, 4861
Arias Dávila, Pedro, 2403
Arias de la Cerda, Diego, 994
Arista, Mariano, 2826
Armas y Céspedes, José de, 2907
Arráiz, Antonio, 3813
Arriaga, Camilo, 2802
ART
General, 4987. Bibliography, 944, Catalogues, 901, 902, 904, 905, 946, 1019, 1025, 1032, 1049, 1062, 1153, 1173, 1174. Exhibitions, 902, 903, 904, 906, 910, 1020, 1025, 1032, 1049, 1069, 1151, 1176, 1177. Minor, 922, 923, 945, 969, 991, 1177. *See also* Anthropology, cultural—Art and architecture; Architecture; Graphic arts; Painting; Sculpture *and under names of countries and geographical areas.*
Assis, Joaquim Maria Machado de, 4279, 4307, 4357
ATLASES. *See* Maps.
Auer, Väinö, 306
Avendaño, Diego de, 2752
Avilés, Gabriel, 2790a
Ay, Manuel Antonio, 2807

BRITISH COLONIES
Bahamas, Anthropology, 254. *British Guiana,* Anthropology, 338, 339, 580, 581. *British Honduras,* Anthropology, 41, 83, 107, 181; Geography, 1963. *British West Indies,* Geography, 1966, 1971; Language, 407. *Carriacou,* Anthropology, 496. *Dominica,* Anthropology, 428–431; Language, 430, 431. *Falkland Islands,* General, 2048; Geography, 2048. *Jamaica,* Anthropology, 257, 453–459; History, 455, 459; Sociology, 453, 454, 459, 4924a, 4979. *St. Lucia,* Anthropology, 259, 260; History, 259; Language, 486; Music and dance, 487. *Tobago,* History, 2307. *Trinidad,* Anthropology, 475–483; History, 2307, 2308; Music and dance, 478–480. *See also* West Indies; Caribbean Area.
British Honduras. *See* British Colonies.
Brown, William, 2989
Brunet, Marta, 3808
BUCCANEERS, FILIBUSTERS, AND PIRATES, 2435, 2440.
Bueno, Cosme, 2758, 3711
Butler, Horacio, 1027

Caballero, Lucas, 3035
Cabrera, Geles, 1064
Cáceres, Núñez de, 3098
Camaño, Joaquín, 2786c
Cambaceres, Eugenio, 3809
Campo, Ángel de, 3658
Cannabrava, Euryalo, 4306
Cantillana, Suárez de, 2780
CARIBBEAN AREA
Anthropology, 207, 250, 251, 255, 258, 263–265, 404. Economics, 1262. Government and politics, 2209. History, 2350, 2439, 2440, 2444, 5069. Language, 265. Social welfare, 3559a. Sociology, 4949.
Carlos I (V), 2419
Caro family, 3830
Caro, Miguel Antonio, 4864
Carpentier, Alejo, 4720
Carranza, Venustiano, 2825, 2863
Carrera, José Miguel, 2990, 2991
Carrillo, Carlos A., 1717
Carrillo Puerto, Felipe, 4223
Carrión, Bartolomé, 993
Carrión, Cachot, Rebeca, 349
Carvajal, Luis de, 2504
Carvajal, Rodrigo de, 3739
Carvalho, Antônio Maria de, 3209
Carvalho, Vicente de, 4314
Casacuberta, Juan Aurelio, 4242
Casal, Julián del, 4146
Casas, Bartolomé de las, 2410, 2442, 2445, 2456, 2457, 2480, 2740
Casas, Ignacio Mariano de las, 958
Cass, Lewis, 2961
Castellanos, Julio, 1049
Castellví, Marcelino de, 1974
Castera, Ignacio de, 978
Castilla, Ramón, 3074–3079

Castillo Armas, Carlos, 1340, 2270–2271a
Castro, Ignacio de, 3719
Catalano, Eduardo, 921
CATHOLIC CHURCH. *See* Church-State relations; History—Ecclesiastical; Inquisition; Missions and missionaries; Sociology —Religion.
Cavalcanti, Emiliano di, 1190
Celso Júnior, Afonso, 3269
CENTRAL AMERICA
General, 2872. Anthropology, 188, 226, 400, 658a, 667a, 682, 689–690, 712a. Art and architecture, 900. History, 2483, 2563–2573, 2840, 2869–2873. Language, 226, 658a, 667a, 682, 689–690, 712a. Music, 188.
César, Roberto Cerqueira, 1178
Céspedes, Carlos Manuel de, 2346
Cetina, Gutierre de, 3709
Chi, Gaspar Antonio, 2548
CHILE
Anthropology, 323–328, 553, 688. Art and architecture, 900, 940–943, 1037–1040. Economics, 1255, 1311, 1312, 2265, 4562, 5062. Education, 1658, 1703, 1704, 4606. Description and travel, 5051. Geography, 2026–2033, 2049. Government and politics, 2260–2265. History, 2772–2779, 2990, 2991, 3025, 5071. International relations, 2821, 3437. Labor, 3521, 3524. Language, 688, 3638, 3660, 3669, 3677. Law, 4511, 4522, 4523, 4535, 4562, 4606. Literature, 3700, 3706, 3708, 3819, 3820, 3826, 3854, 3906, 3909, 3926–3929, 3933, 3935, 3940, 3945, 3946, 3956, 3959, 3961, 3978, 3991, 4058, 4059, 4097, 4098, 4102, 4110, 4112, 4124, 4134, 4143, 4232, 4237, 4270, 5071. Music and dance, 4722. Philosophy, 4752, 4780, 4800. Social welfare, 3579, 3580. Sociology, 4948.
Chocano, José Santos, 4141
CHURCH-STATE RELATIONS
General, 2260. Latin America, 2201. Argentina, 1701, 3017. Chile, 4515. Colombia, 3042. Costa Rica, 2297a. Ecuador, 2268. Mexico, 2284, 2531, 2541.
Cieza de León, Pedro, 2757a
Cisneros, Juan Francisco, 1078
CITIES, 2109 (Brazil). *See also* History—Local; Sociology—Urban.
CLIMATE
Bolivia, 2024. Brazil, 2104, 2105. Chile, 2031. El Salvador, 1955.
COATS OF ARMS, 2794 (Argentina).
Codazzi, Agustín, 1975, 3030
CODICES. *See* Anthropology, cultural — Native sources.
Coelho Netto, Paulo, 5025
COFFEE. *See* Commodities.
Coleti, Juan Domingo, 2703
COLOMBIA
Anthropology, 276–283, 335, 412, 566–573, 650, 656, 658a, 660, 660a, 661, 661a, 663–665a, 677–678, 679, 679a,

688a, 701a, 712a, 713, 2706a. Art and architecture, 917, 944–952, 1076. Description and travel, 3100, 5053, 5060. Economics, 568, 1313–1319, 4580. Education, 1651. Geography, 1973–1986. Government and politics, 2298a. History, 1981, 1984d, 2325, 2331, 2483, 2703, 2706a, 2708a–2720, 2723–2728, 2730–2737a, 2975, 2977, 2987, 3026–3049, 3100. Labor, 3500, 3517. Language, 281, 650, 656, 658a, 660–661a, 663–665a, 677–678, 679, 679a, 688a, 701a, 712a, 713, 3625, 3635, 3643, 3647, 3653, 3679a. Law, 4577, 4580. Literature, 3722, 3723, 3733, 3830, 3848, 3920, 4010, 4107. Music and dance, 660. Philosophy, 4864, 4870b. Social welfare, 3612. Sociology, 4927, 4932, 4941, 4968, 4984.

COLONIZATION
Latin America, 27, 4933. Argentina, 4934. Brazil, 2113, 2115, 2117, 2118, 2119, 3249, 3259, 4936. Ecuador, 4938. Guatemala, 2878. Haiti, 2955. Mexico, 2848. Peru, 2039a.

Columbus, Christopher, 2405–2407, 2445, 2457, 2472, 2484

Columbus, Diego, 2585

COMMERCE. See Trade.

COMMODITIES
Coffee—Brazil, 2084, 2089, 2095, 2105, 2112, 2128. Guatemala, 2358, 2877.
Cotton—Colombia, 1978. Mexico, 1527, 2803.
Petroleum—Argentina, 2215, 2215a, 4596. Bolivia, 4598. Brazil, 1444, 2107. Chile, 2030. Guatemala, 4597. Mexico, 1509, 1547–1550.
Sugar—Brazil, 1410, 1413. Colombia, 2733a. Cuba, 1328. Mexico, 1493. Nicaragua, 1345.
Miscellaneous—Alcohol, 1409, 1413. Cacao, 2103. Guano, 2040, 2044. Henequen, 1473. Maguey, 1503. Mate, 1414. Paper, 1432. Potatoes, 2420. Pulque, 1503. Railway cars, 1533. Sheep, 2014. Shoes, 1463. Textiles, 1522. Timber, 1403. Wheat, 1417, 1555.

COMMUNICATIONS
Brazil, 1419. Venezuela, 3092.

COMMUNISM
Latin America, 3505. Bolivia, 2239. Chile, 2264. Colombia, 3027. Guatemala, 2269, 2272, 2274–2276.

Comomfort, Ignacio, 2800, 2801

Concolorcorvo, 3711

CONFERENCES, CONGRESSES, MEETINGS
Americanists, 751. Anthropology, 752. Economics, 1252, 1469. Education, 1750, 1752, 4757. Indian, 4908. Philosophy, 4751, 4757, 4758. Sociology, 4904. See also Inter-American conferences and meetings.

CONSTITUTIONS AND CONSTITUTIONAL LAW

General, 4498, 4500, 4503. Latin America, 2203, Argentina, 2226, 4501, 4506. Brazil, 3210. Costa Rica, 2294a. Cuba, 4502. Guatemala, 2273, 4499. Mexico, 2277, 2867, 4497, 4504, 4505. Peru, 3073. Uruguay, 2293, 2294.

Contreras, Rodrigo de, 2563

Córdova y Salinas, Diego de, 2751

Coreal, François, 2703

Correia, Raimundo, 4354

Cortés, Hernán, 762, 2461, 2484, 2522, 2541a, 2556, 2562

Cortés de Madariaga, José, 2979

Cosa, Juan de la, 2718

Cosme, Luiz, 4707

Costa, Cláudio Manuel da, 4324

Costa, Francisco Lobo da, 4317

Costa, Lúcio, 1180, 1182

COSTA RICA
Economics, 1320–1324. Education, 1651, 1705, 1706. Geography, 1958, 1961. Government and politics, 2294a, 2297a. History, 2311, 2874. Language, 3644, 3684. Law, 1324. Literature, 3644, 3803. Social welfare, 3558, 3610. Sociology, 4935, 4952.

COTTON. See Commodities.

Cravo, Mário, 1190

CREOLE LANGUAGE
Dominica, 430, 431. Haiti, 440.

CRIME AND CRIMINALS
Mexico, 4530. Peru, 4483. Venezuela, 4991.

Crowder, Enoch A., 2929

Cruxent, José María, 354c

Cuauhtémoc, 2521

CUBA
General, 2368. Anthropology, 252, 256, 423–427, 764. Art and architecture, 900, 1013, 1041–1043. Economics, 427, 1325–1329. Education, 1707–1710, 4772. Geography, 1970. Government and politics, 2295a, 2299. History, 2303, 2309, 2312–2314, 2316, 2324, 2337, 2341, 2346, 2347, 2350, 2351, 2368, 2468, 2576–2578, 2903–2941, 3814, 3832, 4248. Labor, 3525. Language, 423, 424, 3665, 3668, 3674. Law, 4476, 4502, 4510, 4519, 4542, 4572, 4603. Literature, 426, 2904, 2911, 2912, 2914, 3814, 3914, 4011, 4077, 4079, 4116, 4128, 4133, 4136, 4146, 4200, 4240, 4248, 4268. Philosophy, 4756, 4772, 4773, 4775, 4786, 4801, 4860. Music and dance, 4720. Social welfare, 3581, 3582. Sociology, 4900, 4959, 4961.

Cunha, Euclides da, 3287, 4304, 4342

Cunha, Gastão de, 3272

Curaçao. See Netherlands Colonies.

DANCE. See under names of countries.

Darío, Rubén, 4123

Debret, Jean Baptiste, 1172, 1174, 1175

Debreton, Joachim, 1175

Deceliers, Pierre, 1160

Delgado, Claudio, 2931

Delgado González, Juan, 2916

Gerchunoff, Alberto, 2213a, 3815
Gilij, F. S., 2703
Giorgi. Bruno, 1190
Gnattali, Radamés, 4707
Gómez, Juan Gualberto, 2920a
Gómez, Juan Vicente, 3091, 3964, 3968
Gómez, Máximo, 2910, 2923, 2933, 2939
Gómez, Pedro, 1008
Gómez Carrillo, Enrique, 3853
Gómez Farías, Valentín, 2835
Gonzaga, Chiquinha, 4707
Gonzaga, Tomás Antônio, 4324
González, Juan Francisco, 1040
González, Juan Vicente, 3813
González, Pedro Antonio, 4124
González Suárez, Federico, 336, 337
González Torres, Manuel, 3744
González Valencia, Ramón, 3049
Gorostiza, Carlos, 4255
Gorostiza, Manuel Eduardo de, 4249, 4256
Gould, Alice B., 2406
Gould y Quincy, Alicia B., 2406
GOVERNMENT AND POLITICS
　General — Latin America, 2204–2208, 2265, 5063. Argentina, 2210a–2213, 2214–2216, 2222, 2223, 2224, 2229, 2230, 2235, 3006. Bolivia, 2242, 2244. Brazil, 2245a–2247, 2250–2253, 2256, 2258. Caribbean area, 2209. Chile, 2261, 2262. Colombia, 2298a, 3036, 3038, 3040, 3041. Cuba, 2299. Dominican Republic, 2296a, 2297. Ecuador, 2266. El Salvador, 2295. Guatemala, 2270, 2275. Mexico, 2279, 2280, 2283. Paraguay, 2286, 2287. Puerto Rico, 2298. Venezuela, 2296, 5061.
　Administrative organization — Argentina, 2999. Brazil, 2249, 2259, 2259a. Mexico, 2281–2283. Uruguay, 2292.
　Army and politics—Argentina, 2223. Brazil, 2245, 3271. Chile, 2262. Paraguay, 2285.
　Dictatorship and revolution — General, 2200, 2207. Argentina, 2211, 2217, 2219, 2221, 2225, 2232, 2233. Brazil, 2255. Ecuador, 4964. Guatemala, 2271, 2271a. Western Hemisphere, 2201a.
　Legislative—Argentina, 2210.
　Municipal—Brazil, 2248, 2254, 2257.
　See also Constitutions and constitutional law; Political parties.
Gramcko, Ida, 4142
GRAPHIC ARTS
　Latin America, 910. Argentina, 1031. Brazil, 1162, 1172. Colombia, 952. Cuba, 1042, 1043. Mexico, 963, 967, 980, 1051, 1059.
Gros, Jean Baptiste Louis, 1066
Guarnieri, Camargo, 4707
GUATEMALA
　Anthropology, 43, 72, 92, 99, 100, 101, 122, 134, 166, 169, 170, 172, 173, 209, 493, 699a, 758, 765, 767, 956. Art and architecture, 953–956. Economics, 1340, 1341, 2877, 4567. Education, 1711–

1713. Description and travel, 5049, 5057. Geography, 1952, 5049. Government and politics, 2269–2276. History, 2352, 2353, 2565–2567, 2569, 2570, 2876, 2878. International relations, 3420, 3421, 3425, 3432. Labor, 490, 3510. Language, 699a, 1952, 3627. Law, 4499, 4567, 4597. Literature, 3853, 3900, 3907, 3934, 3981, 4054, 4068, 4087, 4215. Music and dance, 4701. Philosophy, 4865. Social welfare, 3590, 3591. Sociology, 4928.
Guayasamín, Oswaldo, 1045
Güell y Renté, José, 2911
Güemes, Martín, 3001
Guerrero, Práxedis G., 2802
Guevara, Luis de, 2563
GUIANAS
　History, 2729. *See also* British Colonies *and* Netherlands Colonies.
Guignard, Alberto, 1190
Güiraldes, Ricardo, 3645, 4007, 4013
Gusinde, Martin, 801
Gutiérrez de la Fuente, Antonio, 3078
Gutiérrez Nájera, Manuel, 3828, 4144
Guzmán, Antonio Leocadio, 3089
Guzmán, Nuño de, 2523, 2538
Guzmán Blanco, Antonio, 3089
Guzmán de Rojas, Cecilio, 1035

HAITI
　Anthropology, 261, 262, 408, 421, 432–452. Art and architecture, 1046, 1047. Economics, 1361. Government and politics, 438. History, 438, 439, 2315, 2340, 2345, 2348, 2471–2473, 2579–2590, 2726, 2902, 2954–2958. Labor, 444. Language, 440. Literature, 4450–4460. Philosophy, 4781, 4870a, 4870d. Social welfare, 3592, 3593.
Haring, Clarence H., 2414
Haya de la Torre, Víctor Raúl, 3402
HEALTH—General, 400. Mexico, 461.
Henna, Julio, 2960
Heredia, José María, 4133, 4136
Heredia, Nicolás, 2913, 2919
Heredia, Pedro de, 1980
Hernández, José, 3645
Herrán, Pedro Alcántara, 3028
Herrera y Reissig, Julio, 4131
Herrera y Tordesillas, Antonio de, 2403
Hidalga, Lorenzo de la, 965
Hidalgo y Costilla, Miguel, 2847, 2854
Hill, George W., 4921
HISTORIOGRAPHY
　General, 2354, 2409–2411, 2446, 2706. Argentina, 2994. Colombia, 2712. Cuba, 2347. Guatemala, 2569. Haiti, 2345, 2957. Venezuela, 2712.
HISTORY
　General — Latin America, 2330, 2334, 2339. Argentina, 2222, 2232. Brazil, 3218, 3222, 3231, 3240, 3241, 3246, 3270. Central America, 2872. Chile, 2261, 2263. Colombia, 1984d, 2325,

2331. Costa Rica, 2311, 2874. Cuba, 2303, 2347, 2932. Dominican Republic, 2348, 2349, 2588, 2942–2942b, 2946, 2949, 2949a. Haiti, 439, 2340, 2949, 2949a, 2954, 2956. Honduras, 2355. Mexico, 2300, 2369, 2800, 2801, 2820, 2825, 2828, 2836, 2852. Nicaragua, 2302, 2563. Puerto Rico, 2968. Trinidad, 2308. West Indies, 2305, 2338.

Conquest—General, 2413, 2453, 2455, 3715, 3722. Chile, 2777, 2778a. Colombia, 280, 1980, 1981, 2714. Florida, 3724, 3737. Mexico, 2512, 2516, 2520, 2533, 2534, 2535, 2550, 3714, 3731, 3732. Peru, 2757a, 2777, 3730.

Diplomatic—General, 2444, 2790a. Brazil, 3224, 3251, 3282. Central America, 2880. Cuba, 2941. Cuba-Catalonia, 2914. Dominican Republic, 2947. Dominican Republic-Spain, 2950, 2952, 2952a. Mexico, 2812. Mexico-Spain, 2845. U.S.-Chile, 2821, U. S.-Haiti, 2958. U.S.-Mexico, 2811, 2816, 2818, 2832, 2839, 2841, 2853, 2859. U. S.-Nicaragua, 2879. U. S.-Panama, 2870. Venezuela, 3104.

Discovery—General, 2404–2406, 2409–2411, 2416, 2467, 2700, 2702. Chile, 2777, 2778a. Colombia, 2718. Peru, 2777.

Ecclesiastical—General, 2401, 2404, 2416, 2448, 2449, 2469. Brazil, 1154, 1167, 3203, 3220, 3228. Chile, 2773. Colombia, 3042, 3043. Dominican Republic, 2364, 2589, 2590, 2951. Mexico, 2321, 2534, 2541, 2541a, 2813. Peru, 2766, 2770. Venezuela, 3088.

Economics—General, 2310, 2408, 2414, 2419, 2424–2426, 2432, 2458, 2461, 2463, 2466, 2471, 2472, 2490. Argentina, 2796, 2995. Bolivia, 2750, 2771. Brazil, 2750. Chile, 2778, 2779, 3025, 5062. Colombia, 2716, 3029, 3047. Cuba, 2350, 2913. Guatemala, 2352, 2353, 2877. Jamaica, 455. Mexico, 1496, 1501, 1553, 1566, 2408, 2502, 2803, 2827, 2866. Middle America, 2840. Peru, 2742–2742b, 2761, 2767, 2779, 3066. Puerto Rico, 2961. Texas, 2806. Venezuela, 2721a.

Emigration to the New World—General, 2488. Argentina, 2786c. Uruguay, 2786c.

European backgrounds, 2424–2426, 2448, 2469, 2527, 2791.

Expeditions, 2301, 2503, 2512, 2513, 2517, 2523, 2557, 2571, 2594.

Independence movements—General, 2983, 2986. South America, 2980, 2985. Argentina, 2981, 2989, 3000–3003, 3005, 3008, 3011, 3014–3016. Bolivia, 3021. Chile, 2990, 2991, 3023–3025. Central America, 2875, 2883. Colombia, 2363, 2987. Cuba, 2904, 2907a, 2912, 2915–2919, 2920, 2920a, 2921. Dominican

Republic, 2942a, 2944, 2948, 2953. Haiti, 2580, 2586, 2957. Honduras, 2875. Mexico, 2868, 5048. Paraguay, 3058a. Peru, 2981, 2982, 2987, 3066, 3067, 3069. Puerto Rico, 2961a, 2965, 2967, 2969a. Uruguay, 2785, 2981, 3080–3084. Venezuela, 268, 3090, 3093, 3101, 3103–3108.

Indians — General, 2401, 2443, 2450, 2706a. Argentina, 2781, 2996. Chile, 2775. Colombia, 2706a, 2712a, 2717, 2725, 2730. Guatemala, 2570. Honduras, 2572. Mexico, 464, 2511, 2519, 2521, 2522, 2525, 2537, 3714. Paraguay, 2795, 2797. Peru, 2741, 2745, 2747a, 2757, 2765, 2765a, 2768b, 3063, 3719. St. Lucia, 259, 260. U. S., 286, 2318, 2544. Uruguay, 2781. Venezuela, 2367, 2708, 3102.

Intellectual — General, 2489. Argentina, 2786. Brazil, 1796, 3202, 4782. Chile, 2260, 2772. Colombia, 2325, 3026. Cuba, 2341, 2346, 2909, 2912, 2919a, 2921, 2922, 2935. Guatemala, 1711, 2567, 2876. Mexico, 1717, 2284, 2541a, 2542a, 2560, 2805, 2847, 2854, 2864, 4789. Peru, 2758, 2763, 3070, 4798. U. S., 2356. Venezuela, 3087, 4784.

Colonial government and institutions—General, 2415, 2431, 2453–2455a. Argentina, 2784, 2789, 2790, 2799. Brazil, 1167, 3242, 3258. Colombia, 951, 2711, 2725, 2735. Cuba, 427. Dominican Republic, 2584. Ecuador, 2756. Guatemala, 2570. Mexico, 977, 2336, 2504, 2507, 2510, 2511, 2522, 2525, 2526, 2530, 2531, 2538, 2540, 2549, 2551. Peru, 996, 1003, 2740a, 2744, 2749, 2754, 2760, 2761, 2761a, 2767. Puerto Rico, 2592, 2593. South America, 907, 916. Venezuela, 2722.

Colonial legislation—General, 2423, 2431, 2441, 2443, 2458, 2725, 2741. Chile, 2774. Uruguay, 2787.

Local—Argentina, 2792d. Bolivia, 2750, 2752a, 2753. Brazil, 1162, 1163, 3200, 3211, 3216, 3219, 3220, 3221, 3225, 3226, 3227, 3232, 3236, 3237, 3238, 3252, 3253a, 3254, 3257, 3281. Chile, 2773. Colombia, 2719, 2723, 2724b, 2731a, 2733, 2734, 3032, 3039, 3045, 3048, 5053. Cuba, 2312, 2351, 2368, 2578. Dominican Republic, 2579, 2585, 2951. El Salvador, 2565. Guatemala, 2564, 2878. Mexico, 978, 2327, 2332, 2360, 2361, 2500, 2501, 2505, 2506a, 2518, 2529, 2539, 2541, 2542, 2543, 2545, 2546, 2547, 2548, 2553, 2561, 2819, 2837, 2846, 2849, 2857, 2860, 2866, 3818. Peru, 2738, 2746, 3065. Puerto Rico, 2359, 2969, 2969a. U. S. 2317. Venezuela, 3102. West Indies, 2575.

Medicine and pharmacy—Brazil, 3239. Colombia, 2703. Cuba, 2576, 2903,

Lana, João de, 1170
LAND
Latin America, 4939, 4940. Brazil, 1405, 2121, 4930, 4931. Colombia, 2712a, 4932. Grenadines, 496. Guatemala, 1340. Mexico, 1956. Middle America, 409. Peru, 2741. *See also* Soils.
LANGUAGE. *See* Spanish language; Portuguese language; Creole language; Anthropology, cultural — Indian languages and linguistics.
Larra, Carlos Manuel, 331
Lars, Claudia. *See* Brannon de Samayoa, Carmen.
Laserna, José de, 2982
LATIN AMERICA
General, 2204, 4908, 5063. Anthropology, 1–28, 47, 207, 408, 653a, 675a, 702a, 721a, 722a, 723, 751, 752. Art and architecture, 900, 904–906, 913–916, 1015, 4987. Economics, 1250–1262, 3519, 4493, 4564. Education, 22, 1650–1660, 5066. Geography, 1900, 1901. Government and politics, 2200–2209, 2248, 2265. History, 2321, 2330, 2334, 2417. International relations, 3400–3455, 4270, 4271. Labor, 3501, 3502, 3505, 3511, 3519, 3526. Language, 26, 653a, 675a, 702a, 721a, 722a, 723. Law, 3508, 4475, 4477–4479, 4481, 4486, 4493, 4520, 4525–4546, 4564, 4590, 4595, 4600. Literature, 3808, 3809, 3833, 3838, 3840, 3849–3851, 4201, 4247, 4267, 4268. Music and dance, 4700, 4702. Philosophy, 4751, 4757, 4759. Social welfare, 3508, 3551–3613. Sociology, 4906, 4907, 4914, 4920, 4925, 4933, 4935, 4939, 4940, 4955, 4978, 4981, 4983, 4987, 4990, 4992. *See also* Caribbean Area; Central America, Middle America; South America; Spanish America; West Indies; *and names of individual countries.*
Latorre, Mariano, 3819
LAW
Commercial, 1253, 1254, 1309, 1335, 1349, 1350, 1416. Copyright, 4520. Legal terminology, 4481. Property, 1340, 4523. Roman law, 4482. Textbooks, 4490, 4511, 4512, 4529, 4535, 4536, 4553, 4591. *See* Law section. *See also* Constitutions and constitutional law; Education—law; Housing; Labor —law; Philosophy—ethics and law; Social welfare—law.
Lecuna, Vicente, 5037
León, Juan Francisco de, 2721a
León, Nicolás, 768
León Pinelo, Antonio de, 3750
Lerdo de Tejada, Sebastián, 2841
Lerma, García de, 1980
Levi, Rino, 1178, 1180
Lewinsohn, Richard 1418
LIBRARIES
Argentina, 3019. Brazil, 3206. Italy, 2482.

Mexico, 2319, 2329. U. S., 2339, 2344, 2486, 2823, 2862, 3213.
Lima, Jorge de, 4336
Lind, John, 2833
Lisbôa, Antônio Francisco, 3214
LITERATURE, BRAZILIAN (Studies)
General, 3225, 4278, 4300, 4301, 4304, 4309, 4311, 4312, 4319, 4323, 4326, 4327, 4329, 4331, 4333, 4336, 4341, 4348, 4355, 4356.
Drama and theaters, 4302, 4318, 4322, 4344, 4353.
Literary magazines, 4275, 4277, 4280, 4281, 4283.
Poetry, 4284, 4314, 4317, 4320, 4321, 4323, 4332, 4336, 4340, 4350, 4351, 4354, 4401.
Prose fiction, 4303, 4323, 4334, 4335, 4345, 4347, 4349.
LITERATURE, HAITIAN (Studies)
General, 4457, 4460.
Drama and theaters, 4452, 4453.
LITERATURE, SPANISH AMERICAN (Studies)
General—Spanish America, 3800, 3801, 3808, 3809, 3827, 3840, 3849, 3851. Argentina, 3809, 3815. Bolivia, 3822, 3845. Chile, 3819, 3820, 3826, 3854. Colombia, 3848. Cuba, 2907, 2934, 3832. Ecuador, 3802. Mexico, 2817, 3816, 3825, 3831, 3838, 3839. Venezuela, 3813, 3817, 3844, 3851.
Drama and theaters—General, 3729, 4201, 4242, 4247. Argentina, 4201, 4224, 4228, 4231, 4245, 4246, 4250, 4255. Chile, 4201, 4237, 4242. Cuba, 4240, 4248. Mexico, 2817, 3727, 4225, 4234, 4241, 4243, 4244, 4249, 4251, 4252, 4256. Paraguay, 4201. Peru, 4201, 4254. Puerto Rico, 4238, 4239. Uruguay, 4201. Venezuela, 3742, 3744, 4253. *See also* Plays.
Literary magazines — Argentina, 3810. Mexico, 3828, 4135, 4808. Peru, 4138.
Poetry—General, 4081, 4085. Argentina, 2782, 4086, 4118, 4120, 4126, 4127, 4140. Bolivia, 3726, 4132. Chile, 3706, 4112, 4124, 4134, 4143. Colombia, 3722, 3723, 4107. Cuba, 2904, 2911, 4128, 4133, 4136, 4146. Dominican Republic, 4113. Ecuador, 3704. El Salvador, 4119. Mexico, 2858, 3705, 3707, 3712, 3713, 3720, 3721, 3747, 4093, 4121, 4122, 4125, 4129, 4135, 4137, 4144, 4147. Peru, 4138, 4139, 4141. Uruguay, 4117, 4130, 4131. Venezuela, 3841, 4142, 4145. *See also* Verse, books of.
Prose fiction—General, 4005. Argentina, 4007, 4013. Chile, 3946. Colombia, 4010. Cuba, 4011. Mexico, 3710, 3716, 3717, 4004. Uruguay, 4008, 4009. Venezuela, 4003, 4006, 4012. *See also* Novels *and* Short stories.
See also names of individual authors.

WITHDRAWAL